AF809335

MOHAMMEDAN THEORIES OF FINANCE

WITH AN

Introduction to Mohammedan Law and a Bibliography

BY

NICOLAS P. AGHNIDES

AMS PRESS
NEW YORK

COLUMBIA UNIVERSITY
STUDIES IN THE
SOCIAL SCIENCES

166

This Series was formerly known as
Studies in History, Economics and Public Law.

Reprinted with the permission of Columbia University Press
From the edition of 1916, New York
First AMS EDITION published 1969
Manufactured in the United States of America

Library of Congress Catalogue Card Number: 72-82246

AMS PRESS, INC.
NEW YORK, N. Y. 10003

PREFACE

THE *raison d'être* of this dissertation is found in the intrinsic interest of its subject and in the fact that this subject up to the present time has never been treated in its entirety and for its own sake. There is indeed some literature bearing upon it in European translations of Mohammedan legal text-books, but the treatment of finance in these text-books is naturally terse and incidental and covers but a portion of the entire subject. Hamilton's English translation of the *Hidāyah* is a case in point. The few chapters in it bearing on finance are at times very inaccurate — a defect explained by the fact that the translation was made from a Persian translation of the original Arabic instead of direct from the original—and lack all historical perspective. Moreover, they do not give a full insight into the arguments invoked in support of the particular views. The translations into the other European languages unfortunately cannot lay claim to greater perfection, the chief difference among them being their varying degree of accuracy.

In this dissertation an attempt has been made to give a comprehensive exposition of the Mohammedan financial theories in their entirety with especial emphasis when possible on the reasons underlying them. To this end all the available primary sources have been used and the divergent views which they contain frequently cited. A body of ancient theories, however, no matter how fully set forth, would convey but little meaning to the modern mind, unless the origin of those theories were indicated and their practical bearings pointed out. These two last needs are met by

Parts I. and III., Part II. being devoted to the theories themselves.

The general purpose of Part I. is to explain the terms and concepts of Part II. More particularly, with a view to settling the question of the origin of Mohammedan financial theories, it attempts to determine the degree to which those theories, as a matter of theoretical possibility, were subject to foreign influences. Its title, ***Introduction to Mohammedan Law***, seems at first blush to bear no relation to these purposes. The connection, however, becomes at once clear when it is remembered that Mohammedan financial theory is but an integral part of ***fiqh*** or Mohammedan law in general. An explanation of the origin of *fiqh* is, therefore, also an explanation of the origin of Mohammedan financial theory. According to the Mohammedan doctors *fiqh* has been derived from the revealed sources of the Koran and the Prophetic conduct or ***sunnah*** exclusively, in conformity with a body of principles called *uṣūl-al-fiqh*. This construction would seem to preclude any foreign influence in the development of Mohammedan law. It was, therefore, to these principles collectively called *uṣūl-al-fiqh* that we had to turn to determine how far they allowed foreign ideas to enter *fiqh*.

The three conventional parts of the Mohammedan treatises on *uṣūl-al-fiqh* are: (1) an introduction on the interpretation of terms (*tafsīr wa ta'wīl*); (2) an explanation of the principles (***arkān*** or *uṣūl*) on the basis of which Mohammedan law (*fiqh*) is derived from the above mentioned revealed sources; (3) an exposition of the values (***aḥkām***) or legal provisions so derived. Of these parts, the first and third have been practically omitted. The first, because as regards the question of the extent to which foreign influences were allowed to enter the structure of *fiqh*, it is, in comparison with the second, of negligible importance; the third, because it is not quite relevant to the purpose in view. However, inasmuch as a secondary purpose of Part I. is to offer a background for the understanding of Part II., an exception to the rule was made in incorporating from this third part the chapter entitled *Classification of the Sharī'ah Values.* The two purposes mentioned will not account for every line of Part I., but it was considered expedient, at the risk of adding to the length of the book, to make Part I. a fairly comprehensive introduction to Mohammedan law. The absence of such an introduction in any language, more than warranted, in the author's opinion, the few additional pages which might have been spared the reader.

The purpose of Part II., the main part of the book, is to present in an orderly and clear fashion the views and opinions of the Mohammedan doctors in regard to financial theory. Part II. concerns itself, accordingly, with theory exclusively, purely descriptive and historical matter being carefully avoided. The reader should, therefore, remember that, whether or not included within quotation marks, the views expressed in Part II. are merely the views of the Mohammedan doctors and as such they need not always coincide with the facts, nor agree with the conclusions reached in Part III.

The purpose of Part III., finally, is to inquire into the origins of Mohammedan financial practice and trace out its relation to Mohammedan financial theory. Part III., then, tests by the light of history the conclusions reached in Part I. as to the theoretical possibilities.

The doctrines and views brought together in this book are, it must be borne in mind, the orthodox, particularly the Hanifite, and to a less extent, the Shafiite and Malikite ones. The views of other schools are only occasionally mentioned, not only because they have enjoyed but scant recognition, but also because the sources concerning them are few and inadequate. In quoting the views of the doctors, the source of each view has been indicated whenever it was considered important or was found in only one or few of the sources. In most cases, however, it was deemed sufficient to indicate the sources consulted collectively, either at the beginning of the section or the end of the paragraph. In referring to the sources a shorter title, usually the one employed by the Mohammedan doctors, has been used. The full title of each reference will be found in an alphabetical list at the end of the book. As an aid to the reader, the gist of the discussion has been indicated by the words printed in bold faced type. It is hoped that this device and the analytical table of contents and topical index that have been supplied will permit ready reference to any part of the discussion.

In transliterating the Arabic words the object has been to reproduce exactly their spelling, but only to approximate their pronunciation. Therefore, in order to avoid confusion for those ignorant of Arabic, the inflective Arabic endings, except in the case of certain pronouns, have been omitted. As regards the method of transliteration itself, the one followed by most European orientalists has been adhered to, barring a few slight modifications making for greater simplicity and better conforming to the peculiarities of English. Thus, instead of the two usual diacritical signs, the point and the dash, only the dash has been used. *Gh* has been replaced by *g*, and *u* (standing for silent *waw* as in *quam*) by *w*. The pronouncing value of the different letters is approximately as follows: *y* is to be pronounced always as a consonant as in *year*; *g* as *gh* in *Buckingham*; all the single consonants, whether or not underlined, must be pronounced as in English; *th* as in *thorn*; *dh* like *th* in *then*; *sh* as in *should*; *kh* like *ch* in the Scottish word *loch*; the signs ' and ' may be ignored; all the vowels are to be pronounced as in

French, the accented ones longer. Consecutive consonants have been set off by a hyphen, when necessary, to indicate that they are not to be pronounced as one letter. In general, combinations of words used currently as single names, as *uṣūl-al-fiqh* or *bayt-al-mal*, have been treated as single words. Furthermore the article *al* has always been united to the word it defines. Where capitals or bold faced type are used the accents are omitted.

The author wants to take this opportunity to express his thanks to all those who have aided him in his work, and particularly to Professor R. J. H. Gottheil. He feels especially grateful to Professors H. R. Seager and V. G. Simkhovitch for assistance with the proofs and to Professor E. R. A. Seligman, but for whose encouragement this work might never have seen the light. His thanks are also due to the authorities of the Columbia University Library and the New York Public Library for the special facilities which they have afforded him. But for the rich collection of Oriental books of the New York Public Library, the preparation of this dissertation in this country would have been well-nigh impossible.

The discussion for Christian readers of Mohammedan institutions, because of the long and bitter animosities that have separated Christians and Mohammedans, is a matter of great delicacy. The writer has sought to treat with absolute impartiality all of the topics that he has considered and trusts that the fact that he was reared as a Christian has been so fully offset by his strong Mohammedan sympathies that he has attained this aim. It is sincerely hoped that all the sources consulted have been given due credit and that the instances are not many where accuracy, the chief aim of the author, has been missed. In such instances, the pioneer character of the work will perhaps be considered sufficient ground for indulgence.

CONTENTS

PART I

The Background—Introduction to Mohammedan Law and Bibliography

PAGE

CHAPTER I

Preliminary Concepts

CHAPTER II

The First Basis of Fiqh: the Koran

CHAPTER III

The Second Basis of Fiqh: the Sunnah (Prophetic Conduct)

PAGE

CHAPTER V

Preliminary Considerations

CHAPTER VI

The Kharaj or Land-Tax

CHAPTER VII

The Jizyah or Poll-Tax

PAGE

CHAPTER VIII

Other Sources of Revenue

B. *Expenditure*

CHAPTER IX

The Public Treasury and the Mohammedan Counterpart of a Budget

CHAPTER X

Expenditure of the Zakat Taxes (Religious Revenue)

CHAPTER XI

Expenditure of the Secular Revenue

PAGE

PART I

INTRODUCTION TO MOHAMMEDAN LAW AND BIBLIOGRAPHY

CHAPTER I

Preliminary Concepts

The word **shari'ah** is the general name given to the Mohammedan dispensation and is defined by the doctors as "that which would not be known had there not been a divine revelation."[1]

This definition of *sharī'ah* is broad enough to include the revelations made by the Hebrew Prophets and Jesus, but their revelations are considered valid only in so far as they have been confirmed by those made through Mohammed. The latter therefore are the *sharī'ah* par excellence. A second corollary from the above definition is that only what is expressly stated in the divine revelations, or may be inferred from them by analogy, properly comes under *sharī'ah.* Matters determined by intellectual processes remain, therefore, outside, *e. g.*, the obligation of belief in God or the Prophets is outside of *sharī'ah* because it is a matter to be established intellectually.

Inasmuch as the prescriptions contained in the *sharī'ah*, to use a judicial analogy, serve as evidences for the establishment of *sharī'ah* values, they have been called by the doctors "**shari'ah evidences**" (*adillah shari'yyah*). With reference to the source from which these evidences are obtained, the doctors have distinguished four types of *sharī'ah* evidences, namely, the Koran, the *sunnah*, the *ijmā'*, and the *qiyās*.

[1] *Tawḍīḥ*, p. 21.

A **shari'ah value** (*hukm shar'i*) is defined as the quality "determined as a result of divine revelation," *e. g.*, the fact of a human act like lying being prohibited in the *sharī'ah* is its *sharī'ah* value.[1]

The science which derives the *sharī'ah* values from the *sharī'ah* evidences is the "**science of fiqh**," or simply *fiqh*, and the person conversant with this science is the *faqīh*.

Fiqh has been **defined** by Abu Hanīfah in a general way as "the self's knowledge of what is to its advantage and disadvantage." This definition, it will be observed, is very broad and includes matters of conduct (*'amaliyyāt*) as well as matters of belief (*i'tiqādiyyāt*), and of ethics (*wijdāniyyāt*). Some have restricted *fiqh* only to matters of conduct, such as civil transactions (*mu'āmalāt*) and religious ritual (*'ibādāt*).

Fiqh has been **defined also** in a specific way as "the deduction of the *sharī'ah* values relating to conduct from their respective particular (*tafsīlī*) evidences." By the use of the term "*sharī'ah*" it is intended to leave out intellectual and perceptual values, such as the obligation of belief in God and the Prophets. The word "conduct" excludes points of theory, *e. g.*, that the *ijmā'* is a lawful evidence for the establishment of *sharī'ah* values. "Deduction" excludes knowledge acquired from a *mujtahid*, instead of by direct inquiry into the evidences. According to this, a person is not called a *faqīh* when he only knows the *sharī'ah* values. He is called a *faqīh* only if he has himself, by personal inquiry and thought, deduced those values. This

[1] The Arabic word *hukm* (plural, *ahkām*) is used in various slightly different meanings which no single English word would exactly render. At least two words will be used to express the Arabic *hukm*, the word value, as in this case, and the expression "legal result". For example, when the doctors say that the *hukm* of a sale is the transfer of ownership in a thing from the seller to the purchaser, they mean only to describe the legal result of a sale.

definition is according to the Shafiite doctors. The Hanifite definition and the one adopted in the modern Ottoman civil code (*majallah*), ignore the way in which this knowledge has been obtained. Consequently the mere knowledge of the *sharīʿah* values is *fiqh*, and the person who has this knowledge is a *faqīh*. In other words, a *faqīh* need not be a *mujtahid*.[1] Finally, the term " particular " indicates that the premises which *fiqh* uses are not directly obtained from the four *sharīʿah* evidences, namely, the Koran, the *sunnah*, the *ijmāʿ*, and the *qiyās*. These evidences, as they stand,

[1] This division between the Shafiites and the Hanifites is only a phase of a more fundamental division among the doctors concerning the definition of science in general. One group of doctors holds that knowledge without an understanding of the underlying reasons is not science (*ʿilm*) but narration (*ḥikāyah*). The other group contends that, in addition to the above meaning, science also means the mere knowledge of the rules (*masāʾil*) as well as the ability (*malakah*) to recall to, or bring before the, mind (*istiḥḍār*) those rules. For instance, they say, when it is claimed that a person knows syntax, it is only meant that he has the ability to bring before the mind the rules of syntax, not that he actually remembers them. The first group replies that, although science may also mean, as contended by the second group, the mere knowledge of the rules, or the mere ability to recall those rules, it is so only when that knowledge or that ability is coupled with a proper understanding of the reasons.

There has also been a dispute as to what exactly is meant by the word ability in this connection. Some say, it is the ability to know all the rules of the science, either by recalling to the memory what has already been stored away in it, or by discovering (*istiḥṣāl*) what is as yet unknown. It is not, they add, the ability to recall only, known as actual intellect (*ʿaql bi 'l-fiʿl*), nor is it the ability to discover only, known as potential intellect (*ʿaql bi 'l-malakah*). For if the latter were the case, a person who has not as yet learned a single rule of a science, although he has the ability to discover those rules, would have to be called a scientist. In the *al-aṭwal* it is stated that the ability to recall what has already been learned is sufficient. The ground for this view is that it is not an uncommon thing for sciences to be in a state of development. In such cases a knowledge of the entire subject-matter is out of the question, but such knowledge of it as has been already acquired may properly be called science. (*Tech. Dict.*, pp. 2-3.)

are too general (*ijmāli*) and are not available for the purposes of *fiqh*, until after they have been reduced by a particular science to logical propositions, each relating to one particular set of values.

This particular science, which prepares its premises for *fiqh*, is the so-called science of **usul-al-fiqh,** literally, **the science of the bases of fiqh**. It has been called so, because the four *sharī'ah* evidences above-mentioned which form its subject-matter, are in the last analysis, the four bases on which the deductions of *fiqh* rest.

The science of **usul-al-fiqh** has been **defined** by the doctors as "the science of the principles whereby one reaches *fiqh* in the true way." [1] The definition needs explanation.

Uṣūl-al-fiqh discusses only those principles which are immediately necessary for reaching *fiqh*, in other words, it does not concern itself with less immediate subjects, like language and syntax, or dogmatics (*kalām*), although they too are necessary. On the other hand, the expression "in the true way" is intended to exclude controversial subjects.

The **function of usul-al-fiqh** is then to prepare the premises which are to be used in *fiqh* in establishing the *sharī'ah* values in particular cases. Thus, *uṣūl-al-fiqh* provides for *fiqh* as premises certain universal propositions (*qawā'id kulliyyah*) to be used by *fiqh* in deriving the provisions of the law applicable to particular cases. For example, *uṣūl-al-fiqh* tells that under such and such conditions *ijmā'* constitutes an evidence for the establishment of a *sharī'ah* value. *Fiqh* takes this proposition as a premise and deduces from it the conclusion that the practice *e. g.*, of *istiṣnā'*,[2] is lawful because there is an *ijmā'* to that effect. Or, again, *uṣūl-al-fiqh* tells us that under cer-

[1] *Tawḍīḥ*, p. 27.

[2] *Istiṣnā'* is placing an order with an artisan.

tain conditions analogy (*qiyās*) is a lawful means of establishing a *sharī'ah* value.

In short, *usūl-al-fiqh* discusses the *sharī'ah* evidences, that is, the bases of *fiqh*, in so far as they may be used as evidences for the establishment of the *sharī'ah* values, and the *sharī'ah* values in so far as they are deduced from the *sharī'ah* evidences, but it does not discuss what the *sharī'ah* values are in particular cases, that being the function of *fiqh*.

The component parts of *usūl-al-fiqh* and *fiqh*, as well as the position of these two disciplines among sciences in general will be made clear by the following classification outlined by the Hanifite doctors.[1]

The established sciences (*'ulūm mudawwanah*) are:

I. Intellectual (*'aqliyyah*), acquired through the exercise of the intellect and the senses;

II. Traditional (*naqliyyah*), acquired by way of tradition. The contrast is thus that between, what we would call the speculative and the historical sciences.

The **traditional sciences** are:

1. The literary or instrumental (*āliyyah* or *lisāniyyah*),
2. The *sharī'ah* sciences.

The **sharī'ah sciences** are:

1. fundamental (*aṣliyyah*), pertaining to the
   (a) reading of the Koran,
   (b) interpretation of the Koran (*tafsīr*),
   (c) *ḥadīths* or traditions;
2. deduced (*mustanbaṭah*), comprising
   (a) dogmatics (*i'tiqādiyyah*), *i. e.*, the science of the unity and the attributes of God, (*kalām* or *uṣūl-al-dīn*, or *al-fiqh al-akbar*, or *'ilm al-tawḥīd wa'l-ṣifāt*),

[1] *Cf. Farā'id*, p. 2, fn.; also Savvas, chap. ii, p. 8.

(b) the practical[1] (*'amaliyyah*) or *fiqh* sciences.

The **practical** or **fiqh sciences** comprise:

1. The science of the bases of *fiqh* (*'ilm uṣūl-al-fiqh*),
2. The science of the applications of *fiqh* (*'ilm furū' al-fiqh*, or simply *fiqh*).

Finally, **fiqh** relates to

1. human acts which are entirely a matter of divine rights (*ḥuqūq allah*), namely, (a) prayers (*ṣalāt*), (b) fasting (*ṣawm*), (c) legal alms (*zakāt*), (d) holy war (*jihād*), covering war and peace, the latter including the fiscal and other relations of the Moslem state to its non-Moslem subjects, and (e) pilgrimage to Mecca;
2. human acts which are entirely a matter of private rights (*ḥuqūq 'ibād*);
3. human acts of a mixed nature, namely, the tithe (*'ushr*).

[1] By "practical", the doctors mean three different things: (1) That which relates to practice, as opposed to what is merely academic. In this sense, logic, practical medicine, and the science of tailoring, are all practical, because they all relate to practice, either mental, as in the case of logic, or physical, as in the case of the others. (2) "Practical" in philosophy means the science of things made by man, as distinguished from theoretical which means the science of things whose existence is outside the reach of human power and will. In this sense, logic is theoretical, because its subject-matter, the mental processes, is not a human institution; *fiqh* is practical, because its subject-matter, namely, human acts, is a matter of human will and power. (3) Applied to the arts, "practical" refers to those whose mastery depends on experiment and practice, as contrasted with "theoretical". In this last sense, *fiqh*, syntax, logic, practical medicine are theoretical because their acquisition does not depend on practice; the art of tailoring, however, is practical. In the first sense practical is more general than in the second, for while logic is practical in the first sense, it is not so in the second. Likewise, practical in the second sense is more general than in the third sense, because *fiqh* is practical in the second sense but not in the third, since practice is not necessary for its learning. (For more information on the divisions of science and on the so-called "eight heads" (*al-ru'ūs al-thamāniah*) to which every author must conform, see *Tech. Dict.*, Introduction).

The second of these three classes, namely, the human acts which concern individual rights alone, may be acts of

(1) the living (*aḫyā'*), that is,
  (a) marriage and divorce (*munākaḫāt*),
  (b) civil or commercial transactions (*mu'āmalāt*),
  (c) transgressions (*'uqūbāt*);

(2) the deceased (*amwāt*), that is matters relating to inheritance (*farā'iḏ*).

It is thus seen that *fiqh* and *usūl-al-fiqh* constitute the two branches of the so-called practical sciences which are the counterpart of the dogmatic, the two making up the deduced *sharī'ah* sciences.

The above table also points out the relative position of Mohammedan finance. It will be observed that in the above scheme, *zakāt*, which comprises the taxes paid by the Moslems, is a matter of religious obligation and is differentiated from the taxes paid by the non-Moslems. The latter come under the caption of "holy war." In other words, the taxes paid by the non-Moslems are based on the relation between conqueror and conquered, rather than on that of the state to its citizens, or of God to His worshippers, as in the case of *zakāt*.

CHAPTER II

The First Basis of Fiqh: The Koran

The word **Koran** literally means, reading, recitation. It is technically called the Book, and is **defined** as "that which has been transmitted to us (*i. e.*, the Mohammedans) by way of *mutawātir*, between the two covers of the holy *Muṣḥafs* (*i. e.*, copies of the Koran collected and edited during the califate of 'Uthmān)." [1]

The Koran is the Holy Scripture of the Mohammedans and, according to the doctors, consists of the very words of God as they were revealed through the angel Gabriel [2] to the Prophet Mohammed during his prophetic career, at first at Mecca and later at Medina.[3] The different stages of this career, as might be expected, find their reflection in the Koran. Indeed the **revelations** contained **in the Koran** may be usefully **divided into two classes**—those revealed during the Prophet's stay in Mecca and those revealed after his arrival in Medina.

Before the last event, Mohammed did not intend to teach a new religion but, according to his own account of the matter, merely to bring his people to the worship of the one true God, whose commandments the Hebrew prophets before him had preached to their peoples.[4] Therefore, the

[1] *Tawḍiḥ*, p. 36.

[2] For full details concerning the various views as to the actual way in which Gabriel communicated the Koran to the Prophet, consult *Tech. Dict.*, pp. 1161 *et seq.*

[3] *Cf.* Gazāli, p. 100.

[4] Juynboll, p. 3.

verses revealed in Mecca, especially the oldest of them, all enjoin upon the Meccans belief in the resurrection, the last day of judgment, and the final reward or punishment of human acts in the world to come.

After thirteen years of effort in Mecca, the Prophet had utterly failed and was forced to give up home and kindred and work among the tribes of Medina. This rupture of the Prophet with his native city and kinsmen and his pact at 'Aqabah with outsiders, under the existing Arabian social conditions, had political as well as religious significance. Probably it was the identification of the movement with political motives that was the most potent factor in bringing about the phenomenal success of Islam in Medina during the last ten years of Mohammed's life.

The Mohammedans call the flight of Mohammed from Mecca to Medina *Hijrah* (literally, flight) and have fittingly chosen it as the beginning of their era. The *Hijrah* ends the first unsuccessful period of Islam in Mecca and ushers in the **Medinian period** during which it may be said that Islam knew nothing but success. In this second period, Islam was no longer the purely religious and passive little group which it was in Mecca, but a vigorous religious and political organization which could defend itself and was eager to expand. What is more natural, therefore, than that this great change in the material conditions of Islam and the success, which it began to enjoy in Medina, should react upon the very nature of the movement and be reflected in the verses revealed during this second period? There could not be a more eloquent witness of this transformation than the following quotation from the Arab historian of Mohammed. Ibn Hishām: [1]

Before the pact of allegiance at 'Aqabah, the Prophet was

[1] Ibn Hishām, p. 313.

not permitted to go to war, nor to shed blood; he was commanded [by God] only to call people to God, to be patient under persecution, and to turn away from the ignorant . . . but when the Quraysh [*i. e.*, the Meccans] rebelled against God, . . . denied His Prophet, tormented and exiled those who followed Him, who believed in His unity and His Prophet, and who clung fast to his religion, God permitted His Prophet to fight and to revenge himself for their oppression, and tyranny.

The **revelations** of the second period, therefore, relate principally to questions of war and internal organization, such as spoils, *zakāt*, marriage, inheritance, usury, transgressions, *etc.* The general characteristic of these revelations is that they are casual, for they were revealed as the circumstances required. They were never meant to be, and they are **not, a well-rounded system of law.** They nevertheless form one of the cornerstones on which the elaborate edifice of *fiqh* has been gradually erected.

During the life of Mohammed the Koran was in a scattered form, there being no complete **collection of all the revelations.** As, however, many of the Companions of the Prophet, who knew by heart shorter or longer passages of the Koran, fell dead in battle after the death of the Prophet, it was feared that some of the holy passages might be forever lost.

The first successor of Mohammed in the leadership of Islam, Abu Bakr, charged a young man by the name of Zayd Ibn Thābit, who had formerly served as scribe to the Prophet himself, to make a written collection of all the revealed passages. Out of the existing notes, as they had been inscribed on scraps of paper, palm-leaves, flat bones, stones, *etc.*, and by reference to the memories of reliable persons, Zayd gathered together as many as possible of the scattered revelations. The first collection was probably intended for the personal use of Abu Bakr and received no official character.

A truly **official codification of the Koran** was first made during the califate of 'Uthmān, the third calif. This was undertaken as a result of disputes over the readings of certain verses. The work was again entrusted to the hands of Zayd Ibn Thābit, this time in collaboration with several other persons. When they had completed the work, 'Uthmān ordered the destruction of all previous Koran collections, and had copies of the new and official Koran sent to the different provinces of the Moslem empire. This **collection of 'Uthman** has come down to our own times unchanged and is the **only authentic text**. Concerning its genuineness no doubt can be entertained.[1] Furthermore, it can be accepted as a complete collection, at least as complete as was humanly possible. The Shiites, chiefly a political sect, have always claimed that the verses referring to the special sanctity of 'Ali, the fourth calif, and his family were intentionally left out. This accusation has no foundation in fact. For, if such had been the case, the contemporaries of Mohammed who were still alive would have seen to it that those verses were included or have complained about their omission; but even the enemies of 'Uthmān accepted his edition of the Koran as absolutely authoritative, thus affording ample proof of its genuineness.

The Koran text is divided into 114 chapters of unequal length, arranged according to their length, the longest coming first. A chronological arrangement would result in very much the opposite order. Each chapter is called a *sūrah*.[2] Most of the *sūrahs* pertain to more than one subject. Each *sūrah* consists of a certain number of verses

[1] Juynboll, p. 9.

[2] Juynboll, p. 9. A word of Hebrew origin meaning number, also a number of written lines.

called *āyah* (literally, sign, miracle). It is claimed that every *āyah* is a sign of wonder.

The revelations contained in the Koran were not all revealed on one occasion, but at long intervals and in response to special needs. Mohammed by no means resorted to Divine revelation in order to decide every case that came up for solution. Tradition tells us that the Prophet, especially in Mecca, only in extremely rare cases and upon the reiterated requests of his most influential followers made up his mind to ask God for a revelation. The case of 'Omar is cited who had to apply several times before obtaining a revelation.[1] The Koran consequently is fragmentary and often mystical in its sense, with frequent allusions to contemporary events and persons, and can only be understood fully on the basis of a complete knowledge of the circumstances which surrounded its revelation. This fact explains the origin of *'ilm al-tafsīr*, *i. e.*, the science of the **interpretation of the Koran**, and the reason for the many voluminous commentaries that were written upon it.

The **commentaries** on the Koran form an important part of Mohammedan literature. They comment on the holy text from every point of view, grammatical, literary, religious, legal, *etc.* Furthermore, they give the history that attaches to each verse and go more or less fully into the legal prescriptions that follow from it. There are also commentaries compiled with one single purpose, *e. g.*, from the grammatical or the literary viewpoint alone. The more favored are those dealing in a compact form with all of these viewpoints. The one written by al-Bayḏāwi is probably the most serviceable of all.

[1] Hurgronje, "Le droit musulman", pp. 5-6.

CHAPTER III

THE SECOND BASIS OF FIQH: THE SUNNAH

SECTION I

General Considerations

FROM the very beginning, the conduct of the Prophet served as a standard as much as the Koran itself. In fact, we have seen that the Koran was revealed to the Prophet in the course of years, and that the Prophet, rather than decide every case by applying to God for a revelation, would solve many of them by his own proper judgment. Such judgments were not respected the less on this account.

Mohammed was not only the transmitter of the Koran but he also interpreted and completed it. The only difference between the ordinary expressions of the Prophet and his revelations consists in the fact that, whereas the former are divine in content alone, the latter are divine in form also. According to the *Mīzān* [1] the ground for this view is afforded by the Koran itself in the verse: "and we have revealed to you the exhortation (*i. e.*, the Koran) in order that you may explain to men what has been revealed to them." The Prophetic conduct then is as important a source of *fiqh* as the Koran itself, and indeed, when later that the Koran in point of time, supersedes it.

The word sunnah literally means way, custom, habit of life. Technically [2] it is defined by the canonists as utter-

[1] P. 45.

[2] *Sunnah* has also another techincal meaning in reference to religious duties, namely, that which is recommended although not obligatory. See, chapter on Classification of the *Sharī'ah* Values.

ances of the Prophet (other than the Koran) known as *ḥadīths*,[1] or his personal acts and acts or sayings of others tacitly approved by him.[2]

A hadith is to be carefully distinguished from a sunnah, although some jurists have claimed that they are identical. *Sunnah* is the custom or *mores*, which was prevalent in the Arabian community, with regard to a religious, social, or legal matter. After the advent of Mohammedanism the old customs of the Arabs were partly modified by the conduct of the Prophet, and to a lesser degree, of his companions. This change, however, only affected the content, for the *sunnah* still continued as a rule of conduct. A *ḥadīth*, on the other hand, is a statement of the Prophet. A *sunnah* may be embodied in a *ḥadīth*, but is not itself a *ḥadīth*. Thus Aḥmad Ibn Hanbal says concerning a *ḥadīth*: "*fi hadha 'l-ḥadīth khams sunan*," *i. e.*, "in this *ḥadīth* there are five *sunnahs*." It is also possible for a *ḥadīth* to contradict the *sunnah*.[3]

Opposed to the concept of *sunnah* is that of **bid'ah**, *i. e.*, innovation, departure from the established *sunnah*. Just as conformity to the *sunnah* is commendable, so innovation is to be condemned. The Prophet has said: "the worst of things are the newly made [*i. e.*, contrary to the *sunnah*], for such things are innovations, and every innovation is a deviation from the right way, and every deviation leads into the Fire."

Such a theory of social control, although expedient from the standpoint of religious conservatism, naturally limits the possibility of social readjustment. Later, the canonists were

[1] The word *ḥadīth*, literally means saying and may apply to a saying of any person, but usually it means a saying of the Prophet unless otherwise indicated.

[2] *Tawḍiḥ*, p. 359.

[3] Goldziher, *M. Studien*, vol. ii, p. 11; *cf. Tawḍiḥ*, p. 362.

compelled to modify it by the fiction that all **innovations** are not blameworthy and that some **may be praiseworthy**. At an early date Mālik said about an innovation, "*ni'mat al-bid'ah hadha*" *i. e.*, "this innovation is good." [1]

The theory that the *sunnah* is a supplement to the Koran and even supersedes it in case of contradiction when later in time, gave the **sunnah** a **predominant** position as a source of law. Such a theory amounted to no less than a shifting of the center of gravity from the Koran to the *sunnah*. For it meant that if there were unintelligible or contradictory passages in the Koran, or if the *sunnah* contradicted the Koran, the decision rested with the *sunnah*.

These circumstances naturally served as so many inducements to the unconscientious and the ambitious to invent and circulate false traditions in order to support their political or other schemes. As time went on and the Companions of the Prophet began one by one to pass away, it became relatively easier to put **false traditions in circulation**, and the number soon became very large. Some were even so unscrupulous as to ascribe to the Prophet statements referring to litigations that had arisen after his death. A certain Ibn Abu 'Awga confessed before his execution in 155 H. that he had put in circulation 4000 false *ḥadīths* [2] In this matter of falsifications the *ḥadīth*-teachers of Kūfah became especially notorious.

This zeal for circulating false *ḥadīths*, however, is to be contrasted with the **great caution which characterized the Companions** of the Prophet and other pious Moslems.[3] The biographies of Ibn Sa'd offer us many a remarkable example of this kind. *E. g.*, people who had long been

[1] Goldziher, *M. Studien*, vol. ii, p. 26.

[2] Kremer, p. 481.

[3] Goldziher, "Kämpfe", p. 860.

in the company of 'Abdāllah Ibn Mas'ūd relate that they scarcely ever heard him report a *ḥadīth,* but when he did so, his forehead perspired from anxiety, while his cane shook in his hand, and even his dress betrayed the trembling of his body. Furthermore, he qualified his statements with all sorts of limitations. This was also true of the other Companions. They were afraid that in repeating the words of the Prophet they might unwittingly add to or subtract from them.

This state of mind explains why **in the beginning the hadiths** were **not written** down. For, if distortion of a *ḥadīth* in saying it was so dreadful, how much more so in writing it. Therefore a *ḥadīth* was not considered canonical unless it was kept in memory and orally handed on.[1] This does not mean that writing was not used at all. From the very first, writing was resorted to, but only as an aid to the memory, and when a *ḥadīth* was written, it was destroyed as soon as committed to memory. Nevertheless the writing down of *ḥadīths* became general early in the first century of the *Hijrah.*

The study and preservation of the *ḥadīths* had a great fascination for the early Moslems, who often traveled long distances to hear *ḥadīths* from a renowned teacher. The instruction and transmission of the *ḥadīths* in time developed into a special discipline called *'ilm al-ḥadīth, i. e.,* **science of the hadith.** Its rules[2] were more or less exacting and

[1] Goldziher, *ibid.,* p. 862; *cf. M. Studien,* vol. ii, p. 196; Juynboll, p. 15; Kremér, p. 475.

[2] The rules mentioned in the following sections represent the views of the authorities on *uṣūl-al-fiqh* (*uṣūliyyūn*) and do not always coincide with those of the *ḥadīth*-teachers (*muḥaddithūn*) inasmuch as the former are interested in the *ḥadīths* primarily as a source of law. When there is a variance between them, the Shafiite authorities generally are likely to side with the *ḥadīth*-teachers and the Hanifites to hold the opposite view. This is because the Hanifites emphasized the

formed some sort of a critical method to check and eliminate the false *ḥadīths*.

There are six collections of *ḥadīths* in the making of which it was attempted to be critical and to include only reliable (*ṣaḥīḥ*) *ḥadīths*. They were all compiled in the third century of the *Hijrah* and are considered standard works. They are denominated briefly as " the six books " (*al-kutub al-sittah*) or **the six sahihs**, *i. e.*, the six reliable collections. Two of them,[1] namely that by al-Bukhāri († 256/870) and the one by Muslim († 261/875) are especially esteemed. The reason for this lies in the fact that by the time they were compiled some of the most bitterly fought questions had been almost settled and the structure of orthodoxy fairly established. These two collections therefore represented in a way the current views and found ready and general acceptance. As in the case of the Koran, voluminous commentaries were written on the *sunnah*, as well. Among the most well-known is the commentary of al-Qasṭallāni on the *ṣaḥīḥ* of al-Bukhāri.

SECTION II

The Different Kinds of Sunnah with Respect to Transmission

From the viewpoint of " continuity " (*ittiṣāl*), *i. e.*, the completeness of the chain of transmission from the last trans-

speculative elements in the law, whereas the Shafiites laid emphasis on the *ḥadīths*. For full information concerning the science of *ḥadīths* see the Introductions in the commentaries of al-Qasṭallāni and al-Nawawi on al-Bukhāri and Muslim respectively. The latter is on the margin of the former. (Qasṭallāni, pp. 2-46 and 2-60.)

[1] The other four collections are those made by Ibn Mājah (+ 273/886), Abu Dāwūd (+ 275/888), al-Tirmidhi (+ 279/892), and al-Nasā'i (+ 303/915). (Juynboll, fn. 2, p. 20; *cf.* Goldziher, *M. Studien*, vol. ii, pp. 254 *et seq.*).

mitter all the way back to the Prophet,[1] the canonists have distinguished four kinds of *sunnah*,[2] the first three being "continuous" and the fourth "discontinuous."

The "continuous" (*muttaṣil*) report (of the *sunnah*) includes:

(1) **The Mutawatir.** It is the report of a people numerically indefinite (*la yuḥṣa 'adaduhum*)[3] whose agreement upon a lie is inconceivable, in view of their large number, reliability (*'adālah*), and diversity of residence.[4] According to one view, the name *mutawātir* applies only to the report which inspires confidence by virtue of the large number of its reporters. According to this view a report would not be called *mutawātir* if its content is believed on other grounds,

[1] *Tech. Dict.*, p. 1507.

[2] By *sunnah* here is meant only the sayings of the Prophet. The doings of the Prophet are dealt with separately (*Kashf*, p. 679), but the principles here mentioned must also apply to them, because the only difference between the two would be, that in one case we have the sayings of the Prophet, and in the other, we have the sayings of the persons who witnessed the doings of the Prophet. The doctors, in speaking of the different kinds of *sunnah*, speak of them advisedly as divisions of the report (*khabar*) in order to include the reports of both the sayings and the doings of the Prophet. (*Cf. Tawḍiḥ*, p. 358; *Talwiḥ*, p. 359.)

[3] The Arabic word *aḥṣa* means, to count, reach the last number, collect into an aggregate by numbering, comprehend (see Lane, under *ḥaṣa*). According to the *Talwiḥ* (p. 359) the expression *la yuḥṣa* (meaning, cannot be collected into an aggregate by numbering) used in the above definition means, it cannot be made a matter of record (*la yad-khul takht al-ḍabṭ*), and in this sense it is opposed to *qawm maḥṣūr*, meaning, a body of people whose number can be made a matter of record, for example, people congregated within four walls. The *Talwiḥ* further states that no definite number is required for the *mutawātir* (*cf. Kashf*, p. 681). In other words, the expression *la yuḥṣa* must not be taken to mean, too many to be counted.

[4] *Tawḍiḥ*, p. 358; Pazdawi, p. 681; Shawkāni, p. 44; *Minhāj*, vol. ii, pp. 77 *et seq.*; *Tech. Dict.*, pp. 1471-2.

e. g., when the report states a matter of axiomatic knowledge (*ḏarūrah*) or when it is believed on grounds of reason.[1]

Various **conditions** must be met before a report may be classed as *mutawātir*. Only three of these are considered necessary (*ṣaḥīḥ*) and are as follows: [2]

(a) The number of the reporters must be large enough to preclude ordinarily (*'ādah*) an agreement among them to spread a false report.[3] Some attempted to fix a minimum varying from as low as 4 up into the hundreds. According to one view, the number required varies with the character of the reporters, as well as the content of the report; the number therefore need not be large, since even the report of a single person, such as a prophet, may engender positive knowledge; moreover, the report of a religious leader may be worth more than that of 10,000 people, *e. g.*, if the latter pretended to report concerning God. It is exactly on this account, the upholders of this view go on to say, that the *mutawātir* has been defined by some doctors (*muḥaqqiqūn*) as the report of those who cannot ordinarily be lying, whether one or more. This view is confirmed by what is related of al-Pazdawi, namely, that he, at one time, considered as *mutawātirs* reports originally transmitted by single Companions, but later spread and reported by many.[4] According to the *Kashf*[5] "the number is not confined to any definite figure, but the mere fact that a number inspires knowledge is a sufficient test of its adequacy . . . the proof that the number is not confined to any one figure is that we consider" a report as *mutawātir* without actually determin-

[1] Shawkāni, p. 44.

[2] *Tech. Dict., loc. cit.*

[3] *Cf. Kashf*, p. 681.

[4] Pazdawi's later opinion is the one according to which the *mutawātir* has been first defined.

[5] P. 681.

ing a definite number, "for if we should impose upon ourselves the knowledge of a number, we would not be ordinarily able to find a way" of ascertaining the true number, since it is constantly changing and its determination is humanly impossible.

(b) The reporters must base their reports on sense perception. If, therefore, a great congregation of people should report that the universe has been created, for example, their report would not constitute a *mutawātir*.

(c) The above conditions must have been met from the origin of the report to the very end.

The conditions which are not considered necessary (*fāsid*) are: that the reporters should be Moslems and just; that they should live in the same locality and belong to the same race and religion; or as the Shiites claim, that they should include among themselves the "infallible" (*al-ma'ṣūm*);[1] or finally, as the Jews claimed, that they should be people deprived of power (*ahl al-dhillah*), as these could not conceivably agree upon a lie through fear of the consequences.

How are we to tell that the conditions have been met? Those who believe that the *mutawātir* does not engender axiomatic (*ḍarūri*) knowledge, hold that a report may not be claimed as a *mutawātir* except after ascertaining that the conditions have been actually met. On the other hand, those who believe that the *mutawātir* engenders axiomatic knowledge, hold that the mere fact that a report has inspired conviction is normally a proof that the conditions have been met.[2] According to the *Kashf*[3] the sufficiency

[1] For example, the sect of Hishām Ibn al-Hakam believe that the *imāms* or leaders of the Moslem community are infallible, in the sense that they cannot commit a mistake or sin. (Bagdādi, p. 50.)

[2] *Tech. Dict., loc. cit.*

[3] *Loc. cit.*

of the number of the transmitters is inferred, if their report has inspired knowledge, for this indicates that the number was complete before God.

What is the Value (*ḫukm*) of the mutawatir? The majority agree that the *mutawātir* engenders positive knowledge (*yaqīn*) and that the person who denies this is a profligate (*safīh*). Some said that the *mutawātir* is open to doubt inasmuch as the report of each transmitter by itself is liable to be false, but this is evidently nonsense and heresy, since it would cast doubt upon the very existence of the prophets and their miracles which we at present can learn about only through reports.[1] There is difference of opinion as to whether the knowledge engendered by the *mutawātir* is axiomatic (*ḏarūri*) or merely inferential (*istidlāli*, or *naḏari*). According to al-Taftāzāni,[2] axiomatic knowledge is that which occurs in the mind through intuition and not as a result of reflective thought (*naḏar*). Inferential is its opposite.[3]

Those who claim that the *mutawātir* creates axiomatic knowledge, support their view by the argument that, if it were inferential, it would not engender knowledge in the mind of children and the weak-minded, since the latter do not possess the ability to make inferences.[4] Their opponents reply that the knowledge of the truth of a report, among others, implies a knowledge of the normal impossibility of

[1] *Kashf*, p. 683.

[2] *Tech. Dict.*, p. 882.

[3] **Axiomatic** has also a more general meaning, *i. e.*, the knowledge which occurs in the mind independently of human will, such as a person's knowledge of his pain and pleasure. In this sense, axiomatic is opposed to "acquisitional" (*iktisābi*) which applies to the knowledge that requires some initiative on the part of the knower, as, for example, in the case of perceptual or intellectual knowledge.

[4] *Minhāj*, vol. ii, p. 80.

an agreement upon a lie among the transmitters of that report, as well as a knowledge of the absence of incentives for such an agreement; but these are nothing but cases of inference; hence the knowledge engendered by the *mutawātir* is inferential. The first side answers that such preliminary notions as are necessary are only incidental, and occur in the mind readily without any special thought or effort.

When the reports of several transmitters answer the description of *mutawātir* but differ from one another, only their common meaning is considered *mutawātir*.[1]

Examples of *mutawātir* are the passages in the Koran, and the *sunnah* concerning the number of prostrations, the rates of *zakāt, etc.*

(2) **The Mash-hur** (literally, widespread). This is a report originally supported by a few individuals (*āḥād*),[2] but later spread and transmitted by a numerically indefinite people whose agreement upon a lie is inconceivable, these people being the generations succeeding to the Companions. In other words, it is necessary that the diffusion of the report should have taken place in the first or second generation after Mohammed, not later. According to the orthodox view, the *mash-hūr* stands higher than the "individual;" and its non-acceptance entails error, but not heresy.[3] The *mash-hūr* engenders conviction but not positive knowledge (*yaqīn*).

(3) The "**individual**" report (*khabar al-wāḥid*). This is the report transmitted by one or two or even more, pro-

[1] *Minhāj*, vol. ii, p. 89.

[2] Their number may be one or more provided it falls short of that required for the *mutawātir*. Some call the *mash-hūr mustafīḍ*, if there were at least three individuals.

[3] Pazdawi, p. 688.

vided their number falls short of that required for the *mutawātir*. The value (*ḫukm*) of this report is, that though it does not establish positive knowledge, it creates obligation for conduct. This is the Hanifite view. Some claimed that it does not create obligation for conduct since it does not engender knowledge, as conduct may be based on knowledge alone. Conversely, some *ḥadīth*-folk expressed the view that the " individual " report engenders knowledge since it creates obligation for conduct. The Hanifites support their view by evidences from the Koran, the *ijmā'* and reason.

The " **discontinuous** " report (*al-khabar al-munqaṭi'*).[1] This is the report in whose continuity of transmission, unlike that of the former three reports, there is a break.

" Discontinuity " may be either formal (*ẓāhir*) or real (*bāṭin*).[2]

(a) " **Formal discontinuity**." This occurs when the continuity of transmission is not complete all the way back to the Prophet, as in the case of an unsupported report (*mursal*),[3] that is, when there is failure to mention the chain of transmitters, as, for example, when some one says, " The Prophet said so and so," without supporting (*isnād*) his statement by saying " So and so related to us, on the authority of so and so, on the authority of the Prophet." The unsupported reports (*mursal*) of the Companions are accepted unanimously, since they are reputed to be based on direct hearing (*simā'*) from the Prophet himself. The un-

[1] *Tawḍīḥ*, p. 367; Pazdawi, p. 722.

[2] *Tawḍīḥ*, p. 367.

[3] According to the usage of the *ḥadīth*-teachers, *mursal* means a report, none of the transmitters of which has been mentioned; *musnad* (supported) is used for the opposite. On the other hand, the report is called *munqaṭi'*, if only one transmitter is omitted, and *mu'ḍal*, if more.

supported reports of the second and third generations are not accepted by al-Shāfi'i, except when their "continuity" is established in some other way. However, such reports are considered by the Hanifites and by Mālik to be superior to supported reports (*musnad*). They are thought to be superior because it is customary that the just man (*'adl*), when he is convinced about the truth of a report and its support, omits the support and links it directly to the Prophet, saying "The Prophet said;" but when he is not convinced about it, he refers it to the person from whom he heard it.[1] Thus, a certain Hasan is reported to have said:[2] "Whenever four of the Companions agreed before me on a *ḥadīth*, I used to ascribe it directly to the Prophet." Similar statements were made by others.

(b) "**Real Discontinuity**." This happens when the report contradicts an evidence stronger than itself, such as, for example, the Koran or the *mutawātir*, or when there is a defect in the transmitter (*nāqil*).

Contradiction, the first kind of "real discontinuity," may occur in the following four ways: (1) when the report contradicts the Koran; (2) when it contradicts the "established *sunnah*" that is the *sunnah* based on the *mutawātir* and the *mash-hūr*; (3) when an "individual" report has not reached the degree of *mash-hūr*[3] in spite of the fact that there is a general need for such a report; (4) when it has been denounced by the Companions.

When it contradicts the Koran, the report is overruled in every case. There is invoked for justification of this overruling the following *ḥadīth*: "After my death the *ḥadīths* will multiply; when therefore a *ḥadīth* is related to

[1] Pazdawi, p. 724.

[2] *Kashf, ibid.*

[3] *Taqrīr*, vol. ii, pp. 295-7; *Talwīḥ*, p. 371.

you, compare it with the Book of God and when it agrees with it, accept it; but if it contradicts it, reject it." The above view is the Hanifite one. The Shafiites have thought differently. When the report contradicts the "established *sunnah*," again it is overruled.[1]

Similarly following the opinion of al-Karkhi,[2] an "individual" report is brushed aside when it has failed to reach the degree of the *mash-hūr*, or to receive recognition by widespread use,—all this notwithstanding the fact that there is a general need for the report, in that it relates to a matter of frequent occurrence. For example, the *ḥadīth*, according to which the first verse of the opening chapter of the Koran must be read aloud in prayer, is not considered obligatory. The argument is that if the *ḥadīth* were true, it would not have failed to attain wide circulation or general use, considering that it concerns a matter of everyday occurrence like prayer. The mere fact that it remained an "individual" report is a presumption of its unreliability. However, the majority of writers on *uṣūl-al-fiqh*, as well as al-Shāfii and all the *ḥadīth*-folk hold that such "individuals" are valid, if they otherwise conform to the rules.[3]

Finally, denunciation of the "individual" report by the Companions is sufficient to cause its rejection.

The second kind of "real discontinuity" occurs when

[1] It must be remembered here that when we speak of contradiction between a report and the Koran, or between a report and the *sunnah*, we mean specifically the "individual" report only, not the *mutawātir* or the *mash-hūr*. (*Cf.* chapter on Abrogation and Conflict of the Evidences; also Pazdwai, p. 728.

[2] *Kashf*, p. 736.

[3] Riad Ghali, in his dissertation on the *sunnah* (pp. 191-3) gives a quite different version on this point. Unless it is due to the sources he used, though this is unlikely, it must be the result of his misunderstanding of the Arabic expression *fi 'l balwa al-'āmm* used by the doctors in this connection.

there is a **short-coming in** the **person of** the **transmitter**, namely: (1) when he is "unknown" (*mastūr*), *i. e.*, when it is not known whether he is just or impious, although the first three generations are an exception to this rule; (2) when he is impious (*fāsiq*); (3) when he has not attained the age of, or is not endowed with, complete understanding, as in the case of minors, the weak-minded (*ma'tūh*), the careless (*muggaffal*), and heretics (*sāhib al hawa*).[1]

SECTION III

Qualifications Regarding the Transmitter as Such [2]

The transmitter (*al-rāwi*) is of two kinds, the "well-known" (*al-ma'rūf*) and the "unknown" (*al-majhūl*). The "well-known" is one known to have transmitted many *hadīths*, whereas the "unknown" is one who is not known to have transmitted more than one or two *hadīths*.

(1) **The "well-known" transmitter.** He is of two kinds: the one who is also a *faqīh*, besides being a transmitter, and the other who is only a transmitter.

(a) The well-known transmitters who are also *faqīhs*. As such are considered the first four Califs, 'Abdāllah Ibn Mas'ūd, 'Abdāllah Ibn 'Abbās, Ibn 'Omar, Zayd, Mu'ādh, Abu Mūsa al-Ash'ari, 'Aīshah, and others. The *hadīths* reported by these are accepted whether or not in accordance with *qiyās*.

(b) The "well-known" transmitters who are not *faqīhs*. These are those who like Abu Hurayrah are reputed for their justice and careful record-taking. The *hadīths* reported by these are accepted if in accordance with *qiyās*. In the contrary case they are abandoned, because these transmitters, not being *faqīhs*, may have taken a wrong record.

[1] *Tawdīh*, p. 372.

[2] *Tawdīh*, p. 362; Pazdawi, pp. 758 *et seq.*

If however, their reports are in accordance with one *qiyās* and at variance with another, they are not abandoned.

(2) **The "unknown" transmitter.**

(a) If the *salaf* [1] have transmitted a *ḥadīth* on the authority of an "unknown" transmitter and testified to the truth of this *ḥadīth*, the *ḥadīth* is then considered like those of the non-*faqīh* "well-known" transmitters.

(b) If the *salaf* have desisted from denouncing the *ḥadīth* after its communication to them, it is like the *ḥadīths* of the "well-known" transmitters, for silence when speech is necessary is equivalent to assent.

(c) If some have accepted and others denounced it, and at the same time trustworthy people have transmitted it on his authority, it is accepted, if in accordance with *qiyās*; though if not in accordance it is rejected.

(d) If his *ḥadīth* has been rejected by all the *salaf* (*mustankar*), it is abandoned.

(e) If it is not known whether the *salaf* have accepted or rejected it (*mustatir*), the *qiyās* overrules it, and conduct in conformity with it is not obligatory, but only permissible (*jā'iz*).

SECTION IV

Conditions of Retention and Transmission [2]

RETENTION. (1) The **transmitter must possess** complete **understanding** obtained only on coming of age.

(2) The **conditions of retention** (*ḍabṭ*) **must be fulfilled.** These conditions are the proper hearing of a report from beginning to end, as well as the thorough understanding of

[1] **Salaf** means literally the predecessors, and technically (see *Tech. Dict.*) those of the predecessors who are followed as authority, *e. g.*, the Companions are *salaf* for Abu Hanīfah.

[2] *Tawḍīḥ*, p. 376; Pazdawi, p. 758.

its meaning, in addition to its retention until it is passed on (*adā'*) to others. The perfection of retention is reached, when the retention of the form and the literal meaning of the report is coupled with a thorough understanding of its legal meaning as well. The hearing (*simā'*) is considered proper when the *ḥadīth*-transmitter reads the *ḥadīth* in the hearing of the listener and the latter repeats it and then says: "Is it as I have repeated it?" the teacher replying, "Yes." Writing or delegation (*risālah*) is deemed equivalent to actual addressing.

The retention may be effected by committing the *ḥadīth* or report to the memory, or to a record. In the beginning, the former was regarded as the ideal way (*'azīmah*); but later the second method came to supplant it.

TRANSMISSION. Some *ḥadīth*-teachers will not allow transmission of the sense alone, but the majority of the doctors hold the opposite view. Of course, they all agree that literal transmission is to be preferred. The transmission of the sense of the Koran is allowed only to the *mujtahid*.

In the **transmission of the sense** the following points must be borne in mind:

(a) If the sense is clear (*ẓāhir*) the transmission is allowed to the person who knows the language.

(b) If the sense is clear but the word is liable to have another meaning as well, as in the case of a universal (*'āmm*) term liable to restriction (*takhṣīṣ*), or when there is the probability of a metaphorical meaning, then the transmission is allowed to the *mujtahid* alone.

(c) When a term may have several literal meanings (*mushtarak*), or its meaning is hard to understand, or mystical, only the literal transmission is allowed.

(3) The **transmitter must possess justice** (*'adālah*), that is, he must refrain from the commission of capital sins

(*kabīrah*) and must not persist in the commission of venial sins (*ṣagīrah*).

(4) The transmitter **must be a Moslem.** This requirement is because the fanaticism of a heretic might be apt to prejudice Islam, and not as we might suppose because all other religions do not uniformly prohibit lying.

SECTION V

The Impeachment of Hadīths

The impeachment (*ṭa'n*) of a *ḥadīth* may originate with the transmitter himself or elsewhere.

(1) When the **impeachment originates with the transmitter** himself, it may be express or implicit. It is **express,** when the person claimed to be the transmitter of a *ḥadīth* angrily repudiates the fact of his transmission, calling the person who claimed it a liar, or when he contents himself with a mere denial of his transmission. In the first case, the *ḥadīth* is considered by the majority as void, but opinion is divided on the second case.[1]

It is **implicit** when; (a) the transmitter acts or counsels in opposition to his own *ḥadīth*. In such case the *ḥadīth* is null, unless it be that he had acted thus before transmitting the *ḥadīth*, or that the date of his transmission is not known; (b) he acts according to some only of the possible meanings of the *ḥadīth*. This amounts to the impeachment of its other meanings. (c) He neither acts in accordance with his *ḥadīth*, nor contrary to it. It is still a case of impeachment, because to refrain from doing what is commanded is equivalent to opposition to it.[2]

(2) When the **impeachment originates elsewhere**: (a)

[1] Pazdawi, pp. 779 *et seq.*; *cf.* Ghali, pp. 195 *et seq.*

[2] Ghali, p. 205.

it comes **from the Companions.** In such case, the *ḥadīth* is void, if in all probability it was known to them, but it remains valid, if the probability is that it was unknown to them, *e. g.*, if the *ḥadīth* referred to a chance occurrence; (b) it comes **from the hadith-teachers.**[1]

The impeachment of the *ḥadīth*-teachers may be of two kinds. It may be indefinite,[2] and then it is not taken into consideration. Or it may be based on a legally admissible ground, and then the *ḥadīth* is ruled out. It is necessary, however, in this last case, that the accuser be not tainted with party spirit and enmity, otherwise his accusation is ignored. According to al-Pazdawi,[3] the accusations of the heretics against the Sunnites, and of the Shafiites against some of the early Hanifites, have been set aside for this last reason. According to the same author, there are about 30 to 40 legitimate ways of impeachment.[4]

Finally, when the *ḥadīth* is **impeached by some** and **accepted by others,** the *ḥadīth* is not considered void, if the number of its defenders is at least equal to that of its denouncers, unless it be that the defenders are not acquainted with the facts.[5]

SECTION VI

Are the Rules Concerning the Sunnah an Adequate Guarantee of Its Reliability

It must be remarked at the beginning that the **preceding rules** are **ultimately intended for religious purposes**, and

[1] Pazdawi, p. 786; *cf.* Ghali, p. 207.

[2] For example, the accuser says, "This *ḥadīth* is abandoned, or is not authentic, or its transmitter is not just," *etc.*, without explaining the grounds on which he bases his impeachment.

[3] P. 795.

[4] *Cf. Tawḍiḥ*, pp. 378 *et seq.*; *Taqrīr*, vol. ii, p. 258.

[5] Ghali, p. 213.

therefore they are subject to the limitations of all religious reasoning, no matter how scientific it may appear. For instance, the rules in question **have** almost **nothing to say concerning the subject-matter** of the *ḥadīths*. Thus a *ḥadīth* which claims the occurrence of things existing only in the wildest imagination would be accepted as genuine, if all the mechanical rules concerning its transmission were conformed to, since no higher criticism would be exercised as regards its content. It follows that a considerable material of miraculous nature could easily find its way into the *sunnah*. It further follows that *ḥadīths* invented with the object of supporting political or other interests could be readily incorporated in the *sunnah*, if only they were put in circulation by prominent and influential persons, such as the Companions.

Let us briefly inquire how far the rules mentioned in the preceding sections would serve to check an accidental or even an intentional falsification of the *sunnah*. First let us examine the *mutawātir* and the *mash-hūr*.

By definition it would seem as if the *mutawātir* were absolutely above doubt. Even a perfunctory examination into the conditions deemed necessary by the doctors will show that this is not so. Theoretically speaking, the **mutawatir need not necessarily be superior to** the **mash-hur**, or conceivably, even to the " individual." This may, at first blush, seem to be a preposterous assertion, but it will not be hard to prove. According to definition, the only difference between the *mutawātir* and the *mash-hūr* is that the *mutawātir* attained wide circulation from the time of the Companions, whereas the *mash-hūr* became widespread only in the next two generations. In other words, during the lifetime of the Companions the *mutawātir* supposedly had a wide circulation which the *mash-hūr* lacked. But the entire issue depends upon what the doctors mean by a wide circulation (*tawâtur*), for if it could be shown that a *mutawâtir* may have been transmitted by as few transmitters as a given *mash-hûr*, the superiority of the *mutawâtir* to the *mash-hûr* as regards the two given reports would forthwith become imaginary. We have, in fact seen, that the doctors have been unanimous in declaring that the number of the transmitters of a *mutawâtir* need not be a fixed number. They do not commit themselves to a minimum even as low as 4. One report, as noted above, goes so far as to ascribe to al-Pazdawi the view that the report of a single Companion might spread and become a *mutawâtir*. We need not, however, make use of this extreme position. According to the orthodox definition, a report transmitted originally, *e. g.*, by 10 or more, may be no more than a *mash-hûr*, or if it did not later attain great diffusion, merely an "individual," whereas one transmitted by fewer than 10 may be a *mutawâtir*. It is not then, so much the number of the reporters, at any rate, the original reporters, that decides whether a report shall be considered a *mutawâtir*, but rather it is the fact that a report appeals as genuine. If a report is accepted, that very fact indicates that the number was sufficiently large. Al-Bukhâri, in the *Kashf*, plainly implies that the *mutawâtirs* were not so classed, because after a special inquiry the numbers of their reporters were found to be sufficient, but because in the first place they had appealed as genuine and received recognition. His justification for it is that it is impossible actually to determine the number because it is constantly growing. Besides, he finds it unnecessary, for he assumes that God would not cause a report to call forth conviction, had the number of its reporters been insufficient.

Clearly then a report classed as *mutawâtir* might have been originally transmitted by the same number or even possibly a smaller number of transmitters, than a *mash-hûr* or even an "individual." The fact is that, the various reports transmitted from the Prophet have not been accorded hierarchical precedence, as statements of fact, on the basis of a previous inquiry into the circumstances which surrounded their transmission. On the contrary, this precedence first appeared as a matter of usage, and only later after some of the reports had already attained great diffusion, has an attempt been made by the doctors to differentiate them into classes. Viewed in this light, the difference between the *mutawātir* and the *mash-hūr* reduces itself to one of wide circulation, not so much during the earliest stage of transmission by the Companions, but chiefly during later stages. The reports which referred to matters of common occurrence or general interest, or accorded with the current views and practices, at once spread and became common knowledge, whereas other reports less favorably circumstanced, did not spread so rapidly, or even at all. Of course, the rapid diffusion of a report, in itself, constitutes a considerable guarantee that the report is true, but as already hinted, the diffusion and favorable reception of a report might have been due to the fact that the report fitted in with the current tendencies and practices. A *mutawātir* of this last type evidently would not be any more reliable, as a statement of fact, than a report which being less fortunate became only a *mash-hūr*, since the original transmitters of both reports might have been as numerous or as trustworthy.

It is therefore easy to understand the psychology of the doctors who, on the one hand, imply that the number must be large, and on the other hand, carefully avoid committing themselves to any sort of a minimum. They were indeed laboring under difficulties. They could not ignore the number of reporters and the matter of diffusion, for when they made their classifications the main distinction among the different reports was the varying extent of their respective diffusions. But they could not also ignore the fact that some *mutawātirs* might have been originally transmitted by no more transmitters than others, which they had classed only as *mash-hūrs*. Hence they only imply the matter of diffusion, and as regards the actual definition of the extent of that diffusion, in other words, the number of the transmitters, they take refuge in indetermination by using the ingenious expression *la yuḫṣa*.[1] Thanks to this expression they could always claim that the number might have been larger than any given number, and in fact, as we saw, they did not concern themselves with its actual determination. This expression appears to have caused the doctors some inconvenience, also, as would seem to have been the case from the following quotation from the *Kashf*.[2] "The majority held the view that numerical indefiniteness is not a necessary condition, for if the pilgrims or the congregation of a mosque should report an event which kept them from the pilgrimage or the prayer, their reports would still produce knowledge, although they may be definite in number." If one is to believe the following quotation from the same work, even the spiritual fathers of this as well as of certain other expressions, providing for the Islam, justice, *etc.*, of the transmitters, did not seriously mean them, but rather used them as a means to silence their opponents: "The *shaykh* (*i. e.*, al-Pazdawi) adverted to these meanings (*i. e.*, the provisions concerning the indefiniteness of number, *etc.*) because they are best fitted to remove all doubt and to refute adversaries, not because they are real conditions . . ."

As regards the "individual," this too, like the *mash-hūr*, theoretically speaking, may have been transmitted by as

[1] *Cf. supra*, under *Mutawātir*.

[2] P. 681.

many original transmitters as the ***mutawātir***, the only difference in that case being their varying diffusion in later times. But this is true only in theory. Doubtless in practice, the "individual," which constitutes by far the greatest portion of the ***sunnah***, has been, generally speaking, transmitted by one or few transmitters. But the "individual" is the report which, in distinction from the two previous, is considered by the doctors, as a report equally liable to be true or false, according as its reporters are just or impious. It is therefore only to the individual that the rules set forth in the previous sections concerning "discontinuity," transmission, transmitters and impeachment, apply.

Are the rules concerning the "individual" sufficient to check falsification? The answer can hardly be in the affirmative, since they almost entirely ignore the content and are mainly concerned with the "continuity" of transmission all the way back to the Prophet. A *ḥadīth* is declared reliable if its chain of transmission is unbroken. But even this simple rule is not always adhered to. Thus according to the Hanifites and to Mālik, the *ḥadīths* transmitted by the first three generations may have a broken or no chain of transmission.[1] This view is justified on the ground that the first three generations were just. Al-Shāfi'i takes exception to this view as regards the last two generations.

The only rule which goes into the substance of the matter at all, is that concerning the justice of the transmitters. But the conception of justice is very mechanical. A man is considered just, if to the knowledge of outsiders, he has not committed one of the so-called capital sins. Moreover, as regards the first three generations[2] it is not necessary actually to determine whether even this minimum of requirement has been met. They are assumed to be just.

[1] *Cf. supra*, under "discontinuity."

[2] *Cf. supra*, *mastūr*.

The **rules concerning the impeachment of hadiths** are not less subject to criticism. Even the fact that a person angrily repudiates having transmitted a certain *ḥadīth*, has not been deemed sufficient cause for setting aside that *ḥadīth*. Then, too, one can always disregard an impeachment on the ground that it has been actuated by partisan motives. Finally, the requirement that a *ḥadīth* must not contradict the Koran or the "established *sunnah*"[1] is not a sufficient check, because not only would it apply to a very small proportion of *ḥadīths*, but also, as we have seen, the *mutawātir* or *mash-hūr* are not necessarily superior to the "individual."

The foregoing discussion conclusively shows that, even if we assume that all the rules have been obeyed, the mere fact that a *ḥadīth* has found a place in the approved collections, the *ṣaḥīḥs*, by no means proves its genuineness. Unless otherwise confirmed, there is always a theoretical possibility that it might have been forged. The Mohammedans themselves have recognized this possibility, since most of them agree that the "individual" produces only probable knowledge (*ẓann*),[2] and since the majority would discourage swearing on the truth of the *ṣaḥīḥs* excepting those by al-Bukhāri and Muslim. Compare also the following statement in the *Tahdhīb*[3] by 'Omar Ibn Habīb, who in defense of the *ḥadīth*-transmitters against impeachment, is supposed to have said to the Calif Hārūn al-Rashīd: "Were the companions of the Prophet liars, then the [entire] *sharī'ah* would become null (*bāṭil*) and the legal provisions (*aḥkām*) [derived from it] should be rejected." In other words, there was a certain reluctance in later times

[1] *Cf. supra*, "real discontinuity."

[2] Nawawi, on the margin of Qasṭallāni, pp. 29-30.

[3] Pp. 446-7.

to brand well-known *ḥadīth*-transmitters of the first three generations of Islam, as liars, because of the fear, that if this were allowed in principle, the evil might go too far.

It must be said in conclusion that the preceding considerations represent only theoretical possibilities, and that the question whether and how far these possibilities have become actualities is largely a matter of how far the actual circumstances offered inducements for making use of the possibilities. Doubtless, the latter, relatively speaking, were few and affected only a small proportion of the entire *sunnah*. It may therefore be said that, **in general**, the *mutawātir* is certainly superior to the *mash-hūr*, and the latter to the "individual," and that for the most part, the **collections of sunnah** considered by the Moslems as canonical **are genuine** records of the rise and early growth of Islam.[1]

[1] *Cf.* Juynboll, pp. 16-19.

CHAPTER IV

The Third Basis of Fiqh: The Ijma

The first two bases of *fiqh* which we have already examined are called by the doctors the two "primary" evidences of *sharī'ah*, as distinguished from the next two evidences of *ijmā'* and *qiyās*, considered in the last analysis as solely derived from, and based on, the two former primary evidences of the Koran and the *sunnah*. But these two latter sources are often involved and contradictory, especially when they are referred to for the solution of novel cases. What guarantee is there, then, that the law has been rightly understood? It is precisely the *ijmā'* that has enabled the canonists to get around this difficulty. Ultimately, the other sources receive their final sanction from the *ijmā'*. It alone can put an end to doubt. When the Mohammedan community has reached an *ijmā'*, that is, a unanimity of opinion concerning a divine prescription, its opinion is infallible.

The doctors have found **justification for ijma'** as a source of law, both in the Koran and the *sunnah*. The Koran says: "It is thus that we have made of you a nation of the right mean"; [1] and in another instance: ". . those who turn away from the Prophet and who do not follow the way of the believers." [2] What else can the way of the believers be, it was argued, but the consensus of the Mohammedan community? On the other hand, the Prophet has said:

[1] Chap. 2, verse 137.

[2] Chap. 4, verse 115.

"My people (*ummah*) shall never agree on an error." Al-Shāfi'i justifies *ijmā'* on the basis of a *ḥadīth* in which the Moslems are enjoined to go with the community. He explains that while isolated individuals are subject to error, the Moslem community as a whole is immune.[1]

Some doctors have **denied** the **legitimacy** of **ijma'** on the two following grounds: (1) It is impossible to ascertain the existence of *ijmā'*, because the *mujtahids*, living at any given period, cannot in fact be numbered, for among them there are those who have not achieved fame, or even possibly women who have reached the degree of *ijtihād* and, being women, escape observation. Even granting that they could be known and numbered, it is impossible to ascertain the consensus of their opinions, since some may have spoken contrary to their inner beliefs. (2) The famous *ḥadīth* concerning Mu'ādh does not mention the *ijmā'* as an evidence, and it would have certainly referred to it, if it were such.[2]

Only later was this dogma of the infallibility of the Mohammedan community raised by the canonists into an elaborate piece of epistemological theory, after it had existed in practice for a very long time. For instance, in the *Risālah* of Al-Shāfi'i which is the first treatise on *usūl-al-fiqh*, the theory of *ijmā'* is as yet far from being elaborate: the whole chapter hardly occupies a page.[3] The first appearance of *ijmā'* is probably to be traced in the city of Medina, among the Companions of the Prophet. After his death, they were the ones to decide all points of difficulty, since they had had the "blessing" of companionship and conversation with the Prophet and, so to speak, had got

[1] *Risālah*, p. 65.

[2] From the *Waraqāt*, quoted in Goldjiher, *D. Zahiriten*, p. 33.

[3] *Risālah*, p. 65.

into the spirit of the new religion. When, therefore, the Companions could agree on a point, their consensus would be accepted by the rest of the community as conclusive. After the Companions, this leadership in religious matters passed to the next generation, the so-called Followers (*tabi'ūn*) and from them to the generation of jurists and *ḥadīth*-teachers who followed them. When these latter differed on a point, they naturally referred to the views and practices of the Companions and Followers; and if their views and practices could be shown to have been unanimous, their points would be made so much easier. What is more natural, therefore, than that under such incentives there should develop the theory of *ijmā'*?

The significance of *ijmā'* in the Mohammedan law can hardly be overestimated. By its means, not only is controversy on many points forever done away with, but also, when new situations have been met by analogy or otherwise, the Moslems may be assured that they are not getting away from the old basis and drifting into heresy.

Notwithstanding the unifying influence of *ijmā'*, there remained indeed always a certain residuum of divergence of opinion on some minor questions on which no consensus could be attained; but this was construed by the canonists to be an indication of God's grace to His people, for there is an *ijmā'* on this very point too, namely, that such divergence is not to be deprecated, because it is a sign of God's grace. This *ijmā'* is based on the *ḥadīth* in which the Prophet said: "The difference of opinion in my community is an indication of grace from God's part."

Al-Sha'rāni, who apparently dislikes the idea of having in the *sharī'ah* any divergence of opinion (*khilāf*) whatsoever, has taken the extreme position of claiming that, in reality, there is no such divergence in the *sharī'ah*; and he attempts to prove his contention by the following ingenious argument: The whole of the *sharī'ah* provisions may be reduced to two categories, commandments and prohibitions, each of which admits of a double construction,—one for the case of want of excuse (*'azīmah*), and the other for the case of excuse (*rukhṣah*). The apparent contradiction and divergence of provisions and views in the *sharī'ah*, is then only a consequence of the fact that while some of these provisions and views refer to cases of want of excuse, others refer to cases of excuse. The believer, however, should not try to benefit from this situation by following the less rigorous prescriptions which are only meant for cases of excuse, when he possesses no real excuse.[1]

The various theories and views of the doctors concerning *ijmā'* may be briefly summed up as follows:[2]

Ijma' is **defined** as "the consensus of the Mohammedan *mujtahids* of any period concerning a *sharī'ah* value." This definition excludes both the non-Mohammedans and the non-*mujtahids*.

The **formal cause** (*rukn*) **of ijma'**.[3] The *ijmā'* is reputed to have taken place whenever there has been a consensus. The consensus may either be *'azīmah* or simply *rukhṣah*. The *ijmā'* is said to be *'azīmah* when the *mujtahids* have spoken with one another concerning the opinion in question or acted according to it. The *ijmā'*, on the contrary, is said to be *rukhṣah*, when some have discussed or acted according to an opinion, and the rest have kept silent, although the matter has been communicated to them and there has passed enough time for consideration. According to some doctors and to a report from al-Shāfi'i, the consensus is not deemed to take place when some of the

[1] *Mīzān*, pp. 4, 8 *et seq.*

[2] *Tawḍīḥ*, pp. 425 *et seq.*; Pazdawi, pp. 946 *et seq.*

[3] Formal cause here is used in the Aristotelian sense.

mujtahids have kept silent. The others reply that it is very difficult for all the *mujtahids* to express opinions, neither is it customary to do so. Moreover, they say, silence when speech is necessary amounts to oral assent.

Who is eligible for ijma'? The opinion must be considered of every *mujtahid* who is not impious and heretical. It must however be remarked that a person need not be a *mujtahid* if the matter to be determined by *ijmā'* is one that does not require judgment (*ra'y*), if, for example, the matter to be decided is the transmission of the Koran or one of the obligations considered fundamental in all religions, such as the five prayers, and the *zakāt*. For an *ijmā'* to occur on these matters, it is necessary that both the *mujtahids* (*khawāṣṣ*) and the laymen (*'awāmm*) should reach agreement. Consequently, if one layman should disagree on them the *ijmā'* would fail to occur, " but this has never happened." [1] If on the other hand, the matter to be determined is one that requires reflection and judgment, such as, for example, the determination of the specific legal provisions concerning sales and marriage, then it is necessary that only the *mujtahids* should agree. The *ijmā'* therefore would not be affected if some of the laymen should disagree; as a matter of fact, " they do agree when all the *mujtahids* have agreed upon a point." In this chapter we are concerned only with the *ijmā'* of the *mujtahids*.

Some have claimed that only the Companions qualify for *ijmā'*. Others have said that the relatives (*'itrah*) of the Prophet alone are entitled to this privilege. On the other hand, Mālik is said to have claimed this for the people of Medina exclusively. But, according to al-Pazdawi, none of these supplementary qualities are necessary, and all the Mohammedans are equal in this respect.

[1] *Kashf*, p. 959; *Tawḍīḥ*, p. 433.

The Conditions of Ijma'. The Hanifites hold that the "lapse of the period" (*inqirād al-'asr*), *i. e.*, the passing away of all those qualified to express an opinion on the matter in question after their previous agreement upon it, is not necessary, but Al-Shāfi'i claimed that they should all pass away while persisting in their agreement. The Hanifites reply that, once the *ijmā'* is reached, any later addition or change is not valid.

Some have **claimed** that the **ijma' must not concern a question already discussed** by the Companions; but, according to a report from Muhammad Ibn al-Hasan (a disciple of Abu Hanīfah), the *ijmā'* of every period on a point on which the former generations have had divergence of opinion is valid, provided that one of the views then debated is accepted and confirmed, for there cannot be reached an *ijmā'* on a new opinion. However, concerning matters on which there has been no previous controversy, an *ijmā'* may be arrived at on any opinion whatsoever.[1]

The value (*hukm*) **of Ijma'.** The value of *ijmā'* is that a legal prescription based on an *ijmā'* is considered to be positive (*yaqīn*), and therefore, non-conformity with it entails heresy. After the attainment of an *ijmā'* on a point, further controversy on that point is barred, and the point becomes acquired forever, unless it be abrogated (*naskh*) in accordance with the following rules.

Abrogation of Ijma'.[2] The abrogation of an *ijmā'* is possible only by another *ijmā'* of a similar class. Thus an *ijmā* of the Companions can be repealed only by another *ijmā'* of the Companions; and likewise, the *ijmā's* of the second generation may be abrogated by other *ijmā's* of the same generation or of following generations, because the *ijmā's* of generations later than that of the Companions are all considered of the same weight.

[1] Pazdawi, p. 967.

[2] Pazdawi, p. 982.

The Basis (*sanad*) **of Ijma'.** According to the majority of the doctors, an *ijmā'* cannot be reached except upon evidence, because to mention only one reason, in religious matters, opinion without evidence is erroneous (*khaṭā'*), " since evidence is what gets us to truth and without evidence there would be no getting to it." Some said that the *ijmā'* without authority, (*i. e.*, one in which the constituent opinions have not been based upon a *sharī'ah* evidence) may still be valid, because God would certainly lead His community to the right view, and because, if it were necessary that the *ijmā'* should require authoritative justification, there would be no longer any use for the *ijmā'* as an independent evidence. The other side replies that this is not true, since the Prophet himself did not speak except through inspiration or by deduction from the divine revelations, and that therefore it behooves the community that it should preferably speak on the basis of evidence. Furthermore, they say, it is necessary that there should be evidence, since opinion based on prejudice or conjecture is proper only to heretics. Finally, they deny that there would no longer be any use for *ijmā'* as an independent evidence, because, as they point out, upon the reaching of an *ijmā'* further controversy on the point is not allowed, since the *ijmā'* establishes the point in a way that does not admit of doubt. Consequently, the authority or evidence for the opinions which make up an *ijmā'* may be a probable evidence (*dalīl ẕanni*) such as *qiyās*; or it may be an " individual " report; or it may be a positive evidence, such as a verse of the Koran or a *sunnah* of the *mutawātir* type. The Zahirites, Shiites and certain of the Mu'tazilites have claimed that the only valid basis for an *ijmā'* is positive evidence.

The Transmission of Ijma'. This is subject to the same rules as that of the *sunnah*.

CHAPTER V

THE FOURTH BASIS OF FIQH: THE QIYAS

SECTION I

General Considerations.

A hot controversy had to be waged before *qiyās* or legal analogy was generally admitted to be a lawful means for establishing *sharī'ah* values. There is no doubt that from the time of Mohammed analogy was resorted to in order to provide for the solution of cases which were left unsettled by the two revealed sources of the Koran and the *sunnah*. That such was the case is amply proved by the *ḥadīths* invoked by the upholders of *qiyās*, as will be seen below. Besides, this is also what reason would lead one to expect, for what can be more natural than to judge by analogy rather than to dismiss a case, when the texts fail?

Of course in the earliest period, no special rules as yet had developed concerning the use of analogy and the latter was practised in a loose way, varying from person to person according to temperament, and so offering more or less free scope for the play of personal opinion. However, as this new principle was practised in an informal way, no one realized its significance. But presently the conditions changed. Islam in the meanwhile quickly spread beyond the limits of Arabia, northward into Syria, and eastward into Mesopotamia and 'Irāq, where, owing to the peculiar agricultural and social conditions, it met with private-law relations essentially different from those of Arabia. How could the Mohammedan judges decide matters for which the Arabian social and legal traditions offered no parallel whatever? They necessarily had to use their personal opinion in the form of *qiyās*, though always trying to follow the spirit of the sacred texts.[1]

This material factor in the growth of Islam occasioned **two distinct tendencies in Mohammedan law.** The jurists of Medina and Mecca, living in the cities in which Islam had had its origin and early development and which were saturated with *ḥadīth*-associations, laid emphasis on the preservation and study of the *ḥadīths*, and in deciding legal questions they referred to them as their standard. This they could easily do, because the cultural and legal conditions under which those *ḥadīths* had been uttered by the Prophet still remained practically the same and so the *ḥadīths* and local customs would be sufficient to decide the legal questions that might arise, without resorting much to the use of analogy.

But it cannot be said that this was true of the jurists of the conquered countries outside of Arabia, especially of 'Irāq. In 'Irāq the conditions were different and the jurists who lived there, being away from the home of the *ḥadīth*-lore and facing new situations, from the very first used and had to use personal opinion (*ra'y*) much more extensively. They were therefore called **ra'y-folk** (*ahl-al-ra'y*), in distinction from the jurists of Hijāz who were known as the **hadith-folk** (*ahl-al-ḥadīth*).

This difference in tendency between the two groups of jurists grew to be more and more marked as time went on and eventually culminated in the famous **controversy between the hadith-folk and the ra'y-folk.** Unfortunately

[1] Goldziher, *d. Zahiriten*, p. 6.

the historical sources do not throw enough light on the different phases of this struggle but nevertheless some of them may be determined.

Thus it is fairly certain that until Abu Hanīfah's appearance upon the scene, the opposition between the two sides was mild; it assumed the form of a violent controversy only after Abu Hanīfah's epoch-making innovation. This we may infer since there are no *ḥadīths* to the contrary, and since all the existing *ḥadīths* refer to Abu Hanīfah and his disciples as the persons at whose door the blame should be laid for introducing into the law the non-revealed new element of personal opinion (*ra'y*). This innovation of Abu Hanīfah, which launched the controversy, consisted in his attempt to codify the Mohammedan law, for the first time using *qiyās* avowedly as a basis.

So long as the use of *qiyās* was not given a formal recognition, but was resorted to occasionally when judgments were rendered, no controversy broke out. It was, however, a very different matter when Abu Hanīfah openly declared *qiyās* to be a legitimate basis of law, and proceeded to codify the law using *qiyās* as one of his bases. This was an unmistakable challenge and the *ḥadīth*-folk accepted it. Apparently the *ḥadīth*-folk were willing to allow the use of *qiyās*, if it were to be applied in an informal way when the situation called for it, but disliked to have *qiyās* put down on paper as a principle of legislation. Thus according to the *Mīzān*,[1] Mujāhid is said to have told his disciples: "Do not write down on my authority the opinions I give—only the *ḥadīths* are written down—for I may revoke tomorrow all the opinions I form today."

One great reason why there was such bitter opposition to *qiyās*, was because **qiyas** was **identified with ra'y** (per-

[1] P. 47.

sonal opinion).[1] It was thought that the use of *qiyās* would result in the setting aside of the revealed texts to make room for *ra'y*. But in the eyes of the conservative *ḥadīth*-folk the use of *ra'y* was almost as bad as unbelief. Thus, al-Sha'bi said: "*Ra'y* is like carrion; you use it as food only when you are in extreme need of it" and in another instance, "May God curse '*a ra'ayta*'", '*a ra'ayta*' being the formula used in introducing a question for a legal opinion. Ja'far al-Sādiq said: "The greatest test that shall befall the Moslem community will be the people who will decide (*yaqīsūna*) matters by their opinions (*ra'y*) and will forbid what God allowed and allow what God forbade." [2]

The two features peculiar to the use of *ra'y* which the **hadith-folk disliked** most, seem to have been, first, the habit of the *ra'y*-folk to imagine **unreal cases** in order to determine their legal solutions; **and**, second, their **scholastic subtleties.** This may be seen in the epigrammatic ridicule heaped on Abu Hanīfah by the poet Musāwir,[3] and in the following quotations. Thus Hafṣ Ibn Giyāth said about Abu Hanīfah: "He is the most informed of people on things that have not existed and the most ignorant of people on things that have existed." Likewise, Mālik, when asked whether he had seen Abu Hanīfah answered:[4] "Yes, I saw a man who, if he told you that he could make this column into gold, would do it by his arguments." In the same spirit al-Shāfi'i said: "I liken the *ra'y* of Abu Hanīfah to nothing but the rope of a witch, who stretches it in one

[1] Al-Shāfi'i considers *ijtihād* and *qiyās* as identical (*Risālah*, p. 66, l. 3; *cf.* also *Kashf*, p. 988).

[2] *Mīzān*, p. 46.

[3] *Agānī*, vol. xvi, p. 169.

[4] Abu 'l Maḥāsin, p. 404.

direction, and you see it yellow, and stretches it in another direction, and you see it red." [1]

The **hadith-folk**, on the contrary, had no liking for abstract speculation, but **would only concern themselves with concrete cases.** One of them, Masrūq, when a question was put to him, would say, "Has the case already happened?", and if answered in the negative, would remark, "Then let me alone with the answer until the case shall have really happened."

In order to discredit the methods of the *ra'y*-folk, the *ḥadīth*-folk invoked many *ḥadīths* supposedly uttered by the Prophet in condemnation of the use of *ra'y*. Moreover, they claimed that *ra'y* was synonymous with *hawa*, meaning a rash opinion formed under the influence of passion and prejudice. However, this is not true, because in common parlance, the word meant just the opposite.[2]

In identifying qiyas with ra'y in this controversy, the **hadith-folk have** really **injured their cause**, since the recognition of *qiyās* as established by Abu Hanīfah would only curb the use of independent opinion (*ra'y*) rather than foster it, as they feared. Formerly there were no strict rules concerning the exercise of personal opinion, and the personal views of the judge might easily color his reasoning.

[1] Goldziher, *d. Zahiriten*, p. 20.

[2] The successive **changes in the meaning of the word fiqh** (literally, judgment, understanding), originally a synonym of *ra'y*, singularly reflect the phases of the conflict in question. Thus *fiqh* was first used in the sense of interpreting the revealed texts (Goldziher, *d. Zahiriten*, p. 19); then it was contrasted with *ḥadīth*, as in the expression "conversant with the *ḥadith* and the *fiqh*" (*ahl-al-ḥadīth wa 'l-fiqh*); *al-Shāfi'ī* uses *'ilm* to denote the knowledge of the revealed sources; finally, after the subsiding of the controversy, we find *fiqh* used to mean the science of law in general, and therefore, in order to distinguish the science of *ḥadith* in particular, the expression *fiqh al-ḥadīth*, *i. e.*, the *fiqh* of *ḥadīth*, is used.

After the introduction of *qiyās* the reasoning of the judge was limited by the rules of *qiyās* which kept it more within the scope of the revealed sources. The best proof for this is probably afforded by Abu Hanīfah's own action when he introduced a new principle to supply the need which resulted from the limitation of personal opinion due to the introduction of *qiyās*. This new principle, which consisted in the free use of personal opinion in the place of *qiyās* when public necessity would call for such a procedure, is called *istiḥsān*.

Taken all in all, this controversy was largely a matter of quibbling over words, for, as a matter of fact, both sides made free use of personal opinion,[1] although one must admit that the *ḥadīth*-folk would exhaust the possibilities of their system before committing themselves to the use of *qiyās*. Thus it is related of Ahmad Ibn Hanbal, that he used to say: "A weak *ḥadīth* is better for us than the *ra'y* of people."[2] Hafṣ Ibn 'Abdāllah al-Nīsābūri († 209, H.) is said to have boasted that during a judgeship of 20 years he never once used *qiyās*. But he must have been an exception. Abu Hanīfah, on the contrary, had no such dread of *qiyās* and would use it rather than countenance an *ḥadīth* of suspicious origin. This difference of attitude towards the use of *qiyās*, accounts for the small number of *ḥadīths* said to have been used by Abu Hanīfah, as contrasted with the 28,000, or more, alleged to have been accepted in the *Musnad* of Aḥmad Ibn Hanbal.

It is no surprise therefore that **qiyas** has been **admitted into most of the schools** that were recruited from the ranks of the *ḥadīth*-folk, and formed the by-products of the controversy. The person who took the first step in this di-

[1] *Cf.* Goldziher, *d. Zahiriten*, p. 36; *Mizān*, p. 53, l. —9.

[2] *Mizān*, p. 50.

rection and who is chiefly responsible for the clearing-up of the situation and the ending of the controversy, is al-Shāfi'i, the founder of the Shafiite school. Notwithstanding that he was reared in the center of the *ḥadīth*-lore, he came out squarely for the lawfulness of *qiyās*, though he was very careful to state in his *Risālah*, the first treatise on *uṣūl-al-fiqh*,[1] that *qiyās* must be strictly based on the revealed sources, and the *ijmā'*.[2] However al-Shāfi'i strongly condemned the principle of *istiḥsān*. Yet he could not dispense with a principle which should act as a safety valve in cases of emergency, any more than Abu Hanīfah could. So al-Shāfi'i was forced to introduce the principle of *istiṣḥāb*, and to allow greater latitude in the determination of the "effective" cause (*'illah*) for purposes of *qiyās*.

The Malikite school fared no better than the others, for it, too, has adopted an analogous principle, the *istiṣlāḥ*.

We are now ready to examine the various principles and rules concerning the use of *qiyās*, which have been elaborated[3] by the followers of Abu Hanīfah, like al-Pazdawi, and al-Karkhi, and which may be found in all the treatises on *uṣūl-al-fiqh*.[4]

The **definition of qiyas** is "to extend [*ta'diyah*] the [*sharī'ah*] value from the original case [*aṣl*] over to the

[1] According to the *Tah-dhib* (p. 60), the *Risālah* was written by request and approved by all.

[2] *Risālah*, pp. 65, 66, 69, 82.

[3] It must not be thought that the detailed **principles of qiyas** as we find them in the treatises on *uṣūl-al-fiqh* have all been **elaborated** by Abu Hanīfah. Probably he did not do more than lay down a few working principles, and the rest were completed by his successors. This is borne out by the fact that the treatises on *uṣūl-al-fiqh*, only very seldom (*cf. Tawḍīḥ*, p. 469, where a certain view is ascribed to Abu Hanīfah), indicate the persons responsible for the opinions cited, or else ascribe them to **later doctors**, like al-Pazdawi, al-Karkhi, and al-Marīsi. (*Kashf*, pp. 1014, 1020, 1021, 1023, 1035.)

[4] *Tawḍīḥ*, p. 444 *et seq.*; Pazdawi, p. 986 *et seq.*

subsidiary [*far'*], by reason of an 'effective' cause [*'illah*] which is common to both cases and cannot be understood from the expression [concerning the original case] alone."[1] For example, if a certain act (*aṣl*) has been prohibited in the Koran or the *sunnah*, other acts (*far'*) common with that act in regard to the "effective" cause (*'illah*) for which the prohibition has been decreed, are likewise prohibited. It is necessary, however, that the acts to which the value is extended, should not be included in the meaning of the prohibitory expression, explicitly or implicitly, for in that case they would be prohibited by virtue of the prohibitory expression itself, and not by virtue of *qiyās* thereon.

According to al-Pazdawi,[2] the **justification of qiyas** is that "all the Companions of the Prophet and all the Followers as well as the righteous people [*ṣāliḥūn*] and the theologians have unanimously agreed that *qiyās*, through use of personal opinion [*ra'y*] on the basis of the *sharī'ah* principles" in order to decide undetermined cases, is a lawful source of law. The Zahirites, who were *ḥadīth*-folk, and others, held that *qiyās* is not a legal evidence (*ḥujjah*) and that action upon it is null and void. Some of them based their dissent on the ground that *qiyās*, being a case of exercising reason, may not constitute evidence. Others contended that while reason may constitute evidence in intellectual matters it may not do so in *sharī'ah* matters. Still others maintained that resort to reason should be only in cases of emergency and that no such emergency could be said to exist in the case of *qiyās*, since *qiyās* could be substituted for by *istiṣḥāb-al-ḥāl*.

According to the *Kashf*[3] the whole **dispute about qiyas**

[1] *Tawḍiḥ*, p. 444.

[2] P. 990.

[3] P. 990.

turned on the following **two points:** (1) whether *qiyās* was lawful in intellectual matters; and (2) whether it was lawful in *sharī'ah* matters. The *Kashf* goes on to say that all the Companions and the Followers as well as the majority of the jurists and theologians considered *qiyās* lawful in both cases; that, among others, all the Shiites and the Khārijites allowed the use of *qiyās* only in *sharī'ah* matters; and that the Hanbalites sanctioned its use only as regards the applications of *fiqh,* in view of the need for it in cases concerning which the Koran was silent, but denied its lawfulness as regards the determination of intellectual matters.

The opponents of qiyas argued in detail as follows: [1]

(1) **From the Koran:** [2] " We have sent down to you the Book, as an explanation for every thing." To consider *qiyās* as an additional evidence would be to consider the Koran insufficient.

(2) **From the sunnah:** the Prophet said: " The affairs of the sons of Israel have continued to prosper until there multiplied among them the children of the war captives, for these have measured (*qāsū*) what did not exist on the basis of what did exist, and so they have erred and led others into error."

(3) **From reason:** there is doubt about the " effective " cause (*'illah*) for which a *sharī'ah* value has been established, because the revealed texts do not mention the causes, and consequently one cannot know what to use as a basis for *qiyās*. Furthermore, God is not worshipped according to the dictates of reason. Are there not in fact, divine prescriptions which cannot be grasped by human understanding, as for instance, the " stated quantities " (*muqad-*

[1] *Cf. Tawḍiḥ,* p. 446.

[2] Chap. 16, verse 91.

darāt) such as the number of prostrations in prayer; and are there not prescriptions which even contradict reason?

To these **the defenders of qiyas answered** as follows:

(1) **From the Koran:**[1] "Consider, oh ye possessors of eyes," and consideration here means the comparison of things similar.

(2) **From the sunnah:**[2] "The *ḥadīths* proving the legitimacy of *qiyās* are innumerable." Thus when Mohammed sent Mu'ādh to Yaman, he asked him what principles he would use in administering justice. Mu'ādh answered that he would decide upon his personal opinion (*ra'y*) in case no provisions were to be found, either in the Koran or the *sunnah*. Upon this the Prophet said: "Thanks to God that He has directed the delegate of His Prophet to that opinion in which the Prophet of God finds pleasure." Again, when the Prophet sent Abu Mūsa to Yaman, he said: "Judge upon the Book of God, and if you do not find in it what you need, upon the *sunnah* of the Prophet, and if you do not find in that, then use your own opinion." Moreover, the conduct of the Companions, and their conversations and discussions bear this out still more forcibly. In fact, it is established by *mutawātirs*[3] that they used *qiyās*, especially in their councils on the matter of succession, where

each spoke using his own opinion until the matter was finally settled according to what 'Omar said in the way of opinion and *qiyās*, when he remarked, "Are you not going to be satisfied as regards worldly matters, with the man with whom the Prophet was satisfied as regards matters of religion? ", and they agreed upon his opinion notwithstanding the fact that the question of succession

[1] Chap. 59, verse 2.

[2] Pazdawi, p. 998.

[3] *Kashf*, p. 1000.

to the califate is of the utmost importance. Again, when the Companions held a council, for determining the penalty of the wine-drinker (*shārib*), 'Ali said: "When one drinks he gets drunk, and when he gets drunk, he raves, and when he raves, he accuses falsely," hence the same penalty must apply to the drinker as to the false accuser.

(3) **From reason:** [1] the allegation that it is not allowed to establish values on the basis of probable evidence is not valid, for in matters which human understanding cannot grasp, probability is sufficient for purposes of conduct. "Besides," they said, "do you not yourselves use *qiyās* to determine the direction (*qiblah*) of the Ka'bah, or to fix the amount of damage to be paid for destroyed property?" The other side replied that these cases were exceptional, because the original obligation, (for example, the thing destroyed), could no longer be discharged *per se*, and because these cases related to individuals' rights (*ḥuqūq 'ibād*). Moreover, there was a possibility of determining them by means of the senses and reason, for instance, through a journey, or the positions of the stars.[2]

SECTION II

Is it Lawful to Investigate the "Effective" Causes of Divine Prescriptions? [3]

We have seen that *qiyās* is the extension of a *sharī'ah* value from the original case (*aṣl*) (concerning which a prescription has been revealed) to a new case, because the latter has the same cause as the former. In other words, no use of *qiyās* can be made before the specific cause of a prescription has been actually determined. Take, for in-

[1] *Tawḍīḥ*, p. 450.

[2] *Tawḍīḥ*, p. 447.

[3] Pazdawi, p. 1013 *et seq.*; *Tawḍīḥ*, p. 464.

stance, the prohibition of usury concerning the six articles, namely, gold, silver, corn, barley, dates, and raisins. Now, if it can be found that the specific cause (*'illah*) of the prohibition is a certain feature of these articles, say, their being measured by weight, then all other articles measured by weight would also be covered by the prohibition. Such an inquiry into the "effective" causes of the divine prescriptions is called by the doctors *ta'līl al-uṣūl*. There have been different views concerning the legitimacy of such a procedure.

One view is that the divine prescriptions do not possess an "effective" cause except when there is evidence to that effect. The people who hold this view argue that the determination of the cause of a divine prescription is like the use of the metaphorical meaning of a word, instead of its proper meaning, but that is allowed only upon evidence. Besides, if each attribute (*waṣf*) were taken as a separate cause, what one attribute included another would exclude, and if all the attributes together were taken as one cause, they would be combined only in the original case (*manṣūs-'alayh*), thus barring the use of *qiyās*. On the contrary, if one of the attributes is set down as the causal one, it involves doubt, since some other one may have been the cause. For instance, if every one of the qualities possessed by the six articles above mentioned is considered as a separate cause of the prohibition, then one of these qualities, for example, being a foodstuff, would bring under the prohibition apples, also a foodstuff, but would exclude plaster, whereas the attributes of being measured by volume or weight (*qadr*) [1] and being a genus (*jins*) would give a different result. Again, if all the qualities taken together are considered to be the one single cause of the prohibition,

[1] *Tech. Dict.*, p. 1179.

then only the six articles mentioned would be the prohibited ones, and the door of *qiyās* would be closed, since no other articles would combine all those qualities. Finally, if only one of the attributes were taken as the cause, there is no guarantee that some other attribute is not the cause. Consequently, unless there is special evidence to indicate which attribute is the causal one, the best thing to do is to refrain (*waqf*) from attempting to determine the cause.

A second view is that every attribute which can possibly be regarded as a cause, and to which a value may properly be attached, is considered a cause except when an express statement (*naṣṣ*) or *ijmā'* points to the contrary. The people who hold this view insist that every attribute may be an actual cause, excepting when there is an obstacle; for example, when the various attributes contradict one another, or when there is an express statement or *ijmā'* to the contrary. Their argument is that *qiyās* is one of the evidences of the *sharī'ah*, that its evidential function would have been defeated if each attribute had not been considered as a separate cause, and that there is no reason for not so considering it, unless there is a real obstacle. Thus, they grant that all the attributes together cannot be considered as a single combined cause but, they say, it is quite possible to consider each attribute as a separate cause, and it is not true, as has been claimed, that this involves contradiction, since they would allow it only in so far as there is no contradiction involved.

A third view is that the divine prescriptions do have causes, but that the right thing to do is to determine only one attribute as the "effective" cause of a prescription, provided that the attribute singled out as the causal one is so designated by a specific evidence. The people who hold this view argue that since all the attributes together may not be a single cause, (as this would make *qiyās* impossible), it becomes clear that one of the attributes must be the causal one, unless there is evidence that more than one attribute are causes; but as it is not known which of the attributes is the causal one, there is need for a specific evidence to designate one as the distinctly causal attribute. Apparently this is the view of al-Shāfi'i. However, his disciples held that the proper conduct concerning the divine prescriptions was to accept (*ta'abbud*) them with devotion, and not to attempt to determine causes.

A fourth view, the generally accepted Hanifite view,[1] is that the prescriptions are presumed to have a single cause which must be determined, unless there is an obstacle to its determination, as for example, in the case of prescriptions concerning "stated quantities" (*muqaddarāt*) with respect to ritual and punishments. However, one may not proceed to determine the cause of a prescription, unless there is previous evidence to show that the prescription actually has a cause; and even then a further evidence is needed, in order to determine which of the several attributes is the cause of the prescription. The argument for this view is that all divine prescriptions do not have a cause, and that a specific evidence is needed to show that the prescription in question actually has a cause. Some Hanifites held that there is no need for such specific evidence when there is already evidence to show which of the attributes of the thing prohibited is the causal one, since evidently a prescription cannot have a causal attribute and yet not have a cause.

SECTION III

How to Determine the "Effective" Cause

We have seen that most of the doctors have agreed that not all the attributes of the thing forbidden or recommended

[1] *Tawḍiḥ*, p. 465; *Kashf*, p. 1014.

may be considered as causal, whether taken together or singly, but that only one or more of them are the causes. These particular attributes must be determined by some evidence, because all the doctors agree that one may not at random hit upon some of the attributes as the causal ones.[1]

According to the majority of the doctors, in order **to be** the **cause** for a prohibition or permission, **an attribute, must be "convenient"** (*munāsib*), that is, it must be such that, when joined with the value, it would result in the accruing of a benefit or the removal of a damage, the benefit and the damage viewed from the standpoint of the *sharī'ah*. Fasting, for example, is useful to mankind from the standpoint of the *sharī'ah*, in subduing the animal nature, though harmful from the medical viewpoint.[2] According to the *Kashf*[3] the attribute is "convenient," if it is like the attributes considered "convenient" by the early Moslems, "who used to consider as causes those attributes which were proper to the values." Again, according to the *Kashf*, Al-Gazāli held that an attribute is "convenient," if the connection of the value to it would lead to a useful purpose (*maṣlaḥah*); for example, in the case of the prohibition of wine-drinking, the "convenient" attribute is the property of wine to destroy reason. According to others, that attribute is "convenient" which appeals to reason as the proper one.[4]

Besides being "convenient," **the attribute must also be "effective"** (*mu'ath-thir*) if its use for *qiyās* is to be obligatory (*wājib*), but it is valid (*ṣaḥīḥ*) to apply a *qiyās* on the basis of an attribute which is only "convenient," without being "effective."[5] According to some of the

[1] *Kashf*, p. 1070.

[2] P. 1072.

[3] *Talwīḥ*, p. 473.

[4] Shawkāni, p. 200.

[5] *Talwīḥ*, p. 475; *Kashf*, p. 1073.

Shafiites,[1] the attribute need not be "effective," but it is sufficient if it occurs to one's mind that it is the one needed. However, in this case, as a matter of precaution one should also refer to the sources (*uṣūl*), in order to make sure that no contradiction to them has been incurred. On the other hand, some Shafiites said that this reference to the sources is to be made first, and if the attribute used as causal is found to contradict no principle of the sources, it is considered as the cause.

The **Hanifites, by** saying that the attribute must be "**effective," mean** that in the Koran, the *sunnah* or the *ijmā'* this very attribute or another of the same genus (*jins*), should have been indicated as an "effective" cause for the very value (*ḥukm*) in question or another value of the same genus.[2] By genus, here is meant the proximate genus (*jins qarīb*).

The doctors have distinguished **four types of "effectiveness"** (*ta'thīr*) :[3]

(1) **The very same attribute** has been indicated in the sources as "**effective" cause for the very same value.** This almost amounts to an application of the original prescription, since the only difference between the two cases is that the attribute in one case qualifies one object, and in the other case another object. It is no wonder, therefore, that this kind of *qiyās* is often accepted by its very opponents. An example of this *qiyās* is the following: if it has been established that the cause of the prohibition of usury as regards dates is their being measured by volume (*kayl*), then without any doubt plaster would be like dates; and if, on the other hand, the cause is their being a foodstuff, then

[1] Pazdawi, p. 1074.

[2] Shawkāni, p. 203.

[3] *Tawḍiḥ*, p. 478; *Kashf*, p. 1073.

raisins would be like dates. Here, in both cases we have the very same attribute and the very same value, namely, being measured by volume, or being a foodstuff, on the one hand, and prohibition for reason of usury, on the other hand.

(2) **The very same attribute** has been indicated as **"effective" cause of the genus of the value;** for example, in inheritance the attribute of being a full instead of a half brother is a cause of the value of precedence. By analogy, the very same attribute is made cause, this time not of the very same value, *i. e.*, precedence in matter of inheritance, but of another value of the same genus, namely, precedence in guardianship (*wilāyah*) in marriage, precedence in both inheritance and marriage being a genus of right.

(3) **The genus of the attribute** has been indicated as a **cause of the very same (*'ayn*) value**; for example, when a person has to settle (*qaḏā'*) many debts of prayers (*ṣalāt*) which he has failed to perform in their right times, by analogy, he is released from these debts if he has fainting fits. The analogy is based on the fact that both insanity and menstruation (*ḫayḏ*) have been considered in the sources as "effective" causes for the very same value, namely the cancelling of the obligation of prayer. In other words, the doctors have considered as cause of the value, not one of the two mentioned excuses or attributes, already indicated in the sources as causes, but another attribute of the genus of those two attributes, namely, fainting. This sort of attribute is usually called *mulā'im.*

(4) **The attribute whose genus has been indicated as the cause of the genus of the value.** This is usually called *al-munāsib al-garīb*. An example of this is the cancelling by analogy of the obligation of performing the

[1] *Talwīḥ*, p. 478.

prayers for cause of menstruation (*ḥayḍ*), because an attribute of the same genus, namely being on a journey, has been indicated already as cause for a value of the same genus, namely the cancelling of the superfluous two prostrations in prayer. Here, from the standpoint of performing the prayer, having menstruation or being on a journey are a genus of "inconvenience" (*mashaqqah*), while the cancelling of the prayers and the cancelling of the superfluous prostrations are a genus of alleviation of the law.

The reason **why** the Hanifites require that **the attribute** besides being "convenient" **must also be "effective,"** is because, "the attribute while being 'convenient' may at the same time not have been in and of itself, (*bi-dhātihi*) the cause (*'illah*) of the value, but simply considered as cause by the *sharī'ah*." [1] To the contention of the opposite side that one cannot understand and feel that a certain attribute is the effective cause of a prescription, al-Pazdawi retorts that one observes causation in the physical world, both in language and perception, as for example, when one says, "He broke it and it was broken," or "He beat him and he was hurt," or when one sees the result (*athar*) of the act of the builder in the building,[2] and so by inference one can observe causation in the *sharī'ah* also. Take, for example, the prophetic *ḥadīth* to the effect that she-cats (*hirrah*) are not impure because they are "from those who are around" people all the time. Clearly, in this *ḥadīth*, the attribute of being around all the time is considered to be the cause of the cleanness (*ṭahārah*) of she-cats. In other words, the law regarding the residue of water or food touched by she-cats is alleviated, because of the great difficulty of guarding against their touching the

[1] Pazdawi, p. 1078.

[2] *Kashf*, p. 1079.

food, since they are around all the time. There is, therefore, necessity (*ḍarūrah*) to consider the food touched by she-cats as clean, just as there is necessity to eat a dead corpse when on the point of starvation.

Of the above-mentioned four types of qiyas, the first three are admitted by all the upholders of *qiyās* to be lawful, but there is dispute as to the fourth. However, it also, is lawful in the generally accepted view (*mukhtār*) because it expresses more than mere probability (*ẓann*).[1] The first three types are called *mulā'im* and the fourth *garīb*.

The Hanifites who hold that in order for a *qiyās* to be *wājib*, the attribute must be "effective," reject as unlawful the kind of causes designated as *ṭardi* (*'ilal ṭardiyyah*), which are used by others and are not "effective."[2] The people who use this last type of causes, namely the so-called *aṣḥāb-al-ṭard*, retort and say, that it is not necessary that the "effectiveness" of an attribute (*ta'thīr al-waṣf*) should have been indicated in the sources, but that the mere concomitance (*iṭṭirād*) of the value and the attribute is an evidence on the part of the sources (*shahādat al-aṣl*) that the attribute is the cause of the value; and further, that it is not true that the early doctors (*salaf*) have always applied the *qiyās* on the basis of "effective" causes. The argument of these people is that *qiyās* is valid on the basis of every attribute, and that each one of the several attributes is assumed to have been expressly stated (*naṣṣ*); for example, if wine has been forbidden, it is as if every one of the attributes of wine has been expressly forbidden; that the so-called *sharī'ah* causes (*'ilal*) in reality are not causes of the values which attach to them, but simply signs (*imārah*) of them, the real cause of all values being God

[1] *Kashf*, p. 1074; *Talwīḥ*, pp. 477-8.

[2] *Kashf*, p. 1085; *Talwīḥ*, p. 485.

the Almighty; that therefore one need not look for evidence that they are the "effective" causes.[1]

We need not examine here the various other methods used by small and less known groups. Let it suffice to describe only two of them. (1) The **method of tard or dawran**, which consists in considering an attribute as cause of the value, simply if every time the attribute was present or absent, the value also was present or absent, irrespective of whether there is an indication in the context to show that the attribute was meant to be the cause of the value. (2) The **method of masalih mursalah or istislah** used by the Malikites. This consists in considering an attribute as causal, although there may be no evidence to show that it was either approved or disapproved by the *sharī'ah*.[2]

SECTION IV

The Conditions of Qiyās[3]

There are four conditions of *qiyās*:

(1) That the **value** (such as prohibition) which is about to be extended to a new case, **should not be** expressly **limited to** the **original case.** Thus while the testimony of Khuzaymah, by himself, is legal evidence, it may not be argued by way of *qiyās* that the testimony of another single individual would likewise be accepted as legal evidence.

(2) That the **value of** the **original case should not have been itself against** the rules of **analogy.** Such is supposed to be the case, either when the mind cannot understand the value in question, such as for example, the number of prostrations in prayer; or when it is against the laws of

[1] Pazdawi, p. 1086.

[2] *Cf. supra*, Other Principles of Legislation; for more details see *Tech. Dict.*, pp. 1366-1372.

[3] Pazdawi, pp. 1021 *et seq.*; *Tawḍīḥ*, p. 451.

qiyās, as when fasting is not invalidated by eating through inadvertence, although *qiyās* would require that the fast should be considered broken by every thing that enters the body. It may not be therefore argued that because eating through inadvertence does not break the fast, by analogy, eating by mistake or accident, also should not break the fast.

(3) That the value whose extension to a new case is sought, should be a shari'ah value established by virtue of the Koran, the sunnah, or the ijma', but not another *qiyās*: that the value in the process of transition to the new case should undergo no change; that the new case be similar to the original case in the quality to which the value attaches; and finally, that concerning the new case (*far'*) there should have been no separate prescription (*naṣṣ*). Ibn Shurayh̲, the Shafiite, and others have held that *qiyās* is allowed also in case of names. For instance, they have argued that because grape juice is called wine whenever it has reached the stage of fermentation, the name wine may be applied to any drink which is in a similar stage, for example, to the drink *nabīdh*. The majority of the doctors however, have objected to the application of *qiyās* in matters of terminology, because there is no connection between the name of a thing and the thing itself, and so nothing can be pointed out as the cause of a name. But *qiyās* is allowed only in cases where one can determine a cause. An example of the second requirement is the following. Because eating through inadvertence during the fast does not legally break the fast, the Shafiites have argued by analogy that eating by mistake (*khaṭā'*) or by threat, also must not break the fast. The Hanifites replied that inadvertence (*nisā'*) is a natural shortcoming against which a person cannot guard, but mistake and threat may be avoided by excess of care or by appeal to the government. Therefore, applying the value (in this case, nullity ascribed to the act of eating

through inadvertence) to the other two acts would be changing it, for it would have been attached to avoidable acts, while it is intended to apply only to unavoidable acts like those due to inadvertence. This case is also an illustration of the third requirement, namely that the qualities to which the value attaches (inadvertence, on the one hand, mistake and threat, on the other) should be similar, but evidently they are not in this case, because the former is unavoidable and the latter two are not so.

(4) That the application of **qiyas, should not result in the altering of a prescription** (*naṣṣ*), because this would be altering the divine prescription on the basis of personal judgment. An example of this is found in the case of false accusation, which by express prescription is a permanent bar to the acceptance of one's testimony. Al-Shāfi'. has argued by *qiyās*, that because the person punished for other great sins (*kabīrah*) upon repentance may be heard as a witness, in the case of false accusation also repentance should remove the bar to the acceptance of testimony. The Hanifites have replied that the application of *qiyās* to false accusation would amount to altering the divine prescription (*naṣṣ*) which declares that the false accuser shall be forever barred from rendering testimony.[1]

[1] *Kashf*, p. 1051.

CHAPTER VI

Abrogation and Conflict of the Evidences

When there exist in the *sharī'ah* two evidences, one of which refutes what the other establishes, the following cases are possible. (1) Both evidences are of equal strength, but one is later in time; (2) both evidences are of equal strength, but it is not known which is the later; (3) one of the evidences is stronger by virtue of a secondary difference; (4) one of the evidences is stronger by virtue of an essential difference. The first case involves abrogation of one evidence by another; the second is a case of conflict without preference; the third is one of conflict, with preference (*mu'āraḍah ma'-al-tarjīḥ*); the fourth properly speaking, is really not a case of conflict or preference, for these terms are used only when the two evidences are of equal strength.

First Case: Abrogation (Naskh) [1]

Abrogation is the occurrence in the *sharī'ah* of an evidence of later date than another already existing, establishing the opposite of what the earlier one does. The fact that the later evidence seems to mortals a reversal of the earlier is simply because the first evidence was indefinite (*muṭlaq*) as to time limit, and consequently was presumed by them, owing to their ignorance, to be eternal. In reality, the occurrence of an abrogatory evidence denotes only that the eternal law-giver had decreed for the first evidence a

[1] *Tawḍīḥ*, p. 408; Pazdawi, p. 874.

certain time limit finally revealed and made known to mortals by the fact of abrogation.

Abrogation is granted by the Mohammedans in distinction from the Jews who deny it. There have also been Mohammedans who denied it; but al-Pazdawi thinks that such persons may not properly be called so.

Inasmuch as abrogation is nothing but the revelation of the time until which the repealed evidence was to be valid, **only those evidences** may be **abrogated which are** in themselves **capable of time limitation.** Hence the following are not subject to abrogation: (1) provisions concerning the divine attributes of the Creator, which having existed forever, are not capable of non-existence; (2) a provision connected with a circumstance which negates the possibility of time limitation: for example the Mohammedan *sharī'ah* in its entirety can never become abrogated, because the circumstance of Mohammed's being the last of the prophets negates the possibility of its abrogation. Furthermore, the abrogating provision must be later than the abrogated, both of them being *sharī'ah* provisions. Hence the suspension of religious duties because of infirmity or death does not constitute a case of abrogation.

There are **other conditions** which are **not unanimously agreed upon,** some of them being as follows: that the two provisions be of the same genus (*jins*); that there must be some substitute for the repealed provision; that the abrogating provision must be less rigorous than the one abrogated; that a provision cannot be repealed before enough time has passed for persons subject to the law (*mukallaf*) to show their faith (*tamakkun min al-i'tiqād*), although it is not necessary, as some claim, that the time should be long enough for the actual carrying out of the provision. The divine command to Abraham to slay Isaac is a case in point. According to some, it is a case of abrogation, because there passed enough time for Abraham to show his faith, but according to others it is not a case of abrogation.

Only the Koran and the sunnah may be abrogators (*nāsikh*). There may be four ways of abrogation: abrogation of Koran by Koran, of Koran by *sunnah*,[1] whether of the *mutawātir* or the *mash-hūr* kind,[2] of *sunnah* by Koran, and of *sunnah* by *sunnah*. Al-Shāfi'i has maintained that the abrogation of the Koran by the *sunnah*, and *vice versa*, is not valid.

As regards the ijma', some Hanifites and the Mu'tazilites held that the *ijmā'* can repeal the Koran and the *sunnah*. According to the majority of the doctors, however, this cannot be, since *ijmā'* is unanimity of opinion and opinion may not set a time limit to the prescriptions of the *sharī'ah*. Besides, if the *ijmā'* occurred after Mohammed's time, it is unanimously admitted that there cannot be abrogation after that time, and if it occurred in Mohammed's time, inasmuch as there could not then be an *ijmā'*, except upon his opinion, it would not really be a case of *ijmā'*, but of *sunnah*.

Finally, **as regards qiyas**, it evidently may not repeal the Koran or the *sunnah*, since its function is to extend their prescriptions to cases lying outside the prescripts of the Koran and the *sunnah*. Some held the opposite view.

SECOND CASE: CONFLICT WITHOUT PREFERENCE (MU'ARADAH)[3]

When there is a conflict between two verses of the Koran, or between one verse and a pair of verses, or between one

[1] According to the *Tawḍīḥ* (p. 416), the *sunnah* does not abrogate the text of the Koran "but only its legal value (*ḥukm*), for the Koran and the *sunnah* are alike only from the viewpoint of being an evidence for values, but not in form also, since the Koran alone is divine in form."

[2] *Tawḍīḥ*, p. 417.

[3] *Tawḍīḥ*, p. 531; *cf.* Pazdawi, p. 796.

sunnah and a pair of *sunnahs*, or between one *qiyās* and a pair of *qiyāses*, it is a case of conflict between equals, since strength does not consist in number, and consequently the single verse, *sunnah*, or *qiyās* is not necessarily set aside to make room for the pair.

In the event of a **conflict,** if **between qiyases,** one or the other is preferred according to one's convictions. If, however, the conflict is **between two verses** or two readings of the Koran, **or two sunnahs,** whether sayings or doings of the Prophet, **or a verse and a sunnah,**[1] and it is not known which of the conflicting evidences is the later in time, (otherwise it would be a case of abrogation) **one proceeds as follows:** if it is possible to reconcile them, by reference to their value (*ḫukm*), subject-matter, or time, it is done, otherwise, the conflicting evidences are set aside, and other evidences are referred to. For example, if the conflicting evidences are verses of the Koran, reference is made to the *sunnah* and, if no provision is found in the *sunnah*, to *qiyās* and the sayings of the Companions. Similarly, if the conflict is between two *sunnahs*, then *qiyās* and the sayings of the Companions are referred to. In going from the *sunnah* to *qiyās* and the sayings of the Companions, two courses are possible. According to those who place the sayings of the Companions before *qiyās* in every case, reference is first made to the sayings, and if no provision is found in them, to *qiyās*. But according to those who hold that the sayings of the Companions, in regard to points that can be established by *qiyās*, are nothing but *qiyāses*, one may refer on such points to either, according to his convictions.

There cannot be a conflict **between** the **ijma' and** another decisive evidence (*dalīl qaṯ'i*), namely, the **Koran and** the

[1] It is only the *sunnah* of the *mutawātir* and the *mash-hūr* type that is meant here, for the "individual" can never conflict with the Koran or the other two kinds of *sunnah*.

sunnah, since a valid *ijmā'* may not be reached in contradiction to them.

THIRD AND FOURTH CASES: CONFLICT OF EVIDENCES UNEQUAL BY VIRTUE OF A SECONDARY OR AN ESSENTIAL DIFFERENCE

The inequality may be in the content or in the support (*matn wa sanad*). **Inequality in the content** arises when the proper sense of a word is contrasted with its metaphorical, or the explicit sense is contrasted with the implicit, *etc.* **Inequality in the support** happens when the *mash-hūr* is compared with the "individual," or the report of the transmitter who is a *faqīh* is compared with the report of a transmitter who is not a *faqīh*, or a *qiyās* which is based on a cause (*'illah*) expressly stated in the sources is contrasted with one whose cause is only hinted at. In case of inequality, the stronger evidence is always preferred to the weaker, for example, the *mash-hūr* to the "individual." The laws of determining the stronger evidence in each case have been carefully defined by the doctors in the treatises on *uṣūl-al-fiqh*.

CHAPTER VII

Other Principles of Legislation

SECTION I

Istihsan [1]

We have been examining so far the four bases of *fiqh*, namely the sources of law which are accepted by all of the four important orthodox schools as lawful, and which constitute, as it were, the sources par excellence. There are however other principles of legislation accepted by only a few of them, which need to be briefly explained.

Foremost among these principles is *istiḫsān*, advocated by the Hanifites alone. The word means literally, to hold something for good, right. According to the treatises on *uṣūl-al-fiqh*, **istihsan technically denotes** the abandonment of the opinion to which reasoning by analogy (*qiyās*) would lead, in favor of a different opinion supported by stronger evidence. Such a departure from *qiyās*, may be based on evidence found in the *sunnah*, or the *ijmā'*, on necessity (*ḏarūrah*), or on what the upholders of *qiyās* claim to be another kind of *qiyās* which, though it does not so readily occur to the mind as the first *qiyās*, in reality is stronger than it.[2] Departure from *qiyās* in the three former

[1] Pazdawi, p. 1122 *et seq.*; *Tawḏiḫ*, p. 493 *et seq.*

[2] In the usage of writers on *uṣūl-al-fiqh*, *istiḫsān* generally means this last kind of *istiḫsān*, namely, the *istiḫsān* based on another *qiyās*, whereas in the books on *fiqh* it denotes the former three kinds. As we are concerned with questions of *uṣūl-al-fiqh*, *istiḫsān* shall mean the *istiḫsān* of the fourth kind, unless otherwise indicated.

cases is held by all four schools to be legitimate. For example, *salam* (sale of future goods for present cash) and location (*ijārah*),[1] though both contrary to *qiyās*, being sales of non-existing goods, have been justified by the *sunnah*; or *istiṣnā'* (placing an order with an artisan), although contrary to *qiyās* for similar reasons, has been justified by *ijmā'*.

However, departure from one *qiyās* in favor of another *qiyās*, that is, in favor of **istihsan**, has been **a subject of** hot controversy and bitter **attack**, especially **on the part of al-Shafi'i**, and his disciples. This attack has been justified by the allegation that *istiḥsān* is no more nor less than a setting aside of the revealed sources in favor of the personal opinion of the canonist. The Hanifites have strongly denied this accusation. Thus the author of the *Kashf*[2] expresses himself on the matter as follows:

Some of the false accusers among the Moslems have attacked Abu Hanīfah and his disciples because they abandoned *qiyās* for *istiḥsān*, and said, "The *sharī'ah* evidences are the Book, the *sunnah*, the *ijmā'*, and the *qiyās*, and the *istiḥsān* is a fifth principle recognized by Abu Hanīfah alone" . . . and it is related of al-Shāfi'i that he exaggerated in denying *istiḥsān*, for he said, "Who uses *istiḥsān* places himself in the place of God as legislator," but all this is attack without examination . . . and learn that the opponents have not blamed Abu Hanīfah for the *istiḥsān* based on evidence in the *sunnah*, or the *ijmā'*, or on necessity, for the abandonment of *qiyās* on these evidences is granted by all unanimously, but they have blamed him only for the *istiḥsān* based on opinion, [but it is not true that this latter *istiḥsān* is based on opinion, since] according

[1] Location is considered as a case of sale of non-existing goods because the benefits from the use of the object leased accrue only in the future.

[2] P. 1123.

to us it is only one of two *qiyāses*, and not a different thing invented by way of passion and without evidence. Doubtless when two *qiyāses* oppose each other one of them must be preferred [for conduct in accordance with it] when a preference is possible, and [the *qiyās* preferred] is called *istiḥsān*, in order to indicate that it is the better fitted of the two [for conduct in accordance with it] in that it is stronger than the other *qiyās*.

Another doctor, al-Pazdawi, says: [1]

Inasmuch as according to our school the cause is a cause for the value, we have named that which is weak, *qiyās*, and that which is strong *istiḥsān*, meaning by it that it is a more commendable *qiyās*, and we have preferred the second, even though it is non-apparent, to the former which is apparent,[2] for importance belongs to the strength, [of causal "effectiveness"] and not to its appearance. Do they not see that this world is apparent, and the next world non-apparent, and yet the non-apparent is preferred by virtue of the strength of its "effectiveness," that is, its permanence, eternity, and excellence, and the apparent [*i. e.*, the present world] is abandoned for the weakness of its "effectiveness" [*athar*]? Likewise the *qiyās* lapses when it is in conflict with the *istiḥsān*.[3]

[1] P. 1126.

[2] The Hanifite doctors, who claim *istiḥsān* to be a kind of *qiyās*, in order to avoid confusion distinguish it from the *qiyās*, whose laws we have already examined, by calling the former apparent (*jali*), and the *istiḥsān* non-apparent, (*khafi*) *qiyās*.

[3] The *Tawḍīḥ* (p. 493) has the following to say on this matter: "Some people have denied the validity of conduct on the basis of *istiḥsān*, because of ignorance about it; for if they oppose the name, there can be no discussion on terminology, and if they oppose the meaning of it, it is nonsense similarly, because by *istiḥsān* we (*i. e.*, the Hanifites) mean an evidence of the number of evidences unanimously accepted (such as the *sunnah*, *etc.*) which occurs in opposition to the apparent *qiyās*, . . . and there is no sense in denying it; in fact, such opposing evidence may be either a *sunnah*, . . . or finally a non-apparent *qiyās*. . . ."

In order to pass judgment on the merits of the case put forth by each side, we must examine first what is really meant by *istiḫsān*, and then inquire into its actual working in one or two cases.

The Hanifites are profuse in saying that, what they mean by istihsan, is that one of two qiyases which, although somewhat more obscure than the other, is preferred because it is stronger in its causal "effectiveness." They further add that the mere fact that it is called *istiḫsān*, a contraction of the expression *qiyās mustaḫsan*, meaning "the *qiyās* which is preferred," indicates that it is a case of choosing between two *qiyāses* and not of introducing a new principle, as the Shafiites claim.

A close inquiry into the treatises on *uṣūl-al-fiqh* will disclose that the word *istiḫsān* is not used to indicate only the *qiyās* that has been preferred but that, on the contrary, the name applies to some new kind of a principle—a principle different from *qiyās*, at least as the latter has been understood by the doctors—which is called *istiḫsān*, whether or not it is preferred to *qiyās*.[1] This point has been raised by the very defenders of *istiḫsān*.[2]

The fact is that istihsan, as originally introduced and used by Abu Hanifah, was no more nor less than a resort to personal opinion as influenced by considerations of public welfare. When the Shafiites attacked this principle on the ground that it meant a setting aside of the revealed texts, the disciples of Abu Hanīfah felt themselves forced

[1] The following quotation from the *Tawḍiḫ* (p. 496) fully bears this point out: "By an intellectual division, each [*qiyās* and *istiḫsān*] is divided into strong and weak in causal "effectiveness," and in case of conflict, istihsan is not preferred to qiyas except in one single case, namely, when the *qiyās* is weak in its causal "effectiveness." and the *istiḫsān* is strong. As regards the other three cases, the *qiyās* is preferred to the *istiḫsān*.

[2] *Kashf*, p. 1123.

to show that such was not the case, and being able in scholastic methods, they put forward the contention that *istihsān* was nothing but another kind of *qiyās*, which was called *istihsān* because, being stronger, it was preferred to the other. But at the next moment, they are forced to contradict themselves by saying that *istihsān* is not always preferred to *qiyās*. This is nothing less than an admission by implication on their part, that *istihsān* is not the same thing as *qiyās*.

That Abu Hanīfah and his earliest disciples did not consider *istihsān* as a kind of *qiyās*, and that the above contention is really an afterthought, is **borne out by** statements quoted in the **Hanifite books themselves.** Thus al-Bukhāri states in the *Kashf* [1] that the Hanifites disagreed about the meaning of the *istihsān* which Abu Hanīfah advocated. Some said that it is a departure from one *qiyās* to another and stronger *qiyās*.[2] Others said it is the limitation of *qiyās* by some evidence stronger than itself. Abu 'l-Hasan al-Karkhi, who preceded al-Pazdawi by over a century [3] is quoted as having said: " *Istihsān* is to depart from judging in a case according to what has been judged in analogous cases, and to judge to the contrary on account of a stronger reason (*li wajh aqwa*) which renders necessary the departure from the former." [4] This quotation from al-Karkhi seems to express the real situation before the later writers had as yet woven into it their own refinements. The mere fact of a disagreement about the meaning in which Abu Hanīfah used *istihsān* is very significant. It shows that Abu Hanīfah did not use the word in any techni-

[1] P. 1123.

[2] This is the view held by al-Pazdawi and the later doctors.

[3] Al-Karkhi died in 340 of the *Hijrah*, while al-Pazdawi died in 482.

[4] *Kashf, loc. cit.*

cal sense. Had that been the case, like so many of his views it would probably have been placed on record. The fact is that he used the word *istihsān* in its usual meaning, namely that of abandoning *qiyās* for an opinion thought more subservient to the social interests. In the *Kashf* there is a quotation to bear this out. According to it, Abu Hanīfah has said on certain occasions, " I have abandoned *istihsān* for *qiyās*." He evidently meant by *istihsān* something different from *qiyās*. Similar statements are found in Abu Yūsuf's *Kitāb-al-kharaj*.[1] Finally, al-Shāfi'i condemning *istihsān* says[2] " If one were allowed to ignore *qiyās*, the people of opinion [*ahl al-'uqūl*] who are not informed on *'ilm* [namely, the knowledge of the revealed texts] would then have been allowed to express opinion on matters in regard to which there is no prescription in the revealed texts, according to what seems to them proper (*istihsān*)"; but this is not allowed. Now if Abu Hanīfah meant by *istihsān* a kind of *qiyās*, it is very likely that al-Shāfi'i would have referred to it. We may, therefore, be certain that the contention made in regard to *istihsān* being a kind of *qiyās*, is only a fiction, invented by later Hanifite doctors. Even if we grant this fiction to be true, *istihsān* still is a liberating principle, as will become clear from the following:

To take up first the contention that *istihsān* is a kind of *qiyās*, it may be answered that **it is true that** in the last analysis **istihsan is a sort of** judgment by **analogy, but** one in which the causal attribute (*'illah*), is not determined in quite the same way prescribed in the treatises on *usūl-al-fiqh*, but is somewhat **far fetched.** The very name of *khafi* (concealed, subtle) given to this kind of *qiyās* by the

[1] P. 109, l. 1; p. 112, l. —5; p. 117, l. —5; *cf.* also *al-Jāmi' al-Sagir*, p. 17, l. —5; p. 72, l. 2.

[2] *Risālah*, p. 70, l. 1.

doctors, suggests this. But in applying a *qiyās* the most important thing is the basis on which the *qiyās* will be made, namely, the *'illah*, and if you once grant the right of departure from the accepted principles in determining this *'illah*, with the aid of a little scholastic ability, one can prove almost anything on earth. A few examples will illustrate the point.[1]

Judging **by analogy the food touched** (*su'r*) **by wild birds should be unclean** (*najs*), because the food touched by wild beasts is unclean, and wild birds are like wild beasts, both being unclean for eating. However, judging **by istihsan,** the food touched by wild birds is **clean** (*ṯāhir*). The argument is as follows. The quadrupeds, when they touch food, inevitably leave a part of their saliva in the remainder and pollute it, because the saliva is secreted from the flesh and is unclean like it. In the case of the birds, however, this is not true, because they take the food by means of their beak, which is a hollow bone and has no saliva in it. So, although apparently, the food touched by the latter should by analogy also be unclean, a closer inquiry reveals the fact that it is not polluted. Indeed the animals are not unclean as such, for it is allowed to use them and sell them, and if they were unclean, in and of themselves, like pigs, their use and sale would have been likewise forbidden. Moreover, if the bones of dead animals are considered clean, how can the bones of living animals be considered unclean? In other words, the uncleanness resides in the flesh alone, and the food they have touched has been considered unclean because of its admixture with the unclean, but this does not happen in the case of the birds.

How many nice distinctions must be made in order to reach the above conclusion? It must first be proved that the

[1] *Kashf*, p. 1126; *Tawḍīḥ*, p. 493.

'illah is the admixture with the unclean. Second, that it is only the flesh that is unclean, not the beak, horn, *etc.* Yet one might just as readily argue that the latter are more, or just as much unclean as the flesh; or, assuming for the sake of argument, that contact without some theoretical minimum of admixture is possible, that mere contact is sufficient to pollute.

To cite **another example of istihsan,** if two parties to an act of *salam,* (sale of future goods for present cash), disagree in regard to the length (*dhirā'*) of the thing sold (*muslam-fīh*), according to *qiyās,* each party may require an oath from the other (*taḥāluf*), because they have dis agreed about something claimed by virtue of an act of *salam.* According to *istiḥsān,* they do not require an oath, because they have not disagreed on the thing sold, but on its quality, which does not require the giving of an oath to each party. " However, if we examine closely, we see that they are not disagreeing on the very thing sold, but on its quality, for they have disagreed about the length. But the length is a quality, because when the length is greater, the dress made out of it is better, unlike the case of measure by volume, (*kayl*) or by weight. Since the measure by length is a quality, disagreement on the length does not necessitate *taḥāluf.* This meaning, namely, that the length is a quality, is more subtle, than the other, and judgment based on it is called *istiḥsān,* as distinguished from *qiyās.*" [1]

The argument here is that a shortage in length is different from one in weight or volume, because in the latter two cases the buyer may make up the shortage by buying more of it, whereas in the case of length, although he may still buy more, he cannot use this last increment as profitably. For instance, assuming the object bought to be cloth, a shortage

[1] *Tawḍīḥ, idem.*

in the length would affect the quality of the dress to be made out of it. Now, although this is true in general, it **is based on many assumptions.** In the first place one might question whether this consideration of length was entirely relevant to the point at issue, namely, the taking of an oath by both parties. Again, one might contend that there are cases where it is not possible to buy the part wanting, and then volume and weight would be like length.

These two concrete cases clearly illustrate, **how easily** the **argument may be twisted** to arrive at conclusions as different as prohibition and permission. This is not saying, that the Hanifite doctors have been consciously twisting their arguments, or that it is at all necessary to do that, in order **to get the desired result.** As a matter of fact, what happens is that one starts out with a certain predisposition inspired by existing practices and social needs or by *a priori* considerations, and the rest takes care of itself without consciousness on the part of the thinker.

SECTION II

The Other Principles

ISTISLAH. We have already referred to this principle in discussing *qiyās*. **It consists in prohibiting or permitting a thing** simply **because it serves a "useful purpose"** (*maṣlaḥah*), although there is no express evidence in the revealed sources to support such action. *Istiṣlāḥ*, has been called by some, "independent deduction" (*istidlāl mursal*), or simply "deduction" (*istidlāl*). Al-Gazāli defines *istiṣlāḥ*, as the establishment of a legal principle (*ḥukm*) for which there is no evidence in the sources, but which is recommended by reason as advantageous. According to al-Khuwārizmi, "useful purpose" (*maṣlaḥah*) means the protection and preservation of the objects of the *sharīʿah*, by warding off mischief from humanity. The "useful purpose" has been divided into three kinds.

(1) **The "useful purpose" which meets an absolute necessity** (*ḏarūri*). Such is supposed to be the case, in the following five instances called *al-kulliyyāt al-khams*: (a) preservation of life (the law of tallion); (b) protection of property (prescriptions like the cutting off of one's hand for theft); (c) preservation of the offspring (prohibition of adultery); (d) preservation of faith (the killing of the apostates [*murtadd*] and holy war); (e) finally, preservation of reason: the prohibition of alcoholic drinks is based on this ground.

(2) **The "useful purpose" which** meets no absolute necessity but **is merely expedient** (*ḥāji*). For example, the institution of location (*ijārah*) is based on this.

(3) **The "useful purpose" which serves** an end like the promotion of **good morals** (*taḥsīni*).[1]

The principle of *istiṣlāḥ* is used by the Malikites, the other schools having prohibited its use. However, the Malikites claim that all the schools have used it.[2] According to al-Juwayni, Mālik carried this principle too far, so that for purposes useful in appearance only, he made legitimate the taking of life, and the confiscation of property, although there was no evidence in the revealed texts to confirm such a procedure.

ISTISHAB. This principle has been introduced by al-Shāfi'i. According to it, when the existence of a thing has been once established by evidence, even though later some doubt should arise as to its continuance in existence, it is still considered to exist. It is called *istiṣḥāb al-ḥāl*, if the present is judged according to the past, and *istiṣḥāb al-*

[1] Shawkāni, p. 201.

[2] *Majmū'*, p. 67.

mādi, if the converse is the case. This principle is admitted by Abu Hanīfah also, but only to refute an assertion (*dawa*), that is, as an instrument of defence, (*daf' dawa*) and not to establish a new claim (*dawa*). According to al-Shāfi'i, however, it may be used for both purposes. The Hanifites hold that the establishment of the existence of a fact is no evidence of its continuance in existence and therefore, they say, the continuance of the Mohammedan *sharī'ah* after the death of Mohammed does not rest on the principle of *istishāb*, as the Shafiites claim, but on the *hadīth* that the Mohammedan *sharī'ah* will never be abrogated.

The principle of **istishab** is **a limited principle.** It only applies to cases where there is no evidence obtainable, and at best, establishes the continuance of a fact in existence, which was already proved to have existed.[1] Nevertheless, in the extended scope given to it by al-Shāfi'i, it acquires considerable importance, especially in questions of *fiqh*.

THE SUNNAH OF THE COMPANIONS. The **sunnah of** the **Companions** of the Prophet has been a source of great importance. **Theoretically** this *sunnah* is not **binding** upon the Mohammedans, except **in so far as it is based on that of the Prophet.** When the conduct of the Companions is based upon their personal judgments, it is considered equivalent to *qiyās*, and the canonist is free to accept or reject it. However this theoretical restriction has no importance in practice, since one can always claim that the *sunnah* of the Companions was based on that of the Prophet. This is confirmed by the divergence of view, concerning the meaning of the word *sunnah* when it occurs by itself (*mutlaq*), that is, when there is no indication to show whether it is the *sunnah* of the Prophet or of his Companions which is meant.

[1] *Tawdih*, p. 527.

We have seen in discussing the classification of the *sharī'ah* values, that many held the view that the word *sunnah* may mean both the *sunnah* of the Prophet and that of his Companions. It would seem that in actual practice usually no distinction was made between the two *sunnahs*, and that the writers on *uṣūl-al-fiqh* attempted to draw such a distinction, only because they were driven by the logical necessities of the case. Hence one may without hesitation say that **in practice the sunnah of the Companions has exercised great influence** on the development of the Mohammedan law. One may easily convince himself of this by a reference to the *fiqh* books where a great number of decisions have been based on the *sunnah* of the Companions. This is also borne out by the great number of traditions found in the *ḥadīth* collections, bearing on the *sunnah* of the Companions.[1]

The **views of the canonists** on this subject may be **summarized** as follows:[2]

(1) The *sunnah* of the companions is by unanimous opinion (*ijmā'*) binding on those points concerning which, though generally known, no opposition has been made on the part of the Moslems.

(2) Their *sunnah* is not binding on the points on which they have disagreed among themselves. There is an *ijmā'* on this opinion.

(3) There is disagreement as to the binding force of their *sunnah* on the points on which it is not known whether they have agreed or disagreed: according to al-Shāfi'i their *sunnah* on such points is not binding, because it cannot have been based on direct hearing from the Prophet, and because the Companions in their *ijtihād*, like other canonists, are

[1] *Cf.* Sprenger, p. 2.

[2] *Tawḍīḥ*, p. 384.

liable to error. But according to Sa'īd al-Barda'i, their *sunnah* is binding, because the Prophet has said: " My Companions are like the stars, no matter whom from among them you follow, you will be going the right way," and because most of the sayings of the Companions are based on what the latter have heard from the Prophet. Moreover, the Companions have witnessed the circumstances of the revelations, have been pioneers in the religion, and have had the blessing of conversation with the Prophet. According to al-Karkhi, the *sunnah* of the Companions is binding only as regards those points which cannot be otherwise cleared up by *qiyās*, as such points must have been based on direct hearing from the Prophet, unless they be lying, which is inconceivable. But their *sunnah* is not valid as regards points which may be established by *qiyās*, since the Companions like others may err in their *qiyāses*.

As regards the **Followers** (*tābi'iyyūn*, or *tābi'ūn*), that is, the generation following the Companions, their sayings are like those of the Companions, if they have expressed them during the time of the latter, for by the tacit confirmation of the Companions, they have become like them.[1]

Custom.[2] Custom (*'urf, 'ādah*) may be general (*'āmm*) or special (*khāṣṣ*). Each of these may either be in opposition to the sources (*naṣṣ shar'i*) or to the statements (*naṣṣ*) occurring in the recognized books of the school (*ẓāhir-al-riwāyah*); or on the contrary, it may be in accordance with them. If the latter is the case, there is no room for discussion; if however custom is in opposition to them the following cases are conceivable.

(1) **Custom is in opposition to the revealed texts,** (*naṣṣ shar'i*). In such a case, **if** the **opposition is absolute,**

[1] *Cf.* Pazdawi, p. 944; *Tawḍīḥ*, p. 383.

[2] Ibn 'Abidīn, vol. ii, pp. 114 *et seq.*

so much so that to follow the custom would amount to an abandonment of the text, then there is no doubt that **custom must be set aside. If** however the opposition is **not absolute,** if for example the text is general and the custom opposes it in some of its applications, or if the custom, instead of opposing the text opposes only a *qiyās* based on it, **preference is given to** the **custom, if general,** as was the case in *istiṣnā'* or in entering a bath without specifying the time to be spent therein.[1] Custom however is set aside, if not general.

(2) **Custom** is **in opposition to the text of the books recognized** in the Hanifite school **as standard** (*ẓāhir-al-riwāyah*). The texts of these books are either directly based on an unequivocal statement (*naṣṣ*) in the revealed sources, and then it is the same as in the preceding case; or they are merely the opinions of the doctors. Inasmuch as many of these opinions have been based by the *mujtahids* on the customs of their times, it is permissible to depart from them if the customs have meanwhile changed. It is necessary, however, in doing this to exercise great circumspection and care. In this last case, it is immaterial whether the custom is general or special, because both of them take precedence over the texts of the books.

Previous Dispensations.[2] According to some, these continue in force so long as they have not been abrogated. Others hold that they are not binding, unless there is evidence to the contrary. Still others claim that these

[1] Both in *istiṣnā'* and in entering a bath, analogy would require that the acts should be considered imperfect (*fāsid*): in the case of sale, because there is opposition to the principle that the thing sold must be already in existence at the time of sale; in the case of location, because the time during which the location is to run must be known. However, in both cases the analogy of the text has been overruled because of a custom to the contrary.

[2] *Tawḍīḥ*, p. 383; Pazdawi, p. 932.

were meant for the people, time and place for which they were revealed. The opinion generally accepted by the Hanifites is that previous dispensations, in view of their great distortion at the hands of their votaries, are **valid** for the Moslems **only in so far as they have been confirmed by the Mohammedan shari'ah.**

CHAPTER VIII

Classification of the Sharī'ah Values

The author of the *Tawḍīḥ* [1] reduces the various kinds of *sharī'ah* values (*ḥukm*) to the following classes:

A *sharī'ah* value may or may not consist in a correlation (*ta'alluq*) between one thing and another, as when we say that A is, or is not, the cause or condition of B.

When the value does consist in a correlation of one thing with another,[2]

(1) if that which is so correlated is contained in the thing to which it is correlated, it is called its **rukn** (formal cause), *e. g.*, the offer and acceptance of the two parties to a sale are the *rukn* of sale, because they are included in the act of sale;

(2) if the thing so correlated is not contained, but is external to the thing to which it is correlated, then,

(a) if it has been indicated in the revealed sources as the "effective" cause (*mu'ath-thir fīh*) of the latter thing, it is called its "**effective**" **cause** (*'illah*);

(b) if it is not so, and,

- (1) if on the whole it leads to the other thing, it is called its **sabab** (occasion, cause),
- (2) if it does not lead to it, and,
  - (a) if the other thing is dependent upon it, it is called a **condition** (*sharṭ*), and
  - (b) if the other thing is not dependent upon it, it is called a **sign** (*'alāmah*) of the other thing.

[1] Pp. 561 *et seq.*; *cf. Talwīḥ, ibid.*

[2] *Tawḍīḥ*, p. 561.

When the value does not consist in a correlation of one thing with another, it is either a quality of an act by a legally responsible person (*mukallaf*), such as the quality of an act being allowed (*ibāḥah*) or prohibited (*ḥurmah*) in the *sharī'ah*; or it is the effect (*athar*) of such an act, such as ownership and indebtedness, which are the effects of the acts of purchase and borrowing respectively.

When the value is a quality of an act, two cases are possible:

(1) The **emphasis** is either **laid on** the "**worldly consideration,**" for example, when we speak of the validity (*ṣiḥḥah*) of an act of worship, we are primarily thinking of the act as freeing the worshiper from the obligation of performing that particular worship again. In other words, we are emphasizing what the doctors call "worldly consideration,"[1] although we may be thinking, in a secondary way, also of the "religious consideration," namely, the acquisition of merit (*thawāb*) which the act results in.

(2) Or the **emphasis** is **laid on** the "**religious consideration,**" for example, when we speak of an act being *wājib* (obligatory), we are primarily thinking of the act as resulting in religious merit (*thawāb*), although we may be thinking of the act, in a secondary way, also as securing freedom from an obligation (*tafrīg al-dhimmah*).

From the standpoint of the "worldly consideration," the value of an act is said to have,

(a) **validity** (*ṣiḥḥah*), if the act results in the realization

[1] By "**worldly consideration**" the doctors mean, in matters of worship (*'ibādāt*), the freeing of the person from the obligation of performing the particular act of worship, say, ablution, and in temporal matters (*mu'āmalāt*), the securing of the various intentions and objects which pertain to those temporal matters, such as, for example, the acquisition of property or its alienation pertaining to the worldly acts of purchase and sale respectively.

of the "worldly consideration;" for example, a sale is valid (*ṣaḥīḥ*) if it results legally in the transfer of ownership from the seller to the buyer;

(b) **nullity** (*buṭlān*), if it entirely fails to secure the realization of the "worldly consideration;" such an act is called null (*bāṭil*);

(c) **imperfection** (*fasād*), if the formal cause (*rukn*) and the conditions (*sharā'iṭ*) of the act are conducive to the realization of the "worldly consideration," but its outward qualities (*awṣāf khārijiyyah*) are not so conducive; the act then is said to be *fāsid*.[1]

From the standpoint of the "religious[2] consideration," values are either **'azimah** (ideal) or **rukhsah** (actual). They are said to be *'azīmah*, when they are considered *a priori* and in their original rigor, without reference to any attenuating circumstances in life, which may soften their rigor or even entirely suspend them. They are the law as intended in the first instance by the lawgiver. They are said to be *rukhṣah* (literally, concession) when they are considered with reference to the attenuating circumstances of life.

Human acts, according to the *'azīmah* values which attach to them, are **grouped in the following** categories

[1] From the standpoint of "worldly consideration" as pertaining to temporal matters (*mu'āmalāt*), one may further distinguish between acts, which are contracted (*mun'aqid*) or uncontracted (*gayr-mun'aqid*), authorized (*nāfidh*) or unauthorized (*mawqūf*), binding (*lāzim*) or non-binding (*gayr-lāzim*).

[2] Some doctors have claimed that the several *sharī'ah* values distinguished from the standpoint of "worldly consideration" may be all reduced to some one of the values distinguished from the religious standpoint. Thus, they said that when a sale is claimed to be valid (*ṣaḥīḥ*), it is only meant that the purchaser may exercise on the thing purchased all the rights of ownership, such acts on his part being *mubāḥ*. Others contended that these values, properly speaking, are not *sharī'ah* values at all. (*Talwīḥ*, p. 563.)

which shade off into one another from the "imperative" (*fard*) to the "indifferent" (*mubāh*).

(1) The **fard** (imperative) is the act whose value, called *faradiyyah*, has been established by a *sharī'ah* evidence about which there is no doubt. The legal effect (*hukm*) of the *fard* is that it must be given absolute faith and self-surrender and that it must be executed. Failure to believe in it entails unbelief, and failure to execute it causes impiety (*fisq*).

Conversely, the commission of the *fard* results in the acquisition of religious merit (*thawāb*). *Thawāb* technically means title to "divine mercy and pardon, and to the mediation of the Prophet."[1] Examples of the *fard* are faith (*īmān*), performance of the daily prayers, giving of *zakāt*, pilgrimage to Mecca, *etc.*

The **fard**, and for that matter, the *wājib* also, is **divided into two kinds:** (a) The **fard 'ayn** (personal *fard*); it is the act which every one must personally perform. The performance of the daily prayers, and the giving of *zakāt* are of this kind. (b) The **fard kifayah** (social *fard*); it is the act which every person is under obligation to perform, until a sufficient number of persons have performed it, the rest being then absolved from the obligation of performance. The reward (*ajr*) in such case, belongs to those who performed the act, but the rest are not punished for its omission. If however no one should perform the act, then they are all punished. An example of this is the obligation of holy war (*jihād*). Every Moslem is under obligation to wage it, until a sufficient number of Moslems have done so.

(2) The **wajib** (obligatory) is the act whose value, called *wujūb*, has been established by a *sharī'ah* evidence concerning which there is doubt. The giving of alms for

[1] *Tech. Dict.*, p. 171.

breaking the fast is of this kind. The value (*hukm*) of the *wājib* is that it must be executed like the *fard*, although it need not be given absolute faith as the latter. Al-Shāfi'i merged the *fard* and the *wājib* into one single category, calling it by either one of the two names, and defining it as "that whose commission is rewarded and omission punished." Both the *fard* and the *wājib* admit of divine pardon.

(3) The acts which are not obligatory to the degree of being *fard* or *wājib*, and whose commission is still rewarded and is preferable to their omission, though the latter does not entail divine punishment, are said to be (a) **sunnah**,[1] if they are the way habitually followed in the religion (*al-tarīqah al-maslūkah fi 'l-dīn*), **namely**, if they are **acts** that were **performed by** the **Prophet habitually**.[2] According to the Hanifites, *sunnah*, unless there is an indication to the contrary (*al-sunnah al-mutlaqah*), may mean habitual acts performed by both the Prophet and the Companions, but al-Shāfi'i held that it can only mean acts performed by the Prophet.[3] The **sunnah** is **of two kinds: sunnat-al-huda**, also called *al-sunnah al-mu'akkadah*, such as the *adhān* (calling the public to prayer) and *jamā'ah* (prayer in public under the leadership of an *imām*), whose omission is evil and abominable (*makrūh*); and **sunnat-al-zawa'id**, such as the personal ways of the Prophet in dressing, walking, and sitting, whose omission is not abominable. According to the *Technical Dictionary*,[4] Sadr-al-sharī'ah classed as *sunnat-al-huda* the Prophetic acts pertaining to

[1] *Sunnah* in this sense must not be confused with *sunnah* in the sense of one of the four bases of *fiqh*. *Sunnah* in the latter sense may and does include prescriptions of every category.

[2] *Cf.* Pazdawi, p. 628.

[3] *Tawdih*, p. 566; *Tech. Dict.*, p. 704; Pazdawi, p. 630.

[4] P. 705.

worship (*'ibādah*), and as *sunnat-al-zawā'id*, those not so pertaining to worship (*'ādah*). *Sunnah*, as will be observed from the above, applies primarily to acts performed in the process of worship (*'ibādah*). This explains the fact that some held *sunnah* to mean that which is supererogatory in worship.[1]

(b) They are said to be **nafl**, if they are **acts** that the Prophet **performed at one time** and **omitted at another** time. The *nafl* is less obligatory than the *sunnat-al-zawā'id*, and like *sunnah*, *nafl*, too, applies primarily to acts of worship, that are supererogatory, namely, acts of worship that are neither *farḏ*, nor *wājib*, nor *sunnah*. *Nafl* is also used in the more general sense of acts of worship that are neither *farḏ*, nor *wājib*, and in this sense it includes *sunnah*. An example of the *nafl* is to perform more prostrations in the prayer, or to give more than the legal rate of *zakāt*. The omission of the *nafl* is not abominable. The *nafl* is also called *mandūb*, *taṯawwu'* and *mustaḫabb*, and the quality of an act being *mandūb* or *mustaḫabb* is called *nadb*, or *istiḫbāb*, respectively.

(4) The **mubah**, or *jā'iz*, or *ḫalāl* (the indifferent) is the act whose commission is not rewarded but whose omission is not punished.

(5) The **makruh** (abominable, odious) is the act whose omission is preferable to its commission. It is of two kinds: (1) The **makruh karahat-al-tanzih** (that which has been considered abominable for purposes of keeping pure). This kind is nearer to the *mubāḫ* than to the next category, that is, its commission is not punished but its omission is rewarded though by a lower reward than that of the next category. (2) The **makruh karahat-al-tahrim**

[1] *Tech. Dict.*, *ibid.*

(abominable to the degree of prohibition). This kind is nearer to the *ḥarām*, that is, its commission results in deprivation of the privilege of intercession and in other disadvantages, excepting punishment in fire. Muḥammad Ibn al-Hasan considers this kind as identical with the following one. In his view, an act is *ḥarām*, whose omission is based on evidence of which there is no doubt, otherwise it is *makrūh karāhat-al-taḥrīm.*[1]

(6) The **haram**, (prohibited) or *maḥẓūr*, is the act whose commission is punished and omission rewarded.

The rigor of the above prescriptions is subject, as already hinted, to **the softening influence of the rukhsah**, which according to Ibn 'Abbās, is an alms of God which one must not refuse.[2] For instance, if a Mohammedan is compelled to deny his faith, he is permitted to do so, although the *'azīmah* would be for him to persist in his faith until death. The excuse in this case is the right of a person to live. In certain cases, it is even obligatory to make use of the benefit of *rukhṣah*, while in others it is only commendable (*mandūb*) or indifferent (*mubāh*). An example of the first case would be to eat a dead corpse, when on the point of starvation. An example of the second, would be to reduce the length of prayer during a journey, and of the third, to break fast while journeying.

With reference to the performance of the preceding various categories of prescriptions, the following distinctions have made made:

(1) **Ada'** is the performance of the obligation *per se* (*'ayn*), whether or not a time has been specified in the revealed sources for its performance.

(2) **Qada'** is the performance of a similar (*mithl*) obli-

[1] *Tawḍīḥ*, p. 566.

[2] Goldziher, *d. Zahiriten*, pp. 68–9.

gation, instead of the identical obligation, as in the first case. The above is according to the Hanifites. The Shafiites use these terms only in regard to the performance of prescriptions for whose obligation a time limit has been specified. They mean by *adā'* the performance of the obligation at the time set for it, *qadā'* being its performance after such time. Moreover, they distinguish a third kind, *i'ādah* (repetition), which means a second performance of the obligation at its set time, the first performance having been non-valid for some reason or other.

CHAPTER IX

Ijtihad or the Exercise of Independent Thought[1]

The word **ijtihad** means literally the exertion of great efforts in order to do a thing. Technically it is **defined** as "the putting forth of every effort in order to determine with a degree of probability a question of *sharī'ah*." It follows from the definition that a person would not be exercising *ijtihād* if he arrived at an opinion while he felt that he could exert himself still more in the investigation he is carrying out. This restriction, if conformed to, would mean the realization of the utmost degree of thoroughness. By extension, *ijtihād* also means the opinion rendered. The person exercising *ijtihād* is called *mujtahid*, and the question he is considering is called *mujtahad-fīh*.

It becomes clear from the definition, that the **mujtahad-fīh must be a question of sharī'ah.** In other words, intellectual problems, such as the createdness (*ḥudūth*) of the universe, the existence of a Creator, the sending of prophets, *etc.*, cannot properly constitute a subject of *ijtihād*, because in these there is only one correct view, and all holding a different view are wrong. **Furthermore,** the subject of *ijtihād* **must not be one on which there is positive evidence** (*dalīl qaṭ'i*). Consequently, one may not exercise *ijtihād* on matters such as the *wujūb* (obligation) of the "pillars of faith" (*e. g.*, the performance of the five prayers or the giving of *zakāt*), or such as the prohibition of adultery, murder, wine-drinking, usury, theft. These are evident truths of the *sharī'ah*, based on explicit statements

[1] *Kashf*, p. 1134; *Tawḍīḥ*, p. 554; *Taqrīr*, vol. iii, p. 291.

(*naṣṣ*), and concerning them the whole Moslem community is of one opinion (*ijmā'*). A wrong *ijtihād* concerning such questions would be outright sin, "and we are concerned here with the kind of *ijtihād* where wrong opinion does not entail sin."[1] In other words, the person who is qualified to be a **mujtahid** may exercise *ijtihād* only in regard to questions on which there is no positive evidence. In such cases he **may be right or wrong,** but, should he be wrong, he is not considered a sinner. On the contrary, "he is excused and rewarded, since his obligation is only to exert himself, and this he has already done, but he could not reach the truth on account of the obscurity of its evidences."[2] **If** the **mujtahid is wrong** notwithstanding the fact that the evidence is clear he is not excused, for obviously he is wrong "by reason of a fault of his, and because he did not do his best in exerting himself, and therefore **he is punished.**"[3] As regards the *mujtahid* who is wrong in the fundamentals of religion, his failure may be a case of simple error (*ḍalāl*) or of unbelief (*kufr*). Some claim that error in the fundamentals of religion does not entail sin.

According to al-Māwardi, the scope of *ijtihād* after the Prophet's death includes eight separate heads. Seven of these consist in the interpretation of the revealed texts, by some method such as analogy. and the eighth is the derivation of a meaning from other than the revealed texts, *e. g.*, by reasoning. A few of the **rules concerning ijtihad are as follows:**

The *mujtahid* is under a "personal obligation" (*farḍ 'ayn*) to exercise *ijtihād* in regard to matters concerning

[1] Gazāli, vol. ii, p. 354.

[2] *Talwiḥ*, p. 560.

[3] *Ibid.*, *cf.* also, Gazāli, vol. ii, p. 357; *Tawḍiḥ*, p. 559.

himself, for in such matters he is not allowed to follow (*taqlīd*) the opinion of others.

A *mujtahid* is likewise under a " personal obligation " to exercise *ijtihād* for others when the matter does not admit of delay.

When a person asks for the opinion of a *mujtahid* in order to meet a situation, the exercise of *ijtihād* concerning that situation becomes a *farḍ kifāyah* obligation upon all the *mujtahids*, and especially the *mujtahid* whose opinion was requested. When any one of these *mujtahids* renders an opinion upon the matter, the rest are absolved from the obligation, but if, notwithstanding the clearness of the question, they all refrain from rendering an opinion, they all become sinners. They are, however, excused if the question is ambiguous, but in such cases they must continue their investigation until they solve it.

When the *mujtahid* is asked to give his opinion on a case that has not as yet occurred, or when he considers such a case of his own accord, the obligation to render the opinion is not of the *farḍ* but only of the *mandūb* category.

The *mujtahid* is not allowed to change his opinion concerning the same case, although he may render a new and different opinion in the future concerning an identical case.

The **conditions pertaining to the mujtahid** are the following: The *mujtahid* must know many sciences and have many attainments. He must know the sciences of Koran, its legal and literal meanings, its divisions, and, some say, he must remember even the textual words, though others claim that the ability to trace them is sufficient. He must know the science of the *sunnah*, the ways of its transmission,[1] the texts and meanings (if transmitted in meaning).

[1] Al-Taftāzāni says that owing to the great distance of time it is now impossible to know all about the transmitters and that therefore it is enough to rely on *ḥadith*-collections like that of al-Bukhāri (*Talwīḥ*, p. 555).

the logical values of the terms, whether they are universals or particulars, *etc.* Finally he must know the laws of *qiyās* and *ijmā'*, *etc.* Yet all this is not enough. The *mujtahid* must possess a perfect character. He must be "just," a man of good faith and right intentions, and truthful. These virtues are not presumed to exist in a person who merely believes in the religious truths; he must practise them. He is assumed to practise them when he does not commit capital sins (*kabīrah*), when he fulfils his religious duties, and when he does not persist in the commission of venial sins (*ṣagīrah*). Therefore the person who does not practise his religious duties, although he may believe in them (*fāsiq*), may not be a *mujtahid.* The man whose thoughts are tainted by heresy (*bid'ah*) is also excluded, for heresy would warrant a presumption of injustice. In short, only the person who is learned, pious and orthodox, may be a *mujtahid.*[1] A detailed statement of all these requirements given by al-Gazāli constitutes a formidable array of sciences and practices, but dogmatic theology is not included in them.

It must be kept in mind that a **combination of all these virtues** is **necessary only for** the person who intends to be a **full mujtahid** (*mujtahid muṭlaq*, or *mujtahid fi 'l-sharī'ah*) *i. e.*, a *mujtahid* who may express an opinion on every question of the *sharī'ah.* Hence, one is allowed to enter the rank of *mujtahids* (*manṣab al-ijtihād*), although one has mastered only a part of the required sciences, provided that one exercises *ijtihād* only on questions falling within that part. For instance, if one knows only the laws of *qiyās,* though he may not know the science of the *sunnah*, or if he knows only the subject of inheritance, he may form an opinion on points included in the field known to him, since it is not necessary for the jurisconsult (*mufti*) to be able

[1] *Cf.* Ostrorog, p. 48.

to answer every question. Thus it is related of Mālik that he was asked forty questions concerning thirty-six of which he answered: "I do not know." Similarly, the Companions and all the great *mujtahids* have not answered every question that was put to them. However, some doctors have questioned the legitimacy of the "splitting" (*tajazzi*) of *ijtihād*, that is whether a person should be allowed to reach independent opinions within the branch of *fiqh* which he has mastered, if he is not acquainted with the entire subject of *fiqh*.[1]

The majority hold that the **limited mujtahid** is **not entitled to independence of opinion outside of his specialty** and like the *muqallids* must apply to a *mujtahid* for an opinion on such matters. This applies only in case the "splitting" of *ijtihād* is granted to be legitimate; in the contrary case, the limited *mujtahid* must rely on the opinion of the full *mujtahid* even on points falling within his own specialty.[2]

The **legal effect** (*ḫukm*) **of ijtihad** is that the opinion rendered is probably right, though there is the possibility of error. Therefore, *ijtihād* in the fundamentals of religion has been forbidden. One sect, the Mu'tazilites, hold that *ijtihād* is always right.

According to the degree of independence and scope of research which the **mujtahids** have shown, they have been **classified** by later Hanifite[3] doctors in the following groups:

(1) **The full mujtahid** (*mujtahid fi 'l-shar'*). The *mujtahids* of this type have established a legal system

[1] It will be noted that this dispute is another form of the time-honored argument over the relative values of general education and specialization.

[2] *Taqrīr*, vol. iii, p. 344.

[3] Ibn 'Abidīn, pp. 11 *et seq.*

(*madh-hab*) of their own and are called founders of schools (*ṣāḥib madh-hab*). Abu Hanīfah, al-Shāfi'i, Mālik, and Aḥmad Ibn Hanbal belong in this group. Each of these has originated a different system of *uṣūl-al-fiqh*.

(2) The **mujtahids "within the school"** (*mujtahid fi 'l-madh-hab*). These are the disciples of the former, like Abu Yūsuf, Muḥammad Ibn al-Hasan, Zufar, *etc.* They have determined the law in the particular cases (*furū'*), applying the principles (*uṣūl*) established by their master, and have at times disagreed with him in the particular applications of the law but never in the principles.

(3) The "**mujtahids on particular questions**" (*mujtahid fi 'l-masā'il*), like al-Khaṣṣāf, Abu Ja'far al-Taḥāwi, Abu 'l-Hasan al-Karkhi, Shams-al-a'immah al-Halwāni, Shams-al-a'immah al-Sarakhsi, Fakhr-al-islām al-Pazdawi, Fakhr-al-dīn Qādīkhān. These have not opposed the founder of the school, either in the principles or in the particular applications (*furū'*) of the principles, but have contented themselves with determining the law in regard to particular cases which the former had left undetermined, using, however, the principles established by the former. All the preceding three classes have been called *mujtahids*, but the following four are usually denominated as *muqallids*, *muqallid* being the opposite of *mujtahid*.

(4) The so called "**ashab al takhrij**," like al-Rāzi, *etc.* These are not able to form *ijtihād*, but, being well-conversant with the principles and the particular applications decided by the former, indicate which view is correct in cases of ambiguity or contradiction.

(5) The so-called "**ashab al-tarjih**," like Abu 'l-Hasan al-Qudūri and the author of the *Hidāyah*. These, when there are several views on the same point, indicate which is the correct view, by means of the use of some such expression as "this is correct" (*ṣaḥīḥ*), or "the *fatwa* is rendered according to this view" (*'alayhi al-fatwa*).

(6) The doctors who can distinguish between the weak and the strong, the reliable (*ẓāhir-al-riwāyah*) and the unreliable, *etc.* They are the authors of " the esteemed texts " (*al-mutūn al-mu'tabarah*), like the *Kanz*, the *Mukhtār*, the *Wiqāyah*, and the *Majma'*. They include in their books only the views that have been considered reliable.

(7) the class of the *muqallids* who lack the powers of the preceding and " do not distinguish between the lean and the fat, right and left, but on the contrary get together whatever they find."

It must be remarked here that this classification apparently is not intended by the doctors to indicate merely that the *mujtahids* have been classed in this or that group because they have shown only that much independence of thought, for it implies a gratuitous assumption that the later *mujtahids* could not show greater independence of thought. This is another symptom of that peculiar habit of mind which resulted in the fiction which has been termed by the Moslem doctors " the closing of the door of ijtihad " (*insidād bāb al-ijtihād*). This fiction consists in the belief that after the era of the full *mujtahids* (*mujtahid muṭlaq*) who founded the schools, no more *mujtahids* of that calibre appeared, and according to some there is not even the possibility that such might appear.[1]

This belief, which is a later development, is partly due to the fact that the founders of the schools were men of great ability and thoroughness who had practically exhausted the various logical alternatives which offered themselves for speculation within the limitations set by the revealed texts. The later doctors had many views to choose from, but there was little to add. They, therefore, seized upon the existing material and elaborated it, filling

[1] Juynboll, p. 34, fn.; *cf. Taqrīr*, vol. iii, pp. 339-40.

in the gaps left by the masters. By far the most important factor, however, in bringing about this acquiescence with what was said and done by the previous generations, and in bringing about this voluntary surrender of independence of thought, must have been the fact that, after the crystallization of the various conflicting views into distinct systems and schools and the acceptance of the same by the majority of society, the future trend of thought was then and there determined along existing lines. As time went on, people as a matter of course ranged themselves under the banner of the school that was predominant in their district. This was especially true as, owing to the doctrine of *ijmā'*, once an agreement was reached on a certain point, further discussion of that point was automatically barred.

But, while there is a historical basis for this fiction, there is **no justification for it in theory.** Even those who accept this fiction, will be careful to indicate by their wording that this closing of *ijtihād* is not necessitated by theory, but merely is a result of the absence of full *mujtahids*. Thus Haydar Effendi, a modern Turkish authority on *Fiqh*, in his *Durar al-Hukkām*,[1] says that the door of *ijtihād* was not closed (*sadd*) by an external cause but that it closed of itself (*insidād*) through mere absence of *mujtahids*. According to theory, the *mujtahid* is not only free in his thinking but is bound to be so, and there is no *a priori* reason why a person today might not be able to combine in himself the necessary qualities required by the Mohammedan doctors themselves.

It is not therefore a matter of surprise to find among **earlier doctors** strong statements **condemning this belief** and refuting it by theoretical arguments.[2] For example,

[1] Vol. iv, p. 671.

[2] Shawkāni, p. 235.

al-Zarkashi [tenth century of the *Hijrah*], expressing great astonishment that such a belief should have arisen at all, says:

If they [*i. e.*, the people entertaining this belief] are thinking of their contemporaries, it is a fact that they have had contemporaries like al-Qaffāl, al-Gazāli, al-Rāzi, al-Rāfi'i, and others, all of whom have been full *mujtahids*; and if they mean by it that their contemporaries are not endowed and blessed by God with the same perfection, intellectual ability and power, or understanding, it is absurd and a sign of crass ignorance; finally, if they mean that the previous writers had more facilities, while the later writers had more difficulties, in their way, it is again nonsense, for it does not require much understanding to see that *ijtihād* for the later doctors (*muta'ākhirūn*) is easier than for the earlier doctors. Indeed the commentaries on the Koran and the *sunnah* have been compiled and multiplied to such an extent that the *mujtahid* of today has more material for interpretation than he needs.

Similar views have been expressed by al-Shāfi'i and others.[1] The writings of the *mujtahids*, like the *mujtahids* themselves, have been grouped by later Hanifite doctors in three main classes.[2]

(1) The so-called **Usul** (bases) **or Zahir-al-riwayah** (of reliable transmission) **or Zahir-al-madh-hab** (the established doctrines of the school). These are the views and opinions, of Abu Hanīfah and his disciples Abu Yūsuf, Muḫammad ibn al-Hasan, also Zufar and Hasan Ibn Ziyād, which have been recorded in the books called by the same name, *i. e., Kutub Zāhir-al-riwāyah*. These books are the *Mabsūṭ*, the *al-Jāmi' al-Kabīr*, the *al-Jāmi' al-Sagīr*, and the *al-Siyar al-Kabīr*, all of them written by Muḫammad Ibn al-Hasan, Abu Hanīfah's disciple.

[1] *Cf.* also Ibn Hazm, p. 212.

[2] Qāḍizādah, p. 14.

(2) The so-called **al-Nawadir.** These are the views and opinions of the above doctors recorded in other than the above mentioned books, such as the *al-Kīsāniyyāt, al-Hārūniyyāt, al-Jurjāniyyāt,* and *al-Raqqiyyāt,* of the same Muḥammad, the *Amāli* of Abu Yūsuf, the books written by Hasan Ibn Ziyād, Zufar, *etc.*

(3) Finally, the **Waqi'at,** namely the views of later *mujtahids,* like 'Iṣām-al-dīn Ibn Yūsuf, Ibn Rustam, Muḥammad Ibn Samā'ah, Abu Sulaymān al-Jurjāni, Abu Hafṣ al-Bukhāri, *etc.* The first book of this kind was the *Nawāzil* of Abu 'l-Layth al-Samarqandi. It was followed by al-Nātifi's *Kitāb Majmū' al-Nawāzil wa 'l-Wāqi'āt.* Later writers compiled works in which they put together the views contained in these earlier books. Qāḏīkhān is one of these writers. The best compendiums of the opinions of the first class (*uṣūl*) are the *Kāfi,* and the *Muntaqa.* A commentary on the *Kāfi* has been written by al-Sarakhsi, in a work entitled *al-Mabsūṭ.* It is a large book in thirty parts and has been very extensively used in Part II. of this study.

The opposite of *mujtahid* is **muqallid and** of *ijtihād* is *taqlīd.* **Taqlid** is **defined** as the servile acceptance of another's opinion without evidence. According to this definition everybody who is not a *mujtahid* would be a *muqallid.* Some have held that the name of *muqallid* applies only to a *mujtahid* who follows the opinion of another *mujtahid,* or to a layman who follows the opinion of another layman, but not to a layman who follows the opinion of a *mujtahid,* because, these people argue, the mere fact that the person from whom an opinion is requested is a *mujtahid* is conclusive evidence for the layman who applies to him. Likewise, they say, it would not be a case of *taqlīd* to follow the views of the Prophet. Shawkāni establishes a more relevant distinction when he says that *taqlīd* applies only in case one follows the opinion of another person, but that it is not a case of *taqlīd* when one applies to another person to determine a point of fact. Therefore it is not *taqlīd* if a layman applies to a *mujtahid* in order to find what the law is on a certain point.

The **lowest scale in the hierarchy of intellectual freedom** is **occupied by the** so-called **'ammis or illiterate.** These naturally possess even fewer rights than the *muqallids*, for while the *muqallids* can refer to the law-books and ascertain the views of the doctors, the *'āmmis* do not even possess the minimum of knowledge required for that, and must apply to the *mujtahids* or the *muqallids*, if they are in doubt concerning a point.

The process by which the mass **of** the illiterate are instructed in law is **ifta**, which means the act of answering a question concerning a point of law. The act of asking for such an answer is called *istifta* and the answer so given is called *fatwa* (plural, *fatāwi*). The person giving the *fatwa* is called *mufti* and the person asking for it is called *mustafti*.

There has been considerable divergence of opinion as to the amount of learning a person must possess in order to qualify to give *fatwas*, but the generally accepted opinion is that **a mufti must be a mujtahid. A person however is allowed to give fatwas by quoting [1] the opinions of others**, provided he conforms to the rules concerning transmitters (*rāwi*).[2] Such a person, according to the *Fatḫ*, when asked about a point, must not give his answer as final;

[1] The expressions used in the law-books to indicate that a certain opinion is recommended by the author of the book for being quoted as *fatwa* are the following: *'alayhi al-fatwa* (according to this is the opinion rendered) *wa bihi yufta* (according to this the *fatwa* is rendered); *wa 'alayhi al-'amal al-yawm* (according to this is conduct at present) *wa huwa al-ṣaḥīḥ* or *aṣaḥḥ* (this is the correct view), *etc.*

[2] *Fatḫ*, vol. vi, p. 360; for full details concerning the *muftis* consult *'Alamkiriyyah*, vol. iii, pp. 380 *et seq.*; *Baḥr*, vol. vi, pp. 292 *et seq.*; *Majma'*, vol, ii. p. 120; *Durar*, p. 717; *Durr*, p. 8; Qāḍīzādah, p. 16.

for example, he must not say, " The answer of your question is this," but on the contrary, he must relate the various opinions on the point, as for example, "Abu Hanīfah said on this point so and so," and leave it to the *mustafti* to follow the opinion that appeals to his intuition as the correct one. The author of the *Fatḫ* here interjects the opinion that, although it is advisable for the person giving the *fatwa* to quote all the opinions on the point, it is not necessary to do so, it being permissible to mention only one of them. The same author goes on to say that, inasmuch as the person giving the *fatwa* is not a *mujtahid* but simply a transmitter and narrator, he must see to it that he is quoting correctly. This last point is considered to have been insured if the narrator knows the complete chain of transmitters from himself back to the original *mufti*, or quotes the *fatwa* from a well-known book that is circulating in the hands of the public, such as the books of Muḫammad Ibn al-Hasan. According to al-Rāzi, such books are equivalent to a report of the *mutawātir* or *mash-hūr* type. If, however, at the present time there should be only a few copies of a rare manuscript in existence, it would not be lawful to give a *fatwa* on the basis of an opinion recorded in them, ascribing it for example to Abu Yūsuf or Muḫammad Ibn al-Hasan, because these copies have not attained wide circulation and reputation (*lam tashtahir*) in our time and place. It is all right, however, if these opinions have been quoted in a well-known book like the *Hidāyah* or the *Mabsūṭ*, since it would then be a case of relying on these latter books.

While the *muftis* who are not *mujtahids* have no liberty of thought and must simply quote others, **the muftis who are mujtahids**[1] are **conceded** by the jurists the **right to depart from** the **opinion of** the **founder of** the **school,** and,

[1] Strictly speaking, the name *mufti* applies only to the *mujtahids*.

in general, to exercise independence of judgment as far as their learning will allow.[1] But almost as early as the time of the disciples of Abu Hanīfah, one can detect the origin of that peculiar state of mind which gratuitously assumes that jurists of great calibre of mind are no longer to be met and so it has been the current view for a long time to consider the *muftis* and the judges as mere *muqallids* or *mujtahids* of the most limited scope of research. Consequently special rules have been elaborated as to the precedence of doctors' opinions in giving a *fatwa* or rendering a judgment.[2]

Special rules have been established also concerning taqlid and the duties of the 'ammis (ignorant) who have to apply to the *muftis* in order to find out what the law is. Reference will here be made only to a few of them. According to Abu 'l-Khaṯṯāb, the duty of an *'āmmi*[3] is to apply to the *mujtahid* for the solution of his difficulties, but he must see to it that he applies to a person whom he knows to possess the ability for that work, either because the latter has reputation for science or piety, or because he has been recommended to him. Consequently he must not apply to a person whose condition is unknown to him, although some claim that he may. Some hold that the educated person is obliged to follow the opinion of a *mujtahid* only when he feels convinced about the soundness of the latter's arguments. It has been a matter of dispute as to whether in intellectual matters, that is matters which are outside of the *sharī'ah* sciences, *taqlīd* is legitimate or obligatory. When

[1] It will be remembered that a *mujtahid* need not be of the full rank and that he is bound to know only as much as he needs for the determining of the particular question he is interested in.

[2] For full details see *'Alamkiriyyah*, vol. iii, pp. 383-387; *cf. al-Fatāwa al-Kubra*, vol. ii, p. 212.

[3] *Majmū'*, p. 140.

there are two *muftis*, the *'āmmi* must apply to the more learned of the two, although some say that he may apply to either. When a person asks for a *fatwa* from two *muftis* he follows the one whose opinion appeals to his intuition as the more correct, although according to the *Fatḫ* [1] he may also follow the one whose opinion does not so appeal to his intuition. For, he says, the intuition (*mayl*) of the ignorant is of no account. When an *'āmmi* has followed the opinion of a *mujtahid* on a point, by unanimous opinion, he may not any longer follow the opinion of another *mujtahid* on the same point, though he may do so in a new case.

There has been **discussion** as to **whether an 'ammi should follow a definite school** [2] in all particulars, some saying yes, others saying no. The argument of the latter is that the Companions of the Prophet did not blame people for following opinions other than their own. The first side argues that after the establishment of the four schools, affiliation with one of them is necessary.

May one in certain particulars **depart from the doctrines of** the **school to which he has pledged allegiance?** [3] Some say he may, others say he may not, and still others say he may not if he has already acted according to his own school. Finally, others say, if the case has already occurred, he may not change, otherwise, he may. This last view has been followed by Imām-al-ḫaramayn. According to al-

[1] Vol. vi, p. 360.

[2] Shawkāni, p. 253.

[3] In the *Taqrīr* (vol. iii, p. 351) it is said that the opinion of later generations is that the *'āmmi* cannot properly claim affiliation with a school and say, "I am a Hanifite or a Shafiite," because following a certain school implies a minimum of discriminating intelligence and acquaintance with the literature of that school, and the illiterate does not possess even that knowledge.

Qudūri, he may change his school if he is convinced that the school he wants to follow is stronger than his own school in regard to that particular case, otherwise he may not. But others say he may change if the new school is not less rigorous than his own school; and, according to others, he may change if the new school pleases him better, and he does not do it merely for fun, provided, however, that by so changing he is not setting at nought what he has already done in accordance with his school. However, in the opinion of some, one becomes impious (*fāsiq*) by picking out from each school what is most agreeable to him, for example, the drinking of *nabīdh* (a kind of wine) from the school of 'Irāq, temporary marriage (*mut'ah*) from that of Mecca, *etc.* The author of the *Taqrīr* sees no objection to this practice.

It will readily be seen that notwithstanding the minute dispositions that we have been briefly examining, there are often cases where the believer may be at a loss as to what is the right thing for him to do. For example, when a person has asked for a *fatwa* from two *muftis*, how is he to tell which one of the two he must follow? Or, supposing that he is in the wilderness and wants to pray, but does not know in which direction Mecca lies (*qiblah*), how can he satisfy his conscience that he has performed his religious duties completely? These difficulties are removed by the process of *taḥarri*.[1]

Taharri [2] technically means the determination of a fact, which it is impossible to ascertain, by means of intuitive conviction. A person is said to resort to *taḥarri* when he turns to his heart, that is, to his intuitive faculty in order

[1] *'Alamkīriyyah*, vol. v, p. 569; *Mabsūṭ*, vol. x, p. 185; *Ja'mi'*, p. 133.

[2] Some jurists restrict the use of the word *taḥarri* to questions of religious ritual (*'ibādāt*) and use the word *tawakh-khi* concerning civil transactions (*mu'āmalāt*).

to find the truth. Resort to this method is allowed when the thing desired to be known is involved in doubt (*shakk*),[1] and other evidence is not available, since in such a case it is the only means of getting at the truth. The legal effect (*ḫukm*) of *taḫarri* is that action based upon it is valid (*ṣawāb*) in the eyes of the *sharī'ah*. The application of the principle of *taḫarri* concerning the payment of *zakāt* will be seen in Part II.

[1] The jurists define doubt (*shakk*) as the state of mind in which knowledge and ignorance just balance each other, and, on the other hand, they mean by *ẓann* (presumption) the case in which the side of knowledge overbalances ignorance, though without any evidence in its support.

CHAPTER X

THE FIQH SCHOOLS AND THEIR FOUNDERS

THE violent discussions which raged in the early period of Islam in regard to religious and legal questions such as the use of *qiyās*, or political issues like the califate, resulted in groupings along certain lines. **The groupings along the line of fiqh,** have been the ones which **have received most** recognition and **adherence.** Consequently they have been practically the only groupings to spread and survive to our own day, and are known as the *fiqh madh-habs* or schools. The differences between these schools, although they primarily relate to matters of law, are by no means confined to them, since they bear on subjects as far apart as metaphysics and politics. In fact, they relate to all the various subjects on which the *sharī'ah* has had something to say, namely to every matter which in those times excited human interest.

The most important of the **fiqh schools** have been the ones founded by Abu Hanīfah, Mālik, al-Shāfi'i, Ahmad Ibn Hanbal, Dāwūd Ibn 'Ali, al-Awza'i, Sufyān al-Thawri, and Abu Thawr. Each one of these is considered a full *mujtahid*, and is supposed to have had his own system of theory and applications of *fiqh*. They have all been reckoned as **orthodox** and they have considered one another as such. They are to be distinguished from the so-called Shiites and Khārijites, *etc.*, who are looked down upon by the former as heretical.

According to al-Bagdādi,[1] the **origin of** this distinction between **orthodoxy** and heresy is based among other things on the following statement of the Prophet:

> "Verily, it shall happen to my community (*ummah*) what happened to the sons of Israel. The sons of Israel split up into 72 sects, and my community shall split up into 73 sects, namely, one more than their sects; all of these sects shall go into the Fire excepting one single sect." They said: "Oh Prophet of God, which is the one sect that will stay away from the Fire?" He replied: "The sect in which I and my Companions have belonged."

The test of orthodoxy then is to hold the same views as the Companions. Using this test, al-Bagdādi says[2] that in his days only the *faqīhs* and theologians who belonged in the so-called orthodox body (*ahl al-sunnah wa 'l-jamā'ah*) could be considered as living in accordance with the Companions, and that the remaining such as the Rāfiḍites, Qadarites, and Khārijites, were heretical.

The content of orthodoxy, as explained by the same author in a long chapter,[3] consists in agreement on 15 heads or "pillars," as he terms them. Each of these "pillars" must be understood by every adult person of mature understanding. These "pillars" include fundamental (*uṣūl*) and secondary (*furū'*) questions. On the fundamental questions, he says, all the orthodox Moslems have been at one, though they have differed on the secondary; but, he adds, their differences have not been in the nature of error (*ḍalāl*) or impiety (*fisq*).

These fifteen pillars embrace **a wide range of subjects:** among others, questions of metaphysics, such as matter,

[1] Pp. 4-5.

[2] P. 304.

[3] Pp. 309 *et seq.*

accidents and essences; dogmatic theology, such as the existence, unity, attributes and names of God, the createdness of the universe, the prophets, and their miracles; worship, such as the observation of the five "pillars" of Islam; *fiqh;* public law, such as the question of the califate, *etc.* Those who do not believe in the above al-Bagdādi would consider as outside of the orthodox body, though they may still be Moslems.

Who is called a Moslem? According to al-Bagdādi [1] this question has been variously answered. Some said, every person who believes in Mohammed as a prophet belongs in the Moslem community (*millat al-islām*). The Karāmites said,—every person who says, "There is no God but God, and Mohammed is the prophet of God" is a Moslem. Still others said,—every person is a Moslem, who believes in the five prayers and in their being said with the face turned toward Mecca. Al-Bagdādi, however, would call a person Moslem, only if he believed in the createdness of the universe, the unity, eternity, justice and wisdom of its Creator, and would not liken others to God, nor deny any of His attributes; believed in the prophecy and mission of all the prophets, and in the truth of the prophecy of Mohammed, as well as in his mission to all nations; believed in his teachings and the Koran as the source of divine revelation; finally, if he believed in the obligation of the five prayers, the giving of *zakāt*, the fast of *Ramaḏān*, and the pilgrimage to Mecca. The person who observes all the above is a Moslem; if he furthermore abstains from any heresy (*bid'ah*) that involves unbelief, he is a Sunnite (orthodox) Moslem. If on the contrary, he commits a heresy, one of these two cases is possible: (1) The heresy is of the nature committed by the Bāṯinites,

[1] Pp. 220-223.

Bayānites, Mugīrites, Manṣūrites, Janāḥites, Sabbābites, or Khaṭṭābites (subdivisions of the Rāfiḍites); or the Hulūlites; or those who believe in the transmigration of souls; or the Maymūnites or Yazīdites (both subdivisions of the Khārijites); or the Hāïṭites or Himārites (subdivisions of the Qadarites); or it consists in the prohibition of what the Koran permitted by name, and *vice versa*. In such cases he does not belong in the Moslem community (*millat al-islam*). (2) His heresy is of the nature committed by the Zaydites and Imāmites (subdivisions of the Rāfiḍites); or most of the Khārijites; or the Mu'tazilites, Najjārites, Jahmites, Dirārites, and Mujassimites. In this case he is considered a Moslem in certain respects, but is considered to be outside of the Moslem community in other respects. For example, like other Moslems, he is buried in the Moslem cemetery, he receives a share in the spoils of war, and he may enter a Moslem mosque to pray in it. However, it is not allowed to a Sunnite Moslem to pray over his dead body, nor to pray under his leadership (*al-ṣalāt khalfahu*), nor to eat his sacrifice; neither may a Sunnite marry women of his sect, or offer him a Sunnite woman in marriage. In brief, al-Bagdādi, distinguishes **three classes of Moslems**, the Moslems who are Sunnites, those who are merely Moslems, and finally those who are Moslems only in name, but not in reality, such as the Maymūnites and Hulūlites. Al-Bagdādi includes the former two classes in the list which he made out to bring the number of sects in the Mohammedan community up to 73, but he excludes from the list the third class of nominal Moslems.

According to the *Technical Dictionary*,[1] **the Prophet defined Islam** as consisting in the observance of "the five pillars," namely, the testimony that there is no God but

[1] P. 696.

God and that Mohammed is his Prophet, the five prayers, the *zakāt*, the fasting during the month of Ramaḏān, and the pilgrimage to Mecca. In other words, **Islam is the external submission,** and differs from **iman** (faith) which means **the internal submission.** This distinction is also acknowledged by al-Bukhāri, though there are those who have considered the two terms synonymous. The **opposite of iman is kufr,** meaning unbelief. According to the view that *īmān* means internal submission only, *kufr*, or unbelief, would not exclude a person from Islam. The majority of *faqīhs* and theologians are agreed that Moslems do not become unbelievers (*kāfir*) by erring in the fundamentals of religion (*usūl al-dīn*), that is, in dogma. When a Moslem errs in other than dogma, if he can justify his opinion by some evidence (*burhān*), he is saved (*nāji*); and even if he bases his opinion on the erroneous view of another person (*taqlīd*) he is still saved, according to the majority view. According to one opinion, Moslems are allowed to call other Moslems *kāfirs* by way of retaliation for the same insult.

The reason why certain groups of Moslems have been considered as heretical is not because they differed in the application or even the theory of *fiqh*, since the orthodox sects will be found to differ among themselves almost as much. It is mainly because of differences on **theological and political issues,** for these were the principal issues which led to their secession from the main body of Moslems.[1] It goes without saying that the heretical Moslems have their own legal systems,[2] but they do not interest us here because we shall be concerned only with the orthodox doctrines.

The **differences between** the various **orthodox schools,**

[1] Goldziher, *Vorlesungen*, pp. 237-239.

[2] *Cf.* Juynboll, pp. 31-32.

as already anticipated in the chapters on *Ijmā'* and *Ijtihād*, **relate chiefly to the applications of fiqh**, for we have seen that in the theory of *fiqh* (*uṣūl-al-fiqh*) they practically all follow the same principles. Al-Sha'rāni has likened the several orthodox schools to so many roads, all leading to the same goal. Thus they have never called one another heretical (*kāfir*), and they usually allow a shifting of allegiance from one orthodox school to another. Of the many schools, which existed, only six, all of them orthodox, have been able to obtain a following. They are known as the six "followed" (*matbū'ah*) schools, and are the Hanifite, Malikite, Shafiite, Hanbalite, and those of al-Thawri and Dāwūd. The first four are the ones which have had the largest following and have survived to our own day; the last two could not survive beyond the seventh century of the *Hijrah*. The rest of the orthodox schools have had little or no following. Here are the most important of the orthodox schools.

The Hanifites. The founder of this school is **Abu Hanifah** Na'mān Ibn Thābit (80/699-150/767).[1] His grandfather was brought from Persia to Kūfah as a slave and later obtained his freedom. According to the historian Ibn Khallikān,[2] Abu Hanīfah was born early enough to have met with four of the Companions, namely, Anas Ibn Mālik, 'Abdāllah Ibn Awfa who resided at Kūfah, and two others, but that he never saw them nor obtained from any of them traditions respecting the Prophet. His disciples have claimed the contrary. According to the same author, Ja'far Ibn Rabī'ah said that he had attended the lessons of Abu Hanīfah during five years and never met a man who would remain silent as long as he; but that when he was questioned

[1] This notation signifies the dates 80-150 *Hijrah* and 699-767 A. D.

[2] Vol. iii, p. 556.

on [a point of] jurisprudence he would launch out into a flux of words, copious as a torrent. Also that in the art of drawing conclusions from analogies (*qiyās*) he was a master of the highest rank.[1] Abu Hanīfah was a man of independent means and perfect character. He devoted his life to the study of religion and law, delivering lectures in Kūfah to his private circle of students. His opinion on legal matters was universally sought after. He left no works except a small book on dogmatics and belief called *al-Fiqh al-Akbar*. His so-called *Musnad* has been compiled by one of his students and contains the *ḥadīths* used by the master.

It was **Abu Hanīfah** who **occasioned** the famous **controversy regarding** the **use of opinion** (*ra'y*) in legislation, and this activity on his part brought upon him bitter attacks. The charge made by his enemies was that he emphasized the speculative elements at the cost of the *ḥadīths*, whereas his disciples rightly maintained that he used *qiyās* only when he could not find a provision in the *ḥadīths*. The truth is that "Abu Hanīfah did not constitute an exception in the use of *qiyās* but that they all acted alike."[2] We have already seen in the chapter on *Qiyās* how much truth there was in the allegation that *qiyās* meant the introduction of the use of *ra'y*; on the contrary, *qiyās* curbed the inordinate and lawless use of *ra'y*, as it was then practised on all sides. It is true that Abu Hanīfah also introduced the principle of *istiḥsān* which was really a case of using *ra'y*, but all the schools were guilty of that practice. The only difference between Abu Hanīfah and the rest was that Abu Hanīfah was conscious of what he was doing and was not afraid of openly admitting it, while the others did the same thing in a more or less concealed way. The work

[1] *Ibid.*, vol. iii, p. 559.

[2] Luknawi, Introduction, p. 27; *Mīzān*, p. 54, l. 10.

of Hanīfah can hardly be over-estimated, for he made the first attempt to codify the Mohammedan law, using *qiyās* as one of his bases. In doing this Abu Hanīfah incidentally evolved a theory of law (*uṣūl-al-fiqh*) for the first time. Abu Hanīfah's work was supplemented and completed by his intimate circle of disciples especially Abu Yūsuf, and Muḥammad Ibn-al-Hasan.

Abu Yusuf, Ya'qūb Ibn Ibrāhīm, (113/731-182/799), was by far the most important disciple of Abu Hanīfah. He was the one who wrote out the principles laid down by the master [1] and occupied in relation to him a position very similar to that which Plato did in relation to Socrates. Abu Yūsuf held office as Chief Justice in Bagdad under the well-known calif Hārūn-al-rashīd, who sought his advice on the most important affairs of state. In answer to certain questions of the Calif concerning taxation, and other matters of public law, Abu Yūsuf wrote his famous *Kitāb al-Kharāj*, a valuable essay on those subjects.

Imām **Muhammad Ibn al-Hasan** al-Shaybāni (135/752-189/804-5) was the younger of the two disciples but by far the keener. Ibn Khallikān [2] says the following:

When the *imām as-Shāfī* went to Bagdad, Muhammad Ibn al-Hasan was there, and they both met frequently and discussed points of law in the presence of Hārūn-ar-Rashīd. Al-Shāfi'i was (*afterwards*) heard to say: "I never saw a person who, when questioned on a point which required reflection, did not betray some uneasiness by his countenance; but I must except Muhammad Ibn al-Hasan." He said again: "The information which I learned by heart from Muhammad Ibn al-Hasan would suffice to load a camel."

[1] It is stated in the *Mizān* (p. 48) that when Abu Hanīfah decided a point of law and all the doctors of his city were agreed upon it, he said to Abu Yūsuf, "Write it down".

[2] Vol. ii, p. 590.

Muhammad compiled the applications of the principles laid down by the master into a *corpus juris*, which served as a basis for many future books on the applications of *fiqh*, and the commentaries, and constitutes the most authoritative source-book for the Hanifite doctrines.

The **Hanifite school** is one of the most, if not the most, important of the four orthodox schools, and **counts many adherents.** It owes its reputation mainly to the Ottoman Turks, who have officially adopted it. It has followers also in other lands where Turkish influence prevails. Furthermore it has spread in Central Asia, Turkestan, Bukhara, Samarqand, and Hindustan. The Hanifite principles are, by far the most humanitarian of all, concerning the treatment of non-Moslems, war captives, slaves, the law of retaliation, *etc.*

The Malikites. This is the school founded by **Malik** Ibn Anas (95/713-4-179/795) of Medina. Mālik was considered as a representative of the *ḥadīth*-folk, notwithstanding the fact that he, too, used *qiyās*, although perhaps to a less extent than Abu Hanīfah. This is borne out by an examination of his collection of *ḥadīths*, called *al-Muwaṭṭā'*, the first orderly collection of law, where Mālik based his legal decisions partly on his personal opinion. Notice this statement by 'Abdāllah Ibn Qa'nab.[1]

I went to Mālik Ibn Anas, in his last illness and saluted him; I then sat down and, perceiving that he wept, I said: "O Abu 'Abdallah; what maketh thee weep?" and he answered, "O Ibn Qa'nab, why should I not weep? By Allah! I wish I had been flogged and reflogged for every question of law on which I pronounced an opinion founded on my own private judgment."

Having lived and acted in the city of Medina, the home of

[1] Ibn Khallikān, vol. ii, p. 548.

the *ḥadīth*-lore, Mālik occupies a conspicuous place in the teaching of *ḥadīths*. Thus it is stated in the *Tah-dhīb*[1] that according to al-Bukhāri, the most reliable chain of transmission is, 'Mālik, from Nāfi', from Ibn 'Omar,' but according to Abu Manṣūr al-Tamīmi it is 'al-Shāfi'i, from Mālik, from Nāfi', from Ibn 'Omar, from the Prophet.' Mālik's teachers were Nāfi', a client of Ibn 'Omar, Muḥammad Ibn al-Munkadir, Abu 'l-Zubayr, al-Zuhri, 'Abdāllah Ibn Dīnār, Abu Hāzim. Mālik had many disciples who taught *ḥadīths* on his authority, among others, al-Awza'i, Al-Thawri, Ibn 'Uyaynah, Al-Layth Ibn Sa'd, Ibn al-Mubārak and al-Shāfi'i. Mālik was well-versed in the study of the Koran and the *sunnah*, and served as official jurisconsult (*mufti*). This last circumstance may explain the fact that Mālik was the first one to break away from the purely casuistic practices of his predecessors and to attempt to formulate the principles underlying the *ḥadīths* and the customs of Medina, and to arrange them topically. The very name of *Muwaṭṭā'*, which he gave to his book, suggests the nature of the work done. The word means that which has been made smooth, even.

The **school of Malik** naturally **found** much **favor in** his native city of **Medina and** in the **western part of** the **Mohammedan world,** namely, in Morocco, Algeria, and Tunis, as well as in the so-called *Magrib* (meaning West), which included Spain, when that country was under Mohammedan rule; also in the other parts of Africa where Islam had already been accepted, and in upper Egypt, where at present it has many followers.

The Shafiites. This school was founded by **al-Shafi'i,** Muḥammad Ibn Idrīs (150/767-204/820). He was born in Gaza and he died in Old Cairo. He taught in Bagdad for

[1] P. 531.

a time and later in Egypt. The Mohammedans consider al-Shāfi'i, as the vindicator par excellence of the *ḥadīths*, although to the impartial critic this view does not seem quite well founded, if it is to mean that he did not use *ra'y* at all. In fact the difference between Abu Hanīfah and al-Shāfi'i was more in appearance than in reality. Al-Shāfi'i freely admitted the lawfulness of the use of *qiyās* and, as we have already seen, his method of determining the "effective" cause for purposes of *qiyās* was looser than that of Abu Hanīfah. It is true that al-Shāfi'i objected to the principle of *istiḥsān* introduced by Abu Hanīfah, but he himself introduced the principle of *istiṣḥāb* which, supplemented by the greater liberty of action afforded by his looser method in *qiyās*, would be as effective a means of introducing personal opinion as the *istiḥsān* of Abu Hanīfah. But this is true only as a theoretical statement, because it may be fairly said that in practice al-Shāfi'i preserved more faithfully the spirit of the *ḥadīths* and used them more extensively. It is easy to understand why it should be so, if it is remembered that al-Shāfi'i was of pure Arab origin and studied *fiqh* in Mecca, and in Medina under Mālik, the champion of the *ḥadīth*-lore. The following quotation from the *Risālah* [1] will well illustrate his tendency to hark back:

God has not given it to any one after the death of the Prophet to express opinion except on the authority of the knowledge (*'ilm*) that came before him, and such knowledge consists in the Book, the *sunnah*, the *ijmā'*, and the sayings and doings (*āthār*) of the Companions, and then, as I have explained, in *qiyās* upon the basis of the preceding, and it is not allowed to any one to use *qiyās* until he has learned what has occurred before him in the way of practices (*sunan*) and sayings of the predecessors, and the *ijmā's* and differences of the people, as well as the Arabic language.

[1] P. 70.

Al-Shāfi'i was very brilliant, and, according to Ibn Khallikān,[1] he

> stood unrivalled by his abundant merits and illustrious qualities; to the knowledge of all the sciences connected with the book of God, the *Sunnah*, the sayings of the Companions, their history, the conflicting opinions of the learned, *etc.*, he united a deep acquaintance with the language of the Arabs of the Desert, philology, grammar, and poetry; . . .

Aḥmad Ibn Hanbal, one of al-Shāfi'i's disciples, is quoted as saying, "al-Shāfi'i was to mankind, what the sun is to the world, and health to the body; what can replace them?"

In contrast to Abu Hanīfah who was of a scholastic type of mind and liked hypothetical speculation, al-Shāfi'i was rather averse to, and probably not so skilful in subtle distinctions, and therefore relied on the revealed sources whenever he could find in them the desired provisions. The following verses composed by al-Shāfi'i bear this out: "The more experience instructs me, the more I see the weakness of my reason; and the more I increase my knowledge, the more I learn the extent of my ignorance."[2]

In short, al-Shafi'i was an eclectic,

> who came when the law books were already completed into elaborate systems, and the laws sifted and laid down in a hard and fast way. He studied the schools of the forerunners and learned from the most prominent doctors; he disputed with the ablest and profoundest and examined their teachings, and later on worked out from them a method which combined the Book, the *sunnah*, the *ijmā'*, and the *qiyās*, and so he did not confine himself to one or the other of these sources, as was the case with others.[3]

[1] Vol. ii, p. 569.

[2] *Ibid.*, vol. ii, p. 572.

[3] *Tah-dhib*, p. 62.

The above quotation from a disciple of al-Shāfi'i, al-Nawawi, although somewhat exaggerated, gives a good idea of the work done by al-Shāfi'i.

The avowed **object of al-Shafi'i was to reconcile fiqh and tradition,** and to those concerned he seemed to have succeeded in doing this (*jama'ahu bayn al-fiqh wa 'l-sunnah*). This explains the circumstance that when al-Shāfi'i appeared in Bagdad, there followed a rapid conversion to his school. The most prominent disciples and followers of al-Shāfi'i were Aḫmad Ibn Hanbal, Abu 'l-Thawr, al-Za'farāni, al-Tabari, al-Māwardi, Imām-al-haramayn, and others.

According to the *Tah-dhīb*[1] al-Shāfi'i wrote 113 works bearing on interpretation (*tafsīr*), *fiqh*, literature, *etc.* The works relating to *fiqh* are, the *Risālah*, the *Kitāb al-Umm*, the two *Jāmi's* and *Mukhtaṣars* of Muzani, the *Mukhtaṣar* of Rabī', *etc.* The most renowned commentaries upon al-Shāfi'i's writings are the *Ta'līqs* of Abu Hāmid al-Isfarā'ini, al-Tabari, and al-Māwardi.

At present, **the followers of this school are found** in the Strait settlements, the Malayan districts of Siam, the coast of Hindustan, (Malabar and Coromandel), in Southern Arabia, especially in Hadramut, in Baḫrayn, on the Persian Gulf, in certain Central Asian districts, in Dagistan, and in the German East-African colonies. Finally, some Mohammedans in Syria follow the Shafiite doctrines in the field of private life only. This is also true of those found in Arabia and Egypt.

The Hanbalites. This is the school founded by **Ahmad Ibn Hanbal** (164/780-241/855). Aḫmad was a disciple of al-Shāfi'i and, next to Dāwūd al-Zāhiri, he was the staunchest opponent of the *ra'y*-folk. He makes use of *qiyās* very little, and bases his system mainly on the sacred

[1] P. 67.

texts. He is uncritical in the selection of his *ḥadîths*, of which he compiled about 28,000 in his *Musnad*. He was a very conservative theologian, and got into trouble on that account. His followers are found now in Central Arabia, the inland districts of 'Omān, and on the Persian Gulf. The others are few in number and are scattered in out-of-the-way localities, in a number of Central-Asian cities, and in the country populations of some isolated Syrian villages.[1]

The Zahirites. This is the school founded by **Dawud Ibn 'Ali** († 270/883-4), who threw *qiyâs* overboard and adhered to the letter (*al-ẓâhir*) of the Koran and the *ḥadîths*, hence his name *al-ẓâhiri*. His school at one time spread westward as far as Spain, when that country was under the Mohammedans, but at present it boasts no adherents.[2]

Al-Awza'i, 'Abd-al-raḥman Ibn 'Amr Abu 'Amr, born in Baalbek, (88/757-157/774) was another founder of a school. He was reputed for his ascetic tendencies and good character, and was called the *Imâm* of Syria. He had followers even in *Magrib*, before it went over to the school of Mālik. Among his contemporaries were Sufyān, Mālik, Ibn al-Mubārak, and others. According to Hiql, who was the most reliable of the persons who quoted al-Awza'i, the latter decided 10,000 and according to another version, 80,000 legal questions.[3] 'Abd-al-raḥman Ibn Mahdi said: "The *imâms* of *ḥadîth* are four, al-Awza'i, Mālik, Sufyān al-Thawri, and Hammād Ibn Zayd."

Al-Thawri, Abu 'Abdāllah Sufyān Ibn Sa'îd of Kūfah was another full *mujtahid*. Among those who quoted him

[1] Juynboll, p. 29; Kremer, p. 499.

[2] Juynboll, p. 25; Goldziher, *d. Zahiriten*, p. 27; Kremer, p. 500.

[3] *Tah-dhib*, p. 384.

were, Mālik, al-Awza'i, and others. He was well-known for his piety, and his thorough knowledge of the *ḥadīths*. Thus Abu 'Aṣim said: "Al-Thawri is the Commander of the Believers in the matter of *ḥadīths*." [1]

[1] *Tah-dhib*, pp. 286-8.

CHAPTER XI

Concluding Remarks

In Part I. we have attempted to give a comprehensive view of Mohammedan law, as a background for the understanding of Part II., as well as for an intelligent determination of the extent to which non-revealed or external elements have gone into the making of *fiqh* or Mohammedan law. Thus in a preliminary chapter we saw that the word *sharī'ah* was the generic name given to the ensemble of religious truths taught by Mohammed; that *fiqh* was the body of legal prescriptions concerning human conduct which was derived from the *sharī'ah*; and finally, that *uṣūl-al-fiqh* was the connecting link between *fiqh* and *sharī'ah*, since it denoted the discipline which derived the former from the latter. In the following chapters we examined the four sources or bases from which *fiqh* was derived by *uṣūl-al-fiqh*, and which were accepted by the four most important *fiqh* schools. These four sources, the reader will readily remember, were the Koran, the *sunnah*, the *ijmā'* and the *qiyās*. In the course of these chapters special emphasis was laid on the discussion of the rules concerning the transmission of the *sunnah*, and of the principles regarding the investigation of the reasons for the divine prescriptions for purposes of reasoning by analogy. In the next chapter we took up the question of the relative importance of these four sources and the degree to which they overruled one another. We then examined the principles of legislation accepted by only one or more schools, and we treated the principle of *istiḥsān* or personal opinion, owing to its importance, in a separate section. A special chapter was devoted to a brief, though comprehensive, exposition of the various classes of *sharī'ah* values. We next inquired into the principles governing the exercise of independent thought (*ijtihād*) as well as the transmission of others' opinions and the duties of the illiterate (*'āmmi*) when they want to determine the law on concrete cases. To complete the discussion, in the last chapter, information was given concerning the most important orthodox schools of *fiqh* and the origin and content of orthodoxy.

A close examination of the **Mohammedan legal system,** even if one should confine himself to what little of it may be learned from the preceding chapters, will at once reveal its **highly mechanical** nature. Like all systems which lack the evolutionary outlook on life, it works under the assumption that social phenomena, complex as they are, may be reduced to hard-and-fast rules to which the intricate and nondescript situations of real life must fit themselves as best they can. Under the plea that reality (*bāṭin*) cannot be known but to God alone,[1] and that for the purposes of law, the outward signs (*ẓāhir*) of reality may be treated as reality itself, the latter is entirely lost sight of, and so the whole discussion is carried on in terms of the signs of reality instead of of reality itself. Of course, the signs correspond to reality only in what the statisticians would call the mode of the cases, and the chances of this correspondence become fewer and fewer as one gets further and further away from the initial premises.

To cite one instance, we saw that a matter so subtle as the exercise of independent thought (*ijtihād*) has been reduced to mechanical laws. For example, the doctors have ruled that one may not exercise independence of thought until he

[1] *Cf. Risālah*, p. 69, l. 1.

has met certain requirements. Of course such a rule is all right in so far as it encourages thoroughness, but it is fatal in at least two ways: (1) it shuts off contributions likely to come from persons who have not as yet met all the requirements, and (2) it excludes those that might come from outsiders who, being engaged in other studies, have likewise failed to fulfill the requirements. It is the familiar case of the conservative theologian who cries halt to the scientist when the latter "steps over the line."

The most fatal consequence of a mechanical system, however, is the excessive feeling of confidence and certainty into which it lulls its adepts. When to all appearances the complex and organic relationships of social life have been reduced to law and order, one cannot help getting into a false sense of security and optimism. Such a state of mind, acts like a selective screen that shuts off those stimuli, which if let through might expose the deceptiveness of the appearances. The Mohammedan legal system offers a good example of optimism carried too far. It inspires its adepts with the feeling, that at no point in the process, from the divine inception of the law down to the detailed legal provisions in the *fiqh*-books, or to the carrying-out of these provisions by the believers, is there any weakness where doubt might enter. Thus to the Mohammedans it is a matter of certainty that the Koran and the *sunnah* are genuine expressions of the divine will. Of course there is a possibility that their meanings may have been misunderstood, but the believer need have no misgivings on this point. For if a passage concerning the meaning of which there is doubt is one on which an *ijmā'* has been reached, certainty is assured by that fact; and if no *ijmā'* has been reached, his conscience may still be set at ease by resort to intuition (*taḫarri*), since the fact that one of the constructions appeals to the intuition is sufficient guarantee of its truth. Finally, if the question were raised that the law, although well understood, is misapplied, resort to intuition would again remove all doubts.

In the light of the above it is easy to understand why the Mohammedan doctors claim with great optimism that the various bases used in deriving the law from the *sharī'ah*, may all be reduced to the four bases of *fiqh*[1] previously mentioned, and that the latter in turn are based on and justified by the Koran and the *sunnah*, the two primary and genuine sources. Let us now critically inquire how true this assertion is and how far the primary sources are revealed, namely, how far they represent genuine records of the Prophetic utterances and conduct, and how far the other sources would in theory exclude external and, especially, intellectual influences. In taking as our basis of comparison the revealed sources we must consider them in their entirety, although it is a fact that they have gone through an evolution considering that they have reached their completion only at the death of the Prophet, that is, in the course of nearly a quarter of a century. Doubtless during this long period external, that is, non-Arabian influences, have made themselves felt, but their effect on the revealed sources in the life-time of the Prophet has indeed been very insignificant, compared to what it has been on the Mohammedan law since the Prophet's death.[2] Then too, there is an added reason for taking as our basis the revealed sources in their entirety, because if we should pass the natural limit afforded by the death of the Prophet, we would not know where to stop, and our inquiry would have to be pushed far back into preislamic history. Viewed from this standpoint, the various bases of *fiqh* are as follows:

[1] *Cf. Taqrīr*, vol. ii, p. 212.

[2] In Part III. we shall see to what influences the revealed sources have been subject as regards finance.

The Koran. There is little doubt that the Koran is on the whole a faithful record of the statements of the Prophet, modern scholars being agreed on this point.

The Sunnah. Unfortunately we cannot say the same thing concerning the *sunnah,* not only because it is a matter of historical record that falsification and invention of *ḥadīths* were extensively practised, but also because, as we have seen, the rules concerning the transmission of the *sunnah* are by no means a sufficient guarantee of its truth. Moreover, we know that one did not need to resort to falsification to support his claims when there could be found a justification for them in the *sunnah* of the Companions, since the *sunnah* of the latter was almost as binding as that of the Prophet.[1] It would not therefore be too rash to assume that certain new elements have found their way into *fiqh* in the garb of *sunnah.* In this respect the *sunnah* of the Companions acquires especial importance when we recall that the spread of Islam throughout Syria, Mesopotamia, 'Irāq and Egypt was completed in a very short time even before many of the Companions had died, for it means that most of the new situations which Islam faced in its expansion, received their solution at the hands of the Companions themselves. Of course this solution, as we shall see later in Part III., was almost always in the way of sanctioning the existing practices and institutions. In other words, by the time the *sunnah* reached its final and settled form in the famous collections of al-Bukhāri, Muslim, and others, many a foreign institution and idea had already found its way into Mohammedan law, either through sanction by the Companions or even through falsification of the *sunnah.*

The process of absorption from outside and adaptation

[1] *Cf. supra,* Classification of the *Sharī'ah* Values.

to changing conditions inside by no means stopped after the crystallization of the *sunnah* into the famous *ḥadīth*-collections, as has just been indicated, but went on as before, though this time through the medium of the remaining sources of legislation, such as *ijmā'* and *qiyās*.

The Ijma' may serve to introduce into the law new elements in two ways: (1) In so far as its constituent opinions consist in *qiyāses, ijmā'* would naturally be as good as *qiyās*. In fact it would be somewhat more effective than *qiyās*, since the evidential force of *ijmā'* is based mainly on the fact of the consensus rather than on the merits of the individual *qiyāses*. (2) *Ijmā'* in many cases would be another form of sanctioning custom. For example, if one doctor should express an opinion in approval of a recent custom, and the others should keep silent, we would have an *ijmā*. Thus we know that the legal institution of *istiṣnā'* was introduced into the law by way of *ijmā'*.

Qiyas. It is evident that in matters of analogy the question whether or not you are departing from your prototype, depends on whether or not the basis of analogy, namely, the causal attribute (*'illah*) is in accordance with the spirit of the prototype. Even if we should disregard the extreme views relative to the determination of this *'illah* and confine ourselves to the orthodox views, we would still find it to be true that they offered no adequate guarantee that in applying *qiyās* the revealed texts were not departed from. Take for instance the prohibition of wine-drinking. In order to make a *qiyās* on its basis, in the first place, the cause of the prohibition must be determined. Right here there would be an opportunity for displaying a great deal of scholastic subtlety whereby to determine as cause exactly that attribute of wine-drinking which would best serve the end in view. For instance, supposing that there is in the sources no prohibition against gambling and that we want to bring this under the prohibition, it would be easy to do it by considering as the cause of prohibition in the case of wine-drinking a quality of the latter which is also common to gambling, for example, excitement. But there is no need to go to even that much trouble, for it is not necessary that gambling should have precisely the quality which was the cause of prohibition in the case of wine-drinking. It is sufficient if gambling has a quality which, while not the very same quality, is of the genus of the quality which was the cause of prohibiting wine-drinking. For instance, one might say that wine-drinking had the quality of causing drunkenness, and gambling, excitement, and that both of them were of the genus of evil, and that consequently gambling came by analogy under the prohibition. It is true that the genus must be a proximate genus, but this does not materially affect the situation, for one might say that the cause was a genus of intellectual evil, in that they both disturbed the mental processes temporarily, or that it was a genus of financial evil, *etc.* Even this does not exhaust the possibilities, for just as in the case of the causal quality one may take the proximate genus instead of the very same quality, so also in the case of the value sought to be applied to the new case, one may apply a value of the same genus instead of the identical value. Thus arguing that prohibition is a genus of restriction one might only restrict gambling instead of entirely prohibiting it, as was the case with wine-drinking. It must be admitted here that the above examples represent somewhat strong cases, yet they are by no means exaggerated. In general one would not have to stretch things so far, for the purpose in hand would be much better served by using a more liberal principle like *istiḥsān*.

Istihsan, taking it in the sense used by the Hanifites, doubtless is a more effective means than *qiyās* for introducing new elements, since in its case the rules for determining the cause are even subtler than in the case of *qiyās*, and consequently afford greater possibilities. All that is needed is to discern in the new element whose introduction is desired some quality that is shared by a matter already approved or prohibited by the sources and the object is achieved.

The principle of **istislah**, made use of by the Mālikites, is probably the most effective of all, since it dispenses with the necessity of finding for its use a justification in the sources.

Custom, as will be recalled, is another important source of legislation, since in matters which are not mentioned, in the sources, according to the Hanifites, it is a direct source of law. To a certain extent custom is a source of law even in matters which are mentioned in the sources; moreover, custom supersedes the doctors' opinions when these have been based on custom and it has meanwhile changed. The significance of this last point will be fully grasped when it is remembered that the doctor's opinions are largely based on custom.

Space will not be taken to discuss the principles concerning the interpretation of texts (*tafsir wa ta'wīl*), since they are of slight importance in relation to the question of the extent to which foreign influences may have been allowed to influence Mohammedan Law. Suffice it to say that some doctors who did not acknowledge *qiyās* achieved practically the same result through a process which they called interpretative.

Without further illustrations, the preceding discussion proves beyond doubt, that so far as theory is concerned, there was practically no check to the introduction into *fiqh* of foreign institutions and ideas.[1] Indeed, in Part III. we shall find this to have actually been the case as regards

[1] *Cf.* Kremer, pp. 532-547.

finance which, as we have seen in Chapter I., is an integral part of *fiqh*. If, therefore, *fiqh* has been on the whole an independent development, especially in its later stages of growth, it is not because there was a theoretical obstacle to non-revealed external influences, but simply because there were not enough of the latter.

BIBLIOGRAPHY

The following bibliography is intended for use in the study of Mohammedan law directly from the Arabic sources, and, therefore, works on the subject written in European languages, as a rule, are not indicated, since a very good account of them may be obtained from the works of Juynboll and, especially, of MacDonald. The chief aim in writing this bibliography is to give a *vue d'ensemble* of the literature and to furnish prospective students with the necessary bearings in approaching the vast subject of Mohammedan law. To this end, the chief works written on the different disciplines that make up, or are preliminary to the study of, Mohammedan law have been explained; works generally referred to and quoted in the sources have been indicated, and, so far as possible, the sources have been presented in a chronological order and their nature briefly explained. Although many books which are not extant in printed or manuscript form have been included, the list is by no means exhaustive, as the object has been selection rather than collection.

The Arabic sources fall into three fairly distinguishable classes: (a) The so-called texts (*matn*) or compendiums (*mukhtaṣar*); (b) the commentaries (*sharḥ*) and glosses (*ḥâshiyah, taqrîr, ta'lîq*); (c) the collections of legal opinions (*fatwa*). The compendiums give in a more or less general way the principles of law respecting concrete cases and are intended to serve as a basis of instruction and as a mnemonic help. As a rule they do not mention the arguments, and do not indicate the views of other schools. As they are intended to be learnt by heart by the students, the ideal that the writers of such compendiums set before themselves is to make them as brief, but also as comprehensive, as possible. Probably the *Mukhtaṣar* of Khalîl has approached this ideal more than any other. Various devices are used to hint, without using more words, whether a certain view was held by the founder of the school (*naṣṣ*) and whether it is an independent view (*qawl*) or merely an application by analogy (*wajh, qawl mukharraj*) of an existing view. The persons responsible for a given view and the view to be preferred out of the many given views are also hinted. The Hanifite usage in this last respect is to cite first the view favored by the writer of the text, unless the text gives the arguments also. In such case, first the views and then the respective arguments are presented,—the view and argument favored, last. While on the whole no established usage has prevailed in this connection, in some instances a fairly common understanding seems to have been reached. A thorough study of this subject would be most helpful for the proper understanding of the sources. Probably the chief distinction between a commentary and a gloss is that a gloss is more sketchy and goes into questions of grammar and syntax more often and more at length. The distinction between so-called *fatwa* collections and works on law proper (*fiqh*), as the words are used by the doctors, is often shadowy. Thus the name *fatwa* collection is given to works, such as the *'Alamkiriyyah*, which by no means answer questions on concrete actual cases but simply give the legal principles on particular points as determined in the first instance by early doctors or as involved in existing *fatwas* on actual cases. These principles, however, are still too general to be applied to actual cases without further interpretation. As it is, the difference of a work on *fatwas* from a work on *fiqh* proper reduces itself to the fact that the latter, besides being somewhat less full as to details, also gives the motives and grounds and is meant to furnish a more or less scientific training whereby one might apply the law to new cases.

The statements occurring in the *fiqh* books of one school concerning views held in another school are not always accurate and must be received with caution. As a rule, greater caution is needed in regard to books that may not strictly speaking be called *fiqh* books, such as the work of al-Māwardi, than would be necessary for a work on *fiqh* proper, such as the *Hidāyah* or the *Minhāj*. Works of the latter type being an object of constant study and comment as well as of actual application have remained, relatively speaking, immune from text corruption. Besides, it is easy to correct any corruptions that may have crept into the text by reference to the source books of the school on which they are invariably based. Works of the former type, however, have not had the benefit of these corrective agncies to the same extent.

Abbreviations and Signs.—Words printed in black-face type indicate the titles under which works have been referred to in this dissertation. Words underlined indicate the shorter names by which persons and books are commonly referred to by the doctors. Dates in parentheses after titles of books and names of persons indicate years of writing and death, respectively. Devotional phrases such as "May He be exalted" or "May God have mercy on him," invariably used by doctors after the mention of God, and persons of note, have been omitted. Where the volume has not been indicated, the first volume is meant, unless another volume has been expressly indicated. A. = Aḥmad; Ism. = Ismā'īl; Ibr. = Ibrāhīm; 'Al. = 'Abdāllah; 'Ar. = 'Abd-al-raḥman; 'Aq. = 'Abd-al-qādir; H. = Hasan; Hu. = Husayn; Su. =

Sulayman; M. = Muḥammad; Yū. = Yusuf; *a.* = *Abu* (father of); *b.* = *Ibn* (son of); *K.* = *Kitāb*. The remaining are self-explanatory.

BIOGRAPHICAL

COMPANIONS AND FOLLOWERS: (1) *Ṭabaqāt al-Ṣaḥābah wa 'l-Tābi'īn* or simply *Ṭabaqāt b. Sa'd* by a. 'Al. M. b. Sa'd al-Zuhri al-Baṣri (230). "The earliest and most comprehensive" (Rieu). (2) *Al-Iṣābah fī Tamyīz al-Ṣaḥābah*, by Shihāb-al-dīn a. 'l-Faḍl A. b. 'Ali b. Hajar al-'Asqalāni (852), the Shafiite. Cairo, 1323. Contains the *Istī'āb al-Ṣaḥābah fī Ma'rifat al-Aṣḥāb* by a. 'Amr Yū. b. 'Al. b. 'Abd-al-barr (463), the Malikite, and the *Usd al-Ghābah fī Ma'rifat al-Ṣaḥābah*, by 'Izz-al-dīn a. 'l-H. 'Ali. b. al-Athīr (-al-dīn) al-Jazari (630), and more, in all 12,279 lives, omitting all but the Companions. Abridged by Jalāl-al-dīn 'Ar. al-Suyūṭi (911) in the *'Ayn al-Iṣābah.*

TRUSTWORTHY REPORTERS (*al-thiqāt*): *K. al-Thiqāt*—by al-Hāfiẓ a. Khātim M. b. Hibbān al-Busti (354).

UNTRUSTWORTHY REPORTERS (*ruwāt*): (1) *Al-Kāmil fī Ma'rifat al-Du'afā' wa 'l-Matrūkīn min al-Ruwāt*—by a. 'Al. A. b. M. b. 'Adi (365). Considered as standard by the doctors. Al-Dāraquṭni asked to compose a work on untrustworthy (*ḍu'afā'*) reporters, answered: "Do you not have the book of b. 'Adi?" "There is sufficient in it; it cannot be augmented." (H. Khal.) The work contains the name of every reporter whose trustworthiness was questioned even if he has already been classed as reliable (*thiqah*). (2) *Mīzān al-I'tidāl fī Naqd al-Rijāl*—by Shams-al-dīn a. 'Al. M. b. A. al-Dhahabi (748). According to b. Hajar, the most comprehensive, except that the author in order to avoid criticism omitted the names of Companions and founders of schools who obtained a following (H. Khal.). Arrangement alphabetical. The *Ṣaḥīḥs*, where the *ḥadīths* reported by these untrustworthy reporters are cited, are hinted.

REPORTERS IN GENERAL: (1) The *Tārīkh*—by M. b. Ism. al-Bukhāri (256). Reporters grouped in classes. (2) *Al-Kamāl fī Ma'rifat* (or *Asmā'*) *al-Rijāl*—by a. M. 'Abd-al-gani b. Abd-al-wāhid al-Muqaddasi (600). Alphabetical list of the reporters mentioned in the six *Ṣaḥīḥs* with biographical notices. The *Tah-dhīb al-Kamāl, etc.*, is an enlargement by Jamāl-al-dīn Yū. b. al-Zaki al-Mizzi (742). "This is a large work, to compose the like of which is believed impossible" (H. Khal.). The work also remarks about the reliability of the reporters. A further abridgment is the *Tah-dhīb al-Tah-dhīb* by b. Hajar (852). A still further abridgment by b. Hajar is the *Taqrīb al-Tahdhīb*, with additions. Lith. Dihli, 1320. Gives full names, places, dates of death and degrees of reliability.

TRADITIONISTS (*Huffāẓ*): *Tadhkirat al-Huffāẓ*—by Shams-al-din M. b. A. al-Dhahabi (748). Haydarabad. It gives lives of students of *ḥadīth* whose function is to decide whether a certain reporter is reliable, *etc.*

GENERAL—(1) *Tarīkh 'Ulamā' al-Andalus*, by a. al-Walīd 'Al. b. M. al-Azdi b. al-Faraḍi (403). Ed. Fr. Codera, Bibl. ar. hisp., vols. vii-viii, Matriti, 1890. Gives briefly in alphabetical order lives of 1,642 doctors, jurists, *etc.* of Spain. Indexes on persons, books and places appended. Scanty in bibliographical information. A continuation of this work is the *Al-Ṣilah fī Akhbār A'immat al-Andalus* (534), by a. al-Qāsim Khalaf b. 'Abd-al-malik b. Bashkwāl al-Qurṭubi (578). Ed. Fr. Codera, Bibl. ar. hisp., vols. i-ii, Matriti, 1883. (2) *Tārīkh Bagdād*—by a. Bakr A. b. 'Ali al-Khaṭīb al-Bagdādi (463). A celebrated extensive history, particularly of the learned men, of Bagdad. (3) *Ṭabaqāt al-Fuqahā'*, by a. Isḥaq Ibr. b. 'Ali al-Shīrāzi (476), the Shafiite. It gives the lives of the jurists among the Companions and Followers and those of the founders of schools and their disciples. (4) *Bugyat al-Multamis fī Tārīkh Ahl Rijāl al-Andalus* (592), by a. Ja'far A. b. Yahya al-Ḍabbi al-Qurṭubi. A completion and continuation of the *Jadhwat al-Muqtabis, etc.* by a. 'Al. M. b. a. Naṣr al-Humaydi (488). (5) *Irshād al-Arīb ila Ma'rifat al-Adīb*, known as *Mu'jam al-Udabā'* or *Ṭabaqāt al-Udabā'*, by Yāqūt b. 'Al. al-Rūmi (626). E. J. W. Gibb Memorial Series. Leyden, 1907. Gives lives of literary persons, such as grammarians, lexicographers, genealogists, Koran readers, chronicle writers, historians, copyists, and famous scribes. Gives lives of jurists in so far as they have been literary writers, such as, *e. g.*, al-Shāfi'i. (6) *K. Wafayāt al-A'yān wa Anbā' Abnā' al-Zamān*—by Shams-al-dīn A. b. M. b. Khallikān (672), the Shafiite. Cairo, 1892, 2 vols. (b. Khall.) (with the *Shaqā'iq* on the margin). English translation by M. G. de Slane (**Ibn Khallikan**) in 4 vols. Paris-London, 1843-7. A celebrated work giving lives of persons of note in every line. Omits Companions and early califs as too well-known. Alphabetical with respect to real names. Many supplements have been written, among others the *Fawāt al-Wafayāt* by M. b. Shākir al-Kutubi (764), who claims to have also supplied omissions mentioned. (7) Tah-dhīb *al-Asmā' wa' l-Lugāt*—by a. Zakariyā' Yahya b. Sharaf al-Nawawi (676), the Shafiite. Ed., F. Wüstenfeld, Göttingen, 1849 (first part only). A very frequently quoted, useful work. First part (*qism*) gives the proper names, and the second part the common names and technical terms occurring in the Shafiite *fiqh* books, *Mukhtaṣar al-Muzani, Muhadhdhab, Tanbīh, Wasīṭ, Wajīz*, and *Rawḍah*. Alphabetical with respect to real names, surnames, *etc.*, grouped in separate sections. The lives given are mostly of Companions and Followers, with a few of the leading jurists of different schools, chiefly the Shafiite. (8) *Al-Nujūm al-Zāhirah fi Mulūk Miṣr wa 'l-Qāhirah*—by **Abu 'l-Mahasin** Jamāl-al-dīn Yū. b. Tagrībirdi (874). Ed. F. G. Juynboll, Lugd. Batav., 1855-61 (as far as year 365). Gives useful information in connection with necrologies. (9) **Husn al-Muhadarah** *fi Akhbār Miṣr wa 'l-Qāhirah*—by Jalāl-al-dīn al-Suyūṭi (911). Cairo, 1299. A many-sided history of Egypt, giving short notices on the *mujtahids* (pp. 161-88) and jurists (pp. 224-74) who lived in Egypt, with their works mentioned. (10) *Nafḥ al-Tīb min Guṣn al-Andalus al-Raṭib wa Dhikr Wazīr-ha Lisān-al-dīn* b. *al-Khaṭīb*—by a. al-'Abbās A. b. M. al-Maqqari al-Tilimsāni (1041), the Malikite. Ed. R. Dozy, *etc.*, Leyden, 1855-61. A large work giving, among other matter, lives of Spanish doctors who traveled eastward and doctors who traveled to Spain, and mentioning names of many books, with some bibliographical information. The arrangement of the book follows no order. The indexes at the end unsatisfactory.

HANIFITE—(1) *Al-Jawāhir al-Muḍī'ah*, by Muhyi-al-dīn 'Aq. b. a. al-Wafā' al-Qurashi al-Miṣri (775). Contains many mistakes because it is the first work of its kind; "therefore the man should be excused" (H. Khal.). Supplement: *Al-Guraf al-'Aliyyah fi Tarājim Muta'akhiri al-Hanafiyyah*, by Shams-al-dīn a. 'Al. M. b. 'Ali b. Tūlūn (955). Contains about 1,200 lives, mostly of eighth, ninth and tenth centuries (Rieu). Condensation by Ibr. b. M. al-Halabi (956), the Hanifite, including only jurists who left works and whose names are mentioned in the books. (2) *Tāj al-Tarājim fi Tabaqāt al-Hanafiyyah*—by a. al-Faḍl Zayn-al-millah wa'l-dīn al-Qāsim b. 'Al. b. Quṭlūbuga (879). The work deals only with jurists who left writings—in all, 330 persons. (3) *Al-Shaqā'iq al-Nu'māniyyah fi Ulamā' al-Dawlah al-'Uthmāniyyah*—by Mawla A. b. Muṣṭafa Tashkeuprizādeh (968). Constantinople, 1851-2, with additions and supplements by Majdi and 'Aṭā'i (Flügel). Also printed on margin of *Wafayāt* by b. Khallikān. The work contains about 600 lives. It was written in order to save from oblivion the doctors (*'ulamā'*) who lived and flourished in the Ottoman Empire. Many supplements were written. H. Khal. speaks in the highest terms of a supplement in 7 vols. by Aṭā'-allah New'īzādeh. (4) *Tabaqāt al-Ulamā' al-Hanafiyyah*, by 'Ali Tchelebi b. Imru'-allah Qinālīzādeh (979). Gives in brief lives of 231 persons, in 21 classes. (5) *Katā'ib A'lām-al-Akhyār min Fuqahā' Madh-hab Nu'mān al-Mukhtār*, also called *al-Katā'ib al-Kaffawiyyah*, by Maḥmūd b. Su. al-Kaffawi (990). It treats of the Hanifite doctors "from the Prophet down" to his own time, giving lists of their teachers and students (*'an'anāt*), peculiar legal opinions as found in famous *fatwa* collections, their works, and other relevant information. An esteemed work. An abridgment of it is the *Al-Fawā'id al-Bahiyyah fi Tarājim al-Hanafiyyah ma' al-Ta'līqāt al-Saniyyah 'ala 'l-Fawā'id al-Bahiyyah*, by a. al-Hasanāt M. 'Abd-al-ḥayy al-Luknawi (1304). Kazan, 1321; Cairo, 1324. (6) *Al-Tabaqāt al-Saniyyah fi Tarājim al-Hanafiyyah*, by Taqi-al-dīn b. 'Aq. al-Tamīmi al-Gazzi (1005-10), with an introduction. Alphabetically arranged with respect to real names (*asmā'*). Separate sections for ethnic (*ansāb*) and honorary names (*alqāb*). "This is the most excellent of the works composed on the lives of Hanifites (*ahl al-ra'y*): It contains the lives of the *Shaqā'iq* and later works until his time, namely 993, the year of its completion" (H. Khal.). (7) **Flügel**, G., "Die Classen der hanefitischen Rechtsgelehrten," *Abhandl. der philol. hist. Classe der königl. sächs. Ges. der Wiss.*, vol. iii.

SHAFIITE—(1) *Tabaqāt al-Shāfi'iyyah*, by Tāj-al-dīn 'Abd-al-wahhāb b. A. (b.) al-**Subki** (771). Cairo, 1324. Overflowing with information (H. Khal.). Intended by the author to include the name of every jurist named in the current books of his time. Often quotes long passages from their works and relates at length debates, *etc.* Alphabetical (not strictly) with respect to real names (*asmā'*) within each group, except that jurists whose name is Aḥmad, then those whose name is Muḥammad, are treated first. First group gives Al-Shāfi'i's personal disciples; the other groups consist of jurists who died within same century. There is an abridgment of it by himself. (2) *Qalā'id al-Fuḍalā' wa 'Uqūd al-Jumān* (769)—by Jamāl-al-dīn a. M. 'Abd-ar-rahīm b. al-H. al-Isnawi (772). Alphabetical with respect to names or surnames by which jurists are commonly known. Based on the work of b. al-Salāḥ and others. (3) *Tabaqāt al-Shāfi'iyyah*—by Taqi-al-dīn a. Bakr b. A. b. (Qāḍi) Shuhbah, al-Dimashqi (851). It gives lives of those "whose names are widespread and about whom the student needs to know," as the author claims. Treats in 29 classes of 20 years each; alphabetical within each class. (4) Wüstenfeld, H. F., "Der Imâm el-Schâfi'i, seine Schüler und Anhänger." *Königl. Gesel. d. Wiss. zu Göttingen, Abdanl.*, vols. 36-37. Based on the works of al-Nawawi, Al-Subki, al-Isnawi, b. Shuhbah, b. Khallikān, al-Maqrīzi, al-Suyūṭi, *etc.*

MALIKITE—(1) *Tartīb al-Madārik wa Taqrīb al-Masālik li Ma'rifāt A'lām Madh-hab Mālik*—by al-Qāḍi 'Iyāḍ b. Mūsa al-Yaḥṣabi (544). An esteemed work that is much quoted. (2) *Al-Dībāj al-Mudhahhab fi Ma'rifat A'yān Ulamā' al-Madh-hab*, also *Tabaqāt al-Mālikiyyah*—by Burhān-al-dīn Ibr. b. 'Ali b. Farḥūn (799). Fez, 1892. An elegant work (H. Khal.). Supplements: (a) *Tawshīḥ al-Dībāj wa Hilyat al-Ibtihāj*—by Badr-al-dīn M. b. Yahya al-Qarāfi (975 or 1008). (b) *Kifāyat al-Mukhtāj ila Ma'rifat man Laysa fi 'l-Dībāj*—by A. Bāba b. A. al-Tunbukti al-Sanhāji (1032). Author claims to have also supplied omissions of the *Dībāj*. (*Cf.* "Les Tabakât Malekites" by E. Fagnan in **Homenaje** *à D. F. Codera*, Zaragoza, 1904.)

HANBALITE—(1) *Tabaqāt al-Hanbaliyyah* (513), by al-Qādi a. 'l-Hu. M. b. M. al-Farrā' al-Bagdādi (526). Supplemented first down to 750 by Zayn-al-dīn a. al-Faraj 'Ar. b. A. b. Rajab (795) down to 750, then by Yū. b. H. al-Muqaddasi, down to 871. (2) *Al-Manhaj al-Aḥmad fi Tarājim Aṣḥāb al-Imām Aḥmad*—by 'Ar. b. M. al-'Umari al-'Ulaymi (927), the Hanbalite. Detailed work on famous Hanbalites down to his time, supplying many omissions of the former.

SHI'ITE—*Majālis al-Mu'minīn* (996), by Nūr-allah b. Sharīf al-Husayni al-Shūshtari. A frequently quoted work.

BIBLIOGRAPHICAL

(1) *K. al-Fihrist*, or *Fihris al-'Ulūm* (377), by a. 'l-Faraj M. b. Isḥāq al-Warrāq al-Bagdādi. Ed. G. Flügel, Leipzig, 1871. A list of the Arabic books written up to 377 topically arranged with occasional bibliographical details. Good for earliest writers. (2) *Fihrist Kutub al-Shī'ah*, by a. Ja'far M. b. al-H. al-Tūsi (459), the Imamite. Ed. A. Sprenger. Bibl. Ind., nos. 60, 71, 91, 107. Calcutta, 1853-5. Gives list of Shi'ite works. According to the *Iktifā'*, it includes the *Naḍad al-Iḍāḥ* of 'Alam al-Huda on famous Shi'ites. (3) **Fihrist** *ma Rawāhu 'an Shuyukhihi min al-Dawāwīn al-Muṣannafah fi Durub al-'Ilm wa Anwā' al-Ma'ārif*, by a. Bakr M. b. Khayr **al-Ishbili** (575). Ed. Fr. Codera and J. R. Tarrago, Bibl. ar. hisp., vols. ix-x, Caesaraugustae, 1894-5. A list of more than 1,400 book-titles topically arranged with full lists of their transmitters but scant bibliographical information. There is a chapter on the many *Fihrists* transmitted down by the author. (4) *K. al-'Ibar wa Dīwān al-Mubtadā' wa 'l-Khabar fi Ayyām al-'Arab wa 'l-'Ajam wa 'l-Barbar, etc.*, by a. Zayd 'Ar. b. M. b. Khaldūn al-Magribi (808), the Malikite; the *Muqqaddamah*, vol. i, pp. 363-77 (**Ibn Khaldun**). Būlāq, 1284. Contains a valuable bibliographical and critical review of the literature of the religious and other sciences. (5) *Miftāḥ al-Sa'ādah wa Miṣbāḥ al-Siyādah*, by a. 'l-Khayr A. b. Muṣliḥ-al-dīn Muṣṭafa Tāshkeuprizādeh (968), the Hanifite. It describes the subject-matters of 150 disciplines indicating the well-known books pertaining to each. Drawn upon by H. Khal. (6) *Risālah fi Tabaqāt al-Masā'il*, by 'Ali Tchelebi Qinālī-zādeh (979) (also b. al-Hinnāli). It explains main types of Hanifite legal literature. Probably does not contain very much more than Ibn 'Abidīn and H. Khal. *Cf.* Ahlwardt, no. 4868. (7) *Kashf al-Zunūn 'an Asāmi al-Kutub wa 'l-Funūn* (**H. Khal.**), by Muṣṭafa b. 'Al. Kātib Tchelebi Hāji Khalīfah (1068). Ed. with Latin translation by G. Flügel, Leipzig, 1835-58. Excepting Malikite works, it gives a nearly exhaustive list of Arabic (also Turkish and Persian) books alphabetically arranged according to titles, with a long introduction on science, its definition, purpose, division, *etc.*, and with learned reviews of the

different sciences and their literatures in their proper places. (For inst., *'ilm fiqh* under *fiqh*, *'ilm uṣūl-al-fiqh* under *uṣūl-al-fiqh*, *etc.*) Profuse in giving dates of death and bibliographical information. In connection with basic works are given the commentaries, abridgments, versifications, etc. **(8)** D'Ohsson, M. de M., *Tableau général de l'empire ottoman*, Paris, 1787. Pp. 17, 290 give a short list of *fatwa* collections and a description of the seminaries (*madrasah*) in Turkey and the text-books used, respectively. **(9)** *Sharḥ al-Manẓūmah al-Musammāt bi 'Uqūd Rasm al-Mufti*, by M. Amīn Efendi, known as **Ibn 'Abidīn** (1250), the Hanifite. Printed in a collection of his essays entitled *Majmū'ah Rasā'il Ibn 'Abidīn*. Constantinople, 1325. Pp. 10-52. Gives valuable information about the original Hanifite sources and the meanings of the terms used by Hanifite doctors in connection with the transmission of early opinions. **(10) Vincent,** M. B., *Études sur la loi musulmane. Législation criminelle.* Paris. 1842. Gives historical, bibliographical information on early important Malikite works of law (pp. 31-62). **(11)** Harington, J. H., Esq. (1828), "Remarks upon the Authorities of Mosulman Law." in his *An Elementary Analysis of the Laws and Regulations* (of Bengal), *etc.*, vol. i, Calcutta, 1805-17. Bibliography of Hanifite works with especial reference to India. **(12)** Morley, W. H. (1860), *An Analytical Digest* (of cases decided in the Supreme Courts of India). New series, vol. i, introd. London, 1852. **(13)** Sircar, Shama Ch., *The Muhammadan Law*, Tagore Law Lectures. 1873 and 1874. Calcutta, 1873 and 1875. Bibliogr. of Hanifite (pp. 18-63) and of Shi'ite works (pp. 167-74). **(14) Kremer,** A. von, *Culturgeschichte des Orients unter den Chalifen.* Vienna, 1875-7. Chapters on law, pp. 470-547, and science and literature, vol. ii. 396-484. Also goes into origin of *fiqh*. **(15)** Chauvin, Victor, *Bibliographie des ouvrages arabes ou relatifs aux Arabes publiés dans l'Europe chrétienne de 1810-85.* Vols. i, ii, iii. Liège, 1892, 1897, 1898. Topical treatment. Very scholarly. Quotes tables of contents. **(16) Ahlwardt,** W., *Verzeichniss der arab. Hss. der königl. Bibliothek zu Berlin.* Berlin, 1887. Topical treatment. Gives list of the works or commentaries bearing on a subject. Valuable work. **(17)** Hurgronje, C. Snouck, **Mekka,** Haag. 1889. Vol. ii, pp. 249 *et seq.* On methods of instruction in seminaries in Mecca and a few of the works used, with a critical evaluation of same. **(18) Goldziher,** I., *Muham.* (**M.**) **Studien.** Halle. 1889-90. Contains a chapter (vol. ii) on *ḥadīth* literature. The book is a masterly study of the entire subject of *ḥadīth*. **(19) Rieu,** Ch., *Supplement to the Cat. of the Arab. Mss. in the Br. Museum.* London, 1894. Topical treatment. Rich in bibliographical information. **(20)** Hughes, T. B., *A Dictionary of Islam*, 2d ed., London, 1896. Gives bibliography of Hanifite and Shi'ite works under Law and Tradition. **(21)** *K.* **Iktifa'** *al-Qunū bima Huwa Maṭbū' min Ajall al-Ta'ālīf al-'Arabiyyah fi 'l-Maṭābi' al-Shar-*

qiyyah wa 'l-Garbiyyah, by Edward Findik, Cairo, 1896. A list of the important Arabic works published in Europe and the Orient. Its bibliographical notices often based on Haji Khalīfah. They are at times original. **(22) Savvas**, Pacha, *Étude sur la théorie du droit musulman.* 2nd ed., Paris, 1902. Pp. 150-60. Bibliography of Hanifite works, with special reference to those used in instruction in seminaries in Turkey. **(23)** Sachau, Ed., *Muham. Recht nach Shafit. Lehre* (**S.**), Stuttgart and Berlin, 1897. Vol. xvii of *Lehrbücher des Sem. für orient. Sprachen zu Berlin.* A bibliography of Shafiite books. For a long, constructive criticism of same by C. Snouck Hurgronje (**H. on S.**), see *Zeitschrift der deutschen morgenländischen Gesellschaft* (*Z. D. M. G.*), Leipzig, vol. 53, esp. pp. 143-150. **(24) Brockelmann,** Carl, *Geschichte der arab. Litteratur.* Weimar, 1898-1902. A list of extant Arabic works with accounts of existing Mss., years of publication, short biographical notices, dates of birth and death, and occasional bibliographical information. Commentaries, abridgments, *etc.*, are given in connection with the basic works to which they relate. Arrangement chronological within general topics. An indispensable manual. **(25)** MacDonald, D. B., *Development of Muslim Theology, Jurisprudence and Constit. Theory.* New York, 1903. Contains a good annotated bibliography on works (esp. European) on Islam in general. **(26)** *Institutes of Mussalman Law*, by A. F. M. Abdur Rahman. Calcutta, 1907. Annotated bibliography on Hanifite works (pp. lv-lxi), chiefly based on Harington and Morley. **(27)** Heidborn, A., *Manuel de droit public et admin. de l'empire ottoman.* Vienna, Leipzig, 1908. Pp. 275 *et seq.* A complete list of books used at present in seminaries in Turkey. **(28)** Norès, Ed., *Essai de codification du droit musulman algérien (statut personel).* Algiers, 1909. Bibliography on Malikite law works. Pp. ix-xxv. **(29) Juynboll,** Th. W., *Handbuch des islam. Gesetzes nach der Lehre der schafiit. Schule nebst einer allgem. Einleitung.* Leiden-Leipzig, 1910. A compact and useful work with many references on each topic. Also contains a list of the chief European and orthodox Arabic works on Moh. law. **(30)** *The Encyclopedia of Islām.* Ed. by M. Th. Houtsma, *etc.* Leyden, 1913. Covers geography, ethnography and biography of Mohammedan peoples. Published as far as the letter H. **(31)** Carusi, Prof. Ev., *Sui rapporti fra diritto romano e diritto musulmano.* Rome, 1913. Extract from *Atti d. Soc. Ital. per il Progresso d. Scienze*, VII, *Riunione-Siena, settembre*, 1913. Makes critical remarks on European works on Muh. law.

LEXICOLOGICAL

NAMES OF PERSONS—**(1)** *Al-Mushtabih fi Asmā' al-Rijāl*—by Shams-al-dīn a. 'Al. M. b. A. al-Dhahabi (748), the Shafiite. Gives spelling of ambiguous real names, ethnic names, surnames (*kunyah*) and honorary names (*laqab*). (**2**) *Lubb al-Lubāb fi Taḥrir al-Ansāb*, by Jalāl-al-dīn 'Ar. b. a. Bakr al-Suyūṭi (911), the Shafiite. Leyden, 1851. Gives spelling of *nisbahs*, *i. e.* names of tribal, family, or local relation. Condensed from the *Lubāb* of b. al-Athīr., with additions.

NAMES OF PLACES—(1) *K. Mu'jam Ma Ustu'jima*, by a. 'Ubayd 'Al. b. 'Abd-al-'azīz al-Bakri (487). Ed. F. Wüstenfeld, Göttingen, 1876. According to R. Dozy, as quoted by Wüstenfeld, it is unique in completeness and accuracy and beyond comparison. The work gives the spelling of names of towns, villages, countries, stations, mountains, rivers, wells, *etc.*, occurring in *ḥadīths*, histories, and poems, with situations indicated. Quotes respective verses. (**2**) *Mu'jam Marāṣid al-Iṭṭilā' 'ala Asmā' al-Amkinah wa 'l-Biqā'*, by Yāqūt b. 'Al. al-Rūmi (626). Ed. T. G. J. Juynboll, Leyden, 1850-64. Condensed from the *Mu'jam al-Buldān* of the same author. (**3**) General dictionaries such as the *al-Qāmūs al-Muḥīṭ* of M. b. Ya'qūb al-Fīrūzābādi (817), the Shafiite, and esp. its commentary, the *Tāj al-'Arūs*, by al-Sayyid M. Murtaḍa al-Zabīdi (1206), the Hanifite. Both are alphabetical with respect to 3d, then 1st and 2d letters of the root. (**4**) *Bibl. Geographorum Arabicorum*. Ed. M. J. De Goeje, Lugduni Batavorum, 1870-94. Contains indexes of places and peoples. (**5**) The *Onomasticon Arabicum* to be shortly brought out in connection with the *Annali dell' Islam* by L. Caetani. It is to contain over 200,000 items, and may fairly be expected to dispense with all other works of its kind.

COMMON NAMES—(I) **Koran**: *Mufradāt Alfāẓ al-Qur'ān*, by a. 'l-Qāsim al-Hu. b. M. al-**Rāgib** al-Iṣfahāni (502). Cairo. Alphabetically arranged and very serviceable. Quotes verses and traditions.

(II) **Tradition**: *Al-Nihāyah fi Garīb al-Hadīth wa 'l-Athar*, by Majd-al-dīn a. 'l-Sa'ādāt al-Mubārak b. M. al-Jazari **ibn al-Athīr** (606). Cairo, 1311. Two vols. Based on the standard works of a. 'Ubayd al-Qāsim al-Harawi (223), 'Al. b. Muslim b. Qutaybah (276), a. Ubayd A. b. M. al-Harawi (401) on both the Koran and the *ḥadīth*, and M. b. a. Bakr al-Iṣfahāni (581), with additions. Alphabetical with respect to roots. Quotes the entire *ḥadīth* where the word is found. Very easy of reference and full of valuable information. A condensation with additions is the *Al-Durr al-Nathīr*, by Jalāl-al-dīn al-Suyūṭi (911). Printed on the margin of the *Nihāyah*.

(III) **Law**—(1) *Garīb al-Fiqh*, by a. Manṣūr M. b. A. al-Azhari (370). Explains words used by Shafiite jurists. It is "a standard" (*'umdah*) in this respect. (H. Khal.) (**2**) **Mafātīḥ** *al-'Ulūm*, by a. 'Al. M. b. A. al-Khuwārizmi al-Kātib (ca. 365-87). Ed. G. van Vlotten, Leyden, 1895. Gives in brief explanations of technical terms used in sciences and arts (such as *fiqh*, dogmatics, syntax, tax and other administration [*kitā-*

bah], music, and chemistry) in separate chapters analytically arranged. Very valuable. (**3**) *Al-Mugrib fi Tartib al-Mu'rib*, by a. 'l-Fath Nāṣir b. 'Abd-al-sayyid al-Muṭarrizi (610), the Hanifite. Haydarabad, 1328. A condensed alphabetical arrangement of his own *al-Mu'rib*. Explains words and locutions used in Hanifite works on *fiqh*, such as the *Muntaqa* of al-Hākim al-Shahīd, the *Tafsir* of al-Qudūri, the *Mukhtaṣar* of al-Karkhi, *etc.*, in a rather non-technical fashion. (**4**) The second part (*qism*) of the work: **Tah-dhib** *al-Asmā' wa 'l-Lugāt*, by Yahya al-Nawawi (676). *Cf. supra*, p. 160. (**5**) *Al-***Misbah** *al-Munir fi Garīb al-Sharḥ al-Kabīr*, by A. b. M. al-Muqri al-Fayyūmi (770), the Shafiite. Cairo, 1305. Explains the words used in al-Rāfi'i's commentary on the *Wajīz*, with additions. Gives many locutions, but in spite of its name is more like a general than a technical dictionary. (**6**) *Al-Ta'rīfāt*, by 'Ali b. M. al-Jurjāni, al-Sayyid al-Sharīf (816), the Hanifite. Cairo, 1321 (with an appendix on Sūfi terms). A well-known work giving brief definitions of technical terms only, such as are found in books on law, *ḥadīth*, syntax, *etc.* (**7**) *Maqālīd al-'Ulūm fi 'l-Hudūd wa 'l-Rusūm*, by the same author. Gives technical terms of 21 sciences. (**8**) *Ishārāt ila ma Waqa'a fi Kutub al-Fiqh min al-Asmā' wa 'l-Amākin wa 'l-Lugāt*, by a. Tāhir M. b. Ya'qūb al-Fīrūzābādi (817). Explains proper names and terms of *fiqh* books. (**9**) *Al-Hidāyah al-Kāfiyah*, by M. b. al-Qāsim al-Rashshā' (894), a commentary on a work on legal definitions by M. b. M. b. 'Arafah al-Wargami (803), the Malikite. (**10**) *Ta'rīfāt*, by a. Yahya Zakariyā' b. M. al-Anṣāri (926), the Shafiite. Brief definitions of the technical terms used in dogmatics (*uṣūl-al-dīn*) and *fiqh*. (**11**) *Kulliyyāt al-'Ulūm*, by a. 'l-Baqā' al-Hu. al-Kaffawi (1094), the Hanifite. Būlāq, 1281. Arrangement hardly alphabetical as claimed by author. At times very long, esp. as regards rules of grammar and syntax; at other times brief and non-technical. (**12**) *Kashshāf Iṣṭilāhāt al-Funūn* (**Tech. Dict.**) (1158), by M. 'Ali b. 'Ali al-Tahānawi, the Hanifite. Ed. A. Sprenger, Bibl. Ind., Calcutta, 1862. Explains technical terms by long quotations from standard works. Contains an introduction on definition, subject-matter, etc., of sciences. (**13**) *Ta'rīfāt al-Funūn wa Tarājim al-Muṣannifīn wa Manāqibuhum*, by M. al-Aqkermāni (around 1160). (**14**) Among general dictionaries the *Muḥīṭ al-Muḥīṭ*, by Buṭrus al-Bustāni (1883), Bayrut, 1867, is particularly helpful in giving summary definitions of technical terms. Also the *Qaṭr al-Muḥīṭ*, an abridgment of the former by the author himself.

KORAN COMMENTARIES

(**1**) *Tafsīr al-Qur'ān*, by a. Ja'far M. b. Jarīr al-Tabari (310), Cairo, 1321. "The entire Mohammedan community is agreed that its like has not been written" (al-Nawawi, in H. Khal.). "The most excellent and the greatest of Koran commentaries" (Al-Suyūṭi, *ibid.*). It is the basic authority. It goes into the motives (*wajh*) of the opinions and indicates those that deserve preference; also goes into questions of syntax (*i'rāb*) and legal deductions (*istinbāṭ*). Contains an analytical table of contents. Index by H. Haussleiter, entitled *Register zum Qorankommentar des Ṭabari* (Kairo, 1321), Strassburg, 1912. It gives the page for each verse. **(2)** *Al-Kash-shāf 'an Haqā'iq al-Tanzil*, by a. al-Qāsim Maḥmūd b. 'Umar al-Zamakhshari (538). Ed. Nassau Lees, *etc.*, Calcutta, 1856. Determines the meanings chiefly from standpoint of syntax and rhetoric, and is Mu'atazilite in its theology (*'aqā'id*) (*cf.* Ibn Khaldūn). "The author of the *Kash-shāf* is the sultan of this art (*i. e.*, rhetoric), and therefore his book flew to the East and the West" (al-Suyūṭi, in H. Khal.). The "best" glosses by Sharaf-al-dīn al-H. b. M. al-Tayyibi (743), who refutes from the Sunnite standpoint (H. Khal.). **(3)** *Mafātīḥ al-Gayb*, known as *al-Tafsīr al-Kabīr*, by Fakhr-al-dīn M. b. 'Umar al-Rāzi (606). An unfinished large work. Author wrote it to disconcert some of "the jealous persons" who would not believe a statement of his to the effect that 10,000 propositions could be derived from the hidden meanings of the opening chapter of the Koran (H. Khal.). It is full of singular views (Ibn Khallikān, in H. Khal.). It is full of the views of the philosophers. Some say that there is in it every thing but a Koran commentary (*Itqān*, p. 917). **(4)** *Anwār al-Tanzil wa Asrār al-Ta'wil*, by Nāṣir-al-dīr a. Sa'īd 'Al. b. 'Umar **al-Baydawi** (685?). Ed. H. O. Fleischer, Leipzig, 1846. Abridged from the *Kashshāf*, as regards syntax and rhetoric, from *al-Tafsīr al-Kabīr* as regards Philosophy and Dogmatics, and from *Tafsīr al-Rāgib* as regards etymology, the mysteries of essences (*ḥaqā'iq*) and subtle points. The work is from the Sunnite standpoint and has enjoyed great favor as a text-book and an object of comment. (H. Khal.) It is still used in the seminaries (*madrasah*) in Turkey. The work distinguishes itself by a summary treatment of all the viewpoints. The best commentary on it was written by Muṣliḥ-al-dīn Muṣṭafa al-Qūjawi (951) in 8 vols. **(5)** *Tafsīr al-Jalālayn*—begun by Jalāl-al-dīn M. b. A. al-Maḥalli (864), and completed by Jalāl-al-dīn 'Ar. b. a. Bakr al-Suyūṭi (911), the Shafiites. "Small in size but great in meaning, for it is the core of the marrow of Koran commentaries." (H. Khal.) Also still used in Turkey.

SCIENCE OF KORAN INTERPRETATION (*'Ilm al-Tafsīr*)

*Al-***Itqan** *fi 'Ulūm al-Qur'ān*, by Jalāl-al-dīn al-Suyūṭi (911). Bibl. Ind. Calcutta, 1857. The work is based on the author's own *al-Taḥbīr* (or *Takhbīr?*) *fi 'Ulūm al-Tafsīr* (an enlargement of the *Mawāqi' al-'Ulūm min Mawāqi' al-Nujūm*, by Jalāl-al-dīn al-Bulqīni and of a smaller work by al-Suyūṭi's teacher, a. 'Al. Muḥyi-al-dīn al-Kāfīji) and on the *al-Burhān fi 'Ulūm al-Qur'ān* of Badr-al-dīn M. b. 'Al. al-Zarkashi (794). It was intended as an introduction for the exhaustive Koran commentary he began writing, the *Majma' al-Baḥrayn* and *Maṭla' al-Badrayn*, which apparently he did not complete. The *Itqān* "is the most useful of his works" (H. Khal.). It is meant by the author to serve the same function with respect to the Koran as the books on the so-called sciences (*'ulūm*) of *ḥadīth* do with respect to the *ḥadīths*. It is in reality a more or less general treatment under separate topics (*naw'* or *'ilm*) of the material scattered through general and special commentaries. There are 80 such topics in the *Itqān*, *e. g.*, on abrogated verses, on verses revealed in peace and war time, on verses of the *mutawātir* type, on Koran commentators, *etc.*

KORAN CONCORDANCE, Flügel, G. L., Concordantiae Corani Arabicae, Leipzig, 1842. Very serviceable.

TRADITION (*Ḥadīth*)

(1) *Al-Muwaṭṭā'*, by a. 'Al. Mālik b. Anas (179). **(a)** Recension of Yahya b. Yahya al-Maṣmūdi (234) (**Muwattā'**). Lithogr. Dihli, 1302. It contains ±1,720 *ḥadīths*. **(b)** Recension of M. b. al-Hasan (189), the Hanifite, with a long introd. and copious notes by a. al-Hasanāt 'Abd-al-hayy b. M. al-**Luknawi**. The latter recension is shorter, containing often Muḥammad's own views. (*Cf.* Goldziher, *M. Studien.*) There are about 16 recensions, that of Yahya being considered as the standard one. The *Muwaṭṭā'* is said to be the first compilation of *ḥadīths*, though different views have been also held. It is properly speaking a work of law, the *ḥadīths* mentioned in it being invoked in support of the author's views. It contains many *ḥadīths* of the *mursal* and *munqaṭi'* rank. Al-Shāfi'i is related to have said concerning the *Muwaṭṭā'*, that after the Koran it is the most reliable book. Later Shafiites say that this statement was made before the writing of the six *Saḥīḥs* and is no longer true. **Commentary** by M. b. 'Abd-al-bāqi al-**Zarqāni** (1122). Cairo, 1280. An esteemed commentary. **(2)** *Musnad al-Imām Aḥmad*, by A. b. M. b. Hanbal (241). This is the most famous collection of the *musnad* type, i. e. a collection where ḥadīths transmitted, *e. g.*, by the same Companion are classed together without respect to content. (For a review of the Cairo edition of this work by I. Goldziher, see *Z. D. M. G.*, vol. 50, pp. 465 *et seq.*) The work is said to contain about 30,000 *ḥadīths*. "It is a worthy work and one of the sources of Islam" (H. Khal.). The work, as it is, is extremely difficult of reference. **(3)** *Al-Jāmi' al-Saḥīḥ*, known as *Saḥīḥ al-Bukhāri*, by a. 'Al. M. b. Ism. al-Bukhāri (256). Ed. L. Krehl (vols. i-iii), Th. W. Juynboll (vol. iv). Leyden, 1862-8. This work is of the type called *muṣannaf*, *i. e.*, a collection of *ḥadīths* arranged in chapters according to content. It is the first of the well-known six *ḥadīth* collections considered reliable (*ṣaḥīḥ*) and canonical. This one, after the Koran, is the most reliable (*ṣaḥīḥ*) book of Islam. Al-Bukhari mentions in his work all the chains of reporters (*ṭuruq*) by which *ḥadīths* have been transmitted. For this purpose he visited all the centers where Companions lived. He does not, however, include a *ḥadīth* unless all its reporters are agreed on it. Many *ḥadīths* are repeatedly mentioned (al-Nawawi, in H. Khal., and Ibn Khaldūn). The work is said to contain 9,000 *ḥadīths*, 2,800 being repetitions. According to Ibn Khaldūn, the Malikites of his time considered that no commentary worthy of this work had yet been written and that the Moslem community owed to the author this debt. H. Khal. remarks that perhaps this debt has been acquitted by the following three **commentaries** written since then: (a) *Fatḥ al-Bāri*, by A. b. 'Ali b. Hajar al-'Asqalāni (852), the Shafiite, with an introduction. Well known. One of the largest commentaries on the work, in 10 parts. (b) *'Umdat al-Qāri*, by Badr-al-dīn a. M. Maḥmūd b. A. al-'Ayni (855), the Hanifite. Based largely on the former, with additional matter. Not so widespread as the former. (c) *Irshād al-Sāri li Sharḥ Saḥīḥ al-Bukhāri*, by Shihāb-al-dīn A. b. M. al-Khaṭīb al-**Qasṭallāni** (923), the Shafiite. Būlāq, 1304-5, in 10 vols., with an introduction on *'ilm ḥadīth* and al-Bukhāri. Also based on the *Fatḥ al-Bāri*. **(4)** *Sunan al-Dārimi*, by 'Al. b. 'Ar. al-Dārimi (255). This work has a long introduction calculated to support the *ḥadīth*-folk side in the controversy about the use of personal opinion in law. Then, too, it contains fewer *ḥadīths* and avoids details. Probably these facts explain why this work has not been included among the six canonical collections, though it enjoys great esteem. Two other important *ḥadīth* compositions which likewise failed are the *Sunans* of 'Ali b. 'Umar al-Dāraquṭni (385), and A. b. al-Hu. a. Bakr al-Bayhaqi (458), the Shafiites. The works of al-Bayhaqi were much esteemed by the Shafiites. **(5)** *Jāmi' al-Saḥīḥ*, by a. al-Hu. Muslim b. al-Hajjāj al-Nīsabūri (261), the Shafiite. The second of the "Six books." This work found especial favor among the Moslems of the Magrib (West), some of whom went as far as placing it above the *Saḥīḥ* of al-Bukhāri (Ibn Khaldūn). Muslim followed the plan of al-Bukhāri, except that his arrangement is better. He mentions a given *ḥadīth* in one place only. Muslim quotes *ḥadīths* from 625 traditionists whose *ḥadīths* al-Bukhāri would not quote. His requirements are said to be somewhat less rigorous than those of al-Bukhāri. **Commentaries:** (a) *Al-Mu'allim bi Fawā'id K. Muslim*, by a. 'Al. M. b. 'Ali al-Māziri (536), the Malikite. Treats also of *'ilm-al-ḥadīth* and *fiqh*. (b) *Ikmāl al-Mu'allim fi Sharḥ Muslim*, by al-Qāḍi 'Iyāḍ b. Mūsa al-Yaḥṣabi (544), the Malikite. It is an enlargement of the former. (c) *Al-Minhāj fi Sharḥ Muslim b. al-Hajjāj*, by Yahya b. Sharaf al-**Nawawi** (676), the Shafiite, with an introduction on *'ilm al-ḥadīth*. Contains matter found in the two previous, and more (Ibn Khaldūn). Published on margin of Qasṭallāni. **(6)** *Sunan* *a. Dāwūd*, by a. Dāwūd Su. b. al-Ash'ath al-Sijistāni (275), the Shafiite. This is a *ḥadīth* collection of the *Sunan* class. The works of this class treat the *ḥadīths* only in so far as they constitute a rule of conduct (*sunnah*). They differ from the *Jāmi's*, which include *ḥadīths* of every description. The author says that out of 500,000 *ḥadīths* he had written down, he incorporated in his book 4,008. This is the third of the "Six Books" passed as canonical, the other three being in order of esteem the *Sunan* books of al-Tirmidhi, al-Nasā'i and b. Mājah. According to Ibn Khaldūn these four are less exacting than the first two, including also *ḥadīths* of a rank below the *ṣaḥīḥ* and *ḥasan*. **(7)** *Jāmi' al-Saḥīḥ*, also called *Sunan al-Tirmidhi*, by a. 'Isa M. b. 'Isa al-Tirmidhi (279), the Shafiite. Goldziher thinks that the word *Jāmi'* better fits this work. **(8)** *Sunan b. Mājah*, by a. 'Al. M. b. Yazīd b. Mājah al-Qazwīni (273). Also one of the "Six Books." The following works, which, written later, superseded the foregoing for purposes of reference and instruction, are based on the foregoing and consist in re-arrangement, compilation, comment, and re-hash. **(9)** *Sunan al-Sagīr*, called *al-Mujtabi*, by a. 'Ar. A. b. Shu'ayb al-Nasā'i (303), the Shafiite. Condensed by the author from his larger work, the *Sunan al-Kabīr*. **(10)** *Al-Jāmi' bayn al-Saḥīḥayn*, by a. 'Al. M. b. a. Naṣr al-Humaydi al-Andalusi (488), a disciple of 'Ali b. Hazm, the Zahirite. A noted work combining the two first *Saḥīḥs*. **(11)** *Maṣābīḥ al-Sunnah*, by Hu. b. Mas'ūd al-Farrā' al-Bagawi (516 or 510), the Shafiite. Contains 4,485 or, in another version, 4,719 *ḥadīths*. Omits supports (*asānīd*) and groups the *ḥadīths* of *ṣaḥīḥ* rank separately from those of *ḥasan* rank, indicating those of inferior rank. This work enjoys great esteem. **An enlargement:** *Mishkāt al-Maṣābīḥ* (737), by a. 'Al. M. b. 'Al. al-Khaṭīb al-Tibrizi, the Shafiite. A standard work in India. English translation by A. N. Matthews, Calcutta, 1809-10. **(12)** *Tajrīd al-Siḥāḥ al-Sittah*, by Razīn b. Mu'āwiyah al-'Abdari (535). Combines all the Six Books, and follows al-Bukhāri as regards chaptering (*abwāb*). Does not comment on the *ḥadīths*. **(13)** *Jāmi' al-Uṣūl*, by Majd-al-dīn Mubārak b. M. b. al-Athīr al-Jazari (606), the Shafiite, with introduction on *'ilm al-ḥadīth* and biographies of the Prophet and his Companions. Combines the previous work and the Six Books, omitting the supports save the name of the Companion or the person directly reporting from the Companion. Comments on difficult (*garīb*) *ḥadīths*. Arranged in chapters alphabetically disposed. Sources indicated by letters. **Abridgments:** **(a)** *Tajrīd al-Uṣūl*, by Sharaf-al-dīn Hibat-allah 'Abd-al-rahīm b. al-Bārizi al-Hamawi (738), the Shafiite. Omits comments and grammatical and syntactical remarks. **(b)** *K. Taysīr al-Wuṣūl ila Jāmi' al-Uṣūl*, by 'Ar. b. 'Ali b. al-Dība' al-Shaybāni al-Zabīdi (944), the Shafiite. Cairo, 1330. An elaboration and, according to the author, an improvement of the abridgment just mentioned. "The best of the abridgments" (H. Khal.). Much used by students. **(14)** *Mashāriq al-Anwār al-Nabawiyyah min Siḥāḥ al-Akhbār al-Muṣṭafawiyyah*, by Raḍi-al-dīn al-H. b. M. al-Sagāni (or Sāgāni) al-Hindi (650). Contains 2,246 *ḥadīths* of the *ṣaḥīḥ* rank. Much commented upon. Al-Subki is quoted in the *Tadrīb* (p. 6) as having said: "The final goal [in the study (*'ilm*) of *ḥadīth* for some people] is the study of the *Mashāriq al-Anwār;* therefore, if they rise as high as the *Maṣābīḥ* of al-Bagawi, they believe that they have reached the degree of *muḥaddiths*." **(15)** *Jam' al-Jawāmi'*, by Jalāl-al-dīn 'Ar. b. a. Bakr al-Suyūṭi (911). Combines the Six Books, several *Musnads*, and others, and is intended by the author to exhaust the entire field of *ḥadīths*. The author abridged it in his *al-Jāmi' al-Sagīr*, which he supplemented in the *Zawā'id*. A compilation and **arrangement** of all the three is the **Kanz** *al-'Ummāl fi Sunan al-Aqwāl wa 'l Af'āl*, by 'Ali b. Husām-al-dīn, al-Muttaqi (975), the Indian. Haydarabad, 1312-14. Eight parts. According to the numbering on the margin, it contains 46,681 *ḥadīths*, cast in books (*Kitāb*) (in the conventional manner of the *fiqh* books), alphabetically arranged. Probably the easiest of reference. A **condensation** of it by its author is the *Muntakhab Kanz al-'Ummāl, etc.* Printed on the margin of the *Musnad* of Ahmad. About one-third reduced. A useful feature of both works is the separate treatment of the *ḥadīths* pertaining to the Prophetic conduct (*af'āl*).

SCIENCE OF TRADITION

(*'Ilm* or *'Ulūm* or *Uṣūl* or *Muṣṭalaḥ al-Hadīth*)

(1) (*Ma'rifat*) *'Ulūm al-Hadīth*, also called *Funūn al-Hadīth* and *Uṣūl al-Hadīth*, by a. 'Amr 'Uthmān b. 'Ar. b. al-Salāḥ (643), the Shafiite. The first work on the subject which achieved a classical fame. Contains 65 topics (*naw'*). **Commentaries:** **(a)** *Al-Taqyīd wa 'l-Iḍāḥ, etc.*, by 'Abd-al-rahīm b. al-Hu. al-'Irāqi (806); **(b)** by 'Izz-al-dīn M. b. Jamā'ah (819); *etc.* **Abridgments:** by Badr-al-dīn M. b. Jamā'ah (733), Ism. b. 'Umar b. Kathīr (774), and others, the most famous of them being the next work. **(2)** *Al-Taqrīb wa 'l-Taysīr li Ma'rifat Sunan al-Bashīr al-Nadhīr*, by Yahya b. Sharaf al-Nawawi (676). It is a second abridgment of a first abridgment of that work by the same author, entitled *K. al-Irshād* (*li-Ma'rifat Hadīth Khayr al-'Ibād*). The *Taqrīb* was translated into French by M. Marçais and was published in the *J. Asiatique*, 1900-1901, 9éme série, vols. 16, 17, 18. The preface gives useful information on bibliography, *etc.* **Commentaries:** **(a)** By 'Abd-al-rahīm al-'Irāqi (806); **(b)** M. b. 'Ar. al-Sakhāwi (902); **(c)** **Tadrib** *al-Rāwi fi Sharḥ Taqrīb al-Nawawi, by* Jalāl-al-dīn 'Ar. b. a. Bakr al-Suyūṭi (911). Cairo, 1307. The work is also intended as a commentary to the works of b. al-Salāḥ and others. It is full of information. **(3)** The *Manẓūmah* of A. b. Faraḥ al-Ishbīli (699).

Also called *Garām Ṣaḥīḥ*, these being the words with which the work begins. It is a love-poem in 20 verses, containing about 40 technical terms. It begins thus: "My longing is true (*ṣaḥīḥ*) and the desire for you is overcoming (*mu'ḍil*)," *etc.*, the words *ṣaḥīḥ* and *mu'ḍil* being also technical terms. A commentary of this is the *Zawāl al-Taraḥ fi Sharḥ Manẓūmat b. Faraḥ*, by 'Izz-al-dīn a. 'Al. M. b. Jamā'ah al-Kināni (816). Ed. by F. Risch as a Leipzig dissertation with notes. Leyden, 1885. **(4)** *Al-Khulāṣah fi Ma'rifat* (or *Uṣūl*) *al-Hadīth*, by Sharaf-al-dīn Hu. b. M. al-Tayyibi (743). An "able compendium" (H. Khal.). Condensed from the works of b. al-Salāḥ, al-Nawawi, al-Qāḍi b. Jamā'ah, with additions from the *Jāmi' al-Uṣūl, etc.* **(5)** *Al-Alfiyyah* (or *al-Tabṣirah wa 'l-Tadhkirah*), by Zayn-al-dīn 'Abd-al-rahīm b. al-Hu. al-'Irāqi (806), the Shafiite. It is a condensation of the work of b. al-Salāh in *rajaz* verse. A **commentary** on it is the *K. Fatḥ al-Bāqi li Sharḥ Alfiyyah al-'Irāqi*, by a. Yahya Zakariyā' al-Anṣāri (926), the Shafiite. **(6)** *Nukhbat al-Fikar fi Iṣṭilāḥ Ahl al-Athar*, by A. b. 'Ali b. Hajar (852), with a commentary by the same. Cairo. 1323. Marçais finds b. Hajar's treatment more scientific. A much annotated work. **(7)** *Bayqūniyyah*, by Tāhir b. M. al-Bayqūni (ca. 1080). A poem in 34 *rajaz* verses containing about 35 terms. Used by students in the Azhar and the Algerian seminaries. There is a **commentary** on it by M. b. 'Abd-al-bāqi b. Yū. al-Zarqāni (1122). **(8)** The introductions of the commentaries of al-Qasṭallāni and al-Nawawi on the *Saḥīḥs* of al-Bukhāri and Muslim, respectively, mentioned before, contain useful matter bearing on this subject.

THE PRINCIPLES OF LAW (*Uṣūl-al-fiqh*)

(1) Risālah, by M. b. Idrīs al-Shāfi'i (204). Recension of al-Rabī' b. Su. al-Murādi. Būlāq. 1321. Said to be the first work on *uṣūl-al-fiqh*. *Cf.*, however, the *Fihrist* (p. 204) where M. b. al-H. is said to have written on "*Uṣūl-al-fiqh*," "*Ijtihād al-Ra'y*" and "*Istiḥsān*." The *Risālah* represents the transition stage in the differentiation of this science from *fiqh*. In many parts it reads like a Shafiite work on *fiqh*. A most valuable source. Commented upon, among others, by M. al-Qaffāl al-Shāshi (507).

(2) *Taqwīm al-Adillah*, by a. Zayd 'Al. b. 'Umar al-Dabūsi (430), the Hanifite. "Best of works written by the earliest writers" (Ibn Khaldūn). Al-Dabūsi completed the elaboration of the laws of *qiyās* (*ibid.*). Commented upon by 'Ali al-Pazdawi (482) and others.

(3) *Al-Mu'tamad*, by a. al-Hu. M. b. 'Ali al-Baṣri (436), the Mu'tazilite. A large work used as basis by later writers. The *Mu'tamad* is a commentary on the *'Ahd* by 'Abd-al-jabbār b. A. al-Asadābādi Qādi al-Quḍāt (415), chief of the Mu'tazilites, but Shafiite as to *fiqh*. (Ibn Khall., Subki, vol. iii, p. 220.)

(4) *Al-Burhān*, by a. al-Ma'āli 'Abd-al-malik b. 'Al. al-Juwayni Imām al-Haramayn (478), the Shafiite. Shows independence of view. "A pride of the Shafiites" (Subki). Style very involved. The work, though by a Shafiite, was commented upon by Malikites such as 'Al. al-Māziri and a. al-H. al-Anbāri. They attack the author where he is at variance, *e. g.*, with a. al-H. al-Ash'ari. They, however, depend on his works exclusively as regards dogmatics. (Subki, vol. iii, p. 264.)

(5) *Al-Waraqāt*, by the same Imām al-Haramayn. It is a small compendium intended for beginners. This work found great favor among the Shafiites and was commented upon by many (also by Hanifites), among others by Jalāl-al-dīn M. b. A. al-Mahalli (864), with glosses entitled *Qurrat al-'Ayn* (953) by M. b. M. *al-Khaṭṭāb*, the Malikite.

(6) *Kanz al-Wuṣūl ila Ma'rifat al-Uṣūl* or *Uṣūl al-Pazdawi*, by Fakhr-al-islām 'Ali b. M. al-**Pazdawi** (482), the Hanifite. "Best of works written by later writers and exhaustive" (Ibn Khaldūn). This is a work of classic reputation among Hanifites. It gives the arguments at length. Style is at parts difficult. **Commentaries:** (**a**) **Kashf** *al-Asrār*, by 'Abd-al-'azīz b. A. al-Bukhāri (730). Constantinople, 1307. "The largest, most profitable and clearest commentary" (H. Khal.). This commentary with its text is indispensable for critical research into history of *uṣūl-al-fiqh*. Later Hanifite works are chiefly based on these two. (**b**) *Al-Kāfi*, by Husām-al-dīn al-Hu. b. 'Ali al-Signāqi (710). (**c**) *Al-Taqrīr*, by Akmal-al-dīn M. b. Mahmūd al-Miṣri al-Bābarti (786), the Hanifite.

(7) *K. al-Uṣūl*, by Shams-al-a'immah a. Bakr M. b. A. al-Sarakhsi (483). Must be a valuable source. The *K. al-Istiḥsān*, by the same, is printed in his *Mabsūt*, vol. x, pp. 145-85. After some valuable general remarks on nature of *istiḥsān*, the author argues at length for its application in practical cases, chiefly in connection with modesty.

(8) *Al-Mustaṣfa*, by a. Hāmid M. b. M. al-Gazzāli (505), the Shafiite. Būlāq, 1322. A valuable work used as basis for later compilations. Original in arrangement. It goes into the arguments. According to Ibn Khaldūn, the *Burhān* and the *Mustaṣfa*, on the one hand, and the *'Ahd* and *Mu'tamad*, on the other, are the four best basic works on *uṣūl-al-fiqh* written from a dogmatic (*mutakallim*) standpoint, namely, in a purely speculative way without reference to the applications of the principles in the field of *fiqh*.

(9) The works of M. b. 'Al. **b. Tumart** al-Mahdi (524), the founder of the Almohades dynasty (*dawlat al-muwaḥḥidīn*), with biographical extracts on b. Tūmart and a critical introduction by I. Goldziher. Algiers, 1903. These works chiefly bear on questions of *uṣūl-al-fiqh* and dogma, and represent a reaction to the speculative and secular tenden-

cies of the four orthodox schools. The point of view is akin to that of the Zahirites.

(10) *Al-Mahsul*, by Fakhr-al-din M. b. 'Umar al-Razi b. al-Khatib (606), the Shafiite. A condensation of the four works mentioned (Ibn Khaldun), especially the *Mustasfa* and the *Mu'tamad*, which, according to al-Isnawi (*Minhaj*, p. 4), he transfers bodily by pages, apparently because he "used to commit them to memory." Unlike the *Ahkam*, the *Mahsul* does not indulge in argumentation (Ibn Khaldun; *cf.* H. Khal.). **Abridgments:** **(a)** *Al-Tahsil*, by Siraj-al-din a. al-Thana' Mahmud b. a. Bakr al-Urmawi (682), the Shafiite. The author abridged the *Tahsil* from the *Mahsul* "in order to supply" the great demand for abridgments. Enjoyed widespread use. **(b)** *Al-Hasil min al-Mahsul*, by al-Qadi Taj-al-din M. b. Hu. al-Urmawi. An abridgment of the *Mahsul* (by about one-tenth) as to words rather than meaning, as the author claims. **(c)** **Minhaj** *al-Wusul ila 'Ilm al-Usul*, by 'Al. b. 'Umar al-Baydawi (685?), based on the *Hasil*. According to Jamal-al-din b. H. al-Isnawi (772), the Shafiite, who wrote a **commentary** on it, the *Nihayat al-Sul* (printed with the *Minhaj* on the margin of the *Taqrir*), most of his contemporaries depended exclusively on the *Minhaj* on account of its small size and attractive style. (This is the *Minhaj* referred to in Part I of this dissertation. The *Minhaj* referred to in Part II is on *fiqh* by al-Nawawi. *Cf. infra*, p. 188.) **(d)** *Tanqih al-Fusul fi 'l-Usul*, by Shihab-al-din A. b. Idris al-Qarafi (684), the Malikite. Based on the *Mahsul* and the *Ifadah* of al-Qadi 'Abd-al-wahhab, the Malikite. Favored by beginners and much commented upon.

(11) *Al-Ahkam*, by a. al-H. 'Ali b. a. 'Ali Sayf-al-din al-Amidi (631), the Shafiite. A condensation of the four basic works mentioned. The author indulges in argumentation (*tahqiq*) and illustrations from the applications (*tafri'*) (Ibn Khaldun). **(a)** An **abridgment** of the *Ahkam* is the *Muntaha al-Sul wa 'l-Amal fi 'Ilmay al-Usul wa 'l-Jadal*, by Jamal-al-din a. 'Amr 'Uthman b. 'Umar, b. al-Hajib (646), the Malikite. **(b)** *Mukhtasar al-Muntaha* or *Mukhtasar b. al-Hajib*, by same. Abridged from the former. This second abridgment enjoyed great popularity and was annotated by Malikites as well as Shafiites. **Commentary** by 'Adud-al-din 'Ar. b. A. al-Iji (756), the Malikite. Constantinople, 1310. Text begins by "*Qal*," commentary by "*Aqulu*." Considered to be one of the best.

(12) *Al-Muntakhab fi Usul-al-Madh-hab*, known as *al-Muntakhab al-Husami*, by Husam-al-din M. b. M. al-Akhsikati (644). A text free of superfluous matter and well arranged with its divisions (*fusul*) indicated, and containing nice points; therefore very much sought after. **Commentary:** *al-Tahqiq*, by 'Abd-al-'aziz b. A. al-Bukhari (730), written after the completion of his commentary on al-Pazdawi's work on *uṣūl-al-fiqh.*

(13) *Badī' al-Niẓām,* by Muẓaffar-al-dīn A. b. 'Ali b. al-Sā'āti (694), the Hanifite. An "elegant compendium" condensing the works of al-Amidi and al-Pazdawi (H. Khal.). Ibn Khaldūn says that the leading doctors of his time currently used it for reading and that many commentaries were written on it.

(14) *Manār al-Anwār,* by a. 'l-Barakāt 'Al. b. A. Ḥāfiẓ-al-dīn al-Nasafi (710, 720), the Hanifite. An esteemed compendium, the most used of the author's works. Numerous **commentaries** were written on it. The most widely known of these is the *Sharḥ al-Manār* by 'Abd-al-laṭīf b. 'Abd-al-'azīz b. Firishtah b. al-Malak (around 830). **Glosses** thereon by Muṣṭafa b. M. Azmīzādeh (ca. 1040). An abridgment of it is the *Mukhtaṣar al-Manār,* by b. Habīb al-Halabi (808). (See *infra,* no. 21.)

(15) Al-**Tawḍīḥ** *fi Hall Gawāmiḍ al-Tanqīḥ,* a commentary, by 'Ubayd-allah b. Mas'ūd b. Tāj-al-sharī'ah b. Sadr-al-sharī'ah al-Awwal al-Maḥbūbi (747), the Hanifite, on his own compendium entitled *Tanqīḥ al-Uṣūl.* An elegant text of classical fame. It is based primarily on the work of b. al-Hājib, the *Maḥṣūl,* and especially the *Uṣūl* of al-Pazdawi. It is a schematic arrangement of those works ably carried out. The author claims priority for his arrangement. The best of its commentaries is the al-**Talwīḥ** *fi Kashf Haqā'iq al-Tanqīḥ* by Sa'd-al-dīn Mas'ūd b. 'Umar al-Taftāzāni (792), the Shafiite. Kazan, 1301.

(16) *Jam' al-Jawāmi',* by Tāj-al-dīn 'Abd-al-wahhāb b. al-Subki (771), the Shafiite. A very comprehensive compendium of great reputation "collected from the flowers of 100 works," containing the cream of the author's commentaries on the *Minhāj* and the *Mukhtaṣar* of b. al-Hājib. A thorough-going **commentary** by Jalāl-al-dīn al-Maḥalli (864). **Glosses** by 'Ar. al-Bannāni al-Magribi (1198) and notes by 'Ar. al-Sharbīni (20th cent.). Cairo, 1309. One of the text-books used in the Azhar.

(17) *Al-Taḥrīr,* by M. b. 'Abd-al-wāhid b. al-Humām (or Hammām or Humām-al-dīn) al-Sīwāsi (861), the Hanifite. Treats both Hanifite and Shafiite views with arguments. Its style is involved. **Commentary:** *Al-***Taqrīr** *wa 'l-Taḥbīr,* by his student M. b. M. b. Amīr al-Hājj al-Halabi (879). Būlāq, 1316-17. **Abridgment:** *Lubb al Uṣūl,* by Zayn al-'Abidīn b. Nujaym al-Miṣri, who rearranged it in the Hanifite order.

(18) *Mirqāt al-Wuṣūl fi 'Ilm al-Uṣūl,* by M. b. Farāmurz Munla Khusrew (885), the Hanifite. **Commentary:** *Mir'āt al-Uṣūl* by the author himself. An elegant commentary containing the early views with original additions; the names of 14 works on *uṣūl-al-fiqh* are given in the introduction (H. Khal.). Both works are still used in the seminaries in Turkey. **Glosses** by Mawla Hafīd Efendi (1098) and notes by Su. al-Izmīri (1102). Būlāq, 1262; Stamboul, 1304.

(19) *Majāmi' al-Ḥaqā'iq*, by a. Sa'īd M. al-Khādimi (after 1200), with his own **commentary** on it, the *Manāfi' al-Daqā'iq*. One of the works on *uṣūl-al-fiqh* used in seminaries in Turkey. "Unquestionably the most methodical and complete of text-books (classiques)" (Savvas).

(20) *K. Irshād al-Fukḥūl*, by M. b. 'Ali b. M. **al-Shawkani** (1255), Cairo, 1909. A modern topical summary exposition of the views held by doctors of different schools, with arguments. The author indicates the views that deserve preference, showing some independence of opinion.

(21) **Majmū'** *Mutūn Uṣūliyyah*. Damascus, al-Hāshimiyyah (ca. 1324). A collection of the following four compendiums: **(a)** *Mukhtaṣar al-Manār* (see *supra*, no. 14), by Zayn-al-dīn a. al-'Izz Ṭāhir b. H. b. Habīb al-Halabi (808), the Hanifite, pp. 3-26; **(b)** *Waraqāt* (see *supra*, no. 5), pp. 27-39. **(c)** *Tanqīḥ al-Fuṣūl* (see *supra*, no. 10), pp. 40-79. **(d)** *Qawā'id al-Uṣūl wa Ma'āqid al-Fuṣūl*, by Ṣafi-al-dīn al-Bagdādi (739), the Hanbalite, pp. 80-154.

THE APPLICATIONS (*Furū'*) OF LAW (*Fiqh, Fatāwa*)

I. Hanifite

(1) *K. al-Kharāj*, by Ya'qūb b. Ibr. a. **Yusuf** (182) (or **Kitāb al-Kharāj**). Būlāq, 1303. It is a valuable treatise on financial and political questions addressed to the calif Harūn-al-rashīd.

(2) *Kutub* **Ẓahir-al-riwayah**, or *Ẓāhir-al-madh-hab*, or *al-Uṣūl*. They are the source-books of the Hanifite school and were written by M. b. al-H. al-Shaybāni (187). According to b. al-Humām, unless M. indicates the contrary, the views stated in these books are the views of a. Hanīfah and a. Yū., as well as his own (Ibn 'Abidīn, p. 19). They are the following: **(a)** *Al-Mabsūṭ*, also called *al-Aṣl*. The recension of a. Su. al-Juzjāni is considered to be the best. Apparently this work was dictated by a. Yū. and compiled by M., with additions. This view is confirmed by al-Sarakhsi (*Mabsūṭ*, part xvi, p. 129), who says: "The work was composed (*aṣl al-taṣnīf*) by a. Yū. and put together (*ta'līf*) by M., and therefore it was considered as a composition (*taṣnīf*) of M." The different parts of the *Mabsūṭ*, known as "Book of so-and-so," were composed separately, and the name *Mabsūṭ* (extended) was given them when they were combined. When, therefore, the doctors say, "M. said in the book of so-and-so," they only mean one of those "books." The style of the *Mabsūṭ* is said to be verbose with repetitions. Many commentaries were written on the *Mabsūṭ*, among others by Shams-al-a'immah 'Abd-al-'azīz b. A. al-Halwāni (or Halwā'i) (448) and Shaykh-al-islām a. Bakr Khwāharzādah (482). The latter is known as *al-Mabsūṭ al-Bakri* (or *al-Kabīr?*) (Ibn 'Abidīn). (b) **Al-Jāmi' al-Sagīr.** (Printed on the margin of Yūsuf.) Is said to contain 1,532 propositions. A greatly esteemed work. Judges and *muftis* were required to learn it by heart as a condition of appointment. It indicates the authorities. Its arrangement and chaptering were made later. According to the *Baḥr* as quoted by Ibn 'Abidīn (p. 19), every book of M. bearing the title *al-Sagīr* has had the approval of a. Yūsuf, and, on the contrary, books bearing the title *al-Kabīr*, such as *al-Jāmi' al-Kabīr*, or *al-Muzāra'ah al-Kabīr* were never submitted to a. Yū. (For more details, see Ibn 'Abidīn and H. Khal.) The most well-known of the many **commentaries** on it are (i) by Fakhr-al-Islām al-Pazdawi (482); (ii) Fakhr-al-dīn al-H. b. Manṣūr al-Uzjandi Qāḍikhān (592). When the doctors say, "Qāḍikhān said so and so in the *al-Jāmi' al-Sagīr*," they mean the commentary in question (Ibn 'Abidīn, p. 17). These commentaries are mixed with the text. (c) *Al-Jāmi' al-Kabīr.* According to H. Khal., it contains principles (*mutūn al-dirāyāt*) and niceties in legal deduction (*laṭā'if al-fiqh*). Many **commentaries.** Also versifications. Two supplements were written to this work by M. b. al-H., the *Al-Ziyādāt* and the *Ziyādat al-Ziyādāt.* These, too, were much commented upon. (d) *Al-Siyar al-Sagīr wa 'l-Kabīr.* The last of M.'s works. Written after his departure from 'Irāq. The author, owing to his dispute with a. Yūsuf, in quoting him does not mention his name, but says: "A trustworthy person (*thiqah*) informed us" (H. Khal.). The *Siyars* treat the subject of *Jihād.* Many commentaries were written.

(3) *K. al-Hiyal al-Shar'iyyah*, by a. Bakr A. b. 'Umar al-Khaṣṣāf (261), Cairo, 1316 (b. Tūmart, p. 32). The most well-known of the works written on lawful tricks. Al-Khaṣṣāf also wrote a *K. al-Kharāj* for the calif al-Muhtadi; the best known of the works on the duties and functions of the judges, the *K. Adab al-Qāḍi*, and a standard work on pious foundations, the *K. Aḥkām al-Waqf.*

(4) *Al-Mukhtaṣar fi 'l-Fiqh*, by a. Ja'far A. b. M. al-Taḥāwi (321). In two sizes. Follows the arrangement of the *Mukhtaṣars* of al-Muzani. Many commentaries were written on it.

(5) *Al-Kāfi fi 'l-Fiqh*, by M. b. M. al-Marwazi al-Hākim al-Shahīd (334). This work combines the works of M. b. al-H. already mentioned, and is an authority for determining the views of a. Hanīfah and his two disciples. A famous **commentary** on it is the **Mabsut** (vol. ii) by

Shams-al-a'immah a. Bakr M. b. a. Sahl al-Sarakhsi (483), Cairo, 1323, in 30 parts. There are many *Mabsūṭs*, but when the word occurs without any qualification this work is meant. The commentary is mixed with the text. The work was dictated by the author in prison. He says in the preface that, seeing that many of his contemporaries engaged in controversy or subtle dialectics, or subordinated legal (*fiqh*) considerations to philosophical ones, he attempts to base the legal principles on legal considerations pure and simple. The arguments used by later doctors almost always are found in the *Mabṣūt*.

(6) *Al-Muntaqa*, also by al-Marwazi. It has disappeared in later times. (H. Khal.) The author is to have culled his work from about 300 sources, such as dictations, (*Amāli*) and works of the *Nawādir* class. Apparently the *Muntaqa* is designed to make use of the legal determinations of the *Nawādir* class which were not included in the *Kāfi*. The secret of its disappearance may lie in this fact.

(7) *Al-Mukhtaṣar fi 'l-Fiqh*, by a. 'l-H. 'Ubayd-allah b. al-H. al-Karkhi (340).

(8) *Mukhtaṣar al-Qudūri*, by a. 'l-Hu. A. b. M. al-Qudūri, al-Bagdādi (428). Kazan, 1896. A compendium of very great reputation. It is referred to as "The Book." It has been said that the person who commits it to memory becomes secure from poverty, and that the person who studies it under a pious teacher and invokes upon him on the completion of his studies God's blessing, acquires as many *dirhams* as there are legal determinations (*masā'il*) in the book. These are said to be 12,000. (H. Khal.) Some of its commentaries are: (a) by A. b. M. al-Aqṭa' (475). (b) *Zād al-Fuqahā'*, by M. b. A. al-Isbījābi (ca. 530). (c) *Al-Mujtabi*, by Najm-al-dīn Mukhtār b. Maḥmūd al-Zāhidi (658), author of the *Qunyat al-Munyah*. (d) *Al-Yanābi' fi Ma'rifat al-Uṣūl wa 'l-Tafāri'*, by Badr-al-dīn M. b. 'Al. al-Shibli (769). (e) *Al-Sirāj al-Wahhāj*, by a. Bakr b. 'Ali al-Haddādi al-'Abbādi (800). (f) *Al-Jawharah al-Nayyirah*, abridged from the former by the same author. Well known. (g) *Jāmi' al-Muḍmarāt wa 'l-Mushkilāt*, by Yū. b. 'Umar al-Sūfi al-Kāruzi. (h) *Al-Bayān*, by M. b. Rasūl al-Mūqāni.

(9) *Al-Muḥīṭ*, known as *al-Muḥīṭ al-Raḍawi* or *al-Muḥīṭ al-Sarakhsi*, by Raḍi-al-dīn M. b. M. al-Sarakhsi (544). In three sizes. Unless there is indication to the contrary, the name stands for the large size of this *Muḥīṭ* as distinguished from the next *Muḥīṭ*. The author gathered together in his work all the legal determinations (*masā'il*) with their motives and meanings. He first mentions the cases of the *Mabsūṭ*, then the *Nawādir*, then the *Al-Jāmi'*, then the *Ziyādāt*.

(10) *Al-Muḥīṭ al-Burhāni fi 'l-Fiqh al-Nu'māni*, by Burhān-al-dīn Maḥmūd b. A. b. al-Sadr al-Shahīd al-Bukhāri b. Māzah (ca. 570). This *Muḥīṭ* is sometimes confused with the previous, which is the

more standard of the two. This is a larger work than the previous, utilizing the works of M. b. al-H. as well as the legal decisions arrived at by later jurists (*fatāwa* and *wāqi'āt*), such as his own father. It often gives the arguments.

(11) *Badā'i' al-Sanā'i' fi Tartīb al-Sharā'i'*, by Alā'-al-dīn a. Bakr b. Mas'ūd al-**Kasani** (vol. ii) (or al-Kāshāni) Malik al-Ulamā' (587). Cairo, 1327. Apparently it is based on the *Tuhfat al-Fuqahā'* of his teacher Ala'-al-dīn M. b. A. al-Samarqandi, who according to the author is the only jurist who before him took pains to arrange (*tartīb*) the legal material. The arrangement of the work is highly schematic. It quotes the views of al-Shāfi'i, and sometimes of Mālik, with their arguments, mentioning the Hanifite arguments last.

(12) *Al-***Hidāyah** (vol. ii), by Shaykh-al-islām Burhān-al-dīn 'Ali b. a. Bakr al-Marginānī (593). It is a commentary on the author's own *Bidāyat al-Mubtadi*. One of the most esteemed Hanifite compendiums. Concerning it, it has been said in a verse that, like the Koran, it abrogated (*naskh*) its predecessors. The work may be said to be a commentary on the *al-Jāmi' al-Sagīr* and on the *Mukhtaṣar* of al-Qudūri, on which two works is based the *Bidāyat al-Mubtadi*. The author, as a rule, mentions the opinion and argument of Abu Hanīfah after that of his disciples, unless it be that he sides with the latter. When the author says, "He said in the Book (*kitāb*)," he means al-Qudūri. When the latter disagrees with the *al-Jāmi' al-Sagīr*, the author expressly indicates the difference. Al-Shāfi'i's differences and the arguments of each side are mentioned. **Commentaries:** (**a**) *Al-Nihāyah*, by his disciple Husām-al-dīn Hu. b. 'Ali al-Signāqi (710); (**b**) *Mi'rāj al-Dirāyah*, by Qiwām-al-dīn M. b. M. al-Bukhāri al-**Kāki** (749). Gives the opinions of the four *Imāms*, their grounds, the old and recent views, *etc.* (**c**) *Gāyat al-Bayān*, by Amīr Kātib b. Amīr 'Umar al-Itqāni (758). (**d**) *Al-***'Inayah** (vol. ii), by Akmal-al-dīn M. b. Maḥmūd al-Bābarti (786). Esteemed in Turkey and one of the best. It is an abridgment for purposes of instruction of his own larger *al-Nihāyah*. Contains useful analytical summaries. (**e**) **Fath** *al-Qadīr* (vol. ii), by Kamāl-al-dīn M. b. 'Abd-al-Wāhid b. al-Humām (861). Esteemed for its independence of view. The *Fatḥ al-Qadīr* was condensed by Ibr. al-Halabi with criticisms. (**f**) *Al-***Kifayah** (vol. ii), by Jalāl-al-dīn b. Shams-al-dīn al-Khawārizmi al-Kurlāni. The *Hidāyah*, the *Fatḥ al-Qadīr* and the *Kifāyah*, with the *'Ināyah* and the glosses of Sa'd-allah b. 'Isa Sa'di Tchelebi or Sa'di Efendi (945) on the margin, have been printed together. Cairo, 1901, 9 vols.

(13) *Al-Farā'iḍ al-Sirājiyyah*, by Sirāj-al-dīn a. Tāhir M. b. M. al-Sajāwandi (towards end of 6th cent.). This, with its commentary *al-Sharīfiyyah*, by al-Sayyid al-Sharīf 'Ali b. M. al-Jurjāni (804), are the standard works on inheritance.

(14) *Al-Hawi al-Qudsi*, by al-Qadi Jamal-al-din A. b. M. al-Gaznawi (600), called so because written in Jerusalem (Quds). In three parts, on (i) dogma (*uṣūl-al-dīn*), (ii) *uṣūl-al-fiqh*, and (iii), by far the largest, *fiqh* proper.

(15) *Wiqāyat al-Riwāyah fi Masā'il al-Hidāyah*, by Burhān-al-dīn (-sharī'ah) Maḥmūd b. Sadr-al-Sharī'ah al-Awwal 'Ubayd-allah al-Maḥbūbi (around 680). A compendium based on the Hidāyah, with omission of the reasons and indication of the right views, made for the benefit of his grandson, 'Ubayd-allah b. Mas'ūd. **Commentaries: (a)** By 'Ubayd-allah b. Mas'ūd al-Maḥbūbi (747). This is the most well-known of the commentaries. **(b)** By 'Abd-al-laṭīf b. 'Abd-al-'azīz b. al-Malak (around 830). **Abridgment:** *al-Nuqāyah* or *Mukhtaṣar al-Wiqāyah*, by 'Ubayd-allah b. Mas'ūd b. Tāj-al-sharī'ah Maḥmūd b. Sadr-al-sharī'ah al-Thāni al-Maḥbūbi (747). A well-known **commentary** on the latter is the **Jami'** *al-Rumūz*, by Shams-al-dīn M. al-Quhistāni (950). Kazan, 1315-16. It is used as basis for rendering *fatwas* in the countries east of the river Oxus (*ma warā' al-nahr*) (H. Khal.). Ibn 'Abidīn, however, would not allow the use as basis for *fatwas* of books like the *Jāmi'*, the *Durr* and the *Ashbāh*, which besides being later compilations are often very concise, and at times cite views which have found no favor (*marjūḥ*) in the school, or even views of other schools. The *Jāmi'* gives no arguments but is rich in details. Printed with the *Jāmi'* is an introduction to it by **Qadizadah** Sharīf Makhdūm b. 'Abd-al-rahīm al-Bukhāri.

(16) *Al-Mukhtār* (*li 'l-Fatwa*), by a. al-Faḍl Majd-al-dīn 'Al. b. Maḥmūd al-Mawṣili (b. al-Buldaji) (683). Another of the esteemed texts. *Al-Ikhtiyār* is a commentary on it by the same author. It gives the motives.

(17) *Majma' al-Baḥrayn wa Multaqa al-Nahrayn*, by Muẓaffar-al-dīn A. b. 'Alī b. al-Sa'ati al-Bagdadi (696). An "esteemed" text, based on the *Mukhtaṣar* of al-Qudūri and the *Manẓūmah* of al-Nasafi (537), with additions. Extremely concise, hence easy to commit to memory, but difficult of understanding (H. Khal.). It indicates the differences of Abu Hanīfah's disciples as well as those of al-Shāfi'i and Mālik by some clever device, such as the use of the nominal instead of the verbal sentence, *etc.* **Commentaries: (a)** By the author himself. **(b)** *Al-Manba'*, by A. b. Ibr. al'Unnābi (767). **(c)** By 'Abd-al-latīf b. al-Malak. Much used.

(18) *Kanz al-Daqā'iq*, by Hāfiẓ-al-dīn a. 'l-Barakāt 'Al. b. A. al-Nasafi (710). An abridgment of his own *al-Wāfi* (modeled after the *Hidāyah* and commented upon by the author himself in the *Kāfi*). One of the esteemed texts (*mutūn mu'tabarah*), namely the texts which are based on *Zāhir-al-riwāyah* sources only (Ibn 'Abidīn, pp. 36-7). **Commen-**

taries: (**a**) *Tabyin al-Haqa'iq*, by Fakhr-al-din 'Uthmān b. 'Ali al-**Zayla'i** (743). Bulaq, 1313-15. Very esteemed. It inquires at length into the differences of al-Shāfi'i and refutes his arguments from the Hanifite standpoint. With **glosses** by Shihāb-al-din A. b. Yūnus al-**Shilbi** (947), printed on the margin. (**b**) *Ramz al-Haqa'iq*, by a. M. Mahmūd b. A. al-'Ayni (855). (**c**) By Mu'in-al-din M. b. Ibr. Mulla Miskin al-Harawi (before 960). Used in instruction in the Azhar. **Glosses** thereon by M. a. al-Su'ūd al-Misri entitled **Fath-*allah* al-Mu'in** embodying the glosses of A. b. M. al-Hamawi. Gives the *fatwas* of later times and is rich in details. (**d**) *Al-***Bahr** *al-Ra'iq* (vol. ii), by a. Hanifah al-Thāni (the second) Zayn-al-'ābidin (or *din*) b. Ibr. b. Nujaym al-Misri (970). Cairo, 1893, 8 vols. One of the most esteemed of later works. The author gives briefly the motives, makes many keen inquiries (*tahrir*) and incorporates the principles involved in new *fatwas*. The preface contains a list of the author's sources. The 8th vol. contains the *Takmilah* of M. b. Hu. al-Tūri, covering the parts of the *Kanz* left uncommented-upon by Zayn-al-'ābidin. Printed on the margin is the **Minhat** *al-Khāliq* by M. Amin b. 'Abidin. Explains the difficulties only. (**e**) *Al-Nahr al-Fa'iq*, by Sirāj-al-din 'Umar b. Ibr. b. Nujaym al-Misri (1005). Completed until the chapter on *habs* in the book on *Qada'*.

(**19**) **Durar** *al-Hukkām* (883), by M. b. Farāmurz b. 'Ali Mulla Khusrew (885). A commentary on his own *Gurar al-Ahkām*. Constantinople, 1299. Enjoys especial favor in Turkey. Used in seminaries. The author shows independence of opinion. This fact explains why Ibn 'Abidin (pp. 36-7) would not place it among the esteemed texts. **Commentaries and glosses:** (**a**) By Qinālizādeh (979). (**b**) *Naqd al-Durar*, by M. b. Mustafa al-Wānqūli (1000). (**c**) Glosses by Mustafa b. Pir M. 'Azmizādeh (1040). Very esteemed. (**d**) By Ismā'il b. 'Abd-al-gani al-Nābulusi (1062). Very extensive in 12 vols. (**e**) By H. al-Shurunbulāli, (1069). (**f**) *Nata'ij al-Nazar fi Hawāshi al-Durar*, by Nūh Efendi b. Mustafa (1070). (**g**) By Mustafa b. 'Uthmān al-Khādimi. (**h**) *Safinat al-Durar*. Compiled by some seminary teachers (*mudarris*) from *fatwa* collections and commentaries on the *Hidāyah*. Turkish translation by Su. b. Weli al-Anqirawi.

(**20**) *Multaqa al-Abhur*, by Ibr. b. M. al-Halabi (956). Contains the determinations of al-Qudūri, the *Mukhtār*, *Kanz*, *Wiqāyah*, and partly the *Majma'* and the *Hidāyah*. It indicates the views to be preferred (*asahh*). At present it is the standard Hanifite text (*matn*). A **commentary** on it is the **Majma'** *al-Anhur*, by 'Ar. b. M. Sheykhzādeh (1078). Constantinople, 1308. An all-round well-known commentary. This commentary is known as *Dāmād* and used in seminaries in Turkey (H. Khal., vol. vi, p. 608; Heidborn). A **Turkish Translation** by Hamidi Rāgib with a commentary by M. al-Mawqūfāti.

(21) *Al-***Ashbah** *wa 'l-Naẓā'ir*, by Zayn-al-'ābidīn b. Nujaym (970). Cairo, 1904. The only Hanifite work where general legal principles are discussed for their own sake and not incidentally to the legal determination of cases. Probably the best source for obtaining a knowledge of the extent to which Hanifite legal discussion becomes strictly scientific. Author is not a pioneer in this respect (*cf.* H. Khal., p. 313), for he admits to have followed the examples of Tāj-al-dīn al-Subki (771), the Shafiite. The work treats, in seven sections (*fann*), of general principles (*qawā'id kulliyyah*, extensively drawn upon in the *Majallah*), similarities, differences, niceties, legal tricks, *etc.* An arrangement of it under the usual *fiqh*-book chapters is the *K.* **Ithaf al-Absar** *wa 'l-Baṣā'ir bi Tabwīb K. al-Ashbāh, etc.*, by M. a. al-Fatḥ. Alexandria, 1289.

(22) *Tanwīr al-Abṣār wa Jāmi' al-Biḥār* (995), by Shams-al-dīn M. b. Al. al-Gazzi al-Timirtāshi (1004). It combines the standard texts. Ibn 'Abidīn does not consider it as an esteemed text. **Commentaries:** (**a**) *Minaḥ al-Gaffār*, by the author himself. (**b**) *Al-***Durr** *al-Mukhtār* (1071), by Alā'-al-dīn M. b. 'Ali al-Haṣkafi (1088), *mufti* at Damascus. Bombay, 1309. Condensed from his larger commentary (10 vols.), *Khazā'in al-Asrār wa Badā'i' al-Afkār*. Very concise and full of details. Utilizes new *fatwas*. A **commentary** on this work is the *Radd al-Mukhtār* by M. Amīn b. Abidīn (1252). This work may be said to be the last word in the authoritative interpretation of Hanifite law. It shows originality in attempting to determine status of present practical situations, as a rule, shunned by others. Author shows a complete mastery of his subject. Very much used in Turkey, less in India.

(23) *Arāḍi Qānūn-nāmeh-si Sherḥi*. A commentary in Turkish on the Ottoman land code by Hu. **Husni,** late professor in the Imperial Law School of Constantinople. Constantinople, 1324. The Ottoman land code promulgated as law in 1274 is a compromise between the rules of *fiqh* and customary law.

(24) **Majallah** *Aḥkām 'Adliyyah*. It is an official Turkish codification of Hanifite law made in 1285 by a special Committee (*Mejelleh Jem'iyeti*) under the chairmanship of Aḥmed Jewdet Pāsha. It represents the last stage in the development of Hanifite doctrines. The committee's report is worth reading. **Commentary: Durar al-Hukkam** *Sharḥ Majallat al-Aḥkām*, by Khōja Emīn Efendi Zādeh 'Ali Haydar. Constantinople, 1330, 4 vols. (In Turkish.) It is the best and most scholarly work of its kind. Used as text-book at the Constantinople Law School and by lawyers and judges.

(25) **Fara'id** *al-Farā'iḍ*, by Maḥmūd As'ad b. Emīn Seydi Shehri, professor at the Imperial Law School at Constantinople. A work in Turkish on inheritance based on the *Sirājiyyah*. Constantinople, 1326.

FATWA COLLECTIONS: (1) *K. al-Nawāzil*, by a. al-Layth Naṣr b. M. al-Samarqandi (376). Said to be the first work combining the legal determinations (*masā'il*) of later doctors (*mashā'ikh*), such as M. b. Shujā' al-Thalji, M. b. Muqātil al-Rāzi, M. b. Salamah (278), a. Bakr al-Iskāf, and *al-faqīh* a. Ja'far M. b. 'Al. al-Hinduwāni (362). The work also contains, under the heading of *'Uyūn al-Masā'il*, legal opinions reported from early doctors (*aṣḥāb*) which were not recorded in *Zāhir-al-riwāyah* or other sources.

(2) *Majma' al-Nawāzil wa 'l-Wāqi'āt*, by a. al-'Abbās A. b. M. al-Nāṭifi (446). A work of similar nature.

(3) *Al-Wāqi'āt*, or *al-Wāqi'āt al-Husāmiyyah*, by Husām-al-dīn (or Husām) 'Umar b. 'Abd-al-'azīz b. Māzah al-Sadr al-Shahīd al-Bukhāri (536). Combines the two previous with the *fatwas* of a. Bakr M. b. al-Faḍl and the *Fatāwa Ahl Samarqand*, indicating the sources by letters. Also by same author, the *al-Fatāwa al-Ṣugra* and *al-Kubra*, which latter, judging from the identity of contents (*cf.* H. Khal. under *Wāqi'āt* and *Fatāwa Kubra*) is probably the *Wāqi'āt* under another name.

(4) *Khulāṣat al-Fatāwa*, by Tāhir b. A. Iftikhār-al-dīn al-Bukhāri (542). Combines the *fatwas* of later *mujtahids* and those of the founders.

(5) *Dhakhīrat al-Fatāwa*, or *al-Dhakhīrah al-Burhāniyyah*, by Burhān-al-dīn Maḥmūd b. A. b. al-Sadr al-Shahīd b. Māzah (ca. 570). An esteemed work. According to the author, it contains the *fatwas* rendered by al-Sadr al-Shahīd Husām-al-dīn and by himself in his youth and, later, during his stay at Samarqand, with additions from the *Nawādir* and later sources (H. Khal.).

(6) *Al-Fatāwa al-'Attābiyyah*, or *Jāmi' al-Fiqh*, by a. Naṣr A. b. M. al-'Attābi (586).

(7) *Fatāwa Qāḍīkhān*, also called *al-Khāniyyah*, by Fakhr-al-dīn al-H. b. Manṣūr al-Uzjandi al-Fargāni Qaḍīkhān (592). Calcutta, 1835, 4 vols. A standard work of enduring reputation. The *Vade Mecum* of judges and *muftis*. Author draws upon the views of later doctors, as recorded in the *fatwa* collections mentioned, as well as those of the founders of the school recorded in the *Zāhir-al-riwāyah* and the *Nawādir*, in giving the legal answer to cases of common occurrence. Hence a mine of information for sociological study. In case there are many views by later doctors, he only mentions two, his preference first.

(8) *Al-Tajnīs wa 'l-Mazīd*, by Burhān-al-dīn 'Ali b. a. Bakr al-Margīnāni (593). Author claims to have carried the arrangement of al-Sadr al-Shahīd's work on *fatwas* (apparently his *Wāqi'āt*) further, by classifying (*tartīb*), also the particular opinions within the books

(*kutub*), and to have enlarged it with additions from other sources. The work enjoyed wide use owing to its serviceableness. Author also wrote the (*K.*) *Mukhtār(-āt) al-Fatāwa(-Nawāzil)*.

(9) Al-Fatawa *al-Zahīriyyah*, by Zahīr-al-dīn a. Bakr M. b. A. (619). Contains the most needed cases.

(10) *Al-Fatāwa al-Walwālijiyyah*, by a. 'l-Makārim Zahīr-al-dīn Isḥaq b. a. Bakr al-Walwāliji (710). Condensed from the *fatwas* of Husām al-Shahīd, with additions.

(11) *Khizānat al-Muftiīn*, by al-Hu. b. M. al-Sam'āni (740). Indicates the accepted views, contained in previous sources, omitting controversial matters.

(12) *Al-Fatāwa al-Tātārkhāniyyah*, by 'Alim (al-A'lam) Ibn Alā'-al-dīn (about 800). (*Cf.* Ahlwardt.) It is a great work combining the *Muḥiṭ al-Burhāni*, the *Dhakhīrah*, the *Khāniyyah*, and the *Zahīriyyah*, with an introduction on science (*'ilm*). Arranged according to the chapters of the *Hidāyah*. Written by order of the ruler Tātārkhān; hence the name. Ibr. al-Halabi (956) extracted from it the *fatwas* that were not mentioned in current *fatwa* collections.

(13) *Jāmi' al-Fuṣūlayn*, by Badr-al-dīn Maḥmūd b. Ism. (or Isrā'īl) Qāḍi Simāwnah (ca. 818). Combines the *Fuṣūl al-'Imādi* (by 'Abd-al-rahīm b. a. Bakr al-Marghīnāni; around 670) and *Fuṣūl* (M. b. Maḥmūd) *al-Ustrūshani* (632), with additions and nice points. It deals with the practical part (*Mu'āmalāt*) of *fiqh* only and is used by judges in particular.

(14) *Al-Fatāwa al-Bazzāziyyah*, or *al-Jāmi' al-Wajīz*, or *Fatāwa al-Kardari*, by M. b. M. al-Bazzāzi al-Kardari (827). It contains the "cream" of previous works and is relied upon. Abu 'l-Su'ūd, the mufti, when asked to compile a collection of the important *fatwas*, is said to have answered: "Would I not be ashamed of the author of *Bazzāziyyah* when he has written his book?—for it is a venerable collection containing the points of importance, as is proper."

(15) *Fatāwa Zayniyyah* are in reality essays on matters of practical interest (such as the status of the lands of Egypt, *istiṣḥāb*, land concessions, *Kharāj*, *etc.*) by Zayn-al-'ābidīn b. Ibr. b. Nujaym al-Miṣri (970) as collected and arranged by his son A., with additions.

(16) *Fatāwa a. al-Su'ūd*, by a. al-Su'ūd M. b. M. al-'Imādi (982-3). In Turkish. Lived in the reign of the sultan Su., the Magnificent. His *fatwas* throw light on adaptation of *sharī'ah* to practical requirements, particularly as regards land. A collection of the same by Weli al-Askelibi Weli Yekān, also containing *fatwas* by others, is current (H. Khal.).

(17) *Mugni al-Mustafti' an Su'āl al-Mufti* (or *al-Fatāwa al-Hāmidiyyah*), by Hāmid Efendi b. M. al-Qūnawi (985). (But *cf.* Ahlwardt.) A practical work, but too long. An extract with modifications is the

Al-'Uqud al-Durriyyah *fi Tanqih al-Fatawa al-Hamidiyyah*, by M. Amin b. 'Abidin (1258). Būlāq, 1300. Ibn 'Abidin draws upon his previous works, such as the *Radd al-Mukhtār, Minhat al-Khāliq*, and Essays (*Rasā'il*). A useful work, in the form of questions and answers.

(18) *Fatāwa Khayriyyah*, by Khayr-al-dīn b. A. al-Fārūqi al-Ramli (1081), collected by his son and one of his students. 2d ed. Būlāq, 1300. Consists in reasoned answers to actual questions.

(19) *Wāqi'āt al-Muftīin*, by 'Aq. b. Yū. Qadri Efendi (after 1088). Būlāq, 1300. A compact guide for common cases as settled by previous authorities.

(20) *Fatāwa al-Anqirawi*, by Shaykh-al-Islām M. b. Hu. al-Anqirawi (1098). Gives most of the accepted decisions and is relied upon by doctors and jurists.

(21) *Fatāwa 'Ali Efendi*, by Shaykh-al-Islām 'Ali Efendi Jatāljawi (1103). Constantinople, 1323. (In Turkish.) Well known. Consists in actual *fatwas*. Contains the arguments derived later by Sālih b. A. al-Kaffawi from the Arabic sources. Printed on the margin are the *Fatāwa Fayḍiyyah* by Shaykh-al-islām Fayḍ-allah Efendi.

(22) *Al-Fatāwa al-***'Alamkīriyyah**, compiled upon the order of the sultan Muhyi-al-dīn 'Alamkīr Ewrenkzīb (ruled from 1069-1118) by a commission under the chairmanship of Shaykh Niẓām. Calcutta, 1243. The work is meant to be exhaustive and to dispense with the need to refer to other *fatwa* collections. It enjoys in India the highest esteem.

(23) *Fatāwa 'Abd-al-rahīm*, by Shaykh-al-islām Menteshzādeh 'Abd-al-rahīm Efendi al-Bursawi (1128). Constantinople, 1827. An esteemed large collection in Turkish. Contains many *fatwas* on modern matters such as the agrarian relations.

(24) *Fatāwa Hammādiyyah* (1241), by Mawlāna a. 'l-Fath Rukn b. Husām al-Nākūri. A compact work of the *'Alamkīriyyah* type. It gives in preface a long list of sources.

II. Shafiite

(1) *K. al-***Umm** (vol. ii), by M. b. Idrīs al-Shāfi'i (204). Recension of al-Rabī' a. M. b. Su. al-Murādi. Būlāq, 1321. There is also a recension by al-H. al-Za'farāni, one of al-Shāfi'i's Bagdad disciples, which has gone into oblivion. The *Mabsūt* referred to by the *Fihrist* must be the old Bagdad version of the *Umm*, since the chapters tally. Apparently the *K. al-Hujjah* which al-Shāfi'i is said to have composed in Bagdad (*Tah-dhīb*, p. 61) is another name for the recension of al-Shāfi'i's Bagdad teachings. In the long list of the works ascribed to al-Shāfi'i in Yākūt neither title is mentioned. Evidently these names were given by al-Shāfi'i's students when they collected his teachings. The *Umm* is a valuable source for the study of law. It is full of *ḥadīths* and contains many repetitions. There are abridged recensions (*mukhtaṣar*) of al-Shafi'i's doctrines by Al-Rabī', a. Ya'qūb al-Buwayṭi, and a. Ibr. Ism. b. Yahya al-Muzani (264). The *Mukhtaṣar* of al-**Muzani** is the most widely known of them. It is printed on the margin of the *Umm*. Al-Nawawi speaks of it as one of the five widely-used books at his time, the other four being the *Muhadh-dhab*, the *Tanbih*, the *Wasīṭ* and the *Wajiz*, to be mentioned later. The *Mukhtaṣar* of al-Muzani hardly deserves its name, for it is still large, often literally quoting the *Umm*. Many **commentaries** were written on it, notably by a. al-Tayyib al-Tabari, M. b. A. al-Shāshi, and Zakariyā' b. M. al-Anṣāri. There is a smaller compendium by al-Muzani, called *Nihāyat al-Ikhtiṣār*, where he often indicates his own views, which in many instances disagree with those of al-Shāfi'i (Subki, p. 244). The opinions of al-Shāfi'i cited in the *Umm* and the other recensions of his teachings in Egypt are called his recent (*jadīd*) opinions in distinction from his older views (*qadīm*) contained in recensions of his teachings in Bagdad, such as the *K. al-Hujjah*.

(2) *Al-Hāwi al-Kabīr*, by a. al-H. 'Ali b. M. al-Māwardi (450). An exhaustive treatise of *fiqh*. A condensation of it is the author's *al-Iqnā'*. Al-Māwardi is said to have written the *Iqnā'* upon the order of the calif al-Qādir-bi-'llah in competition with al-Qudūri, the Hanifite, a. M. 'Abd-al-wahhāb b. M.. the Malikite, and a Hanbalite. The story says that al-Māwardi was the winner. (Yāqūt, vol. v, p. 408.)

(3) *Al-Aḥkām al-Sulṭāniyyah*, by the same al-**Mawardi**. Ed. Max Enger, Bonn, 1853. This is a justly renowned work giving the description of an ideal state. Some of the subjects it covers are not to be found elsewhere, as the author himself points out in his conclusion. The treatment is schematic and clear-cut, as regards content, in many cases, closely following upon al-Shāfi'i's *Umm*. The views of a. Hanīfah and Mālik are mentioned. The motives are not, as a rule, gone into. Strictly speaking, it is not a work of *fiqh* proper. In so far as it treats questions of *fiqh*, it does so from the standpoint of the state. The first part of the work (the first 107 out of 432 p.) has been translated into French by L. **Ostrorog**, Paris, 1901-6.

(4) *Al*-**Tanbih**, by a. Isḥaq Ibr. b. 'Ali al-Shīrāzi (476). Ed. A. W. T. Juynboll, Leyden, 1879. A well-known compendium which may be said to have eclipsed its predecessors, though itself has had a similar fate. Clear and detailed. The best known of the **commentaries** on it is that by Badr-al-dīn M. (b. Bahādur) b. 'Al. al-Zarkashi. *Al-Muhadh-dhab fi 'l-Madh-hab* is another well-known work of al-Shīrāzi, formerly much used. It gives the arguments and difficult points.

(5) *Nihāyat al-Maṭlab fi Dirāyat al-Madh-hab*, by a. 'l-Ma'āli 'Abd-

al-Malik b. a. M. 'Al. al-Juwayni, Imâm-al-haramayn (478). An extensive work in 40 parts, "such as has not been composed in Islam its like" (Ibn Khallikan in H. Khal.). (H. on S.)

(6) *Al-Basiṭ*, by Hujjat al-islâm a. Hâmid M. b. M. al-Gazzâli (505). Based on the *Nihâyat al-Maṭlab* of his teacher Imâm-al-Haramayn. *Al-Wasîṭ al-Muḥîṭ bi Aqṭâr al-Basîṭ* is a condensation of the former by the author himself. One of the five books referred to by al-Nawawi as being in use. *Al-***Wajiz**, by the same author; a condensed compendium based on the former, with additions. Cairo, 1317. Also one of "the five books," and the best known of his works on *fiqh*. It is an excellent schematic summary of all the Shafiite views, independent (*aqwâl*) or deduced (*wajh*), the authors responsible for them not being mentioned. The differences of al-Muzani, a. Hanîfah and Mâlik are indicated by letters. The best known of the **commentaries** on the *Wajîz* is the *Fatḥ al-'Azîz 'ala K. al-Wajîz*, by a. al-Qâsim al-Râfi'i (623). *Al-Rawḍah*, by al-Nawawi, is an abridgment of it.

(7) *Iḥyâ' 'Ulûm al-Dîn*, by the same al-Gazzâli. Bûlâq, 1289. Although it contains many chapters of *fiqh*, the book is not strictly a book on *fiqh* but has a larger scope. It is meant by the author as a plea for the regeneration of religion, and represents a reaction against its increasing secularization. It gives valuable sidelights into existing conditions. It treats in four parts (*rub'*), questions of worship (*'ibâdât*), personal manners, character, and social relations. "It has been said about this book that if the books of Islam were destroyed except the *Iḥyâ'*, it would dispense with those destroyed" (H. Khal.).

(8) *Al-Taqrîb fi 'l-Fiqh*, or *Mukhtaṣar a. Shujâ'* (also called *Gâyat al-Ikhtiṣâr*), by a. Shujâ' A. b. al-H. al-Iṣfahâni (593). Brief and clear. The most widely-spread Shafiite compendium (S.). **Commentaries:** (**a**) *Al-Iqnâ' fi Hall Alfâẓ a. Shujâ'*, by M. b. al-Khaṭîb al-Sharbîni (977). (**b**) **Fath al-Qarib** *al-Mujîb fi Sharḥ Alfâẓ al-Taqrîb*, also called *Al-Qawl al-Mukhtâr fi Sharḥ Gâyat al-Ikhtiṣâr*, by M. b. al-Qâsim al-Gazzi (981). Publ. with French translation by Van den Berg, Leyden, 1895. It is elementary, explaining chiefly questions of grammar and syntax. Used by students in Java. **Glosses** on it by Ibr. b. Qâsim al-Bâjûri (1278). Cairo, 1901. They consist in his lectures in the Azhar and are used as text-book. Author wrote his glosses because the previous glosses by Ibr. b. M. al-Birmâwi (1106), known as al-Muḥash-shi (S.), though complete, contained difficult passages. Goes at length into grammatical and syntactical details. Very useful for beginners. (For criticism of Bâjûri by Hurgronje, *cf. De indische Gids*, 1884.)

(9) **Minhaj** *al-Ṭâlibîn*, by Muḥyi-al-dîn a. Zakariyâ' Yahya b. Sharaf al-Nawawi (676), an improved abridgment of the *Muḥarrar* by a. 'l-Qâsim 'Abd-al-karîm b. M. al-Râfi'i (623), a well-known work based on the works of al-Gazzāli (H. on S.). It is a standard, concise, clear text of great fame. It indicates by a clever terminology (see its preface) the original views (*naṣṣ* or *qawl*) of al-Shāfi'i as well as the views (*wajh, qawl mukharraj*) deduced by his followers by analogy. Publ. by Van den Berg with a French translation. Batavia, 1882-84. **Commentaries: (a)** By Jalāl-al-dīn M. b. A. al-Maḥalli (864). Goes into the arguments. **(b)** *Tuḥfat al-Mukhtāj li Sharḥ al-Minhāj*, by A. b. M. b. Hajar (973). Cairo, 1290. **(c) Mugni** *al-Mukhtāj ila Ma'rifat Ma'āni Alfāẓ al-Minhāj*, by M. b. al-Khatīb al-Sharbīni (977). Cairo, 1308. A fairly exhaustive, useful work, giving in a concise manner most of the matter found in other commentaries. It indicates the views that have found acceptance and gives briefly the motives, but does not go into syntax and grammar. **(d)** *Nihāyat al-Mukhtāj ila Sharḥ al-Minhāj*, by Shams-al-dīn M. b. A. al-Ramli (1004), with **glosses** printed on the margin by A. b. M. 'Abd-al-razzāq al-Rashīdi (wrote in 1086) and a. al-Diyā' 'Ali b. 'Ali al-Shabrāmallisi (1087). Cairo, 8 vols. Indicates clearly the views that have been endorsed by the Shafiite school. By "*qālā*" (they two said) he means the "two *imāms*," namely al-Rāfi'i and al-Nawawi, by "*al-Shāriḥ*" (the commentator), Jalāl-al-dīn al-Maḥalli, and by "*al-Shaykh*," Zakariyā' al-Anṣāri. The *Muḥarrar* and the *Minhāj* with its two commentaries, the *Tuḥfah* and the *Nihāyah*, "are considered as the Law books of the Shafiite school" (H. on S.).

(10) *Manhaj al-Tullāb*, by a. Yahya Zakariyā' b. M. al-Anṣāri (926). An abridgment of the *Minhāj* which itself became classical and is today used in instruction (S.). A well-known **commentary** on it is the *Fatḥ al-Wahhāb* by the author himself. **Glosses** by Su. al-Bajīrmi (1221).

(11) *Taḥrīr al-Tanqīḥ*, by the same Zakariyā', an extract from the *Tanqīḥ al-Lubāb* of a. Zur'ah (b.) al-'Irāqi (826), with some additions, controversial matter being left out. The *Tanqīḥ* itself was a condensation of the *Lubāb* of a. al-H. A. b. M. al-Maḥāmili (415). A **commentary** on the *Taḥrīr* is the *Tuḥfat al-Tullāb* by Zakariyā' himself. **Glosses** thereon: (i) by al-Madābigi (1170); (ii) by 'Al. al-Sharqāwi (1227). Very much favored. Used by students in the Azhar (S.). Printed with notes by al-Sayyid Muṣṭafa al-Dhahabi on the margin. Būlāq, 1891.

(12) *Asna al-Maṭālib*, by the same Zakariyā' al-**Ansari**. A commentary on the *Rawḍ al-Ṭālib* by Sharaf-al-dīn Ism. b. a. Bakr b. al-Muqri (837). Printed with **glosses** by Shihāb-al-dīn a. al-'Abbās A. b. A. al-Ramli (957), Cairo, 1895. Very much like the *Mugni*, though not quite so exhaustive.

(13) *Qurrat al-'Ayn* (982), by Zayn-al-dīn al-Malibāri. A **commentary** on it by the author himself is the *Fatḥ al-Mu'īn*. **Glosses** on it:

I'ânat al-Tâlibin, by Sayyid Bekri a. Bekr Shaṭṭâ', a Mecca professor. Cairo, 1884, 4 vols. Gives the recent *fatwas*. The works of this group are very much used in East Africa and British and Dutch Indias (H. on S.).

FATWA COLLECTIONS: **(1)** *Fatâwa b. al-Salâḥ*, by 'Uthmân b. 'Ar. b. al-Salâḥ (642), collected by his disciples. Very useful. (H. Khal.) **(2)** *'Uyûn al-Masâ'il al-Muhimmât*, by Yahya b. Sharaf al-Nawawi (676), in two sizes. Answers on actual cases. **(3)** *Fatâwa b. Firkâḥ*, by a. M. 'Ar. (b.) Ibr. al-Fazari al-Firkâḥ al-Miṣri (690). **(4)** *Fatâwa al-Zarkashi*, by Badr-al-dîn M. b. Bahâdur al-Miṣri al-Zarkashi (794). **(5)** *Fatâwa al-Ramli*, by Shihâb-al-dîn a. al-'Abbâs A. b. A. al-Ramli (957), edited by his son Shams-al-dîn M. b. A. al-Ramli (1004). Printed on the margin of the *al-Fatâwa al-Kubra*. **(6)** **Al-Fatâwa al-Kubra** *al-Haytamiyyah al-Fiqhiyyah*, by A. b. M. b. Hajar (973). Cairo, 1890, 1308. Answers to actual questions with long arguments.

III. Malikite

(1) (*Al-Masâ'il*) ***al-Mudawwanah*** (vol. ii). Recension of Qâḍi Saḥnûn a. Sa'îd b. 'Abd-al-salâm al-Tanûkhi (240). Cairo, 1323-24. It consists of questions by Saḥnûn and answers by 'Ar. b. al-Qâsim (191), a student of Mâlik for 20 years. These answers as a rule repeat the literal words of Mâlik, though at times they are b. al-Qâsim's own interpretation of the same. The *Mudawwanah* is a revision by b. al-Qâsim of the *Asadiyyah* of Asad b. al-Furât, when it was submitted to b. al-Qâsim by Saḥnûn, who had studied the *Asadiyyah* under Asad. Asad having failed to incorporate the corrections of b. al-Qâsim as found in Saḥnûn's copy, the *Asadiyyah* fell into oblivion. After b. al-Qâsim's death, Saḥnûn incorporated in his copy *ḥadîths* in support of some of the views and improved its arrangement. *Mukhtaliṭah* is another name given to the *Mudawwanah* (*Fihrist al-Ishbîli*, p. 240, seems to confirm this), though in another version it is the name given to the *Asadiyyah* on account of Asad's having studied previously the Hanifite law also. (*Cf.* Ibn Khaldûn, Vincent, *Mudawwanah*, vol. i, p. 12; Kharashi, 'Adawi, vol. i, p. 38.) The *Mudawwanah* is the greatest Malikite authority. Its relation to other books has been likened to that of the opening chapter (*al-Fâtiḥah*) of the Koran. The Malikites by "The Book" mean it. The *Mudawwanah* found special favor among the Mohammedans of W. N. Africa (*Ifriqiyah*) (such as b. Yûnus and al-Lakhmi) (Ibn Khaldûn), who showed great zeal in studying and commenting on it.

(2) *Al-Wâḍiḥah*, by a. Marwân 'Abd-al-malik b. Habîb al-Sulami (238), of Spain, who studied under b. al-Qâsim and spread the Malikite doctrines in Spain. The *Wâḍiḥah* naturally found favor in Spain.

(3) *Al-Mustakhrajah min al-Asmi'ah al-Masmu'ah min Mâlik b. Anas*, known as *Al-'Utbiyyah*, by M. b. A. al-'Utbi al-Qurtubi (255), student of b. Habib. This work superseded the *Wâdihah* and itself became an object of study and comment (Ibn Khaldûn). The commentary on it by M. b. A. b. Rushd (520) deserves mention. It is entitled *K. al-Bayân wa 'l-Tahsil wa 'l-Sharh wa 'l-Tawjih wa 'l-Ta'lil fi Masâ'il al-Mustakhrajah*. (*Cf*. Prof. C. A. Nallino's "Intorno de *Kitâb al-Bayân* del Giuristo Ibn Rushd" in the *Homenaje á D. Fr. Codera*, Zaragoza, 1904.) Arranged in the conventional *fiqh*-book chapters. The author, after citing the questions and Mâlik's answers and *e. g.* the view of b. al-Qâsim, introduces his own view by "*Qâl* M. b. Rushd," supporting it by lengthy arguments. A valuable source-book for determining the development of the school. The *Mudawwanah, Wâdihah* and '*Utbiyyah*, with the *Mawâziyyah* of M. b. Ibr. b. al-Mawâz (281), a student of b. 'Abd-al-Hakam (*cf. Husn al-Muhâdarah*, p. 169), are called *al-Ummahât, i. e.*, the mother books. The last work does not seem to have spread as widely as the others. Ibn Khaldûn does not mention it. Some would add to this list also the following: (a) *al-Majmû'ah*, by M. b. 'Abdûs (260; but *cf*. Brockelmann, p. 177); (b) *al-Mabsûtah*, by a. Ishaq al-Qâdi Ism. b. Ishaq (282), of Bagdad (*cf*. Vincent). All of them are necessarily very long and badly arranged and uncoördinated.

(4) *Tah-dhib*, by a. Sa'id al-Barâda'i. It is a condensation of the *Mudawwanah* and the *Mukhtalitah* which found great favor with the jurists of Ifriqiyyah and superseded its predecessors. (Ibn Khaldûn; *cf*. also b. Tûmart, p. 41.) Al-Maqqari (vol. ii, p. 122) reads as follows concerning a *K. al-Tah-dhib* by al-Barâdha'i al-Saraqusti: "As regards (books of) *fiqh*, the book that is relied upon at present, and the one that is designated by the Malikites as far as Alexandria as the Book, is the *Tah-dhib* of al-Barâdha'i al-Saraqusti." (Brockelman speaks of a *Tah-dhib Masâ'il al-Mudawwanah wa 'l-Mukhtalitah* (372) by a certain Khalaf b. a. al-Qâsim al-Bagdâdi, a student of b. a. Zayd. It may be the same book.)

(5) *K. al-Nawâdir*, by 'Ubayd-allah b. 'Ar. b. a. Zayd al-Qayrawâni (386). It combines the previous works.

(6) *Al-Risâlah* is by the same b. a. Zayd. Cairo, 2d ed., 1905. It is a clear, brief compendium—said to be the first in the Malikite school—covering also questions of catechism and meant to be a guide for the layman. It is a compendium of great authority that has been copied and commented upon more than any other. (Vincent.) The author also wrote a *Mukhtasar*, where he abridged the *Mudawwanah* and the *Mukhtalitah*. (Ibn Khaldûn.)

(7) Abu Bakr M. b. 'Al. b. Yûnus al-Tamîmi al-Saqali (451) wrote a commentary on the *Mudawwanah* where he included the greater part

of b. a. Zayd's *Nawādir*. Ibn Yūnus' originality of thought consisted in indicating (*tarjīḥ*) the views to be preferred.

(8) *K. al-Tabṣirah*, by a. al-H. 'Ali b. 'Al. al-Lakhmi (478). It is a well-known *Ta'līq* on the *Mudawwanah*. Al-Lakhmi's characteristic has been his independence of view (*ikhtiyār*).

(9) *Al-Muqaddamāt al-Mumahhadāt li Bayān ma Aqtaḍat-hu Rusūm al-Mudawwanah min al-Aḥkām al-Shar'īāt wa 'l-Taḥṣīlāt al-Muḥkamāt li Ummahāt Masā'iliha al-Mushkilāt* (**Ibn Rushd, M.**), by a. al-Walīd M. b. A. b. Rushd al-Qurṭubi (520), grandfather of the famous philosopher b. Rushd (Averroes). Cairo, 1907. It indicates the etymology and the justification of the words and meanings of the *Mudawwanah*. Treatment analytical. Ibn Rushd distinguished himself by singling out the true reports (*riwāyat*) from Mālik ('Adawi, p. 41).

(10) Abu 'Al. M. b. 'Ali al-Tamīmi al-Māziri (536), known as the *Imām*. He is another famous doctor who commented on the *Mudawwanah*. Al-Māziri distinguished himself by his generally accepted independent views (*qawl*). Ibn Yūnus, al-Lakhmi, b. Rushd and al-Māziri are the four authorities whose opinions are mentioned and authorship is specified by Khalīl in his famous *Mukhtaṣar*.

(11) *Mukhtaṣar*, by a. 'Amr 'Uthmān b. 'Umar b. al-Hājib (646). This is a compendium that combines all the Malikite views and was much read in the Magrib in the days of Ibn Khaldūn. It was commented upon among others by M. b. 'Abd-al-salām al-Umawi (wrote in 799), b. Rushd, and Khalīl b. Ishaq (the *Tawḍīḥ*).

(12) *Bidāyat al-Mujtahid wa Nihāyat al-Muqtaṣid* (**Ibn Rushd, B.**), by a. al-Walīd M. b. A. b. Rushd al-Qurṭubi, well known as b. Rushd al-Hafīd (the grandson) (595). Cairo, 1329. The work was written by the author in order to enable the jurists to decide cases for which the *sharī'ah* did not provide. It is a masterly analysis of the main issues at law with the views held by doctors of various schools and the grounds underlying their viewpoints ably discussed. The grounds ascribed by b. Rushd to the doctors do not, therefore, always tally with those claimed by them.

(13) *Al-Mukhtaṣar*, by Diyā'-al-dīn a. al-Safā' **Khalīl** b. Isḥaq al-Jundi al-Miṣri (767). Paris, 1318. It is the most famous compendium of the Malikite school, and since its writing virtually the most authoritative summing-up of the Malikite doctrines. Perhaps no compendium has found such favorable reception as this. It is said to contain 100,000 explicit and as many implicit legal determinations. It is an attempt to include in the briefest possible compass the accepted doctrines of the school on the minutest details, the holders of the opinions and the unsettled points being hinted at by a clever use of words as explained in the preface. Probably here lies the secret of

its success despite the fact that the work is involved to an unheard-of degree and absolutely defies understanding. A French translation of the *Mukhtaṣar*, with explanatory phrases thrown in the text, by Perron, in *Exploration scientifique de l'Algérie, Sciences hist. et géogr.*, vols. x-xvi, Paris, 1848-52. **Commentaries:** (**a**) By Tāj-al-dīn Bahrām b. 'Al. al-Damīri (805), in three sizes; (**b**) by a. 'Al. M. b. Yū. al-Mawwāq al-'Abdari al-Garnāti (897), in two sizes. (**c**) *Fatḥ al-Jalīl*, by M. b. Ibr. al-Tatā'i (942). **Glosses** thereon by al-Kharashi (1101). *Jawāhir al-Durar* is another smaller commentary by al-Tatā'i. (**d**) By a. 'Al. M. b. M. al-Khaṭṭāb (953). A large commentary. (**e**) By al-Laqāni (958) on the preface (*khuṭbah*) with **glosses** by al-Zarqāni (1099). (**f**) By a. al-Najā' Sālim al-Sanhūri (1015). (**g**) By 'Ali al-Ujhūri (1066), in two sizes. (**h**) By 'Abd-al-bāqi b. Yū. al-Zarqāni (1099), with **glosses** by M. b. al-Tālib al-Tāūdi (1207). Būlāq, 1307, 8 parts. An advanced commentary going into arguments and quoting views of other commentators (Vincent). Also **glosses** by M. b. al-H. al-Bannāni. (**i**) by a. 'Al. M. al-**Kharashi** (vol. ii) (1101), with **glosses** by 'Ali al-'**Adawi** (vol. ii) (1189). Cairo, 1307. A very well-known commentary. Goes into grammatical and syntactical details. Does not as a rule go into arguments. There is also a larger commentary by al-Kharashi. (**j**) By Ibr. b. Mar'i al-Shabrakhīti (1106), in three sizes. (**k**) By A. b. M. al-Dardīr (1201). Būlāq, 1282. **Glosses** thereon by M. b. 'Arafah al-Dasūqi. Cairo, 1310. Both the commentary and the glosses are very much esteemed. (**l**) By M. 'Alīsh (1299), with **glosses** by himself. Printed in 4 vols. Būlāq.

(**14**) *Tabṣirat al-Hukkām fi Uṣūl al-Aqḍiyah wa Manāhij al-Aḥkām*, by Ibr. b. 'Ali b. Farḥūn al-Andalusi (799). Formerly much used. Intended for judges especially.

(**15**) *Al-Mukhtaṣar fi 'l-Fiqh*, by M. b. M. al-Wargami al-Tūnisi, b. 'Arafah (803).

(**16**) *Tuḥfat al-Hukkām fi Nukat al-'Uqūd wa 'l-Aḥkām*, by a. Bakr M. b. M. b. 'Aṣim (829) of Granada. A celebrated compendium in *rajaz* verse. It is brief and clear. **Commentaries:** (**a**) By M. b. A. Mayyārah al-Fāsi. Cairo, 1897. (**b**) By 'Ali b. 'Abd-al-salām Tasūli Sabrāri. Būlāq, 1256.

(**17**) *Aqrab al-Masālik li Madh-hab al-Imām Mālik*, by a. al-Barakāt A. b. M. al-**Dardir** al-'Adawi al-Azhari (1201). An abridgment of the *Mukhtaṣar* of Khalīl. Though not quite as rich in details as the latter work, it is remarkably clear for a Malikite compendium. **Commentary** by the author himself known as *Sharḥ al-Sagīr*. Būlāq, 1281. Where Khalīl indicates two views, al-Dardīr often gives only the one preferred by him. This work, and the author's and al-Kharashi's commentaries on Khalīl, are used by students in the Azhar (*Iktīfā'*).

Glosses by A. b. M. Al-Sāwi (1241). Named *Bulgat al-Sālik li Aqrab al-Masālik*. Cairo, 1903.

(18) *Al-Majmu' fi 'l-Fiqh*, by M. b. M. al-Sunbāwi al-Amir (1232). A compendium written on the same plan as that of Khalil. **Commentary** and **glosses** by the author himself.

FATWA COLLECTIONS: **(1)** *Al-Mi'yār al-Mugrib wa 'l-Jāmi' al-Mu'rib 'an Fatāwi A'lām Ifriqiyah wa 'l-Andalus wa 'l-Magrib*, by A. b. Yahya al-Wansharisi (914). **(2)** *Fatḥ al-'Ali al-Mālik fi-'l-Fatwa 'ala Madh-hab al-Imām Mālik*, by a. 'Al. M. b. A. 'Alish (1299). 2 vols., Cairo, 1300. The *fatwas* given by the author arranged in the conventional *fiqh*-book chapters.

IV. Other Schools

HANBALITE: *Dalil al-Tālib fi Nayl al-Ma'ārib*, by Shaykh Mar'i, b. Yū. (1033). This is the text used by Hanbalite students in Mecca. (*Mekka*, vol. ii, p. 249.)

SHI'ITE: *Sharā'i' al-Islām* (between 436 and 676), by Najm-al-din Ja'far b. M. al-Hilli a. al-Qāsim. A **commentary** on it is the *Masālik al-Afhām* (964) by Zayn-al-din b. 'Ali al-Shāmi al-'Amili. A French translation of the *Sharā'i'* is A. Querry's *Droit Musulman*, Paris, 1871. N. B. E. Baillie's *A Digest of Moohummudan Law, etc.*, part ii, 2d ed., London, 1887, is based on the same work.

V. Books on Differences of Mohammedan Schools

(*Ikhtilāf al-Madhāhib*)

(1) *Ikhtilāf al-Fuqahā'*, by a. Ja'far M. b. Jarir al-Tabari (310), the Shafiite. Ed. F. Kern, Cairo, 1320. **(2)** *Ikhtilāf al-Fuqahā'*, by a. Ja'far A. b. M. al-Taḥāwi (321), the Hanifite. **(3)** *Raḥmat al-Ummah fi Ikhtilāf al-A'immah* (780), by Sadr-al-din M. b. 'Ar. al-Dimashqi al-'Uthmāni, the Shafiite. Būlāq, 1300 (with the *al-Mizān al-Khiḍriyyah* of al-Sha'rāni). **(4)** *Al-Mizān al-Kubra*, by 'Abd-al-wahhāb b. A. al-Sha'rāni (973), the Shafiite. 2d ed., Cairo, 1318 (the *Raḥmat al-Ummah* on the margin). An **abridgment** of it by the author himself is the *al-Mizān al-Khiḍriyyah.* French translation entitled *Balance de la loi, etc.*, by Perron, Algiers, 1898.

BOOKS ON SECTS (RELIGIOUS AND PHILOSOPHICAL)

(1) *K. al-Farq bayn al-Firaq wa Bayān al-Firqah al-Nājiyah minhum*, by a. Manṣūr 'Aq. b. Tāhir al-**Bagdadi** (429), the Shafiite. Cairo, 1328. **(2)** *K.* (*al-Fiṣal fi*) *al-Milal* (*wa 'l-Ahwā'*) *wa 'l-Niḥal*, by a. M. 'Ali b. A. b. Hazm (456), the Zahirite. Cairo, 1317. Polemical. Goes into lengthy metaphysical and other arguments. "This book is from the

worst of books, and our doctors have never ceased forbidding its study on account of its despise of the Sunnites" (al-Subki as quoted by H. Khal.). (3) *K. al-Milal wa 'l-Niḥal*, **by a. al-Fatḥ M. b. 'Abd-al-karīm al-Shahrastāni (548).** Ed. W. Cureton, London, 1842. Also printed on the margin of the preceding book. A compact work treating of religious and philosophical sects in general in a clear and summary manner. Al-Subki approves of this book. (H. Khal.) (For further details, *cf.* I. Goldziher, "Zur Litteratur des *Ikhtilāf al-Madhāhib*," *ZDMG*, 1884, vol. 38, pp. 669-82; *d. Zahiriten*, pp. 37 *et seq.*; F. Kern, "*Tabari's Ikhtilāf al-Fuqahā'*," *ZDMG*, 1901, vol. 55, pp. 61-95.)

MISCELLANEOUS

(1) *K. al-Agani*, by a. al-Faraj 'Ali al-Iṣfahāni (356). Cairo, 1285. **(2) Bélin,** "Étude sur la propriété foncière," *J. Asiatique*, 1861-62. **(3) Berchem,** Max van, *La propriété territoriale et l'impôt foncier sous les premiers califes*, Genève, 1886. **(4) Bruno,** H., *Régime des eaux en droit musulman*, Paris, 1913. **(5) Caetani,** L., *Annali dell' Islām*, Milano, 1905. A monumental work in course of publication. Published as far as vol. vii (year 32). **(6) Defteri Muqtasid,** by Su. Sūdi; 2d ed., Constantinople, 1307. **(7) Gatteschi,** D., *Real Property, Mortgage and Waqf According to Ottoman Law.* Translated from the Italian by Edw. A. Van Dyck. London, 1884. **(8) Ghali,** R., *De la tradition considérée comme source du droit musulman*, Paris, 1909. **(9) Goldziher,** I., *die* (**d.**) **Zahiriten**, Leipzig, 1884. **(10) Goldziher,** I., "Kämpfe um die Stellung des *Hadīṯ* im *Islām*" (**"Kämpfe"**). *Z. D. M. G.*, vol. 61, pp. 860-72. **(11) Goldziher,** I., **Vorlesungen** *über den Islam*, Heidelberg, 1910. **(12)** Goldziher, I., "Das Princip des *Istiṣḥāb* in der muh. Gesetzwiss.," *Vienna Oriental Journal*, pp. 228-36. **(13)** Goldziher, I., "Muh. Recht in Theorie und Wirklichkeit" *Zeits. für vergl. Rechtswiss.*, vol. viii, pp. 406-23. **(14) Ibn Hisham:** *Das Leben Muhammad's nach Muhammad ibn Ishaq* (151) *bearbeitet von 'Abd-al-malik Ibn Hischam* (218). Ed. F. Wüstenfeld, Göttingen, 1858-60. **(15) Hurgronje,** C. Snouck, "**Le droit musulman,**" *Revue de l'histoire des religions*, 1898, vol. 37, pp. 1 *et seq.*, and 174 *et seq.* **(16)** Hurgronje, C. Snouck, *The Achehnese.* English trans. by A. W. S. O'Sullivan, Leyden, 1906. Based on critical first-hand observation. For bibliogr. information see vol. ii, p. 9. **(17)** Kohler, Dr. J., "Die Wirklichkeit und Unwirklichkeit des islam. Rechts," *Zeits. für vergl. Rechtswiss.*, vol. viii, pp. 424-32. **(18) Maqrīzi,** *K., Al-Mawā'iẓ wa 'l-I'tibār fi Dhikr al-Khiṭaṭ wa 'l-Athār*, by a. al-'Abbās A. b. 'Ali. al-Maqrizi (845). Cairo, 1324-26. **(19)** Margoliouth, D. S., *The Early Development of Mohammedanism.* Lectures delivered in the University of London, New York, 1914. **(20) Padel** et L. Steeg, *De la législation foncière ottomane*, Paris, 1904. **(21) Sprenger,** A., "Eine Skizze der Entwickelungsgeschichte des musl. Gesetzes."

Zeitsch. für vergl. Rechtsw., 1892, vol. x, pp. 1-31. **(22) Worms,** Dr., "Recherches sur la constitution de la propriété territoriale dans les pays musulmans et subsidiairement en Algérie," *J. Asiatique*, 1842-44. **(23) Yahya:** *K. al-Kharāj*, by Yahya b. Adam b. Su. al-Qurashi (203). Ed. Th. W. Juynboll, Leyden, 1896. A valuable source written in the way of *ḥadith* collections. **(24) Young,** G., *Corps de droit ottoman*, Oxford, 1905-6. **(25) Zaydān:** *Tārikh al-Tamaddun al-Islāmi*, by Jurji Zaydān, late editor of the *Hilāl;* 5 vols., Cairo, 1902-6.

PART II

FINANCIAL THEORIES

CHAPTER I

Preliminary Remarks

"Mohammedan," as used in these pages, does not mean every financial theory evolved by a Mohammedan writer; nor does it mean the theories evolved concerning every Mohammedan financial practice. It means only the theories evolved by Mohammedan writers in conformity with the principles of *sharī'ah* on the basis of the financial practices of the early Mohammedan state, particularly during the califship of Omar. In other words, only the financial practices which were sanctioned by usage in the early Mohammedan state and only the financial theories treated in the books of *fiqh* are called "Mohammedan". Financial practices which have not received sanction from the early Mohammedan state or financial theories which have not been based on the *sharī'ah*, even if practiced or written by Mohammedans, remain outside the pale of *sharī'ah* and may not properly be called "Mohammedan". This is in strict accordance with the usage of the Mohammedan writers, who in their works on *fiqh* discuss only the "Mohammedan" theories of finance and do not treat the practices which came into Mohammedan use later, except in terms of summary condemnation.

These **extra-shari'ah practices** made their way into Mohammedan history rather early, and in the course of time entirely displaced the *sharī'ah* practices. The new taxes resulting from the introduction of these practices have been given various designations, such as *hilāli, marāfiq, ma'āwin, mukūs* [1] and *'urfi.* [2]

[1] Maqrizi, p. 167. [2] *Defteri Muqtasid*, p. 22.

Al-Maqrīzi, who in his *Khiṭaṭ* gives a detailed description of the extra-*sharī'ah* taxes in Egypt during his time, states that the revenue of Egypt at that time consisted of the two classes of *kharāji* (*i. e.*, the *sharī'ah* taxes levied on the non-Moslems) and *hilāli* revenue (*māl*), and condemns the latter as instituted "one after another by evil *wālis* (governors)".[1]

The author of the *Defteri Muqtaṣid*,[2] on the other hand, sees no objection to the extra-*sharī'ah* taxes on the part of the *sharī'ah*, when they are not exorbitant. In Mohammedan histories frequent allusion is made in terms of praise to attempts of pious Mohammedan rulers immediately after their accession to power to remove the pernicious practice of extra-*sharī'ah* taxes,[3] but the invariable refrain is that the practice reappeared.[4] Part II concerns itself exclusively with the Mohammedan theories of finance and has nothing to do with the extra-*sharī'ah* taxes.

The various *sharī'ah* sources of revenue discussed by the Mohammedan writers fall into two well-defined classes: the class of **religious revenue** collected from Moslems alone; and the class of **secular revenue** derived primarily from non-Moslems. The religious revenue includes the three *zakāt* taxes constituting the so-called *ṣadaqah* or *zakāt* revenue and the financial contribution for the conduct of holy war and other affairs of public interest. The three *zakāt* taxes are the *zakāt* on flocks and herds, the *zakāt* of gold and silver and the articles of trade, and the *zakāt* of the produce of the earth, or tithe.[5] The secular revenue,

[1] Maqrīzi, p. 166.

[2] P. 24.

[3] *Cf.* Maqrīzi, p. 167, ll. 1, 15, 19; p. 169, l. 10.

[4] *Cf. ibid.*, p. 167, l. 17; p. 169, l. 13.

[5] As this dissertation deals primarily with the Hanifite doctrines, its

on the other hand, comprises the *kharāj* or land-tax, the *jizyah* or poll-tax, the tax on non-Moslem traders, the imposts on spoils, mines, and treasure-trove, and the estates of persons who died intestate and without heirs.

For the sake of clearness, these taxes are discussed under two main divisions, one on revenue, and the other on expenditure; while the subject of public domain, which seemed to belong in neither of these divisions, is treated as a third coördinate division in a chapter bearing that title. The division on revenue includes discussions of assessment and collection, while that on expenditure considers the principles governing the disposal of public funds and the allied topics of public treasury and budget, military stipends, grants, and public records. The sharp distinction between the religious and the secular revenue is indicated by the separate treatment accorded to religious and secular revenue. Owing to the intimate connection between the principles concerning the status of persons and lands, on the one hand, and the *kharāj* and *jizyah*, on the other, the discussion of the latter has been preceded by an explanation of the former. The discussion of spoils, as a source of revenue, is justified by the fact that one-fifth of them belonged to the state, and the remaining four-fifths divided among the soldiers in reality constituted a state expenditure. This is easy to understand if it be remembered that the conduct of holy war was one of the primary functions of the Mohammedan state and the expense for it had to be provided for by the state in some way. Moreover, the four-

internal arrangement has been made to fit those doctrines, and therefore need not always be in accordance with the Shafiite and Malikite views. For instance, according to the Shafiites, and partly to the Malikites also, the taxes levied on mines and treasure-trove are considered as *zakāt*, and should consequently be treated under the *zakāt* taxes rather than under the secular taxes where they have been treated.

fifths so divided might be considered as an advance payment on the pay of the soldiers and a supplement to the military stipends provided by the state.

Finally, in the conclusion, an analysis of the Mohammedan theories of finance is given. In this analysis, the theories are taken entirely at their face value and the deeper philosophy underlying them is not discussed.

CHAPTER II

THE ZAKAT TAXES [1]

SECTION I

General Principles

Zakat literally means growth and increase (as in the phrase *zaka al-zar'*, the crop grew), and, according to some, purity (as in the verse *qad aflaḥa man tazakka*,[2] *i. e.*, verily the pure ones prospered). The tax has been named *zakāt* with respect to the first meaning of the word, because its giving leads to increase of property in this world and growth of religious merit (*thawāb*) in the next: and with respect to the second meaning, because its payment purifies from sins. God said: "Take from their property alms (*ṣadaqah*) in order thus to purify them (*tuzakki-him*) [from their sins]".[3]

Technically **zakat** is **defined** by the Hanifite doctors as "the giving [4] (*tamlīk*), as an act of piety, of a legally

[1] *Majma'*, p. 157; Qudūri, p. 20; *Mabsūṭ*, p. 149; Kāsāni, p. 2; *Hidāyah*, *Fatḥ*, *Kifāyah*, and *'Ināyah*, p. 112; *Durar*, p. 112; *Durr*, p. 131; *Jāmi'*, p. 297; *'Alamkīriyyah*, p. 239; *Baḥr*, p. 216; *Umm*, p. 2; *Wajīz*, p. 79; *al-Fatāwa al-Kubra*, vol. ii, p. 32; Māwardi, p. 195; *Minhāj*, p. 228; Anṣāri, p. 338; Zarqāni, vol. ii, p. 41; Ibn Rushd, *M.*, p. 200; Ibn Rushd, *B.*, p. 225; *Mudawwanah*, p. 2; *Muwaṭṭā*, p. 103; *Kharashi*, p. 51.

[2] Koran, chap. 87, verse 14.

[3] *Ibid.*, chap. 9, verse 104.

[4] "Giving" is used here in the sense of transferring the ownership of a thing.

(*shar'a*) stated portion of one's property to a poor Moslem who is not of the Hāshim family or their clients (*mawla*), in such a way as to preclude for the giver any sort of benefit." [1] *Zakāt* also means the thing so given. *Sadaqah* is another name for *zakāt*. The general usage, however, is to consider *ṣadaqah* as a more generic term applying to the alms whose payment is a *farḍ* (obligation), as well as to the alms the giving of which is entirely voluntary (*taṭawwu'*). In other words, while every *zakāt* is also *ṣadaqah*, only the *ṣadaqah* which is a *farḍ* is *zakāt*. Al-Shāfi'i and al-Māwardi, on the other hand, claim that there is no distinction between the two terms and that they both denote the same thing.[2]

The giving of zakat by Moslems is **a fard** based on evidence found in the Koran, the *sunnah*, the *ijmā'* and in reason. In the Koran *zakāt* is set down as the third faith (*thālithat al-īmān*) as becomes evident from these divine words: "and if they [*i. e.*, the infidels] have repented and performed the prayers and paid the *zakāt*, they are your brethren in religion." [3]

In the *sunnah*, *zakāt* is reckoned as one of the five "pillars of faith". The Prophet said: "Islam has been built on five [things], namely, testimony that there is no God but the God, the performance of the prayers, the giving of *zakāt*, the fast during the month of Ramaḍān, and the pilgrimage to Mecca when one can afford it." [4]

It is justified in the *ijmā'*, because the entire Mohammedan community has agreed upon *zakāt's* being a *farḍ*.[5]

Finally, it is supported by reason, because the giving of

[1] *Majma'*, p. 157.

[2] For details see Part III.

[3] Koran, chap. 9, verse 11.

[4] *Mabsūṭ*, p. 149.

[5] Kāsāni, p. 3.

zakāt is an assistance to the poor and enables them to perform their religious obligations—to help perform a *farḍ* is itself a *farḍ*—and because the giving of *zakāt* purifies one's morals by inculcating habits of generosity and greatheartedness and by eradicating those of niggardliness, since it is a fact that possession of property leads one to greed.[1] According to the *Muḥīṭ*, failure to believe that *zakāt* is a *farḍ* entails unbelief (*kufr*), and refusal to practice it involves the death penalty.[2]

The cause (*sabab*) **of zakat**'s being a *wājib*[3] is the possession in full ownership (*milk tāmm*) of **a productive** (*nāmi*) **nisab** (minimum) of property. This is based on the divine words: "Take from their properties *ṣadaqah*". "Property is a cause of *zakāt* not *per se*, but in so far as it contributes to the wealthiness of the owner, for the Prophet said to Mu'ādh: 'Tell them that God has prescribed for them *ṣadaqah*, to be taken from the rich among them in order to be given to their poor'. But wealthiness results only from the possession of a definite quantity of wealth,

[1] *Ibid.* The *Baḥr* (p. 217) objects to the *sunnah*, and especially to reason being invoked as evidence for *zakāt*'s being a *farḍ*.

[2] *'Alamkīriyyah*, p. 239.

[3] It will be noticed that while in the previous paragraph the giving of *zakāt* was referred to as a *farḍ*, here the cause of *zakāt*'s being a *wājib* only is discussed. Most of the Hanifite texts follow this usage. The commentators explain the discrepancy in two ways: (1) The giving of *zakāt* is called a *farḍ* because it is based on positive evidence (*dalīl qaṭ'i*). On the other hand, it is spoken of the cause of *zakāt*'s being a *wājib* only, because in certain respects it is based on presumptive evidence alone (*dalīl ẓanni*). (*Majma'*, p. 157; *'Ināyah*, p. 113.) (2) In this connection *wājib* is used by extension in the sense of *farḍ*. (*Hidāyah*, p. 112; *Kifāyah*, p. 112; *Baḥr*, p. 217; *'Ināyah*, p. 213.) Certain texts use the word *farḍ* in both instances. (*Durr*, p. 132; Kāsāni, p. 4.) However, this difference of usage affects only the obligation of believing in *zakāt* but not of practising it, since in engendering an obligation for doing a thing the *farḍ* and *wājib* are on a par. (See Part I.)

and this quantity is the *niṣāb*."[1] However, the *niṣāb* becomes a cause only by virtue of productivity, for *zakāt* is a contribution set apart from superfluous property, as may be inferred from this passage in the Koran:[2] "And they shall ask you as to what they shall bestow in alms (*yunfiqūna*). Say, 'The superfluous'."[3] And so the cause of *zakāt* is the productive *niṣāb*, and the *zakāt* is, therefore, referred to the *niṣāb*, as, for example, when we say, "the *zakāt* of cattle". Consequently, when the *niṣāb* is doubled the *zakāt* is also doubled.

Productivity (*numā'*) **is** either **real** (*taḥqīqi*), as in procreation and trade, **or hypothetical** (*taqdīri*), as, for example, in the case where productivity has been possible, though not actual, in that the property has been in the possession of the owner or his agent.[4] Productivity, real or hypothetical, is considered to have existed whenever one of the following three cases is present: (1) when property is gold or silver (*naqdān* or *thaman*); (2) when animals are pastured (*saum*); (3) when property is intended for trade (*niyyat al-tijārah*).[5] According to the *'Alamkīriyyah*,[6] productivity, both real and hypothetical, is further classified into natural (*khilqi*) and artificial (*fi'li*). The first is found in gold and silver, which have been created for trade and in themselves are not fit for the satisfaction of wants. Gold and silver pay *zakāt* whether or not they are intended for trade or personal consumption. Artificial productivity, on the other hand, is found in other than gold and silver,

[1] *Mabsūṭ*, p. 149.
[2] Chap. 2, verse 217.
[3] *Ibid.*, p. 150.
[4] *Majma'*, p. 158.
[5] *Jāmi'*, p. 299.
[6] P. 244. Zaila'i, p. 256.

whenever there is intention of trade or of pasture, provided the intention in each case is borne out by an act of trade or pasture.

Besides being productive, **the nisab must also be owned in full ownership** (*milk tāmm*), that is, ownership (*milk*) combined with possession (*yad*). Consequently, mere possession of property does not subject it to *zakāt*. "For the state of wealthiness does not exist without ownership (*milk*), and the productive property was a cause for *zakāt* only by virtue of contributing to the wealthiness of the owner, and when it fails to do so it is no longer a cause [of *zakāt*]."[1] According to Abu Hanīfah, neither does ownership without possession subject to *zakāt*[2] since the *niṣāb* could not have then been productive. Consequently the wife is not subject to *zakāt* on her marriage price (*ṣidāq*) before she has received it, although she owns it.

The **nisab,** furthermore, **must be over and above what is necessary for the** satisfaction of the primary **necessities of life** (*ḥājah aṣliyyah*), because property destined for such necessities is, as it were, non-existent.

The **nisab,** finally, **must be free of debt** subject to demand of payment by one's fellow-men (*'ibād*),—whether the debt be owing to them or to God,—as distinguished from debts which are not subject to demand on payment by one's fellow-men, such as debts of vow or *ṣadaqat al-fiṭr*,[3] and which, therefore, do not oppose the obligation of *zakāt*. According-

[1] *Mabsūṭ*, p. 164.

[2] *Fatḥ*, p. 113; *cf.* '*Alamkiriyyah*, pp. 241, 245.

[3] *Sadaqat al-fiṭr* is a kind of *ṣadaqah* (also called *zakāt al-fiṭr*) bestowed upon the poor on the festival of breaking Lent. Its chief difference from *zakāt* is that, while its settlement is morally just as obligatory (since it is a *wājib*), it does not come under state control and lies entirely with the person himself. The *zakāt al-fiṭr* is also called *zakāt al-ru'ūs* (*zakāt* of heads) in distinction from the *zakāt* with which we are here concerned and which strikes property.

ing to al-Shāfi'i,[1] indebtedness does not affect the obligation of *zakāt*. According to one Shafiite view, however, indebtedness opposes *zakāt* in the case of non-apparent property. Finally, according to the Malikites,[2] indebtedness exempts (*yusqiṭ*[3]) from the *zakāt* of gold and silver (*'ayn*) and the articles of trade, though not of crops, cattle, and mines. The argument of al-Shāfi'i is that the cause of *zākat* is the ownership of a complete *niṣāb* and the debtor possesses one. Moreover, the debt of a free man attaches to his person and does not encumber his property which he may handle as he pleases and so make productive. The Hanifite argument is as follows: The calif 'Uthmān said in his address in the mosque during the month of Ramaḏān: "Behold, the month of your *zakāt* has come. Whoever has property and debts, let him deduct from what he owns what he owes and pay *zakāt* for the remaining property,"[4] and none of the Companions blamed 'Uthmān for his action. and so it was an *ijmā'* on their part to the effect that there is no *zakāt* on the amount covered by debt. Besides, the debtor is really a poor man and the *zakāt* is paid by the rich alone. Furthermore, the debtor deserves help himself, and there is no reason in taking from him as a taxpayer, for instance, a sheep, and then returning the same to him as a beneficiary of the tax. Finally, it cannot even be properly said that the debtor completely owns the *niṣāb*, since it is affected by the right of the creditor.

[1] *Hidāyah*, p. 118; *Umm*, p. 22; *Minhāj*, p. 261.

[2] Kharashi, p. 106: Dardīr, p. 124.

[3] The word *yusqiṭ* means to cause to lapse, and if its use was advised it would imply that indebtedness does not oppose the operation of *zakāt* in the first place. The Hanifites and Shafiites, however, expressly stand for this last meaning by using the expression *yamna'u wujūbaha*, *i. e.*, the debt prevents the *zakāt* from becoming due.

[4] *Mabsūṭ*, p. 160.

There has been dispute as to whether a debt of zakat should constitute a cause of exemption. According to Zufar, a debt of *zakāt* is like a debt of vow or *kaffārah*,[1] and does not exempt from *zakāt*. In fact, it is canceled in case of death before payment, and therefore is not really a debt. Al-Balkhi establishes a distinction between the *zakāt* due on "apparent" property and that due on "non-apparent" property, holding that only the *zakāt* due on "apparent" property exempts from *zakāt*, because, according to him, only the latter kind of *zakāt* is subject to demand of payment on the part of the public collector. Al-Sarakhsi takes exception and claims that the *zakāt* due on both "apparent" and "non-apparent" property is alike subject to demand of payment. He contends that, during the time of the Prophet and the two califs after him, the *zakāt* of "non-apparent" as well as of "apparent" property was collected by the public collectors, and that the third calif 'Uthmān, in order to remove from the taxpayers the inconvenience and trouble attendant on the investigation of their "non-apparent" properties by evil collectors, limited the jurisdiction of the public collectors to the "apparent" property and delegated the right of collecting the *zakāt* of "non-apparent" property to the property owners themselves; that, therefore, the *zakāt* of "non-apparent" property is still subject to demand of payment (though now by the property owners themselves instead of by the public collectors) and that consequently, the *zakāt* on "non-apparent" property, too, is a cause of exemption. On the other hand, according to Abu Yūsuf, a *zakāt* debt is cause of exemption if the property on which the *zakāt* is due is still intact, but it is not so, if the property has been destroyed, because in

[1] *Kaffārah* is a financial expiation for such sin as the breaking of fast or an oath.

case the property is intact, there is always a possibility that the owner may pass a public collector with that property and so be subject to demand of payment as regards its *zakāt*. It is stated in the *Mabsūṭ* that, when Abu Yūsuf was called upon to show cause for not assenting to Zufar's view, he replied, "What is my cause against a man who makes one pay 400 *dirhams* of *zakāt* for 200 *dirhams* of property!", meaning thereby that according to Zufar a person owning 200 *dirhams* would have to pay after 80 years 400 *dirhams* of *zakāt,* if he had failed to pay the *zakāt* for each year at the end of the same. According to the view which considers a *zakāt* debt as a cause of exemption, the *zakāt* due on the 200 *dirhams* in question would be only one year's *zakāt,* namely 5 *dirhams,* since after the falling due of the first year's *zakāt* the 200 *dirhams* would be affected with the *zakāt* debt of 5 *dirhams* for the first year, and the second year no *zakāt* would be due, the condition of an unobstructed *niṣāb* of 200 *dirhams* being absent.[1] Abu Hanīfah and Muḫammad Ibn al-Hasan hold the same view as al-Sarakhsi.

Al-Shāfi'i,[2] with respect to *sawā'im* animals, says that a previous debt of *zakāt* on them exempts from *zakāt,* but he recommends that advantage should not be taken of this exemption. Finally, according to the Malikites,[3] a debt of *zakāt,* like other debts, exempts from the *zakāt* of gold and silver and the articles of trade only.

A debt of kharaj is like other debts, although according to some this is true only in case the *kharāj* was justified. As regards **tithe debts,** if the crop remains intact, the *zakāt* is not affected by it, since the tithe debt attaches to the crop. Again, if the crop is accidentally destroyed, the *zakāt* is not

[1] *Mabsūṭ,* p. 169.
[2] *Umm,* p. 15.
[3] Kharashi, p. 106; Dardīr, p. 124.

affected, since the tithe debt has in that case lapsed. If, however, the crop was destroyed wilfully, the tithe thereby becomes a personal debt and in such case like other debts exempts from *zakāt*.[1]

According to Abu Hanīfah, Abu Yūsuf, and Muḫammad Ibn Al-Hasan, a debt must have been incurred during the year, but not after it, in order to constitute a cause of exemption as regards the *zakāt* of that year.[2] As regards **debts incurred during the year but since discharged;** according to Muḫammad Ibn al-Hasan, and, in the opinion of Ibn 'Abidīn,[3] according to Zufar, they exempt from *zakāt* and the year begins anew; but according to Abu Yūsuf, and, in the opinion of Ibn 'Abidīn, also according to Abu Hanīfah and Muḫammad, such debts result only in a decrease of the *niṣāb,* not its total disappearance, and consequently the *zakāt* is due when the year is complete. According to the *Baḫr,*[4] debts incurred as a result of suretyship (*kafālah*) are like other debts.

A debt is a cause of exemption whether or not it has fallen due.[5] Consequently the marriage price (*mahr*) stipulated by the husband in favor of his wife exempts him from *zakāt* even if the price is to fall due at a future date (*mu'ajjal*). Some differ on the ground that such debts are not ordinarily demanded. Others hold that they should exempt only in case the husband really intends to settle them when demanded to do so by his wife. Some say that only debts which have fallen due justify exemption.[6] The author of the *Jāmi'* approves of this last view.

[1] *Jāmi'*, p. 300; *'Alamkīriyyah*, p. 242; *Baḫr*, p. 220.

[2] *'Alamkīriyyah*, p. 243.

[3] *Minḫah*, p. 220.

[4] P. 220.

[5] *'Alamkīriyyah*, p. 242; *Baḫr*, p. 220.

[6] *Jāmi'*, p. 300.

When a person owns several *niṣābs* in several kinds of property at the same time that he owes a debt, he makes allowance for the debt as follows. He applies the debt first against the *dirhams* and *dīnārs* (the gold and silver currency), and, if there remains a surplus of debt, against the articles of trade, and if there is still a surplus, against the *sawā'im* animals, beginning with the kind of *sawā'im* animals that is subject to the least amount of *zakāt*, unless they are all subject to an equal amount of *zakāt*, in which case he may first apply the surplus to whichever kind he pleases. The above is true when the collector has called in person for the collection of the *zakāt*, for in the contrary case the property owner may apply the debt against any property he chooses, since he is liable to *zakāt* equally with respect to every kind of property. This is not true, however, of the collector, for he has jurisdiction over the *sawā'im* animals alone, and, therefore, he applies the debt against the currency and collects the *zakāt* of the animals.[1]

According to the accepted Hanifite view the **debt is applied against the property which is subject to zakat** and not against property which is destined for the satisfaction of necessities and is consequently exempt from *zakāt*. However, according to Zufar, it is applied to property of its own genus. Thus a person possessing 200 *dirhams*, a slave and a quantity of borrowed grain, and owing a slave, pays no *zakāt* because the debt is applied to the *dirhams*. According to Zufar the debts of grain and slave are applied to the grain and slave he possesses and a *zakāt* is due on the *dirhams*. Likewise, a person owning a house, a personal slave worth 10,000 *dirhams* and 1,000 *dirhams* pays no *zakāt* if he also owes 1,000 *dirhams*, for the house and slave, far from satisfying his needs, on the contrary, increase

[1] *'Alamkiriyyah*, p. 244; *Mabsūṭ*, p. 184.

them.[1] According to the Malikites,[2] a debt may be applied to gold and silver and the articles of trade with a view to canceling or reducing their *zakāt* only if the *zakāt* payer does not possess other appropriate property against which he may apply the debt in question. By appropriate property here is meant gold or silver extracted from a mine, tithable grain, collectible claims already accrued, or, finally, commodities (*'arḍ*) which he has had for a year and which may legally be sold for the satisfaction of debts, such as clothing, cattle, riding beasts, books of law; but not clothing destined for his person or a house destined for his residence, unless they exceed his needs. Thus a person having forty *dīnārs* and a commodity worth twenty *dīnārs* and owing forty *dīnārs* pays *zakāt* only for twenty *dīnārs* if at the time the *zakāt* falls due he has had that commodity for at least a year and it is worth twenty *dīnārs*.

The conditions of zakat's being a wajib are the following:

(1) Reason (*'aql*) and maturity (*bulūg*), for there can be no responsibility without them.

(2) State of Islam, because the payment of *zakāt* is an act of worship and as such it can validly be performed only by a Moslem.

(3) Freedom of person (*ḥurriyyah*), in order that the provision in the definition of *zakāt* concerning the transferring of ownership (*tamlīk*) by the *zakāt* payer to the *zakāt* beneficiary may be realized, for the slave can not own any property.

Exemptions. As a result of failure in one or more of the above requirements, the following are exempt from *zakāt*:

(1) **The Mukatab,**[3] because though he enjoys the right

[1] *'Alamkīriyyah*, pp. 243, 244. [2] Kharashi, p. 107; Dardīr, p. 124.

[3] The *mukātab* is the slave who obtained from his master the privi-

to dispose of (*taṣarruf*) his goods, he does not completely own them.

(2) **The debtor** subject to demand of payment of his debt on the part of a fellow-man, to the amount of his indebtedness, provided the debt is of the kind above described. Such fellow-man may be the creditor, the *imām* [1] as regards the *zakāt* of "apparent" property, or the debtor himself, as regards the *zakāt* of his "non-apparent" property, such as gold and silver. If, however, the debt is not subject to demand of payment and refusal to pay it does not involve imprisonment, it does not result in exemption. A debt of vow is of this last kind.[2]

(3) **Dimar property,** which has been recovered, for past years. *Dimār* is property which has slipped out of one's possession with little chance of recovery, such as fugitive or stray slaves. *Dimār* property is exempt from *zakāt* according to Abu Hanīfah, Abu Yūsuf and Muḫammad Ibn Al-Hasan (*'indahum*), because the condition of productivity is absent. According to Zufar and al-Shāfi'i,[3] however, *ḏimār* property is subject to *zakāt* for past years, when recovered, because upon its recovery the cause of *zakāt*, namely a complete *niṣāb*, has come into existence. They base their view on the analogy of the traveler. The others invoke the *ḫadīth* of 'Ali, who said: "There is no *zakāt* on *ḏimār* property"; and as regards the analogy of the traveler, they claim that the case is different, because he can still make his property produce through an agent. Fin-

lege of manumission on payment of a fixed price. Such slaves have the right to engage in trade and buy and sell in order to earn the price of their freedom.

[1] That is, the head of the Moslem state.

[2] *Jāmi'*, p. 300.

[3] *Umm*, p. 44; *Minhāj*, p. 260.

ally, according to the Malikites,[1] *ḏimār* property, provided it is gold or silver, when recovered, pays *zakāt* for one year only, even if meanwhile many years should have passed. If it is cattle, then according to the prevalent view the *zakāt* is paid for all past years. As regards trees this is always the case. The following, when recovered, are **examples of dimar property:** slaves—lost, fugitive, or gone astray; property fallen into the sea; property usurped, when there is no evidence to prove that fact; property buried in the country, in a place since forgotten; property seized tyrannically by the sultan; claims publicly disclaimed by the debtor with no evidence to disprove him. However, claims acknowledged by a debtor who is well-to-do, or even in financial difficulties, or who has been declared by a judge insolvent (*mufallas*), are not considered *ḏimār* property, because there is yet a possibility of recovering them. In fact, as regards the debtor who is in difficulties, he may still recover his fortune, and as regards the case of the debtor who has been declared insolvent, according to Abu Hanīfah, such declaration is not valid and debts owed by the insolvent are not lost considering that wealth flows back and forth. Muḫammad Ibn al-Hasan has dissented from Abu Hanīfah as regards the validity of declaring a debtor insolvent, and so he has considered claims owed by an insolvent as *ḏimār*. Abu Yūsuf, while agreeing with Muḫammad as regards the validity of the judgment of insolvency, followed Abu Hanīfah in not considering the debts of the insolvent as *ḏimār* property. The motive in their case was to guard the interests of the poor who are the chief beneficiaries of *zakāt*. Likewise, according to most of the leading doctors (*mashā'ikh*), claims denied by the debtor, if they have been proved by evidence, are not *ḏimār*. However, according to Muḫam-

[1] Khalil, p. 41; *Mudawwanah*, p. 98; Kharashi, p. 84.

mad Ibn al-Hasan they are *ḏimār* and are not subject to *zakāt*, because every judge is not just and all evidence is not reliable. Similarly, claims concerning the validity of which a judge has personal information are not *ḏimār*. However, this is not true at the present time, because the judges now may no longer render judgment on the basis of personal information they may happen to possess. Finally, property which has been buried in a place answering the description of *ḥirz*,[1] such as the house or shop of the owner, is not *ḏimār* even if its exact location has since been forgotten, because it may be recovered by being dug up. According to the *Baḥr* this is also true of property buried in another's house (*ḥirz*).[2] The Hanifite doctors have differed as regards property buried in the owner's garden (*karm*) or field. Some hold that such property is not *ḏimār* considering that it may be recovered by digging. Others take the opposite view because of the difficulty of digging up the entire garden or field; they claim that for this reason also property buried in a large house would be *ḏimār*.

(4) **Also**, for want of productivity, or because of being destined for primary necessities, or for both reasons, the **following articles:** dwelling-houses; wearing apparel; household utensils; slaves employed as servants; riding animals; arms kept for use; food used by one's self and family; articles of adornment, if not made of gold and silver; gems, pearls, rubies, hyacinths, emeralds, and the like; coins of other than gold and silver, if intended for personal expenditure; books and tools. All the preceding articles are exempt from *zakāt* even when they are not destined for primary necessities, and are not actually used—for instance, even when the tools are not owned by people who use them,

[1] *Ḥirz* technically means a place where property is customarily kept, such as one's house, shop, tent, or person.

[2] *'Alamkiriyyah*, p. 245.

provided, however, they are not intended for trade.[1] It must be remarked that the tools (*alāt*) referred to above are the tools which render a use without leaving a trace in the thing on which they have been used. If, however, they do leave a trace in the thing, as is the case with yellow dye or saffron bought by a dyer in order to be used for the dyeing of people's clothing in consideration of a price (*ajr*), they are then subject to *zakāt*, provided their value amounts to a *niṣāb* and a year has passed from the time of their purchase. Likewise subject to *zakāt* is every article (*'ayn*) bought for use in the process of work, if a trace of it remains in the object worked upon. Gall-nut and grease used for the dressing of leather are of this category. No *zakāt* is due on instruments, however, if, as in the case of soap and potash, no trace of them is left.[2]

(5) **Property of minors and the insane,** because, in their case, the conditions of maturity and reason are wanting; and of non-Moslems, because the condition of Islam is wanting. However, according to the Malikites (especially as regards cattle and crops) and also according to al-Shā'fii,[3] minors and the insane are subject to *zakāt*. Al-Shāfi'i's ground is that *zakāt* is an obligation connected with property, irrespective of ownership. The Hanifites, on the other hand, reply that *zakāt* is an act of worship and therefore incumbent only on those who can exercise an option in its discharge.[4]

[1] The reason for this is that *zakāt* is due on property other than *sawā'im* animals or gold and silver only when that property is intended for trade. Consequently an amount of property that is not intended for trade does not pay *zakāt*, merely because it is not destined for primary necessities, no matter how large such amount may be. There is, however, a difference in the disbursement of *zakāt*. There, the possession by a person of a *niṣāb* of books bars him from having a share in the *zakāt* unless he needs to use those books. *Durar*, p. 113.

[2] *'Alamkiriyyah*, p. 242.

[3] *Wajīz*, p. 87.

[4] *Hidāyah*, p. 115.

Insanity is of two kinds, original (*aṣli*) and acquired (*'āriḍi*). It is original, if a person is insane when he comes of age; it is acquired, if he goes insane after coming of age. There is no difference between the two kinds of insanity, except that in the original, according to Abu Hanīfah, the year begins from the date of recovery. Furthermore, according to Abu Hanīfah, the *zakāt* is due on the insane's property if he has had a lucid interval during the year, no matter how short the interval was. According to Abu Yūsuf, however, the lucid interval must be at least more than half of the year, since otherwise insanity would have had predominated over sanity.[1]

The condition of the payment of zakat being a *wājib*[2] **is the lapse of a year** (*ḥawalān al-ḥawl*) over the *niṣāb* of productive property while it is in the proprietor's full possession, provided the conditions of age, freedom, *etc.*, are fulfilled. In other words, if one possesses in full ownership for a year articles coming under the description of *thaman* or *sawā'im*, or articles that he intended to trade in for profit, he pays *zakāt* for those articles at the end of the year, regardless of whether or not they have been actually productive.

The lapse of a year is necessary, "because time is indispensable for productivity to materialize—this time has been fixed by the *sharīah* at one year according to the *ḥadīth*: 'No *zakāt* is due on property before there elapses over it a year', and because productivity during a year is possible" by virtue of the succession of seasons in the course of which prices usually vary.[3]

[1] *'Ināyah*, p. 117.

[2] This condition must not be confused with the condition of "the *zakāt per se*" being a *wājib*, since the *zakāt per se* may have become a *wājib* without its payment being due, owing to the fact that the condition of payment is not yet realized.

[3] *Hidāyah*, p. 113.

According to the Malikites,[1] in conformity with the practice of Medina, in cattle the obligation of *zakāt* does not arise upon the mere lapse of the year but only after the arrival of the collectors, provided there are such who can reach the cattle owners.

With respect to the requirement of the lapse of a year, it must be borne in mind that nothing must supervene during the year which in the technical language is called "**dissolution" of the nisab, or,** what is the same, dissolution of **the year** (*inqiṭā' al-ḥawl*), as in that case there would have to elapse a new year before *zakāt* became due on the new *niṣāb*. Thus according to al-Sarakhsi if one should sell his *niṣāb* of *sawā'im* animals just one day before the completion of the year, whether the price was *sawā'im* animals of the same genus (*jins*), or whether it was wealth of another genus, such as gold and silver currency, the year would be dissolved and another year would have to elapse over the price before a *zakāt* was due on it. According to Zufar, the year is not dissolved if the price was *sawā'im* animals of the same genus. Al-Shāfi'i, on the other hand, claims that the year is not dissolved in either case, because, as he argues, the wealth of the owner has not been affected by the transaction, just as this is the case in the exchange of trade articles against one another. Zufar argues that when the price is of the same genus as the animals sold, the provisions concerning the original animals continue in force as regards their price. Al-Sarakhsi, on the other hand, remarks that the *sawā'im* animals are subject to *zakāt,* in and of themselves (*'ayn*), and not on account of their value as is the case with the articles of trade. Indeed, the *niṣāb* of the *sawā'im* animals, as well as their productivity, is reckoned with respect to the physical identity (*'ayn*) of the

[1] Dardir, p. 115; Kharashi, p. 66.

animals, not their commercial value, and so when they are sold the year is dissolved; for their price, even though it be *sawā'im* animals of the same genus, is no longer the very same animals. In articles of trade the case is different, since there the object in view is not the physical identity of the thing but its value, which is not affected by exchange. Moreover, an exchange in articles of trade is conducive to the realization of the object of trade, namely profit. An exchange in *sawā'im* animals, on the contrary, is subversive of the object in owning *sawā'im* animals—namely, keeping them in permanent possession for their physical produce. The view above ascribed to al-Shāfi'i is his older view (*fi 'l-qadīm*), namely, the view he held during his stay in 'Iraq before his departure to Egypt. The view expressed in the *Umm*[1] apparently is his more "recent" (*fi'l'jadīd*) view, since it is to the contrary effect, namely, that if a person exchanges his *sawā'im* animals against other animals of the same genus or against other kinds of wealth, such as gold or silver, he does not pay *zakāt* on the animals he sold if the sale occurred before the completion of the year, and he pays *zakāt* on the price he received in exchange only after the lapse of a year. However, according to the Malikites,[2] exchange (*ibdāl*) does not dissolve the year if made with the purpose of escaping the *zakāt*—for instance, if made within a month from the completion of the year.

Must the nisab be complete every moment **through the entire year** or may it vary to a certain extent without resulting in the dissolution of the year? According to al-Sarakhsi, the *niṣāb* must be complete at least in the beginning and at the end of the year, and furthermore, at no time must it have entirely disappeared (*inqiṭā'*). According-

[1] P. 20; *cf. Minhāj*, p. 236.

[2] Kharashi, 'Adawi, p. 58; *cf. Mudawwanah*, p. 81.

ing to Zufar, the *niṣāb* must be complete throughout the entire year, and, on the other hand, in al-Shāfi'i's opinion, this is only true of the *sawā'im* animals and of gold and silver (*naqd*), while in the case of articles of trade it is sufficient if the *niṣāb* is complete at the end of the year only. The argument of Zufar is that there is no difference between the different periods of the year and that the condition of a complete *niṣāb* must be present at every period of the year. Al-Shāfi'i joins with Zufar in his argument as regards the *sawā'im* animals and admits that analogy would require that this should be true of the articles of trade also, but remarks that the latter pay *zakāt* on the basis of their value, which it is well-nigh impossible to ascertain for every day in the year. Therefore, for the sake of convenience, he requires that this condition should be met only at the time the *zakāt* falls due, that is, at the end of the year. Al-Sarakhsi, however, argues that a complete *niṣāb* is required in order that the state of wealthiness may be realized. Consequently, it is necessary at the beginning of the year, in order that the year may begin to run, and at the end of the year, in order that the *zakāt* may fall due; but it is not necessary that the *niṣāb* should be complete in the meanwhile, provided it does not entirely disappear. The analogy of *sawā'im* animals (which cease to be *sawā'im* if in the middle of the year they are turned into beasts of burden), invoked by the opponents is not valid, because in that case the *niṣāb* has entirely disappeared; for as soon as the animals have been used as beasts of burden they have forthwith ceased to be *sawā'im* animals, but we have not allowed the destruction of the entire *niṣāb* but only its decrease. Finally, as regards the inconvenience of the appraisal of the articles of trade which al-Shāfi'i alleges, it is not any harder to appraise the articles at the beginning of the year than it is at the end, and there is no great inconvenience in doing so twice a year, at the beginning as well as at the end of it.[1] Consequently, if a *niṣāb* of grape juice should turn into wine and then into vinegar before the completion of the year, the year would be dissolved with respect to the grape juice and a new year would have to elapse before the vinegar would become subject to a year's *zakāt*. If, however, a *niṣāb* of sheep should perish during the year but the wool of the same was worth 200 *dirhams*, the year would not be dissolved, considering that the *niṣāb* was not entirely destroyed. Indebtedness, even when it covers the entire *niṣāb*, does not dissolve the year, although Zufar holds the contrary view.[2]

Property acquired (*istifādah*) **in the course of the year** is added to the *niṣāb* of property already in existence and their *zakāt* is paid together when the year is complete for the *niṣāb* in question. Thus a person who has 200 *dirhams* and acquires 100 more during the year, pays *zakāt* for 300 *dirhams* at the end of the year. If, however, the acquisition is made after the completion of the year, or the property already possessed is not of *niṣāb* quantity, or, finally, the two properties in question are not of the same genus, the above rule does not apply and they are treated separately.[3]

According to al-Shāfi'i additional property acquired during the year is not added to the original *niṣāb*, because it is independent in its ownership and should be independent also in its obligation of *zakāt*, unless the increment consists in

[1] *Mabsūṭ*, p. 172.

[2] *Majma'*, p. 170.

It goes without saying that if the indebtedness continues through the year the *zakāt* does not fall due, because the *niṣāb* must be free of debt. We are concerned here with the indebtedness that disappears before the completion of the year. Such indebtedness does not dissolve the year.

[3] *Jāmi'*, p. 316; *Majma'*, p. 170; *Baḥr*, p. 239.

offspring or in a profit (*ribh*) which has not been liquidated, such as an increase in price which has not been turned into cash (*lam yanidd*). For the profit as well as the offspring are dependent on the original *nisāb* as regards their ownership and must be dependent on it also as regards the obligation that attaches to their ownership. Then, too, it is difficult to follow the rise and fall of prices. The Hanifites reply that the reason why the offspring and profits are added to the original property is their homogeneity, since in their case it is difficult to single out the increment from the original property; and this is also true of every acquisition which is of the same genus as the original property.[1]

It follows from the above that if one should have a *nisāb* of camels and acquire more camels during the year through purchase or gift or otherwise, according to the Hanifites, he adds them together and pays *zakāt* for the whole when the year is complete; but according to the Shafiites, he can do so only if the increment of camels acquired is an offspring of, or an unliquidated profit from, the camels formerly owned—otherwise they are treated separately. According to the *Fath*,[2] in Abu Hanīfah's opinion, the price of animals whose *zakāt* was paid is not added to a *nisāb* of gold and silver already owned, as this would result in double taxation. In Abu Yūsuf and Muhammad Ibn al-Hasan's opinions, however, such price is added, since the reason for so doing, homogeneity, is present. All three of them have agreed that the price of land or of its produce, on which the tithe has been paid, is added to the *nisāb* of gold and silver already possessed.

Finally, according to the Malikites, four cases are distinguished in the acquisition of additional property—two

[1] *Hidāyah*, p. 148; *Minhāj*, pp. 236, 251; Ansāri, pp. 352, 383.

[2] P. 148.

for the case of animals and two for other cases. (1) The case of animals: (a) The additional animals are acquired either as a result of procreation or by the exchange of the original animals against a larger number of animals of the same species, as of camels for camels. In either case the additional animals pay *zakāt* on the basis of the year of the original animals, and it is not necessary that the latter should be of *niṣāb* quantity. (b) The additional animals are acquired in some other way. In such case they pay *zakāt* with the original animals when the latter's year is complete, even if acquired one day before the completion of that year, provided they are of the same genus, and provided the original animals are of at least a *niṣāb* quantity. For should they be fewer, the year begins from the day the *niṣāb* is completed.[1] (2) The case of other property: (a) The increment consists in profit (*ribḥ*) as, for example, from trade, or in the rental of a house or of a slave leased for silver or gold coins for profit. The profit or the rental received is added to the original value, and pays *zakāt* with it, when its year is complete. For instance, if one starting with a capital of one *dīnār* should earn by the end of the year nineteen more, he would pay *zakāt* on twenty *dīnārs*, without having to wait for the completion of a year with respect to the nineteen *dīnārs*. Or if he should rent with that *dīnār* an animal and by re-renting it make nineteen *dīnārs* of rental, a day before the end of the year, the nineteen *dīnārs* of rental are added to the original value of one *dīnār*, and the *zakāt* of the twenty *dīnārs* so resulting is paid when a year has passed from the possession of the original one *dīnār*. (b) The increment consists in what is called *fā'idah*, *i. e.*, silver and gold (currency) acquired in some other way. Such increment pays *zakāt*

[1] Dardīr, p. 112; Kharashi, p. 52; Ibn Rushd, B., p. 247.

after the completion of a year from its date of acquisition. When the increment is less than a *niṣāb* quantity, it is added to later ones, and the year for the whole begins from the date of the completion of the *niṣāb*. Examples of this increment are gifts and other fortuitous acquisitions, the price of property not subject to *zakāt*, rental of trade articles, *etc.*[1]

In reckoning up the nisab, the rule is to add together only articles which belong in the same genus (*jins*). As the *zakāt* of the *sawā'im* animals attaches to their physical identity and not to their commercial value, each physical genus constitutes a separte legal genus, and therefore it is not allowed by *ijmā'*, for instance, in computing the *niṣāb* of camels, to make up the shortage by adding together with the camels sheep or cattle.[2] The articles of trade, on the other hand, are subject to *zakāt* in virtue of their value, and therefore with respect to *zakāt* they constitute one single genus. Consequently the different kinds of trade articles may be added together in order to complete the *niṣāb*. Furthermore, according to Abu Hanīfah, the *niṣāb* of either gold or silver may be completed by the other or even by articles of trade and *vice versa*. However, according to his two disciples, although the *niṣāb* of gold or silver may be completed by adding articles of trade, the converse is not allowed, because in their opinion gold and silver pay *zakāt* in terms of weight and therefore may not be added to articles of trade which pay *zakāt* in terms of value.[3] Thus a bushel of wheat and five *mithqāls* of gold, according to Abu Hanīfah, pay *zakāt* if their total value amounts to two hundred *dirhams*, but according to his two disciples they do not.

[1] Dardīr, p. 119; Kharashi, p. 87.

[2] *Majma'*, p. 170, l. 7.

[3] *Jāmi'*, p. 317.

According to al-Shāfi'i,[1] gold and silver are distinct genera and may not be added together to complete the *niṣāb* of either. However, the *niṣāb* of articles of trade may be completed by such coin (gold or silver) as may legally be used for their appraisal, the year for the whole being reckoned with respect to the coin only. Thus if a person having one hundred *dirhams* buys with fifty an article of trade, and should such article at the end of the year be worth one hundred and fifty, the fifty *dirhams* are added to them and a *zakāt* of five *dirhams* becomes due on the two. According to the Malikites,[2] gold and silver may be added together.

According to Abu Hanīfah **gold and silver are added** together **in terms of** value. According to Abu Yūsuf and Muḥammad Ibn al-Hasan, however, they are added in terms of weight. Consequently, if a person has 10 *dīnārs* worth 150 *dirhams* and also 50 *dirhams,* according to Abu Hanīfah he pays *zakāt* because their value amounts to 200 *dirhams, i. e.,* a full *niṣāb*; but according to the two disciples he does not pay *zakāt* because their weight falls short of a *niṣāb*. Conversely, if a person has 5 *dīnārs* and 150 *dirhams* worth only 7½ *dīnārs,* according to the disciples he pays *zakāt*, for the *niṣāb* is complete in terms of weight—¼ in gold and ¾ in silver; but according to Abu Hanīfah, he does not pay *zakāt*. Some dotcors say that Abu Hanīfah would have addition in terms of value only in case the *niṣāb* would not be complete in terms of weight, and that in this case, according to Abu Hanīfah, the owner would have to pay a *zakāt* of 5 *dirhams*. The author of the *Baḥr,* however, retorts that Abu Hanīfah stands for addition in terms of value in every case, and that the owner in this case would have to pay *zakāt* also according to Abu

[1] *Umm*, p. 34; *Mugni*, p. 387; *Wajiz*, p. 93.

[2] Kharashi, p. 81.

Hanīfah, for although the *niṣāb* might be incomplete if computed in terms of *dīnārs*, it would be complete if computed in terms of *dirhams*—in fact, it would amount to 250 *dirhams* and the *zakāt* due on them would be not 5 but 6¼ *dirhams*. In other words, according to Abu Hanīfah, either metal may be computed in terms of, and added to, the other in order to complete a *niṣāb*.[1] The Malikite view in this respect is like that of the two disciples.[2]

Finally, as regards crops which are subject to the tithe, Abu Hanīfah exempts them from the requirement of *niṣāb*, but his two disciples, Muḥammad and Abu Yūsuf, require the presence of a *niṣāb*. Muḥammad holds that the different genera of grains are not added together. According to him and one report from Abu Yūsuf, they are added together if they may not be exchanged against one another in unequal quantities; otherwise, as for instance in the case of wheat and barley, they may not be added together, and each pays tithe by itself if it amounts to a *niṣāb*. According to another report from Abu Yūsuf they are added together and pay tithe if together they amount to a *niṣāb*,[3] provided that they ripen at the same time, like barley and wheat, because in his opinion the tithe is a charge by reason of the benefit derived from the ground, and when they ripen together they are one single benefit.

According to a report from Abu Yūsuf, when a person has two pieces of land they are treated independently, if the collectors are different, and they are treated as one single piece of land if they both come under the jurisdiction of the same collector. In the latter case, therefore, the *niṣāb* of one piece may be completed by the produce of the other.

[1] *Mabsūṭ*, p. 193; *Baḥr*, p. 247; *Jāmi'*, p. 317; *Fatḥ al-Mu'īn*, p. 393.

[2] Kharashi, p. 81.

[3] *Mabsūṭ*, part iii, p. 3; *cf. Majma'*, p. 176.

However, according to Muḥammad Ibn al-Hasan, the produce of one piece is added to the produce of the other and the *niṣāb* is reckoned with respect to the sum, because the tithe is a charge on the owner and the owner in this case is one and the same person. Al-Sarakhsi adds that Muḥammad must mean simply that the owner as between him and God should pay tithe on the basis mentioned, since in no case the collector of one farm could collect the tithe of a piece of land over which he has no jurisdiction.

According to the Shafiites,[1] the *niṣāb* of one genus may not be completed from another genus, though one species may be added to another. In this last case each species (*naw'*) pays a proportionate part of the entire *zakāt*. Wheat, barley, rice, maize (*dhurah*), beans, lentils (*'adas*), peas (*ḥimmaṣ*), and millet (*dukhn*) are distinct genera. Fruits of the same year may be added together even if they matured at different times. But fruits and crops of one year may not be added to those of another. The Malikites agree with the Shafiites that the different genera may not be added together, but they disagree as to the meaning of "genus". Thus with respect to tithe they consider the so-called *qaṭāni* (literally, sheath-bearers), such as beans, peas and lentils, as one genus, although they admit that with respect to sale they are distinct genera, and consequently may be exchanged against one another in different quantities without involving usury (*riba*). Likewise wheat (*qamḥ*) and barley (*sha'īr*) are one genus. But maize, millet and rice are distinct genera. So are dates (*tamr*), raisins (*zabīb*), and the four oil-bearers (*dhawāt al-zuyūt*), such as olives and sesam.[2]

In reckoning the nisab of cattle jointly owned, each

[1] *Minhāj*, p. 239; *Wajīz*, p. 90; Māwardi, p. 205.

[2] Dardīr, p. 117; Kharashi, p. 74.

share is considered separately. Thus although five camels owned by one person constitute a *niṣāb* and pay *zakāt,* they are exempt from it if owned by two persons, since the share of neither partner amounts to a *niṣāb*. According to al-Shāfi'i, however, such property pays *zakāt* as a whole irrespective of its joint ownership if it is in the state of *khulṭah,*[1] and each of the owners belongs to the category of people subject to the obligation of *zakāt.*[2] On this point Mālik agrees with the Hanifites to the extent of not considering combined properties as one lot unless the share of each amounts to at least one *niṣāb*. In such case the *zakāt* is divided between the two proportionally.

Al-Shāfi'i's ground for his view is the *ḥadīth*: "The separate are not combined and the combined are not separated, for fear of *ṣadaqah*." It is not therefore permissible, he argues, to separate cattle and pay their *zakāt* independently, when they have been together all the time. Moreover, by rearing their cattle together they have had

[1] *Khulṭah* is the state of two properties being so mixed that they cannot be separated. According to the *Muwaṭṭa'* (p. 112), in this connection a state of *khulṭah* exists if the shepherd, the bull (*faḥl*), the watering-pail (*dalw*), and the resting-place (*murāḥ*) are common, even if the two owners can tell their cattle apart—it being a case of joint ownership if they cannot tell them apart. According to al-Kharashi, it is sufficient if three or more, of the above-mentioned four things and the barn (*mabyit*), are common, provided, however, that the two partners have intended the state of *khulṭah* and are both free Moslems, and provided this state has lasted for a year. According to al-Shāfi'i (*Umm*, p. 11), on the other hand, it is a case of *khulṭah* if, for instance, the cattle are jointly owned. If, however, the cattle are not jointly owned but have been merely herded together by the owners, and the cattle of each may be distinguished from those of the other, it is still a case of *khulṭah* if the cattle have had common resting-place (*murāḥ*), pasture, watering-place, and bull (*faḥl*). In either case the state of *khulṭah* must have existed during the entire year. According to the *Minhāj* (p. 235), intention is not necessary.

[2] *Mabsūṭ*, p. 153; *Umm*, p. 12; *cf. Wajīz*, p. 82; Muzani, p. 205.

the benefit of reducing the expense, and it is not unreasonable that they should bear this burden. If therefore the entire *zakāt* should be collected from one of the two partners, or part of the *zakāt* from the property of one and part of it from that of the other, each partner would have a right of recourse to the other (*tarāju'*) for his share of the *zakāt*, provided the amount collected does not exceed the legal rate. For such part of it as has been collected unlawfully the person from whose property it was collected may bring action against the collector only.[1]

The Hanifite argument, on the other hand, is that by the very terms of the divine prescriptions a person is subject to *zakāt* when he owns a certain minimum of property, and therefore in case of joint ownership each partner is liable for his own share. As regards the *ḥadīth* invoked by al-Shāfi'i, the words "separate" and "combined" occurring in it refer to ownership and not to locality, since it is unanimously admitted that the property of the same person, even if scattered in many places, pays *zakāt* as one lot. In other words, the *ḥadīth* only means that it is not allowed to the collector or the property owner to treat a lot of cattle owned by one person as two lots, or lots owned by several persons as one lot, with a view to increasing or decreasing the *zakāt*, as the case may be. Thus it is not allowed to a person, in order to escape the tax of one sheep due on his forty sheep, to split them into two lots of twenty each; neither is the collector allowed, in order to collect a *zakāt* of one sheep, to consider two lots of twenty owned by different individuals as one lot of forty sheep.[2]

Consequently,[3] if one of the partners (*shirkah mufāwa-*

[1] *Umm*, p. 12; Anṣāri, p. 349.
[2] *Mabsūt*, p. 154; *'Alamkiriyyah*, p. 254.
[3] *Mabsūt*, part iii, p. 40.

ḏah, or *shirkah 'inān*) pays (*adā'*) the *zakāt* of the other's share he has no recourse to him for reimbursement. The reason for this is that he had no authority to settle the *zakāt* of his partner, and therefore he loses the money he paid on his account. Especially is this true, because by paying for his partner he has not cancelled the latter's debt of *zakāt* since the *zakāt* debt is discharged only when there is an intention on the part of the person for whose *zakāt* the money is paid. To the *ḥadīth*, "As regards that which concerns two partners (*khalīṭ*), they have recourse to one another (*yatarāja'āni*) equally", invoked by the Shafiites, the Hanifites answer that they, too, believe in one partner's having recourse to the other (*tarāju'*) but they claim that this happens only in case the collector takes the whole of the *zakāt* from the joint property (*akhadha min 'urḍ al-ganam*); in such case each partner has recourse to the other for such part of the other's share of *zakāt* as was collected from his own property, because there is implied permission to the collector on the part of each partner to collect his share of *zakāt* from the common property. For instance, if the collector collects from one hundred and twenty sheep owned by two persons (eighty by one and forty, that is, one-third, by the other), the *zakāt* due on them, namely, two sheep (one on the forty and one on the eighty), the owner of the two-thirds has recourse to the owner of the one-third for one-third of a sheep's value, because one-third of the entire sheep due on his share of forty sheep was paid by his partner, since of the two sheep taken as *zakāt*, he owned only one-third, namely, two-thirds of a sheep.[1]

According to both the Shafiites and Malikites,[2] the state of **khultah** is not limited to the case of animals but **applies**

[1] Kāsāni, p. 30; *Mabsūṭ*, p. 154; *'Alamkīriyyah*, p. 254.

[2] *Minhāj*, p. 235; *Wajīz*, p. 83; Anṣāri, p. 348; *Mudawwanah*, p. 103.

also to crops and fruits, gold and silver, and the articles of trade. The Hanifites again disagree with them except that Abu Yūsuf, as regards crops only, requires the tithe, if the jointly owned produce amounts to a *niṣāb,* because, in his opinion, the tithe is a charge upon the produce itself, not upon the owners of the same, and therefore, as in the case of the produce of *waqf* lands,[1] the tithe is due when the entire produce is of *niṣāb* quantity, irrespective of its joint ownership. On the contrary, Muḥammad Ibn al-Hasan requires that the share of each partner amount to a *niṣāb.*[2]

The lapse of the zakat debt. If the nisab is accidentally destroyed (*halāk*) **after the lapse of the year,** that is, after the *zakāt* fell due, the *zakāt* debt lapses, whether the property was "apparent" or "non-apparent" or whether it had meanwhile been possible to pay the *zakāt.* This view is unanimously adhered to by the Hanifites as regards the case in which the public collector had not yet demanded payment of the *zakāt.* If, however, the collector had demanded payment of the *zakāt,* according to some, the *zakāt* debt still lapses—and this is the view generally accepted; but according to others the debt must be paid (*ḏamān*). Tithe is like *zakāt* in this respect.[3]

According to Al-Shāfi'i, the *zakāt* lapses if the property has been destroyed accidentally before the payment of *zakāt* has been possible (*tamakkun min al-adā'*), but it does not lapse if meanwhile payment of *zakāt* has been possible.[4]

Finally, according to the Malikites,[5] the *zakāt* does not lapse, in case of destruction, if the owner delayed its settle-

[1] *Cf.* Ibn Rushd, *M.*, p. 230; Anṣāri, p. 369.

[2] *Mabsūṭ,* part iii, p. 4.

[3] *Majma',* p. 166.

[4] *Hidāyah,* p. 152; *'Ināyah,* p. 152; *Mabsūṭ,* p. 174; *Minhāj,* p. 268.

[5] Kharashi, p. 130.

ment for more than a day or so, or if, for instance, he took the tithe home, for future settlement, although he could have settled it right away.

The argument of al-Shāfi'i is that *zakāt* is a financial obligation ordained by God and that it does not lapse merely because the property is destroyed, if its settlement in the meanwhile had been possible. He bases this on the analogy of the debt of *ṣadaqat al-fiṭr* and pilgrimage. Indeed, if a person was well-to-do when he started out for pilgrimage, he is not freed from the obligation if his property is later destroyed. Furthermore, he argues that the *zakāt* debt is a divine trust and one becomes responsible for it if he refuses to settle it when it has been demanded by a person who has the right to demand, for instance, a poor person.[1]

Al-Sarakhsi's argument in support of the Hanifite view is that the *zakāt* is a charge on the *niṣāb* and lapses when the *niṣāb* is destroyed; that there is no ground for holding the property owner to liability (*ḍamān*) for his *zakāt* debt, because there is liability only when a right of ownership or possession has been encroached upon, and it cannot be said that in this case the right of the poor to ownership or possession has been invaded; that the analogy of the debt of *ṣadaqat al-fiṭr* and pilgrimages is not valid, because in their case the obligation attaches to the person of the worshiper and not to his property, and hence it continues even after the destruction of the property; then, too, in the case of the *ṣadaqat al-fiṭr* and pilgrimage, property is a condition of their being *wājibs*, not a condition of their payment being a *wājib*, and so when once they have become due owing to possession of property they do not lapse after its destruction; that *zakāt* has been made obligatory for the consolation of the poor, and after the destruction of his prop-

[1] *Mabsūt*, pp. 174-5.

erty the owner is in need of consolation as much as the poor and therefore is not obliged to console others; that *zakāt* is a small contribution from a great quantity of property in order that its payment may not be heavy and for this reason it strikes only productive property so that the hardship involved in its settlement may be offset by the productivity of the property, and that therefore if the *zakāt* were extracted in this case, there would have been exacted other than what was due; finally, that the fact that a poor person has demanded payment of *zakāt* is of no account, because he is by no means the very one beneficiary entitled to the *zakāt* and the *zakāt* payer has the right himself to disburse the *zakāt* to the poor person and it is exactly in order to disburse it to a more deserving poor person that he refused to disburse it to him. The Hanifite doctors of 'Irāq, however, claim that if the owner refuses to disburse the *zakāt* to the public collector he becomes responsible for it in case of destruction, because the public collector, unlike the poor, is entitled to demand payment of the *zakāt*.

If only a part of the nisab has been destroyed accidentally, then only its share of the *zakāt* lapses since the rest can still pay *zakāt*. If, for example, out of 130 sheep all but 40 were destroyed, there would still be due a *zakāt* of one sheep on the 40. The rule in this respect is that the part destroyed is applied first to the *'afw* (the surplus over the *niṣāb*) which does not pay *zakāt*, and if it does not cover the *'afw* entirely, the amount of the *zakāt* to be paid is not affected, since the *niṣāb* has been left intact. But if the destroyed part more than covers the *'afw* and runs over into the *niṣāb*, the excess over the *'afw* is applied to the various *niṣābs* successively, beginning with the *niṣāb* next to the *'afw* until the first *niṣāb* is reached. For instance, if 15 out of 40 camels were destroyed, the various *niṣābs* being 5, 10, 15, 20, 25, 36 and 46 camels, and the intervals between those numbers being the respective *'afws*, the 15 camels destroyed are applied successively to the *'afw* of 4 camels (between 40 and the next ***niṣāb*** of 36), then to the ***niṣāb*** of 36 down to 25, just leaving 25 camels, the ***zakāt*** for which would be a ***bint makhāḍ***. If, instead of 15, 20 camels were lost, then there would be due ***zakāt*** on 20 camels, namely, 4 sheep, and so on. This is according to Abu Hanīfah. According to Abu Yūsuf, the destroyed number applies first to the *'afw* and then to all the remaining ***niṣābs*** proportionately, for instance, in the above case, the 15 camels are applied first to the *'afw* of 4, and the remaining 11 are distributed proportionately among the rest, that is, the remaining 25 camels are subject to a ***zakāt*** of 25/36 of a ***bint labūn***, which is the ***zakāt*** of 36 camels.[1] According to Muḥammad Ibn al-Hasan, however, in the above case, the ***zakāt*** due on the remaining 25 camels would be 25/40 of a ***bint labūn***. This difference of view is due to the fact that while according to Abu Hanīfah and Abu Yūsuf the ***zakāt*** attaches to the ***niṣāb*** alone, according to Muḥammad and also to Zufar, it attaches to both the ***niṣāb*** and the *'afw*. Their argument is that ***zakāt*** is due as a thank-offering for the blessing of property and in this respect the *'afw* is like the ***niṣāb***. The former two reply that there is a ***ḥadīth*** to the effect that ***zakāt*** is a charge on the ***niṣāb*** alone. The ***ḥadīth*** in question is: "For every five camels one sheep, and for the surplus (*'afw*) nothing until ten is reached."[2] The ***Minhāj***[3] is at one with Muḥammad.

So far we have been examining the case of accidental destruction. The case of **wilful destruction** (*istihlāk*) is different because, if the property on which a year's ***zakāt***

[1] *Majma'*, p. 167.

[2] *Ibid.*

[3] P. 268; *Wajīz*, p. 89.

fell due is wilfully destroyed, whether literally or legally, *e. g.*, by exchange, its *zakāt* must be paid (*ḍamān*)[1] irrespective of whether the value received in exchange is still in the hands of the owner or whether it has been accidentally destroyed. This is because, unlike the case of accidental destruction where the *zakāt* debt lapses, in wilful destruction there is no ground for such leniency to the owner since he has wilfully destroyed a property in which the poor had a right. Besides literal destruction, these acts also are considered by the law as wilful destruction: Exchange of *sawā'im* animals against *sawā'im* animals of the same or a different genus, or against gold or silver or articles of trade; and exchange of articles of trade against other than articles of trade. The ground for this is that the *zakāt* of *sawā'im* animals attaches to the animals themselves and not to their value and so their exchange amounts to their literal destruction.[2] In general, exchange of wealth (*māl*) on which a year's *zakāt* has fallen due for wealth that is not subject to *zakāt*, such as slaves intended for personal use, or for no consideration whatever, as in the case of a gift, or for other than wealth (*māl*), such as marriage price, is considered wilful destruction.[3] There has been dispute as to whether it is a case of wilful destruction to keep one's *sawā'im* animals from forage and water until they perish.[4]

It is not however a case of wilful destruction to exchange one article of trade for another, even if the articles ex-

[1] *Ḍamān* legally means that if the property destroyed is of the class of fungible (*mithlī*) goods, it is made good in terms of its like, and if it is of the class of non-fungible (*qīmī*) goods, in terms of its value (*qīmah*).

[2] *Fatḥ*, p. 154; *Durr*, p. 136.

[3] *Baḥr*, p. 236.

[4] *'Alamkīriyyah*, p. 254.

changed are of different genera, unless the price received was inordinately low (*muḫābāt*). In this last case the owner pays the *zakāt* for the reduction made. Thus, if one should buy a trade slave with a 1,000 *dirhams* on which a year's *zakāt* had been due, and the slave should subsequently die, no *zakāt* would be due on the 1,000 *dirhams* or the slave, as the buying of the trade slave is not a case of wilful destruction, and the death of the slave is a case of accidental destruction. It would be a different case, however, if one bought a personal slave, instead of a trade slave, or if the trade slave he received in exchange was worth, say, 500 *dirhams* only. In such case, one would have to pay the *zakāt* for the 1,000 *dirhams*, or in the second case, for the 500 *dirhams* of reduction, such reduction being inordinately great and subject to the suspicion that it was intended for a present. In the exchange of articles of trade the rule is that unless a definite intention is adopted the article received in exchange is considered an article of trade if the article given away in exchange was such. Thus, if a person should exchange 1,000 *dirhams* against a slave—because silver and gold are always articles of trade—the slave is considered a trade slave, unless he was actually intended for personal use.[1] Likewise it is not a case of wilful destruction if one should discharge (*ibrā'*) one's debtor from his debt, or should lend an article (*i'ārah*), or give a loan (*iqrāḏ*) and the property be destroyed in the hands of the borrower.[2]

What has been said above applies only in case the destruction has occurred after the lapse of the year, namely, after the *zakāt* fell due. **Destruction before the lapse of the year,** even though wilful, does not entail any liability for the *zakāt* that was yet to fall due on the part destroyed,

[1] *Fatḫ*, p. 154.

[2] *Baḫr*, pp. 235-6.

and the *zakāt* is paid only for the part that will be on hand at the end of the year, provided the other conditions have been met. However, according to the Malikites,[1] if a person wilfully destroys (*ibdāl*) his cattle before the lapse of the year in order to escape paying their *zakāt* he nevertheless pays it if there is presumptive evidence of his intention, *e. g.*, if he destroyed the cattle within a month from the completion of the year.

A second way in which the zakat may lapse after it becomes due is by the death of the property owner without a will directing the settlement of the *zakāt* from the third of his estate. This is the Hanifite doctrine. The view of al-Shāfi'i is that the *zakāt* debt of the deceased person may be collected from the entire estate whether or not he left a will to that effect.[2]

Finally, according to the Malikites,[3] the *zakāt* of cattle as well as of crops, *i. e.*, apparent property, is collected from the whole estate even if the deceased left no will to that effect, but the *zakāt* of non-apparent property is not collected from the estate, because, unless there is evidence to the contrary, the presumption is that the deceased paid it himself. If, however, the deceased acknowledged his debt of *zakāt* during the last year of his life and willed its payment, then it is paid from the entire estate; if, without such acknowledgment, he willed its payment, it is paid after the payment of the three more preferential debts for funeral, *etc.*, from the one-third of the estate as to which according to Mohamedan law a will is valid; finally, if he acknowledged but did not will it, the heirs are advised to pay the *zakāt* but may not be forced to do it.

[1] Kharashi, pp. 57-8.

[2] Kāsāni, p. 53; *Mabsūṭ*, p. 185; *Minhāj*, p. 262.

[3] Kharashi, p. 130; vol. v, pp. 425-6; 'Adawi, vol. v, p. 425.

Al-Shāfi'i's argument is that the Prophet in one of his sayings likened the claim of God to the claim of a fellow-man; and since the latter may be collected from the estate of a deceased person, the *zakāt* debt may also be collected. Moreover, after one's death his personal obligations devolve upon his property and they must be discharged by the heirs from the estate. Al-Sarakhsi, on the other hand, argues that there is a *ḥadīth* to the effect that a person's property, outside of such part of it as has been consumed or disposed of by will by the deceased in a charitable way, becomes the property of his heirs; that in a case of conflict between a claim of God and a claim of a fellow-man, the latter is given precedence; furthermore, that the *wājib* consists in the act of giving, not in the thing given, and therefore cannot be discharged by the heirs; moreover, that the giving of *zakāt* is an act of worship and as such must be accompanied by the intention of the worshiper, which in this case is impossible, since the intention of the heirs cannot replace that of the deceased, unless the deceased willed to that effect; for the heirship of the heir is not based on his consent but is enforced on him by the law.

If the death occurred during the year, the year is dissolved, and a new year must elapse before a *zakāt* is due on the property inherited. According to al-Shāfi'i, the year is not dissolved, and, therefore, the time passed before the death is taken into account by the heirs in determining the completion of the year in the discharge of the *zakāt* dues of the inherited property.

According to al-Kāsāni,[1] **a third cause for the lapse of the zakat debt**, after it becomes due, is apostasy (*riddah*). This is the Hanifite and Malikite[2] view. Al-Shāfi'i holds that apostasy is not a cause of lapse. In other words, if

[1] Kāsāni, p. 53. [2] *Wajiz*, p. 87.

the apostate should return to Islam, according to the Hanifites he is not obliged to pay the *zakāt,* but according to al-Shāfi'i he must pay it. Al-Shāfi'i's argument is that the apostate is able (*qādir*) to perform (*adā'*) the obligation but that because a condition of performance is his being a Moslem he is not held to perform it until after he returns to Islam. He bases this on the analogy of the person who, though unclean, is able to perform the obligation of prayer, but may not do so until after he has purified himself. The Hanifite argument is that Islam effaces what was before it, and that the apostate is not fit (*ahl*) to perform an act of worship or to be subject to an obligation of worship, and hence upon his apostasy the obligation lapses forthwith.

May the owner sell his sawa'im animals after a year's **zakat has fallen due on them?** The Hanifite answer is "Yes". The argument is that the fact that a property is affected with a divine right (*ḥaqq allah*) constitutes no bar to its sale; that an act of sale is valid so long as the seller owns the thing he sold and is able to deliver it to the purchaser, and that both these conditions are fulfilled in the present case; that finally, the *zakāt* due on a property need not be paid out of that very property, since the owner may discharge it otherwise. When therefore the collector presents himself after the sale, analogy requires that he should collect the *zakāt* from the seller and have no lien on the animals, since by sale they have become the property of the purchaser and no *zakāt* is due on them as yet. Moreover, the seller is obliged to pay the *zakāt* because by selling the animals he has destroyed the right of the poor. Although analogy requires the above, this case is judged according to *istiḥsān* which requires as follows: If the collector comes before the two parties to the sale have parted, he has the option either of collecting the *zakāt* from the very animals in question (and in that case the purchaser has action against the seller for the *zakāt's* share of the price) or of collecting the *zakāt* from the seller and letting the buyer keep the animals. However, according to Muhammad Ibn al-Hasan, the question turns on whether or not the animals have been taken away before the collector appeared. If the collector appeared after the animals have been carried away, he does not collect anything from the animals but applies to the seller. If he comes before, he may collect the tax in kind from the animals, for the purchaser begins to be responsible (*ḍāmin*) [1] for (losses affecting) the things bought only after he has carried them away. As regards property subject to tithe, it is immaterial whether or not the parties have parted or carried the thing sold away, because tithe attaches to the produce of the earth independently of its ownership, whereas the *zakāt* attaches to the owner, not the thing owned.[2] According to the Shafiites,[3] the sale is null and void to the amount of the *zakāt*, though valid as regards the balance.

The tribe of Taglib, notwithstanding that they were Christians, were treated in a preferential way in that they were subject, like Moslems, to *zakāt*, though at a double rate. In all other respects their *zakāt* is subject to the same rules as that of the Moslems. Thus their minor children are exempt from the *zakāt* and their women pay the same *zakāt* as their men. There is, however, a report from Abu Hanīfah through Hasan according to which their women are not subject to *zakāt* because the tax paid by the Taglib tribe, although named *zakāt* in deference to their Arab blood, is in reality *jizyah*, and women do not pay *jizyah*.

The doctors all agree in considering the *zakāt* paid by

[1] In other words, while the goods sold continue to be at the seller's risk, they are legally considered to be his property, and consequently the *zakāt* due on them may be collected from them in kind.

[2] *Mabsūt*, p. 173.

[3] *Minhāj*, p. 269.

this tribe as a kind of *jizyah* and in fact it is appropriated like the *jizyah*. One reason for this is that when this tribe was required by the calif Omar to pay the *jizyah* as a tribute, they prevailed on him by invoking their Arab blood and got his consent instead of the *jizyah* to pay the *zakāt* at a double rate. Omar is said to have told them: "This is your *jizyah*, but call it what you will: its meaning is *jizyah* in our regard and we shall place it with the *jizyah*."[1] Another reason is that the tax paid by them is not in reality *zakāt* because the giving of *zakāt* is an act of worship which the Taglib race is not fit to perform. A third reason is that *jizyah* is a fine for infidelity, and this is what happens here. When the Taglib tribesmen become Moslems they cease to pay the double rate. The clients (*mawāli*) of the Taglib tribe, like other infidels, pay the *jizyah* and do not share in the privilege extended to the tribesmen themselves.

According to the *Mabsūṭ*, the compact made with the Taglib tribe may not be broken by any Moslem state. Indeed, the calif 'Ali, at one time when the tribe had lost its power, desired to break the compact, but the Companions, 'Ali being among them, agreed in a council that it is not in the power of any one to break it. According to Muḥammad Ibn al-Hasan the compact derives its main strength from the fact of *ijmā'*. Moreover the Prophet said that whatever the calif Omar did is well done.

The persons who became **converts to Islam** while they were **in the enemy land** (*dār al-ḥarb*) and remained there for years before they came to the Moslem country are not held to the payment of their *zakāt* debt for past years, even if they should have known that as Moslems they were under obligation to pay *zakāt*. The reason for this is that during

[1] *Mabsūṭ*, p. 178; *Majma'*, p. 170.

that time they were not under the protection of the Moslem state. However, as between them and God, such persons are recommended to settle their *zakāt* obligation. If, however, they did not know of the obligation of *zakāt,* they are not under any obligation to settle it, although Zufar holds the contrary view. Indeed Zufar has analogy on his side, since by conversion to Islam one accepts all the obligations of Islam and one's ignorance of these obligations is an excuse only as regards sins, but may not in any way operate to remove an obligation which has been contracted owing to the fact that its cause (*sabab*) was present.

We have, however, judged by *istiḥsān* and said, "The contraction of a *sharī'ah* obligation depends upon the communication of the same. Does he not see that the people of Quba [a suburb of Medina] continued to say their prayers facing Jerusalem after the direction in prayer (*qiblah*) had been changed towards the Ka'bah, and this was allowed to them because they had not been informed of the change. Indeed one is subject to the divine obligations in the degree of possibility only, and there is no possibility of carrying out an obligation before it has been communicated, and so it is as if the divine commandment did not exist so far as he is concerned." [1]

It cannot be said that the fact of the diffusion (*shuyū'*) of a *sharī'ah* prescription may be considered as tantamount to its actual communication, for in the enemy world the law of Islam does not spread.[1]

The **persons who have belonged in the camp of Harijites** for years and have later returned to the fold of Islam likewise are not held to the payment of *zakāt* for past years, even as regards their apparent property. However, as between them and God, they are enjoined to settle an obligation which has fallen upon them.

[1] *Mabsūṭ*, p. 181.

SECTION II

The Zakāt of Sawā'im or Flocks and Herds [1]

According to al-Sarakhsi,[2] the *zakāt* of animals is treated first, because the Prophet in his letters deferred to them first, and cattle were considered by the Arabs, who were cattle raisers, as the most honored property, and because the legal provisions concerning the *zakāt* of cattle are unanimously agreed upon.

Sawa'im, plural of *sā'imah,* literally **means** any animal that is pasturing. Technically, however, the word *sawā'im* does not apply to animals that are pastured in order later to be used for riding (*rukūb*) or carrying loads (*haml*), because such animals never pay *zakāt*. Thus animals used as beasts of burden are not considered *sawā'im* even if they are actually pastured every eight out of twelve months; neither does *sawā'im* apply to animals pastured in order to be later sold for profit (*tijārah*), because such animals pay *zakāt* as articles of trade but not as *sawā'im* animals, the rules concerning the two being very different. The term *sawā'im* then applies to animals pastured for some other purpose, for instance, for their milk (*darr*) and offspring (*nasl*) or in order that they may grow fatter. Al-Kāsāni, however, does not consider animals pastured for flesh (*lahm*) to be *sawā'im*, on the ground that they do not bear any offspring which is the very quality in virtue of which *sawā'im* animals are considered to be "productive". The *Jāmi'* in this connection remarks that as productivity is a concealed (*khafi*) matter the *sharī'ah* substitutes the fact of pasture

[1] *Majma'*, p. 161; *Hidāyah*, p. 126; *'Alamkīriyyah*, p. 248; *Mabsūṭ*, p. 150; *Minhāj*, p. 228; *Mudawwanah*, p. 66; *Zarqāni*, p. 54; *Muwaṭṭa'*, p. 109.

[2] *Mabsūṭ*, p. 150.

in its stead and whenever the latter is present considers the former to be also present.[1]

Only animals pastured for at least more than half of the year are considered *sawā'im*. They need not be pastured through the entire year, for cattle owners cannot avoid feeding their cattle on provender (*'alaf*) during the days of snow and cold. If, therefore, an animal is fed on provender during half or more of the year it is not a *sawā'im* animal and is exempt from *zakāt* unless it is subject to it as an article of trade. If an animal intended for trade is pastured for six or more months during a year it does not become *sawā'im* unless it was also intended to be made *sawā'im*. On the other hand, if the owner of *sawā'im* animals intends to use them at work or feed them on provender, they do not cease to be *sawā'im* until he actually carries out his intention. If, therefore, the year should pass by before he did so the animals pay *zakāt* as *sawā'im*. If a person buys animals for trade and afterwards turns them into *sawā'im*, the year is considered to run from the time they became *sawā'im*.[2]

Al-Shāfi'i [3] says that an animal is *sawā'im* if it subsists on pasture and does not involve for the owner expense for provender. According to him, beasts carrying water (*nawāḏiḥ*) or oxen used for ploughing or camels used for transportation purposes are not *sawā'im* and do not pay *zakāt*, even if they are kept idle and pastured for the greater part of the year, because *sawā'im* are the animals pastured all their lifetime (*dahrahu*). Likewise, beasts of burden (*'awāmil*), even if they are sometimes pastured and some-

[1] *Baḥr*, *Minḥah*, p. 229; Kāsāni, p. 30; *Jāmi'*, pp. 299, 307; *Mabsūṭ*, p. 165; *'Alamkīriyyah*, p. 248; *Hidāyah*, p. 147; *Majma'*, p. 161.

[2] For the relation of intention to act, *cf. infra*, pp. 271, 272.

[3] *Umm*, p. 20; Muzani, p. 217.

times used as work animals, or sheep sometimes fed on provender and sometimes pastured, are not *sawā'im* and "I would not take anything from their owners, although if the animals were mine, I would pay their *ṣadaqah,* if God will, and I should prefer that the person who owns them should do so."

Both the Hanifites and the Shafiites are agreed that **animals are subject to the zakat** of animals **only when they are sawa'im,** although they differed in their definition of the word *sawā'im*. Mālik and al-Layth, on the other hand, held that animals are subject to *zakāt* even if they are used for work, whether or not they are *sawā'im*. According to some Malikites, Mālik requires animals to be *sawā'im* as a condition to paying *zakāt* only in the case of sheep. Mālik's argument is that whether or not the animals are actually pastured they are by quality pasture animals and the fact of their prevention from being so does not take them out of the denomination *sawā'im.*[1] Al-Sarakhsi, however, replies that the Prophet explicitly said: "For five of *sawā'im* camels, . . ." which means that there is no *zakāt* on animals that are not *sawā'im*. Moreover, according to a *ḥadīth* reported by Ibn 'Abbās, the Prophet said: "There is no *ṣadaqah* on the animals used for work (*'awāmil*) and as beasts of burden (*ḥawāmil*)." Furthermore, only that property is subject to *zakāt* which is sought for its physical produce, not its use. Is it not true in fact that dwelling-houses and personal slaves do not pay *zakāt,* and that animals used at work are sought for their use and not for their physical produce? Again, if the animal is fed on forage there is no *zakāt* on it because the expense is great for the owner, and the reason why *sawā'im* animals are subject to *zakāt* is that their maintenance is so inex-

[1] Zarqāni, vol. ii, p. 56; *cf.* Ibn Rushd, *M.*, p. 244; Ibn Rushd, *B.*, p. 231, l. —8; *Muwaṭṭā',* p. 110, l. 6; *Mudawwanah*, p. 73, l. 14.

pensive. Therefore no *zakāt* is due when there is great expense because evidence in the sources shows that the smallness of the expense is an "effective cause" (*athar*) of the obligation of *zakāt*. Thus the Prophet said: "In what has been watered by heaven the tenth, and in what has been watered by buckets or water wheels half of one-tenth."[1] On the other side, al-Shāfi'i, in justifying his view against the Malikites, says: "There were water-carrying animals in the time of the Prophet and his successors and I have not heard any one relate that the Prophet collected from them *ṣadaqah*, or that any one of his successors did so."[2]

The blind, the emaciated, the young, the sick, the lame, **etc.,** are **treated like the sound** ones **in reckoning the nisab** of the *sawā'im* animals, though they are not accepted in payment of *zakāt*. There is a *ḥadīth* to this effect from Omar. People had complained to him to the effect that the collectors counted the weaklings in reckoning the *niṣāb*, but refused to accept the same in payment of *zakāt*. Omar answered that the collector was to count them in reckoning the *niṣāb* but was not to receive them in payment, just as he was not to take as *zakāt* the *sawā'im* that were nursing their young (*rubba*), those fattened for their flesh (*akīlah*), the pregnant, and the rams of the sheep (*faḥl al-ganam*), in order to strike a happy medium. Al-Sarakhsi observes that the last-mentioned animals are the most prized ones among cattle dealers and that they are not taken as *zakāt* in obedience to the *ḥadīth*: "Beware of (taking) the best part of people's property". In other words, just as the interest of the property owner is protected by not taking the choice animals, so is the interest

[1] *Mabsūṭ*, p. 165.

[2] *Umm*, p. 20.

of the poor considered by not taking the young and the sickly, although they are all counted in reckoning up the *niṣāb*.[1]

According to al-Zāhidi, only domestic animals are included in reckoning the *niṣāb*, **the wild and the cross** between the two being **disregarded.** This view is approved of in the *Majma'*. However, as it is stated in the *Muḥīṭ*, the status of a cross depends on that of the mother and if the mother was domestic the offspring is considered domestic. This is also the view taken by the author of the *Durr*.[2] According to al-Shāfi'i, the cross between domestic and wild do not pay *zakāt* because, while one side requires the payment of tax the other exempts from it, and it is a principle of law that in cases of conflict one must construe in favor of exemption. The Hanifite reply is that the cross normally is like its mother and follows its status so much so that the owner of the mother owns its offspring also. This is because the sperm of the father legally becomes destroyed (*mustahlak*) by that of the mother and so the offspring comes from her.[3] According to the Malikites,[4] the cross are exempt from *zakāt* in both cases.

While an animal must answer the description of *sawā'im* in order to pay the *zakāt* of *sawā'im* animals, every *sawā'im* animal is not subject to it, since it is only the *sawā'im* animals specified in the *sunnah* which pay the *zakāt* of *sawā'im* animals. These animals are treated in the lawbooks under the following heads.

The Zakat of Camels (*ibl*). The lowest *niṣāb* in camels being 5 camels, no *zakāt* is due on fewer than 5. The *zakāt* on 5 camels up to 9 is one goat (*shāt*) of medium

[1] *Mabsūṭ*, p. 172; *Muwaṭṭā'*, p. 113; *cf.* *Minhāj*, pp. 234-5.

[2] P. 135.

[3] *Mabsūṭ*, p. 183.

[4] Kharashi, p. 52.

size. All the *ḥadīths* bearing on this point are at one, and so the doctors have been unanimous on it.[1] The proportion of 1 goat on 5 camels is based on their valuations in accordance with the rate prescribed in the *ḥadīth*: "Give one-fourth of one-tenth of your property", for in those days the goat sold at 5 *dirhams* and the *bint makhāḍ* (a camel) at 40 *dirhams*. Consequently, 1 goat for 5 camels would be in the proportion of 5 for 200 *dirhams*. The Arabian and the cross between the Arabian and the foreign camels are alike with respect to *zakāt*. The rates for more than 9 camels are as follows:

For 10 camels and more up to 14 inclusive, 2 goats.

For 15 camels and more up to 19 inclusive, 3 goats.

For 20 camels and more up to 24 inclusive, 4 goats.

For 25 camels and more up to 35 inclusive, 1 *bint makhāḍ*, *i. e.*, a female camel colt in her second year.

For 36 camels and more up to 45 inclusive, 1 *bint labūn*, *i. e.*, a female camel colt in her third year.

For 46 camels and more up to 60 inclusive, 1 *ḥiqqah*, *i. e.*, a female camel colt in her fourth year.

For 61 camels and more up to 75 inclusive, 1 *jadha'ah*, *i. e.*, a female camel in her fifth year.

For 76 camels and more up to 90 inclusive, 2 *bint labūns*.

For 91 camels and more up to 120 inclusive, 2 *ḥiqqahs*.

From 120 up to 144 the process is started over again according to the Hanifites, namely, one goat for every 5 camels after the 120th camel, plus the 2 *ḥiqqahs* for the 120. Thus for 125 up to 129, 2 *ḥiqqahs* and 1 goat, and so on up to 144. And for 145 up to 149, 2 *ḥiqqahs* and 1 *bint makhāḍ*, and for 150, 3 *ḥiqqahs*.

After 150, the process of calculation is again repeated from the beginning as follows:

[1] *Mabsūṭ*, p. 150.

From 150 up to 174, 3 *ḥiqqahs* plus 1 goat for every 5 camels after the 150th.

From 175 up to 185, 3 *ḥiqqahs* plus 1 ***bint makhāḍ***.

From 186 up to 195, 3 *ḥiqqahs* plus 1 ***bint labūn***.

From 196 up to 200, 4 *ḥiqqahs* or, if the owner pleases, 5 ***bint labūns***.

The same applies on every 50 camels after the 150th, namely, for 205 up to 209, 1 goat together with the 4 *ḥiqqahs* or 5 ***bint labūns***, *etc.*[1]

The above is according to the Hanifites. Al-Shāfi'i held that as soon as 120 is reached, the *zakāt* is computed at the rate of 1 *ḥiqqah* for every 50, and 1 ***bint labūn*** for every 40, the fractions being neglected. Thus from 121 to 129 the *zakāt* would be 3 ***bint labūns***, and for 130 camels, 1 *ḥiqqah* and 2 ***bint labūns*** up to 139, and for 140, 2 *ḥiqqahs* and 1 ***bint labūn***, and so on accordingly. Mālik, on the other hand, claimed that as soon as 120 is exceeded by at least 10, the *zakāt* is computed at the rate of 1 ***bint labūn*** for every 40 and 1 *ḥiqqah* for every 50, the intervals being omitted. Thus, according to him, after 120, nothing is due for the excess until 130 is reached, the *zakāt* on 130 being 1 *ḥiqqah* and 2 ***bint labūns***. The ground for the Shafiite and Malikite views as against that of the Hanifites is a letter of the Prophet on the *ṣadaqah* related by Ibn Omar, where it was written: "When the number of the camels exceeds 120, then for every 40 a ***bint labūn***, and for every 50 a *ḥiqqah*". Mālik, however, construed the excess over 120 referred to in the *ḥadīth* to mean such a number only as would just bring the total number of camels under one or the other or both of the two rates, that is, just result in the total number of camels being a multiple of 40 or 50 or both. Mālik consequently considered free from *zakāt* any excess

[1] *Majma'*, p. 162.

which fell short of such a number, that is, an excess of from 1 to 9, in other words the interval from 120 to 129. Al-Shāfi'i, on his side, construed the excess to mean any number after 120. The ground for the Hanifite view, on the other hand, is among others the following *hadīth* of Qays: "I said to Abu Bakr Ibn Muhammad Ibn 'Amr Ibn Hazm: 'Show me the letter on the *sadaqah* which the Prophet wrote to 'Amr Ibn Hazm', and he showed a letter written on a leaf (*waraqah*) reading: 'When the camels exceed 120, the rates are started over again, and for what is below 25 the *zakāt* is in sheep, one sheep for every 5 camels.'"[1] Moreover there are reports of the *mash-hūr* type from 'Ali and Ibn 'Abbās to the effect that after 120 the process is repeated. Therefore as regards the excess after 120, the process is repeated according to the *hadīth* of 'Amr Ibn Hazm and the *hadīth* of Ibn Omar invoked by the others is applied to the greater excess which brings the number up to 200. As between the unit of fifties (*khamsīnāt*), including the sub-units of one sheep for every five camels, *etc.*, provided for in the *hadīth* of 'Amr Ibn Hazm and the units of forties and fifties suggested in the *hadīth* of Ibn Omar, the former has been chosen because it is an essential principle in *zakāt* that in dealing with large numbers the *nisāb* should be one and definite.

From the fact that the names *bint makhād, bint labūn, etc.*, mentioned in the *hadīths* are names of female animals, it has been inferred that only females can lawfully be accepted for the *zakāt* of camels and that males are only taken at their market value.[2]

The Zakat of Oxen or Bulls and Cows (*baqr*).[3] *Baqr* is

[1] *Mabsūt*, p. 152; *cf. Fath*, p. 131.

[2] *Majma'*, p. 162.

[3] *Majma'*, p. 163; *Hidāyah*, p. 133; *Minhāj*, pp. 232-3; Māwardi, p. 198; Kharashi, p. 55.

a generic term meaning the whole bovine genus, both male and female. Buffaloes (*jāmūs*) are considered a species of *baqr*. The fact that a person who swore not to eat *baqr* flesh, upon eating buffalo flesh does not become a perjurer must not lead one to think that buffaloes are a different genus. It is simply owing to the fact that buffaloes, being rare, do not occur to the mind. If, therefore, they were not rare it would be a case of perjury. In the case of *baqr* the male as well as the female are accepted in payment of the *zakāt* because, unlike the case of camels, where the females are prized more, in *baqr* as well as in sheep, there is no premium on females.

[1] No *zakāt* is due upon fewer than 30 heads of *baqr* and upon 30 and more up to 39, the *zakāt* is 1 *tabīʿ* or 1 *tabīʿah*, *i. e.*, 1 male or female calf in the second year, and according to Khalīl, in the third year. And upon 40, 1 *musinn* or 1 *musinnah*, *i. e.*, a male or female calf in the third year, and, according to Khalīl, in the fourth year. This is based on a *ḥadīth* according to which the Prophet ordered Muʿadh to collect the *zakāt* of the *baqr* in the way mentioned. However, this *ḥadīth* does not mention how many heads of *baqr* are free from the tax after 40 is reached. Therefore there is dispute on this point. According to Abu Yūsuf and Muḥammad Ibn al-Hasan, and also a report from Abu Hanīfah, there is no *zakāt* on the excess until 60 is reached. The Shafiite and Malikite views are to the same effect. According to another report from Abu Hanīfah, through Hasan, after 40 up to 49 there is no *zakāt*, and for 50, 1 *musinn* and 1/4 of a *musinn* or 1/3 of a *tabīʿ*. However, according to a third report from Abu Hanīfah, cited in a *Zāhir-al-riwāyah* source (*riwāyat al-aṣl*),[2] the excess over 40 until 59 pays *zakāt* proportionally, *i. e.*, 2½ per cent of a *musinn*

[1] *Mabsūt*, p. 186. [2] *Cf.* Ibn ʿAbidīn, p. 16.

per head. Thus 41 heads of *baqr* would pay a *zakāt* of 1 *musinn* plus 2½ per cent of a *musinn*. The ground for this view is that the exemption of the *'afw* from *zakāt* is based on a provision (*naṣṣ*) which is contrary to analogy and exceptional and therefore limited to the case concerning which it was made. Consequently in this case the decision is rendered according to analogy and so the excess over 40 up to 59 pays *zakāt* at a proportionate rate. The two disciples, on the other hand, based their view on the *ḥadīth* according to which the Prophet ordered Mu'ādh not to collect any *zakāt* from the intervals (*awqāṣ*) between *niṣābs*, and so they have interpreted the interval between 40 and 60 as the one referred to in the *ḥadīth*. Some interpreted the word *awqāṣ* to mean the young.

For 60 up to 69 the *zakāt* is 2 *tabī's* or *tabī'ahs*.

For 70 up to 79 the *zakāt* is 1 *musinn* or *musinnah* and 1 *tabī'* or *tabī'ah*.

For 80 up to 89 the *zakāt* is 2 *musinns* or *musinnahs*.

For 90 up to 99 the *zakāt* is 3 *tabī's* or *tabī'ahs*.

For 100 up to 109 the *zakāt* is 1 *musinn* or *musinnah* and 2 *tabī's* or *tabī'ahs*.

For 110 up to 119 the *zakāt* is 2 *musinns* or *musinnahs* and 1 *tabī'* or *tabī'ah*

For 120 up to 129 the *zakāt* is 3 *musinns* or *musinnahs* or 4 *tabī's* or *tabī'ahs*.

And so on, after 60, at the rate of 1 *tabī'* or *tabī'ah* for every 30 and 1 *musinn* or *musinnah* for every 40 heads of *baqr*, in the intervals between successive multiples of 30 or 40 or both, for every additional 10 heads a *musinn* or *musinnah* being substituted for the *tabī'* or *tabī'ah*.

The Zakat of Sheep and Goats (*ganam*).[1] *Ganam* in-

[1] *Majma'*, p. 163; *Mabsūṭ*, p. 182; *Hidāyah*, p. 135; *Minhāj*, p. 233; Māwardi, p. 199; Kharashi, p. 56.

cludes sheep (*ḏā'n*) and goats (*ma'az*) of both sexes. The ground for the *zakāt* of *ganam* is the *ḥadīth*: "There is no owner of *ganam* who did not give its *zakāt* but that he will be knocked down for it on a level ground the Day of Judgment and the *ganam* will trample over him with his hoofs and will strike him with his horns," and "Let me not find any one of you come on the Day of Judgment with a sheep (*shāt*) on his shoulder that is bleating and say: 'Oh Mohammed, Oh Mohammed!' for I will say to him: 'I will not let you have from God any thing. Did you not hear it when we told you about it?'"[1]

According to the Hanifites, as well as the Shafiites and the Malikites, there is no *zakāt* on fewer than 40 heads of *ganam*. And upon 40 and more up to 120 heads, the *zakāt* is 1 *shāt*.[2]

Upon 121 and more up to 200, the *zakāt* is 2 *shāts*.
Upon 201 and more up to 399 the *zakāt* is 3 *shāts*.
Upon 400 and more up to 499 the *zakāt* is 4 *shāts*.
Upon 500 and more up to 599 the *zakāt* is 5 *shāts*.

And so on, at the rate of one *shāt* for every additional 100 heads after 500, fractions being neglected. The above rates are based on letters concerning the *ṣadaqah* rates written by the Prophet and the calif Abu Bakr, and there is *ijmā'* on these rates.[3]

In reckoning up the *niṣāb* of *ganam*, the sheep and goats are counted alike, but in the payment of their *zakāt* there is some difference between the two. The youngest ganam which are subject to *zakāt* and are accepted as lawful payment for it are the *thanis*, *i. e.*, one year old *ganams*, not

[1] *Mabsūt*, p. 182.

[2] *Shāt* is a generic term applying to sheep as well as to goats, although in common usage it means sheep.

[3] *Hidāyah*, p. 135.

the *jadha's, i. e.*, young *ganam* under one year and above six months old. This is the *Zāhir-al-riwāyah* view. However there is a report from Abu Hanīfah through al-Hasan to the effect that, although only the *thanis* of goats are accepted in payment of *zakāt*, in the case of sheep both the *thanis* and the *jadha's* are accepted. This is the *gayr Zāhir-al-riwāyah* view. This is also the view of Abu Yūsuf and Muḥammad Ibn al-Hasan. The ground for this view is the *ḥadīth*: "We have a right on the *jadha'* and the *thani*." Moreover the *jadha's* of the sheep are lawful for sacrifice, and hence for *zakāt* also. The ground for the first view is a *ḥadīth* of the calif 'Ali, to wit: "In *zakāt* only the *thanis* and what is older is taken". Furthermore the lawfulness of the *jadha'* in sacrifice is not to the point, because there it is based on a special prescription (*naṣṣ*) which is against analogy and therefore cannot be extended to the case of *zakāt*. Besides, the *jadha'* mentioned in the *ḥadīth* in regard to sacrifice refers to the *jadha'* of camels. The author of the *Fatḥ*[1] observes that although the first view is *Zāhir-al-riwāyah*, the second view which allows the acceptance of the *jadha'* is to be preferred. According to the *Durr*,[2] the *jadha'* may be accepted at its appraised value.

According to the prevalent Shafiite view,[3] the *zakāt* of *ganam* is paid in terms of one-year-old sheep (*jadha'ah*) or two-year-old goats (*thaniyyah*). On the other hand, according to the Malikites,[4] it is paid in terms of one-year-old sheep or goats.

According to the **Hanifites,** as well as the Malikites, in *ganam* **both sexes** are **acceptable for payment** as *zakāt*, but

[1] P. 136.

[2] P. 136.

[3] *Minhāj*, pp. 229, 233; *Wajīz*, p. 80.

[4] Kharashi, p. 56.

in al-Shāfi'i's opinion, males are lawful payment only when the entire *niṣāb* consists of males, because males alone cannot procreate but are acceptable in the latter case because the *zakāt* must be a part of the *niṣāb*. The Hanifite argument is that the word *shāt* occurring in the *ḥadīth* applies to both sexes.[1]

When the sheep and goats are mixed together, it is unanimously agreed that they are to be counted indiscriminately in reckoning the *niṣāb*. This is also true when buffaloes and *baqr* are mixed together. According to the Hanifites, the *zakāt* is taken from animals of average value when the two species are mixed. There are two views on this point by al-Shāfi'i. One view is that the *zakāt* is taken from the size that predominates because importance always attaches to the predominant. The other view is that one of large size and one of small size are appraised and their average is computed; then an animal of that value is taken as *zakāt*, both sides being thus considered.[2]

The Zakat of Horses (*khayl*).[3] Horses, **when males and females are together,** pay *zakāt*, according to Abu Hanīfah, if they are *sawā'im*. The owner has the option of paying a *dīnār* for each horse without regard to the requirement of *niṣāb*, or of appraising them and, if their value amounts to a *niṣāb*, of paying at the rate of 5 *dirhams* for every 200 *dirhams*. This view has been preferred by the authors of the *Majma'*, *Hidāyah*, *Mabsūṭ*, *Badā'i'* and by al-Qudūri. However, according to Abu Yūsuf, and Muḥammad Ibn al-Hasan, as well as al-Shāfi'i, there is no *zakāt* on horses. In the *fatwa* collection of Qāḏīkhān the opinion of the latter has been recommended. It must be remarked here that

[1] *Mabsūṭ*, p. 183; *cf. Minhāj*, p. 234.

[2] *Ibid.*

[3] *Majma'*, p. 164; *Mabsūṭ*, p. 188; *Fatḥ*, p. 137.

although Abu Hanīfah favors ***zakāt*** on horses, he leaves the payment to the voluntary choice of the owner, the state having no right to collect it by force. According to the *Mabsūṭ*, the ground for this is the fact that horses are objects of great desire and instruments of warfare and that therefore greedy persons would wrest them from their owners if they knew of their existence.

If there are only male horses they are, by unanimous opinion, exempt from tax, although a report from Abu Hanīfah points to the contrary. **If,** however, **they are all female,** there are two views on the matter from Abu Hanīfah; according to one, they pay *zakāt*, but according to the other they do not.

It is stated in the *Majma'* that Abu Hanīfah's view to the effect that horses are subject to *zakāt* applies only in case the horses have been pastured for their offspring (*nasl*), for if they were pastured for riding or transportation or the conduct of holy war, they are exempt from the tax, and if they are pastured for trade, they pay the *zakāt* of trade, not that of *sawā'im* animals. This last point is agreed to also by al-Shāfi'i.[1] The ground for the view of the disciples and al-Shāfi'i are the *ḥadīths*: " There is no *ṣadaqah* on the Moslem for his slave and his horse (*faras*) ", and, " I have pardoned my community (*ummah*) from the *ṣadaqah* of the horse and the slave ". Moreover, there is *ijmā'* to the effect that the *imām* cannot collect the *zakāt* of horses by force. Then, too, according to Abu Hanīfah himself the *zakāt* of horses is in terms of value and not in kind, but it is a well-known principle that the *zakāt* of *sawā'im* animals is in kind. Al-Shāfi'i further adds that the Prophet never collected *zakāt* from horses. Abu Hanīfah's argument, on the other hand, is that according to Ibn al-Zubayr, quoting

[1] *Umm*, p. 22.

Jābir, the Prophet said: "For every *sawā'im* horse (*faras*) [1] 1 *dīnār* or 10 *dirhams*, and there is nothing on horses stationed in forts (*murābaṭah*) ". Furthermore, the calif Omar wrote to Abu 'Ubaydah ordering him to collect *zakāt* from the *sawā'im* horses at the rate mentioned. Again, in the time of Marwān a council of the Companions was held on this matter and in it Abu Hurayrah said: " There is no *ṣadaqah* on a man for his horses and slaves ". Marwān then said to Zayd Ibn Thābit: " What do you say, oh, Father of Sa'īd? " and Abu Hurayrah, wondering at Marwān, said: " I am relating a *ḥadīth* of the Prophet, and he says: ' What do you say, oh father of Sa'īd?' " Zayd, thereupon, observed that Abu Hurayrah was telling the truth but that the Prophet only meant the horses of the warriors, and that horses kept for their offspring were subject to *zakāt* at the rate above mentioned. Al-Sarakhsi says that the reason why the *ḥadīths* concerning horses are not widespread is because horses in those days were very much honored and used in war only; and that the *zakāt* is collected in value because the poor cannot use it as such since according to Abu Hanīfah the flesh of horse is not lawful for eating.

As regards the two views of Abu Hanīfah concerning mares when they are alone, the ground for one is that the productivity of horses consists in their offspring and is therefore absent when the mares are alone. The ground for the other view is that mares may produce offspring by the use of a borrowed stallion (*faḥl*). Finally, the ground for Abu Hanīfah's view that male horses when they are alone do not pay *zakāt* is the fact that male horses by themselves cannot produce offspring, and their value does not increase with age as is the case in other animals, neither is their

[1] *Faras* is a generic term applying to male and female as well as to Arabian and foreign horses.

growth in flesh of any account since their flesh may not be eaten.

As regards the option of the owner between the two rates, it is based on a *hadīth* from the Prophet as well as the practices of Omar and Zayd Ibn Thābit. Some said that this applies only to the Arab horses because they all have about the same value, that consequently in other horses the *zakāt* is paid at the rate of five for two hundred on the basis of their appraised value. However, the author of the *Majma'* observes that if this applies to the Arab horses which are higher in price it ought to apply *a fortiori* to non-Arab horses. Still others say, that it applies only to horses having the same value, and that horses varying in value pay the *zakāt* on the basis of their appraised value.

Mules (*bigāl*) **and asses** (*hamīr*) do not pay the *zakāt* of *sawā'im* animals even if they are *sawā'im,* but they pay like other things the *zakāt* of trade if they are intended for trade. The ground for this is the fact that asses and mules in spite of their large numbers are not pastured in most of the cities, and, in law, importance attaches only to the predominant and the general. "Therefore there is no *zakāt* on them but God, may he be praised and exalted! knows better the right." [1]

According to the *Majma',* there is a *hadīth* to the effect that asses do not pay *zakāt,* and that if asses do not pay mules also must not pay, since they are the offspring of asses.

The Zakat of the Young.[2] There is no *zakāt* on the young of camels (*fasīl,* plural *fuslān*) and the young of sheep and goats (*hamal,* plural *hūmlān*) [3] and of cows (*'ijjawl,* plural *'ajājīl*) which are under one year of age.

[1] *Mabsūt,* p. 189.
[2] *Majma',* p. 165.
[3] *Durr,* p. 136, l. —12.

That is to say, if a man were to purchase twenty-five camel colts or forty kids or thirty calves, all under one year old, or if the same were given to him as a gift and one complete year passed from the time of acquisition, still no *zakāt* would be due on them until a year passed from the day they became one year old.[1] This is according to Muḥammad Ibn al-Hasan and the last opinion of Abu Hanīfah. In this connection Abu Yūsuf is quoted as saying:

> I went to see Abu Hanīfah and said to him: "What do you say concerning a person who owns forty lambs (*ḥamal*)?" He said: "One grown sheep (*shāt*) is due on them." Then I said: "Perhaps the value of that one sheep will equal that of most of the lambs or of all of them." He reflected for a while and said: "No, one of the lambs is taken." I said: "Are then lambs taken as *zakāt*?" He thought a while and said: "No, in that case nothing is due on them."

Some of the doctors dismissed this story as too childish to be true of Abu Hanīfah. Others, however, objected to a similar construction claiming that the report was too widespread (of the *mashhūr* type) to be set aside and that under the circumstances the right thing to do was to explain the matter as best they could. And so they said that Abu Hanīfah was merely trying to see if Abu Yūsuf, his disciple, had learned the art of discussion and when he saw that he had, he expressed the view he really believed in. Zufar's and Mālik's views are at one with the first view of Abu Hanīfah, but the views of Abu Yūsuf and al-Shāfi'i agree with his second view, namely, that the young pay *zakāt*, but that it is one of the young that is taken as such.[2]

[1] *Fatḥ*, pp. 139-140.

[2] *Cf.* Māwardi, p. 199; *Wajīz*, p. 82; *Minhāj*, p. 235; *Muwaṭṭa'*, pp. 113-4; Kharashi, pp. 52, 56.

Some remark that the foregoing difference in reality turns on the question as to when the year begins to run, not whether or not lambs pay *zakāt,* since by the end of the year when *zakāt* is due they cease to be "lambs". Others, however, observe that the difference turns on the question of the continuation of the year, namely, if the sheep should bear young during the year and perish before its completion, whether or not their year continues with respect to their young. If, however, among the young there are grown-ups, be it only one, then both young and old are counted in reckoning up the *niṣāb,* although the young are not accepted for *zakāt,* and if the *niṣāb* is complete the *zakāt* is due. Thus, if there are 39 lambs and one grown-up sheep, the sheep is taken as *zakāt* after the lapse of a year. But if the sheep dies after the completion of the year, then according to Abu Hanīfah and Muḥammad, the rest are exempt from *zakāt* since it became due by virtue of the sheep, but according to Abu Yūsuf there is due on them a *zakāt* of 39/40 of a lamb.[1]

SECTION III

The Zakāt of Gold and Silver and the Articles of Trade[2]

Some texts treat this section under the general caption of "*zakāt* of commercial capital" (*zakāt al-māl*) as distinguished from "*zakāt* of *sawā'im*".[3] Other texts treat it under several captions, such as "*zakāt* of gold and silver", or "*zakāt* of gold" and "*zakāt* of silver", and "*zakāt* of articles of trade".[4] However, they all agree that the

[1] *Fath,* p. 141.

[2] *Majma',* p. 168; *Mabsūt,* p. 189; *Hidāyah,* p. 158; *Umm,* p. 33; Māwardi, p. 206; Kharashi, p. 81; Dardīr, p. 118.

[3] *Cf. Durar,* pp. 115, 118; *Durr,* p. 138; *Hidāyah,* p. 158; *Mabsūt,* p. 189.

[4] Qudūri, p. 22; *Umm,* pp. 33, 34, 39, *etc.*

zakāt of *sawā'im* animals is a tax on the animals by reason of their physical identity (*'ayn*), while, on the contrary, the **zakat of the articles of trade**, and, according to the Hanifites only, also of gold and silver, is **due by reason of** their **commercial value** (*qīmah*). Consequently in the articles of trade the meaning of productivity is considered with reference to their value just as in the *sawā'im* it is considered with reference to the animals as such (*'ayn*).[1] Notwithstanding that the *zakāt* is by reason of the value, not the physical identity (*'ayn*), according to the Hanifites, the *zakāt* of a given article nevertheless attaches to its physical identity. With respect to the articles of trade al-Shāfi'i remarks that the *zakāt* attaches to their value because it became due by reason of it.[2] The Hanifites answer that although the *zakāt* obligation attaches to one's trade property by reason of its commercial value (*ṣifat al-māliyyah*), inasmuch as a given piece of property has a physical identity of its own, the *zakāt* which fell due on that piece of property attaches to its physical identity.[3]

According to the Hanifites, the *zakāt* of trade is given preference in case of **conflict between the zakat of trade and the zakat of sawa'im.** Thus if a person has *sawā'im* camels which he bought for trade, the camels pay the *zakāt* of trade only. Al-Shāfi'i[4] agrees that the same property pays one *zakāt* only but he holds that in such case it is the *zakāt* of *sawā'im* that must be paid, unless the *niṣāb* of camels, considered as *sawā'im*, is not complete, for in that case they pay *zakāt* as articles of trade if their value amounts to a *niṣāb*. The argument of al-Shāfi'i is that the *zakāt* of

[1] *Mabsūṭ*, p. 190.

[2] *Umm*, p. 33.

[3] *Mabsūṭ*, p. 191, l. —10.

[4] *Cf. Umm*, p. 41, l. 20; *Minhāj*, p. 253; *Wajīz*, p. 95.

sawā'im is a stronger obligation because the entire community has agreed that it is a *wājib* and because it is based on clear, revealed statements (*naṣṣ ẓāhir*). Since the weak may not conflict with the strong, when a property is subject to *zakāt* both as *sawā'im* and as an article of trade, it pays *zakāt* as *sawā'im* only. Moreover in the preference of the *zakāt* of *sawā'im* there is advantage for the poor, because the *zakāt* of *sawā'im* is collected by the collector whereas the *zakāt* of trade property is paid by the owners themselves "and often they do not pay it". The Hanifite argument, on the other hand, is that as soon as animals are intended for trade, the purpose of pasture and the cause (*sabab*) of the *zakāt* of *sawā'im* cease to exist. For the productivity of the *sawā'im* is physical and necessitates that the animals be permanently retained in one's ownership, but the intention of trade militates against this, and so the animals in reality cease to be *sawā'im*. On the contrary, they become trade property both in appearance (*ṣūrah*) and in reality (*ma'na*) and therefore the *zakāt* of trade is given preference. However, the right to collect this *zakāt* of animals still belongs to the state collector, irrespective of whether they are subject to the *zakāt* of *sawā'im* or of trade because they are always apparent property and stand in need of the *imām's* protection.[1] The Malikite[2] view on this point is like the Shafiite, for according to the Malikites the *zakāt* of trade applies to such articles only as are not subject to *zakāt* by reason of their physical identity.

The classes of goods subject to the *zakāt* of wealth are:

(1) Gold (*dhahab*), whether bullion or wrought.

(2) Silver (*fiḍḍah*), whether bullion or wrought.

(3) Articles of trade (*'urūḍ al-tijārah*).

[1] *Mabsūṭ*, p. 170.

[2] Kharashi, p. 99; 'Adawi, p. 99; Dardir, p. 121.

Gold and Silver. The *niṣāb* of gold is 20 *mithqāls*[1] and the *niṣāb* of silver is 200 *dirhams*. The rate of *zakāt* both in gold and silver is one-fourth of one-tenth of the *niṣāb*, *i. e.*, one-half *mithqāl* in 20 *mithqāls* of gold and 5 *dirhams* in 200 *dirhams* of silver.

There is no *zakāt* for less than 20 *mithqāls* of gold and 200 *dirhams* of silver because of the *ḥadīths*: " There is no *zakāt* on gold until its value amounts to 200 *dirhams*," and " There is no *zakāt* on silver until it reaches 200 *dirhams* and when it reaches 200 *dirhams* the *zakāt* on it is 5 *dirhams*."

[1] A *mithqāl* literally means any measure of weight. In general usage it denotes the weight of a piece of gold weighing 20 *qīrāṭs*. A *qīrāṭ* is the weight of 5 medium-sized grains of barley whose husk has not been removed but whose projecting ends have been cut off. The *mithqāl* is then 100 grains. This is according to the later canonists and to the weight system of Hijāz and most of the cities. According to the earlier writers and to the weight system of Samarqand, a *mithqāl* is 6 *dāniqs*, a *dāniq* 4 *ṭassūjs*, a *ṭassūj* 2 *ḥabbahs*, and a *ḥabbah* 2 grains; in other words, a *mithqāl* is 96 grains, or 19 *qīrāṭs* and 1 grain, instead of the 100 grains or 20 *qīrāṭs* of the former version. *Dīnār* literally means a round gold coin, and technically a *mithqāl's* weight of such coins. Likewise *dirham* literally means a round silver coin, and technically the weight of such a coin. There have been various versions concerning the weight of a *dirham* in terms of a *mithqāl*, a *dirham* being, according to these estimates, 1/2, 6/10, 9/10 of, or 1 *mithqāl*. Later in the time of the calif Omar the weight of the *dirham* was fixed at 7/10 of a *mithqāl*. This last ratio is called the septimal weight (*wazn sab'ah*) and is the weight used in *zakāt*. (*Tech. Dict.*, p. 500; *Majma'*, p. 169.) According to certain doctors in *zakāt* it is the weight of each locality that is taken into consideration. (*Jāmi'*, p. 311.) For the Shafiite and Malikite views on the matter, see *Minhāj* (p. 244), Māwardi (p. 206) and Kharashi (p. 81). According to the *Mabsūṭ* (p. 190), at the time of the Prophet, the *dīnār* was valued at 10 *dirhams*; in other words, 1 *mithqāl* of gold was worth 10 *dirhams* of silver. There are various versions concerning the weight of a *dirham* in terms of a *mithqāl*, but the version generally accepted is that a *dirham* was ½ of a *mithqāl*. The value of gold, then, in relation to that of silver seems to have been as 1 to 5, or, according to the most extreme version, as 1 to 10. In Hamilton's English translation of the *Hidāyah*, the *dirham* is valued at about 2 pence sterling.

After the first 20 *mithqāls* and 200 *dirhams*, the *zakāt* for every additional 4 *mithqāls* and 40 *dirhams* is 2 more *qīrāṭs* of gold and 1 more *dirham* of silver respectively. If the additional amount after the 20 *mithqāls* or 200 *dirhams* is below the above-mentioned quantities, according to Abu Hanīfah there is no *zakāt* on it. According to Abu Yūsuf and Muḥammad Ibn al-Hasan, as well as al-Shāfi'i,[1] and the Malikites,[2] such additional quantity even if less than 4 *mithqāls* and 40 *dirhams* respectively is subject to a proportional amount of *zakāt*, namely, at the rate of one-fourth of one-tenth. The ground for this view is the *ḥadīth* of 'Ali: "and for what is beyond 200, accordingly," and also the fact that *zakāt* is a return of gratitude for the blessing of property, and therefore, although in the beginning the *niṣāb* is necessary in order that the state of wealthiness may be realized, when the *niṣāb* is once complete, any excess, no matter how little, operates to increase the state of wealthiness to a corresponding degree and therefore it must pay *zakāt* proportionally, without regard to *niṣāb* requirements.[3] Abu Hanīfah, on the other hand, in support of his view invokes among others the *ḥadīth*: "For every 200 *dirhams*, 5 *dirhams*, and for every 40 *dirhams*, 1 *dirham*," where the *niṣāb* of 40 *dirhams* is mentioned after that of 200 and apparently is meant as a secondary *niṣāb* which is to come into operation after the first *niṣāb* of 200. Moreover, in the case of *sawā'im* animals there was after the first *niṣāb* an interval (*waqṣ*) exempt from *zakāt* and it is reasonable that there should be one in gold and silver also. Finally, the *ḥadīth* of 'Ali invoked by the opponents has never been traced (*marfū'*) to the Prophet. Al-Shāfi'i, in answer to the argument derived from the analogy of *sawā'im* animals

[1] *Cf. Wajīz*, p. 92.

[2] Kharashi, p. 81.

[3] *Mabsūṭ*, pp. 189-90.

with respect to the intervals which do not pay *zakāt*, says that in the animals this must necessarily be so in order to avoid forced partnership between the state and the *zakāt* payer in cases where the *zakāt* would be a fraction of an animal. The *'Ināyah*, on the other hand, retorts, on the ground of administrative expediency, that if in silver, for example, an excess of fewer than forty *dirhams* were taken into account the determination of the *zakāt*, and certainly its payment, would be very difficult and often impossible owing to the incommensurate numbers and the minute fractions that would result from such a procedure.[1]

In regard to the *zakāt* of gold and silver the following points must be borne in mind:

(1) From the standpoint of *zakāt*, **bullion** (*tibr*) **gold and silver is like wrought** or coined (*'ayn*) gold and silver,[2] such as the *dirhams* and *dīnārs* or the ornaments, decorations, and plate made of them. Gold and silver wrought for purposes of decoration and personal adornment pay *zakāt* as bullion, whether or not they are used by women, whether or not the amount used is excessive, and finally, whether they are kept for purchase of necessaries (*nafaqah*), for personal adornment or for trade. According to Mālik, gold and silver do not pay *zakāt* if used for lawful purposes. There is also a report from al-Shāfi'i to the same effect. The use of gold and silver by women for personal adornment is considered lawful. On the other hand, men as a rule may not use either of the two metals for personal adornment, excepting silver seals, gold nose rings and silver-covered arms. Gold and silver plate, however, is forbidden for both sexes.[3] The ground for the Malikite and Shafiite view is that gold or silver used

[1] *Hidāyah* and *'Ināyah*, p. 160.

[2] *Jāmi'*, p. 311.

[3] For details see Kharashi, p. 86; Dardīr, p. 119; Māwardi, p. 207; *Minhāj*, p. 244; *Umm*, p. 35; *Wajīz*, p. 93.

in the ways mentioned, is, like one's personal clothing, intended for everyday use which is a lawful purpose. The Hanifite argument is that they are productive property and must pay *zakāt*. The productivity here consists in the fact that, unlike clothing, gold and silver are by nature intended for trade.[1]

(2) In determining whether or not the *niṣāb* is complete and a *zakāt* is due (*wujūb*) it is the weight and not the value or number (*'adad*) that is taken into account. Thus if one should have a golden or silver pitcher weighing ten *mithqāls* or one hundred *dirhams* but owing to its artistic value worth twenty *mithqāls* or two hundred *dirhams* it is not subject to *zakāt*.[2] This point is agreed upon unanimously. There is, however, difference of opinion as to payment. According to Abu Hanīfah and Abu Yūsuf it is still the weight that serves as basis. Zufar claims that the value and Muḥammad Ibn al-Hasan contends that the one that is more favorable to the poor serves as a basis. Thus if one should give in payment of *zakāt*, instead of five good *dirhams*, five spurious ones worth four good ones, the *zakāt* debt is discharged, according to the two first doctors, since the weight in both cases is the same, but according to the others it is not. If, on the other hand, he should give four good *dirhams* worth five bad ones in the place of five bad ones, there is still due a fifth *dirham*, but according to Zufar, who takes into consideration the value, the entire debt is discharged. The above applies only when a *zakāt* debt is paid in terms of its own genus, for it is admitted unanimously that when the *zakāt* debt is paid in terms of another genus, it is the value that is taken into consideration. The Shafiites and Malikites[3]

[1] *Majma'*, p. 169.

[2] *Baḥr*, p. 244; *Jāmi'*, p. 311; *Majma'*, p. 168; *'Alamkīriyyah*, p. 251.

[3] *Cf. Umm*, p. 34; Kharashi, p. 81.

take into consideration always the weight only, for according to them gold and silver pay *zakāt* by reason of their physical identity and not their value.

(3) If **gold or silver** be **mixed with an alloy** (*gishsh*),[1] it is considered as pure if the alloy is less than half the content. For instance, if one should possess *dīnārs* and *dirhams* which contained more than fifty per cent of gold and silver respectively they would pay *zakāt* as gold and silver at the full rate. If the alloy just equals the nobler metal, it does not then pay as gold and silver, although some say that it still pays the full rate, and others, that it pays only a half rate. Finally, if the alloy predominates over the gold or silver, the article is considered to belong in the class of *'urūḍ* and as such it pays *zakāt* according to value, if it comes under the description of an article of trade or is used as currency (*thaman rā'ij*). This is in case the gold or silver cannot be separated to pay *zakāt* independently according to weight, for in such case the precious metal is legally deemed to be destroyed. Consequently, if the gold or silver can be separated, according to most doctors, it pays *zakāt* by weight. According to others, however, if the article was intended for trade it pays the *zakāt* of trade according to value, even if the gold or silver can be separated.[2] According to one view, in gold and silver coins it is not necessary actually to separate the precious metal and it is sufficient if it is known that they contain a *niṣāb* weight of the metal in question. According to the Shafiites,[3] alloys pay *zakāt* for the precious metal they contain only in case the latter by itself amounts to a *niṣāb* weight.

[1] *Jāmi'*, p. 312.

[2] *Fatḥ al-Mu'īn*, p. 390.

[3] *Minhāj*, p. 244; *Umm*, p. 33; *Mugni*, p. 380.

When **gold is mixed with silver** instead of with an alloy, if the gold predominates over the silver, then the entire contents are taxed as pure gold. If, on the contrary, the silver predominates, then each pays *zakāt* separately if of *niṣāb* weight.[1] According to the Shafiites,[2] when gold and silver are mixed together it is not allowed to pay *zakāt* for the whole as pure gold, since the *zakāt* of silver is not discharged unless it is paid in silver. If the weight of each metal is not known, *e. g.*, if a vase is made of silver and gold, 600 *dirhams* of one and 400 of the other, but it is not known which, then the *zakāt* payer may proceed to determine the matter, as in the case of other alloys, by melting, *etc.*, or if he is of age and is paying his own *zakāt*, he may, in order to avoid sin, resort to extreme precaution (*iḥtiyāṭ*) and pay *zakāt* of gold for 600 *dirhams*, and also *zakāt* of silver for 600 *dirhams*.

According to al-Haytami,[3] in case of alloys, **if the zakat payer does not know the amount of zakat** which **he must pay**, he resorts to the opinion of two experts or determines it by the method of water displacement. If neither way is possible, he has the option of melting the article and paying the *zakāt* of the precious metal, or paying the *zakāt* for the *niṣābs* of which he is sure (*tayaqqana*) and, by way of precaution and in order to avoid committing a sin (*iḥtiyāṭ*), also for the *niṣābs* of which he is not positive. This, however, applies only in case the *zakāt* payer is paying his own *zakāt*, for, if he is paying the *zakāt* of his ward (*maḥjūr 'alayh*), he has no right to resort to extreme precaution and pay for the *niṣābs* of which he is not positive. In fact this is the way of procedure: he consults two experts and pays

[1] *Durr*, p. 138; *'Alamkīriyyah*, p. 251.

[2] *Mugni*, p. 380; Anṣāri, p. 377; *Wajīz*, p. 93.

[3] *Al-Fatāwa al-Kubra*, vol. ii, pp. 34-5; *cf. Umm*, p. 34; *Wajīz*, p. 93; *Mugni*, p. 380; Anṣāri, p. 377.

according to their opinion; or he determines the proportion of the precious metal by means of its water displacement. If these two methods are not possible, he melts a small part of the article, if that is possible. If, however, the amount of the metal can only be determined by melting the whole of the article or an important part of it, either method resulting in a decrease of the value of the article, he pays the *zakāt* only for the *niṣābs* of which he is positive but not for those about which he is doubtful.

The **weight of** the **precious metal** is **determined by water in two ways:** (1) The article in question is immersed in a vessel containing water and the level of the water is marked. Then equal weights of the precious metal and of the alloy in question are immersed and the level of the water is again marked for each. If the mark for the article is, for instance, equally distant from the other two marks, then the alloy and the precious metal are half and half, and similarly for other proportions. (2) The article in question, which, for example, weighs 10 *dirhams*, is immersed in the water and the level is marked. Then the weight of the precious metal and of the alloy which will displace the water to the same level are successively determined. If then the weight of the precious metal is 12 and of the alloy 8 *dirhams*, it is clear that the proportion is half and half.

Articles of Trade (*'urūḏ al-tijārah*).[1] The Arabic word for article is *'urūḏ*, plural of *'araḏ*, or *'arḏ*, meaning wealth in general except gold and silver. According to Abu 'Ubayd, *'urūḏ* applies to every thing which is not measured by volume or weight and is not animal or real estate (*'aqār*). The author of the *Fatḥ*[2] approves of the first definition because every thing except gold and silver may become an article of trade and pay *zakāt* as such. This

[1] *Majma'*, p. 169; *Umm*, p. 39; Zarqāni, p. 51.

[2] P. 165.

is also the Malikite view.[1] The author of the *Majma'*, on the other hand, finds the first definition too broad and prefers the second, but is willing to allow for animals and include them in the definition, since animals also, even when they are *sawā'im*, may become articles of trade. Whatever may be the views of the Mohammedan doctors on the meaning of the word *'urūḏ*, it seems clear that it covers every article except gold and silver, since every article except those two may become an "article of trade" and pay *zakāt* as such. In other words, even real estate comes under *'urūḏ*, for as the author of the *Durr*[2] rightly remarks, the fact that a piece of land subject to *kharāj*, for instance, does not pay the trade *zakāt*, does not prevent it from being an article of trade, since it is merely the result of the desire not to have the same article subject to two taxes at the same time.

According to al-Shāfi'i, the *zakāt* of trade articles is based on the practice of the califs Omar I. and Omar II.[3]

All articles which come under the description of *'urūḏ*, whether or not they are otherwise subject to *zakāt*, as *sawā'im* animals, and mules and asses, are subject to the *zakāt* of trade as soon as they become "articles of trade". An article technically becomes one of trade if there has been with regard to it an **intention of trade** coupled with an act to bear the intention out. This requirement is because of the general legal principle that, intentions, in order to be effective, must be coupled with and, so to say, perfected by an act. The word act is here used in a technical sense, meaning the commission of an act as well as its omission. Either one of these two kinds of acts may complete the intention. According to the *Fatḫ*,[4] the rule in this respect is

[1] Kharashi, p. 99.
[2] P. 138.
[3] *Umm*, p. 39.
[4] P. 124.

that in the acts of omission (*a'māl al-turūk*) mere intention is sufficient, but that in acts of commission (*a'māl al-jawāriḥ*) mere intention is not sufficient for the act to be considered complete but that the intention must be coupled with an act. For example, a person who is resident (*muqīm*) may not be legally considered as a traveler (*musāfir*) if he merely intends to undertake a journey, while a person who is already traveling becomes a resident by merely intending so. There has been a difference of opinion among the Hanifite doctors as to whether the act needed to complete the intention of trade may be any act or whether it must be exclusively an act of trade, an act of trade being exchange of wealth against wealth for profit. For instance, if a person acquires some property through gift intending it for trade, according to Abu Yūsuf the property becomes an article of trade, because the intention has been coupled with an act, namely, the acceptance of the gift. According to Muḥammad Ibn al-Hasan, however, the property does not become an article of trade because the intention has not been coupled with an act of trade. The ground for the first view is that, properly speaking, intentions should be effective by themselves, even though unaccompanied by an act, because the Prophet said: "The intention of the believer is better than his act". However, as intentions, being mental, are concealed, they cannot become in the nature of things effective unless borne out by an act. The ground for the other view is that an intention of trade, for example, does not become evident unless the act which is to bring out the intention is also one of trade. The net result of these differences is summarized in the '*Ināyah* [1] as follows:

(1) What is inherited, even though intended for trade, does not by unanimous opinion become an article of trade,

[1] P. 125.

because in this case the act is wanting. This becomes clear when it is remembered that in Mohammadan law inheritance is compulsory and takes effect without and in spite of the will of the heirs who cannot refuse to be heirs.

(2) What is acquired against a consideration of wealth (*māl*), *e. g.*, through purchase, location (*ijārah*) or loan.[1] Such acquisitions become articles of trade if intended for trade, since there would then be in them both the intention and the act of trade. This is also unanimously agreed upon.

(3) What is acquired for a consideration that is not wealth (*māl*), such as the prices of marriage (*mahr*) divorce (*khul'*), and composition from the right of retaliation for murder (*badal al-ṣulḥ 'an dam al-'amd*), or what is acquired for no consideration at all, such as gifts, alms and legacies. According to Abu Yūsuf wealth acquired in these ways comes under the description of articles of trade if intended for trade, but it does not so come according to Muḥammad Ibn al-Hasan.

According to the Shafiites,[2] only property acquired for a consideration, even though one of a non-financial nature, such as marriage and divorce, may become an article of trade by being so intended. The Malikite view is like the Shafiite except that it requires the consideration to be financial, *i. e.*, other than marriage, *etc.*[3]

According to the *Fath*,[4] the above applies only to articles in regard to which an intention of trade is valid, namely, articles other than land, for in land intention of trade is not valid. If, therefore, a person should buy a *kharāj* or tithe land in order to trade in it, he does not pay for this land the *zakāt* of trade but only tithe or *kharāj* because it is not lawful to tax a person twice by reason of the same

[1] *Durr*, p. 134.

[2] *Minhāj*, p. 251; *cf. Umm*, p. 40.

[3] Kharashi, and 'Adawi, p. 99.

[4] P. 125.

cause,—ownership of land in this instance. However, according to Muḥammad Ibn al-Hasan, a tithe land bought for trade pays both the *zakāt* of trade and the tithe. According to al-Shāfi'i,[1] land may become an "article of trade" and pay the *zakāt* of trade, provided there is not grown on it a crop which is subject to tithe, as in that case only tithe is levied on it.

The intention [2] must be present at the time of the act, otherwise it has no effect. If therefore one should buy a slave and later intend him for trade, the slave does not become a slave of trade until he is actually traded in (*taṣ-arruf*), because only then will the intention and the trade have been coupled together.

If there was no intention whatever at the time of purchase, the article is considered to have been intended for personal use (*qunyah*), for the presumption is that an article, unless expressly intended for trade, is bought for personal use.[3] On the other hand, an article intended for trade becomes an article of trade even if it was also intended to be used personally, or rented (*gallah*) meanwhile before its sale.

An article of trade continues to be so until it is intended for other than trade, whereupon it at once ceases to be an article of trade, although the intention to trade has not been confirmed by an act, because in this case the act is one of omission (of trade) and therefore mere intention is sufficient.[4] If afterwards he intends again to trade in that article, it does not become an article of trade until after it has been actually disposed of.

The **intention of trade may** also **be implied.** For ex-

[1] *Umm*, p. 41; Muzani, p. 244; *cf. Wajiz*, p. 96.

[2] *Jāmi'*, p. 312; *Durr*, p. 134; *Umm*, p. 40; Kharashi, p. 99.

[3] Kharashi, p. 99.

[4] *Cf. Umm*, p. 40.

ample, if one buys an article with a trade article, or if one rents his house which was intended for trade for an article, the articles received constitute articles of trade even if they have not been intended for trade.[1] Concerning the case of articles received as the rental of articles intended for trade, however, there is also a report to the contrary. The theory in this case is that as the article given away was one of trade the price obtained for it becomes substituted (*badal*) for it and so no new intention of trade is necessary.

A few examples from the *'Alamkīriyyah* [2] will make clear what is meant by intention of trade. Thus if one should buy brass pots in order to rent them he does not pay *zakāt* on them just as he would not pay *zakāt* on houses intended for renting. Similarly if a spice grocer should buy glass bottles or sacks in order to rent them to the people there is no *zakāt* on them because they are bought for their use and not for trade. Likewise the baker by buying wood or salt for baking is not subject to *zakāt*, but if he buys sesame and makes it into bread he pays *zakāt* for it. However, if a person other than a trader buys food for a trade slave he owns, he does not pay *zakāt* for it. A trader (*muḏārib*), on the other hand, would do so.

Mālik, unlike the Hanifites and al-Shāfi'i, distinguishes between the person who buys things for speculation (*irtiṣād al-aswāq*) by selling them when he thinks the price is highest, and the person who, like the store-keepers, buys and sells (*man yudīru mālahu*) without waiting for speculation.[3] According to Mālik the merchant who turns over his stock without waiting (*al-mudīr*), assigns a month of the year as the time for the payment of his *zakāt* and in

[1] *'Alamkīriyyah*, p. 244; *Durr*, p. 134.

[2] P. 253.

[3] *Muwaṭṭa'*, p. 109; *Mudawwanah*, pp. 11, 14; Kharashi, p. 101; Zarqānī, p. 52; *Mabsūṭ*, p. 190, l. —9; Ibn Rushd, *M.*, p. 212.

this month he appraises his trade stock and adds to the total the claims he expects to collect and pays *zakāt* for the whole. If however he is merely a speculator (*muḫtakir*), he does not pay *zakāt* for the articles he bought with the intention of selling later for profit every year but only once for all when he turns them into cash by sale,—even if meanwhile many years should have passed from the time of their purchase. Just as in the case of merchandise he does not pay *zakāt* until he has sold them, so in claims, he does not pay *zakāt* on them until he has collected them. This is based on the *ḥadīth*: " There is *zakāt* only on the produce of the land (*ḥarth*), on gold and silver (*'ayn*), and on animals." In other words there is no *zakāt* on the articles of trade and the claims until they have become gold or silver by sale and collection, respectively. This distinction between the two kinds of trade, however, applies only to the *zakāt* of trade articles and such claims as have not arisen in consequence of loans (*qarḍ*), for with respect to the *zakāt* of loans (of gold and silver), traders and others are alike.[1]

According to Abu Hanīfah the **articles of trade are appraised** in gold or silver coins (*naqd*) according as one or the other way is the more profitable to the poor, that is, according as the *niṣāb* is attained by appraising in terms of one or the other. Some said that the advantage of the poor is considered even when the *niṣāb* is reached by appraising in terms of either, namely, that it is appraised in terms of the more current (*arwaj*) of the two, and that if both have the same degree of currency, the owner has the choice of appraising in either.[2]

According to Abu Yūsuf, if the article was bought for coins (*naqd*) it is appraised in terms of that coin, and if it

[1] *Mudawwanah*, p. 11; Kharashi, p. 101, l. 10.

[2] *'Alamkīriyyah*, p. 252.

was bought for other than coin, it is appraised in terms of the most common (*aglab*) coin. However, according to Muhammad Ibn al-Hasan it is appraised in terms of the most predominant (*aglab*) currency in every case.[1]

According to the Shafiites,[2] articles of trade, if bought for currency (*naqd*), are appraised in terms of that currency, otherwise they are appraised in terms of the common (*gālib*) currency. If there are two such currencies, the appraisal is made in terms of the currency which results in a complete *niṣāb*. If the *niṣāb* is reached in either case, the appraisal is made in terms of the more profitable of the two, or at the owner's choice.

In appraising in terms of coins, the appraisal is made only in terms of coins which themselves are subject to *zakāt*, namely, coins in which the precious metal predominates.[3] Furthermore, the appraisal is made in terms of the currency of the town where the property subject to *zakāt* is situated. If such property is situated in the desert the appraisal is made in terms of the currency of the nearest town.[4]

Claims (*duyūn*).[5] According to Abu Hanīfah, claims are strong (*qawi*), medium (*wasaṭ*), or weak (*ḍa'īf*). Strong claims are those which have arisen in consideration of an article of trade or a loan, that is, property which would have paid *zakāt* at the end of the year if left in the creditor's ownership. Medium claims are those that arise in consideration of property which would not have paid *zakāt* if left in the creditor's ownership, *e. g.*, personal clothing or the rental derived from a personal slave. Weak

[1] *Majma'*, p. 169.

[2] *Minhāj*, p. 252.

[3] *'Alamkīriyyah*, p. 251, l. —9.

[4] *Majma'*, p. 169.

[5] *Majma'*, p. 159; *Mabsūṭ*, p. 194; *Jāmi'*, p. 301.

claims, finally, are those that arise in consideration of other than wealth (*māl*), such as the price of marriage or divorce, or arise for no consideration at all, such as inheritance and bequests.

In **strong claims,** the *zakāt* is due at the end of the year, whether or not collected, but its payment is made only after every collection of a minimum of 40 *dirhams* or more at the rate of 1 *dirham* for every 40 *dirhams* collected.

In **medium claims,** in one report from Abu Hanīfah, the *zakāt* is still due at the end of the year but its payment becomes obligatory only after a *niṣāb* of 200 *dirhams* has been collected, at the regular rate of 5 for 200 *dirhams*. In another report from him, there is no *zakāt* on such claims until they have been collected and a year has passed.

In **weak claims** the *zakāt* is not due until a *niṣāb* of 200 has been collected and a year has elapsed.

According to Abu Yūsuf and Muḥammad Ibn al-Hasan, however, all claims are alike excepting those consisting of the price of manumission (*badal kitābah*) and the price of blood (*al-diyat 'ala 'l-āqilah*). If they are of *niṣāb* quantity and the year has elapsed the *zakāt* becomes due on them, but it is not paid before collection. When, however, part of it is collected, no matter how little, its *zakāt* is paid. As regards the two claims which formed an exception to the rule, their *zakāt* is due only after a *niṣāb* has been collected and a year has elapsed. This difference of opinion between the disciples and Abu Hanīfah arises from their different method of classifying claims. The disciples classify the claims into absolute (*muṭlaq*) and defective (*nāqiṣ*), and consider as absolute all but the two claims mentioned.

The above controversy applies only in case the creditor does not have in his possession other wealth (*māl*) when he collects the claim, for in that case, by unanimous opinion, he adds the claims collected to the wealth he already possesses and pays their *zakāt* together with that of the wealth in question.

According to al-Shafi'i all claims are alike subject to *zakāt* which must be paid when the year has elapsed, even if the claims have not been as yet collected. His argument is that the creditor's property became a claim by his will and through an act of his and therefore there is no reason for delaying the right of the poor, by requiring another year to elapse after their collection. The Hanifite reply is that the claims before collection are not as yet in the *zakāt* payer's possession, and therefore he is not obliged to pay their *zakāt* until after he has collected them, just as the wayfarer is not required to discharge the *zakāt* of property he left at home, except as he gradually receives it. According to the *Minhāj*,[1] the view above ascribed to al-Shāfi'i is his more recent view, and applies only to claims of gold and silver and commodities (*'ārḏ*), but not to claims of animals, nor to debts which may be repudiated (*gayr lāzim*), such as the price of manumission. The *zakāt* of the claims in question is paid when due before their collection, provided the claims are already due and their collection is possible, for if their collection is not possible by reason of the debtor's being in poverty or otherwise, they are like usurped property, namely, their *zakāt* is paid after their collection. If the debts have not yet fallen due (*mu'ajjal*), the prevalent Shafiite view is that they are like usurped property, but some hold that their *zakāt* is paid as soon as it falls due, even though before their collection.

Finally, **according to Malik** and his followers,[2] there are three classes of claims: (1) Those accruing in consideration of property which is not trade property, such as prop-

[1] P. 261.

[2] *Mudawwanah*, pp. 16, 18, 27-8; Dardīr, pp. 121-3; Kharashi, pp. 93-9, 101; Ibn Rushd, *B.*, p. 249.

erty bought for personal use, or inherited or received as gift, or such as the price of manumission or blood. These claims are not subject to *zakāt,* since the original property in consideration of which they have accrued is not subject to *zakāt.* But if a *niṣāb* of these claims is collected and remains in the possession of the creditor for a year, it pays *zakāt* as any other property would, provided the claim collected consists of gold or silver. (2) The claims accruing in consideration of trade property or in consequence of loans of gold or silver. These claims are subject to *zakāt* for one year only, even if in the interim before their collection, from the time their *zakāt* was last paid on the original property, or from the time such property was acquired by the creditor, there elapsed several years. But this *zakāt* is not discharged until after a *niṣāb* of the claim has been collected. When once a *niṣāb* has been collected and its corresponding *zakāt* paid, the *zakāt* of later collections, no matter how little they are, is paid as they are collected, even if meanwhile the *niṣāb* first collected should have been disposed of or lost. For instance, a person who loaned 40 *dīnārs* after possessing them for 6 months pays no *zakāt* on the 20 *dīnārs* which he recovers after 5 months, until after he has possessed them for another month to complete the year. If he should recover them after 5 years, he at once pays the *zakāt* of the 20 *dīnārs.* If, on the contrary, he should recover after 5 years, first 5, then 5, which he spends and then 10, he pays immediately *zakāt* for the 20 for one year only, and if later he should recover another *dīnār,* he at once pays its *zakāt,* even if meanwhile the 20 *dīnārs* should have been spent. In the same case, if instead of loaning the entire 40 *dīnārs* he had only loaned 20, and meanwhile paid *zakāt* on the remaining 20, he would then have to pay *zakāt* for any collection he made, even if it be one *dīnār,* and even if the 20 *dīnārs* he had kept were meanwhile destroyed. The same would be true if he had loaned the entire 40 *dīnārs*, but had meanwhile acquired 20 *dīnārs* which he had in his possession for one year and had paid *zakāt* on them. If, on the other hand, he had acquired only 10 instead of 20 *dīnārs*, he would not pay *zakāt* on his collections until after he had collected 10 *dīnārs* from his claim, and paid *zakāt* on the 20. In other words, the principle here is that before he begins to pay *zakāt* on his collections, he must have had in his ownership at least 20 *dīnārs*, for an entire year, whether all of these 20 *dīnārs* have been collected from the claim or whether they have come into his possession otherwise. It must be stated that the above applies only if the receipts were in gold or silver. (3) The claims of the second class, excepting those arising from loans of gold and silver, when they have accrued to merchants, such as the storekeepers (*mudīr*), who buy and sell their stock without waiting for a rise in price in order to speculate. Such persons pay the *zakāt* of their claims yearly together with the *zakāt* of their stock in trade, irrespective of whether or not they have collected them, provided, however, that these claims are already due and their collection is possible. If the claims are not yet due, or if they are due but consist of commodities, their *zakāt* is paid on the basis of their market value.

If the creditor delays the collection of his claims in order to avoid the payment of *zakāt* he pays *zakāt* for every year which elapsed before its collection, unless the claim arose in consideration of no property or property that is not considered wealth (*māl*), such as the price of manumission.

According to the *Durr*,[1] if the creditor, after the lapse of a year, waives his claim he does not pay *zakāt* for it, whether it was strong or weak.

[1] P. 139.

Rentals and Wages (*ujrah*). There are three reports from Abu Hanīfah concerning the *zakāt* of rentals and wages. According to one report, he likened them to the marriage price, in that both are not the price of wealth itself, but of its use. In a second report, he likened them to the price of every-day clothing, in that, like it, they are not subject to *zakāt*. In a third report, the most reliable of all, the rental of a business office or the wages of a trade slave have been likened to the prices of the same. Consequently, according to this report, whenever 40 *dirhams* are collected on account of the rental or the wages, their corresponding *zakāt* is paid, just as in the case of the price of trade articles. In other words, Abu Hanīfah considered the price for the use of a thing similar to the price for the thing itself.[1] If, however, the rental is derived from a house which is not intended for trade, and the wages from a slave who is not intended for trade, then no *zakāt* is paid on them until a year has passed after their collection.

According to the Shafiites,[2] the *zakāt* is paid on such part of the rental collected as has already accrued. For instance, if a person should rent a house for two years for 40 *dīnārs* and receive them, he pays *zakāt* at the end of the first year for the 20 *dīnārs* only, because the other 20 *dīnārs* have not accrued to him yet and might be reclaimed by the tenant if, for example, the house should be destroyed at the end of the first year.[3]

SECTION IV

The Zakāt of the Produce of the Earth or the Tithe[4]

[1] *Mabsūṭ*, p. 196; *Fatḥ*, p. 123.

[2] *Minhāj*, p. 263; Anṣāri, p. 357.

[3] For the Malikite view on the matter, see *supra*, pp. 223-5.

[4] *Majma'*, p. 175; *Fatḥ*, p. 186; *Jāmi'*, p. 325; *Durr*, p. 142; *Durar*, p. 122; *'Alamkiriyyah*, p. 260; *Umm*, p. 29; Māwardi, pp. 202-5; *Minhāj*, p. 238; Zarqāni, p. 67; *Mudawwanah*, p. 105; Dardīr, p. 116.

The Hanifite doctors treat tithe under *zakāt*[1] because they consider tithe as the *zakāt* of the produce of the earth. Some of them have nevertheless raised the **question as to whether tithe is really a kind of zakat.** A few maintain that tithe was called *zakāt* because, in the opinion of Abu Yūsuf and Muḥammad Ibn al-Hasan, as in *zakāt* so in tithe also, the conditions of *niṣāb* and lapse of year are required.[2] The author of the *Majma'* objects to this construction and claims that the tithe was called *zakāt* because it was disbursed like *zakāt*. The author of the *'Ināyah* says that the extension of the name *zakāt* to tithe is by way of metaphor.[3] The author of the *Fatḥ*,[4] on the other hand, puts a strong plea for the identity of *zakāt* and tithe. He remarks that tithe is *zakāt*: so much so that it is disbursed the same way as *zakāt*, and that the most that can be said concerning the controversy over the nature of *zakāt* is that it turns on the question whether or not certain of the conditions of *zakāt* apply to certain kinds of *zakāt*. But he adds that whatever the answer to that question may be, it evidently does not prevent tithe from being a kind of *zakāt*. The Hanifite doctors are nevertheless unanimous in saying that

Some Hanifite texts treat tithe under the caption of *Zakāt* of the Produce of the Earth (*zakāt al khārij*), while others treat it under that of *Zakāt* of the Crops and Fruits (*zakāt al-zurū' wa 'l-thimār*). Aside from cases like the foregoing, the Hanifites, even those who consider tithe as identical with *zakāt*, use the word *'ushr* (tithe) in order to refer to the tithe; and, on the other hand, when they use the word *zakāt* they mean by it the *zakāt* of animals, gold and silver, and articles of trade only. The Shafiites and Malikites, on the contrary, denote by *zakāt* the tithe, as well as the other kinds of *zakāt*: and so, when they want to distinguish the tithe from the others they use some such expression as *zakāt* of crops and fruits, or *zakāt* of produce (*ḥarth*).

[2] *Majma'*, p. 175.

[3] *'Ināyah*, p. 186; *Fatḥ al-Mu'īn*, p. 401.

[4] P. 186.

there is a difference between the two, namely, that while *zakāt*,—that is, the kinds of *zakāt* so far treated,—is an act of worship pure and simple, tithe is primarily a financial charge (*ma'ūnah*) although it participates in a way in the nature of worship; and that this is the reason why tithe was treated last of all. From this rather important difference follow certain minor ones, such as, that unlike *zakāt*, tithe is levied on property owned by minors, insane persons, *waqfs, etc.* In many respects, however, the tithe is like the *zakāt*. It might be advanced as a general proposition that unless the doctors indicate the contrary, the presumption is that tithe is like *zakāt*, especially as regards its religious aspects, and that the differences between the two are practically limited to the political and financial field, such as the state's right of collection.[1] The Shafiites and Malikites, on the contrary, both treat and consider the tithe as an integral part of, and identical with, the *zakāt*. Consequently, what they say on "*zakāt*" applies equally to the tithe and to the other kinds of *zakāt*.[2]

The **tithe is a fard by reason of evidence found** in the Koran, the *sunnah*, the *ijmā'*, and reason. (1) In the Koran: there are the verses: "and on the day of its harvest give its right (*i. e.*, the right that attaches to it)",[3] and: "Bestow alms from the choice part of what you have earned and we have made grow for you from the ground."[4] Although some claim that the *zakāt* is collected after the harvest and therefore the right mentioned in the verse refers

[1] *Fatḥ al-Mu'īn*, p. 401; *Baḥr*, p. 255; *Kifāyah*, p. 172; Kāsāni, p. 37; *cf.* also *Defteri Muqtaṣid* (p. 54) on nature of "tithe" paid by *dhimmis*.

[2] *Cf.* Māwardi, pp. 204-5; *Minhāj*, p. 238; *Wajīz*, p. 90; Kharashi, p. 71.

[3] Koran, chap. 6, verse 142.

[4] Koran, chap. 2, verse 269.

to the alms given to the poor at harvest, the majority have agreed[1] that it refers to the *zakāt*. The ground advanced by those who hold the opposite view is the fact that the verse in question was revealed in Mecca before the *zakāt* was yet made a *fard*. (2) In the *sunnah*: there is the *hadīth*: "In what has been irrigated by Heaven, one-tenth, and in what has been watered with buckets or waterwheels, one-half of one-tenth." (3) In the *ijmā'*: the entire Moslem community has agreed on tithe's being a *fard*. (4) It follows from reason: as in the case of *zakāt*, the giving of tithe to the poor is an act of gratitude for the blessing of property, and, furthermore, it enables the poor to perform their religious obligations and inculcates in the giver habits of generosity while it destroys those of niggardliness.[2] Al-Shāfi'i[3] bases the tithe on the practice of the Prophet, who took *sadaqah* from wheat, barley, and maize (*dhurah*).

The cause of tithe being a *wājib* is the actually productive land—unlike the *kharāj* whose cause is the absolutely productive land, whether actually or only potentially so. Therefore the tithe is due only when there is a produce, so much so that when the produce is destroyed by an act of God, the tithe lapses.

According to Abu Hanifah, the **produce** of the earth as well as the fruits of wild trees are **subject to tithe,** no matter what their quantity is and **irrespective** of whether the requirements **of nisab,** durability, and lapse of a year have been met. Hence green vegetables pay tithe though they may not be preserved for a year.[4] According to Abu

[1] *Cf.* Baydāwi: Yahya, pp. 88 *et seq.*

[2] Kāsāni, p. 53.

[3] *Umm*, p. 29.

[4] *Durr*, p. 142.

Yūsuf and Muḥammad Ibn al-Hasan, however, the tithe is levied only on such produce of the earth as may be conserved for at least a year without much care and management, and amounts to at least a *niṣāb*. Therefore, in the opinion of the disciples, garlic, onions, apples, plums, green vegetables and other produce which cannot be preserved for a year, do not pay tithe at all. On the other hand, produce that may be preserved for a year, such as dates, grapes, grains, *etc.*, pays tithe only in case it amounts to 5 *wasqs*,[1] —if it is the kind of produce measured by *wasqs*. For if it is the kind of produce that is not measured by *wasqs*, such as cotton, saffron and sugar, it pays tithe, according to Abu Yūsuf, if its value amounts to the value of 5 *wasqs* of the least valuable produce measured by *wasqs*, *e. g.*, millet, and according to Muḥammad, if its quantity amounts to five times the highest unit of measure by which produce of its kind is measured. Thus cotton pays tithe when it amounts to 5 *ḥimls*, and saffron when it amounts to 5 *manns*, the *ḥiml* and the *mann* being the highest units of measure by which cotton and saffron are respectively measured. The ground for Abu Yūsuf's view is that since the *sharī'ah* specifications in regard to quantity cannot be applied here literally, one figures out on the basis of value, as was done in the case of articles of trade, and the value of the least valuable produce is taken into consideration in order to benefit the poor. The ground for Muḥammad's view, on

[1] The *wasq* (also *wisq*) is a measure of capacity, about a camel's load, holding 60 *ṣā's*, of the kind used by the Prophet, each *ṣā'* being 4 *mudds*. The *mudd* being, according to the people of 'Irāq and Abu Hanīfah, 2, and, according to the people of Hijāz and al-Shafi'i, 1⅓ *raṭls* (or *riṭls*), the *wasq* is 480 and 320 *raṭls*, respectively. *Ḥiml*, a measure of weight, is 300 *manns* (plural: *amnān*). The *mann* (also *mana*, plural: *amnā'*) is 2 *raṭls* (*raṭl* also being a measure of weight), the *raṭl* 12 *uqiyyahs* (plural: *awāqi*), or 20 *istārs*, or 128 *dirhams* (septimal weight). The *uqiyyah* used in *ḥadīths* is 40 *dirhams*. (*Cf.* Māwardi, p. 203; *Minhāj*, p. 238; Kharashi, p. 71).

the other hand, is that the *wasq* was considered a basis for produce measured by *wasq,* because the *wasq* was the highest unit of measure in that produce, and therefore the spirit of the law requires that for produce that is not measured by *wasqs* the highest unit of measure applicable to it be considered.

There is no tithe on firewood, Persian cane and dry herbage (*ḫashīsh*), because ordinarily they are not grown as a means of deriving profit from the ground. They would therefore be subject to tithe if the land were specially used for growing them. Sweet rush and sugar cane are, however, subject to tithe. Palmboughs and straw, grains that are not sown for their own sake, such as the seeds of cucumbers and melons, and secretions from trees, such as resin and tar, are likewise exempt from tithe. Olives and safflower and their seeds however pay tithe.

Of fruits, **according to the Shafiites,**[1] only dates and grapes, and of crops, only those grown by men and stored away as food pay tithe, provided they amount to at least 5 *wasqs,* excepting rice, *etc.,* where the *niṣāb* is 10 *wasqs* in order to allow for the husk. The crops which pay tithe are wheat (*ḫinṭah*), barley (*sha'īr*), rice, lentils (*'adas*), millet (*dukhn*), beans (*bāqilā'* or *lūbiyā'*), peas (*ḫimmas*), maize (*dhurah*), and their varieties, and according to the older view of al-Shāfi'i, also olives, saffron, honey, *etc.* **According to the Malikites,**[2] the tithe is levied only on dates and grapes, the grains (*ḫabb*), and the oil-bearers (*dhawāt al-zuyūt*), provided they amount to at least 5 *wasqs,* no allowance being made for the husk (*qishr*). The grains include 14 kinds, the 7 so-called sheath-bearers (*qaṭāni*),

[1] *Minhāj,* p. 238; *Wajiz,* p. 90; Māwardi, pp. 202, 204; *Mugni,* p. 372; Anṣāri, p. 367; *Umm,* p. 29.

[2] Kharashi, p. 71; Dardīr, p. 116.

such as beans, peas, and lentils, as well as wheat (*qamḥ*), barley, rice, millet, maize, and their varieties. The oil-bearers include olives, sesame, *etc.*

According to the Shafiites and the **Malikites,**[1] following the Prophet's precedent, **dates and grapes are appraised** by the state as soon as they become ripe and proper for eating; and the owners are required to pay their tithe later in dry dates (*tamr*) and raisins (*zabīb*). The Hanifites and others opposed this practice on the ground that it is a curtailment of the owner's rights and because the precedent of the Prophet concerned the dates of the people of Khaybar who were Hebrews and could not therefore apply to the *zakāt* of Moslems, the only *ḥadīth* that might support such a construction being open to impeachment. Moreover, appraisal is in reality an exchange of fresh dates which are yet on the trees against dry dates to be delivered in the future and involves a difference of quantity (*tafāḍul*) as well as a term sale (*nasī'ah*), both of which are forbidden as usurious (*riba*).[2] Al-Shāfi'i justifies this practice on the

[1] *Umm*, p. 27; *Minhāj*, p. 241; *Wajīz*, p. 92; Māwardi, p. 203; Kharashi, p. 78; Ibn Rushd, *B.*, p. 244; Dardīr, p. 117; *Muwaṭṭa'*, p. 117.

[2] *Riba* (surplus) is technically defined as the excess stipulated in favor of only one of the two parties to an exchange of wealth (*māl*) for wealth without a consideration (*'iwaḍ*). This excess may consist in the granting of a term for delivery (*nasī'ah*) or, in the exchange of homogeneous goods only, in an excess of volume (*kayl*) or weight (*wazn*). Thus exchange of gold for gold or silver to be delivered in the future, and exchange of gold for gold, or of silver for silver in unequal quantities are usurious acts. Usury is forbidden in the *sunnah* with regard to 6 definite articles, which are interpreted variously. The Hanifites interpret them as the articles sold by volume (*makīl*) or weight (*mawzūn*). The Shafiites take them to mean gold and silver and foodstuffs (*maṭ'ūmāt*). Finally, according to the Malikites, inequality in quantity is forbidden with respect to gold and silver and sustaining foodstuffs (*muqtāt*) that are stored away for future use (*mudakhkhar*), and future delivery, with respect to gold and silver and foodstuffs. (*Tech. Dict.*, p. 593; Qudūri, p. 45; *Fatḥ al-Qarib*, p. 314; Ibn Rushd, *B.*, vol. ii, p. 106; Dardīr, vol. ii, p. 14.)

ground that it inures to the interests of both sides, since by it the owners are allowed to eat their fruits when they are fresh yet or to sell them and fetch higher prices, and, on the other hand, the beneficiaries are secured a tithe on the entire produce. According to al-Māwardi, the owner after the appraisal may assume responsibility for the tithe on the basis of the appraisal and be free to dispose of his fruits as he pleases or he may refrain from doing so and in that case the produce is a sort of trust which he may not touch until he has paid its tithe. According to the prevalent Shafiite view the owner is not responsible for the tithe on the basis of the appraisal, unless he has expressly assumed this responsibility, but certain Shafiites expressed the view that it is not necessary expressly to stipulate this and that by the very fact of appraisal the owner becomes responsible for the tithe. The Malikite view seems to agree with the latter view. No allowance is made in the appraisal for the fruits that may be eaten by the owner or by birds and animals and a single appraiser is sufficient.

For produce which was irrigated by rain or running water, and for wild fruits, **the rate of tithe** is one-tenth of the produce. On the contrary, for crops watered by water-buckets or waterwheels, the rate is one-half of one-tenth.[1] In either case the rate applies before deduction of the expenses of production, for the *ḥadīth* on which the rate of tithe is based does not allow for any such deduction.

According to Abu Hanīfah, the amount eaten from the produce before the deduction of the tithe is also taxed, but according to another report from him, no tithe is received for the amount consumed by the owner if the amount was reasonable. According to Abu Yūsuf the amount necessary for one's own and one's family's food is exempt from

[1] *Cf. Minhāj*, p. 240; Kharashi, p. 71.

tithe, but, according to Muhammad Ibn al-Hasan, nine-tenths of what he consumed is taxed. Finally, according to al-Timirtāshi, one is not allowed to consume anything at all before paying his tithe, but others say that this applies only when he is determined not to pay his tithe, for if he sincerely intends to pay his tithe, he may consume nine-tenths of the crop, although it is preferable that he should not.[1]

It is not necessary that the produce should have been attended to in order that it may be subject to tithe, therefore the tithe is due on the produce of land that is not owned by any one, and also on fruits that have grown in the wilderness without any one's having cared for them. However, according to Abu Yūsuf and al-Hasan, no tithe is due on them, because they constitute free goods and become the property of the first comer. Al-Timirtāshi says that such produce and fruits pay tithe if they have enjoyed the protection of the *imām*.[2]

The **tithe is due on** the produce of *waqf* lands as well as on the **lands of** the **minors**, the insane, the *mukātabs*, the slaves who have permission to trade (*ma'dhūn*), and the persons who are indebted; but according to al-Shāfi'i, the land of the *mukātab* and *waqf* lands whose beneficiaries are not definite persons are exempt from *zakāt*. His reason for this is that tithe is a kind of *zakāt* and is levied with respect to the owner of the property. The Hanifite argument is that like *kharāj* (land-tax) tithe is a charge on the productive land and that therefore it strikes the produce, no matter who the owner is.[3]

Honey, like the produce of the earth, is **subject to tithe**,

[1] *Jāmi'*, p. 325.

[2] *Jāmi'*, *ibid.*; *Majma'*, p. 176; *Durr*, p. 142.

[3] *Mabsūṭ*, part iii, p. 4; *cf.* Anṣāri, p. 349.

according to Abu Hanīfah, no matter how small or how large its quantity. There are many *ḥadīths* from the Companions to show that the Prophet, and later the califs, levied the tithe on honey. There is also a *ḥadīth* from the Prophet, reading, " In honey one-tenth ". Al-Shāfi'i, in his more recent view, and Mālik exempted honey from tithe on the analogy of silk. The Hanifite reply is that silk-worms eat leaves which are not subject to tithe, unlike the bees which collect the honey from flowers and fruits on which there is a tithe. However, the author of the *Majma'* remarks that flowers are not subject to tithe.

According to Muḥammad Ibn al-Hasan, honey pays tithe only when it amounts at least to 5 *faraqs,* because the *faraq* is the highest unit of measure used for measuring honey. On the other hand, in Abu Yūsuf's opinion honey pays tithe when it amounts to 10 *qirbahs,* because of a *ḥadīth* to that effect.[1]

Crops and fruits as well as honey are **subject to tithe only if** they have **grown** or have been collected **on tithe land** or tithe mountain, or, as the *Durr* observes with respect to honey and wild fruits, even on land that is not tithe land, provided it is not also *kharāj* land, such as mountains and deserts, but in no case may the land be *kharāj* land. Honey collected in *kharāj* lands pays neither tithe nor *kharāj*,[2] because the produce of *kharāj* lands is subject to *kharāj*, and were the tithe also levied, it would be subject to two taxes at the same time.[3]

According to al-Shāfi'i, the tithe is due even on produce grown on *kharāj* land, because in his view there is no in-convenience in the collection of two taxes from the same

[1] A *faraq* (plural, *afrāq*) is 36 *raṭls* (*cf. al-Mugrib*). A *qirbah* (water-skin) is 50 *manns.*

[2] *'Ināyah*, p. 191.

[3] Kāsāni, p. 57; *Majma'*, p. 177.

object at the same time. His ground for this view is that *kharāj* and tithe are different charges as regards nature, cause, and object, and therefore there is no incompatibility between them. Indeed the difference of their natures needs no special mention and as regards their cause, the cause of tithe is the produce and that of *kharāj*, the productive land, and finally, the object of tithe is the produce and that of the *kharāj*, the legal personality (*dhimmah*) of the owner. The Hanifite reply is that the Prophet said: "The **tithe and** the **kharaj are not combined** on the land of the Moslem" and that none of the Moslem *imāms*, whether just or tyrannical, ever levied other than the *kharāj* on the lands of Sawād. Moreover, the cause of the tax in both cases is the same, namely, the productivity of the land; and just as the *zakāt* of *sawā'im* and trade may not be levied on the same object so the *kharāj* and tithe may not be levied on the same piece of land.[1] Mālik's view of the matter is like that of al-Shāfi'i.[2]

There is no tax on the habitations (*dār*) and the cemeteries even if they should belong to the *dhimmis*, because the calif Omar exempted them from taxation. If, however, a person, whether a Moslem or a *dhimmi*, transforms his habitation into a garden, he pays *kharāj* in every case if he is a *dhimmi*, and if he is a Moslem, he pays tithe if he waters his garden with tithe water, and *kharāj* if he waters with *kharāj* water.

There is no tithe on springs of tar and naphtha, and on salt found in tithe land, nor is there a *kharāj* on them when they are found in *kharāj* lands, since they may not properly be called the produce of land. Some hold that springs legally are the dependency (*taba'*) of their imme-

[1] Kāsāni, *ibid.*

[2] *Mudawwanah*, p. 105; *cf.* Kharashi, p. 7?.

diate vicinity (*harīm*) as regards payment of *kharāj*. The immediate vicinity of springs, if the land is one of tithe and produce is actually grown on it, pays tithe, and if it is *kharāj* land, and fit for cultivation, pays *kharāj*, whether or not it is actually cultivated, since the cause of *kharāj* is potential rather than actual productivity.

As in the case of *zakāt*, the obligation of **tithe lapses** when the produce is destroyed accidentally. When part of the produce is destroyed, according to Abu Hanīfah, the rest pays tithe proportionately. According to his two disciples, if the part destroyed together with the remaining part amounts to a *niṣāb*, the tithe is collected, otherwise it is not. According to a report from Abu Yūsuf, the remaining part by itself must amount to a *niṣāb*, otherwise it does not pay tithe. If a part or the whole of the produce has been destroyed by the owner wilfully, then he pays its tithe. In this matter the Shafiites [1] and the Malikites make no distinction between the tithe and the *zakāt* in general. Apostasy, as in *zakāt*, is another cause for the lapse of the tithe obligation although al-Shāfi'i held the opposite. Contrary to al-Shāfi'i, death of the owner, according to the Hanifites, is a third cause for the lapse of the tithe, unless the deceased had willed its payment, provided, however, that the produce was destroyed by him already. For if the produce is still in existence, as mentioned before, the tithe is collected from it according to the *Zāhir-al-riwāyah* report.[2] The ground for this view is the fact that the produce is owned jointly by the poor and the heirs and that the death of the owner is no reason for the lapse of the tithe. There is, however, a report from Abu Hanīfah through Ibn al-Mubārak to the contrary.[3]

[1] *Minhāj*, p. 268.

[2] Kāsāni, p. 65.

[3] *Mabsūṭ*, part iii, p. 50.

If a person rents a tithe land and cultivates it, according to Abu Hanīfah, the tithe is upon the landowner, whether it be more or less than the rental. Abu Yūsuf and Muḥammad Ibn al-Hasan, on the contrary, hold that the tithe is paid out of the produce by the tenant. Their argument is that tithe is a charge on the produce and the produce in this instance belongs to the tenant, the person who rented a land without a consideration (*musta'īr*) being in this respect like the tenant. Abu Hanīfah replies that the tax is a charge for the use of the land, and the use here belongs to the landowner, since he is entitled to the rental, which is the price of the use of the land. In other words, the tenant enjoys the use of the land in consideration of the rental he has paid, and so he is not subject to tithe any more than the purchaser of the produce is. Moreover, tithe is a charge on productive land, and the land here does not belong to the tenant. It is however a different case if the land was leased to a Moslem for no consideration, because the tenant in that case enjoys the use of the land for no consideration whatsoever, and because the tithe, being due only when there is a real benefit (*manfa'ah*), is not to be paid when there is no produce. If, however, the land was leased without a rental to a *dhimmi*, the tithe is paid by the landowner, because tithe is a kind of *ṣadaqah* and may not be paid by an unbeliever, and because the landowner by renting his land to a *dhimmi* has destroyed the right of the poor and must be responsible (*ḍāmin*) for it. Zufar, following the analogy of *kharāj* lands, said that the tithe is always paid by the landowner even when the use of the land is allowed without a rental to a Moslem.[1]

The members of the **Taglib tribe**, men, women and children, pay a double rate, *i. e.*, two-tenths for the tithe

[1] *Mabsūṭ*, part iii, p. 5; *cf.* Māwardi, p. 206.

lands they own, according to Abu Hanīfah and Abu Yūsuf, but in Muḫammad Ibn al-Hasan's opinion, only one-tenth is collected from them if the lands were bought from Moslems, because, in his view, the tithe is a charge on the land and its amount does not change with the owner.[1]

[1] *Majma'*, p. 177.

CHAPTER III

Collection and Discharge of the Zakat

Section I

The Collectors

In the earliest period of Islam, according to the Hanifite doctors, there was no distinction between the different kinds of property as regards the jurisdiction of the state tax collector to demand the settlement of their *zakāt*. This state of affairs is said to have continued from the time of the Prophet until the califship of 'Uthmān who " delegated the matter of payment (*adā'*) to the property owners because he feared that they would be subjected to inconvenience and trouble in the inspection of their property by evil collectors." Since then property subject to *zakāt* has been distinguished into the two classes of **apparent** (*amwāl ẓāhirah*) **and non-apparent property** (*amwāl bāṯinah*). Apparent property consists of the animals [1] and of such " non-apparent " property as has become " apparent ". Non-apparent property, on the other hand, consists of the remaining classes of property subject to *zakāt*, namely gold and silver and the articles of trade, so long as they have not become

[1] Although later doctors (*cf. 'Ināyah*, p. 171; *Majma'*, p. 172, *etc.*) in this connection use the word *sawā'im*, implying thereby that animals other than *sawā'im*, for instance, animals kept for trade, are not apparent property, al-Sarakhsi (*Mabsūṭ*, p. 170) expressly states that such animals are apparent property. Al-Kāsāni (p. 35), by using in this connection the word *mawāshi* (animals), seems to hold the same view; on the Shafiite side, al-Māwardi (p. 195) and the *Mugni* (p. 401) do likewise use *nawāshi*, and *na'm* (animals) respectively.

"apparent". It will be noticed that no mention is made here of the tithe. This is because, as already explained in the section on Tithe, the Hanifites[1] consider tithe more or less different from *zakāt* proper, using *zakāt* to denote in particular the *zakāt* of animals, gold and silver, and articles of trade. The Hanifites do nevertheless assimilate tithe, so far as the owner's right to disburse it himself and the state's right to collect it are concerned, with the *zakāt* of apparent property.[2] Thus the *Kifāyah* quoting from the *Tafārīq* says that the owner may himself disburse his tithe and the *zakāt* of his apparent property to the poor, as between him and God, although the *imām* in both cases collects the tax from him again. There is, however, a difference between the two, namely, that while the *imām* may not collect the *zakāt* by force, he may do so with the tithe. In such case the tithe obligation is discharged both as towards God and the state but the owner earns no religious merit for having failed to pay his tithe of his own free-will. In the case of *zakāt,* however, the *imām* has no right to collect by force, for should he do so, the *zakāt* obligation of the owner remains nevertheless undischarged.

According to the Shafiites,[3] apparent property consists of animals (*na'm*), crops and fruits (*mu'ash-sharāt*), and mines; non-apparent property, on the other hand, consists of gold and silver (*naqdān*), articles of trade, and treasure-trove.[4]

[1] *Bahr*, p. 255; Kāsāni, p. 37; *Fath al-Mu'īn*, p. 401. The last work, however, in another passage (p. 373) quotes Nūh Efendi to the contrary, namely that crops and fruits are apparent property.

[2] *Kifāyah*, p. 172; Kāsāni, p. 37.

[3] *Mugni*, p. 401; Māwardi, p. 195.

[4] The discrepancy between the two schools is due to their different interpretations of the meaning of *zakāt* as explained in the chapter on Public Treasury.

The *zakāt* of the animals is collected by special collectors called *sā'i* (plural *su'āt*). The *zakāt* of non-apparent property, on the other hand, is disbursed by the owners themselves directly to the *zakāt* beneficiaries, unless the non-apparent property has become "apparent" by being taken out of the cities into the country, in which case their *zakāt* may no more be disbursed by the owners themselves to the beneficiaries but must be paid to the public collectors stationed on the highways, the *'āshirs,* who have equal jurisdiction over both apparent and non-apparent property which passes under their inspection.

The right of the state itself to collect the *zakāt* in order later to disburse it to its lawful beneficiaries, according to the Hanifite doctors, is based on the protection (*ḥimāyah*) afforded by the state to the property. In the case of animals, state protection is needed all the time and therefore their *zakāt* must be always paid to the collector. As regards articles of trade and other non-apparent property, "when the Moslem takes his stock of trade out into the country he needs the protection of the *imām* and therefore the latter has the right to collect the *zakāt* from him".[1]

According to al-Māwardi,[2] the jurisdiction of the collector of *ṣadaqah* taxes (*wāli al-ṣadaqā*), although he accepts the *zakāt* of "non-apparent" property when the property owners pay it to him of their own accord, and assists them in setting it apart, is limited to the *zakāt* of apparent property which the property owners are ordered to pay him. There are two views concerning the meaning of this order, if it is issued justly. One view is that the order constitutes for the property owners a *wājib* obligation and that therefore they may not themselves pay the *zakāt* directly to the

[1] *Mabsūṭ*, p. 199.

[2] Māwardi, pp. 195, 196.

poor, and if they do so, their *zakāt* obligation is not settled. According to the author of the *Mugni*,[1] the owner, when ordered, should for the sake of loyalty pay the *zakāt* of his apparent property to the *imām* even if the latter should be tyrannical, for the author adds that by being tyrannical the *imām* does not forfeit his rule. The second view is that the order constitutes only a *mustaḥabb* obligation and is merely meant to exhort the owner to loyalty (*iẓhāra li 'l-ṭā'ah*). If, therefore, he himself pays the *zakāt* directly to the poor, his *zakāt* obligation is discharged.

In short, according to the Hanifites, within the cities, the *zakāt* of non-apparent property is disbursed by the owner himself directly to the beneficiaries of *zakāt*, or, if he so chooses, to the collector. If non-apparent property is taken outside of the city into the country, it becomes apparent and, as in the case of other apparent property, its *zakāt* must then be paid to the public collector and may not be disbursed by the owners directly to the beneficiaries. Finally, the *zakāt* of animals must always be paid to the collector. Al-Shāfi'i, in his more recent view,[2] contends that the *zakāt* of animals may be paid by the owners directly to the beneficiaries, for instance, to the poor, because the poor for whom the *zakāt* is paid have a right in property subject to *zakāt*, and when the *zakāt* has been given directly to them this right (*ḥaqq*) will have reached its destination; under these conditions the *zakāt* debt must therefore be considered settled exactly as the price of a thing bought would have been settled if the buyer gave the price to the principal of the agent rather than to the agent from whom he bought it. Moreover, since the collector collects the *zakāt* in order later to disburse it to the poor, and the owner by himself disbursing it to the poor has spared the collector that

[1] P. 402.

[2] *Minhāj*, p. 264.

trouble, no action would lie against the owner on that score.[1] Moreover, according to al-Shāfi'i, as quoted in the *Umm*,[2] the disbursement of *zakāt* by the owner himself is even to be recommended on the ground that the owner in this way can better assure himself that his *zakāt* obligation is "discharged" as between him and God. However, according to the *Mugni*,[3] it is preferable that the owner pay his *zakāt* to the *imām* if the latter is just, rather than that he disburse it himself or through an agent, because by paying his *zakāt* to a just *imām* he is positively freed from his obligation, whereas by disbursing it himself he incurs a risk, for should he disburse it to the wrong person his *zakāt* obligation would remain "undischarged". Then, too, by paying the *zakāt* to the *imām* he makes it possible to distribute the *zakāt* among a larger number of beneficiaries. Some Shafiites hold that the *zakāt* must be disbursed to the *imām* in every case, even if the *imām* is tyrannical. Still others hold that it must in every case be disbursed by the owner himself, not only because in this way the owner may disburse his *zakāt* to his kin and neighbors, but also because he earns additional merit for disbursing it himself. Al-Sarakhsi, in reply to al-Shāfi'i, says that the property owner has no more right to invalidate the right of collection which belongs to the *imām* by the authority bestowed on him by the *sharī'ah,* than has the person who is subject to the poll-tax to settle it himself to the warriors who are the beneficiaries of that tax. There are two grounds for this. One ground is that the *zakāt* is a divine right (*ḥaqq allah*) pure and simple, that its collection belongs only to the person whom God appoints as His vicar for the

[1] *Mabsūṭ*, p. 161-2.

[2] P. 19.

[3] P. 402.

collection of divine rights, namely, the *imām,* and that therefore the owner's debt is not canceled until he has paid his *zakāt* to the *imām.* Therefore, even if it should be known that he settled his *zakāt* debt once to the poor, he is required to pay it again. Moreover, in this case the *zakāt* obligation is not settled even as between him and God, for the *imām* has a voice in the disbursement of the *zakāt* to its beneficiaries and the property owner, by himself paying it to them, has rendered void the *imām's* right in this respect. The other ground is that although the collector is an agent of the poor and the latter have a right in the *zakāt* collected, yet with respect to the collection of *zakāt* the collector is so much their master (*mawla*), that the poor do not have the right themselves to demand the payment of *zakāt* by the owners, and the owners are not obliged to settle their *zakāt* debts to them if they so demand. Should they do so in fact, their position would be like that of a person who paid his debt to a minor himself rather than to his guardian. According to this second ground the owner's obligation of *zakāt* is settled as between God and himself, if he pays it to the poor. Therefore if it should be known that he actually paid his *zakāt* debt to the poor, he is not required to pay it again, unlike the person who paid his debt to the minor himself, for the minor is not legally fit to receive payments while the poor are fit to receive the *zakāt* even though they may not demand its payment.[1]

The distinction in theory between apparent and non-apparent property is recognized also by the Malikites. However, as regards collection, the Malikites virtually consider all *zakāt* property as apparent in contrast with the Shafiites who almost go to the other extreme. Thus, unlike al-Shāfi'i who, as we saw, recommends the disbursement of *zakāt*

[1] *Mabsūṭ*, p. 162.

to its beneficiaries by the owners themselves, the Malikites,[1] with a view to avoiding praise and insuring secrecy, recommend the disbursement of *zakāt* through an agent (*nā'ib*), that is, the state, especially if the *zakāt* payer is ignorant of the law or the *imām* is just. In fact the Malikites require the owners to disburse to the *imām* when he is just even the *zakāt* of their non-apparent property.

The person who fails to pay his zakat (*tārik al-zakāt*) is not killed for it, but his *zakāt* is collected from his property by force. If, however, the collection of the *zakāt* by force is not possible, then he may be proceeded against by military force until the *zakāt* is collected, even if that should eventually lead to his being killed.[2] This was done by the calif Abu Bakr with the tribes which had refused to pay the *zakāt* after the Prophet's death. The fighting of the "refusers" (*māni'*) of *zakāt* is lawful according to either of the two constructions put on the "order" to pay the *zakāt* above mentioned, because by refusing to submit to the just orders of the authorities they have committed treason. Abu Hanīfah disapproves of fighting in case the property owners undertake themselves to settle the *zakāt* to the poor directly.

The above applies as regards the *zakāt* of apparent property only,[3] for in the case of non-apparent property, the owners may themselves settle their *zakāt* dues. They are nevertheless rebuked (*ankara 'alayhi*) if they fail to do this, the right of censure in this case belonging to the public inspector (*muḥtasib*), since the collector has no jurisdiction over non-apparent property. It might, however, be argued that this right belongs to the collector because, although he

[1] Kharashi, pp. 124, 130.

[2] Māwardi, p. 380.

[3] Māwardi, pp. 415-6.

has no jurisdiction in this case, the obligation of the property owners is discharged should they pay the *zakāt* to him. The punishment (*ta'dīb*) of the property owner depends upon the peculiar circumstances of the case, for if he claims that he settles his *zakāt* in secret he is believed.

According to the Hanifites,[1] the state may resort even to war in order to collect the *zakāt* of apparent property. Moreover, according to a quotation from the *Tafārīq* in the *Kifāyah*,[2] if it is understood that the people of a city do not pay the *zakāt* of their non-apparent property, they are ordered to do so, and those among them who are known to fail in settling their dues are beaten and, according to the *Ishārāt*, put in prison until they pay them. Finally, according to Mālik, the owners should make no distinction between the *zakāt* of their gold and silver (*nāḏḏ*) for which the *imām* does not send and the *zakāt* of their cattle and crops and fruits for which the *imām* does send; but should settle both when the *imām* is just. Consequently if the *imām* knows positively that they are not paying the *zakāt* of gold and silver, he may take it from them.[3] According to later Malikites,[4] the *zakāt* of both apparent and non-apparent property is paid (*dufi'at*) to the *imām*, who collects it by force and even by war. If no property of the person who refuses to pay his *zakāt* can be found, the *imām* may put him in prison if he is known to possess wealth.

[5] **If the collector is unjust and tyrannical** in the collection of *zakāt* but just in its distribution among its beneficiaries, the concealment of property from him is allowed. If, on the other hand, the collector is just in the collection

[1] Yūsuf, p. 45.
[2] P. 172.
[3] *Mudawwanah*, pp. 44-5.
[4] Kharashi, p. 130.
[5] Māwardi, p. 209.

of *zakāt* but unjust in its distribution, the concealment of property from him is then a *wājib* obligation, and the payment of *zakāt* to him is not allowed.

If a person conceals[1] **the zakat** of his property from a just collector, he collects it later when he discovers it, and he then inquires into the cause of concealment. If the *zakāt* was concealed because the property owner wanted himself to pay his *zakāt* to the poor, the collector does not punish (*ta'zīr*) him. If, on the contrary, he hid it in order to defraud God, the collector punishes him, but he does not fine him by charging him a higher rate of *zakāt*. Mālik says that the collector in such case receives half of the property as fine because of the *ḥadīth*: "If a person fraudulently withholds his *zakāt*, I will receive the *zakāt* and half of his property as a fine of God." However, the *ḥadīth*: "There is no other right against the property (of the Moslem) except *zakāt*" indicates that the other *ḥadīth* is not to be taken literally and that it is merely meant to warn against defrauding.

In the appointment of a collector there are three possible cases: (1) The collector may be empowered both to collect and to disburse; (2) He may be empowered to collect the *zakāt* but forbidden to distribute it among its beneficiaries. The person, however, who appointed the collector becomes a sinner by causing a delay in the distribution of the *zakāt*, unless he appoints another person for distributing the same. (3) His power may be indefinite, that is, he may be neither specifically empowered to distribute the *zakāt* nor forbidden to do so. He is then entitled both to collect and to distribute the *zakāt*.

[2] The collector, to be a full-powered collector (*'āmil al-*

[1] Māwardi, pp. 208, 380.

[2] Māwardi, p. 196.

tafwīḍ), must be a free man, a Moslem, just, and conversant with the law on the *zakāt*, but, if he is to be only an "executive" (*munaffidh*) collector who is directed by the *imām* how much he is to collect, he need not be conversant with the law concerning the *zakāt*. It is permissible to appoint as collector a person who may not lawfully receive a share from the proceeds of *zakāt*, namely, a person from the Prophet's relations, but such persons receive their pay from the share of *maṣāliḥ*.

[1] The full-powered collector in collecting the *zakāt* follows his own judgment (*ijtihād*) on disputed points of law. He does not follow the judgment of the *imām* or of the property owner. Neither is the *imām* allowed to prescribe the amount he is to collect. If, however, he is an executive collector, he follows on disputed points the judgment of the *imām*, but not of the owners, and it is the duty of the *imām* to tell him what he is to collect. Such a collector is in reality a messenger (*rasūl*) of the *imām* for carrying out his judgments. Therefore he may be a slave or a *dhimmi*, subject however to these conditions: He may not be appointed for the collection of *zakāt* in general, because slavery and unbelief are incompatible with the exercise of authority, but he may be appointed for the collection of *zakāt* as regards a particular piece of property whose amount and *zakāt* liability are known. If, however, the amount of the property whose *zakāt* is to be collected or the amount of the *zakāt* due on it is not known, then it is not permissible to appoint as collector a *dhimmi*, because he would have been entrusted with a property concerning which his report (*khabar*) is not valid. However, in this case it is permissible to appoint a slave as a collector because the report of a slave is valid.

[1] Māwardi, pp. 200-2.

If the collector is late in presenting himself for the collection of *zakāt* which has already fallen due, the property owners wait for him in case they have heard that he is coming and that he is occupied for the moment with others, because the collector cannot possibly attend to every one at the same time. However, the property owners themselves settle their *zakāt* if the collector is late with respect to all of them and exceeds the usual delay limit, because the obligation of the owners to pay the *zakāt* to the collector is conditioned upon the possibility of so doing and lapses when this is impossible. In this last case, namely, when the owner himself pays his *zakāt* to the poor, he acts according to his own judgment if he is a *mujtahid*; but if he is not one, he asks for the opinion of the *faqīh*, in whom he trusts, for he is not obliged to ask for the opinion of a *faqīh* whom he does not trust. If he asks two *faqīhs* for their opinions and one of them expresses the opinion that he must pay the *zakāt*, and the other, that he is not under obligation to pay it, or one holds the view that he must pay more than the other advises him, the Shafiite doctors have disagreed as to which of the two opinions should be followed, some holding that the more unfavorable of the two must be applied, others contending that the person who asks for the advice may follow whichever opinion he chooses.

When the collector presents himself after the property owner has acted upon his own judgment or upon another's view, and the collector's opinion happens to be different in that it requires the payment of *zakāt* or of more of it, the opinion of the colector is followed if it is still possible to do so, otherwise the view of the property owner is accepted. If, on the contrary, the property owner's judgment requires more than that of the collector, the owner as between him and God is obliged to pay the *zakāt* according to his own judgment, since by his judgment he has confessed the right of the poor in his property.

If the property owner contends that the property was destroyed before he had become responsible for its *zakāt*,[1] he is believed, but the collector may, if doubting his honesty, put him on oath.

With respect to grapes or dates which were appraised,[2] if the owner contends that they were destroyed, he is believed upon oath if the cause of destruction he invokes is concealed (*khafi*), as theft, or open (*ẓāhir*) and well-known; but, according to the more prevalent view, he is required to produce evidence if it is not well-known. If, on the other hand, he claims that the appraiser was unjust or that he made a mistake, his plea is rejected if the injustice or mistake claimed is too great to be true, such as one-fourth of the entire amount; otherwise, according to the more general view, he is believed.

If the property owner admits to the collector the amount of his zakat dues but does not tell him about the amount of his entire property, the collector may take the owner's word and collect accordingly without requiring him to exhibit his property.

If[3] the owner of cattle fixes their number at a figure, he is believed, if trustworthy; otherwise the animals are counted by being made to pass through a narrow passage. The owner is likewise believed if he contends that the young were born after the year and should not pay *zakāt*. In such cases he may also be sworn by way of precaution though not as a matter of law (*istiḥbāba*). In other words, should he refuse to swear he is nevertheless excused.

According to al-Haytami,[4] the word of the property

[1] According to the Shafiites, as we already saw (*Minhāj*, p. 268), the owner becomes responsible for the *zakāt* by not disbursing it as soon as it became possible (*tamakkun*) to do so.

[2] *Minhāj*, p. 242; *Mugni*, p. 378.

[3] *Minhāj*, pp. 236, 237; *Mugni*, pp. 370, 371.

[4] *Al-Fatāwa al-Kubra*, vol. ii, p. 34.

owner as to the amount of his *zakāt* is taken only in case he is himself positive about it, and in such case it is well to put him on oath if there is ground for suspicion. If, however, the property owner is only guessing, his conjecture is not taken into account, the amount being determined otherwise.

[1] If the property owner contends that he paid (*ikhrājaha*) his *zakāt* directly to the poor, his word is accepted, if the collector had not arrived on time when the *zakāt's* payment became possible; but the collector, if he has suspicions, may require him to take oath. According to one view, the *zakāt* is collected from the owner if he refuses to take the oath, but according to another view, it is not. If, however, the owner contends having himself disbursed his *zakāt* notwithstanding the arrival of the collector on time, his word is not accepted if it is said that the owner is obliged to pay his *zakāt* to the collector, but his word is accepted if it is said that the payment of *zakāt* to the collector is only a *mustaḥabb*.

If the property owners claim to have paid the collector their *zakāt*, and the collector denies it, the disbursed owners are sworn to the truth of their claim and released from their dues.

[2] If the collector, whether of the full-powered or the executive type, confesses having received the zakat from the owners, his word is accepted during his tenure of office, but there are two views concerning the acceptance of his word after his dismissal from office. Those who hold that the payment of *zakāt* to the collector is a *mustaḥabb* say that his word is still accepted, but those who hold that the payment of *zakāt* to the collector is a *wājib* obligation say that his word after dismissal from office is not accepted, and that independent evidence must be presented to prove

[1] Māwardi, p. 209.

[2] Māwardi, p. 209.

the point; that furthermore, even though he be just, he is not also allowed to bear witness to the payment of the *zakāt*.

[1] **If** the property **owner** has suspicion about the proper disbursement of his *zakāt* and **asks to watch** the **collector disburse** it, the collector is not obliged to grant his request, because by paying it to the collector the property owner becomes free from his *zakāt* obligation, and therefore should the collector ask him to be present at the disbursement of the *zakāt* he is not obliged to do so.

The **collector is not allowed to receive bribes or gifts** from the property owners, for the Prophet said: "The gifts of the collectors are a case of fraud".

If the **collector appears to have been unfaithful** (*khiyānah*) the right to remedy the evil belongs to the *imām* and not to the property owners. In this case the beneficiaries do not have a right of action, but as "persons in need" (*taẕallum dhawu al-ḥājāt*) they may lodge a complaint with the proper authorities. They are, however, barred from testifying against the collector because of the suspicion attaching to them. As regards the testimony of the property owners against the collector, if it relates to the collection of *zakāt* from them it is not admissible, but if it relates to the disbursement of *zakāt* to others than its beneficiaries it is admitted.

According to the Hanifites, if the Moslem or *dhimmi*[2] **traders** who pass the *'āshirs* **claim** that **they do not owe zakat or toll** on their goods, either because the year has not elapsed or the goods are not articles of trade, or because

[1] Māwardi, pp. 214-7.

[2] The *dhimmi* traders are treated by the *'āshirs* exactly like the Moslem traders, excepting the case where the *dhimmis* claim themselves to have disbursed the tax to its beneficiaries. This is because the toll levied on the *dhimmis* is not *zakāt* but a regular tax disbursed by the state itself. The *ḥarbi* traders are treated in a different way, as will be explained in the next section on the *'Ashirs*.

they are in debt or have already settled their dues to another *'āshir*,—provided however there was another *'āshir* during the year,—or if the Moslem traders claim that they settled in the city directly to the poor the *zakāt* of their non-apparent property, they are believed if they support these statements by taking oath and they consequently do not pay *zakāt*. For they are trustees in regard to their *zakāt* debt and, as such, their word is taken if supported by an oath. Abu Yūsuf claims that, as in the case of other acts of worship, their statements are taken to be true and they need not be sworn to. Some say that a claim of indebtedness is not accepted unless the debt covers the entire property, but the author of the *Majma'* observes that it is immaterial whether the debt covers the entire property or a part of it provided only it affects the *niṣāb*.[1]

Likewise, if the trader claims that his goods are from Marw (*marwi*) or from Harāt (*harawi*), the *'āshir* may not open the goods in order to inspect them, if by so doing he is likely to injure them. In such case he collects the tax in accordance with the sworn statement of the trader. This is based on a *ḥadīth* of the calif Omar to that effect.[2]

The Moslem trader has to pay the *zakāt* again if he claims that he settled the *zakāt* of his trade goods to the poor outside of the cities, because he is entitled to do this only within the cities, not in the country, since there the property needs the protection of the state and the right of collection therefore belongs to the state. For the same reason, the *zakāt* has to be paid over again if the Moslem trader claims that he settled the *zakāt* of his *sawā'im* animals to the poor, no matter where, because the collection of the *zakāt* of *sawā'im* animals both in the cities and in the country belongs to the state.

[1] *Majma'*, p. 172.

[2] *Mabsūṭ*, p. 200.

All the above applies also as between the **owner of sawa'im animals** and the collector (*sā'i*) who calls at his residence for their *zakāt*; namely, the owner is believed upon oath if he says that the year has not elapsed or that the animals are covered by debt, or if he says that the animals are not his or that he settled the *zakāt* to another collector; but his claim is rejected if it is to the effect that he gave his *zakāt* to the poor directly. Al-Shāfi'i differs on the last point.[1]

According to the *Zāhir-al-riwāyah* view, when the owner claims to have settled his *zakāt* dues to another collector, **it is not necessary** for him **to present a written receipt** from the other collector, but his sworn statement is considered sufficient; provided that there was in fact another collector during that year. However, according to a report from Abu Hanīfah through Hasan Ibn Ziyād, the tax payer must prove his statement by presenting the respective receipt (*barā'ah*). The ground for this second view is that the custom of collectors is to give a receipt when they collect the *zakāt* and therefore unless the owner presents this receipt the presumption is against him and his word is not accepted; just as the claim of the mother to have borne a child is not accepted even if sworn to by her, unless testified to by the midwife. The ground for the other view, which is the one generally accepted by the doctors, is that although the receipt is a written instrument, people's writings look similar, and sometimes it happens that the tax payer forgets to take the receipt along, or loses it, and that therefore the decision may not be made to depend on the receipt.

When the tax payer is obliged to pay the tax over again for one reason or another, it is the second payment that constitutes a payment of the *zakāt*, the first payment being

[1] *Mabsūt*, p. 161.

a *nafl*. Some say that the *zakāt* is the first sum paid, and that the second is a fine.[1]

Finally, according to Malik,[2] both the practice and the opinion of the doctors of his time is to the effect that people should not be oppressed in the matter of *ṣadaqah* but that whatever they give should be accepted. According to later Malikites, when the owner claims to have disbursed his *zakāt* directly to the poor, or contends that he is exempt from it by reason of indebtedness, he is believed only as regards the *zakāt* of non-apparent property, the settlement of which is entrusted to his loyalty, but his plea is rejected as regards the *zakāt* of apparent property. However, following a statement of Mālik, the owners are believed in their statements to the effect that they do not have other property and are not put on oath, even as regards apparent property.

According to Khalīl,[3] if the number of one's cattle, when they are actually counted, turns out to be different from the number previously reported to the collector (*sāʿi*), the latter collects the *zakāt* on the basis of the actual number if he had not previously believed (*ṣaddaqa*) the cattle owner's report. If, however, he had believed his report, he still collects on the basis of the actual number if that number is lower than the one reported. If, on the contrary, it is higher, according to one view of the matter the actual number, but according to another view, the number reported is taken as basis. This difference of view is a consequence of the difference of view on the question whether or not the fact of the collector's believing the cattle owner's report has the legal force of judgment by a judge and may therefore replace the facts

[1] *Jāmiʿ*, p. 319.

[2] Kharashi, p. 130, also pp. 80, 106; *Muwaṭṭā'*, p. 115; Zarqāni, vol. ii, p. 62.

[3] *Kharashi*, p. 70.

themselves. Al-Kharashi thinks that the tax should still be collected on the basis of the actual number. If the grapes or dates which were appraised are later destroyed by accident (*jā'iḫah*) this fact is taken into consideration. If the appraisal turns out to be too high, no reduction is made unless this is proved by the owner. If, on the contrary, it turns out to be too low, the owner is advised to pay tithe on the basis of the actual produce, but he may not be forced to do so.[1]

[2] **If the collector admits having received the zakat** but claims to have disbursed it to the beneficiaries, while the latter deny it, the collector's word is accepted because he is a trustee with regard to *zakāt*; but the denial of the beneficiaries is likewise accepted to the extent that they are considered still to be "poor" and entitled to *zakāt* as beneficiaries.

If the collector denies that he has received the zakat he is released upon making oath. If in such case some of the property owners testify in favor of those claiming the payment of their *zakāt* dues to the collector, their testimony is not admitted if it is after the collector's denial, and the institution of legal proceedings between them; but if it happens before, their testimony is heard and the collector is sentenced to make restitution of the amount claimed to have been paid to him. If in such case the collector after the testimony claims to have disbursed the *zakāt* to its beneficiaries he is not listened to, because he has belied his claim by his previous denial; and, on the other hand, if the beneficiaries testify in his favor, saying that they received it from him, they are likewise disregarded.

If the zakat is destroyed in the hands of the collector before its disbursement to its beneficiaries, the collector is not liable to damages unless it is due to his neglect or fault.

[1] Kharashi, p. 80.

[2] Māwardi, pp. 215-7.

If the collector by mistake disburses the **zakat to other than its beneficiaries** he is not liable for damages if he disburses it to persons whose status is concealed, such as well-to-do persons; but if he disburses it to persons whose status he might have known, such as slaves and the Relations, opinion varies. If it is the property owner who makes this mistake, opinion varies as regards disbursement to those whose status is not apparent, but as regards persons whose status is apparent, he is universally held to be liable for damages. The collector is treated with greater leniency because he is occupied with so many more people.[1]

SECTION II

The 'Ashirs or Collectors on the Public Road

The *'āshirs* are the collectors stationed by the *imām* on the public road in order to collect the *zakāt* of Moslem traders, as well as the tolls imposed on the *dhimmi* and *harbi* traders who pass him. The institution of *'āshirs* and the rules pertaining to their authority are based on the precedent established by the calif Omar, who appointed *'āshirs* and instructed them to collect from Moslem traders two and one-half per cent and from *dhimmi* traders five per cent, and who when asked " How much shall we collect from the *harbis*? ", said: " How much do the *harbis* collect from us? " When he was told that they collected ten per cent, he said: " Collect from them ten per cent." According to another report, he said: " Collect from them the rate that they collect from us "; and when further asked, " If it is not known what rate they collect? ", he answered: " Collect from them ten per cent." [2]

[1] Concerning the proper authorities invested with the right of appointing the collectors and other officials, the persons who may be so appointed, the duration of their tenure of office, the determination of their salaries, the manner in which they are appointed, and their right to appoint substitutes, see Māwardi, pp. 360-6. For the audit of their accounts, see *infra*, pp. 498-9.

[2] *Mabsūṭ*, p. 199; Yūsuf, p. 76.

The **Shafiites**[1] **condemn the institution of 'ashirs**, as applied to traffic within the Moslem world, as unjust and unlawful. They consequently do not allow the levy of tolls (*'ushr*, plural, *'ushūr*) from *dhimmi* traders who travel within a Moslem country from one city to another, unless it is so stipulated. Likewise it is not allowed to levy tolls on the *ḥarbi* traders unless it is so stipulated. The rate of the toll is fixed by the *imām* who may, and should, entirely remit it if that would induce the importation of commodities which are greatly needed by the Moslems. However, both the *dhimmi* and the *ḥarbi* traders may not be allowed to enter the Hijāz territory for trade purposes unless their trade is needed or a toll is stipulated. If the toll is based on the price, it is not collected until after the sale. When it is collected, a receipt is given, and it is not collected again during that year. Non-traders do not pay a toll, even when they enter the Hijāz.

According to the Malikites,[2] the levy of tolls from infidel traders is justified by the practice of Omar. Thus Mālik says that if a *dhimmi* of Egypt goes to Syria for trade, or if a Syrian goes to 'Irāq, or a trader of 'Irāq to Medina or Yaman, he is subject to a toll when he sells or buys wares; but that when once he has paid a toll he is not taxed further should he buy or sell again, until he has left the city and returned once more.

The Malikite doctrine as summarized by al-Dardīr is as follows: The *dhimmi* traders pay a toll of ten per cent on the wares they sell or purchase in other than their own districts (*iqlīm, ufq*), even if they should return (*ikhtalafū*) to a district several times in a single year, for the toll is levied in consideration of the benefit derived from the trade

[1] Māwardi, p. 359; Anṣāri, vol. iv, p. 218; *Wajīz*, vol. ii, p. 201; *Minhāj*, vol. iii, p. 278; *Mugni*, vol. iv, p. 288; *cf. Umm*, vol. iv, p. 193.

[2] Dardīr, pp. 205-6; *cf. Mudawwanah*, p. 40; Zarqāni, vol. ii, pp. 51, 75.

and the benefit recurs every time the *dhimmi* returns for trade. At each time, however, the toll is collected only once, even if he should buy and sell during that time repeatedly. In case of purchase, the toll is collected in kind, but in case of sale it is collected in specie from the price, and consequently no toll is collected if the goods are not sold. In order to induce the importation of foodstuffs to Mecca and Medina and the adjoining country, the rate of the toll in those cities was only five per cent of the price. If the *dhimmi* traders buy goods in one city and sell them in another city, both cities being within the same district, for instance, in Syria or Egypt or the Byzantine country (*rum*) or the Magrib, they are subject to no toll whatever. Unless otherwise stipulated, the *ḥarbi* traders pay as toll ten per cent of their wares, whether or not they sell them. This toll is not repeated if they travel from one district to another within the Moslem world, for with respect to the *ḥarbis* all Moslem districts are like one single district. The toll, however, is repeated if they had meanwhile returned to their country and are coming back from it; for upon their return to their country the effect of the *amān* which was given to them before ceases.

The *'āshirs* must be distinguished from the *sā'is* who are the collectors of the *zakāt* of *sawā'im* animals and go about in the country calling on the owners of *sawā'im* animals for their *zakāt* dues; as the word *sā'i*, literally runner, indicates. As opposed to these special terms, *muṣaddiq* means any collector of *zakāt*, within or without the cities; so does *'āmil*, literally, agent. On the other hand, the expression *wāli al-ṣadaqāt* denotes the authorities entrusted with the collection and disbursement of the *zakāt* taxes.[1]

The Hanifite views concerning the powers and duties of

[1] *Cf.* Anṣāri, p. 395; *Mugni*, vol. iii, p. 102.

the *'āshir* are as follows: The *'ashirs* are entitled to collect the zakat of both apparent and non-apparent property which comes under their jurisdiction, although they are primarily appointed to collect the *zakāt* of non-apparent property and the tolls imposed on the non-Moslem traders. The jurisdiction of the *'āshirs* as regards the *zakāt* of non-apparent property (which is normally outside of governmental jurisdiction), is based on the fiction, already referred to, that non-apparent property becomes apparent property when it is taken outside of the cities into the country where it is exposed to the danger of robbers and hence needs the protection of the state; which in consideration for the protection it affords acquires the right itself to collect the *zakāt*. Al-Sarakhsi [1] observes that this (fiction) holds even more truly as regards the non-Moslems because they are more exposed to the danger of robbers.

The *'āshirs*, therefore, in reckoning up the *niṣāb*, have no right to count non-apparent property that the traders may happen to possess elsewhere, but may count the property in question only when the owners have it with them. They may, however, count apparent property found elsewhere, because apparent property remains such, no matter where situated.[2]

In accordance with the *ḥadīth* of the calif Omar already referred to, the rates are two and one-half per cent for the Moslems, but five per cent for the *dhimmis*, owing to the fact that they need protection from robbers more than the Moslems. Unlike the Moslems, who must pay the *zakāt* of their trade articles whether or not they pass an *'āshir*, the *dhimmis* are subject to this toll of five per cent only in so far as they come under the jurisdiction of an *'āshir* by

[1] *Mabsūṭ*, p. 199.

[2] *Mabsūṭ, ibid.; Jāmi'*, p. 318; *'Alamkīriyyah*, p. 257.

traveling for trade.[1] This difference is due to the fact that while the tax collected by the *'āshirs* from Moslems consists in their *zakāt* dues, the one collected from the *dhimmi* is in reality only an *octroi* duty. Except for these two differences the *dhimmis* are treated like the Moslems in every respect. According to the doctors, the *dhimmis* by paying a double tax have earned a right to this equality of treatment.

As regards the harbi traders, the *'āshir* collects from the property they have with them at the rate of ten per cent, provided their property amounts to a *niṣāb* and the *'āshir* does not know the rate collected from the Moslems by the *ḥarbis* in their country but only knows the fact of collection. If, however, the *'āshir* knows the rate paid by Moslems in the land of *ḥarbis*, he then collects from the *ḥarbis* the same rate, whether it be little or much, in order to get even with them. According to the *Fatḥ*,[2] it is only with respect to the rate of the tax that the principle of reprisal (*mujāzāt*) holds true, since the right of collecting a tax at all (*aṣl al-akhdh*) is based on the fact that the *ḥarbis* during their sojourn in Moslem territory enjoy the protection of the Moslem state and so come under its taxing power. If the *ḥarbis* are collecting as a tax from Moslem traders the whole of their property, the *'āshir* does not collect the whole of the *ḥarbis'* property but leaves with them enough to enable them to return home. Some say that in such case the whole should be taken in order to dissuade the *ḥarbis* from doing the same thing to the Moslems, but the *Fatḥ* replies that this would be unjust after the *ḥarbis* have been given a pledge (*amān*) of safety when they entered the Moslem territory, and that therefore the Moslems should not do it simply because the *ḥarbis* do, for leaving a person without

[1] Yūsuf, p. 76.

[2] P. 175.

any means for returning home, after having given him a pledge of safety, would practically amount to murdering him. The *Hidāyah* applies the principle of reprisal also as regards the requirement of *niṣāb*, for according to it, if the *ḥarbis* tax any quantity, the Moslems also do the same. In another view of the matter, however, the *ḥarbis* are never taxed when their property is little, because they will need it for food and for satisfying other wants, and because the property, being little, does not need protection from robbers.

If, finally, the *ḥarbis* collect no tax from Moslem traders, then likewise the *'āshir* does not collect a tax from the *ḥarbis*, " for the fact that they have given up their oppression (*i. e.*, collecting taxes from Moslems) while they have the power, is on their part an exercise of favor toward us, but we (*i. e.*, Moslems) are more fit to be possessed with virtues than the *ḥarbis*." [1]

The children and women of the *ḥarbis* are exempt from tax on condition that similar treatment is accorded to Moslems by the *ḥarbis*.

If the *ḥarbi* traders claim that they have debts or that the year is not complete, their statements are not accepted and they must pay the tax even if those assertions would be proved.[2] Some say that this applies only in case the practice of the *ḥarbis* is not known or, if it is known that they do not accept similar statements made by Moslem traders in their country. If therefore it is known that they accept such statements, their statements then are accepted by the *'āshirs* and they are exempted from the tax.[3] If, however, the *ḥarbi* claims that a certain person is his child or *umm walad* (mother of a child, *i. e.*, a slave whose child was

[1] *Fatḥ*, p. 175.

[2] *Fatḥ*, p. 174.

[3] *Jāmi'*, pp. 319-20.

acknowledged by her master as his own), his words are believed and he does not pay tax on them, because the fact that he is a *harbi* does not preclude his having children or his acknowledging as his own the children of his slaves.

If the *harbi* passes the *'āshir* for a second time before the lapse of a year from the first time, he is taxed again if he had returned to his country in the meantime, and this would be true if he passed the *'āshir* ten or more times during a single day, provided that each time in the meanwhile he had returned to his own country, because the tax is collected from him in consideration of the *amān* (pledge of protection) given him when he entered the Moslem territory, and the effect of the *amān* ceases as soon as he returns to the country of the *harbis*. The *amān* in fact has to be renewed every time he enters the Moslem territory.

Consequently, if the *harbi* has not returned to his country during the year he is not taxed again during that year. According to the *Jāmi'*,[1] what is said concerning the last case applies if the *harbis* act the same way in regard to the Moslems or if it is not known how they act, for if it is known that they act differently they receive a similar treatment at the hands of the Moslems.

If the dhimmi passes the 'ashir with wine he is taxed for its value if he intended to trade in it. **If** however **he passes** the *'āshir* **with pigs** he is not taxed. According to al-Shāfi'i, wine and pigs are not taxed, because they do not possess a value, but Zufar holds that they do possess a value for the *dhimmis* and must therefore pay a tax. Finally, Abu Yūsuf says that they pay a tax if they are found together,—in such case the pigs being considered as an appendage (*taba'*) to wine; but if they come under the *'āshir's* jurisdiction separately, only the wine

[1] P. 320.

is taxed. The Moslem is never taxed for his wine. The skins of dead animals are treated like wine, because both may be converted into wealth (*māl*),—the former by being turned into vinegar and the latter by being tanned for use as leather. Pigs, however, do not constitute wealth in any case. Moreover, wine and skins being fungible goods, the collection of a part of their value as a tax is not collection of the thing itself, but, pigs being non-fungible (*qīmi*) goods, the collection as a tax of part of their value is collection of a part of the pigs themselves (*'ayn*), which are forbidden to Moslems. The value of the skins and the wine is ascertained from a *dhimmi* and according to another view from two *dhimmis* who became Moslems or from two Moslems who, having for a time practised impiety (*fisq*), have later repented. However the *Majma'* remarks that the value of goods changes with time and place and that there is difficulty in finding two persons of these types at the time of need.

According to Abu Hanīfah, if a person should pass the *'āshir* with **perishable goods,** like fruits, fresh dates, vegetables, milk, *etc.*, the *'āshir* does not collect their tax but orders the owners themselves to pay it to the poor. According to Abu Yūsuf and Muḥammad Ibn al-Hasan, the *'āshir* collects the *zakāt* on them, since they are like other goods as regards need for protection from robbers. Abu Hanīfah's argument is that the *'āshir* collects as *zakāt* a part of the *niṣāb* in order to disburse it to the poor, but that in this case there are no poor to whom he may disburse immediately, and that he cannot do so later because by that time the goods will have perished. Therefore, the best thing to do under the circumstances is to order the owners themselves to pay their *zakāt* dues directly to the poor.[1] The above applies also to the case of *dhimmis* and *ḥarbis*.

[1] *Mabsūṭ*, p. 204; *'Alamkiriyyah*, p. 259.

The **'ashir does not collect zakat from the mukatab** or the minor who passes him, since his property is not subject to *zakāt*. Likewise, he does not collect *zakāt* from slaves for goods (*biḍā'ah*) of their masters which they happen to possess for trade unless their masters are with them. If, however, the goods do not belong to the master, but are the slave's own stock earned by him by trading with the permission of his master (*ma'dhūn*), the slave does not pay *zakāt* on them if he owes money to the entire value of his goods. If he does not owe any debts, the *'āshir* collects *zakāt* if his master is along with him. If, however, the master is not present, then according to Abu Hanīfah, as quoted in the *al-Jāmi' al-Sagīr*, the *'āshir* still collects the *zakāt*, but in the opinion of Abu Yūsuf and Muḥammad Ibn al-Hasan, he does not.[1]

According to Abu Hanīfah's first view, **if the mudarib passes the 'ashir** with trade stock (*māl muḍārabah*), the *'āshir* collects *zakāt* from it; but according to his later view, the *'āshir* does not collect *zakāt*. The later view is also shared by his disciples. Al-Sarakhsi observes that although he does not know whether Abu Hanīfah changed his view concerning the case of the slave who was allowed by his master to trade, the analogy of the *muḍārib* would lead one to expect that Abu Hanīfah would exempt the slave also. The ground for the first view, according to which the *muḍārib* is subject to *zakāt*, is that he has rights in the trade stock like those of a proprietor, since he has a share in the profit. The ground for the other view is that he is a trustee concerning the trade stock which belongs to the principal (*rabb al-māl*) and that although he has the right to trade in it he does not have authority to settle its *zakāt*, especially as the settlement of *zakāt* to be valid must be accompanied

[1] *Mabsūṭ*, p. 201; *cf. Al-Jāmi' al-Sagīr*, p. 21.

by intention. The slave, however, trades in the stock for his own proper benefit and differs from the *muḏārib* by virtually owning his profits.

In regard to *'āshirs,* the members of the Taglib tribe are like the *dhimmis.*

SECTION III

The Discharge of the Zakāt Obligation (General) [1]

The **condition determining** the **validity** (*ṣiḥḥah*) **of** the **payment of zakat** is that the payment be coupled with the intention that it is to discharge the *zakāt* rather than some other obligation. For *zakāt* is an act of worship and as such is not valid unless so intended. The intention may

[1] The distinction between *zakāt* as a predominantly religious obligation and *zakāt* as a predominantly political obligation must always be borne in mind. The Mohammedan doctors, when they want to refer to the settlement of the *zakāt* as an obligation to God as distinct from that to the state, use the word *ajzā',* which means "to satisfy," "to serve instead of." This word has been rendered by the English "discharge." It is only when settlement of *zakāt* as an obligation to the state is accompanied by its discharge as an obligation to God that the *zakāt* payer earns religious merit (*thawāb*). While the payment of *zākat* to the state collector carries with it normally also its discharge as a religious obligation, this by no means always follows. Thus, although the payment of *zakāt* to tyrannical governments frees the *zakāt* payer from the political obligation, in the opinion of some doctors it does not carry with it the "discharge" of the *zakāt,* which should therefore be paid over again by the owners directly to the proper beneficiaries secretly if they are to be freed from the religious obligation also. The doctors indicate when the two obligations do not go together, and when they fail to do so it may be presumed that they coincide. The question of the discharge of the *zakāt* obligation acquires special significance when the *zakāt* may be and is disbursed to its beneficiaries directly by the owners, since in such cases the political obligation is not present and the "discharge" of the *zakāt* obligation is the only point at issue. The first two sections of this chapter relate chiefly to the settlement of the political obligation, while the last three, particularly the last two, sections concern chiefly the "discharge" of the religious obligation.

accompany the act of payment, whether it be made to the *zakāt* payer's agent (in order to be paid by him to the poor) or directly to the poor themselves. The intention may also follow the act of payment, provided it be made while yet the property remains intact in the hands of the poor. If, however, the property had been destroyed in the hands of the poor before the *zakāt* payer intended it for the settlement of his *zakāt* debt, his *zakāt* debt is not discharged and the amount has to be paid over again. Finally, the intention may accompany, instead of the actul payment of *zakāt*, its setting apart from the *niṣāb* by the property owner for its future payment. Thus if one sets apart from his *niṣāb* on which a year's *zakāt* falls due, an amount equal to the *zakāt* intending it for such, and later pays it to a poor person without intending it again at the time, the *zakāt* debt is discharged.

The generally accepted view is that it is not necessary for the discharge of the *zakāt* debt, that a poor person should know that what was given him was intended for *zakāt*. If therefore one should give a poor person money as a present or a loan, but intend it for *zakāt*, the *zakāt* debt is duly discharged. According to the *Fatāwa* 'Ali Efendi,[1] in giving the *zakāt* it is preferable to do it in public (*iẓhār*), unlike alms (*taṭawwuc*), which should preferably be given in secret.

If one should give the poor as alms (*ṣadaqah*) the whole of the *niṣāb* without intending it for the discharge of his *zakāt*, the *zakāt* is nevertheless discharged. Although it is necessary that the intention of *zakāt* should be present, and although analogy requires that the part of the *niṣāb* intended for the *zakāt* debt should be specified, the act is valid, judging by *istiḥsān*. In fact, intention is essential

[1] P. 14.

in order to distinguish an act of piety from an habitual act, and in the giving of alms there is already an intention of obtaining the divine good will. The requirement that the property given in settlement of *zakāt* must be definitely known is, on the other hand, met, in that the portion intended for *zakāt* is defined through the fact that the entire *niṣāb* (which includes the *zakāt*) has been defined. Zufar, following analogy, held the contrary view; for he argued that inasmuch as the *farḍ* and the *nafl* are both *sharī'ah* obligations, it is necessary to specify whether it is the *farḍ* (*i. e.*, the *zakāt*) or the *nafl* (*i. e.*, the alms) whose discharge is intended.[1]

However, according to Abu Yūsuf, if one should give as alms a part of the *niṣāb*, that part's share of the *zakāt* is not discharged, because there is no sign that the part given is intended to include its share of the *zakāt*, in view of the fact that the entire *zakāt* may be settled from the remaining part and that it cannot therefore be known how much of the debt was intended to be settled in the part given. According to Muḥammad Ibn al-Hasan the *zakāt* of the part given as alms is included in it and discharged; this is because he considers that the obligation of *zakāt* is proportionately distributed throughout the entire *niṣāb*, and that when part of it is given as alms its share of *zakāt* is included and discharged.

If, however, one gives the *niṣāb* or part of it, intending it for the settlement of some other *wājib* than the *zakāt*, then only that *wājib* is discharged, and the *zakāt* debt has to be settled separately.

The **Shafiites and Malikites**[2] alike require the presence of intention at the time of setting apart (*'azl*) one's *zakāt*

[1] *'Ināyah*, p. 126.

[2] *Minhāj*, p. 265; *Wajīz*, p. 87; *Umm*, p. 18; Kharashi, p. 126.

for future disbursement or of actually disbursing it. According to the Shafiites, it is not necessary in giving the *zakāt* to intend it for the *zakāt* of a definite article, the *zakāt* in such case applying to *zakāt* due on any article. According to the Malikites, should the part set apart for *zakāt* be destroyed before its disbursement to the poor, the *zakāt* debt is nevertheless discharged.

May the **intention of the sultan** or his agent replace that of the *zakāt* payer, when the latter, forced to pay his *zakāt* dues, fails to observe the requirement of intention? The question is answered differently by different authorities. According to the prevalent Shafiite view[1] the intention of the sultan or his agent is sufficient. The Māli-kite[2] view is to the same effect. According to both schools, the intention of the guardian replaces that of his ward who is a minor or insane.

Finally, the Hanifite[3] views on the matter are as follows: According to al-Taḥāwi, if the *imām* collects the *zakāt* by force and disburses it to its lawful beneficiaries, the *zakāt* obligation is discharged. According to the accepted view, (*mufta bih*) in such cases the *zakāt* is discharged only as regards apparent property over which the *imām* has jurisdiction even if he should fail to disburse it to its beneficiaries. In the *Khāniyyah* the validity of such a view is questioned on the ground that intention is entirely absent. One doctor observes that the *zakāt* is not collected by force but that the owner is told to pay it of his own will. The *Durr*, while agreeing with the premise of the last view remarks that the difficulty may be avoided by forcing the cattle owner,

[1] *Umm*, p. 19; *Minhāj*, p. 265; *Mugni*, p. 403; *Wajīz*, p. 87.

[2] Kharashi, p. 130; Dardīr, p. 128.

[3] *Baḥr*, p. 227; *Durr*, p. 137; Shilbi, p. 257.

through imprisonment, to pay his *zakāt* of his own accord; for, it is argued, duress does not preclude consent.[1]

May the settlement of the **zakat** debt **be delayed** or must it be made immediately after the *zakāt* falls due? According to Abu 'l-Hasan al-Karkhi the property owner becomes a sinner by delaying the settlement of his *zakāt* debt. It is related that according to Muḥammad Ibn al-Hasan the person who delays the settlement of his *zakāt* debt without an excuse is no longer acceptable as a witness. Muḥammad made a distinction between *zakāt* and pilgrimage and did not allow delay in *zakāt* because in doing so the rights of the poor would be encroached upon. On the other hand, according to Abu 'Abdāllah al-Balkhi, it is permissible to delay the payment of *zakāt*, because the divine commandment concerning the giving of *zakāt* is indefinite as to time limit (*muṭlaq*). According to a report from Hishām, Abu Yūsuf held the same opinion on the ground that while pilgrimage must be rendered at a certain season and one may not know whether he shall live until the next season, by the delay of *zakāt* no harm is done because any time is fit for its discharge.[2]

It is stated in the *Majma'*,[3] however, that according to the opinion at present generally accepted the immediate (*fawr*) settlement of the *zakāt* is necessary. By immediate settlement is meant that the obligation must be settled at the earliest opportunity.

According to the Shafiites,[4] the *zakāt* must be disbursed

[1] The doctors are concerned about the discharge of the *zakāt* obligation because, unless it is discharged, the amount collected would not be the *zakāt*, and the state would have confiscated a Moslem's property without just cause.

[2] *Mabsūṭ*, p. 169.

[3] P. 157.

[4] *Minhāj*, p. 264; *Wajīz*, p. 87.

to its beneficiaries as soon as possible (*tamakkun*). According to al-Shāfi'i,[1] the settlement of *zakāt* is considered possible (*tamakkun min al-adā'*) if the owner can actually disburse it to the collector or the *zakāt* beneficiaries, or, as the *Minhāj* puts it, if the property and the beneficiaries or the collector are present, provided, according to the *Mugni*, that the owner is not occupied with an important religious or worldly function, such as prayer or eating, respectively. If only one beneficiary is on hand, he is given his particular share, and is not made to wait until the required number of beneficiaries has appeared. According to the *Wajīz* one does not commit sin by delaying disbursement in order to disburse his *zakāt* to a more deserving person or to his kin, but if the property meanwhile should be destroyed he makes good the *zakāt*. In the case of property situated elsewhere, the disbursement of *zakāt* is considered to have been "possible" as soon as a time long enough to reach the property in question elapses. The Malikite[2] view is analogous.

May the zakat debt be settled before it has yet become due (*ta'jīl*)? According to the Hanifites this is allowed. According to Mālik, however, an obligation may not be settled before it has fallen due. According to the prevalent Malikite doctrine,[3] although anticipation is abominable, it is nevertheless allowed as regards cattle, gold and silver, and, with respect to professional traders (*mudīr*) only, also in trade articles before their sale, and debts before their receipt, provided the debts have not arisen from loans. Such anticipation may not, however, be by over a month. Al-Sarakhsi, in support of the Hanifite view, invokes the example of the Prophet who received in advance

[1] *Umm*, p. 44; *cf. Minhāj*, p. 264; *Wajīz*, p. 89; *Mugni*, p. 401.

[2] Kharashi, p. 126.

[3] Kharashi, p. 128.

from al-'Abbās the *zakāt* of two years, and argues that the *zakāt* is due when there is a productive *niṣāb*, and that the lapse of the year is only in order to give time for the payment of the debt and may be disregarded without affecting the obligation. However, it is not allowed to anticipate the payment of the *zakāt* if there is not already a complete *niṣāb*. According to al-Shāfi'i, anticipation of *zakāt* is allowed only for one year. According to Zufar, anticipation of *zakāt* for more than one *niṣāb* is not allowed, though it may be allowed for more than one year. If after the anticipation of the *zakāt* it turns out that at the end of the year the amount anticipated does not fall due, according to al-Sarakhsi the *zakāt* receiver may not be forced to return the part that has not fallen due. According to al-Shāfi'i, if at the time of discharge it was made clear to him that he would have to reimburse such part of the *zakāt* as would not have fallen due at the end of the year, it may be taken from him; otherwise the taxpayer has no right to demand restitution of the *zakāt* paid. Al-Sarakhsi remarks that *zakāt* is paid to the poor as an offering to God and may not be reclaimed afterwards.[1]

The **conditions necessary for the anticipation of zakat** are summarized in the *'Alamkīriyyah*[2] as follows: (1) At the time of anticipation the year should have already begun to run on at least one complete *niṣāb*. (2) The *niṣāb* or *niṣābs* for which the *zakāt* has been anticipated must be complete at the end of the year. (3) The original *niṣāb* should not disappear entirely in the interval. An example of anticipation for one year for many *niṣābs* would be the payment in advance of *zakāt* for one thousand *dirhams* for one year by one having two hundred *dirhams*. If this per-

[1] *Mabsūṭ*, pp. 176-8; *cf. Umm*, p. 17; *Minhāj*, p. 266; *Wajīz*, p. 87.

[2] P. 247.

son in the course of the year acquired more wealth or made profits so that at the completion of the year he was possessed of one thousand *dirhams,* the anticipation would be valid and the *zakāt* of the one thousand *dirhams* for the year past discharged. If, on the contrary, at the completion of the year he was still possessed of two hundred *dirhams* only, the anticipation would not be valid, and should he acquire more money after the year, he would have to pay its *zakāt* when a year passed after its acquisition. If one should pay in advance *zakāt* for two thousand *dirhams* while he possessed only one thousand and intended the additional *zakāt* of one thousand *dirhams* for the second one thousand *dirhams* he would come by during the year or, failing that, for the *zakāt* of the original one thousand *dirhams* for a second year, it would be valid.

The **anticipation of tithe** is not allowed with respect to what has not yet been sown, or to fruits that have not yet appeared. Abu Yūsuf, contrary to Abu Hanīfah and Muḥammad Ibn al-Hasan, allows anticipation in fruits whose pollen has not appeared (*qabl ẓuhūr al-ṭalʿ*), and crops which have not grown (*qabl al-nabāt*). Abu Yūsuf's ground is that the fruits and the crops will grow of themselves by mere lapse of time. The argument of the others is that anticipation is not valid unless the cause (*sabab*) of tithe is present, but that the palmtrees, for instance, evidently are not the cause of tithe, for the owner may cut them down without incurring responsibility for the tithe. The anticipation of the tithe of what has not yet been sown is, however, unanimously held to be void, because land, in and of itself, is not the cause of tithe, but a special act is needed, namely, cultivation, before there may be any question of tithe.[1]

[1] *Mabsūṭ*, part iii, p. 11; *'Alamkīriyyah*, p. 261.

According to the Shafiites,[1] anticipation is not allowed before the fruits have ripened or the grains have hardened. Some Shafiites express the opinion that anticipation is allowable after the grains have appeared and before they have as yet hardened. Still others, with respect to grapes and dates, hold that anticipation is not allowable before they have been dried; this view apparently is preferred by al-Gazzāli, who mentions it first, if one might so infer from the analogy of the Hanifite usage. According to the Malikites, anticipation in fruits and crops is not allowed.[2]

In the settlement of the *zakāt* debt the **substitution of values** (*daf' al-qiyam*) is allowed. Thus one may pay three fat sheep instead of four medium-sized ones or pay, instead of bushels of wheat, their value in *dirhams*. Al-Shāfi'i holds that this is not lawful because it would result in the setting aside of the express *sharī'ah* prescription (*naṣṣ*).[3] Consequently he does not allow substitution so long as it is possible to pay the very thing due as *zakāt*. According to the Malikites, substitution of values, except as between gold and silver, is unlawful.[4] The *Fatḥ*,[5] in reply to al-Shāfi'i, says that the cause of the divine prescription (*naṣṣ*) is the desire to provide for the poor the sustenance (*rizq*) promised them by God. Indeed, the Almighty promised a sustenance to every one, but he gave to some the means of acquiring it, such as trade, while he deprived others of all means; accordingly he commanded the rich to give them from God's property a certain proportion as *zakāt*. Since this is the cause of the prescription and

[1] *Minhāj*, pp. 266-7; *Wajīz*, p. 87.

[2] Kharashi, p. 128.

[3] *Hidāyah*, p. 144; *Majma'*, p. 166.

[3] *Hidāyah*, p. 144; *Majma'*, p. 166; *Umm*, p. 19.

[4] Kharashi, p. 125.

[5] P. 144.

the kinds of property specified for payment as *zakāt* by no means exhaust the needs of the poor, the specifications of the *sharī'ah* are interpreted in a liberal way, and the payment of the value is considered as the main object in view. It is not therefore a setting aside of the divine prescription (*naṣṣ*) by the process of *ta'līl* for purposes of analogy, as some have claimed, but on the contrary if it is at all a case of analogy, it is one of establishing by analogy all the various implied prescriptions (*naṣṣ*) in regard to the divine promise to provide a sustenance to every poor man; therefore it is only a case of setting aside the construction that the divine prescription regarding the payment as *zakāt* of certain definite animals precludes the payment of their values. The Hanifite construction then, instead of being a case of analogy, is merely one of interpretation (*madlūl*) of the divine prescription. Indeed, this construction is suggested by the context of the divine prescription. Consequently the value of the identical thing due as *zakāt* is not a substitute (*badal*) for that thing (*aṣl*)—since in that case the substitute could be paid only when the original thing was not in existence,—but both the original thing and its value are equally obligatory. The **zakat payer** therefore **has** the **option between four things:** (1) He may pay the very thing due as *zakāt, e. g.*, the sheep or wheat. Or, even if he should possess the very thing due, he may pay its value in one of the following three ways: (2) He may pay an older animal and be reimbursed by the collector for the difference. (3) He may pay a younger animal and make up the difference to the collector. (4) Finally, he may pay the exact equivalent of the thing due as *zakāt*; for instance, he may pay three fat sheep in lieu of four middle-sized ones, or their value in money.

It must be pointed out that when the *zakāt* debt is paid in terms of an equivalent the latter may not differ from the original debt in quantity in order to allow for a difference in quality between them, if they are fungible (*mithli*) goods of one and the same genus.[1] For example, it is not allowed to pay, in settlement of a *zakāt* debt of four bushels of wheat of medium quality, three bushels of good quality; or to give, in lieu of two dresses of inferior quality, one dress of better quality, although the three bushels of good wheat may be worth the four bushels of inferior quality, or the one superior dress may be worth the two inferior ones. The reason for this is that when articles subject to the prohibition of usury are exchanged for one another, no allowance may be made for a difference in quality between them if they are both of the same genus. Such articles are exchanged in equal amounts only. Zufar held the opposite view, arguing that the prohibition of usury applies only as between man and man, not God and man, as is the case in *zakāt*.

While the *zakāt* payer has the four options mentioned, the collector may nevertheless refuse to accept the second alternative, namely, that of being paid more than the *zakāt* and of reimbursing the difference, but he may not refuse the other three. According to the author of the *Badā'i'*,[2] the collector may refuse only when the *zakāt* payer offers in payment of his *zakāt* debt a fraction of an article, for instance, a part of a *ḥiqqah,* instead of a *bint labūn*. Others say that the above four options belong to the collector, but this view is not generally accepted.

According to Abu Yūsuf and Muḥammad Ibn al-Hasan, when the *zakāt* payer pays the value, instead of the very thing due as *zakāt*, **he pays its value on the day of payment,**[3] but according to Abu Hanīfah, he pays its value on

[1] *Mabsūt*, p. 203; *Jāmi'*, p. 313.
[2] *Majma'*, p. 166.
[3] *Cf.* Kharashi, p. 125.

the day on which the *zakāt* fell due (*yawm al-wujūb*). Other canonists hold that in the case of *sawā'im* animals one may pay the animal itself or its value on the day of payment, and in the case of other than *sawā'im* animals, the thing itself or its value on the day on which the *zakāt* fell due. However, when one settles in any of these ways, he may no longer change to another, *e. g.*, in paying the *zakāt* of two hundred measures of wheat worth two hundred *dirhams* on the day of *wujūb* (that is, when the *zakāt* fell due) the owner may give five measures of wheat, and this is not controverted, or according to Abu Hanīfah, he may give five *dirhams* instead, even if the price of wheat should meanwhile have changed, but according to his two disciples, if the price on the day of settlement should be four hundred *dirhams*, he pays ten *dirhams*. The same is true of the *sawā'im* animals.[1]

If the property on which zakat fell due is dayn, as distinguished from *'ayn*,[2] its *zakāt* may be settled in terms of *'ayn* wealth. Thus a person having a claim of two hundred *dirhams* on which *zakāt* is due, may give, in settlement of the same, five *dirhams* in cash, because *dayn* as compared with *'ayn* is defective (*nāqiṣ*) and the *'ayn* is complete

[1] *Jāmi'*, p. 313.

[2] **Dayn** means wealth, the payment of which attaches as a liability to a legal person (*dhimmah*), as the result of a transaction (*'aqd*) or a loan, or as damages for property destroyed (*istihlāk*). *Dayn* by extension also means the class of goods called *mithli* (fungible); that is, goods whose price (*thaman*) in sale is determined on the basis of weight (*wazn*), or volume (*kayl*), or number (*'adad*), and among the various units of which there is no difference of value due to human art (*Tech. Dict.*, pp. 502, 1343). The definition of *dayn* given in the *Majallah* (art. 158) in a way combines these two meanings. According to it, a stated portion of a heap of wheat is *dayn* before it has been set off. **'Ayn** is the opposite of *dayn* in the last sense, meaning that which is definite and has a bodily existence. Thus, in the above example, the said portion becomes *'ayn* by being set off.

(*kāmil*), and the settlement of the defective in terms of the complete is valid. On the contrary, the settlement of the complete *'ayn* in terms of the defective *dayn* is not valid, and, therefore, the *zakāt* debt is not discharged if a person wants to pay the *zakāt* of two hundred *dirhams* which he possesses (*i. e.*, *'ayn*) in terms of the five *dirhams* which a poor person owes him (*i. e.*, the *dayn*); namely, by absolving him from the debt intending it for his own *zakāt* debt on the two hundred *dirhams*. Finally, as regards the settlement of the *zakāt* of *dayn* wealth in terms of *dayn* wealth, if the wealth on which *zakāt* is due is of the kind of *dayn* which becomes *'ayn* it is not valid; otherwise it is valid. Thus if a person has five *dirhams* owed him by a poor person and two hundred *dirhams* by another person, he cannot settle the *zakāt* of the two hundred by making a present of the five to the debtor as alms, because the two hundred *dirhams* will become *'ayn* when collected, and the settlement of the *zakāt* of *'ayn* wealth in terms of *dayn* is not valid. An example of the opposite case would be that of a person who wanted to settle the *zakāt* of two hundred *dirhams* owed him by another by making a present of those *dirhams* to the debtor and intending it for his *zakāt* debt. However, this is allowed only in case the debtor is a poor person, although there is also a view to the contrary. It goes without saying that the *zakāt* of *'ayn* wealth is discharged if paid in terms of *'ayn* wealth; if, for instance, one pays the *zakāt* of two hundred *dirhams* he possesses by paying five out of those two hundred.[1]

If the **rebels and schismatics**, *i. e.*, Moslems who refuse to acknowledge the authority of the *imām*, collect once from the Moslems the *zakāt* of their *sawā'im* animals, or the tithe, neither is collected again from the owners by the

[1] Kāsāni, pp. 42-3.

imām when he recovers control over them. This is because taxation is based on protection and in this instance the *imām* has failed to protect them. However, a person taxed by the *'āshir* of the rebels once is taxed again by the *'āshir* of the Moslems, for it was his own fault, and not that of the *imām*, to have passed the *'āshir* of the rebels.[1] According to the *Majma'* the taxes are not collected by the *imām* even if the rebels had not collected them. However if the *zakāt* taxes collected by the rebels have not been disbursed by them to their lawful beneficiaries, the property owners, as between them and God, should repeat their *zakāt* dues by paying them secretly to the poor. In one opinion of the matter, the *zakāt* and the tithe obligations are discharged even if the proceeds have not been disbursed to their lawful beneficiaries because in that case the sin belongs to the authorities.[2]

Some express the view that *zakāt* paid to rebels and in general to any tyrannical person, if paid with the intention of *zakāt*, is discharged also as between God and man and therefore need not be paid again by the owners. It is argued that the rebels and tyrants are in reality poor in view of the fact that they would be reduced to poverty if they restored the properties which they seized unjustly, and that the *zakāt* after all has been paid to its lawful beneficiaries.[3] The author of the *Hidāyah*, however, expresses

[1] *Majma'*, p. 173.

[2] *Majma'*, p. 167; *Hidāyah*, *'Ināyah*, and *Fatḥ*, p. 150; Kāsāni, p. 36.

[3] The Hanifite doctors (Kāsāni, p. 36; *Fatḥ*, p. 151) in this connection cite a certain *fatwa* according to which it was declared lawful to pay the *zakāt* to 'Ali Ibn 'Isa, a governor of Khurāsān, on the ground that if he offered damages for the many injustices he had committed he would be a poor man. The case of a governor of Balkh is even more interesting. This governor having committed perjury, had to offer expiation (*kaffārah*). A *fatwa* was given that in his case the expiation should consist in fasting. Thereupon the governor is said to have begun crying, saying to his attendants: "They tell me: 'What you

the view that the *zakāt* should be repeated even if the taxes paid were intended for it. According to the *Fatḥ*, this is necessary because the person who collects the *zakāt* should know why he is collecting it, or, perhaps, because the *zakāt* has not been disbursed to its lawful beneficiaries.

In the *Durr* [1] it is stated that there is a dispute as to whether the above applies to the *zakāt* of non-apparent property as well; the view recommended in the *Mabsūt* being that they are alike. This is also the view expressed in the *'Ināyah*. In the *Fatāwa* 'Ali Efendi,[2] it is stated that the **custom duties paid nowadays** by Moslem traders cancel the *zakāt* dues of the latter if they are intended by them for those dues.

According to al-Haytami,[3] to the question whether the *zakāt* obligation is discharged **in case the imam seizes property unjustly** and the owner intends it for his *zakāt* dues, the reply is made that the obligation is discharged if the *imām* knew his intention. It is added, however, that in case the *zakāt* is collected by other than the *imām* it is not necessary that the latter should know the intention of the owner. With regard to **the imposts** (*mukūs*) **of later Moslem states**, al-Haytami says that they constitute a payment of *zakāt* only if they are collected under the name of *zakāt* and intended by the owners for their *zakāt* dues; that consequently the so-called *'ushūr* taxes of later times are in reality extra-*sharī'ah* taxes (*mukūs*), and do not re-

owe [before God] in the way of restoration [for injustice committed] is more than what you own, and therefore your expiation (*kaffārah*) is that of a person who owns nothing.'" (According to the law, the expiation for perjury for people who have the means is to free a slave or to feed or clothe ten poor persons; on the contrary, for those who cannot afford this, it consists in fasting for three consecutive days. *Cf. Durar*, p. 335.)

[1] P. 137.

[2] P. 15.

[3] *Al-Fatāwa al-Kubra*, vol. ii, p. 48.

sult in the discharge of the *zakāt* obligation even if so intended.

According to al-Māwardi,[1] **if** the *zakāt* **collector is tyrannical in collecting** the *ṣadaqah* **but just in disbursing** it, the *zakāt* obligation is discharged when the *zakāt* is given to him. Conversely, if he is just in collecting it but unjust in disbursing it, the obligation is not discharged as between God and the owner—whether the collector collects the *zakāt* by the consent of the owner or whether he collects it by force. In such case the owner must pay the *zakāt* over again to its lawful beneficiaries. According to the Malikites,[2] this applies only in case the owner paid the *zakāt* of his own accord. According to Mālik, the obligation is discharged and the owner need not repeat it.[3]

According to al-Shāfi'i,[4] **if after** the **disbursement of zakat** by the public distributor (*qāsim*) **to a person, it appears that such person was not a lawful beneficiary,** the *zakāt* is taken back from him to be disbursed to the proper person, but the *zakāt* obligation of the owner remains discharged whether or not the collector fails to take the *zakāt* back. In case of failure the collector is not liable for damages because he is only a trustee in this matter. The Malikite[5] view is similar. If in the above case it is the owner himself who is disbursing the *zakāt*, according to al-Shāfi'i, in one view of the matter, he must take the *zakāt* back in order to disburse it to the right person, and if he fails to do so, he must pay the *zakāt* over again to the right person if his obligation is to be discharged. In the other view, the

[1] Māwardi, p. 209.

[2] Kharashi, p. 128.

[3] *Cf. Mudawwanah*, p. 45.

[4] *Umm*, p. 63.

[5] Kharashi, p. 128; 'Adawi, *ibid.*

owner, too, like the collector, need not repeat the *zakāt*; for by paying it to a person whom he thought to be a lawful beneficiary he has fulfilled his obligation. The Malikite view is again similar. Moreover, according to the Malikites, if a person disburses his *zakāt* to a person who he believes (*ẓann*) is not a beneficiary of the *zakāt*, and later it appears that he was a beneficiary, his obligation is discharged; but the *zakāt* payer becomes a sinner by having paid his *zakāt* to one believed to be the wrong person.[1]

SECTION IV

The Place of Intuition (Taḥarri) in the Discharge of the Zakāt Obligation[2]

When the *zakāt* is disbursed directly by the *zakāt* payer himself, rather than by the state, the question whether or not the obligation is discharged depends on whether the person to whom the *zakāt* was disbursed was a lawful beneficiary of the *zakāt*. If the *zakāt* payer is in doubt as to this last point, he may as a precaution resort to his intuition (*taḥarri*) for determining it. In this connection the following four cases are conceivable:

(1) The *zakāt* payer gives the *zakāt* to a person, without at all doubting the latter's financial need, and without resorting to the process of *taḥarri*, or asking some one about it. In this case the *zakāt* obligation is lawfully discharged (*ajzā'*) and the payer is rewarded by God for it, provided it does not appear later that the person to whom the *zakāt* was given was rich. This is because the act of a Moslem is construed to be valid until the contrary appears to have been the case. Besides, the presumption is that the person

[1] For the rules to determine the right person for disbursing the *zakāt*, see *infra*, under Expenditure of *Zakāt* Taxes.

[2] *Mabsūṭ*, part x, p. 186; *'Alamkiriyyah*, vol. v, p. 569.

who received the *zakāt* is poor, for man is born poor and is assumed to remain so until there is evidence to the contrary. Consequently, the *zakāt* obligation is considered to have been discharged until it becomes evident that the person who received the *zakāt* was rich, and in that case the *zakāt* must be paid again.

(2) The *zakāt* payer is seized with doubt concerning the status of the person to whom he intends to pay his *zakāt*, either because that person looks like a rich man or because the *zakāt* payer inclines to the belief that he is rich. However, notwithstanding his doubts, he settles his *zakāt* to him. In this case the *zakāt* obligation is not legally discharged, because after once doubting his poverty, it was the duty of the payer to turn to his intuition in order to reach the truth. Having failed to do this, he has forfeited the privilege of presumption granted him by the law. If, however he finds out later that the man was poor, his payment of *zakāt* becomes valid in spite of the fact that he omitted to resort to *taḥarri*. This is because the purpose of *taḥarri* is the determination of truth, and when that purpose has been achieved in some other way the obligation of *taḥarri* lapses.

(3) The *zakāt* payer is in doubt and to clear his doubts resorts to the process of *taḥarri*. His intuition tells him that the man is rich, yet in spite of it he settles his *zakāt* to him. Clearly in this case the obligation is not discharged and must be fulfilled over again, unless the *zakāt* payer finds out that the man was really poor, in which case he need not pay the *zakāt* over again. This is the view generally accepted, although some Hanifite doctors believe that Abu Hanīfah and Muhammad Ibn al-Hasan required the *zakāt* to be repeated.

(4) The *zakāt* payer resorts to the process of *taḥarri* and the conviction dawns upon him that the person is poor, and thereupon he pays the *zakāt* to him. It is considered a case

of resort to *taḥarri* if the taxpayer without actually consulting his intuition pays his *zakāt* to a person sitting in line with the poor, or dressed like a poor man, or if he gives his *zakāt* to one after his begging for it. In such cases whether or not it is later found out that he actually was poor, the *zakāt* obligation is by unanimous opinion discharged. According to Abu Hanīfah and Muḥammad the obligation remains discharged, even if it later appears that he was rich. Abu Yūsuf held that the *zakāt* must be paid over again. It is stated in the *'Alamkīriyyah* that in such case the person who received the *zakāt* must return it to the *zakāt* payer who, in case the *zakāt* is not returned, acquires only the *thawāb* of kindliness but not that of *ṣadaqah*. The argument of Abu Yūsuf for dissenting from the others is that when later it appears that the *zakāt* receiver was rich, the *zakāt* payer's previous intuition to the contrary patently appears to have been erroneous, and may no longer be taken into account, and that consequently the *zakāt* must be paid over again. Moreover, the decision of a case through intuition is valid only in case the rights of third parties are not involved, which is not true in the present case, the poor having a right in the *zakāt*. The others reply that the *zakāt* payer had discharged the obligation imposed on him by the *sharī'ah* and there is no more ground for requiring a repetition of the *zakāt*, than when nothing is discovered about the *zakāt* receiver's status. In fact, the *zakāt* payer is obliged to pay his *zakāt* to the person who, in his opinion, is poor, but this person need not be poor in reality also, since that is impossible to ascertain. Indeed one sometimes cannot tell his own financial state, and how can he be expected to tell that of others! Furthermore, a *sharī'ah* obligation never exceeds human capacity, and in this case the utmost the *zakāt* payer can do is to determine the state of the *zakāt* receiver by means of inferences based on his appearance, or the fact of his sitting in line with the poor, or his begging for alms and the like, or, if such circumstances are not at hand, by resorting to his intuition, the only remaining means at his disposal. Besides, when later it appears that the *zakāt* receiver was in reality rich, it is no longer of any avail, since by unanimous opinion the *zakāt* payer may not recover the *zakāt* or its equivalent from the *zakāt* receiver, and therefore it would be entirely unjust to require him to settle the same obligation twice over. The above applies also in case the *zakāt* receiver turns out to be the *zakāt* payer's father or son, or according to a *Zāhir-al-riwāyah* report, even a Hāshimite or a *dhimmi*. The *zakāt* likewise remains discharged if the *zakāt* receiver appears to be the slave or *mukātab* of a rich person. If however the *zakāt* receiver proves to be the *zakāt* payer's own slave or *mukātab*, by unanimous opinion the *zakāt* must be paid over again, since a condition of *zakāt* is that it must be "given" (*i'ṭā'*), but this does not happen until the thing given ceases to be the *zakāt* payer's own property.

SECTION V

The Use of Cunning in the Discharge of the Zakāt Obligation [1]

According to the Hanifite doctors, **resort to cunning** (*ḥīlah*), in order to invalidate the right of a third person, or to involve it in doubt or confuse it, is unlawful and **abominable,** but resort to cunning in order to escape from engaging in an unlawful act, or in order to be able to do an act which is legitimate (*ḥalāl*) is a good deed. According to Abu Yūsuf, resort to cunning is permissible even in order merely to avoid incurring an obligation (*imtinā' 'an al-*

[1] *'Alamkīriyyah*, vol. vi, pp. 559-62; *Mabsūṭ*, pp. 166-7; *cf.* part xxv, p. 209; *Majma'*, p. 161.

wujūb) before the obligation has been as yet contracted. The use of cunning is justified by the following verse of the Koran:[1]

"Take in thy hand a bundle of dry herbs and strike with it, and do not break an oath." This was advice given to Job, who had sworn that he would beat his wife by inflicting on her a hundred stripes. All the Hanifite doctors agree that the tenor of the above verse has not been abrogated (*naskh*) by a later prescription.

The Hanifite **doctors** have **disagreed as to** the **legitimacy of resorting to cunning** in order to avoid the payment of **zakat.** According to Muḫammad Ibn al-Hasan such a practice is abominable, because it results in the prejudice of the poor and because the giving of *zakāt* is an act of worship and it does not befit a believer to try to avoid it. Abu Yūsuf, however, holds the opinion that there is nothing to condemn in such a practice because it merely consists in an attempt to avoid the incurring of an obligation, and therefore it does not result in the prejudice of third parties, since their rights accrue only after the obligation has been incurred. Moreover, he argues, one is sometimes afraid that he may not be able to carry out a divine commandment and that he may so become a rebel, and in such cases it is advisable to avoid coming at all under the commandment in question, since to avoid a sin is itself an act of submission. For instance one may avoid getting rich in order to be free from the obligation of performing the pilgrimage or paying *zakāt*. What is therefore blameworthy is the avoiding of *zakāt* after it has once been contracted, but not before it has as yet been incurred. The view of Muḫammad is the one generally accepted.

The doctors are then unanimous in holding that the **zakat**

[1] Chap. 38, verse 43.

may not be avoided after it has once been incurred. Abu Yūsuf himself severely condemns [1] any attempt to defraud the public treasury.

It is not allowed, [he says], to one who believes in God and the Last Day to refuse the *ṣadaqah* or to alienate his property in favor of a group of people dividing it among them in a way that the share each receives is too little to be subject to *zakāt*, neither is it allowed for any cause or reason to resort to cunning in order to annul (*ibṭāl*) the *ṣadaqah*.

He further cites a report from 'Abdāllah Ibn Mas'ūd according to which the person who refuses to pay his *zakāt* is not a Moslem and is not admitted to say prayers (*la ṣalāt lahu*), and the *ḥadīth* of Abu Bakr: " If they should refuse me a halter (*'iqāl*) of what they used to give the Prophet as *zakāt*, I would indeed fight them when they refused it."

The Hanifite doctors have devised several **ways in which the payment of zakat may be lawfully avoided** by the property owner **before it has as yet become due.** Thus if a person owning two hundred *dirhams* desires to escape paying *zakāt* on them, the method is to give away as alms one of the two hundred *dirhams* just one day before the year has run out in order that the *niṣāb* may be incomplete at the end of the year. The same end is achieved if, instead of giving that *dirham* as alms, he gives it as a present to his minor son, or makes a present to him of the entire two hundred *dirhams*, or spends them on his children.

Again if a person wants to give alms to a poor person by giving up the claim he has on that poor person and to count the same for his *zakāt* dues, he may not do so, because it is an established Hanifite principle that the **zakat** of a definite article (*'ayn*) may not be **paid in terms of a claim** (*dayn*), neither may the *zakāt* of a claim be paid in terms of a dif-

[1] Yūsuf, p. 45.

ferent claim. The following trick, however, offers a way out of the difficulty: the creditor gives the poor an amount equal to his claim on him intending it for the settlement of his *zakāt* debt, and then the debtor, after receiving the *zakāt*, returns it to the creditor in settlement of his debt to him, such procedure being lawful. It is stated in the *Nawādir* that Muḫammad Ibn al-Hasan, when asked about his opinion of this trick, answered that it is preferable to pay one's *zakāt* to one's debtor. In fact the earlier Hanifite doctors used to resort to this trick in regard to their insolvent debtors. The creditor need not be afraid that the debtor after receiving the *zakāt*, may refuse to give it back in settlement of his debt, for the creditor can easily extend his hand to seize the property of his debtor, if such property happens to be of the same genus (*jins*) as the claim he has on him; and should the debtor attempt to prevent him from so doing, he can enforce his point of view by appealing to a judge. Another way of getting at the same result is to tell the debtor: "Name as your agent one of my servants in order to receive this as the *zakāt* of my property, and give him power to settle your debt to me by paying it back to me." When the agent receives the *zakāt* it becomes the property of his principal, that is, the debtor; but being also an agent for the settlement of the debt he pays the sum received back to the *zakāt* payer. Shams-al-a'immah al-Halwā'i (or al-Halwāni) said that when the property owner resorts to this trick it is advisable that the sum given to the debtor should exceed the amount of the debt by a little margin so that after the settlement of the debt there will still be left something in the hands of the debtor, and therefore he will not be tempted to refuse to settle his debt after receiving the money.

If the claim is a **joint claim**, then the other creditor is entitled to his share in the amount received on account. In order to avoid this inconvenience, one first gives the debtor as *zakāt* an amount in cash equal to his share of the claim. Then he gives up his share of the claim, by making an alms of it to the debtor, whereupon the debtor makes a gift of the cash received to the creditor, and in this case the other creditor is not entitled to a share in this cash, because it has not been given in settlement of their joint claim. Another way to obtain the same result is for the debtor to borrow from another person a sum equal to the creditor's share in the joint claim, and give it to the creditor as a gift. The creditor then returns it to the debtor as his *zakāt*, at the same time that he absolves the debtor from his share of the claim, and again the other creditor cannot claim anything from the cash he had received as a gift.

Cunning may be resorted to also with respect to the **zakat of sawa'im animals** as follows: the owner of the *sawā'im* animals exchanges them just one day before the completion of the year for animals of the same or a different genus, and in such case the year is dissolved and he escapes the *zakāt*. Or he makes a present of the animals to a person he trusts and after the completion of the year he takes back his present, and in such case the year begins to run from the date the gift has been revoked and taken back, and so the time that has passed before does not count against him in reckoning the *zakāt*. He may repeat the same trick every year.

It must be remembered that the giving of *zakāt* is valid only if the process involves a transfer of ownership (*tamlīk*) from one person to another. Consequently the *zakāt* obligation is not discharged if a person spends a certain sum of money for a public work (*wujūh al-birr*) or the funeral expenses (*takfīn*) of a poor person. The dodge here is to give the *zakāt* to a poor person and direct him to spend it for the purpose in view. The consequence is that the *tha-*

wāb of the *zakāt* belongs to the *zakāt* payer and that of the construction of the public work or the funeral to the poor person who attended to it. It must be stated here, however, that should the poor person, after receiving the *zakāt*, refuse to apply it to the purpose for which it was intended, the *zakāt* payer would have no legal claim against him.[1]

The Shafiites,[2] likewise, consider such practices abominable[3] if resorted to merely in order to avoid the *zakāt*. They do however allow them if they are necessary, or if the intention of avoiding the *zakāt* is only incidental.

Finally, **according to the Malikites,[4] cunning does not avail** in freeing one from an obligation, either in religious (*'ibādāt*) or in civil matters (*mu'āmalāt*). Thus if a person just before the end of the year makes a present of his property to his son or slave or, as sometimes happens, to his wife, with the intention of taking it back after the end of the year and so escaping the *zakāt* of that year, the *zakāt* is nevertheless collected from him and it is his duty to pay it of his own accord. It is likewise futile to resort to cunning with a view to settling one's *zakāt* in terms of one's claims, *e. g.*, by paying one's *zakāt* to one's poor debtor with the understanding that the debtor will return the *zakāt* as a payment on account of his debt. The later Malikites, however, disagree as regards the case in which the debtor pays back the *zakāt* of his own accord.

[1] *Durr*, p. 145.

[2] Anṣāri, p. 353; *Mugni*, p. 370.

[3] It must be pointed out here that the fact that a practice is considered abominable (*makrūh*) does not detract from its legal validity. It simply means that a person by committing it becomes a sinner.

[4] Dardir, p. 114; *cf.* Kharashi, pp. 57, 59, 61, 119.

CHAPTER IV

The Financial Contribution for the Conduct of Holy War (*ju'l*) and for Other Public Purposes

The word "*ju'l*" literally means compensation for work done, and, more specially, compensation for military services of a substitute, hence also, the financial contribution levied by the *imām* on Moslems who stay away from the war for the equipment of those who join the army. It is related of Omar that he equipped the bachelors at the expense of the married, giving the bachelors the horses of the married. Indeed, Omar was a man of great executive ability and had the interests of the Moslems at heart, for he knew that the minds of married people, unlike those of bachelors, go back to their families, and that they cannot stay away from them for long. In this way married people were enabled to stay with their wives and protect them, and yet participate in the war by means of their horses; and, on the other hand, the bachelors participated in the war in body. Some say that Omar used to do this only with the consent of the persons concerned, and that, failing such consent, he equipped the soldiers from the public funds. The proper view however is that the **imam has** the **right to levy** on the people the amount needed **if there are no available funds** (*māl*) **in the public treasury**, because the *imām* is entrusted with the interests of the Moslems, and if he should fail to equip an army for their defence the infidels would be victorious and seize their properties, children, and lives. It is therefore only wise policy to assess the people of means for raising the necessary funds.[1]

This is also the view held by the later Hanifite doctors.[2] If, however, there are available funds in the public treasury, then it is abominable to levy this impost, since the funds in question are destined for such purposes. Some of the later doctors, such as the authors of the *Hidāyah* and the *Durar*, hold that it is only abominable to levy the impost in case there are no available funds in the *fa'y* treasury, but others reply that if there are, for instance, *ṣadaqah* funds, it is still abominable to levy the impost since the *imām* may finance the campaign by borrowing money from the *ṣadaqah* funds on account of the *fa'y* treasury.

Irrespective of the levy of such an impost by the *imām*, it is **the duty of every Moslem** who has the means, but cannot fight himself, to equip another person who has not the means but can fight. Al-Sarakhsi, in support of this, says that the person who is able to fight needs a large amount of money to equip himself, and, on the contrary, the wealthy person who cannot fight himself needs some one to ward off the evils of the infidels from himself and his property, and therefore there is no harm in Moslems' helping one another. Moreover, the wealthy person by giving the poor fighter his equipment aids him in performing a *farḍ* obligation (*i. e.*, the obligation of holy war) and this is a commendable act on his part. If however the fighters have the means, then it is not proper for them to receive such help, because perfection in the performance of the holy war obligation is reached by participating in it both in person and wealth, and because if he received assistance it

[1] *Mabsūṭ*, part x, p. 20.

[2] *Majma'*, p. 495; *Baḥr*, vol. v, p. 79; *Hidāyah*, vol. v, p. 194; *Durar*, p. 165.

would be as if he performed his religious duty for a pecuniary reward (*ujrah*).[1]

According to al-Sugdi, as quoted in the *Baḥr,* if the person who stays at home (*qā'id*) says to the person who is going out to join the war (*shākhiṣ*): "Take this property and fight with it," it is not a case of being hired for fighting the holy war and is permissible, but if he says: "Take this in order to fight with it," it is a case of being hired and is not allowed.

According to Malik,[2] people in Medina used to practise the giving of *ju'l*; those who stayed at home equipping those who joined the colors. Mālik therefore did not see any objection to its practice as between two stipendiaries of the *Dīwān.* Ibn al-Qāsim, however, disapproves of stipendiaries' sending in their place non-stipendiaries by paying their expenses.

According to the Shafiites, it is not allowed to hire a Moslem to fight, but the stipends which the soldiers receive from the state are not a case of rental. If the *imām* assigns to a Moslem the task of washing a dead Moslem, he is not given a wage if the dead person has no estate and the treasury has no available funds.[3]

Al-Mawardi,[4] in discussing the duties of the public inspector (*muḥtasib*) with respect to the enforcement of acts recommended and prescribed by the *sharī'ah* (*amr bi 'l ma'rūf*), **extends this idea** of forced assessment from the carrying out of the holy war to every undertaking which redounds to the benefit of Moslems as a whole as follows:[5]

[1] *Mabsūṭ,* part x, p. 75.

[2] *Mudawwanah,* part iii, pp. 43-6.

[3] *Wajīz,* vol. ii, p. 189.

[4] Pp. 411-3.

[5] The general nature of the wording used by al-Māwardi would indicate that what he says in this connection applies to all the residents

If the water supply of a city is cut off or its walls are dilapidated, or if needy wayfarers come to it, there is no obligation for the people of the city to restore the supply of the water or build the walls or to aid the wayfarers so long as there are available funds in the treasury. This would also apply if their mosques and worshiping places (*masjid*) were dilapidated. If, however, there are no available funds in the treasury, then the obligation of doing the above rests upon all the people of means (*dhu 'l-miknah*) in general though upon no one of them in particular. Should the people of means undertake these tasks, the public inspector's right to order them lapses, and the former are not required to obtain permission for aiding the wayfarers or rebuilding what has been already demolished. However if they want to demolish what is dilapidated in order to rebuild it, they are not given the above prerogatives if, for instance, the matter concerns the walls of the mosque of all the inhabitants of a city. They must then obtain the permission of the authorities (*wali al-amr*), not of the public inspector; furthermore, they have to offer beforehand guarantee that they will build it. It is not, however, necessary to obtain the permission of the authorities as regards worshiping places of tribes and clans which are not used by many people (*fīma khaṣṣa*). It is the duty of the public inspector to require the people who demolished a building to build it up, but he may not force them to complete buildings begun by them for the first time.

When the persons of means desist from building and repairing the dilapidated buildings, if residence in the city is still possible, or if the water supply, although scanty, is

(*nās*) of the Moslem state, whether Moslems or *dhimmis*. Of course, when the contribution is levied on the *dhimmis* it is a secular impost and the general remarks made concerning religious taxes do not apply to it.

sufficient, the public inspector leaves them in peace. If, however, residence in a city becomes impossible on account of the cutting off of its water supply or the collapse of its walls, the authorities do not allow the residents to abandon their city, if—it being a frontier city—its abandonment would result in the prejudice of the "Moslem world". On the contrary, the persons of means are required to meet the emergency, in the way such untoward contingencies (*nawāzil*) are met. The duty of the public inspector, on his side, is to inform the sultan about the matter and to incite the people of means to meet the emergency.

If, however, the city is not a frontier city whose abandonment would result in the injury of the "Moslem world", the case is easier to deal with. The public inspector in such case has no right to force the inhabitants (*ahlahu*) to rebuild it, because the sultan is more entitled to this right, and if he has the funds, he sees to it that it is rebuilt. But if the sultan does not possess the funds, then the public inspector says to the inhabitants of the city: "You are free to abandon the city or to undertake to do what is necessary for rendering continued residence in it possible". If they undertake to do so, then they are all obligated to give generously what they will. The public inspector has not the right to force any one of them in particular to undertake to give what he would not of his own free will and consent, whether little or much, but he says: "Let each give what is easy for him to give and what pleases him". Those who can give money do so, and those who are not rich offer their services until a sufficient amount has been raised or its raising has been insured by the people of means who have pledged themselves for the amounts agreeable to them. Then the work is begun and each person is held to make good his pledge. Although such pledges are not valid in private relations, in this case they have been considered valid and binding because of the general interests involved. In cases where the interests of all Moslems are involved, the public inspector does not proceed to deal with the situation without previously asking for the permission of the sultan; but it is allowed to begin work without permission, if it is difficult to obtain permission or it is feared that meanwhile the evil will grow.[1]

[1] *Cf. infra*, p. 437; also p. 521.

CHAPTER V

PRELIMINARY CONSIDERATIONS

SECTION I

Classification of Persons [1]

ACCORDING to Mohammedan theory the world at large falls into two parts, the **world of Moslems** (*dār al-islām*) and the **world of foes,** the *ḥarbis*, (*dār al-ḥarb*).[2] An intermediate position may be assigned to the **world of allies** (*dār al-'ahd*), although strictly speaking the ally world is only a temporary stage, since theoretically Moslems are under obligation (*farḍ*) to engage in holy war until all infidels shall have accepted Islam or the status of *dhimmis*.[3] Indeed the *imām* may break the truce he may have

[1] Kāsāni, vol. vii, p. 102.

[2] For details concerning definitions and as to when *dār al-ḥarb* becomes *dār al-islām*, and *vice versa*, consult al-Kāsāni (vol. vii, p. 130), the *'Alamkīriyyah* (vol. ii, p. 330), and the *Technical Dictionary* (p. 466); also al-Māwardi (p. 239). Suffice it to say that the expression *dār al-islām* applies to every land where the *imām* (ruler) of the Moslems holds sway and the Moslems enjoy security, and that the enemy world (*dār al-ḥarb*) becomes moslem world when the *sharī'ah* prescriptions are enforced in it. There is divergence of opinion as to when the moslem world becomes enemy world.

[3] *Cf. Umm*, vol. iv, p. 91; *Wajīz*, vol. ii, p. 186; *Minhāj*, vol. iii, p. 255; *Kanz*, vol. ii, p. 253, no. 5393; Kharashi, p. 406. According to the *Mugni* (vol. iv, p. 193) the obligation of holy war should be fulfilled at least once a year. The "holy war," however, may be only negative and consist in the strengthening of defences instead of in actual aggression.

entered into with the infidels on condition of payment by them of *kharāj* and *jizyah,* if such a course is required by the best interests of Islam, provided however he gives them due notice. Normally therefore the Moslem world is in a state of war with the *ḥarbis* unless this state has been terminated in one of these three ways; namely, conversion to Islam, taking of refuge in the Sanctuary (*ḥarām*), and the giving of *amān*. Of these three ways, only the last need be discussed here. The giving of *amān* consists in pledging security and protection to the *ḥarbis* and may be temporary or perpetual.

(1) **The Temporary Aman** (*amān muwaqqat*). This is of two kinds: the well-known (*ma'rūf*) or informal, and the formal (*muwāda'ah*).

(a) **The Well-known Aman.**[1] Any freeborn Mohammedan, man or woman, may give pledge of protection (*amān*) to a *ḥarbi* or a group of *ḥarbis* or even the entire defensive force of a fortress, and thereupon the *ḥarbis* become *musta'mins* and are not molested, provided they can prove by two witnesses that they have been given *amān*. The *imām* however may repudiate such an *amān* and even punish the Moslem who gave it, if the latter was mistaken in thinking that Moslem interests required such a course.

(b) **The Formal Aman** or Truce Pact (*muwāda'ah*).[2] It is allowed to the *imām* or to a group of Moslems without the *imām's* permission to make truce with the *ḥarbis* (enemy) on condition of payment by them of a certain sum of money or goods, unless they are renegades; such are not given quarter, but have to choose between the sword and Islam. The money received from the enemy is considered as *jizyah* if the enemy agreed to pay it before the be-

[1] *Cf. Wajiz*, vol. ii, p. 194; *Minhāj*, vol. iii, p. 271; Kharashi, p. 420.

[2] The Shafiites and Malikites instead of *muwāda'ah* use *muhādanah* and *hudnah*.

ginning of hostilities; otherwise it is treated as spoils. It is even allowed to conclude a truce pact on condition of payment on the part of Moslems, if such course is indispensably necessary for the furtherance of the Moslem interests. The legal result of the pact is like that of the informal *amān*, namely, the enemy enjoys security from death and captivity, and security of property on the part of Moslems. If a person residing in the country with which the pact has been made, enters the country of the *ḥarbis* and subsequently the latter country is conquered by the Moslems, that person is treated as a *musta'min*. Likewise a *ḥarbi* entering the country of pact with *amān*, is considered a *musta'min* with regard to the Moslem country also if he has not meanwhile returned to the *dār al-ḥarb*. The *imām* may repudiate the pact made if that is conducive to the interests of Islam, provided the enemy is duly notified about it, and in such case there is returned to the enemy a proportionate part of the tribute paid by them. This is based on the precedent of the Prophet, who broke the agreement made between him and the Meccans.[1]

According to the Shafiites, a valid *amān* of either kind may not be annulled by the *imām* unless he suspects treachery.[2] The Malikites agree with the Shafiites as regards the formal *amān* only.[3] The dissolution of the pact takes place at the time set if one has been set. If no time has been set, the pact ends in two ways, namely, by express dissolution by either side, or implicitly, if, for instance, the *ḥarbis* go out on the highways with the permission of their ruler in order to rob Moslems. If the pact is made with the condition that in the country of the enemy the laws of Islam will be enforced, it is equivalent to giving the perpetual *amān*.

[1] *Majma'*, p. 498.

[2] *Minhāj*, vol. iii, pp. 272, 290.

[3] Kharashi, p. 449.

(2) **The Perpetual Aman** called *'aqd dhimmah.* This consists in the acquisition of the status of the *dhimmi,* and may be expressed or implicit, as, for instance, when the *ḫarbi* enters the Moslem state by a temporary *amān,* and exceeds the time limit set by the *imām,* or if no limit has been set, according to the *Mabsūṭ,*[1] when he resides in the Moslem state a year, but according to others, only after a time has been set and has elapsed. Indeed, when a *ḫarbi* enters the Moslem state by virtue of an *amān* the *imām* should notify him, that should he reside a year or more, he would be considered as a *dhimmi* and would be subject to the *jizyah* and the *kharāj.* The author of the *Majma'* approves of the policy of allowing the *ḫarbis* a short stay because in the contrary case trade would stop and the Moslems would suffer by it. If a *ḫarbi* buys a *kharāj* land he becomes *dhimmi* from the time the *kharāj* has been assessed on the land, even if the time previously set has not elapsed. The effect of becoming a *dhimmi* is security of property and life. Indeed in the field of civil transactions the *dhimmis* enjoy the same rights as the Moslems.[2]

In reply to the following question put by certain Moslems, "How may the *dhimmis* be allowed to persist in what is the worst of crimes, *i. e.,* unbelief, by payment of a monetary consideration?", al-Sarakhsi says that the object is not the monetary consideration, but their invitation to the Faith in the most beautiful way. In fact, as a result of the act of covenant (*'aqd al-dhimmah*) the *dhimmi* abandons fighting, and the person who does not fight may not be attacked. Then, too, "the *dhimmi* by living among the Moslems sees the beauties of the Moslem faith and is exhorted to, and often does, accept Islam."[3]

[1] *Majma',* p. 510.

[2] *Cf. Wajīz,* vol. ii, p. 201; *Minhāj,* vol. iii, p. 283.

[3] *Mabsūṭ,* part x, p. 77.

It is not within the power of the Moslem state to break of its own accord the pact of *dhimmah*, but the pact is not binding (*lāzim*) as regards the *dhimmis*.[1] The pact is considered dissolved in three ways: If the *dhimmi* becomes Moslem, because the reason in giving him the status of *dhimmi* was the possibility of his conversion to Islam, and the object in this case has been secured; or if the *dhimmi* returns to the land of *ḥarbis*, for by so doing he becomes like the renegades; except that if he is captured he is made a slave, which is not true of the renegades; or, thirdly, if the *dhimmi* fights the Moslems.

The pact is not broken, however, if the *dhimmis* do not pay the taxes, for it may be due to their poverty; or if they slander the Prophet, for this would only amount to an increase of unbelief, but unbelief was not an obstacle to their acquisition of the status of *dhimmi* in the first place.

The **refusal of a dhimmi to pay the jizyah** is not construed as a breach on his part of the pact of *dhimmah* by virtue of which he acquired the status of *dhimmi*, because the object in view is the *dhimmi's* acceptance of the obligation to pay the *jizyah*, but not its payment *per se*, and so when he refuses to pay the tax, his previous acceptance and the humiliation attendant on it are still there.

In the *Durar* it is stated that there is a difficulty involved in this view, because to refuse to pay the *jizyah* is virtually to state expressly that it will not be paid, as if one said: "I will not pay the *jizyah* in the future", and it is evident that this makes impossible the continuation of the acceptance unless refusal be construed to mean delay and offer of excuses, in which case the difficulty is removed. It may, however, be replied that in consequence of the *dhimmi's* acceptance of the obligation the *jizyah* becomes a debt, as in case of suretyship for wealth, and therefore if the *dhimmi* later says:

[1] *Cf. Wajiz*, vol. ii, p. 197; Kharashi, p. 447.

"I will not pay the *jizyah*", it has no legal effect beyond entailing his imprisonment, as in the case of other debts.[1]

According to the Shafiites,[2] the pact is broken if the *dhimmis* fight the Moslems, or if they refuse to pay the *jizyah* or to obey the Moslem laws, but, unless expressly stipulated, not if they debauch Moslem women or slander the Prophet. Finally, according to the Malikites,[3] the pact is broken in all the four cases mentioned.

Corresponding to the three "worlds", the Moslem, the ally, and the enemy, there are the three classes of persons designated as **Moslems, allies** (*mu'āhid*) and **enemies** (*ḥarbi*); besides, there are the classes of **dhimmis** and **musta'mins.** The *dhimmis* are, as already explained, the *ḥarbis* who have definitely committed themselves to the protection of the Moslems, whereas the *musta'mins* are persons who have come under that protection only temporarily.

SECTION II

Classification of Waters and Lands[4]

Waters are distinguished into tithe and *kharāj* water.[5] **Tithe water** is the water of rivers, seas, and springs situated, and of wells sunk, in the first four[6] classes of tithe lands set forth below, or as the author of the *Hidāyah* puts it, it is water that has not come under the jurisdiction (*wilāyah*) of any person.

[1] *Majma'*, p. 519.

[2] *Minhāj*, vol. iii, p. 286; *Wajīz*, vol. ii, p. 203.

[3] Kharashi, p. 447.

[4] *Majma'*, pp. 178, 512; *Fatḥ*, p. 199, also vol. v, p. 277; *Jāmi'*, p. 328.

[5] This distinction is according to the Hanifites. The Shafiites and Malikites ignore it because, according to them, in determining the kind of tax to be levied on a piece of land, the status of the land-owner and the land is more significant than that of the water used in its irrigation. (*Cf.* Māwardi, pp. 262, 310.)

[6] *'Ināyah*, p. 199.

Kharaj water, on the other hand, is the water of rivers, seas, and springs situated, and of wells sunk, in *kharāj* lands. It includes also the water of rivers dug by Persian kings, such as the river Yazdajard, and the water of springs and canals dug at the expense of the public treasury.[1] Likewise, according to Abu Hanīfah and Abu Yūsuf, the water of the rivers Sayḫūn, Jayḫūn (Oxus), Euphrates, Tigris, and Nile is *kharāj* water, because these rivers are from time to time taken under possession (*yad*), in that in these rivers vessels often are placed alongside one another so as to form a sort of bridgeway on which one may pass across to the other bank. According to Muḫammad Ibn al-Hasan, however, these rivers are tithe rivers because they are not under the protection of any person, but are like the open sea, and because the forming of bridges referred to by the others is rare. According to the *Fatḫ*, the reason why waters which were formerly under the possession of unbelievers become *kharāj* water is because, like the rest of the property of unbelievers, through the fact of conquest, waters, too, become booty of war and like the lands they become objects of *kharāj* when left to the infidels.

Tithe lands are the following:

(1) The entire land of the Arabs, namely, the country extending from the borders of Syria and Kūfah to the farthest point of Yaman, or according to al-Karkhi, the districts of al-Hijāz, Tihāmah, Yaman, Tā'if, and Barriyyah. The land of the Arabs has been considered as tithe land, because the Prophet, and after him the four "righteous" califs, did not impose on it the *kharāj*, and because the payment of *kharāj* involves humiliation, and the lands of the Arabs do not deserve *kharāj* any more than their persons

[1] Kāsāni, p. 58.

deserve slavery. In fact, the *kharāj* is imposed only on lands whose owners may persist in their unbelief, but the Arabs, if they are heathens, have only two alternatives to choose between, namely, Islam and the sword.

(2) As an exception, Baṣrah has been considered tithe land owing to an *ijmā'* of the Companions. Abu Yūsuf says that by analogy Baṣrah should be *kharāj* land because it is a part of *kharāj* country, but that analogy was abandoned in this case in consequence of the practice of the Companions who levied the tithe on the lands of Baṣrah.[1] The Shafiite view is to the same effect.[2]

According to al-Māwardi this view as to the lands of Baṣrah being tithe lands has been justified by the doctors of 'Irāq (*i. e.,* the Hanifites) who follow Abu Hanīfah on two different grounds: the first ground is that the water of the Tigris, which, according to Abu Hanīfah, is *kharāj* water diminishes at ebb time in the vicinity of Baṣrah and that the lands are irrigated at flow time only, that is, from sea water. Al-Māwardi remarks that this reasoning is false in view of the fact that the flow holds the sweet water back from the sea and prevents its mixing with the sea water, and that consequently the lands are irrigated from the water of the Tigris. The second ground is that the water of Tigris and the Euphrates disappears in the Great Swamps (*Baṭā'iḫ*) and loses its character of *kharāj* water since the Great Swamps are not *kharāj* rivers; consequently when the water reappears at Baṣrah, it is no longer *kharāj* water. Al-Māwardi after remarking that this second reasoning is also false, adds that the grounds invoked by the Hanifites as justification for their view on the matter are only pretexts and that their view in reality is based on the *ijmā'* of the Companions.

[1] *Cf.* Zayla'i, vol. iii, p. 272.

[2] *Cf.* Māwardi, p. 310.

(3) All the lands whose owners became Moslems of their own accord and have been allowed to remain in possession of their lands.

(4) All the lands which were conquered by force (*'anwat*) and divided among the victorious Moslem army, or for that matter among any Moslems. This is because it is not fitting to begin with *kharāj* in taxing the land of a Moslem for the first time, and because the tithe is lighter than the *kharāj*, and includes besides an element of worship. According to al-Shāfi'i such lands become booty of war (*ganīmah*) and as such they are divided among the victorious army who pay for them tithe, but never *kharāj*. According to Mālik, however, these lands by the very fact of conquest become common property (*waqf*) of all the Moslems and pay *kharāj* as a rental (*kirā'*).[1] Abu Hanīfah, on the contrary, gives the calif the option of dividing these lands among the army and levying the tithe, or of leaving them to their non-Moslem owners and collecting from them the *kharāj*.

(5) The Habitations (*dār*) of Moslems which have been converted by their owners into gardens, provided they are irrigated with tithe water.[2] If they are watered alternately with tithe and *kharāj* water, they are still tithe lands.

(6) The waste lands (*mawāt*) developed (*iḥyā'*) for cultivation by Moslems with the *imām's* permission; according to Abu Yūsuf, if the lands are situated in a tithe district; but according to Muḥammad Ibn al-Hasan, if the lands have been developed with tithe water.[3]

According to the *Muḥīṭ*,[4] the principle just referred to

[1] Māwardi, p. 254; Kharashi, pp. 426-7; Dardīr, p. 200. See *infra*, under (4) of *Kharāj* lands.

[2] *Majma'*, p. 178.

[3] *Mabsūṭ*, part iii, pp. 57-58. But *cf.* Māwardi, p. 310.

[4] *Jāmi'*, p. 328.

with respect to waste lands developed for the first time applies also to lands previously developed and already subject to *kharāj* or tithe, namely, that if a *kharāj* land is cut off from its *kharāj* water and is watered with tithe water it becomes tithe land, and *vice versa*. The same view is expressed by al-Zayla'i [1] as well as the *Durar*,[2] and the *Durr* [3] except that they restrict this to the Moslem owners only, the non-Moslem owners always paying *kharāj* irrespective of the water they use. The *Fatḥ*, however, restricts this to the case of waste lands first developed by Moslems.[4]

The contention of Abu Yūsuf is that when a piece of land is in a tithe district it legally becomes a dependency (*taba'*) of the district and pays tithe like the rest of the district, exactly as the immediate surroundings of the house are a dependency of the house and, like it, are exempt from taxation. Muḥammad's ground is that it is not proper to begin with *kharāj* in taxing the land of a Moslem for the first time, except when the Moslem voluntarily incurs such treatment by developing his land with *kharāj*, rather than with tithe, water. Finally, the ground for the view expressed in the *Muḥīṭ* is that the tax levied on a land depends on its productivity and the latter on the kind of water used. However, in the case of the non-Moslem owner the water is disregarded, because the payment of tithe is an act of worship which only Moslems can perform. Therefore the non-Moslem owner perforce pays *kharāj* in either case.

According to al-Māwardi [5] a waste land developed for

[1] Vol. iii, p. 271. [2] P. 177. [3] P. 364.

[4] *Fatḥ*, vol. v, p. 280. According to al-Shāfi'i (Māwardi, pp. 262-3, 310), the kind of tax levied on land depends on the kind of land, not of water used, and therefore, contrary to what Abu Hanīfah held, the owner of a tithe land should be allowed to use *kharāj* water, and *vice versa*.

[5] P. 310.

cultivation is subject to tithe irrespective of the water used in its irrigation.

The kharaj lands, on the other hand, are the following:

(1) The Sawād of 'Irāq, namely, the territory included lengthwise between Hadīthah and 'Abbādān, both on the Euphrates, and in breadth between the streams 'Udhayb near Kūfah, and Hulwān. This territory was called Sawād, meaning black, because, owing to its rich flora it appeared black, from a distance. The Sawād is *kharāj* land because Omar in the presence of the Companions imposed on it the *kharāj*.

According to the Hanifites the Sawād was conquered by force and its lands were left in the ownership of their original owners who may therefore sell their lands to one another and in general exercise all the rights of ownership.

The Shafiites,[1] while agreeing with the Hanifites that the Sawād was conquered by force, claim that subsequently the army was induced by proper compensation to relinquish its property rights in the lands of Sawād, which were thereupon made *waqf* for the benefit of all Moslems, and leased in perpetuity (*ijārah mu'abbadah*) to the former owners who thereby, being mere tenants, may not sell or inherit them.[2] Al-Shāfi'i[3] says that the question whether the

[1] *Minhāj*, vol. iii, p. 269; *Wajīz*, vol. ii, p. 193; Māwardi, p. 302.

[2] According to the Hanifite Abu Bakr al-Rāzi, as quoted by al-Zayla'i (vol. iii, p. 272), there are ten different reasons against the Shafiite fiction about the lands of Sawād being held by their cultivators merely on lease. The most important of these reasons are as follows: A lease implies offer and acceptance by the parties, and in this case they are absent; had it been a case of lease, the Companions could not have bought any lands of the Sawād, as they have done; it cannot be a case of lease, for the term and object of a lease must be known, furthermore such term may not be perpetual; then, too, a lease would not lapse on conversion to Islam, but according to al-Shāfi', the *kharāj* lapses on conversion.

[3] *Umm*, vol. iv, p. 193; Muzani, vol. v, p. 192.

Sawād was conquered by force of arms, or acquired through treaty cannot be positively settled in view of the many contradictory *ḥadīths* bearing on the matter. However, he strongly inclines to believe certain *ḥadīths* according to which immediately after the conquest of the Sawād one-fourth of it was divided among one-fourth of the army who received the rentals for 3-4 years until the calif Omar by proper compensation obtained their consent to the return of the lands in order that they might be made *waqf* for the benefit of all Moslems. In refutation of al-Shāfi'i, al-Sarakhsi says the following:

Al-Shāfi'i said in his book: " I do not know just what to say concerning the Sawād of Kūfah, but I will make a guess which is near to knowledge ", but such a statement is contradictory and a sign of ignorance on the part of the person who made it, for how may a guess (*ẓann*) be called knowledge unless one of its two sides predominates on the basis of evidence. Moreover, the conquest of Sawād by force is too well-known to be a secret to any one and there is no need to go to all this trouble, for al-Shāfi'i now says: " Omar made the lands property of the Moslems and made the residents slaves, afterwards allowing them to work on the lands of the Moslems, and the *kharāj* and *jizyah* which he imposed upon them is a kind of impost (*ḍarībah*), exactly as the master arranges with his slave for an impost on his earnings and employs him," and again he says: " He (Omar) set them free as a favor and acquired the ownership of the lands, then he leased them to the (people of Sawād) and the *kharāj* he imposed on them is a rental." However, this is absurd, for their *jizyah* is too well-known to be a secret, and in fact they have been accustomed to sell these lands to one another and inherit them from one another from that time to this, and so we know that the correct view is that of our own doctors, namely, that he (Omar) set them free as a favor and made them a present of their lands and he imposed on them the *jizyah* for their heads and the *kharāj* for their lands.[1]

[1] *Mabsūṭ, ibid; cf. Umm*, vol. iv, p. 192.

According to the Malikites Sawād was conquered by force and by that very fact became *waqf* territory.

(2) Egypt, because when it was conquered by 'Amr Ibn al-'As, Omar imposed on it the *kharāj*.

(3) Syria, because concerning it there is an *ijmā'*. According to the *Fatḥ*[1] the tax collected "at present" from the lands of Egypt and, by analogy, of Syria, is not *kharāj* but in reality a rental, because the lands became property of the state as the owners gradually died without rightful heirs. According to the Malikites,[2] like the lands of the Sawād, those of Syria and Egypt were also conquered by force and are *waqf* lands.

(4) All lands that were conquered by force (*'anwat*) and were not divided among the victorious army but were left to the original owners or given to non-Moslem settlers brought from elsewhere. The Prophet made an exception in the case of Mecca, which city, although conquered by force and left to its owners, was not subjected to *kharāj*. According to al-Shāfi'i,[3] Mecca was conquered by treaty. However, al-Gazzāli[4] and Mālik agree with the Hanifites. According to the *Majma'*, this is because the lands of the Arabs are not subject to *kharāj* any more than their persons are liable to slavery. According to al-Shāfi'i,[5] however, following the precedent of the Prophet with the people of Khaybar and the tribe of Qurayẓah, lands too, like chattel, become the property of the army which conquered them, and after deduction of the state's share of one-fifth they are divided among the army and only pay tithe. However,

[1] *Durr*, p. 364; *Baḥr, Minḥah*, vol. v, p. 114.

[2] Kharashi, p. 426.

[3] *Cf.* Māwardi, p. 284; *Minhāj*, vol. iii, p. 271.

[4] *Wajīz*, vol. ii, p. 194.

[5] *Umm*, vol. iv, p. 193.

the soldiers may of their own accord relinquish their rights in these lands, and then the *imām* makes them into *waqf* and the state collects their rental (*gallah*). According to the Malikites,[1] lands conquered by force of arms by that very fact become *waqf* but are nevertheless left in the hands of their former owners in order that they may better be able to pay the *jizyah*. These lands are subject to the *kharāj*, which in reality is a rental, and being *waqf* lands, they revert to the state, upon the death of their holders. Unlike the lands, the buildings conquered by force, pay no rental, though they also become *waqf*. However, buildings put up by the *dhimmis* on *waqf* ground after the conquest become their private property.

The author of the *Multaqa*, following al-Qudūri, says that these lands do not become tithe lands even when irrigated with tithe water. The author of the *Hidāyah*, on the other hand, quoting the *al-Jāmiʻ al-Sagīr*, says:[2]

"All lands conquered by force and irrigated by rivers are *kharāj* lands, and if they are not irrigated by rivers, but by springs issuing from them, they are tithe lands." The author of the *Fatḫ*, however, remarks that the preceding quotation can refer only to waste lands which were conquered by force from infidels and were first developed by Moslems. Indeed the cultivated lands so conquered, if left to their infidel owners, are *kharāj* lands, even if watered by rain (*i. e.*, tithe water); on the other hand, if such lands were divided among the Moslem soldiery, they are tithe lands, even if watered by rivers (*i. e.*, *kharāj* water).[3] For while it is unanimously admitted that in taxing the infidel for his land for the first time, he is always taxed *kharāj*,

[1] Kharashi, p. 426.

[2] *Hidāyah*, vol. v, p. 280.

[3] But *cf.* Zayla'i, vol. iii, p. 271; *Durar*, p. 176; *Durr*, p. 364.

the Moslem's land is never taxed *kharāj* for the first time unless it be that the Moslem entails upon himself such treatment by his own consent, namely, by developing his land with *kharāj*, instead of with tithe, water.[1]

(5) Lands concerning which the *imām* (*i. e.*, the Moslem ruler) has come to an agreement with their infidel owners that the lands shall be left to them and that they will not be forced to migrate. According to the *'Alamkīriyyah*,[2] the *imām*, if he chooses, may impose on these lands the tithe (*'ushr*) but this is in name only, for such a tax " is in reality *kharāj* and it is for that very reason that this tithe is disbursed like the *kharāj* ". An example of this class are the lands of the people of Najrān who had made an agrement with the Prophet to pay on their lands a fixed amount of *kharāj*. Another example is the tribe of Taglib who had a similar treaty with Omar. Balkh and Sugd are further examples. According to this, the lands of Samarqand should also be *kharāj* lands, but because they were on the frontier, they were made tithe lands for insuring the protection of the frontiers.[3]

In the *Nutaf* it is written that when the *imām* agrees with a Moslem people upon a certain tribute to be paid by them on their lands this tribute is legally a tithe, and if it is less than the lawful rate of tithe the balance must be disbursed by the people directly to the poor. This applies also to agreements made with the infidels if they later become Moslems.[4]

[1] *Majma'*, p. 513; *Fatḥ*, vol. v, p. 280; *Baḥr*, vol. v, p. 113; *Durar*, p. 176; *Durr*, p. 364; *Jāmi'*, p. 328.

[2] Vol. ii, p. 291.

[3] In other words, Moslem soldiers stationed on the frontiers were given in fief *kharāj* lands, and as an inducement to military pursuits they were required to pay on these lands the tithe instead of the *kharāj*, because the former was much lighter and, besides, could be paid to the poor by the soldiers themselves.

[4] *Jāmi'*, p. 330.

According to the **Shafiite view**, as summed up by al-Māwardi,[1] this class of lands are the only ones which pay the *kharāj* and they fall into two classes: (a) The lands whose owners (*ahl*) have evacuated them, so that they came into Moslem hands without fighting. These lands become immobilized (*waqf*) in the general interest of Moslems and are subject to *kharāj*, which is really a rental collected from them forever, even if no time limit was set for it, because the benefit derived from these lands belongs to the entire Moslem community. Moreover, the *kharāj* levied on these lands is not affected by conversion to Islam, and being *waqf* lands, they may not be alienated by sale to private individuals. (b) The lands whose owners have not abandoned them and which by the terms of the agreement are left in the possession (*yad*) of the owners (*ahl*), subject to the payment of *kharāj*. This class is of two kinds: (i) The owners have by the terms of the agreement relinquished their rights of ownership in the lands in favor of the Moslems. These lands become *waqf* (mortmain) in the interest of all Moslems, as was the case with lands whose owners had abandoned them, and the *kharāj* levied on these lands is a rental (*ujrah*) which does not lapse on their conversion to Islam, neither can they validly sell the ownership in the lands (*bay' riqābihim*). However, they are entitled to (the possession of) the lands more than others (*aḥaqq*) so long as they abide by the terms of the agreement and the lands may not be taken away from their possession, whether they persist in their unbelief or are converted to Islam, just as land which was leased may not be taken away from the possession (*yad*) of the tenant. These people by paying the *kharāj* do not become exempt from the *jizyah*, should they acquire the status of *dhimmi*

[1] Pp. 254-6, also pp. 237-9; *cf. Umm*, vol. iv, pp. 103, 193.

by settling (in the "Moslem world"); for they are not allowed to reside for an entire year unless they relinquish the status of ally (*ḥukm al-'ahd*) and become *dhimmis*. They may however reside for a shorter time without paying the *jizyah*. (ii) By the terms of the agreement they preserve their ownership (*milk*) in the lands but pay *kharāj* on the lands in consideration therefor. According to al-Shāfi'i,[1] the *jizyah* to be paid yearly should be a definite sum, for there is no advantage, he goes on to say, in stipulating that the *kharāj* shall be so much *per jarīb* when there is a produce, since crops may fail or be abundant, and so the amount which will be collected is never known. This *kharāj* is of the nature of a *jizyah* which is levied on them so long as they persist in unbelief but lapses upon their conversion to Islam. It is also allowed not to provide for the payment of a *jizyah*. These people may sell their lands to any persons they desire, including Moslems and *dhimmis*. When they sell their lands among themselves, the amount of *kharāj* is not affected, but if they sell them to Moslems, the latter do not pay *kharāj*. If, finally, the land is sold to a *dhimmi*, from one point of view the tax should also lapse, because by being a *dhimmi* the owner remains outside of the scope of the treaty by which the tax was collected, since that treaty was made with the "allies"; but from another point of view the *kharāj* should not be allowed to lapse, because the *dhimmi*, like the allies, is also an unbeliever.

When the *kharāj* lapses with respect to some of the lands by reason of the owners being Moslems (*bi islām ahlihi*), if the *kharāj* was assessed on the basis of area, at the rate of so much silver or grain *per jarīb* of area, the remaining lands pay the usual rate, which is not increased to allow for the part that has lapsed. If, however, the *kharāj* was

[1] *Umm*, vol. iv, p. 104.

assessed as a lump sum without regard to area, according to al-Shāfi'i, the amount which lapsed on account of the owners being Moslems is deducted from the total, but according to Abu Hanīfah the share of such Moslems is not deducted from the total.

According to the Malikites,[1] when a city comes under Moslem rule as a result of a treaty stipulating the payment of a tribute under the name of *jizyah* or *kharāj*, the lands of the city in every case remain in the ownership of the former owners who inherit and may sell them at will. Other points, however, vary according to the terms of the treaty as follows:

(a) The tribute may have been fixed at a lump sum (*ujmilat*) without being distributed over the heads (*riqāb*) or the lands, *e. g.*, at so much *per* tree or unit area. The amount of the tribute in this case does not vary with the increase or decrease of the population of the city, but remains constant, and every one of the people of the city continues to be responsible for the entire tribute until it has been paid. When one of them dies without heirs his lands devolve to his fellow people who become responsible for his tribute. If some of them should become Moslems they become exempt from tribute, but they nevertheless continue to own their lands. According to Ibn Habīb, however, they forfeit their lands when they become Moslems, because the lands are legally immobilized in order to enable them to pay the *jizyah*, and consequently they may not be inherited or sold.

(b) The tribute, on the contrary, may have been distributed over the heads or the lands, or over both. In such case the tribute varies with the number of the heads or the area of the lands. The latter continue to be the property

[1] Kharashi, and 'Adawi, pp. 444-5; Dardīr, p. 204; *cf.* Ibn Rushd, *M.*, p. 280.

of their owners even after conversion, notwithstanding that in such case they become exempt from tribute. Should one of them die without heirs, his lands become *waqf* property of all the Moslems unless it be that he had willed away one-third of such lands. He cannot, however, in the absence of heirs, will more than one-third of his lands. In case the tribute was distributed over the lands, whether or not it was distributed over the heads, the owners and their heirs do not become free from the *kharāj* by selling their lands, but continue to pay it. According to one doctor, in case of sale, the *kharāj* should be paid by the whole community rather than by the seller, and after his death, by his heirs alone. According to a third view of the matter, the *kharāj* should be paid by the buyer.

(6) Waste lands developed for cultivation by *dhimmis* with the state's permission.

(7) Lands granted by the *imām* to the *dhimmis* from the lands conquered from the enemy in consideration of assistance rendered by the *dhimmis* in fighting the enemy.[1]

(8) Waste lands developed for cultivation by Moslems if they have been developed with *kharāj* water, or are situated in a *kharāj* district.

(9) Habitations of *dhimmis* converted into gardens. Also habitations of Moslems converted into gardens, if they are irrigated with *kharāj* water.[2]

If a dhimmi buys a land from a Taglabi, he pays on it the double rate of two-tenths, because according to Abu Hanīfah, as well as his two disciples, Abu Yūsuf and Muḥammad, the rate is doubled in regard to the *dhimmi*, as it is doubled, for instance, when he passes the public collector (*'āshir*). According to Abu Hanīfah, likewise, two-tenths

[1] *Durar*, p. 176.

[2] For details concerning this and the preceding class, see classes 5 and 6 of tithe lands.

is collected if the land is bought by a Moslem, instead of by a *dhimmi*, or if the owner (the Taglabi) becomes a Moslem, because the land was taxed at that rate before and the charge continues as it was. According to Abu Yūsuf, however, the rate is reduced to one-tenth, because the doubling of the rate was due to the owner's being an infidel, and when he is a Moslem the tax should be only one-tenth. Muhammad in this connection agrees with Abu Hanīfah, for he believes in the continuation of the double rate, although he does not believe in the doubling of the rate after it had been one-tenth.[1]

If a non-Taglabi dhimmi buys a tithe land from a Moslem, according to Abu Hanīfah the land becomes *kharāj* land and he pays *kharāj* on it. According to Abu Yūsuf he pays a double rate. According to Muhammad he pays only a single rate. Mālik claims that the *dhimmi* is forced to sell it back to a Moslem. Al-Shāfi'i, according to one report, considers the sale of a tithe land to a *dhimmi* as essentially null and void, but according to another report, the land pays both tithe and *kharāj*. Finally, Sharīk Ibn 'Abdāllah, following the analogy of *sawā'im* animals, said that the *dhimmi* pays for the land no tax whatever. The argument of Mālik is that the right of the poor is attached to the land, but because the property of an infidel is not fit for payment in discharge of this right, the *dhimmi* is forced to sell it back to a Moslem. Muhammad's ground is that the charge attaching to the land does not change with the status of the owner. Moreover, according to one report from him, the single rate of tithe collected from the *dhimmi* is disbursed like the proceeds of *zakāt* to the poor, because the right of the poor was already attached to it. The reason of Abu Yūsuf is that when the

[1] *Majma'*, pp. 177-8.

infidel is subject to the same tax as the Moslem the rate to him is doubled. The reason of Abu Hanīfah, finally, is that productive lands in Moslem states cannot remain untaxed, and that of the two taxes, the *kharāj* and the tithe, the tithe is precluded here because it is a kind of *ṣadaqah*, which the infidel may not pay, and that therefore he is subject to *kharāj*. If the land sold by the Moslem returns to him or to another Moslem through the exercise of the right of pre-emption or option (*khiyār*), or through the sale's being imperfect (*fāsid*), or by virtue of a judgment of dissolution on the ground of a defect (*'ayb*) in the land, it becomes again a tithe land. If, however, the land is returned to its former Moslem owner for a defect without a judgment to that effect, or by reason of a dissolution of the sale by the common consent of the two parties (*iqālah*) then, because such a dissolution is a new sale as regards third parties, the Moslem owner pays *kharāj* on it.[1]

If a Moslem buys a kharaj land from a dhimmi, the land still pays *kharāj*, according to the Hanifites. Mālik says that the land becomes tithe land because *kharāj* involves humiliation and a Moslem is never humiliated either when he acquires a land that is not subject to *kharāj*, or even when, for instance, he buys land already paying *kharāj*. Al-Sarakhsi says that Mālik, in arriving at his conclusion, likened the *kharāj* of heads (*kharāj al-ru'ūs*) to that of lands.[2] But this is not true, not only because the precedents of Ibn Mas'ūd, al-Hasan Ibn 'Ali, and Abu Hu-

[1] *Durr*, p. 143.

The difference between dissolution for defect by a judge and dissolution by the two parties lies in the fact that dissolution by the judge in virtue of the general authority (*wilāyah 'āmmah*) vested in him amounts to an absolute dissolution (*faskh*) of the sale, as if the Moslem seller had never sold his land. Consequently the latter continues to pay tithe on his land.

[2] *Cf. Umm*, vol. iv, p. 193; vol. vii, p. 325.

rayrah, who paid *kharāj* on lands owned by them in the Sawād, point to the conclusion that the *kharāj* must be continued on the land with respect to its new Moslem owner, but also because the humiliation in paying *kharāj* exists only when the *kharāj* is imposed on a land for the first time, but not when it is continued on a land that already was paying it. Just as it is not an humiliation to continue in the status of slavery after conversion to Islam, although it is humiliating to a person to be reduced to slavery after having become a Moslem. As regards the *ḥadīth* invoked by certain opponents to the effect that the Prophet referring to instruments of agriculture said: "These have not entered the house of a people but that they have become degraded", the meaning is only that if Moslems occupy themselves with agriculture, follow the tails of oxen, and so become sedentary and abandon the holy war, their enemies will return to the charge upon them and so humiliate them; it by no means signifies that the payment of *kharāj* is humiliating. The *kharāj* of heads, however, is different because it is humiliating whether assessed in the first place or continued, and therefore if a person paying this *kharāj* becomes a Moslem he ceases to pay it. Al-Sarakhsi adds that all this is based on the customs of the people.[1]

Later doctors[2] distinguished, besides tithe and *kharāj* lands, a **third class of lands called amiriyyah** (also *mamlakat*) lands. These are lands conquered by force or gained by treaty which were not left in the ownership of their former proprietors but were made the property of the public treasury (*bayt-al-māl*). Their proprietors therefore were reduced to mere tenants (*mutaṣarrif*) and paid on the produce of the

[1] *Mabsūṭ*, part iii, p. 5; *cf.* part x, p. 83.

[2] *Majma'*, p. 513. For details, see Bélin, Padel, Gatteschi, and Husni (pp. 19-20).

land a proportional *kharāj* commonly known as tithe (*'ushr*). The tenants do not have the right to sell, or make gift of, or constitute as *waqfs,* their lands unless so permitted by the sultan. Furthermore, if they allow the lands to lie idle for three years they forfeit their rights of tenancy, and the lands are leased again upon repayment of their value. Formerly the right of inheritance was restricted to the male children of the tenant only, his daughters and paternal brothers enjoying only a right of preference to acquire the tenancy rights by payment of the land's value. Later the right of inheritance has by law been considerably extended. The transfer of the tenancy rights in these lands is effected only by permission of the sultan or his representative.[1]

[1] This permission is a matter of form only, being never refused. The legal status of these lands viewed from the standpoint of the *sharī'ah* is not well defined. Thus the concession of the tenancy rights in these lands is not exactly in accordance with the *sharī'ah* principles concerning location (*ijārah*) because the duration and the rental are not known. Turkish *faqīhs* consider it a case of extra-*sharī'ah* or imperfect (*fāsid*) location. (*Cf.* Husni, pp. 24, 93.) Consequently, the lump sum paid at the time of the concession, which is called *ṭāpu*, and is equal to the value of the land, is looked upon as the anticipated part (*mu'ajjalah*) of the future rentals, while the taxes collected yearly as tithe or *muqāṭa'ah, etc.*, are considered as the delayed (*mu'ajjalah*) part of the same. In Turkey the so-called *ijāreteynli waqfs* present another case in which the exigencies of the times have made a departure from accepted principles necessary.

CHAPTER VI

THE KHARAJ OR LAND-TAX [1]

THE word *kharāj* literally means the revenue derived from a piece of land or a slave. Technically it denotes the tax imposed on land, and by extension, it also means the *jizyah*. According to the *Fatḥ*, the proper meaning of the word *kharāj* is the *kharāj* of land, and therefore it may not be construed to mean the *kharāj* of heads (*ru'ūs*), that is, the *jizyah*, unless there is an indication to that effect.[2]

[1] *Majma'*, p. 512; *Mabsūṭ*, part x, p. 79; *Hidāyah*, vol. v, p. 281; *Jāmi'*, p. 330; *Durr*, p. 364; *Durar*, p. 177; *'Alamkīriyyah*, vol. ii, p. 337; *Baḥr*, vol. v, p. 115; Māwardi, p. 253. Unlike the Hanifites, the Malikites and the Shafiites, with the exception of al-Māwardi, do not discuss the *kharāj* beyond summarily indicating the disbursement of its proceeds. As regards the *kharāj* levied on the strength of a treaty, it is easy to explain why they do not discuss it, for the details of its administration in that case did not concern the central Moslem authorities, who were interested in the proceeds only. On the other hand, as regards the *kharāj* levied on lands conquered by force and brought under immediate Moslem administration, we saw that such lands were legally considered as *waqf* property left in the possession of their original owners by perpetual leases in return for the payment of rentals known as *kharāj*. Al-Shāfi'i (*Umm*, vol. iii, p. 240) considers the nature of their holdings in the lands as one of *qabālah*, namely, an undertaking to pay the *kharāj* in return for their cultivation. Later Shafiites (*Tanbīh*, p. 300; *Wajīz*, vol. ii, p. 201; *Mugni*, vol. iv, p. 217; *cf.* Māwardi, p. 303), on the other hand, consider it a case of perpetual lease (*ijārah mu'abbadah*), the *kharāj* levied being a rental pure and simple. Apparently the theory is that such lands are governed by the principles of location (*ijārah*) in general. Probably these facts account for the silence of the two schools on this subject.

[2] *Tech. Dict.*, p. 409.

The *kharāj* is levied only on the lands which come under the description of *kharāj* lands, as explained in the last section, and is of two kinds, the **proportional kharaj** (*kharāj muqāsamah*) and the **fixed kharaj** (*kharāj waẓīfah* or *muwaẓẓaf*).[1]

The Proportional *Kharāj* consists in a proportion of the produce of the ground, like one-half, one-third, one-fourth, or one-fifth of the same. The *Kharāj waẓīfah,* on the contrary, is a fixed charge on the ground, at so much of natural produce or money per unit area or per tree.

The *kharāj* is levied on land irrespective of whether the owner is a minor or adult, free or slave (*mukātab*), man or woman, Moslem or infidel. Consequently if the *dhimmi* owner of the land is converted to Islam, or if he sells his land to a Moslem, the land is still subject to *kharāj*. However, Mālik said that in such case the *kharāj* is remitted exactly as the *jizyah* is remitted.

In the case of **the fixed kharaj the rates imposed by the calif Omar** on the lands of Sawād in 'Irāq constitute the

[1] Max Van Berchem (p. 53), inferring from al-Balādhuri's use of the word *muqāṭa'ah*, distinguishes a third kind of *kharāj*, the **kharaj muqata'ah**. He means by it the *kharāj* paid as a lump sum by certain tributary provinces, especially such of them as were on the border of the Moslem empire and had been able to preserve their autonomy. On the other hand, according to the Persian commentary of al-Māwardi's *al-Aḥkām al-Sulṭāniyyah* (Māwardi, pp. 33 *et seq.* of the notes) the word *muqāṭa'ah* denotes the lump sum agreed upon to be paid yearly to the state by individuals in consideration of (public) lands made over to them by the state. The commentary adds that this procedure was followed as regards waste lands which needed development or villages and estates which needed improvement. The *'Alamkīriyyah* (vol. ii, p. 344) seems to use the word in this second sense when it says that the *imām* may give away, in the form of *muqāṭa'ah, kharāj* lands abandoned by their owners. The standard books on *fiqh* do not discuss either one of these two meanings of *muqāṭa'ah*. The only reference to it which I have come across is in the *Jāmi'* (p. 331) to the effect that the *kharāj waẓīfah* is also called *kharāj muqāṭa'ah*. For definitions of terms pertaining to tax administration, see *Mafātīḥ* (pp. 58-62.)

lawful rates and may not be augmented. These rates were collected from every land fit for cultivation and accessible to water, at the rate of one *ṣā'* of barley or wheat and one *dirham* from every *jarīb* of barley or wheat, and according to al-Shāfi'i, from the wheat four, and from the barley two *dirhams;* and from every *jarīb* of trefoil (*raṭbah*) five *dirhams,* and according to al-Shāfi'i six; and from every *jarīb* of closely planted trees (*karm*), vines and palms ten, and according to al-Shāfi'i eight *dirhams,* but according to al-Māwardi, from the trees ten and the palms eight *dirhams,* and the sugar-cane six *dirhams.*[1] The above taxes concerning trees applied only in case they were closely planted in such a way that cultivation of the intervening space was impossible, for isolated trees growing in cultivated fields were exempt from tax, for the land was then taxed as a cultivated land.[2]

In other than the above cases, namely, in **cases concerning which there is no precedent of the calif Omar,** for instance, in saffron or in gardens (*bustān*),[3] the *kharāj* is assessed according to the tax-bearing capacity (*ṭāqah*) of the lands, and as the limit of tax-bearing capacity (*gāyat al-ṭāqah*) has been fixed by Hanifite doctors at half of the entire produce, in no case may the rate exceed half the entire produce, whether or not the rates were fixed in accordance

[1] Other variants of the above numbers, as found in Abu Yūsuf, al-Māwardi, and al-Balādhuri, are for palms five, vines eight, meadows and cotton plantations five, and for sesame five *dirhams.* According to one report, palms were taxed on the basis of feet, as under the Sassanides, and according to another report, palms were exempt from tax. However, this last report applied to isolated palm trees found in cultivated fields, which were exempt from tax already under the Sassanides (Berchem, p. 50, fn. 1.)

[2] *Fatḥ*, vol. v, p. 282, l. 6.

[3] *Bustān* here means any enclosure of trees sufficiently apart to allow of cultivation in the intervening spaces. It is the opposite of *karm*.

with the precedent of Omar and whether the *kharāj* is fixed or proportional. This is because Omar himself in assessing the rates above mentioned took into consideration the tax-bearing capacity of the land.

If then a land cannot stand the rate of *kharāj* imposed upon it, the rate may be reduced to what it can stand, but it is not allowed in any case to increase the rates imposed by Omar or, for that matter, by another *imām*, in accordance with the rates imposed by Omar, even if the land can stand a higher rate. According to the *Durr*,[1] the *kharāj* may in no case fall short of one-fifth of the entire produce, as it may not exceed one-half of it. If, however, a piece of land is assessed for the first time, according to Abu Hanīfah and Abu Yūsuf, it is still unlawful to assess higher rates than those assessed by Omar, because Omar said to his agents 'Uthmān and Hudhayfah who had assessed the *kharāj* of Sawād: " Perhaps you assessed the land with a rate which it cannot stand?", and they said: " No, on the contrary, we have assessed it with a rate which it can stand, but if we had assessed a higher rate the land could still stand it." These words indicate that the rate may be reduced if the land cannot stand it, but that it may not be increased even if it can stand it, for Omar, although informed that the land could stand more, did not order an increase of rate. According to Muhammad Ibn al-Hasan, however, higher rates may be assessed, since the rates are determined on the basis of the tax-bearing capacity of the land.[2]

According to al-Māwardi,[3] if the crop is one on which there is no legal prescription (*naṣṣ*), it pays the rate prescribed in the *sharī'ah* for the crop that most resembles it in appearance and profits.

[1] P. 365.

[2] *Hidāyah*, vol. v, p. 283.

[3] P. 262.

Al-Māwardi [1] discusses as follows **the factors which determine the tax-bearing capacity** (*ṭāqah*) **of land.** The person who assesses the *kharāj* on a piece of land should consider the capacity of land, which varies according to three factors, each factor affecting the amount of *kharāj* more or less. One of these factors pertaining to the land itself is the quality of the land by virtue of which the crop grown on it is rich, or the defect which causes the produce to be small. The second factor relates to the kind of crop, since grains and fruits vary in price, some fetching a higher price than the others, and the *kharāj* must therefore be assessed accordingly. The third factor pertains to the method of irrigation, for the crop that has been irrigated with water carried on the back of beasts or raised by a water-wheel, cannot stand the same rate of *kharāj* which could be charged on land watered by running water or rain.

The **irrigation of crops** and trees may be effected **in four ways:** Artificial irrigation without the use of any instrument, that is, by means of running water derived from springs and rivers, by turning their course to the field to be watered. This way is by far the most profitable and least expensive, inasmuch as the water is turned on when needed, and turned off when enough of it has been used. (2) Artificial irrigation by means of some instrument, *e. g.*, by water carried on the back of beasts, or by buckets or waterwheels, this way being the most expensive, and the one that entails the greatest hardship. (3) Natural irrigation by means of rain or snow or dew. (4) Irrigation by means of the humidity of soil, or by water concealed underground. In this case the crops and trees are irrigated by means of their roots.

Irrigation by means of conduits falls under the first class if the water used is running water, and under the second

[1] P. 257 *et seq.*

class if not so. Again, irrigation by water derived from wells belongs in the second class if the water is carried on the back of beasts, and in the first if drawn (*ustukhrija*) through conduits.

The assessor of *kharāj*, therefore, in estimating the amount of tax to be assessed on a piece of land, should take into consideration the above-named three factors, namely, the quality of land, the kind of crop, and the method of irrigation. In this way justice is attained, as between the beneficiaries of the *fa'y* and the taxpayer, since neither the latter is overburdened nor the former are prejudiced.

Some have recognized **a fourth factor**, namely the distance of the land from cities and markets, because the price increases or decreases according as this distance is shorter or longer, but this concerns only the case in which *kharāj* is paid in silver (*i. e.*, specie), and does not apply to the collection of the tax in grain (kind), whereas the three factors above-mentioned apply equally in both cases.

When the *kharāj* has been fixed by reference to the above-mentioned principles, it is assessed on the ground according to the most profitable of the following three ways: It is assessed on the area of the land, or on the area of the cultivated portion of the land, or, finally, on the produce as a definite proportion of the same. When the *kharāj* is assessed on the area of the entire land the year used is the lunar year, and if the *kharāj* is assessed on the cultivated area, the year used is the solar year, but if the *kharāj* is proportional, the tax is due when the crop is ripe and the grain ready for consumption.

When any one of these three alternatives has been settled upon, one is not allowed to change[1] it to another but it is

[1] *Cf. Bahr*, vol. v, p. 116.

continued for ever, and hence the tax may not be increased or decreased so long as the land continues to remain the same with respect to its irrigation and advantages (*maṣāliḥ*).

If, however, the land **changes as to** its **method of irrigation and** its **advantages**, then there are two cases conceivable: (1) The change is caused by an act of the landowner, *e. g.*, the productivity of the land is increased by means of water diverted from a river or derived from the ground, or on the contrary, it is decreased owing to negligence in cultivation and defective methods. In this case the *kharāj* is left as it is; not being increased for increased productivity, or diminished for decreased productivity. The owner, however, is reproved, in order that he may cultivate the land so that it may not go to waste. (2) The change has occurred owing to no act of the owner, but by reason of a natural contingency, either to the advantage or the disadvantage of the land: (a) When the change is to the disadvantage, *e. g.*, when the valley subsides, or the river dries up, if repair is possible, it is the duty of the *imām* to use for this purpose the revenue appropriated for works of public utility, namely, from the share of *maṣāliḥ*; and the *kharāj* is remitted to the landowner for the time the land has lain uncultivated. The Hanifite view is to the same effect.[1] If, however, repair is not possible; in case, for instance, the land cannot be cultivated; the *kharāj* is definitively remitted if the land cannot be utilized in some other way, for instance, as a pasture or hunting ground. But if it can be used for some other purpose, then the land pays the rate of *kharāj* levied on similar lands. (b) When, on the other hand, the change results to the advantage of the land, *e. g.*, when the river follows a new course and as a re-

[1] *Cf. 'Alamkiriyyah*, vol. ii, p. 345.

sult, the land is irrigated in the future by running water instead of by artificial means, if the change is not believed to be permanent, the tax is not increased, but if the change is believed to be permanent, then the *imām* increases the tax or desists from so doing according as he hold one or the other course to be in the best interests of both the land owner and the beneficiaries of the tax.

If a piece of land cannot be cultivated every year, but must be allowed to lie fallow every other year, this fact is taken into account when the *kharāj* is first assessed, and one of the following three methods is applied with a view to reconciling the interests of both sides. Half of the regular rate on the cultivated portion is collected on the entire field; or every two *jarībs* are counted as one single *jarīb* in order to allow for the uncultivated portion; or, finally, the full rate is assessed on the cultivated portion only.[1]

According to the *Hidāyah*,[2] if a person without excuse changes from a kind of crop that pays a high rate of *kharāj* to one that pays a lower rate he still pays the higher rate, because he is responsible for the decrease of the rate. The *Hidāyah*, however, does not recommend this view (*la yufta bihi*) because it would give an excuse to tyrants to oppress the Moslems by forcing them to cultivate crops which require great pains.

If a person plants in his farmland vines or fruit-bearing trees, he continues to pay on his land the *kharāj* of crops until the new plants shall have borne fruit, and he then pays

[1] There is in the text a statement to the effect that in such case "one-half of the produce" is taken. This statement was omitted as inconsistent with the previous sentence where it was said that "the whole of the tax is assessed". If the whole of the tax is only one-fifth, one cannot evidently collect "half of the produce." The variants of the text indicated at the bottom of the page confirm the suspicion that the text at this point suffered corruption.

[2] Vol. v, p. 285.

ten *dirhams* per *jarīb*, if the value of the fruits is twenty or more *dirhams*; and if their value is less than this, he pays half of that value, provided it does not fall short of the equivalent of one *qafīz* of grain and one *dirham*, because that is the least rate that a *jarīb* of land pays when its cultivation is possible.

The kharaj is due on land irrespective of **whether or not the owner cultivated the land,** provided that he has been able to do so, because the reason for *kharāj* is the productivity of land, and the owner by not cultivating his land, notwithstanding that it was productive, has deprived the beneficiaries of *kharāj* from their revenue.[1] According to Mālik, the owner pays no *kharāj* if the land was not cultivated, whether or not he had an excuse for not cultivating it.[2] If the owner was unable to cultivate his land because he lacked the means to do so, the *imām* is entitled to lease the land to another farmer by way of *muzāra'ah*,[3] and collect the tax from the owner's share of the produce, or to lease the land to a tenant and collect it from the rental, or, finally, to have the land cultivated at the expense of the public treasury and collect the tax from the owner's share. According to the *'Alamkīriyyah*,[4] a similar course is fol-

[1] *Mabsūṭ*, part x, p. 82.

[2] Māwardi, p. 261.

[3] *Muzāra'ah* is an agreement between the owner of a farm and a farmer that the latter shall cultivate the farm in consideration of a certain proportion of the produce. It is also called *mukhābarah*. The term *muzāra'ah* applies to the cultivation of grains, while the terms *mu'āmalah* and *musāqāt* are used with respect to trees. *Muḍārabah* is the counterpart of the same idea with respect to trade, meaning a partnership between the principal (*rabb al-māl*) who owns the stock and the trader (*muḍārib*) who contributes the labor for a part of the profits. If all the profit is to belong to the capital owner (*mubḍi'*) the transaction is called *biḍā'ah*, and the person who trades with it *mustabḍi'*.

[4] Vol. ii, p. 344.

lowed if the owners abandon their lands, or if one of them dies. However, according to a report from Abu Hanīfah, when the *kharāj* people abandon their lands the *imām* may have them cultivated at public expense, or lease (*muqāṭa'ah*) them, the entire income belonging to the public. If none of the above mentioned courses is possible, the *imām* sells the land and collects the tax from the price, returning the balance to the owner.[1] Should the owner later again be able to cultivate his land, it is returned to him unless, indeed it has been sold.

According to al-Māwardi,[2] if in the above-mentioned case of neglect of cultivation the *kharāj* levied on the land would differ with the kind of crop raised, only the lowest of the possible rates is collected from the owner, for if the latter, instead of entirely neglecting the cultivation, had only raised the crop subject to that lowest rate, he would have been within his right.

According to the *Fatḥ*,[3] there is a reliable report from Abu Yūsuf to the effect that when the owner is unable to cultivate the land, the public treasury should advance him as a loan the necessary funds.

According to al-Māwardi,[4] however, when the owner lacks the means of cultivation, he is told either to lease his land to another person or to forego his possession (*yad*) of the land in order that it may be turned over to a person who can cultivate it; for the land is not allowed to go to waste even if its *kharāj* is paid, because it would then become waste (*mawāt*) land.

According to the *Durr*,[5] all the above applies to the fixed *kharāj* only, provided the owner is not prevented from cul-

[1] *Baḥr*, vol. v, p. 118.

[2] Pp. 261-2.

[3] Vol. v, p. 285.

[4] P. 264.

[5] P. 365.

tivating his land. For if he is so prevented or if the *kharāj* is of the proportional kind, no *kharāj* is due on the land.

In the *Bahr* it is said that since the **kharaj** levied on the lands **of Egypt is** in reality **a rental,** the cultivators (*fallāh*) should not be obliged to pay the *kharāj* when they do not cultivate the land and are not tenants thereof.[1] Furthermore, it is unjust to oppress the farmers when they abandon agriculture and settle in the cities, especially when they do so in order to engage in the study of the *sharī'ah.*

With respect to the present land holders of Syria, Ibn 'Abidīn[2] remarks that, being mere cultivators of the land for a part of the produce (*muzāri'*), they may not lease (*ījār*) their holdings in consideration of a rental (*ujrah*) to be collected by themselves from the lessees (*musta'jir*) over and above what is already paid by the latter to the *imām*. Consequently the above-mentioned practice of the cultivators (*muzāri'*) of the *sulṭāniyyah* (*i. e., amīriyyah*) and *waqf* lands betokens their ignorance, and so " I have rendered a *fatwa* to the effect that it is not lawful ". According to the *Tātārkhāniyyah,* as quoted by Ibn 'Abidīn, the so-called *al-arādi al-mamlakah* (*i. e., amīriyyah*), namely, lands without owners, may be given away to people on condition of payment of *kharāj* by them. This is lawful on one of these two grounds: either the people in question become like owners (*iqāmah maqām al-mullāk fi l'-zirā'ah wa i'tā' al-kharāj*) so far as cultivation and the payment of *kharāj* is concerned; or it is a case of lease (*ijārah*) at a rental equal to the *kharāj*, and in such case, the amount collected from the lessees is *kharāj* as regards the *imām,* though it is rental as regards them. Ibn 'Abidīn concludes from this quotation that the cultivators of Syrian lands

[1] *Bahr*, vol. v, p. 118.

[2] *Minhah*, vol. v, p. 114.

should not pay the tithe (*'ushr*), for if the tax already collected from them is *kharāj*, it is a well-known principle that the *kharāj* and the tithe are never levied on the same land; and if, on the other hand, it is rental, it is again well-known that, according to Abu Hanīfah, the tithe should be levied on the lessor (*mū'jir*)—though according to his two disciples it is levied on the leaseholder—" however, what is collected is not rental in every respect since it is *kharāj* as regards the *imām*. Reflect on it."

If there is in a piece of land a thick wood with plenty of game, no *kharāj* is paid on the land; but if the land is growing reeds or tamarisks or pinetrees or willows or other non-fruit-bearing trees, the owner pays *kharāj* if he can clear the ground and grow crops on it; otherwise he is exempt from the tax. The same principle applies if, instead of trees, there are salt deposits on the land.[1]

If a person owns a village situated on *kharāj* lands, he pays **no kharaj for the houses** and dwellings of the village whether or not he leases them. Likewise, if a person converts part of his habitation situated in a Moslem city into a field, he pays no *kharāj* on the field because the field is considered a dependency of the house and houses are exempt from taxes; but if he turns the whole of his habitation into a field, then he pays for it the *kharāj*, provided it is *kharāj* land. On the other hand, if a person turns his *kharāj* land into a habitation he pays *kharāj* for it.[2] According to al-Māwardi,[3] such part of the land as is covered with buildings which are indispensable should be exempted from the tax.[4]

[1] *'Alamkīriyyah*, vol. ii, p. 345.
[2] *'Alamkīriyyah*, vol. ii, p. 341.
[3] P. 263.
[4] *Cf.* Kharashi, p. 427.

The **kharaj** becomes **due** only **once a year**, even if the land should grow during the year many crops, because the calif Omar collected from the lands of the *dhimmis* only once a year, and because lands in general grow only one single crop during a year, and the law is rather concerned with general cases than with exceptions.[1] Of course this applies to the fixed *kharāj* only, as the proportional *kharāj*, like tithe, is collected every time a crop has been grown.[2]

A **land subject to kharaj does not also pay tithe** under any circumstances according to the Hanifite school, but the other two schools allow the combination (*ijtimā'*) of the two taxes.

The kharaj lapses if the entire crop has been destroyed (*iṣṭilām*) as a result of unavoidable natural forces (*afāt*), such as the subsiding of the land, fire, extreme cold, *etc.* If, however, the crop was destroyed in consequence of avoidable agencies, such as wild birds, or if the crop is destroyed after harvest, the tax is not remitted. Some say that the tax is remitted only if the year is too far spent to allow the farmer to cultivate again. According to the *Fatḥ* this time has been fixed at three months. All the above applies in case the entire crop has been destroyed, for if only part of it has been destroyed the whole of the tax is collected, if the remaining part is still sufficient for the settlement of the tax twice over; however, only half of the remaining part is collected, no matter how little, if such part is less than the *kharāj*. According to the *'Alamkīriyyah*,[3] the leading Hanifite doctors hold the view that the proper thing to do in this last case is to deduct from the remaining produce, before everything else, the

[1] *Mabsūṭ*, part x, p. 82.
[2] *Majma'*, p. 515; *Jāmi'*, p. 330; Māwardi, p. 260.
[3] Vol. ii, p. 345.

expenses of the farmer, and then proceed as explained. The reason for the remission of the tax in case of destruction is that the farmer has been stricken with adversity and deserves assistance, since the opposite policy would result in his extermination. Besides, one of the virtues for which the Persian kings have been praised has been their policy, in case of the destruction of the entire crop, of returning to the owners (*dihqān*) from their treasuries their expenses of cultivation; and therefore, if such expenses are not returned, at least the *kharāj* must be remitted. Moreover, when the entire crop has been destroyed, it has become apparent that the possibility of deriving a benefit from the land has been absent, but the *kharāj* is due only when such possibility has existed.[1]

If the **owner sells his land** during the year, the **kharaj is paid by the buyer** if cultivation is possible during the remaining part of the year; otherwise the *kharāj* is paid by the seller. According to the *Tātārkhāniyyah*, this applies in case the land was sold free of cultivation. For if a land already under cultivation is sold with its crop before it has as yet grown the *kharāj* is in every case paid by the buyer. If, on the contrary, the crop has grown, it is the same as if the land was sold free of cultivation. According to a report from Muḥammad Ibn al-Hasan, if a *kharāj* land is sold successively from person to person so that the land has not been in the possession of any one person for at least three months, no one of the buyers is subject to payment of *kharāj*. In deciding whether there was enough time left for cultivating, the time necessary for the cultivation, according to some doctors, of wheat or barley, and according to others, of any crop, is taken as the basis, but according to the *Wāqi'āt* of al-Nāṯifi, this time is fixed at three months.

[1] *Mabsūt*, part x, p. 83.

According to al-Ramli,[1] **the proportional kharaj** is like the fixed *kharāj* as regards its appropriation, but like tithe in all other respects: namely, in that every produce which may be subject to tithe may be also subject to the proportional *kharāj*, and that it is like tithe a charge on the produce and hence due every time there is a produce. It is claimed, according to the *Jāmi'*, that the proportional *kharāj* is not due if the land has been allowed to lie idle, even if cultivation was possible; that although some hold the contrary, the farmer may consume a reasonable part of the produce before the tax has been paid, the fixed *kharāj* being like the proportional in this respect; that the tax is remitted if the product is destroyed, even though after the harvest; that indebtedness does not exempt from its payment; finally, that the payment of the tax need not be made as soon as the tax falls due, subject, however to the same divergence of view as tithe.

The farmer may bestow alms from his crop before the *kharāj* has been demanded by the sultan, but not after. If the sultan makes to the *kharāj* payer a gift of his *kharāj* debt, it is lawful according to Abu Yūsuf, and unlawful according to Muḫammad Ibn al-Hasan. The view of Abu Yūsuf is the one generally recommended, provided the *kharāj* payer is one of the beneficiaries of *kharāj* revenue. In tithe, however, according to all, the amount constituting the present must be made good to the *ṣadaqah* treasury from the *kharāj* treasury unless the tithe payer was poor. It is allowed to collect the entire amount of the fixed *kharāj* in specie, since the object in view is that the tax should equal the capacity of the land. As in proportional *kharāj*, a charge of debt does not exempt the land from the *kharāj*. Finally, a debt of *kharāj* of either kind does not lapse upon

[1] *Baḫr, Minḫah*, vol. v, p. 116.

the death of the land owner, but is collected from his estate. However, according to the *Mabsūṭ*,[1] if the owner of the *kharāj* land dies before the collection of the *kharāj*, the latter lapses and is not collected from the estate. This is because, like the *kharāj* of heads, the *kharāj* of lands also has the meaning of humiliation. Moreover, it cannot be collected from the heirs, for although they own the land, they could not use it before the death of the deceased.

According to al-Māwardi,[2] **if the kharaj land is leased** with or without a rental, the tax is collected from the land owner, and not from the lease holder; but Abu Hanīfah holds that the tax is paid by the lease holder if the lease was made without a rental, and by the owner in the other case. Abu Hanīfah's two disciples hold the same view as al-Māwardi.[3]

According to Abu Hanīfah,[4] in the collection of *kharāj* the taxpayers must be treated with consideration and justice, and the *kharāj* must be collected in instalments, namely, from each crop must be taken its proportionate share of the year's *kharāj*. For instance, if a piece of land grows two crops, when the first crop is taxed, only half of the year's *kharāj* is collected by the collector if he thinks that the second crop will be as good as the first; and so on for the rest.

If one is unable to pay his kharaj debt[5] he is allowed to delay its payment until his finances improve. Abu Hanīfah says that the *kharāj* is due only when the landowner can pay it, and that it lapses when he is unable to pay it. If, however, a person delays the payment of his *kharāj* debt,

[1] Part iii, p. 50.
[2] P. 263; *cf. Umm*, vol. iii, p. 240.
[3] *'Alamkīriyyah*, vol. ii, p. 340.
[4] *'Alamkīriyyah*, vol. ii, pp. 342, 346.
[5] Māwardi, p. 264.

notwithstanding his ability to pay it, he is put in prison for it, unless there is discovered some of his property. In such case the property is sold and the debt settled out of the sale price, just as this is done for the recovery of ordinary claims. If the debtor has no other property than the *kharāj* land, the *imām*, if he sees fit, sells enough of the land to settle the debt, or he leases the land and settles the debt from the rental and returns the rest to the land owner. According to the *'Alamkīriyyah*,[1] the sultan may keep under control (*ḥabs*) the produce of the land until the *kharāj* is collected.

According to a report from Muḥammad Ibn al-Hasan,[2] if one pays in advance (*'ajjala*) the kharaj of his land for one or two years, it is lawful. If subsequently the land is flooded with water, the *kharāj* is returned to the landowner if it remained intact. According to the *Muntaqa*, the *kharāj* is returned, or reckoned as payment on account of the *kharāj* of the next year.

If the kharaj has been collected once by rebels and schismatics it is not collected again by the *imām* when he recovers control over the taxpayers, for taxation is based on protection and in this instance the *imām* has evidently failed to protect them.[3] The view expressed by al-Māwardi[4] is practically to the same effect.

In settling the *kharāj* in specie,[5] only gold and silver coins which are not mixed with baser metals (*gishsh*) are to be accepted. Again, only those of these coins bearing the impression of the sultan are accepted, because they

[1] Vol. ii, p. 346.
[2] *Ibid.*
[3] *Majma'*, p. 167; *Hidāyah*, p. 150; Kāsāni, p. 36.
[4] P. 225.
[5] Māwardi, pp. 269-72.

alone are reliable and secure from counterfeiting or other source of loss. Consequently, ingots of gold and silver are not accepted, because they are not reliable and may not be depended upon unless tested by melting. If more than one impressed coin of the same degree of purity of metal but of different value be current, and the tax collector demands payment of the tax in terms of the most highly valued of those coins, the tax is settled in its terms, in case such coin is one that has been struck by the sultan of the time, because the contrary course would involve disloyalty. If, however, the coin has been struck by another sultan, then the tax is still settled in it, if the previous landowner has paid in the same coin; otherwise it is tyranny to insist on that particular coin.

The *dirhams* [1] and *dīnārs* are not accepted in payment of *kharāj* if their silver or gold has been reduced (*maksūr*).[2]

As regards **the measure used in the kharaj**,[3] if it is the proportional *kharāj*, it makes no difference what measure is used. If, however, the *kharāj* is of the fixed kind, according to the *'Alamkīriyyah*, the measure used in this con-

[1] The *dirham* used in connection with *kharāj* is the same as is used in *zakāt*.

[2] The doctors disagree as to the propriety of reducing the metal of the coins. Mālik and most of the Medina doctors declare such a practice to be abominable. The Prophet is said to have forbidden the reduction of the size of the coin (*sikkah*). This *ḥadīth* is taken by some to mean a prohibition of turning the coins into bullion, by others, of turning them into plate, by still others, of trimming off the edges of coins with scissors, because in the beginning of Islam coins were counted by tale. Abu Hanīfah and the doctors of 'Irāq, on the other hand, hold the view that such a practice is not abominable. Al-Shāfi'i says that the practice is not abominable if the reduction was required by necessity, otherwise it is a wanton act. Finally Aḥmad Ibn Hanbal approves of it only with respect to coins on which the name of God was not impressed.

[3] Māwardi, p. 272; *'Alamkīriyyah*, vol. ii, p. 339; *Fatḥ*, vol. v, p. 281; *Mafatiḥ*, pp. 14-5, 66-8.

nection is the *ṣā'* which is eight *riṭls*. According to al-Māwardi, when a district is assessed with *kharāj* for the first time the measure of that district is taken as the basis.

Finally, as regards the **measure used for measuring the land**,[1] according to the *'Alamkīriyyah*, the *jarīb* is sixty by sixty cubits, in terms of the cubit of al-Malik, which is seven *qabḏahs*;[2] namely, one *qabḏah* longer than the common cubit, which is six *qabḏahs*. According to the *Kāfi* as quoted in the *Fatḥ*, in measuring the land in every district the measure commonly used there is taken as the basis.

If the **tax collector and** the **land owner disagree** about the status of the land,[3] the former claiming that the land is *kharāj* land, and the latter contending that it is tithe land, in case the contention of either side may be true, the claim of the land owner is given preference; but if he is suspected he must swear as to the truth of his contention in order to clear up the doubt. In such cases of dispute, it may be referred to the public registers (*dīwān*) if their reliability is well-known and the registrars may be relied upon. Disputes of this kind, however, are rare, occurring only on the borders of territories subject to one or the other of the two taxes.

If the **landowner claims that he paid the kharaj**, his claim is not observed although he is believed if he makes a similar statement with respect to the tithe. In such case it may be referred, in accordance with custom, to the public registers concerning the *kharāj*, if they are reliable.

Like the *zakāt* collectors, the **kharaj collectors receive their pay** (*rizq*) **out of the kharaj proceeds**, and this is also true of the pay of the surveyor (*massāḥ*), but there is dis-

[1] For details on kinds of measures, see Māwardi, p. 265.

[2] *Qabḏah* is the measure of the fist, *i. e.*, about 4 fingerbreadths, or nearly 6¼ inches.

[3] Māwardi, p. 263.

agreement as regards the wages (*ujrah*) of the distributor (*qassām*).[1] According to al-Shāfi'i, his wage is taken out of the proceeds of the tithe or *kharāj* collected. Abu Hanīfah, on the other hand, says that the wage is paid in an equitable manner out of the produce before the collection of the tax. Sufyān al-Thawri says that such wages are paid, in the case of *kharāj*, by the sultan and in the case of tithe, by the landowner, and finally Mālik holds that wages relating to tithe are paid by the tithe payer and those relating to *kharāj* are paid half and half by the taxpayer and the sultan.

The **officials of the fa'y revenue**,[2] such as the *kharāj* and the *jizyah*, besides being reliable and active, are **required to possess certain** other **qualities** according to the extent of jurisdiction and power with which they are invested: (1) If they are charged with the assessment and distribution of the *fa'y revenue*, they must possess these four qualities: they must be freemen, Moslems, *mujtahids*, and conversant with arithmetic and surveying. (2) If they have full authority over the collection of tax rates which have already been assessed, they must be freemen, Moslems, and conversant with arithmetic and surveying, but they need not be *mujtahids*; since their duty is only to collect what has already been assessed. (3) If they have limited authority over a specified part of the *fa'y* revenue, then it depends on the duties they have been charged with. If their duties are such that they need to appoint a substitute, they must be Moslems, freemen, and conversant with arithmetic and surveying to the degree required, but they may not be

[1] *Qassām* (distributor) means the official who measures off the tithe or the proportional tax from the entire produce which after harvest was deposited in the barns (*bayādir*). The *massāḥ* (surveyor), on the other hand, is the official who measures the land in order to determine the amount of the *kharāj*. (*Cf.* Berchem, p. 72, fn. 4.)

[2] Māwardi, p. 224; also p. 264.

dhimmis or slaves, because these two are not qualified to exercise authority (*wilāyah*). On the contrary, if they do not need to appoint substitutes, they may be slaves, since they are in this case like messengers (*rasūl*) sent on an errand. **As for their being dhimmis**, it depends on the taxes they are to collect. If they are to collect taxes from *dhimmis*, such as the *jizyah*, and the tolls (*'ushr*) levied on the *dhimmi* traders, they may be *dhimmis*. If, however, they are to collect taxes from Moslems, such as the *kharāj* of lands found in the possession (*yad*) of Moslems, opinion varies.

If the person named collector is not qualified to exercise the authority vested in him and yet collects the tax, the taxpayer is released from his debt if the collector was not forbidden from collecting the taxes, because the collector was authorized to collect the tax from him, although his authority was imperfect (*fāsid*) and he was acting as a messenger. The difference between the collector's authority being valid (*ṣaḥīḥ*) and imperfect (*fāsid*) is that in the first case he may force the taxpayer to pay the tax, and in the second he may not. If the authority of the collector is not only imperfect, but he is also forbidden to collect, he may not then force the taxpayers to pay the taxes, or even collect the same. Should the taxpayers pay the tax to the collector, though knowing that he was forbidden to collect taxes, they are not released from their tax dues; but if they did not know about it, then, according to one view of the matter, they are released, but according to another view, they are not. The same divergence of view exists concerning agents (*wakīl*).

Unike the *zakāt* official, the *fa'y* official may not distribute the *fa'y* revenue he has collected without permission, because while the beneficiaries of *zakāt* have been determined by revealed texts, those of the *fa'y* are determined by the *imām*.

CHAPTER VII

THE JIZYAH OR POLL TAX[1]

THE word *jizyah* is derived from *jaza* meaning compensation, requital for good or evil. This tax owes its name to the fact that it is taken from the *dhimmis* as a punishment for their unbelief in order to humiliate them or, it may be, by way of mercy, as a price for the protection given them by the Moslems.[2]

The collection of the *jizyah* is based on the divine words:[3] " Make war upon such of those to whom a Scripture has been given, as do not believe in God, nor in the last day . . . until they pay by their hands the *jizyah* in order to be humiliated." The *dhimmis* by paying the *jizyah* become entitled to two rights: security from molestation and protection. By virtue of the first right they become safe (*amin*) and of the second, protéges (*maḥrūs*).[4]

According to the Hanifite doctors, the tax is called *jizyah* because it is paid by the *dhimmis* as a compensation (*jaza*) for being spared from death; since by the payment of the *jizyah* the non-Moslems purchase their lives and may no longer be killed. Al-Sarakhsi, in this connection remarks that the infidel who lives in the Moslem state is

[1] *Majma'*, p. 515; *Hidāyah*, vol. v, p. 288; Yūsuf, p. 69; Māwardi, p. 245; *Minhāj*, vol. iii, p. 275; *Mugni*, vol. iv, p. 224; Anṣāri, vol. iv, p. 210; Dardīr, p. 203; Kharashi, p. 441.

[2] Māwardi, p. 246; *cf.* Kharashi, p. 441.

[3] Koran, chap. 9, verse 29.

[4] Māwardi, p. 247.

subjected to the payment of *jizyah* for his humiliation and punishment so long as he persists in his unbelief, and in order to impress him with the degradation of unbelief and the power of Islam. According to him, the **jizyah is taken from the dhimmis in lieu of the assistance** which they would be liable to give if they had not persisted in their unbelief, because, living as they do in the Moslem state, they must be ready to defend it. However, since they do not embrace Islam, they are not fit for such assistance in person because they would be favorably inclined towards the enemy. Consequently, instead of personal service they are required to give part of their wealth, which is spent on the Moslem soldiers who defend the state; and exactly as the poor Moslems take part in the war as footmen, and the rich as horsemen, so the amount of the monetary equivalent collected from the *dhimmis* varies according to their means. Some say that the *jizyah* levied on the *dhimmis* is a rental for residing in the Moslem state, but the former view is preferable; for if the latter view were true, women and children also would be liable to pay the tax, which they are not, because they are not liable for the defence of the country.[1]

The **jizyah** is **levied only on those** who may be admitted into the status of the *dhimmi*, namely, Christians, Jews, both of whom possess a Scripture, and the idolaters and fireworshipers. According to the Malikites,[2] excepting apostates, all persons who may be made slaves, that is, all unbelievers (*kāfir*), even including the Quraysh, may be admitted into the status of *dhimmi*. According to al-Shāfi'i, the *jizyah* may be accepted only from Christians, Jews and fireworshipers, but not from idolaters, inasmuch as the above-mentioned verse refers only to the first two

[1] *Mabsūṭ*, part x, p. 8.

[2] Kharashi, p. 442.

classes, and the Prophet extended its scope to the fireworshipers also; but the idolaters are left out entirely. The Hanifites argue that since the idolaters may be made slaves it should also be allowed to accept the *jizyah* from them, but they admit that this is true only of the idolaters who are not Arabs. The Arab idolaters may not pay the *jizyah*, for the Prophet was sent from among them and the miracles were performed before their eyes. So their persistence in unbelief is of the worst type. By Arabs here are meant the original Arab tribes that are idolaters, and not the Jews and Christians settled among the Arabs or Arabs who have been converted to the Hebrew or Christian religion. The *jizyah* is likewise not accepted from renegades, for these "have turned to unbelief after having once witnessed the beauties of Islam". The Arab idolaters and the renegades have to accept either Islam or the sword, but their wives and children are spared and made slaves.

The *jizyah* is of two kinds:

(1) The **jizyah imposed by** agreement and **treaty**, the amount of which has been fixed by the terms of the agreement and may not be later changed.[1] For example, the Prophet arranged with the people of Najrān that they should pay yearly in two instalments 2,000 *ḥullahs* (a dress of two pieces), each *ḥullah* being worth 40 *dirhams*. According to Abu Yūsuf, this yearly payment is for both their persons and their lands, and the part paid for the persons applies only to the non-Moslem part of the population of Najrān, while the part paid for the lands is collected from every piece of land, even when sold to a Moslem. According to the *'Alamkīriyyah*,[2] the *imām* may require the payment of a lump sum of money or goods without specifying the part to be

[1] *Fatḥ*, vol. v, p. 288.

[2] Vol. ii, p. 350.

paid by persons (*jamājim*) and by lands, or he may so specify. In the former case, the total sum is justly apportioned among the persons and the lands, the part allotted to the persons being *jizyah* and the other *kharāj*. Both of them are distributed among the individual taxpayers according to the principles governing the *jizyah* and *kharāj* in general. If the number of heads decreases or entirely disappears by conversion to Islam or death or otherwise, their share of the tribute is reduced or entirely removed and charged to the lands if the latter can stand it; otherwise it lapses. Should the heads later increase, they gradually resume payment of their full share. A similar course is followed if the lands cannot bear their share of the tribute. In the case of lands, however, should they be entirely destroyed, their share lapses. If, on the contrary, the shares of the lands and the persons were specified by the *imām*, then neither bears the share of the other, should the latter be unable themselves to pay it, but such share lapses until they are again able to pay. Should they become Moslems, the part assessed on the persons lapses, but the fact of conversion has no effect on the part assessed on the lands. Should the *imām* follow a third course and arrange for a tribute on the persons or the lands alone, such an agreement is null and void (*la yaṣiḥḥu*), the sum arranged being distributed as noted above between the persons and the lands.[1]

The Shafiites[2] agree with the Hanifites that the *jizyah* agreed upon in a treaty may not later be changed, but they hold that the rate of the *jizyah* per individual as provided for in the agreement should never fall short of the minimum rate of one *dīnār*. When by such an agreement the

[1] For the Shafiite and Malikite views, see *supra*, pp. 369-372.

[2] Māwardi, pp. 249, 250; *Minhāj*, vol. iii, pp. 279, 281; *Wajīz*, vol. ii, p. 200; Anṣāri, vol. iv, p. 216; *Fatḥ al-Qarīb*, p. 624; *Umm*, vol. iv, p. 101.

infidels retain the ownership of their city or their village, it is recommended to the *imām* to obtain the insertion of a **provision for** the **entertainment of Moslem travelers** who may stop in that city or village. In such case the total number of the days of entertainment during the year, and the number of guests and horses, as well as the length of time individual guests are to be entertained, are specified. As in the case of *jizyah,* the individual assignments are varied according to the wealth of the entertainers. When the individual assignments have not been specified in the agreement, then the people of the city or village themselves make the assignments among themselves. The amount and kind of food to be served the travelers and the quantity of barley to be given their animals are also indicated. The superfluous residences and the churches where the Moslems are to be lodged are also mentioned, in this respect the lodgings of the poor infidels being equally liable. The sojourn of the same individual may not exceed three days, neither may he require medical service nor baths. Furthermore, the infidels are never forced out of their houses in order to make room for Moslem travelers. Some Shafiites say that this burden of entertainment is in lieu of the minimum rate of one *dīnār* in specie, and that consequently it may be converted to its monetary equivalent and collected in specie. Others hold that it is independent of, and over and above, the minimum rate of one *dīnār,* and that consequently the latter may not be reduced to allow for this burden in kind, and that the infidels may not be forced to pay it in specie. If it is converted to specie it becomes a part of the *fa'y* and may be disbursed to the *fa'y* beneficiaries only, although before its conversion any Moslem is entitled to entertainment.

Like the Hanifites, **the Malikites** give power to the *imām* to settle the *jizyah* at any figure. If the amount was not indicated in the treaty, it is collected at the same rates as obtain in regard to *dhimmis* who do not enjoy any treaty rights.[1]

(2) The **jizyah imposed** by the *imām* upon the population of a district conquered **by force of arms.**[2] **The yearly rate** for the rich is forty-eight *dirhams, i. e., four dirhams* per month, for the middle class half of this sum, and for the poor who can earn their living, one-fourth of this sum. The above is based on the precedents of the califs Omar, 'Uthmān and 'Ali, the other Companions having approved of their action. In other words, it is based on *ijmā'*. There is no *Zāhir-al-riwāyah* report concerning the meaning of the terms rich, middle-class and poor, but in the commentary of al-Taḫāwi it is stated that the person who owns 10,000 *dirhams* and upwards is rich, the person owning from 200 upwards is middle class, and finally the person owning less than that is poor. Some say that the person who needs to work in order to earn a living is poor, the person who, though having possessions, works, middle class, and the person who owns enough to afford to be idle, rich. Still others say that the person who has not enough is poor; the person who has enough food for his family and himself, middle class; and the person who has more, rich. The author of the *Ikhtiyār* believes that this point should be settled by the *imām* on the basis of the particular conditions prevailing in each locality.

Al-Shāfi'i has expressed the opinion that the minimum rate of *jizyah* is one *dīnār* or twelve *dirhams* upon every adult, rich or poor, the maximum rate being fixed by the *imām* according to his judgment. According to the *Minhāj*,[2] the *imām* should bargain

[1] Ibn Rushd., *M.*, p. 279; Dardīr, p. 204. [2] *Cf.* Kharashi, p. 443.

[2] Vol. iii, p. 279; *Wajīz*, vol. ii, p. 200; *Mugni*, vol. iv, p. 229.

(*mumākasah*) until he obtains the rate of four *dīnārs* for the rich and two for the middle class. Some say that this bargain may be made only at the time of the agreement, since afterwards the agreement may no longer be changed. Still others hold that it may be made at the time of the agreement, or afterwards, at the time of collection as well. According to Mālik, both the minimum and the maximum are fixed by the *imām*.[1] However, according to Khalīl,[2] the rate of the *jizyah* is fixed at four *dīnārs* or forty *dirhams*, with necessary reductions to allow for poverty.

According to both the Shafiites and the Malikites,[3] if the infidels refuse to pay as *jizyah* more than the minimum of one *dīnār*, the *imām* may not fight them in order to obtain a higher rate, but is obliged to accept that rate. According to Mālik, the *dīnār* is valued at ten *dirhams*. According to most of the Shafiites the *dīnār* is valued at its current market value. According to the Hanifites, however, although the *dīnār* in general is valued at ten *dirhams*, in the case of *jizyah*, following the precedent of Omar, it is valued at twelve.[4]

The jizyah is not imposed upon the children, insane, and the imbecile old people; in other words, persons who do not possess legal responsibility; because they are not fit for assistance in the defence of the state. This is also true of senile old people, and of the blind and cripples. Abu Yūsuf says that the blind and the cripples who have property are subject to the tax, because, although they cannot assist in person, they may do so by their wealth, and because such

[1] Māwardi, p. 249.

[2] Kharashi, p. 443.

[3] *Wajīz*, p. 200; Ibn Rushd, *M.*, p. 279.

[4] *Fatḥ*, vol. v, p. 289.

persons, when they have had a voice in government, are liable to death in time of war. Likewise, the poor who are not engaged in business are exempt from the tax. Also monks who are retired from the world, even if they can work, are not subject to it, because they are not liable to death in time of war. According to Abu Hanīfah and Abu Yūsuf, monks pay the *jizyah* if they can work. Slaves of every description (*qinn, mudabbar, umm walad, ummah,* or *mukātab*) do not pay the *jizyah*, nor is the *jizyah* paid by their masters, who on their account already pay a higher rate of *jizyah* than they would otherwise do. The sick as well are free from the tax. According to al-Shāfi'i,[1] the *jizyah* is levied on every male *dhimmi* who is of age and sane of mind and of free status; the priests, the senile old people, the paralytics, *etc.*, included. The poor who are unable to engage in business are to be ousted from the Moslem country according to one view; in another view, they are exempted from the *jizyah*; however, in a third view they are subject to it like others.

According to the *Ikhtiyār*, if the cause of exemption disappears in the case of the above-mentioned people, excepting the poor, before the tax was yet imposed on them, they become subject to it; but if the cause disappears after the tax was imposed for that year, they are exempt from it for that year, because the cause of exemption is considered with reference to the time of the imposition of the tax.

According to Abu Hanīfah, the **jizyah becomes due** at the beginning of the year, but is collected at the end of the year, two or three days before it runs out; Abu Yūsuf maintains that it should be collected by instalments every two months and Muhammad Ibn al-Hasan, every month, in order that the tax may become more onerous for the tax-

[1] *Umm*, vol. iv, pp. 98, 101; *cf. Wajiz*, vol. ii, p. 198.

payers and more beneficial to the Moslems. The view generally accepted is that it is collected at one time at the end of the year.[1] This is also the opinion of al-Shāfi'i, and the Malikites.[2]

The **jizyah is canceled by conversion to Islam,** by **death,** and, according to Abu Hanīfah, also by **non-collection** (*tadākhul*). It is canceled by conversion to Islam, because the *dhimmi* after this can serve in person for the defence of the state. According to Abu Yūsuf and Muḥammad Ibn al-Hasan, the *jizyah,* like other debts, is collected even if it has been allowed to remain uncollected for many years. Abu Hanīfah's argument in support of the contrary view is that the *jizyah* is imposed by way of punishment, and, like other penalties imposed for the sake of God, it is canceled if allowed to fall into arrears. Besides, from the Moslem standpoint, the *jizyah* is a financial aid to the state in lieu of the bodily assistance every citizen is obliged to tender for the defence of the state, and in collecting the tax for only one year the meaning (*ma'na*) of assistance is realized. Moreover, the main object in levying the tax is the subjection of infidels to humiliation and this object is secured by collecting the tax for the current year only and letting that of the former years lapse.[3]

According to the Shafiites,[4] conversion or death are a bar to the *jizyah* only as regards the future, but such part of it as has already accrued is collected. According to the Malikites,[5] they constitute a bar even as regards arrears.

When the jizyah is collected from the dhimmi he is obliged to stand while the collector is seated, and he must

[1] *Mabsūt,* part x, p. 82.

[2] Kharashi, p. 443.

[3] *Ibid.*

[4] *Minhāj,* vol. iii, p. 280.

[5] Kharashi, p. 443; Dardīr, p. 204; Ibn Rushd., *B.*, p. 327.

wear the distinctive dress prescribed for the *dhimmis*. During the process of payment, the *dhimmi* is seized by the collar and vigorously shaken and pulled about in order to show him his degradation, and he is rebuked in these words: "Oh, *dhimmi*, or, Oh, enemy of God, pay the *jizyah*!", but he is not addressed, "Oh, infidel". The *dhimmi*, therefore, may not pay his *jizyah* by proxy, because this would defeat one of the objects of the tax, namely, his humiliation. However, in the opinion of the two disciples, this is allowed.[1] It should be noted, however, that Abu Yūsuf,[2] far from subscribing to these extreme views of later Hanifites, recommends to the calif Hārūn al-Rashīd gentleness (*rifq*) in the treatment of the *dhimmi*.

Al-Shāfi'i,[3] on the strength of the opinions held by a number of people of knowledge (*'ilm*), concludes that the humiliation referred to in the Koran consists in the submission of the infidels to Moslem rule (*ḥukm al-islām*), and that consequently a people may not be admitted into the status of *dhimmi* except on condition of submission to Moslem law. Some of the later Shafiites hold that the reference to humiliation in question requires that the *dhimmi* should be humiliated literally in paying the *jizyah* by placing it in the balance while he is standing with the head bent and the shoulders stooped and while, on the other hand, the collector, who is seated, seizes the *dhimmi* by his beard and slaps his face on both sides, saying: "Oh, enemy of God, give the right of God". However, the prevalent Shafiite doctrine severely condemns such a construction of the Koranic reference to humiliation.[4]

[1] *Mabsūṭ*, part x, p. 81; *Jāmi'*, vol. ii, p. 577; *Baḥr*, vol. v, p. 121.

[2] Yūsuf, pp. 70, 71, 72.

[3] *Umm*, vol. iv, p. 99.

[4] *Minhāj*, vol. iii, p. 281; *Fatḥ al-Qarīb*, p. 624; *Wajīz*, vol. ii, p. 200; *Mugni*, vol. iv, p. 230.

Finally, according to the Malikites,[1] the humiliation of the *dhimmis* is a matter of obligation (*wujūb*), and, therefore, they may not settle their *jizyah* by proxy; for it is essential that they taste humiliation, and "perhaps they will then decide to get rid of it by becoming Moslems." According to the most extreme view quoted by al-'Adawi, the humiliation of the *dhimmi* is necessary in order to demonstrate their inborn hatred of the Moslems, their refutation of the Prophet, and the fact that if they had the power they would exterminate the Moslems gradually.

[1] Kharashi, p. 443; Dardīr, p. 204.

CHAPTER VIII

OTHER SOURCES OF REVENUE

SECTION I

The Spoils of War[1]

THE word **spoil** (*ganīmah*, plural, *ganā'im*) **technically means** próperty taken by force from infidels during war. Hence property taken from the infidels by Moslems who entered the enemy land without the *imām's* permission is not spoil, because such property has been seized not by force, but by theft. If, however, the Moslems entered the enemy's country in " force " (*bi mana'ah*) then the *imām's* permission is not necessary. The lowest number of raiders that constitutes a " force " is four, or, according to a report from Abu Yūsuf, nine. The case of entering in " force " is clear. As regards the case of permission by the *imām*, the latter by permitting the raid has virtually engaged to assist the raiders in case of need.[2]

According to the Shafiites,[3] all property taken from the infidels while war is going on, even property taken by theft,

[1] *Majma'*, p. 499; *Hidāyah*, vol. v, p. 215; *Mabsūṭ*, part x, pp. 37, 136; *'Alamkīriyyah*, vol. ii, p. 290; Kāsāni, vol. vii, p. 117; *Baḥr*, vol. v, p. 89; *Durar*, p. 167; *Durr*, p. 356; Māwardi, p. 217; *Umm*, vol. iv, p. 64; Muzani, vol. iii, p. 179; *Minhāj*, vol. ii, p. 297; *Wajīz*, p. 290; Dardīr, p. 198; Yahya, p. 3.

[2] *Majma'*, p. 505; *Durr*, p. 359.

[3] *Mugni*, vol. iii, p. 93; Kāsāni, vol. vii, p. 117; *cf. Minhāj*, vol. ii, p. 297; *Wajīz*, p. 290; *Umm*, vol. iv, p. 64.

is spoil. The Malikite view[1] is like the Hanifite. The Malikites give the name of *mukhtaṣṣ* (proper) to property which is neither spoil nor *fa'y*, but belongs entirely to the person who took it, such as property stolen from the enemy.

When the imam conquers a place or a city by force of arms (*'anwat*), he may divide the property taken, whether lands or chattels, after the deduction of the state's share of one-fifth, among the victorious army, since the Prophet had done so with respect to Khaybar. Or the *imām*, if he so chooses, may leave the lands in the hands of their original holders, and impose upon their persons the *jizyah*, and upon their lands the *kharāj*. The *imām's* right to relinquish to the enemy his property applies only to landed property, not to chattels, except in so far as they are indispensable for the exploitation of the lands and the real estates which have been left in the enemy's possession. Thus the calif Omar left the lands and houses of Sawād to the original owners. Or finally, the *imām* may expatriate the original settlers, bring other infidels in their place, and impose on them the *jizyah* and the *kharāj*.

Al-Shāfi'i objects to making a present of their lands to the owners when the lands have been conquered by force, because, according to him, they are a booty of war, in such case, and, like chattels, are the property of the soldiers; he maintains that although the *imām* may set the unbelievers free, or even kill them, if he chooses (for the right of the soldiers to them is not so clear-cut) he has no right to deprive the soldiers of their unquestioned property. The Hanifites reply that the exercise of an option by the *imām* in this case is only in accordance with the interests of the Moslems, for if he distributed these lands among

[1] 'Adawi, p. 426.

the soldiers they would settle down on them in order to cultivate them, and so they would stay away from the holy war and the enemy would then return to the charge upon the Moslems. Moreover, Moslems are often ill-adapted to agriculture. Consequently, if the lands are returned to the unbelievers who are more familiar with this art and are made subject to payment of *kharāj*, the Moslems can devote their time to the holy war. Furthermore there is no prejudice in this for the soldiers' interests, for although in the case of distribution the benefits are more immediate, in the other case they are more persistent. Then, too, future generations also have a right in these lands, and should the lands be distributed among the victorious army, future Moslems would have been wronged.[1]

The imam has also **several options concerning the people themselves** inhabiting the country conquered. Thus he may kill the captives, or he may make them slaves, or he may do them a favor by allowing them to remain free as *dhimmis* of the Moslem state, except when they are Arab idolaters or renegades, who have to choose between the sword and Islam. The captives however may not return to their country, because it would result in the strengthening of the enemy. According to the *Jāmi'*, women and children are not killed, but are made slaves for the benefit of the fighters.[2]

It is not allowed to divide the spoils in the land of the enemy, although Abu Yūsuf says this is permissible. However, if the *imām* does not possess the means of carrying the spoils to the Moslem land he may then divide the spoils provisionally in order that they may be carried to the Moslem land, where they are redivided definitely. In such case the

[1] *Mabsūt*, part x, p. 40; *Umm*, vol. iv, pp. 103-4, 193.

[2] *Cf. Minhāj*, vol. iii, p. 264; Māwardi, pp. 226, 232; Kharashi, p. 410.

soldiers are entitled to wages for carrying the spoils entrusted to them. According to the Shafiites,[1] the spoils are divided in the enemy's country. The fighters and their helpers are equally entitled to a share in the spoils, but not the persons who have not fought. Thus the traders following in the wake of the army are not entitled to a share. The fighters may use the spoils in the land of the enemy before the spoils have been yet divided, if there is need for doing so, *e. g.*, they may use the horses or arms taken from the enemy. As regards forage, wood, oil, perfumes and the like, these may be used by the soldiers even if they should not need them.[2] The fighters, however, may not sell the spoils or appropriate them. Neither may they use them after they have left the enemy's land; on the contrary, they must return to the spoil fund whatever remains in their possession.

The imam may promise (*tanfīl*) [3] the army more than their regular shares in the spoils before the spoils have been taken, and the war has ended, in order to induce them to greater ardor in the fight. Thus the *imām* may promise the soldiers the personal effects (*salab*) of the persons slain by them, or a certain propor ion of the property taken by them. The personal effects of persons who are not killed in war, such as women and children may not be promised, because such a policy would encourage their killing. However it is allowed to promise the personal effects of the traders who follow the enemy or of the *dhimmis* who fight on the side of the enemy. It is not permissible to promise extra shares after the spoils have been taken, unless it be from the fifth set apart as the state's share. The personal effects of the

[1] Māwardi, p. 240; *Wajīz*, p. 291.

[2] *Cf. Minhāj*, vol. iii, p. 267.

[3] *Cf. Wajīz*, p. 290; Kharashi, p. 427.

slain belong in the spoils, if they have not been promised by the *imām* as extra shares; this being also the Malikite view. The Shafiites, however, hold that the personal effects (*salab*) of the killed belong to the soldier who killed him irrespective of whether or not the *imām* had so stipulated.[1]

The spoils are divided among the army after the deduction of one-fifth as the state's share, according to Abu Hanīfah and Zufar, at the rate of two shares to the horseman, and one share to the footsoldier, but according to the two disciples, al-Shāfi'i and the Malikites, at the rate of three shares to the horseman; one for himself and two for his horse.[2] In Abu Hanīfah's opinion, the footsoldiers who bought a horse after entering the land of the enemy, and the horseman whose horse died before the battle are entitled to a full horseman's share. No shares, however, are assigned to mules and animals used for transporting. The slaves, *mukātabs*, minors, women and *dhimmis*, if they have been helpful in bringing about the victory, do not receive a full share, but, at the *imām's* discretion, a small gift (*radkh*) less than four-fifths of a full share.

SECTION II

The Tax on Mines and Treasure-trove[3]

The doctors have disagreed about the nature of the tax levied on mines[4] and treasure-trove. The Shafiites consider this tax as a case of *zakāt*. So do the Hanbalites, who

[1] Māwardi, p. 241.

[2] *Cf. Wajīz*, p. 292; Māwardi, p. 243; Kharashi, p. 432.

[3] *Majma'*, p. 173; *Hidāyah*, p. 178; *Durar*, p. 121; *Umm*, p. 36; *Minhāj*, p. 247; Māwardi, p. 207; *Mudawwanah*, p. 50; Dardīr, p. 124.

[4] Following the usage of the doctors, mine is used in the sense of the mineral produce extracted from a mine, since in that way only a mine becomes an object of taxation.

tax at the same rate as *zakāt,* namely, one-fortieth. The Hanifites, on the other hand, consider this tax as a case of spoils and, as in the rest of spoils impose the rate of one-fifth. Finally, Mālik is said to have held both views.[1] The author of the *Majmā'* says in this connection that according to the Hanifites the proceeds of this tax are disbursed in the same way as the spoils, and that they should have been treated by the author (*muṣannif*) of the text under the section of holy war rather than under *zakāt*, except possibly for the fact that according to al-Shāfi'i this tax is a kind of *zakāt* provided for by special prescription (*naṣṣ*). Al-Zarqāni,[2] likewise, observes that the name *zakāt* is used with respect to this tax by way of metaphor, or because in some cases it is subject to the *zakāt.*

Much of the dispute concerning this tax turns upon the determination of the meaning of the word *rikāz* which occurs in the *ḥadīth*: "And in the *rikāz* one-fifth". According to the doctors,[3] the word *rikāz* means any property buried underground; whether by God, as the mine (*ma'-dan*), or by man, as treasure-trove (*kanz*). The *Fatḥ*[4] says that *rikāz* has both meanings literally (*mushtarak*); but according to the *Hidāyah* and the *Badā'i'*, *rikāz* means literally only a mine.[5] The *'Ināyah* says that God created mines in the Earth on the day He created the Earth. Sa'di Efendi, however, objects to this additional qualification on the ground that it is not known. The *Majma'* remarks that the matter is open to discussion because there is a *ḥadīth*

[1] Qasṭallāni, vol. iii, p. 83.

[2] Vol. ii, p. 47.

[3] *Cf. Mabsūṭ*, p. 211; *Durar*, p. 121.

[4] *Majma'*, p. 173.

[5] The Shafiites and Malikites use *ma'dan* for mine and *rikāz* for treasure-trove only. The Hanifites in general use *rikāz* for both meanings and differentiate treasure-trove by the use of the word *kanz*.

in which the Prophet said that gold and silver were created on the day the Earth was created. The dispute on the meaning of the word *rikāz* has an important bearing because, as al-Qastallāni observes, in case *rikāz* means treasure-trove alone, mines would be exempt from the tax of one-fifth.

Mines. According to the Hanifites, **mines are of three kinds:** those which are solids which may be melted and which admit of imprints, like gold, silver, iron, copper, lead, *etc.*; those which are solids which do not melt and do not admit of imprints, like gypsum, arsenic, coal, *etc.*; those which are liquids which do not become solid, like water oil, *etc.*[1]

In the case of mines of the first kind,—the only kind subject to tax,—according to the Hanifites, the fifth belongs to the state. Al-Sarakhsi, in justification of this, says[2] that the veins in which mines are found have once been like treasures, in the possession of the infidels before they came under Moslem jurisdiction by force of arms, and therefore they are a spoil of war and one-fifth of them belongs to the state.

According to the Hanifites, if a Moslem or a *dhimmi,* whether a freeman or a slave, minor or adult, man or woman, should discover a mine of the first kind, like gold or silver, in a land subject to tithe or *kharāj,* one-fifth of the find is taken as tax, and the remaining four-fifths belongs to the finder, unless he is a *musta'min*; the latter is excepted because he is a *ḥarbi* and the *ḥarbis* are not entitled to a share in the spoils even when they have fought the enemies of Islam with the *imām's* permission. However, according to the *Minaḥ*, the *ḥarbis* and the *musta'mins* in the

[1] *'Ināyah*, p. 179.

[2] *Mabsūṭ*, p. 211.

last case should be entitled to the share agreed upon between them and the *imām*. According to the *Mabsūṭ*,[1] this should also apply in case the *ḥarbi* works a mine with the *imām's* permission.

The finder gets the four-fifths as mentioned only in case the land where the mine was discovered is not private property (*mamlūkah*), for in the latter case, after the deduction of the state's share of one-fifth, the four-fifths belongs to the owner of the land instead of to the finder.

If the find is made in the finder's own habitation, or store, according to Abu Hanīfah, no tax is levied on the find, but in the opinion of Abu Yūsuf and Muḥammad Ibn al-Hasan there is levied a tax of one-fifth on the find because the tenor of the respective *ḥadīth* is general. If, however, the mine was discovered by the finder in his own land (*milk*), there are two different views reported from Abu Hanīfah. The view cited in the *Mabsūṭ* is that no tax is levied, but the view cited in the *Jāmiʿ Sagīr*[2] is to the contrary. The distinction between land and habitation is due to the consideration that land is owned subject to public charges like tithe and *kharāj*, whereas houses are owned subject to no taxes whatever.

According to al-Shāfiʿī, mines do not pay this tax because, like game, they were the property of no one when found, and so they belong to the person who first found and seized (*iḥrāz*) them. Consequently, according to him, mines pay a tax only in so far as they are subject to *zakāt*, namely, if they are gold or silver, provided, however, the *niṣāb* requirements have been met. As regards the lapse of a year, in one view of the matter he requires it, but, in another view, he does not require it, since this requirement is in order that productivity might materialize, and in the case of mines the

[1] P. 215.

[2] *Cf. al-Jāmiʿ al-Sagīr*, p. 22.

whole thing is a product (*numā'*). This second view is the prevalent one.[1] According to the Shafiites, gold or silver extracted from a mine at one time may be added to that extracted at another in order to complete the *niṣāb*, so long as the exploitation of the mine has not been definitively abandoned. The *niṣāb* may be also completed by gold, silver, and articles of trade which the miner may already possess, even if their year has not completely run out. Mines worked by *dhimmis* are not subject to tax, because the tax levied on mines is *zakāt*, which may be levied on Moslems alone.

According to Malik, mines, like crops, are a kind of produce derived from the earth, and therefore if they are gold or silver they pay *zakāt* subject to the requirement of *niṣāb*, though not that of the lapse of a year.[2] According to the Malikites,[3] the *niṣāb* may be completed from gold or silver extracted from the same vein (*'irq*), regardless of continuity of extraction. Once the *niṣāb* has been reached, later findings, no matter how little, pay *zakāt pro rata*. If the mine extracted falls under the description of *nadrah* (literally, rarety), namely, pure gold or silver which does not need smelting, it is considered a treasure-trove (*rikāz*). Consequently, such finds are not subject to *zakāt* but pay the tax of one-fifth levied on treasure-trove, irrespective of the *niṣāb* requirement, even if they are discovered by an infidel or slave. If, however, the extraction of the *nadrah* involves great expense or labor, then, as in treasure-trove, it is subject to *zakāt* as a mine.

According to Abu Hanīfah and Muḥammad Ibn al-Hasan, there is no tax of one-fifth on pearls and amber-

[1] *Wajīz*, p. 96; Māwardi, p. 207.
[2] Ibn Rushd, *M.*, p. 226.
[3] Kharashi, pp. 112-3.

gris, and, in general, on anything taken out of the sea, even if it is gold or sliver, because, being at the bottom of the sea, these things are proof against conquest, but the tax applies to the spoils of war only. Likewise, there is no tax on stones, like turquoise, sapphires, topaz, emeralds, *etc.*, when they are found in the mountains, because the Prophet said: "There is no fifth on stones". Both sea products and stones are taxed, however, if found in the treasure store of the enemy. There is a tax on quicksilver, according to the last opinion of Abu Hanīfah. According to Abu Yūsuf, however, quicksilver is not taxed; but on the contrary, products of the sea used as ornaments, such as pearls, are taxed, since Omar taxed ambergris.[1] According to the Shafiites and the Malikites,[2] none of them pay *zakāt* as such, though they may pay as articles of trade.

Treasure-trove (*kanz*). Treasures are of **three kinds:** Treasures which bear a sign of Islam, such as the sentence of testimony to the existence of one God; those which do not bear any sign; thirdly those which bear a sign of the pre-Islamic age, such as a picture of a god, or the cross.

Treasures of the first kind legally are property lost and found (*luqaṭah*), that is, property owned by a Moslem, and therefore they are not subject to tax. Treasures of the second kind, according to the most reliable Hanifite report (*Ẓāhir-al-madhhab*), are considered to be like those of the third kind, since the presumption (*aṣl*) is that they are of pre-Islamic origin; but some hold that they are like those of the first, because, they argued, treasures found nowadays are probably of Islamic origin, owing to the long standing of Islam.

Finally, treasures of the third kind are subject to a tax

[1] *Hidāyah*, p. 184; *Jāmi'*, p. 319.

[2] *Minhāj*, p. 246; Kharashi, p. 116.

of one-fifth, the remaining four-fifths belonging to the person who found them; provided he is not a *musta'min*, and the treasure has been found in a land which is not owned (*mamlūkah*) by any one, *e. g.*, in the country, or the mountains. It makes no difference whether the finder is adult or minor, free or slave, Moslem or *dhimmi*, man or woman. In case the treasure has been found by a *musta'min*, the entire treasure belongs to the state.

If, however, the treasure has been found in a land owned (*mamlūkah*) by a private individual, according to Abu Yūsuf, the remainder after deduction of the state's share of one-fifth still belongs to the person who found the treasure; but according to Abu Hanīfah and Muḥammad Ibn al-Hasan, it belongs to the person to whom the land was given (*khiṭṭah*) at the time of its conquest, or to his heirs, if they are known, otherwise, following al-Sarakhsi, to the earliest known owner of the land; according to Abu 'l-Layth, however, it belongs to the public treasury; this last view being approved by the *Majma'*. The above applies in case the two parties agree that the thing found is a treasure-trove, for if the owner of the land says that he had himself buried it, his statement is believed after he has sworn to it. The argument of Abu Hanīfah and Muḥammad is that the person to whom the land was given after conquest owns both its surface and what is below the surface, and when later he sells it to others, he transfers the ownership of the surface of the land only, not the inside of it; hence the treasures buried in the land remain the property of the original owner, exactly as the pearl found in the belly of a fish belongs to the person who caught it, not the party who bought the fish from him. The reasons for the view of Abu Yūsuf who in this connection departs from analogy and judges by *istiḥsān*, is that the person who found the treasure is the one who really discovered and occupied it. Besides, it may not be said that the *imām*, in dividing the lands after conquest, also transferred the ownership of the treasures possibly buried in the lands, because the *imām* is just, and such a thing would result in injustice, since all lands are not alike in respect to treasures. Consequently the treasures continue to be property of no one, and the person who discovers them owns them. The others reply that the *imām* is only obliged to be just within the bounds of the possible, and he cannot possibly be so with respect to the treasures; moreover, it is not claimed that the *imām* actually transfers the ownership of the treasures buried in the land, but simply that he prevents other soldiers from encroaching on them and that for this reason they become the property of the person to whom the land including them was given.[1] Mines lying in a piece of land, however, belong to the present owner, because, according to the *Hidāyah*,[2] unlike treasures which are distinct from the land where they are buried and are, as it were, trusts to the land, mines are intimately mixed with the particles of the land, and therefore when the land is sold the mines are also sold.

If a person enters the land of the *ḥarbis* by way of *amān* and finds in the country, that is, in a land which is not owned by any one, a mine or a treasure, (according to some, a mine only), the whole of the find belongs to the finder, since, not being in the possession of any one, no injustice is involved. According to Abu Yūsuf, one-fifth of the find is taken as a tax. If, however, the find is discovered in a house or land owned by a *ḥarbi*, the find is then returned to the owner of the house or the land, since he owns what is in them also. If the finder fails to return the find to its owner, but brings it with him on his return

[1] *Mabsūṭ*, p. 214.

[2] P. 183.

to the Moslem country, the find becomes his property, but it is an impure (*khabīth*) property. With respect to property found by a Moslem in the territory of the *ḥarbis*, the *Fatḥ*[1] observes that, although property found under similar circumstances by a *ḥarbi* in Moslem territory belongs to the Moslem state, property found in the territory of the *ḥarbis* by a Moslem belongs to the latter, because, the land of the *ḥarbis* being one where law does not rule, only actual possession there counts; the Moslem land on the contrary, is one of law, and in the eyes of the law, hypothetical (*ḥukmi*) possession is like actual possession. The above applies in case the Moslem entered the territory of the *ḥarbis* after having obtained *amān* from the *ḥarbis*; for if he entered without *amān* for the purpose of robbing, such property as he finds in the country is not taxed, since the tax is levied on spoils only and this property is not a spoil of war.

According to the Shafiites,[2] treasure-trove of pre-Islamic origin is subject to *zakāt* at the rate of one-fifth, if it consists of gold or silver and is of *niṣāb* quantity. The lapse of a year, however, is not required. Because the tax levied on treasure-trove is *zakāt*, the *dhimmis* do not pay it.

According to the Malikites,[3] treasure-trove of pre-Islamic or doubtful origin is subject to a tax of one-fifth, whether it is in large or small quantity, gold or silver or other than gold or silver, found by Moslems or found by infidels. Treasure-trove is, however, subject to *zakāt* if its unearthing involved great labor or expense, and in such case all the conditions of *zakāt* must be met excepting the one concerning the lapse of a year.

[1] P. 184.

[2] *Minhāj*, p. 248; *Wajīz*, p. 97; Māwardi, p. 207.

[3] Kharashi, p. 113.

SECTION III

The Tax on non-Moslem Traders, and the Estates of Deceased Persons

The tax on non-Moslem traders, whether they are *dhimmis*, or *ḥarbis* who entered the Moslem state with *amān* (*musta'min*) for trade, is collected by the *'āshirs*, who also collect from Moslems, who pass them on the public road, their *zakāt* dues. As the details pertaining to the rates and the method of collection have been already explained in the first two sections of chapter III on Collection, they will not be repeated here.

The estates of deceased persons or the blood price of murdered persons who left no lawful heirs, or left only a husband or a wife, and who have not disposed of these estates by will are a source of negligible importance, and therefore need only to be enumerated here in order to complete the list.[1]

[1] Kāsāni, p. 68.

CHAPTER IX

The Public Treasury and the Mohammedan Counterpart of a Budget

Every property (*māl*) which belongs to Moslems in general and not to any Moslem in particular constitutes a part of the assets (*ḥuqūq*) of the **public treasury (bayt-al-mal)**. It is not necessary that the property should be actually in the vaults (*ḥirz*) of the treasury for it to be considered an asset of the treasury, because the conception of *bayt-al-māl* refers to the destination (*jihah*) of the property, not to its actual location. Therefore every expenditure (*ḥaqq*) which must be incurred in the interests of Moslems in general (*maṣāliḥ al-muslimīn*) is a liability of *bayt-al-māl* and when it is made, it is considered to have been made by it, whether or not it has actually been paid out of the vaults of *bayt-al-māl*; this is for the reason that a revenue which has gone into the hands of the public collectors or has been spent directly by them is really a part of the income and outgo of the *bayt-al-māl* itself, and is therefore subject to the regulations governing the same.

In other words, according to the Shafiite conception, the term "public treasury" applies only to those revenues of the Moslem community or state whose disbursement has not been prescribed by the *sharī'ah* in favor of definite classes of Moslems, but which belong to the Moslem community at large and are disbursed by the *imām*, its lawful head, for the common Moslem interests, namely, in meeting the

[1] Māwardi, p. 366.

general expenses of the state. The " public treasury ", then, does not exhaust the various items of revenue accruing to the Moslem community or state,[1] for a revenue might be a source of income to the state to meet its obligations and yet technically not be a part of the assets of the public treasury. Consequently, the distinction of revenue between these two classes does not mean that because an item of revenue is not an asset of the public treasury it is not also a revenue of the state; in the last analysis it amounts to this, namely, that certain of the activities of the Moslem state, as well as the revenues and the expenses necessary for them, owing to their importance, have been defined and prescribed by the *sharīʿah* itself, while other activities considered less important, and, as it were, matters of course, were left to the discretion of the constituted authorities of the Moslem state. The revenue necessary for these latter activities constitutes the assets of the public treasury.

The Malikites, although they do not expressly state the meaning of *bayt-al-māl*, nevertheless imply by their use of the term,[2] that they hold a similar view of the matter. Finally, the Hanifites, likewise fail expressly to define their position, but the fact that they apply the expression to all the revenue of the state[3] would force one to the conclusion that they mean by it every revenue which accrues to the state, whether or not the *imām* has a free hand in its disbursement.

[1] One may distinguish three kinds of revenue: revenue for the Moslem community proper, such as the four-fifths of the spoils divided among the victorious army; revenue for the state, such as the fifth part of the spoils set apart for the state; finally, there is revenue for the public treasury as distinct from either.

[2] Kharashi, p. 121, l. 3; pp. 127, 427; 'Adawi, p. 123; Ibn Rushd, *B.*, p. 329.

[3] *Baḥr*, vol. v, p. 128; *Majmaʿ*, p. 520; Kāsāni, p. 68.

There are [1] **three distinct classes of revenue** (*māl*) which accrue to the Moslem community or the Moslem state as distinct from the public treasury (*bayt-al-māl*). They are: (1) the **sadaqah or zakat revenue** (*amwāl al-ṣadaqāt*), such as the *zakāt* and tithe; (2) the **booty revenue** (*ganīmah*), namely, the spoils of war; (3) the **fa'y revenue**, such as the *jizyah* and the *kharāj*. The first applies to revenue derived from Moslems, the other two apply to revenue taken from infidels. *Ganīmah* means property taken from the infidels by assault (*'anwat*) with arms in hand, whereas *fa'y* [2] is property given by the infidels "spontaneously (*'afwa*) [3] without fighting and without making horses and riders run." [4]

These three classes of revenue differ [5] from one another as follows: The *ṣadaqah* revenue differs from the other two classes in four respects:

(1) The *ṣadaqah* is received from the Moslems for their purification; the others are taken from the infidels for revenge.

[1] Māwardi, p. 217; *Umm*, vol. iv, p. 63.

[2] *Fa'y* literally means "that which came back," in this instance, as al-Shāfi'i (Muzani, vol. iii, p. 183) remarks, "that which God returned to His people (without fighting on their part) from those who opposed His religion," the theory implied being that property taken as spoils, as a matter of law, belongs to the Moslems. (*Cf.* Berchem, p. 9.) According to some, *fa'y* is spoils taken without difficulty (al-Rāgib). According to Abu 'Ubayd, it is property taken from the enemy after the cessation of hostilities, such property belonging to all the Moslems. According to the *Mafātīḥ* (p. 58), it is the revenue derived from a country conquered by force. According to 'Ali Ibn 'Isa, *fa'y* is more general than *ganīmah* (spoils), applying to everything accruing to the Moslems from the enemy (*Mugrib*, vol. ii, p. 80). Finally, according to the *Miṣbāḥ*, it is the *kharāj* and the spoils.

[3] According to Ibn Rushd, *B.* (p. 325), "through terror and fear."

[4] Cf. Yahya, p. 3.

[5] Māwardi, p. 217; *cf. Umm*, vol. iv, p. 64.

(2) The destination of the *ṣadaqah* has been entirely determined by special provision (*naṣṣ*), whereas that of the others is partly determined by the *imām's ijtihād*.

(3) In the case of *ṣadaqah*, the taxpayers may themselves pay it directly to the beneficiaries, while this is not allowed in the others.

(4) The destination of the *ṣadaqah* is different from that of the others.

As regards the *ganīmah* and *fa'y* revenues, they agree and differ in two points respectively:

(1) The points of agreement: both are taken from infidels, and one-fifth of both is disbursed alike.

(2) The points of difference: *ganīmah* is taken by force of arms (*qahra*), whereas *fa'y* is taken peacefully (*'afwa*), and secondly, the beneficiaries of the four-fifths of the *ganīmah* are different from the beneficiaries of the four-fifths of the *fa'y*.[1]

[2] Of the above three classes of revenue which may accrue to the Moslem community or the state, namely, the *ṣadaqah*, booty, and *fa'y* revenues, the **(four-fifths of) fa'y revenue** is a **part of** the **public treasury** because its disposition is made according to the personal judgment of the *imām*. On the contrary, the **(four-fifths of) booty revenue** is not a part of the treasury—and on this point the Hanifite and Malikite views are at one,—for the beneficiaries of the booty revenue have been prescribed by express revealed provision (*naṣṣ*), and are definite persons, namely, the army who fought the battle, and the *imām* may not dispose of the booty in any other way.

As regards the **fifth** part **of** the **fa'y revenue**, and the

[1] The above is according to the Shafiites. The Hanifite and Malikite views somewhat differ.

[2] Māwardi, p. 367.

state's part of one-fifth of the booty revenue, each consists of three distinct parts: (a) part of it, the Prophet's share, belongs to the treasury, since it is disposed of by the *imām* of the community for the time being according to his own judgment; (b) part of it, namely, the share of the Prophet's relations (*dhawu al-qurba*) does not belong to the treasury, since its beneficiaries are known, and the *imām* has no voice in its disposition; (c) finally, a third part is kept in the treasury as a trust fund on account of the various purposes for which it is destined. This last part consists of the shares set aside for orphans, the indigent, and wayfarers. They receive their shares, if they are present; otherwise their shares are kept for them.

Applying the Shafiite conception of public treasury to the Malikite view,[1] the entire *fa'y* and the state's part of one-fifth of the booty revenue would be assets of the public treasury, for, according to the Malikites, both are disposed of by the *imām* according to his own proper judgment. Finally, applying the same test to the Hanifite views, the entire *fa'y* revenue would be distinctly an asset of the public treasury. On the other hand the state's part of one-fifth of the booty revenue would be outside of the public treasury to the extent that it must be disbursed to definite classes of people, such as orphans; though, in so far as it may be disbursed by the *imām* to any one of those classes exclusively, it might properly be classed as an asset of the public treasury.

Finally, the sadaqah revenue is of two kinds: the *ṣadaqah* revenue levied on non-apparent property, which does not form a part of the treasury's income, since the property owners may themselves disburse their *zakāt* dues directly to the beneficiaries, such as the poor, with-

[1] Kharashi, p. 427.

out resorting to the intermediary of the public collectors; secondly, the *ṣadaqah* revenue derived from apparent property; namely, the tithe and the *zakāt* collected from cattle. This second kind of *ṣadaqah* revenue, according to al-Shāfi'i, is not a part of the treasury, because the beneficiaries are known and the funds may not be disposed of in any other way. Al-Shāfi'i, however, holds two different views concerning the lawfulness of keeping this revenue in the treasury as a trust when it is not possible, for some reason or other, to disburse it to its beneficiaries. His earlier opinion was that such funds should be kept in the treasury as a trust until the appearance of the rightful claimants. Later, al-Shāfi'i abandoned this opinion in favor of his later opinion which is that the treasury may not keep these funds in its vaults as a matter of right, although they may be entrusted to the treasury for safekeeping.

Applying the Shafiite conception of public treasury to **the Hanifite views** concerning the disbursement of *zakāt* revenue from apparent property, we may say that to the extent that such revenue must be disbursed to certain specified classes of people it is not a part of the public treasury, but in so far as the *imām* may disburse it to any one or more of those classes exclusively, and in view of the comprehensive and loose meaning which has been given to those classes, such revenue may properly be said to be a part of the public treasury. The *zakāt* from non-apparent property, however, is in no way a part of the public treasury. What is true of the Hanifites as regards *zakāt* from apparent property is even more true of **the Malikites,** for, according to the latter, the *imām* might disburse the entire *ṣadaqah* revenue to public functionaries exclusively, even if they should be rich. Moreover, as we have already seen, the Malikites practically assimilated the *zakāt* of non-apparent property to that of apparent property by requiring the payment of the former to the state officials.[1]

A detailed **description of the various items of revenue,** classed by the three schools under one or the other of the three classes of revenue above mentioned, follows:

(1) The **sadaqah or zakat revenue** designated in this dissertation under the expression of *zakāt* taxes, according to the Hanifites,[2] consists of the *zakāt* of non-apparent property disbursed to the *zakāt* beneficiaries directly by the owners, namely, the *zakāt* of gold and silver and the *zakāt* of the articles of trade; as well as the *zakāt* of apparent property collected and disbursed by the state, as the *zakāt* of animals, the *zakāt* collected by the *'āshirs* from apparent and non-apparent property of Moslems only, and the *zakāt* of produce or tithe. According to the Shafiites,[3] the tax of one-fifth levied on treasure-trove (*rikāz*) and the tax collected on mines (*ma'dan*) also form a part of *zakāt* revenue. Al-Shāfi'i, in this connection, remarks that whatever is due on a Moslem's property in virtue of a prescription found in the Koran, or the *sunnah*, or an *ijmā'* of Moslem laymen (*'awāmm al-muslimīn,* that is, all Moslems, laymen or *mujtahids*), "its meaning is one, namely, it is *zakāt*, and *zakāt* is *ṣadaqah*, and its disbursement is always one and the same as God divided the *ṣadaqahs*." According to the Malikites, on the other hand, taxes levied on mines and treasure-trove are a part of *ṣadaqah* revenue only in so far as they are levied at the regular *zakāt* rate of one-fortieth.[4]

[1] 'Adawi, p. 120.

[2] *Majma'*, p. 520; Kāsāni, p. 68; *'Alamkīriyyah*, p. 268; *Baḥr*, vol. v, p. 128.

[3] *Umm*, p. 71; *Wajīz*, pp. 96, 97; *Minhāj*, pp. 247, 248.

[4] Kharashi, pp. 111, 113, 427.

(2) **Booty** (*ganīmah*) **revenue** consists of spoils of war, mines, and treasure-trove. One-fifth of the booty revenue is levied by the state as a tax. According to the Shafiites, booty revenue consists of the spoils of war alone. The tax levied on mines and treasure-trove is considered by them as *zakāt*. Finally, according to the Malikites, the tax levied on mines and treasure-trove is considered booty revenue only if levied under the name of one-fifth (*khums*).[1] This tax applies to the treasure-trove, and, in mines, to the gold or silver ingots called *nadrat*, provided the unearthing of neither has involved great expense or labor. In the latter case, treasure-trove, as well as *nadrats*, are subject to *zakāt*.

(3) The **fa'y revenue** consists of the *kharāj*, the *jizyah*, the dresses (*ḥullah*) paid by the people of Najrān, the double rate of *zakāt* paid by the tribe of Taglib, the tolls collected by the *'āshirs* from the *dhimmi* and *ḥarbi* traders, and the estates of *dhimmis* who left no will and no heirs, or only a husband or wife,[2] also[3] the payment for a truce (*hudnah*), property taken from a country whose population has fled, property given to the Moslems by the *ḥarbis* as a gift, property belonging to apostates (*murtadd*), *etc.* The Malikites merge this and the preceding class into one single class so far as disbursement is concerned.[4]

(4) According to the Hanifites, there is a **fourth class of revenue** consisting of property lost and found (*luqaṭah*),

[1] Because the rate of one-fifth is the rate prescribed for the spoils of war, the Malikites, unlike the Shafiites, consider every revenue collected on the basis of such a rate as identical with the revenue derived from the spoils of war.

[2] *Baḥr*, vol. v, p. 127; but *cf. Fatḥ al-Mu'īn*, vol. ii, p. 456; *Majma'*, p. 520; Kharashi, p. 427. On wills of *dhimmis*, see *Majma'*, vol. ii, pp. 564-5; *Fatḥ al-Mu'īn*, vol. iii, p. 546; *Wajīz*, p. 269; Kharashi, pp. 444-5.

[3] *Umm*, vol. iv, p. 77; *Wajīz*, p. 288.

[4] Kharashi, p. 427.

and the estates (*tarakah*) left by Moslems,[1] who leave no heirs, or leave only a husband or wife.[2]

As the appropriation of the first three classes owing to their importance will be discussed separately, only the expenditure of the fourth class will be explained here. The revenue from this source is appropriated for the support of sick people who are poor, and for the buying of their medicines, for the funeral expenses of the dead who leave no estates, for the support of foundlings (*laqīṭ*), for compensation for crimes committed by them, for the support of persons who are unable to earn a living and who do not have a relation on whom their support legally rests, and for similar purposes.[3]

It is the duty of the imam to keep each of the abovementioned four classes of revenue apart from the others in separate treasuries, because each has certain peculiarities of its own. If no property is available in one of them, the *imām* may borrow funds on its account from the others. When he does so; if for instance, he borrows money on account of the *kharāj* treasury from the *zakāt* treasury; he must return the amount borowed from the latter when the *kharāj* is collected, unless the fighters who are beneficiaries of the *kharāj* are poor; in the latter case the fighters by being poor have a share also in the proceeds of *zakāt*, and therefore the amount taken from the treasury of *zakāt* is not really a loan. If, on the other hand, the *imām* borrows

[1] *Baḥr*, vol. v, p. 127; but *cf. Fatḥ al-Mu'īn*, vol. ii, p. 456; also, Kāsāni, p. 68; *'Alamkīriyyah*, p. 268; *Majma'*, p. 520.

[2] When the husband or the wife is the only heir, he or she is entitled to the prescribed share (*farīḍah*) only, the rest devolving to the state. It would, however, be a different matter if the only heir were another relative, say, a sister, for she being of the class of heirs called *ṣāḥib al-radd* (literally, one to whom the balance is turned over), receives also the balance after the deduction of her prescribed share.

[3] *Majma'*, p. 520; Kāsāni, p. 68; *'Alamkīriyyah*, p. 268.

money on behalf of the *zakāt* account from that of the *kharāj* and distributes it to the poor, it does not become a loan on the charge of the poor, because, the *kharāj* being treated like (*lahu ḥukm al-fa'y*) the *fa'y* and the *ganīmah*, which are disbursed to provide for the needs of the Moslems, the poor have a share in them, and if they do not actually receive a share from them, it is only because the proceeds of the *zakāt* revenue are sufficient for their needs.[1]

According to al-Māwardi,[2] if the treasury has to meet two claims,[3] while there are sufficient funds for only one of them, that claim is settled first which is a debt (*dayn*) upon the treasury. If the funds are not sufficient for either claim, then it is allowed to the official in charge to borrow money on account of the treasury in order to settle the debts, if he fears that a contrary policy would result in evils; but he may not borrow money to settle claims which are in the nature of donations (*irtifāq*). When he borrows money, his successor is obliged to pay back the loans as soon as the treasury has sufficient funds. If, on the contrary, the funds of the treasury are more than sufficient for the settlement of the claims, opinion varies as to the manner in which the surplus should be disposed. Abu Hanīfah holds that the surplus must be laid aside in the treasury in order to meet future emergencies, but al-Shāfi'i thinks that the surplus is not laid aside, because the meeting of future emergencies becomes an obligation only after the emergencies have occurred. A similar view is expressed in the *'Alamkīriyyah*, where it is stated that when there is any surplus left it is divided among the Moslems at large,

[1] *'Alamkīriyyah*, p. 268; *Mabsūṭ*, part iii, p. 17; *cf*. p. 18.

[2] P. 369.

[3] Of course, here it is a question of claims which have to be paid out of the same class of revenue.

[4] *'Alamkīriyyah*, p. 268.

and if the *imām* fails to do this, he suffers the evil consequences of his failure. It is the duty of the *imām* to disburse the revenues to their rightful claimants and not to deprive them of their rights. The *imām* and his assistants are not allowed to take from these revenues more than the needs of their families and themselves, and they are not allowed to hoard the revenues. It is recommended that the *imām* and the collector do not advance to themselves their salaries for the coming month, but that they take their salaries only for the current month.

The **dhimmis have no share in the revenues of the treasury,** except when the *imām* sees a *dhimmi* starving from hunger, in which case it is his duty to give him something from the treasury, because the *dhimmi* is residing in the Moslem state and the *imām* is under obligation (*'alayhi*) to keep him alive.[1]

According to al-Shāfi'i,[2] the *imām* may not disburse to *dhimmis* from the *fa'y* revenue, any more than he may do so from spoils and *ṣadaqah* revenue. For all these revenues (*māl allah*) belong to Moslem beneficiaries and "it is prohibited (*ḥarām*) for the *imām*—but God, may He be exalted, knows better—to take a Moslem's right and give it to another, and how (might he give it) to a *dhimmi*!" for whom God assigned no share in any one of those revenues.

There has been difference of opinion among the disciples of al-Shāfi'i[3] on the question as to **whether real estate devolving to the public treasury** by that very fact **becomes immobilized** (*waqf*). Some hold that these estates by becoming a part of the treasury assets become immo-

[1] *'Alamkiriyyah*, p. 260; but *cf.* al-Sarakhsi (*Mabsūṭ*, part iii, p. 19).

[2] *Umm*, vol. iv, p. 102.

[3] Māwardi, p. 336.

bilized in order that their income may be used for the general expenses of the treasury, and that therefore their sale and concession (*iqṭāʿ*) are unlawful.[1] Others hold that they do not become immobilized until they are so constituted by the *imām*, and that hence the *imām* may sell them if he sees fit for the interests of the treasury. The price realized is expended for the general needs of the treasury and for those of the beneficiaries of *faʾy* and *ṣadaqah* who are in need. With regard to the concession (*iqṭāʿ*) of the ownership of such estates, it is said that such concession is lawful since it is lawful to sell them and give away their price to people who are in need and for other general needs approved by the *imām*. In fact, there is no difference between alienating the ownership of real estate and giving away the price realized from its sale. Others contend that such estates may be sold because a sale is a bilateral transaction, but that their concession is unlawful, because that is a case of donation (*ṣilah*) and in the matter of donations, fleeting cash differs from the permanent real estate of which it is the price.

According to the Hanifites, real estate (*ʿaqār*) such as lands devolving to the public treasury becomes, according to one opinion, a perpetual *waqf* (*waqf muʾabbad*),[2] but the general view is that such real estate is like that of the orphan; the authority of the *imām* or the guardian (*walī*) being valid with respect to the real estate of the public treasury or the orphan respectively, only in so far as it is conducive to their interests. According to one view, real estate of the public treasury differs from that of orphans as well as from *waqf* estates in that, unlike them, it may be leased for indefinite terms.[3]

[1] *Cf. Minhāj*, vol. ii, p. 297; *Wajīz*, pp. 248, 289.

[2] *Al-ʿUqūd al-Durriyyah*, p. 176.

[3] *Itḥāf al-Abṣār*, p. 191; *Durr*, p. 364; *Fatḥ al-Muʿīn*, vol. ii, pp. 446-7.

Finally, the Malikite view in regard to real estate conquered by force from the infidels, as we have already seen, is to the effect that such estate by the very fact of conquest becomes *waqf* property.[1]

According to the Malikites,[2] the sale by the state of its waqf estates is unlawful. According to the earlier Hanifite authorities, the alienation by sale of the real estate of orphans, and, by analogy, that of the public treasury is only allowed (1) in case of need for funds which could not otherwise be procured. Later authorities however allow it in six other contingencies; (2) if there is a demand for it at double its value; (3) if the deceased left debts to be settled; (4) if the deceased left a will (*waṣiyat mursalah*) which can only be executed by selling the real estate; (5) if the income from the estate does not exceed its expense; (6) if the estate consists in a house or store whose depreciation is feared; (7) finally, if the estate is in the hands of a person of power (*mutagallib*), and it is feared that he will appropriate it, it may be sold to him.[3]

It is not lawful for the *imām* to buy a land of the public treasury from the agent (*wakīl*) of the latter, but if he

[1] It must be pointed out that while the Shafiite and Hanifite views above quoted refer to any real estate which became an asset of the public treasury, the Malikite view refers only to such estate as has been conquered from the infidels by force (*'anwat*). What the Malikite view is concerning real estate in general, I have been unable to discover, but the fact that the Malikite doctors, speaking of lands of deceased *dhimmis*, refer to their devolving to "the Moslems in general" rather than to their being made *waqf* (Kharashi, p. 427; Ibn Rushd., *M.*, p. 280), as occurs with respect to lands conquered by force, would seem to indicate that according to the Malikites the disposition of such lands is left to the judgment of the *imām*. Such a construction is also borne out by the Malikite policy of allowing the *imām* greater latitude than is customary with the other schools.

[2] Kharashi, vol. v, pp. 94-5.

[3] *Majma'*, vol. ii, p. 571; also vol. i, p. 561; Qudūri, p. 65.

desires to buy a certain land, according to an opinion cited in the *Wāqi'āt*, he first orders the sale of the land to a third party and then buys it from that party. If the conditions of the purchase of a public treasury land are not known, the presumption is that the purchase was valid. It is lawful to constitute a *waqf* of a land bought from the public treasury, and in such case the conditions of the *waqf* founder are valid, and the land is exempt from *kharāj*.

The **liabilities**[1] **of the public treasury are of two kinds:** (1) Liabilities resulting from property kept in the treasury for safe-keeping (*ḥirz*) as trust. Such liabilities are enforceable by the claimants only when the funds are present in the treasury, but the claimants have no action against the treasury when there are no funds. (2) Liabilities arising with respect to revenues which are the treasury's own assets. (a) One part of these **liabilities is incurred for value received** (*badal*), *e. g.*, by way of compensation, for the pay of soldiers, or the price of horses and arms; and these claims may be demanded by the persons entitled to them, irrespective of whether or not there are funds in the treasury. If there are available funds the claims are settled at once. But if there are no funds available, the creditors must wait.

The Shafiites[2] have answered in four ways the question as to whether a person may himself collect from the public treasury funds which came into his hands a claim of his which the sultan had failed to settle. In one view of the matter, he may not take anything for his claim because the funds of the public treasury are the joint property of many persons and he does not know what his share is. A second view is that he takes every day enough for

[1] Mawardi, p. 368.

[2] *Mugni*, vol. iii, p. 88.

the food of that day. A third view is that he takes enough for one year. A fourth view is that he takes his stipend, which is his share. This last view is in accordance with analogy, because the treasury funds are not joint property of the Moslems in the sense in which spoils are the joint property of the army, or the estate of the deceased is the joint property of the heirs, for, unlike the case of spoils and estates, should the person in question die, his heirs are not entitled to his stipend.

According to the Hanifites,[1] if a person who has a claim on the public treasury happens to lay hands on a public fund, he may keep it on account of his claim, so far as his religious duties are concerned, but the *imām* may prevent him from so doing, if he chooses.

(b) The other part consists of the liabilities which have been incurred, for the general interest or by way of assistance (*irfāq*), for no consideration of value whatever. The settlement of these liabilities is conditioned upon the existence of funds in the treasury. Consequently, when there are funds in the treasury these liabilities must be met, and in such case the obligation (*farḍ*) of the Moslems at large in this respect lapses. If, however, there are no available funds in the treasury, the liability of the treasury is *ipso facto* canceled but, if the need to be met by that liability was such that its neglect would affect the entire Moslem community, the liability becomes a *farḍ kifāyah* obligation upon all the Moslems, and ceases to be so only after a sufficient number of them have met the liability. For example, the holy war must be financed by the treasury so long as there are funds in it, but if no funds are available, then the obligation of the treasury ceases to exist by that very fact, and the financing of the *jihād* becomes a duty of the Moslems

[1] *'Alamkiriyyah*, p. 269.

at large, until a sufficient number of them have volunteered to finance and carry out the holy war. If, however, the need to be met by the liability is one whose neglect does not result to the injury of all the Moslems; such as the bad condition of a road which however may be replaced by another road, or such as the cutting-off of a city's water supply for which however another water supply may be substituted; then the obligation of making the necessary repairs is removed from both the treasury and the Moslem community.[1]

[1] See *supra*, pp. 350-353.

CHAPTER X

EXPENDITURE OF THE ZAKAT TAXES [1]

The various **beneficiaries of the zakat taxes** have been determined on the basis of the following Koran verse [2] respecting the disbursement of *ṣadaqah* [3] in general: "Verily the *ṣadaqahs* are for (*li*) the poor, the indigent, the respective public agents, the *mu'allafah qulūbuhum*, and [are disbursed] with respect to (*fī*) the slaves (*riqāb*) and the debtors and with respect to 'the way of God', and the wayfarers."

According to the *Jāmi'*, the beneficiaries of the *zakāt* do not have the right to demand settlement of the *zakāt*, nor may they themselves take the *zakāt* without the *zakāt*

[1] *Majma'*, p. 179; *Hidāyah*, p. 200; *Baḥr*, p. 258; *'Alamkīriyyah*, p. 263; *Jāmi'*, p. 334; *Durr*, p. 144; *Durar*, p. 123; *Mabsūṭ*, part iii, pp. 8-15; *Minhāj*, vol. ii, p. 302; *Mugni*, vol. iii, p. 99; Māwardi, p. 210; *Umm*, pp. 60-80; *Wajīz*, p. 292; Kharashi, p. 116; *Muwaṭṭā'*, p. 115; *Mudawwanah*, pp. 46, 55-61; Zarqāni, p. 63.

[2] Chap. 9, verse 60.

[3] The Mohammedan writers consider *zakāt*, as we have already seen, as a special case of *ṣadaqah*, which by extension applies in general to any disbursement made with a view to earning religious merit (*thawāb*). Inasmuch as the Koranic verse relates to the disbursement of *ṣadaqahs*, in general, the disbursement of *zakāt* is treated by the doctors under the heading of *maṣrif al-ṣadaqāt* (beneficiaries of the *ṣadaqahs*); the principles set forth in this chapter apply, therefore, equally well to other kinds of *ṣadaqah* such as the *ṣadaqat al-fiṭr*, or the *kaffārah*, and the vows. We are, however, concerned here with the *zakāt* only. (*Jāmi'*, p. 334.) It must be pointed out here that the views concerning disbursement held by each school apply only to the revenue considered *zakāt* revenue by that particular school. This remark holds true of the other revenues as well.

payer's knowledge; and when they do so, they may legally be forced to return it, although the *zakāt* payer, as between him and God, is advised to let it go, provided, however, that he does not happen to have relations who need the *zakāt* more. The beneficiaries are in detail as follows:

(1) **The "poor"** (*faqīr*) are those who do not own a *niṣāb* of property, or who own a *niṣāb* of unproductive property, which is entirely destined for the satisfaction of first necessities, or of debts. Hence if a student of law should own books to the value of many *niṣābs*, he is still poor if he needs those books, but should the latter be owned by an ignorant person, he is barred from receiving a share out of the *zakāt* proceeds. What is true of books is also true of artisan's tools. If, however, a student of law has two copies of the same book or two houses and needs only one of them, the extra book or house is taken into account and if its value amounts to a *niṣāb*, its owner is considered rich. Muḥammad Ibn al-Hasan holds that if the rental of the extra house is used for the food of himself and his family, the value of the house is not taken into account in reckoning the *niṣāb*.[1] According to the *Fatḥ*,[2] there are three different **kinds of nisab** which must be distinguished from one another. (1) The *niṣāb* of productive property which is unencumbered with debts; such *niṣāb* subjecting its owner to the obligation of *zakāt*. (2) The *niṣāb* which is not productive or which is encumbered with debts. Such *niṣāb* does not subject to *zakāt*, but bars from participation in the proceeds of *zakāt* if it is not entirely destined for the satisfaction of the first necessities. Thus a person owning several articles of wearing apparel or several household utensils or a horse, is barred from receiving *zakāt* if he does not

[1] *Majma'*, p. 182.

[2] P. 202; *cf.* also *Majma'*, p. 183, l. 1.

need to use all the articles of wearing apparel or the utensils, or if he does not need to ride the horse; otherwise he is poor, and may receive a share. (3) The *niṣāb* which does not bar from participation in the *zakāt*, but bars from begging. This *niṣāb* consists in the possession of sufficient food for a single day after covering one's nakedness, or in the ability to earn one's living even if one should not own a day's food; or as some say, it consists in the ownership of fifty *dirhams*. According to al-Māwardi,[1] if a rich person goes begging and the public inspector knows that he is rich, he rebukes him, but if he merely infers from the fact that he has the signs of wealth, he informs him that begging is not allowed to the rich, but does not rebuke him, for he may in reality be poor. Finally, if he sees an able-bodied man begging, he forces him to work and learn a trade, and if he insists on begging he is punished.[2]

In computing the *niṣāb* to determine whether the owner is poor, according to some authorities the procedure is exactly the same as that to determine whether the property should pay *zakāt*; for example, if the property consists of *sawā'im* animals, the *niṣāb* is considered complete if the number of the animals amounts to the minimum number which pays *zakāt*, irrespective of whether or not their value amounts to two hundred *dirhams*. However, the view generally accepted is that the *niṣāb* is considered complete if its value amounts to two hundred *dirhams*, whether or not it is complete when computed in kind. According to al-Margīnāni, if a person has five camels worth less than two hundred *dirhams*, he is "poor" and is given *zakāt* but, on the other hand, he pays a *zakāt* of one sheep on the camels. This view is based on a *ḥadīth* in which the Prophet defined the

[1] P. 416.

[2] *Cf. 'Alamkīriyyah*, p. 263.

rich as the persons owning two hundred *dirhams*.[1] According to the *'Alamkīriyyah*,[2] it is allowed to give the poor a share from *zakāt* even if they are in good health and are engaged in business (*muktasib*). In the *Mi'rāj*, however, it is stated that although the *zakāt* may be given to such persons, it is not proper for them to receive it, because it does not follow that because the *zakāt* may be disbursed to a person, that person may properly receive it; just as it is not proper for a rich person to receive the *zakāt* although it is allowed to disburse the *zakāt* to him when his state is not known. The *Majma'*,[3] however, remarks that it is allowed to the persons in question to receive *zakāt*, although, as is said in the *Baḥr*, it is preferable that they should not do so.

The **Malikite and Shafiite conceptions of the poor** are more flexible. Thus, according to Ibn Rushd,[4] Mālik says that the question of deciding whether a person is poor is left to the judgment of the *imām*. According to Khalīl,[5] however, the poor are the persons who lack sufficient means (*kifāyah*) to provide for necessities for one year, even if they possess a trade. On the other hand, according to al-Shāfi'i,[6] one is rich not only by possessing wealth, but also by being able-bodied and able to earn a living; and if it is said that one may become sick, it is replied that one may as easily lose his wealth. Consequently, the able-bodied poor who know a trade are not given any assistance unless they need it in order to make a living. Al-Māwardi[7] says that a

[1] *Majma'*, p. 182.
[2] P. 265, l. 5. [3] P. 180.
[4] Ibn Rushd, *B.*, p. 251.
[5] Kharashi, p. 117.
[6] *Umm*, p. 64.
[7] P. 211; *cf. Minhāj*, vol. ii, p. 302.

person may be given assistance from *zakāt* so long as he has not attained the lowest stage of wealthiness (*gina*); that there are persons who can make a living by turning over a capital of one single *dīnār*, while others are unable to subsist on a capital of less than 100 *dirhams*. Therefore the latter must be given more than the former. Finally, there are able-bodied and strong artisans who can make a living without any capital, and these are not given assistance even if they do not possess a single *dirham*. According to the *'Alamkīriyyah*, the *zakāt* is given to the learned poor in preference to the ignorant poor.

(2) **The "indigent"** (*miskīn*) are those who do not have anything, and who need to resort to begging in order to make a living and obtain enough clothing to conceal their nakedness. Al-Shāfi'i, and according to one report, Abu Hanīfah also, define the words "poor" and "indigent" in just the other way, and on the contrary Abu Yūsuf holds that the terms are identical. The Malikite view agrees with the prevalent Hanifite view in considering the "indigent" as the needier of the two. However, according to the *Majma'*,[1] these differences of definition are of no consequence as regards *zakāt*.

(3) **The collectors** (*'āmilūn*) are the persons appointed by the *imām* for the collection of the *zakāt* taxes. The term collector applies to the *'āshirs* and the *sā'is* as well as to other collecting agents. According to the Shafiites,[2] the word *'āmilūn*, besides applying to the *sā'is* who collect the taxes of cattle, applies also to the scribes (*kātib*), the distributors (*qāsim* or *qassām*), the *ḥāshirs* who bring together the property owners or the beneficiaries, the *'arīfs* who inform about the beneficiaries, the *zakāt* keepers (*ḥāfiẓ*), and

[1] P. 180.

[2] *Minhāj*, vol. ii, p. 303; *Wajīz*, p. 292; Anṣāri, p. 395; *Mugni*, vol. iii, p. 102.

the accountants (*ḥāsib*). There is dispute as to whether the *kayyāls* who measure off the *zakāt* dues should come under the class of collectors (*'āmilūn*) and be paid out of the *zakāt* taxes. Judges (*qāḍi*) and governors (*wāli*) and the *imām*, however, are not included in the class and are not paid from the *zakāt* for any services they may have rendered in the collection or distribution of the *zakāt*, because they are appointed to look after the interests of Moslems at large, and are paid from the share of *maṣāliḥ* if they have not offered their services freely. According to the Malikites,[1] the persons who collect (*jābi*) and those who distribute (*mufarriq* or *qāsim*), as well as the scribes and *ḥāshirs*, are paid from the *zakāt*. However, the shepherds (*rā'i*), waterers (*sāqi*), judges, *muftis* and the like are only paid from the *zakāt* when, for some reason, they were not paid from the *fa'y* (*bayt-al-māl*) revenue, which is their usual source of payment. According to al-'Adawi, it is probable that the shepherds and waterers are not paid from the *zakāt* because the *zakāt* as a rule is disbursed to its beneficiaries as soon as it is collected.

There are two views concerning the reward of the collectors. The more generally accepted view is that the collector is paid from the *zakāt* which he has collected an amount which is on the average sufficient for himself and his helpers for the time of their outgoing and incoming, provided that the reward so given him does not exceed the half of the *zakāt* collected, because a half-and-half division is the very essence of justice;[2] according to the *Muḥīṭ*, however, the reward may be as high as three-fourths of the tithe collected.[3] The other view is that the collector is

[1] Kharashi, p. 120.

[2] *Majma'*, p. 180; *'Alamkīriyyah*, p. 264; *Hidāyah*, p. 204; *Durar*, p. p. 123.

[3] *Jāmi'*, p. 335.

given the price of his labor, whatever that price may be, and this view is shared by al-Qudūri.[1]

According to al-Shāfi'i,[2] the collectors are paid at the current rate of wages out of the eighth set apart as the collectors' share. If this share is not sufficient, their wages are made up from the other shares if there is a surplus available, otherwise from the share of the Prophet, or according to al-Māwardi, from the share of *maṣāliḥ*, set apart from the *fa'y* and *ganīmah* revenues.

Finally, according to the Malikites,[3] the wages of the collectors are paid out of the *zakāt* proceeds before anything else, even if they should absorb the entire *zakāt* proceeds.

The collector may be rich, according to all of the three schools, because, as the Hanifites argue, his reward is not meant to be alms, but the price of his services, and since the collector is going to give his time and effort for the work of collection he is entitled to compensation. The collector may not, however, be a Hāshimite, according to all of the three schools; this is because the reward given to the collector is itself, in a way, in the nature of *zakāt*, and the Hāshimites are not entitled to receive *zakāt*; nevertheless, al-Taḥāwi holds the opposite view. If, however, reward comes from other than the proceeds of *zakāt*, according to the *Jāmi'* the collector may then be a Hāshimite.

If a person pays his *zakāt* directly to the *imām*, the collector has no share in it. Similarly if the *zakāt* is lost or destroyed in the hands of the collector, the latter forfeits his right to a share.[4] The collector may take his share in advance before it is yet due, although it is preferable that he should not do so.

[1] *Jāmi'*, *ibid.*

[2] *Umm*, p. 64; *cf.* Māwardi, p. 211; *Wajīz*, p. 295.

[3] Kharashi, p. 120.

[4] *'Alamkīriyyah*, p. 264.

(4) **The "mukatabs"** are the *mukātabs* of others than the *zakāt* payer, even if these other persons are rich; provided they are not Hâshimites. This is according to the Hanifites, who hold that the expression *fi 'l-riqāb* occurring in the Koran verse cited means *fi fakk al-riqāb,* namely, that the slaves are aided in completing the price of manumission (*badal al-kitābah*) in order that they may become free; and not, as Mālik claims, *fi 'itq al-riqāb,* namely, that slaves are bought and set free. The Hanifites take exception to the view of Mālik on two grounds:[1] (a) The obligation of *zakāt* consists in transferring ownership (*tamlīk*) in the thing given as *zakāt* from the giver to the receiver, but this does not happen when a slave is bought and set free with the intention of settling the *zakāt*. (b) The setting free of a slave establishes for the liberator the relation to the slave freed, of a patron to a client (*walā'*), but it is a fundamental principle of *zakāt* that its giving must not redound in any benefit for the giver. Neither of these objections, however, holds true when the *mukātab,* who has the right to trade and to receive and give money, is given, from the *zakāt* funds, a certain sum in order that he may himself apply it towards the price of manumission. According to the *Mudawwanah,*[2] Mālik holds the view that when slaves are bought and set free, the rights of patron accrue to the entire Moslem community.

(5) **The "debtors"** (*gārimūn*) are those who do not own a *niṣāb* over and above their debts and first necessities; thus, it is agreed by all that a person possessing a single month's food worth a full *niṣāb,* over and above his debts, is still entitled to a share. Some say that the word *gārimūn*

[1] Kāsāni, p. 45; *Mabsūt,* part iii, p. 9; *cf. Minhāj,* vol. ii, p. 304; Kharashi, p. 121.

[2] P. 59.

occurring in the verse means the creditor who can not collect his claims from his debtors.[1] According to the *Majmaʿ*, in giving assistance from the *zakāt* the debtors are to be preferred to the poor.

According to the Malikites,[2] debtors are paid from *zakāt* only for debts for which a debtor may be put in prison, namely, debts to fellow-men (*adami*), provided, however, the debtors prove their good faith by applying towards the settlement of their debts such cash as they may have, and by applying the saving they can effect through living in more modest quarters; and, furthermore, provided the debts were not incurred for unlawful ends such as drinking wine or gambling.

Finally, according to the Shafiites,[3] the word *gārim* (debtor) here means not only persons who, incurring debts for lawful personal reasons, are aided only when they cannot settle the debts by their own means, but also persons who incurred debts in the public interest, by becoming surety (*ḥamālah*) or by composing feuds and differences (*iṣlāḥ dhāt al-bayn*). These latter are paid from the *zakāt* even if they are rich. According to the *Jāmiʿ*, al-Zāhidi considers the word "debtors" in this connection to mean those who incurred debts for composing feuds.

(6) **"The way of God"** (*sabīl allah*). According to Abu Yūsuf and a report from Muḥammad Ibn al-Hasan, the expression "the way of God" means persons who by reason of poverty have been unable to join the army of the Moslems for the purpose of holy war. This is the view generally accepted. Such persons deserve a share even when they can engage in business, because if they were re-

[1] *Jāmiʿ*, p. 336.

[2] Kharashi, p. 122.

[3] *Umm*, p. 61; *Wajīz*, p. 293; *Minhāj*, vol. ii, p. 304.

fused a share they would stay away from the war. According to another report from Muḫammad, the expression means pilgrims who, by reason of poverty, have been incapacitated for the completion of their pilgrimage. The ground for the view held in the second report is that a person who was given a camel from this share, was ordered by the Prophet to transport the pilgrims on his camel. The ground of the first view is that although the expression " the way of God " may apply to every act of devotion, when there is no indication in the context, or otherwise, in favor of a specific act of devotion, it applies to the persons who fight the holy war.[1] According to the *Jāmi'*, some say that the expression means the poor persons who committed the Koran to memory; still others say that it means the poor students. According to the *Fatḫ*, however, whatever the meaning of the expression may be, the unanimous opinion is that with the exception of collectors, people of all the classes mentioned, if they are poor, receive a share, and the pilgrims as well.

According to the Malikites,[2] the expression here means the persons who engage in holy war (*jihād*), even if they are rich. However, according to the prevalent view, also judges, jurisconsults, prayer-callers (*mu'adh-dhin*), and other functionaries whose services redound to the benefit of all Moslems are paid from the *zakāt*, provided they do not draw a pension (*rātib*) from the public treasury. In one Malikite view of the matter, the above in reality come within the scope of the expression " the way of God ", for they contribute to " the maintenance of Islam, its reputation and exaltation (*ta'ẕīm*) and to the easing of hearts in that respect ".

[1] *Hidāyah*, p. 205; *Jāmi'*, p. 337.

[2] Kharashi, p. 122.

However, according to al-Shāfi'i and his followers,[1] the expression means the persons who do not draw a pension from the *fa'y* revenue, and yet volunteer to join the holy war, especially such of them as come from the district where the *zakāt* was collected.[2] Such persons are given a share even if they are rich.

(7) **The wayfarers** (*ibn al-sabīl*) are the strangers cut off from their property, and, by extension, all persons who have been cut off from their possessions, even if they should be in their own cities, such as the resident (*muqīm*) who has property away from his home, and the creditor, whose debtor admits his debt but cannot settle it because he is in financial straits. These people do not receive more than they need, and it is preferable that they should borrow the money they need, if they can do so. Like the poor person who becomes rich, the wayfarer, too, is not obliged to bestow as alms the money that is left in his possession from the *zakāt* when he recovers his property.[3]

According to the Shafiites,[4] wayfarers are given enough to complete their journey, even if they have not as yet started on it, provided, however, that the journey is made for a lawful end. According to the Malikites,[5] wayfarers who have property at home are aided only in case they fail to obtain a loan.

(8) **The people called mu'allafah qulubuhum,** literally, people whose hearts have been conciliated. These people were of three classes. One class included those to whom the

[1] *Umm*, pp. 62, 73; *Minhāj*, vol. ii, p. 304; *Wajīz*, p. 294.

[2] According to the Shafiites, as we shall later see more in detail, the fact of being a stipendiary of the *dīwān* bars from participation in the *zakāt*, no matter what class of beneficiary one belongs in.

[3] *Fatḥ*, p. 205.

[4] *Umm*, pp. 62, 73; *Minhāj*, vol. ii, p. 305; *Wajīz*, p. 294.

[5] Kharashi, p. 123.

Prophet used to give from the proceeds of *zakāt* in order to draw them into Islam. Another class consisted of those who, although already converted to Islam, were weak in their faith, and to whom the Prophet gave a share from the *zakāt* in order to strengthen them in the Faith. A third class were those to whom the Prophet gave a share in order to deter them from doing harm. These people were leaders of the Quraysh tribe, and other Arab chiefs. When the Prophet died, these people came to Abu Bakr and asked him to renew the document concerning their shares in the *zakāt*, and he granted their request. Then they came to Omar and informed him of it, whereupon Omar took the document from their hands and tore it up, saying that the Prophet gave them a share in order to draw them into Islam, but that meanwhile God had made His religion to prosper and the only alternative that remained for them was Islam or the sword. Upon this they returned to the calif Abu Bakr and told him of what Omar had done, saying: "Is it you who is the calif, or he?" Abu Bakr replied: "He, if God will", and so Abu Bakr did not blame Omar for what he had done; when the other Companions learned of the happenings, they all approved of them, and in this way an *ijmā'* was reached on the matter. In view of this *ijmā'*, and because Islam now is strong and no longer needs resort to such means for protection, the Hanifites hold that this share has lapsed since the Prophet's death.

According to al-Shāfi'i and his followers,[1] it is not allowable to disburse the *zakāt* to an unbeliever in order to draw him into Islam. It is, however, permissible to disburse it to powerful Moslems if it is expected that this will result in others of their tribe becoming Moslems. The *zakāt* may

[1] *Umm*, pp. 64, 73; *Wajīz*, p. 293; *Minhāj*, vol. ii, p. 303; *cf.* Kāsāni, p. 45.

also be disbursed in order to confirm Moslems in their faith, or to enlist the military assistance of a Moslem people against those infidels or Moslems who refuse (*mānīʿ*) to pay *zakāt*, who, being near that people, can be best brought to submission by them. Al-Māwardi [1] says that although it is not allowed to give the infidels from the *zakāt* in order to draw them into Islam, it is lawful to give them funds for that purpose from the *fa'y*, from the share of *maṣāliḥ*. Mālik says that these people were given a share only when Islam was still weak, and that in his own time Islam was strong and did not stand in need of financial backing, as it did in the days of the Prophet when the Moslems were few and their enemies many and strong. Mālik arrived at this view by using his method of *istiṣlāḥ*.[2] According to later Malikites,[3] the divine prescription concerning this share is still in force and consequently *zakāt* may be disbursed to unbelievers provided it is known that this will lead to their embracing Islam.

The controversy on this subject has largely turned on the question whether it was possible to abrogate a point of law established by the Koran and continued in force until the death of the Prophet by means of an *ijmāʿ* after his death. Those who believed in the abrogation of the Koran and the *sunnah* by an *ijmāʿ* after the Prophet's death, saw no difficulty in the matter. But those who believed the contrary, had to tax their resources to find a justification for it. Thus some say that it is not a case of abrogation by *ijmāʿ*, but one of lapse of a value on account of the termination of its cause. One Hanifite doctor expresses the view that in the time of the Prophet the share was given in order to

[1] P. 212.

[2] Ibn Rushd, *B.*, p. 251; *cf. Mudawwanah*, p. 57.

[3] Kharashi, p. 121.

strengthen Islam; but that now Islam is strong and the same object is served by not giving any share. This view is approved by the *'Ināyah*.[1]

According to the Shafiites,[2] **if a person claims to be a beneficiary of zakat** on the ground that he is poor or indigent, he is believed and in case of suspicion is sworn to the truth of his statements. According to some doctors, he is always sworn. If, however, it is known that he had property although he claims that it was destroyed, he has to prove it. The same applies if he claims that he has a family to take care of. Again, if a person claims a share in the *zakāt* on the ground that he is a wayfarer or a soldier he is believed without oath; he is also believed if he claims a share on the ground of being weak in faith; but if he claims that he is a *mukātab* or a debtor, he is required to produce evidence to that effect, since this can be done in these two cases. If the fact is generally known (*mustafīḏ*), or if the creditor confirms the claim of the debtor, it is as if proved by evidence.

According to the Malikites,[3] persons claiming to be poor or indigent are believed without oath, unless there is reason for suspecting the contrary, in which case they are required to produce evidence. If a person claims an additional share on the ground of having a family, he is believed unless he is a resident of the place where the *zakāt* is being disbursed, for in such case the matter is inquired into. If a person is known to have been well-to-do he is required to show that he has lost his wealth. A person, however, is believed, if he claims bad business. Debtors, must prove their inability to pay, with respect to debts incurred for other than

[1] P. 201; *cf. Fatḥ*, and *Kifāyah*, *ibid.*

[2] *Wajīz*, p. 294; *Minhāj*, vol. ii, p. 305.

[3] Kharashi, 'Adawi, p. 116.

food only, because it is generally hard to prove the amount of food consumed. Al-'Adawi wonders if, when evidence must be produced, one witness would be sufficient, or whether, as in the case of civil procedure, there should always be at least two. On the whole, he seems to favor a more lenient attitude than would be warranted in strictly civil matters.

The Hanifites do not discuss this matter, except in what they say concerning the disbursement of *zakāt* by the owners themselves; in which case, as we saw, they resort to intuition. As regards the disbursement of *zakāt* by the state officials, they evidently intend that the general principles respecting the verification of assertions (*da'wa*) shall be applied.

The method of distribution of the zakat among the various beneficiaries has been a matter of difference of opinion. The Hanifites [1] claim that the *zakāt* may be disbursed to all the classes together, excepting that of the *mu'allafah* whose claims have lapsed; or to any one of them exclusively, even if it consists in one single person. Al-Shāfi'i, on the contrary, expresses the view that the *zakāt* may not be disbursed to one or few classes when there are more of them present, and that the share of each class is disbursed preferably among all its present members, or at least three of them; it being unlawful to disburse to fewer, when there are three beneficiaries present; otherwise the collector or the owner, if it was he who disbursed the *zakāt*, has to make good to the third beneficiary his share.[2] According to the later Shafiites, if the *zakāt* proceeds are sufficient for all the beneficiaries of a class, and their number is easily determinable (*munḫaṣir*), each is given a share, otherwise

[1] *Majma'*, p. 181; *Jami'*, p. 337; *Hidāyah*, p. 205.

[2] *Umm*, pp. 69, 76-7; *Mabsūṭ*, part iii, p. 10.

only three are given a share. This rule does not apply to the collectors who may be fewer than three.[1] Finally, according to Mālik and his followers,[2] as in the case of the Hanifites, the *zakāt* need not be disbursed to all the classes or all the individual beneficiaries present, but is disbursed to the neediest ones, even if they should be in other districts.

Al-Shafi'i's ground is that the Arabic preposition "for" (*li*) occurring in the verse establishes for the beneficiaries a right on the property due as *zakāt*, and, since the names of the various classes are construed in the plural, there may not be fewer than three persons in each class; three being the minimum number for which the plural is used. It is true that the words "poor", "indigent", *etc.*, are defined with the article and the article indicates the entire genus, but since such a meaning cannot have been intended here, they are construed as mere plurals and the articles are ignored. Al-Shāfi'i, in support of his construction, invokes also the analogy of a will, for it is admitted on both sides that if a person wills a sum of money to a number of classes they are all entitled to a share.[3]

On the Hanifite side, al-Sarakhsi invokes the precedent of Omar, and with respect to the analogy of a will, remarks that it pertains to a relation of man to man, where importance attaches to the expression (*lafẓ*) and not the meaning (*ma'na*) because human orders (*awāmir al-'ibād*), unlike divine commandments, may lack a commendable wisdom. The *Hidāyah* says that the preposition "for" (*li*) merely indicates who the beneficiaries are, but it does not establish

[1] *Minhāj*, vol. ii, p. 308; Anṣāri, p. 402; *Wajīz*, p. 295; Māwardi, p. 210; *al-Fatāwa al-Kubra*, vol. ii, pp. 37-8.

[2] *Mudawwanah*, p. 55; Ibn Rushd, *B.*, p. 250; Kharashi, p. 124; Dardīr, p. 126.

[3] *Mabsūt*, part iii, p. 10.

a valid title (*istiḥqāq*) to the *zakāt* in their favor, since the *zakāt* is in reality only a right of God, and the classes mentioned are beneficiaries merely by reason of their poverty. Furthermore, the *Fatḥ* [1] observes that the preposition here only means that the different classes are entitled to the proceeds of *zakāt* as a whole, not that necessarily every individual *zakāt* must be distributed among all the individual beneficiaries, an operation which is, besides, impossible. Moreover, it is a rule of Arabic grammar, that when two plurals are set against one another, as in the phrase, "the people mounted the animals", distribution is meant, namely, that each person mounted one animal; similarly in the case of *zakāt*, each *zakāt* is given to one or a few beneficiaries, but not to all the beneficiaries. The *Fatḥ* adds that this construction holds true even if the preposition "for" (*li*) means what al-Shāfi'i claims it to mean, that is, a title on the *zakāt* in favor of the beneficiaries. Sadr-al-sharī'ah remarks that the article before the words "poor", *etc.*, here may not be construed to mean certain definite (*al-'ahd*) poor, since there is no evidence in the context to bear this out, neither may it mean the entire genus of poor, since this would require that all the *zakāt* of the world should be given to all the poor of the world. Therefore, as is otherwise stated in the *Baḥr*,[2] the defined plural here of necessity and by way of metaphor means the genus at large, and may apply to a single individual of the genus, just as an oath not to buy the slaves applies to a single slave, and renders him a perjurer if he buys a single slave. The author of the *Farā'id*, however, takes exception to this and says that the article before the plural need not necessarily mean a literal universality (*istigrāq ḥaqīqī*) since it may also mean a customary (*'urfi*) universality, as for example, in the phrase,

[1] P. 206.

[2] P. 260.

"the king called together the artists"; where simply the artists of the city or the outlying districts, but not of the entire world, are meant.[1]

The Malikite view on this matter is to the same effect as the Hanifite.[2]

The Shafiite method of distribution of the proceeds of the *zakāt* taxes, as **summarized** by al-Māwardi,[3] is briefly as follows: When the proceeds have been divided among the eight classes, and each has received its sufficiency, they cease to be beneficiaries of *zakāt,* and may no longer claim a share. If, on the other hand, they have not received their sufficiencies, the balance is made up from future proceeds. If the shares of all the classes are more than sufficient for their needs, the surplus is disbursed to the beneficiaries of the nearest city. If the share of some classes is insufficient and of others is more than sufficient, the surplus of the latter is disbursed to make up the shortage of the former classes. If all the eight classes are not present, then the entire *zakāt* is distributed among those present, even if it be one single class; and the shares of the absent are not carried to them, except in the case of the share of "the way of God" which belongs to the fighters who normally reside away from their homes in the frontier cities.

According to the Hanifites, **the giving of zakat must result in the transfer of ownership** (*tamlīk*) in the thing given as *zakāt* from the giver to the receiver. This is considered to be the formal cause (*rukn*) of *zakāt,* in other words, the *zakāt* is not supposed to have been given if this requirement is not met. The reason for this requirement is that the preposition "for" (*li*) which occurs in the Koran

[1] *Majma'*, p. 181.

[2] Kharashi, p. 116.

[3] P. 213.

verse respecting the beneficiaries, indicates that the *zakāt*, when it is given, becomes the property of the person to whom it was given. Consequently, the *zakāt* may not be appropriated for impersonal purposes, such as the building of mosques, bridges, repairing of roads, draining of rivers, *etc.*[1] Likewise, the *zakāt* is not disbursed for fitting out the dead for burial or for paying their debts. Neither is it allowable to give the *zakāt* to the insane or the undiscerning minor (*gayr murāhiq*), unless it be given to his guardian, such as the father; but it may be given to the minor who has reached the age of discernment. For the same reason, a person may not dispose of his *zakāt* in settlement of the price of a slave he has bought, in order to set him free. According to Abu Yūsuf, he may feed (*ibāḥah*) the people of his household, intending this for the settlement of his *zakāt* debt, but according to Muḥammad Ibn al-Hasan he may not do so; however, the accepted view is that of Abu Yūsuf.

Mālik agrees with the Hanifites that the *zakāt* may not be disbursed for the fitting out of the dead for burial or for the building of mosques, on the ground that *zakāt* is not intended for the dead but for the living, such as the poor.[2] What is true of mosques is also true of the construction of bridges, the payment of the salaries of judges and of *imāms*, *etc.*, that is, purposes of public utility (*maṣāliḥ*), because these are not specified in the Koran verse cited. However, the salaries of the functionaries mentioned may be paid from the *zakāt* in case they have not been paid from the public treasury. We already saw that one Malikite view brought such persons within the scope of the expression "the way

[1] There is, however, a way of getting around this difficulty, as explained in the section on cunning, under Collection.

[2] *Mudawwanah*, p. 59; *cf.* Kharashi, pp. 120, 123.

of God". According to the Shafiites, the *zakāt* may not be disbursed to others than those specified in the verse.

Similarly for want of complete transfer of ownership (*tamlīk*), it is not allowed to give the *zakāt* in a way that may result in some benefit for the giver. **It is not** therefore **lawful to give the zakat to one's ancestors and descendants** in direct line, no matter how far up or down, whether legitimate or not, or to one's wife, even if she is divorced and in her waiting term (*mu'taddah*); and further, in Abu Hanīfah's opinion, the wife may not give it to her husband. However, Abu Yūsuf and Muhammad allow it in the last contingency. Neither may one give his *zakāt* to his slaves (*mukātab, mudabbar,* or *umm walad*), even if they should have been partly set free. According to Abu Yūsuf and Muhammad, however, one may give it to his slave if partly set free, because, in their opinion, the setting free of a slave does not admit of division, and a slave partly set free is considered entirely free.

It is not lawful to give the zakat to the dhimmis, because the *hadīth*: "Take it from their rich and give it to their poor", refers only to the poor of the Moslems.[1] Similarly it is not given to the renegade, nor is it proper either that it should be given to those of the innovators (*mubtadi'*) who have incurred unbelief. Zufar expressed the opinion that the beneficiary need not be a Moslem. It is, however, permissible to give to the *dhimmis* other than *zakāt*, such as vows, *kaffārah, etc.*, although, in one report, Abu Yūsuf, would not allow this. The *harbis*, however, may not receive from any one of the various kinds of *sadaqahs*.

According to the Shafiites and the Malikites,[2] *zakāt* funds

[1] This is a case of supplementing the Koran on the basis of a report of the *mashhūr* type.

[2] *Minhāj*, vol. ii, p. 305; *Wajīz*, p. 294; Kharashi, p. 117.

may not be given to unbelievers. The Malikites, however, make an exception as regards the class of *mu'allafah* and the spies.

Likewise **it is not allowed to disburse the zakat to the rich,** because it can clearly be seen from the respective verse that, excepting the collectors and the *mu'allafah,* the cause for the above-named classes being beneficiaries is their poverty, and because there are *ḥadīths* from the Prophet to this effect.[1]

According to the *Badā'i',* in some *fatwa* collections the opinion has been expressed that **students** of law such as the judges and the *muftis,* **may receive the zakat even if** they are **rich,** provided that they exert themselves in acquiring and transmitting knowledge, since by so doing they become unable to engage in business. Ibn 'Abidīn says that he saw a similar view expressed in the *Jāmi' al-Fatāwa,* where it is said that, according to the *Mabsūṭ,* it is not allowed to disburse the *zakāt* to a person who owns a *niṣāb* excepting to the students, the fighters (*gāzi*), and the persons cut off (*munqaṭi'*) from their resources, because the Prophet said: " It is allowed to disburse the *zakāt* to the student of law (*'ilm*), even if he possesses sufficient subsistence for forty years."[2]

According to the Shafiites, the fighters (*gāzi*), the *mu'allafah,* the collectors, and the debtors who have incurred debts for public purposes are not barred from participation in the *zakāt* for being rich. However, no beneficiary of any class is given *zakāt* if he is also a stipendiary of the *dīwān.*[3] According to the Malikites, finally, the *mu'allafah,* the collectors, and the fighters are not barred from *zakāt* for being rich.

[1] *Fatḥ,* p. 209.

[2] *Minḥah,* p. 260; *cf.* 'Adawi, p. 120.

[3] *Wajīz,* p. 292.

Likewise it is not allowed to give *zakāt* to the slave (*'abd*) of a rich person, even if he is of the *mudabbar* or *umm walad* type, because the property of the slave belongs to the master. According to Abu Hanīfah it is also lawful to give the *zakāt* to the slave, if he is indebted for all his possessions and his own value. Abu Hanīfah's two disciples hold the contrary view. The *zakāt*, however, may be given to the *mukātab* and the slave who was permitted to trade (*ma'dhūn*).

Neither is the *zakāt* given to the infants of a rich person. However, according to a *Zāhir-al-riwāyah* report, the *zakāt* may be given to his adult children and wife if they are poor, even though the children's subsistence comes from the father, because it is not customary to consider the child rich merely because the father is rich. Likewise it is lawful to give the *zakāt* to the father of a rich person or the children of a rich woman.[4]

According to both the Shafiites and the Malikites,[1] persons, like the wife or children, whose support legally is upon others, may not be given *zakāt*.

Likewise it is not allowed to give the *zakāt* to certain members of the Hashim family, namely, those who helped the Prophet in spreading Islam, Hāshim being the grandfather of the Prophet. This is based on many *ḥadīths* of which the following one was uttered by the Prophet when he refused to accept the *ṣadaqah* offered him. It is as follows: " Verily the *ṣadaqah* does not become the family of Mohammed, because it is the slops (literally, washwater) of the people." [2] Another *ḥadīth* is the following: [3] " Oh, people of Hāshim, God has not deemed fit for you the wash-

[1] *Durr*, p. 145.

[2] *Minhāj*, p. 303; *Wajīz*, p. 292; Kharashi, p. 125.

[3] *Fatḥ*, p. 212.

[4] Kāsāni, p. 49.

water of the people, but has given you as compensation for it one-fifth of the fifth of the spoils." However, they may be given the *nafl*; namely, what is given over and above the amount prescribed as *zakāt*—or some other *wājib* obligation, such as the *ṣadaqah al-fiṭr*. In other words, if one should give them property intending it for the *zakāt*, the property given is considered as a supererogatory offering, and hence the *zakāt* debt is not discharged. According to the *Majmaʿ*, Abu Hanīfah allowed the disbursement of *zakāt* to these people. In the *al-Athār*, however, it is stated that Abu Hanīfah held two contradictory views on the matter, but that the view which allows the disbursement is preferred, on the ground that the prohibition of disbursement was limited to the Prophet's time. The Hāshimites, in one version, may pay *zakāt* to one another. The clients (*mawla*) of the Hāshimites are treated like themselves, because the Prophet said: "The clients of a prophet are like them." [1]

In paying the *zakāt* to the beneficiaries, the **proper thing is to pay only enough to relieve** them **from** the **necessity of begging** on that day; according to the *Majmaʿ*, however, from the necessity of begging absolutely (*muṭlaqa*), because the object in giving the *zakāt* is to remove the need for begging. It is therefore an abominable practice to give a poor person two hundred *dirhams* or more, unless he has a family, or is in debt; in the latter case it is allowed to give the entire amount of the debt plus an amount less than a *niṣāb*; and in the former case more than one *niṣāb*, provided the share corresponding to each member of the family falls short of a *niṣāb*. If the poor is given a full *niṣāb*, notwithstanding that he is not in debt or has not a family to support, according to al-Sarakhsi, the *zakāt* debt is nevertheless discharged. Zufar says that it is not. Finally, according

[1] *Cf. Minhāj*, vol. ii, p. 305; *Wajīz*, p. 294; Kharashi, p. 120.

to Abu Yūsuf, there is no harm in giving two hundred, but it is abominable to give more than two hundred *dirhams*. Zufar's argument is that when a poor person is given two hundred *dirhams* he comes under the description of a rich man during the act of receiving the money and therefore the *zakāt* is not discharged in that it has been paid to a rich person. Al-Sarakhsi replies that the state of wealthiness depends on ownership but the ownership of the money given accrues to the poor person only after he has received it, and consequently he is poor while he is yet receiving the money, and therefore the *zakāt* debt is discharged. However, because here the state of wealthiness follows upon that of poverty so very closely, it is an abominable practice to pay two hundred *dirhams*, although legally the *zakāt* is discharged, just as it is abominable to pray on a clean spot close to which there is filth, although the prayer is legally valid. Abu Yūsuf's ground is that when two hundred *dirhams* are given to a poor person, a small part of them is already applied (*mustaḥaqq*) to his needs; as the part which remains available is less than two hundred, he, therefore, is not rich.[1]

According to the *Minhāj*,[2] the poor and indigent are never given more than a year's subsistence. But, according to al-Shāfi'i and the majority of his followers, they are given enough for the rest of their probable lives and the amount given is applied to the purchase of real estate, its income to be used by the poor.

It is abominable to transfer the zakat of a property after the lapse of a year **to another town,** even if that town is the home of the *zakāt* payer, since in the settlement of *zakāt* the location of the property, and not the residence of

[1] *Mabsūṭ*, part iii, p. 13.

[2] Vol. ii, p. 306; *cf.* Kharashi, p. 119.

the *zakāt* payer, is taken into account. However, it is allowable to transfer it if the poor of the town to which the *zakāt* was transferred are godlier or more useful to Islam in that they are abler in learning and teaching the *sharī'ah*, or if the *zakāt* payer has transferred the *zakāt* to his relations in that town, or, finally, if the poor of the second town are needier than those of the original. It is said that the best way to settle one's *zakāt* is to pay it first to one's brothers or sisters, then to their children and children's children forever, then to one's paternal uncles, then to their children and children's children forever, then to maternal uncles, then to other relations through females (*dhawu al-arḫām*), then to neighbors, then to the beneficiaries of one's own district, finally to those of one's own town. According to al-Māwardi,[1] if the property owner brings his relations before the collector so that he may disburse his *zakāt* to them, the collector does so, if his *zakāt* has not already been mixed with the *zakāt* of others. If, however, it has been mixed with the *zakāt* of others, then the relations are not entitled to it more than others but the collector nevertheless gives them a share from it, because to a part of it they are more entitled than others. Al-Māwardi says that the transfer of *zakāt* to another town is not allowed unless there are no beneficiaries in the first town. If, however, the *zakāt* is transferred while there are beneficiaries in the original town, then, in one view, the debts of the *zakāt* payers remain undischarged, but in the other view, which is advanced by Abu Hanīfah, they are discharged.[2]

Finally, according to Mālik and his followers,[3] the *zakāt*

[1] P. 214.

[2] Māwardi, p. 213; *cf. Umm*, p. 67; *Wajiz*, p. 295; *Minhāj*, vol. ii, p. 300; *cf. supra*, pp. 335-9.

[3] *Mudawwanah*, p. 46; Kharashi, p. 126.

is distributed among the beneficiaries of the town and its outskirts (*qurb*),[1] *i. e.*, the town where the *zakāt* was collected, unless it be that the *zakāt* was collected from gold and silver and articles of trade. In such case the *zakāt* is distributed in the town where the owner is. If there is an available surplus it may be transferred to another town, preferably a near one. It is even allowed to transfer the greater part of the *zakāt* of a town to another town if the people of the latter town are needier. Mālik allows a person to settle the *zakāt* of property located in Egypt (*Miṣr*) to the poor of Medina.[2]

[1] The word *qurb* (vicinity) is technically defined as the distance from the inhabited part of a town within which one may not shorten (*qaṣr*) one's prayer on the ground of having set out on a journey. This distance is known as *masāfat al-qaṣr*. The inhabited gardens of a city are included within this distance (Kharashi, vol. i, p. 411; 'Adawi, p. 127).

[2] The Hanifite doctors do not state if the rules of this chapter apply in their entirety to all disbursements of *zakāt*, whether made by the *zakāt* payers directly to the beneficiaries or whether made by the state collector. There is no doubt that certain of those rules cannot very well apply in the last case, for instance, the rule concerning the prohibition of paying the *zakāt* to one's father or son, or slave, *etc.* The wording of the texts often suggests whether the rule is meant for both cases or for the case of disbursement by the *zakāt* payer himself. Thus as against the impersonal "the *zakāt* is not disbursed (*la tudfa'*) for building mosques. . . ." there is also used the personal form: "the *zakāt* payer does not disburse the *zakāt* to his ancestry." Excepting, however, those cases where, in the nature of things, the rule must be intended for the case of disbursement by the *zakāt* payer himself, in general the rules set forth in this chapter apply equally well to both cases, since according to the Mohammedan law the public collectors act only as the agents (*nā'ib*) of the *zakāt* payers. This is also borne out by a statement in the *'Alamkīriyyah* (p. 268) which implies that the rules in question apply also in case the *zakāt* is disbursed by the collector after its collection. (*Cf.* also Kharashi, p. 124, l. 6.)

CHAPTER XI

Expenditure of the Secular Revenue

SECTION I

The Booty Revenue[1]

The expenditure of the booty revenue[2] is based on this verse of the Koran:[3] "And know ye, that whatever thing you have taken as booty, a fifth part of it belongeth to (*li*) God, and to the Prophet, and to the near of kin (*dhu al-qurba*), and to the orphans and to the indigent (*miskīn*), and to the wayfarer."

It is stated in the *Mabsūṭ*, that, according to Ibn 'Abbās, during the life of the Prophet **the fifth of the spoils was divided into** five **shares,** namely, one share to God and His Prophet, one to the relations of the Prophet (*dhawu al-qurba*), one to the orphans, one to the indigent, and finally

[1] As the four-fifths of the booty revenue accruing to individual members of the community,—such as the soldiers (in the case of spoils), or the person who extracted the mine, or found the treasure-trove,—has been already treated in the respective sections, in this section we will consider only the part, namely, the one-fifth, accruing to the state. For the disposal of the four-fifths, see *supra*, pp. 409-413, 413-421. *Majma'*, p. 504; *Mabsūṭ*, vol. x, p. 8; *Hidāyah*, vol. v, p. 243; *Wajīz*, pp. 288, 290; *Umm*, vol. iv, pp. 71, 77; *Minhāj*, vol. ii, pp. 293, 299; Māwardi, p. 241; Muzani, vol. iii, p. 192; *cf.* Ibn Rushd, *B.*, p. 315.

[2] Although, following the usage of the Hanifites, reference in this section will be to the expenditure of the fifth of spoils alone, the reader should bear in mind that what is true of the fifth of spoils is true of the fifth of booty revenue in general.

[3] Chap. 8, verse 42.

one share to the wayfarers. Later, after the Prophet's death, the calif Abu Bakr divided it into three shares, namely, the parts for orphans, the indigent and the wayfarers. So did the califs Omar, 'Uthmān, and 'Ali, none of the Companions objecting to this practice. Abu 'l-'Aliyah, on the other hand, said that besides the above-named five shares there should also be set apart **a share for God** to be spent for the Ka'bah, if the division of the spoils happens near it, or for the mosque of a town if the division takes place near it, because these places are connected with God. Al-Sarakhsi objects to this construction, saying that the expression "to God" occurring in the verse is not to be taken in its literal sense, since it is merely meant to be an act of devotion to open a sentence with the name of God.

As regards **the share of the Prophet,** according to al-Sarakhsi, it lapsed after the Prophet's death. Al-Shāfi'i [1] thinks that this share after the death of the Prophet should go to the *imām,* inasmuch as the Prophet took this share in his lifetime in order to use it as gifts for delegations and deputations.[2] Indeed the Prophet said: "It is not allowed for me to take a share from your spoils except the fifth which is again returned to you." The *imām* in this respect is exactly like the Prophet, and therefore he must take this share. The Hanifites reply that the righteous califs did not appropriate this share for themselves and moreover this share belonged to the Prophet by virtue of his being a Prophet, which is not true of the calif. Then, too, when the Companions came together to give the calif

[1] According to the Malikites (Kharashi, p. 427; Ibn Rushd, *B.*, p. 315; *Mudawwanah*, vol. iii, p. 26), the fifth of the spoils is disbursed like the *fa'y* revenue, as will be explained in the next section.

[2] It is stated in the *Umm* (vol. iv, p. 72, l. 1) that Al-Shāfi'i would prefer to have this share disbursed by the *imām* for the strengthening of Islam, *e. g.* for fortifications, arms, *etc.*

Abu Bakr his stipend, they did not give it from this share. Finally there is no reason why the calif should take the place of the Prophet as regards the fifth of the fifth (*i. e.*, the Prophet's share) when it is a fact that he does not, as regards the *ṣafis*, namely, choice spoils like swords, horses, slaves, *etc.*, which the Prophet chose out of the spoils for his own special use.

Finally as regards **the** so-called **share of the Relations,** namely, the descendants of the families of Hāshim and al-Muṭṭalib, according to al-Sarakhsi, this share has been abolished after the Prophet's death. Al-Shāfi'i, on the contrary, says that the relations of the Prophet are gathered together from the corners of the earth and their share is divided among them. Al-Karkhi says that this share lapsed after the Prophet's death only as regards the rich Relations. Al-Taḥāwi, on the other hand, maintains that the share lapsed as regards both the rich and the poor Relations. Abu Bakr al-Rāzi, finally, holds that the Relations were not entitled to this share by virtue of their relationship, but that the Prophet gave them this share in consideration of the assistance (*nuṣrah*) they rendered him, this last view being approved by al-Sarakhsi.

Al-Shafi'i's ground is that the preposition "to" (*li*) occurring in the verse cited establishes ownership, and as the word "relation" does not imply any economic incompetency, the poor and rich are treated alike. It is, however, different with the orphans, for the word orphan implies poverty, and therefore only the poor of the orphans are entitled to a share. Moreover it is a fact that the Prophet gave the Relations a share, and inasmuch as there can be no abrogation (*naskh*) after the Prophet's death, the share stands valid. Finally, the Hanifite contention that the lapse of the share is based on an *ijmā'* of the Companions is not true, because there is a *ḥadīth* from Abu Ja'far Muḥammad Ibn

'Ali who said: "The opinion of 'Ali concerning the fifth was like that of his family but he disliked to oppose Abu Bakr and Omar", and evidently there can be no *ijmā'* while the Family of the Prophet dissent.

Al-Sarakhsi replies that 'Ali agreed with the rest simply because he saw that the truth was on their side, for it is known that he opposed them on many occasions, and that he would have done so in this case also if the right had been on the other side, because 'Ali was a *mujtahid* and a *mujtahid* is not allowed to abandon his own opinion in favor of another's opinion merely because he is ashamed of him. There is, besides, an unconfirmed (*shādhdh*) *ḥadīth* according to which the Prophet said that the share of the Relations was to be given during his lifetime only. Finally, there is a *ḥadīth* according to which the Prophet, referring to the Relations, said: "We have always been like this"; pointing out his fingers which were knit together. This *ḥadīth* shows that the Prophet granted them a share because of the assistance which they gave him, not because of their relationship, for if that had been the case, the Prophet would have given a share to his other relations as well, and not to the descendants of Hāshim and Al-Muṭṭalib alone; it is well to remember that 'Abd Manāf, the originator of the family, besides these two sons had two more, Nawfal and 'Abd Shams. Indeed the Prophet himself explained the matter, saying that he gave a share on the ground of assistance in the way of intimate association, not in the way of fighting; no share was given to 'Uthmān, a descendant of 'Abd Shams, and yet 'Uthmān fought for the Prophet.[1]

To sum up the discussion, according to the accepted **Hanifite view,** the booty revenue is divided into three shares, one to the orphans, one to the indigent and one to

[1] *Mabsūṭ*, part x, pp. 9-14; *Umm*, vol. iv, pp. 72-77.

the wayfarers; the shares of the Prophet and the Relations having lapsed after the Prophet's death. The Relations, however, are entitled to a share in so far as they belong in one of the above classes, and in that case they are given precedence over the rest.[1]

On the other hand, **the Shafiite view** is that the fifth is divided into five shares, namely, the Prophet's, the Relations', the orphans', the indigents', and the wayfarers', and that the Prophet's share after his death is disbursed in the general interest (*maṣāliḥ*) of Moslems; for instance, for buying the provisions of the army, for the building of forts, bridges, for the salaries of the judges and *imāms, etc.* This share is referred to by the Shafiites as the share of *maṣā-liḥ*. The share of the Relations is divided among their poor and rich, minors and adults equally; but the males receive twice as much as the females,[2] because they are entitled to this share by virtue of relationship, with respect to which God said:[3] "To the male the equal of the share of two females". The clients of the Relations, and the children of their daughters are not given a share. The orphans receive a share only in case they are poor, and their share is discontinued on their coming of age. By "indigent" here are meant the indigent from the beneficiaries of the *fa'y* (*ahl al-fa'y*) who are different from the indigent who receive aid from the *zakāt*, since the beneficiaries of the two revenues are different. This is also true of the wayfarers.[4] This last requirement, namely, that by indigent and wayfarers here is meant those from the *fa'y* beneficiaries is because, according to the Shafiites, the fifth part of the spoils is disbursed in

[1] *Majma'*, p. 504; *'Alamkīriyyah*, vol. ii, p. 304.

[2] The passage in the *Mabsūṭ* (part x, p. 9) to the contrary effect must be a mistake.

[3] Koran, chap. 4, verse 12.

[4] Māwardi, pp. 218-9.

the same way as the fifth part of the *fa'y* revenue, which latter may not be disbursed to the *zakāt* beneficiaries.[1] The Hanifites, however, as will be seen in the next section, hold that a fifth part of the *fa'y* revenue is not set apart as in the case of spoils.

According to the Shafiites, **the fifth is disbursed equally** among all the five classes mentioned, but the Hanifites, as in *zakāt*, here, too, hold that the entire fifth may be disbursed to one single class, *e. g.*, the orphans, since the beneficiaries are not entitled to a share, but may simply be given one. Moreover, according to the Shafiites,[2] the four last shares are distributed among all the beneficiaries of the entire Moslem world and not merely among such of them as are found in the district where the proceeds were obtained.

SECTION II

The Fa'y Revenue[3]

According to **the Hanifites**, a fifth part of the *fa'y* revenue is not set apart, as in the spoils, but the whole of the *fa'y* revenue is disbursed for purposes of general utility to the Moslem community (*fi maṣāliḥ al-muslimīn*); such as the stipends of the soldiers, the fortification of cities, the maintenance of stations on the highways for protection from robbers, the dredging of great rivers, the building of dikes, the stipends of the learned (*'ulamā'*), judges, muftis, public inspectors, teachers, students, collectors, governors and their assistants, and in general persons who exert themselves in doing some work for the Moslems in consideration

[1] *Cf.* Māwardi, p. 217; Muzani, vol. iii, p. 179; *Minhāj*, vol. ii, p. 299.

[2] *Umm*, p. 71; *cf. Minhāj*, vol. ii, p. 294.

[3] *Majma'*, p. 520; *Hidāyah*, vol. v, p. 306; *Mabsūṭ*, part iii, p. 17; Kāsāni, vol. vii, p. 116; Māwardi, p. 218; *Umm*, vol. iv, p. 78; Muzani, vol. iii, p. 199; *Minhāj*, vol. ii, p. 293; *Wajīz*, p. 288; Ibn Rushd, *B.*, p. 325; *Mudawwanah*, part iii, p. 26; Kharashi, p. 427.

of a reward.[1] Some say that only the offspring of the soldiers receive stipends, but the opinion generally accepted by the Hanifites is that the offspring of all the classes receive stipends, because the sustenance of the offspring is upon the fathers, and if the offspring were not given their sustenance the fathers would have to go into business and Moslem interests would suffer from it.[2]

According to **the Shafiites**, as in the case of the spoils, one-fifth of the *fa'y* revenue is set apart to be spent like the fifth of the spoils, and the remaining four-fifths are, in the more prevalent view of the matter, disbursed to the army alone, and in another view, to the army as well as for other purposes of general utility to all Moslems.[3]

According to al-Muzani,[4] al-Shāfi'i holds that the four-fifths of the *fa'y* is applied to the payment of the soldiers' stipends, and if there is a surplus it is used for the repair of forts, and the purchase of ammunition and arms, and in general, for the strengthening of the Moslems; any further surplus is divided among the soldiers according to their stipends. Moreover, the stipends of officials, such as judges and religious leaders, employed in the service of the *fa'y* beneficiaries are paid out of the *fa'y*. In other words, according to the prevalent Shafiite view, only the share of the *maṣāliḥ*, namely, one-fifth of one-fifth of the entire *fa'y* is spent for purposes of general utility.[5]

Finally, **according to Malik**,[6] the entire *fa'y* revenue and

[1] According to the *Hidāyah*, the persons who received stipends (*'aṭā'*) in its author's days were the judges, the teachers (*mudarris*), and the *muftis*.

[2] *Mabsūṭ*, part iii, p. 18; *Majma'*, p. 520; *'Alamkīriyyah*, p. 268.

[3] Māwardi, p. 219; *Minhāj*, vol. ii, p. 294; *Wajīz*, p. 289.

[4] Vol. iii, p. 206.

[5] *Minhāj*, vol. ii, pp. 294-6; *Wajīz*, p. 289.

[6] Ibn Rushd, *B.*, p. 325; *Mudawwanah*, part iii, p. 26; Kharashi, p. 427.

the fifth of spoils are a part of the assets of the public treasury and belong to all the Moslems, that is, they are appropriated by the *imām*, according to his judgment, for the stipends of soldiers, the building of forts and mosques, the salaries of judges, the settlement of debts, the marrying of bachelors (*a'zab*), the blood money of wounds, and other purposes of public utility. If the revenue is ample, the Relations (of the Prophet) are paid first, then the remainder of the revenue of each city is disbursed to the *fa'y* beneficiaries of that city, or, to use the wording of the *Mudawwanah*, "to those who conquered the city by assault or by treaty". The poor among these latter are first provided, the amount given to each being sufficient for a year's subsistence. If, on the contrary, the revenue is not sufficient for all, the neediest are paid first. It is lawful to transfer the greater part of the *fa'y* revenue of one city to another if the beneficiaries of the latter city are in greater need. When there is a surplus, it may be transferred to another district, or immobilized, or disposed of otherwise.

Al-Shāfi'i's reason for setting apart the fifth of the *fa'y* is the verse of the Koran:[1] "What God has returned (*afā'a*) as spoils to His Apostle from the people of the towns, belongeth to (*li*) God, and to the Apostle, and to the Relations (*dhu al-qurba*), and to the orphans, and to the indigent, and to the wayfarers". Ibn Rushd says that because the wording of this verse resembles that of the verse concerning the fifth of the spoils, al-Shāfi'i by mistake concluded that the mode of division there mentioned applies to the fifth only, and that consequently a fifth part of the *fa'y* also must be set apart. The division referred to in this verse, however, applies to the whole of the *fa'y*. The same Ibn Rushd[2] remarks that some followed the literal

[1] Chap. 59, verse 7.

[2] Ibn Rushd, *B.*, pp. 315-6, 325.

sense of the verse and held that the entire *fa'y* is disbursed like the fifth of spoils; but that the other side took the specifications of the verse to be merely illustrative (*tanbīh*), not limitative (*ta'dīd*).

Al-Kāsāni[1] says that although there are two reports from Abu Hanīfah on the matter, the more reliable of the two is the one according to which there should be no fifth set apart from the *fa'y*, because the fifth is set apart only in the case of spoils and the *fa'y* is not spoil. There is a *ḥadīth* from Sufyān Ibn Sa'īd to the effect that only in the case of spoils a fifth is set apart and that the *fa'y* is for all Moslems.[2]

According to the Shafiites the fa'y revenue is disbursed to the beneficiaries of fa'y (*ahl al-fa'y*) **exclusively**, exactly as the *ṣadaqah* revenue is disbursed to the beneficiaries of *ṣadaqah* (*ahl al-ṣadaqah*) exclusively. However, according to Abu Hanīfah, either may be disbursed to the beneficiaries of the other.[3] The Malikites[4] on this point agree with the Hanifites.

The beneficiaries, or, literally, the people, of *ṣadaqah* were those who had not migrated,[5] and on the contrary, the

[1] Vol. vii, p. 117.

[2] Yahya, p. 5.

During the lifetime of the Prophet the whole of the *fa'y* belonged to him, and he defrayed from it the subsistence of his family, and the rest he spent in the interests of Moslems in general. (Māwardi, p. 218; Yahya, p. 3; *Wajīz*, p. 289.)

[3] Māwardi, pp. 219-20.

[4] Kharashi, p. 120.

[5] According to the *Mabsūṭ* (part x, p. 6), before the conquest of Mecca it was a *farḍ* obligation upon every Moslem to migrate to Medina in order to learn Islam and join the Moslems in order to aid the Prophet. The people who did this were called the **Emigrants** (*muhājir*). "And they who have believed but have not fled (*lam yuhājirū*) their homes, shall have no rights of kindred with you at all" (Koran, chap. 8, verse 73.) After the conquest of Mecca, this verse

people of *fa'y* were the emigrants who defended the Moslem territory and its sacred places, and who fought the enemy. Formerly the name of *muhājir* (emigrant) used to apply only to those who had left their homes to go to Medina in the quest of Islam, but after the conquest of Mecca this distinction disappeared, and the name came to designate the people of *fa'y* in opposition to the people of *ṣadaqah* who were called *a'rābi* (Bedouin).[1]

There is a *ḥadīth* to the effect that Moslem Bedouins (*a'rāb al-muslimīn*) have no share in the *fa'y* and the spoils unless they fight together with the Moslems. Therefore the Bedouin who has not fought with the Moslems and is not poor, or is engaged in trade or some other work, has no share in the spoils and the *fa'y* until he falls in need; in that case he receives a share with the needy (*ahl al-ḥājah*).[1]

According to al-Shāfi'i,[2] the Prophet used to instruct his armies to tell the persons who became Moslems: "If you migrate, then you shall have what the Emigrants have, but if you remain in your homes, you are like the Bedouins".

According to al-Māwardi,[3] if the imam desires to give

was abrogated by the *ḥadīth*: "There is no migration after the conquest, but only holy war and sincere intention (*niyyah*)." Again the Prophet said: "The emigrant is the person who shuns (*hajara*) the evil and shuns what God forbade." According to Ibn al-Athīr (under the word *hajara*) there were two kinds of migration. The first migration or *hijrah* for which God promised Paradise was the migration to Abyssinia and to Medina. After the conquest of Mecca, the second *hijrah* (migration) came to supplant the former. This second *hijrah* consisted in the Arabs of the desert (*a'rābi*) leaving the desert and joining the Moslem campaigns. This second *hijrah*, however, did not equal in meritoriousness the former. If, without an excuse for so doing, a person returned to his home after migrating, he was considered an apostate. The word *muhājir* (emigrant) came to be used as the opposite of Bedouin (*a'rābi*) (Ibn al-Athīr under *'aruba*).

[1] Māwardi, p. 220.

[2] Yahya, p. 5; *cf.* Muzani, vol. iii, p. 242.

[3] *Umm*, vol. iv, p. 84.

[4] P. 220.

presents to a people from the *fa'y* revenue, he may do so if it will result to the benefit of the Moslems at large.[1] If, however, the present of the *imām*, being in his personal interests only, does not redound to the benefit of the Moslems, then it must be paid out of his own property.[2]

It is allowed to the imam to assign from the *fa'y* **a stipend** (*'aṯā'*) **to his male children,** since they are from the beneficiaries of the *fa'y*. If they are yet minors they receive the stipend given to the offspring of the pioneers (*dhawu al-sābiqah*), and if they are of age,[3] they receive

[1] The Prophet gave 'Uyaynah, on the day of the battle of Hunayn, one hundred camels, al-Aqra' one hundred, and to al-'Abbās fifty camels, but the latter was displeased at the paltriness of his share, and so the Prophet ordered that they give him more until he was silenced.

[2] It is related that a Bedouin came to the calif Omar and recited a poem asking for assistance. Omar was touched by his plea and wept until his tears wetted his beard and he ordered his coat given to the Bedouin, saying that he had nothing else. Al-Māwardi adds that Omar made his present out of his own property and not that of the Moslems, because his present did not involve any benefit for the Moslems at large. Such Bedouins, al-Māwardi goes on to say, belong in the people of *ṣadaqah*, but Omar did not make the present out of the *ṣadaqah* revenue, either because in his poem the Bedouin reproved him, or because the *ṣadaqah* is disbursed to the neighbors and the Bedouin was not one of them. In contrast with Omar, the calif 'Uthmān was reproved by the people for not taking into account the distinction between the two cases and charging all his gifts to the *fa'y* revenue.

[3] It is related of 'Abdāllah, son of Omar, that when he came of age he presented himself before his father and said: "Oh, Father, I have just come of age, assign me then (a stipend)." Omar assigned him 2000 *dirhams*. Then came to him a son of the Helpers (*anṣār, i. e.* the Medina people who became Moslems and otherwise helped the Prophet when he came to their city) who had just come of age, and asked for a stipend, and Omar assigned him 3000. Thereupon 'Abdāllah said: "You assigned me 2000, and you assigned him 3000, and yet his father has not fought the battles you have."—" Yes," answered Omar, "but I saw the father of your mother fight the Prophet, whereas I saw the father of his mother fight with the Prophet, and the mother is worth more than 1000."

the stipend given to soldiers (*muqātilah*) of their rank.[1] It is **not**, however, lawful for the *imām* **to** assign **his female children** a stipend from the *fa'y*, because they are his offspring and are provided for in the stipend of their father.

As regards his **slaves**, as well as the slaves of others, if they are not soldiers, their subsistence is upon their masters.[2] If, however, they are soldiers, opinion varies, as will be explained in the next section. The slaves may be assigned a stipend after they have been set free. It is likewise allowable to assign a stipend for the intendants (*naqīb*) of the beneficiaries of *fa'y*, but not to the officials (*'ummāl*), because the former are from the people of *fa'y*, but the officials only receive a wage for the work they have done.[3]

According to the Hanifites,[4] **if a beneficiary of the fa'y dies in the middle of the year** he forfeits his stipend (*'aṭā'*), because it is a kind of gift (*ṣilah*) on the part of the state and not a debt, and its beneficiary does not acquire a title to it until after he has received it. If, however, he dies towards the end of the year, it is commendable that his stipend should be given to his relations. Shams al-A'immah, on the contrary, holds that nothing is given to his heirs even in case he should die at the completion of the year, since the stipend is a gift, and therefore is not complete before its receipt. If a beneficiary has been given his

[1] The rules concerning the pensions of soldiers are explained in the next section.

[2] But *cf. Mudawwanah*, vol. iii, p. 28.

[3] The *naqibs*, and the *'arifs*, who were just below the *naqibs* and the lowest officers of the army, were appointed from among the people of *fa'y* and served as intermediaries between the state and the soldiers, informing the *dīwān* administration about the condition of the soldiers and the offspring they had to take care of. (*Minhāj*, vol. ii, p. 295; Māwardi, p. 352; Anṣāri, vol. iii, p. 89.) According to the *Wajīz* (p. 289), there was appointed an *'arīf* for every ten soldiers.

[4] *Fatḥ*, vol. v, p. 307.

sufficiency before it became due, and if later he is dismissed, or dies before the end of the year, opinion varies as to whether the stipend should be returned. Muḥammad Ibn al-Hasan holds that it is preferable that it should be returned. Abu Hanīfah and Abu Yūsuf, on the other hand, say that the stipend, being a kind of gift, may not be reclaimed after the death of the person who received the gift.

SECTION III

The Military Stipends[1]

The diwan[2] of the army concerns the registration (*ithbāt*) of the soldiers and their stipend (*'aṭā'*). **A person may be registered** in the *dīwān* of the army **upon the fulfilment of three conditions.** The first condition consists in the possession of the following five qualifications: (1) The person must be adult, for the child belongs in the class of offspring and dependents and may not be registered in the *dīwān* of the army. (2) He must have freedom of status, because the slave is included in his master's share.

[1] Māwardi, pp. 351 *et seq.* The rules set forth in this section, with respect to the disbursement to the soldiers in the way of military stipends of four-fifths of the *fa'y* revenue, are according to the Shafiites. The Hanifites and the Malikites do not devote to this matter any special attention, probably because according to them the *fa'y* revenue, or at least a part of it, need not be disbursed exclusively to the soldiers, as the Shafiites require, but on the contrary may be disbursed entirely for peaceful purposes, such as the salaries of civil functionaries. The Shafiites, as we already saw, allow this in regard to the share of *maṣāliḥ*, that is, in one-fifth of one-fifth of the *fa'y* revenue only. *Cf.* Anṣāri, vol. iii, p. 89; *Mugni*, vol. iii, p. 90.

[2] *Dīwān* means a register, or a government office where administration is carried on. Thus *dīwān al-jaysh* (*dīwān* of the army) means the register or administrative office of the army, and *dīwān al-ṣadaqāt* (*dīwān* of the *ṣadaqahs*) means the registers where the records pertaining to the *ṣadaqahs* are entered, or the office where the registers are kept and the administrative work pertaining to the *ṣādaqahs* is carried on. (Māwardi, p. 343.)

Abu Hanīfah, following the precedent of the calif Abu Bakr, allows the giving of soldiers' stipends to slaves. On the contrary, al-Shāfi'i, following the precedent of Omar, makes freedom a requirement, but allows for the slaves in the way of increased stipends for their masters. (3) He must be a follower of Islam, in order that he may ward off harm from the Moslem community by virtue of his belief and in order that his sincerity and judgment may be depended upon. Therefore, a *dhimmi* may not be registered along with Moslems, and the name of a Moslem is stricken from the register if he becomes a renegade. (4) He must be free from personal defects (*afāt*) which prevent him from participating in fighting. Therefore cripples, the blind, and the one-handed, are barred from registration. The dumb and the deaf, however, are not barred. The lame, if horsemen, are not barred; otherwise they are. (5) He must be courageous in battle and conversant with the art of war.

When the applicant is possessed of all of these five qualities, his registration in the register (*dīwān*) of the army depends upon the fulfilment of two more conditions, *i. e.*, the offer and the acceptance. The offer (*ījāb*) is made by the applicant if he is not engaged in any employment; on the other hand, the offer is accepted by the authorities (*wali al-amr*) if there is need for the services of the applicant, or, to quote al-Anṣāri,[1] "if the funds are ample." If the applicant is well-known and of high standing, it is not proper that he should be described and characterized in the regsiter, but if he is from the ordinary people, then he is described and signalized, and his age, stature, color, and facial features are described and his peculiarities indicated, in order that he may not be confused with others bearing the same

[1] Vol. iii, p. 92. This seems to suggest that every able-bodied person who had no other occupation was enrolled as a soldier and received a stipend from the *dīwān* of the army.

name. The stipendiary is called when the stipends are distributed, and is attached to his *naqīb* or *'arīf* in order to receive his stipends through his intermediary.

After the title to registration in the register has been settled, the next question to solve is the **order of registration.** This order may be general or particular. **The general order** is the order in which the tribes (*qabā'il*) and clans (*ajnās*) are entered in the register, each being entered apart from the other. It is not allowed therefore to enter persons belonging to different groups under one group, or to enter persons coming under a particular group under different groups. This is in order that the call of the register may be in a uniform manner, and that strife and friction may cease. The order of registration differs according as the stipendiaries are Arabs or non-Arabs.

If they are Arabs, their tribes and clans are entered in the order of their relation to the Prophet, as was done by the calif Omar. In this order of registration, one begins with the origin of the lineage (*aṣl al-nasab*); then with the successive generations in the male line (*ma yafra'u 'anhu*). Thus the two main branches of the Arabs, are the 'Adnān and Qaḥṭān folk. The former come before the latter because the Prophet was from among them. On the other hand, among the 'Adnān folk the Muḍar folk precede the Rabī'ah folk. Again, from the Muḍar folk, the Quraysh are given precedence over the rest. Again, among the Quraysh the Banu Hāshim come first. The Banu Hāshim then constitute the pole of the register; after them come in order of relation to the Prophet the adjoining families until the whole of the 'Adnān folk are included.[1]

[1] But *cf.* Anṣāri, vol. iii, p. 90. According to al-Māwardi, the Arabian society is grouped on the basis of relationship in the male line (*nasab*) and, according to the length of lineage with respect to its first founder, each of the two independent main branches (*sha'b*) of 'Adnān and

If, however, the **beneficiaries are not Arabs**, and are not organized on the tribal (*nasab*) basis, then they are united by one of two ties: either by the tie of race (*ajnās*) or by that of home (*buldān*). The Turks and Hindus are examples of the former, and the Daylams (Kurds) of the second. But the Turks and Hindus are further distinguished among themselves by races, and the Kurds by cities. These races and cities then are entered in the register in the following order of precedence. First are entered those who became Moslems first. Then, as in the case of the Arabs, are entered the nearest relatives of the ruler (*wali al-amr*), then those who obeyed him first.

The particular order is the order in which the individuals of the same group are registered. Here the order of preference is according to priority in accepting the Islam. If this test fails the preference is according to godliness (*dīn*), then age, then courage. If the last test also fails, *e. g.*, if all are of the same courage, then the *imām* may draw lots as between them, or use his own judgment.

The **amount of the stipend** should be sufficient to satisfy the soldier's needs, in order that he may refrain from engaging in what may keep him from protecting the Moslem coun-

Qaḥṭān is divided, as it were, into six concentric social layers. The *sha'b* (branch) then includes all those who can be traced to the same remotest lineage. Within the *sha'b* are distinguished the so-called *qabīlahs;* thus the 'Adnān folk comprise the *qabīlahs* of Muḍar and Rabī'ah. Within the *qabīlah* are distinguished the *imārahs*, such as the Quraysh and the Kinānah; within the *imārah*, the *baṭns* like the Banu 'Abd Manāf; within the *baṭn* are the *fakh-dhs*, like the Banu Hāshim. Finally, within the *fakh-dh* are the *faṣīlahs*, like the Banu al-'Abbās, Banu Abu Ṭālib. Each layer contains the following ones, namely, the *sha'b* includes the *qabīlahs*, the *qabīlah* the *imārahs*, the *imārah* the *baṭns*, the *baṭn* the *fakh-dhs*, and the *fakh-dh* the *faṣīlahs*. In the course of time, as the lineage lengthens the various layers become raised to the preceding layer; thus the *qabīlahs* become *sha'bs*, the *imārahs*, *qabīlahs*, *etc.* (*Cf.* Zaydān, vol. iii, p. 34; vol. iv, p. 11; Ibn Khaldūn, pp. 108 *et seq.*)

try. This sufficiency is measured with reference to three circumstances; the number of children and slaves he has to provide for; the number of horses and retinue he stations; thirdly, the place where he lives with reference to the high or low cost of living. In other words, the soldier is assigned an amount sufficient to provide for subsistence and wearing apparel for the whole year, and this amount becomes his stipend.

The **condition of** the **stipendiary** is **examined every year** and if his pressing expenses have increased, his stipend is increased, and *vice versa*. The doctors have disagreed as to whether it is permissible to increase the stipend beyond one's sufficiency. Al-Shāfi'i prevented the increase of the stipend beyond one's sufficiency, even if there should be available funds, because the funds of the public treasury are not disbursed except for necessary expenses. Abu Hanīfah allowed such increase over and above one's sufficiency when the funds are abundant.

The **time of payment** of the stipends is known, and the army expects to be paid when it has acquired title to its pay. This time is fixed according to the time in which the revenues of the public treasury are due. If the revenue is collected once a year the stipends are paid in the beginning of the year. If the revenue is collected twice a year the payment is made twice a year. Finally, if it is collected once a month, the payment is made at the beginning of each month. This is because as soon as there has been collected any revenue it should reach its destination as soon as possible, but the army has no right to demand payment, if the collection has been delayed. If the payment of the stipend is delayed the stipendiaries may legally demand their settlement if there are funds in the treasury. If, on the contrary, the treasury is involved in financial difficulties owing to untoward events which wiped out its revenues or delayed their collection, they then become creditors of the treasury to the amount of their stipends; but they may not legally demand (*muṭālabah*) their stipends from the Moslem ruler, just as the creditor may not demand from his debtor when the latter is in straits.

If the ruler wants to dismiss part of the army for sufficient cause he may do so; otherwise this is not lawful, because the army of the Moslems is for their protection. On the other hand, if a part of the army wants to quit the army, it is allowed if they are no longer needed; but it is not allowed if they are needed, unless they have an excuse. If the soldiers refuse to fight when they are ordered to do so, notwithstanding that they are equal in number to the enemy, they forfeit their stipends; but if they are weaker than the enemy, their stipend is not canceled. If a soldiers' beast is destroyed during a battle the loss is made good to him, but if the beast dies outside of the battle he is not compensated for it. If a soldier's weapons are destroyed in battle, he is only repaid for them if no allowance had been made for them in his stipend. Likewise, when a soldier is detached for a campaign, he is given the traveling expenses, if they have not been allowed for in his stipend. If a soldier dies or is killed in action his stipend is turned over to his heirs.

The **stipend** is **turned over to** the **heirs** if the stipendiary died after the collection of the *fa'y* revenue, even if it should be before the completion of the year. The heirs, however, do not receive anything if the stipendiary dies after the completion of the year but before the collection of the *fa'y* revenue, for the stipendiary acquires a title on his stipend only by the revenue's having been collected.[1]

[1] *Wajiz*, p. 289; Anṣâri, vol. iii, p. 91; *Mugni*, vol. iii, p. 92; for details on the stipendiaries of pious foundations, see *Mugni*, *ibid.*

Concerning the **continuation of** the **subsistence of** his **offspring** out of his stipend from the *dīwān* of the army, the doctors have held two views. One view is that upon the death of the rightful titleholder of the military stipend, the latter is canceled, and the offspring are cared for from the proceeds of the *zakāt* taxes. The other view is that this subsistence is continued to them from the stipends of the deceased soldier in order to induce people to enter the army and to inspire them with courage. According to al-Anṣāri,[1] the subsistence of the wives and children of the stipendiary after the latter's death is continued until his wives and daughters are married and until his sons become independent as to earning their living by becoming registered in the *dīwān* as soldiers, or by other means. The doctors have likewise disagreed on the canceling of the stipend when the stipendiary becomes a cripple. One view is that the stipend is canceled because it was given in consideration of a service which is no longer performed. The other view is that the stipendiary is still given his stipend in order that this may serve as an incentive for volunteering for the army service.

[1] Vol. iii, p. 91; *cf. Mugni*, vol. iii, p. 91.

CHAPTER XII

Tax Grants

Al-Māwardi discusses tax grants under the general topic of grants (*iqṭāʿ*) and distinguishes them from the grant of lands in that the latter is a **grant of ownership** in the land, whereas he holds the former a **grant of the usufruct** (*iqṭāʿ al-istiglāl*).[1]

The grant of the usufruct (*iqṭāʿ al-istiglāl*) is of two kinds, grant of the tithe and grant of the *kharāj*.[2]

(1) **Grant of the tithe.** This is not lawful because the tithe is a kind of *zakāt* in favor of certain persons who at the time of appropriation must possess certain qualities, *e. g.*, poverty, and it is possible that the grantee may not possess the qualities required from the beneficiaries of tithe when he becomes entitled to it. Moreover, the *zakāt* is due upon the fulfilment of certain conditions and sometimes these conditions may be wanting and then the *zakāt* is not due. If, however, the conditions are present and the *zakāt* is due, and furthermore the grantee is entitled to it at the time of payment by possessing the required qualities, such as poverty, it is virtually a case of an assignment (*ḥawālah*) of

[1] Māwardi, pp. 337-341. This chapter is entirely according to the Shafiites.

[2] From the financial standpoint, a grant of tithe or *kharāj* meant that the state instead of itself collecting the tithe or *kharāj*, in order to defray from the proceeds the stipends of the state employees gave the latter a grant of tithe or *kharāj*, that is, the privilege of collecting the tithe or *kharāj* directly from the taxpayers and applying the proceeds to the settlement of their stipends.

the tithe against the person who is to pay it in favor of the assignee. Such an assignment therefore is valid and the payment of the tithe to the assignee is allowed; nevertheless, this does not create for him a title to the tithe until he has actually received it, for the *zakāt* ceases to be the property of the *zakāt* payer only after he has paid it. Therefore, if the assignee is refused the tithe he cannot bring an action against the tithe payer and in such case the tithe collector is more entitled to the collection of the tithe than the assignee.

(2) **Grant of the kharaj.** This differs according as the grantees differ, as follows:

(a) **The grantee is a beneficiary of the sadaqah revenue.** It is not allowable to grant *kharāj* to such, because the *kharāj* is a part of the *fa'y* revenue, and the beneficiaries of the *ṣadaqah* revenue are not entitled to the *fa'y,* just as the converse is true. Abu Hanīfah allowed this because he permitted the disbursement of the *fa'y* to the *ṣadaqah* beneficiaries.

(b) **The grantee is one of the beneficiaries of the share of masalih** who are not assigned stipends from the public treasury. Although these people may be given assistance from the *kharāj* revenue, they may not nevertheless be assigned a regular stipend, for they are the least entitled (*nafl*) to the *fa'y* and get a share only after the rightful claimants of the *fa'y* have received their stipends; what they get therefore comes only from the gifts distributed from the share of *maṣāliḥ*.

When these people are given a share from the *kharāj,* it is legally a case of assignment (*ḥawālah*) and not of grant (*iqṭā'*), and hence two conditions are necessary if it is to be allowed. First, the amount assigned must be fixed and the justification of its donation already present; and secondly, the *kharāj* must have already fallen due, otherwise the assignment is not valid. These two conditions differentiate the assignment from the grant.

(c) **The grantees are** from the class of the beneficiaries of the *fa'y* who are stipendiaries (*murtasiqah*) of the *dīwān*, in other words, **soldiers** (*ahl al-jaysh*). These people are the fittest (*akhaṣṣ*) of all to be grantees of the *kharāj*, for they receive stipends to which they are entitled in consideration of the services they have rendered in fighting the enemies of Islam and in defending its sacred territories. Since a grant to these people is valid, the next thing to consider is the nature of the *kharāj* revenue granted, for it may be of two kinds. It may be in the nature of a poll-tax (*jizyah*), or it may be in the nature of a rental (*ujrah*).

If the kharaj [1] granted is the jizyah, inasmuch as the *jizyah* is not levied forever, but only as long as the taxpayer is persisting in his unbelief, it is not lawful to grant it for a term longer than one year, because the grantee is not assured of its collection after the year. When a grant is made for one year, if it is after the tax has fallen due, it is valid, but if it is made during the year before the tax has yet become due, then there are two ways of looking at the situation: If the condition of lapse of a year in respect to the *jizyah* is considered to have been meant for the convenience of payment, the grant is valid; but if it is said that the lapse of a year is necessary in order for the tax to become due, it is not valid.

If, however, the **kharaj granted is the rental of the ground,** which is due permanently, its grant for a term of more than one year is valid, and it need not be limited to one year. In fact, the grant of this latter kind of *kharāj* may be in one of the following three forms.

[1] The word *kharāj*, besides the land tax, its more common meaning, may also mean any tribute. In this latter sense in which it is here used by al-Māwardi, *kharāj* applies to the *jizyah* as well as to the *kharāj* (land tax) proper.

(a) It may be **granted for a definite number of years,** *e. g.*, ten years. Such a grant is valid if the stipend (*rizq*) of the grantee is known to the grantor, and, furthermore, if the amount of the *kharāj* is known to both grantor and grantee. If, however, the second condition is not present, opinion differs according as the *kharāj* is proportional or fixed. The jurists who have allowed the levy of the proportional (*muqāsamah*) *kharāj* have justified it by considering it to be a case of granting a definite amount of *kharāj*. The jurists who have opposed the levy of the proportional *kharāj* have considered it to be a case of granting an unknown quantity of *kharāj*. If, however, the *kharāj* is of the fixed (*masāḥah*) kind, then, if it is of the kind that does not vary with the kind of crop, the grant is valid, since the amount of the *kharāj* granted is known. The grant is also valid, if the *kharāj* is of the kind which varies with the nature of the crop, but the stipend of the grantee is equal to the amount of the *kharāj* which would be yielded by the highest of the various possible rates, for the grantee has virtually consented to a lesser yield, should that be the case; on the contrary, the grant is not valid, if the grantee's stipend is equal to the yield of the lowest of the various possible rates, for he may possibly get more *kharāj* than his stipend would entitle him to.

If the grantee remains alive during the term of the grant, it continues. If, however, he should die before its expiry, the grant is then considered canceled for the rest of the term, and the *kharāj* right reverts to the treasury. In such case, if the deceased has left offspring they, receive a share from the share of offspring, but not from that of the army; and therefore what they receive is of the nature of public assistance (*sabab*), not of grant. A third contingency is that the grantee should become a cripple after a time. According to those who hold the view that being a cripple does not deprive one of his stipend, he continues to enjoy the grant, but according to the opposite group, the contrary is true.

(b) The **grant** is to be valid during the life of the grantee, and after his death it is **to devolve to his heirs.** Such a grant is void, because it amounts to the alienation of the interests of the treasury, since the treasury's right to collect taxes in this way becomes an inheritable private property. Although such a grant is legally imperfect (*fāsid*), the grantee is nevertheless entitled to the *kharāj* he has already collected and the taxpayers are absolved from their debts; if he collects more than his stipend, he returns the surplus to the treasury and, on the other hand, if he collects less than his stipend, he applies to the treasury for the balance. The sultan in this case announces the voidness of the grant, in order that the grantee may be prevented from collecting, and the taxpayers from paying to him, the *kharāj*; should they do so they would have to pay the *kharāj* over again.

(c) The **grant** is made **for the life** of the grantee. There are two views as to this case: According to those who hold that being a cripple does not constitute a cause for the discontinuance of the stipend, such a grant is valid, but according to those who hold the opposite view, it is not valid.

When a grant is valid, the sultan may still revoke it for the coming year, and in that case the stipendiary applies for his stipend to the *dīwān* of the army. The sultan may not revoke the grant for the current year, if the time of the stipend has come before the *kharāj* has fallen due, because the grantee has already acquired a title on the *kharāj* of that year, considering that his stipend is overdue; but if the *kharāj* has fallen due before his stipend, then the grant may be revoked, because the anticipation (*ta'jīl*) of a future debt, *i. e.*, the stipend, although lawful, is not binding.

As regards the **stipends of others than soldiers**, when these are given a grant of *kharāj*, three cases are possible:

(a) They are persons who, like the public functionaries (*'ummāl al-maṣāliḥ*) and the *kharāj* collectors, receive stipends in payment for temporary services. A grant in consideration of such stipends is not valid, and when it is made it legally constitutes an assignment and assistance (*tasbīb*), which is valid only after the stipend and the *kharāj* have fallen due.

(b) They are persons who receive stipends in consideration of permanent services, but the stipends legally constitute a case of *ja'ālah*.[1] They are the persons connected with religious and pious institutions (*al-nāẓirūn fī a'māl al-birr*), such as the *mu'adh-dhins* (callers to prayer) and the *imāms*, who, without an investiture from the proper authorities, might have offered their services to those institutions voluntarily and without payment for them (*yaṣiḥḥu al-taṭawwu' biha*), but who actually are receiving stipends. A grant of *kharāj* in favor of such persons legally is not a grant, but an assignment.

(c) They are persons who, like the judges and the *dīwān* registrars, receive stipends for permanent services, but whose stipend legally is a wage (*ijārah*) and who can lawfully exercise jurisdiction only by virtue of investiture (*taqlīd*) and legal authority (*wilāyah*). In consideration of their stipends they may be given a grant of *kharāj* for one year, and, according to one view, as in the case of the army, also for more than one year; but according to another opinion this is not lawful, because they may be dismissed from service or shifted to another post.

[1] *Ja'ālah*, according to the Shafiites (*Tanbīh*, p. 149; *Wajīz*, p. 240), is the promise of a compensation for services rendered. The title to the compensation is acquired only after the performance of the work. Although the person undertaking the work is free to cancel the agreement at any time, the person who promised the compensation may do so only before the performance of the work.

CHAPTER XIII

Concerning Public Records

SECTION I

The Public Registers[1]

The accounts (*a'māl*) of taxes (*rusūm*) and dues (*ḥuqūq*) entered (*ithbāt*) in the public registers are subject to the following rules: The jurisdiction of each city is marked out so that there is no overlapping, and moreover the districts (*nāḥiyah*) of each city are entered separately when they are subject to exceptional treatment; this is also true of the individual estates (*ḍay'ah*) of a district when they are treated in an exceptional way, but if all the estates are subject to the same rules, then they are not treated separately.

The way in which the city has been conquered, *e. g.*, whether by assault or peace, is also recorded; and furthermore a record is entered of the status which was given to its lands, *e. g.*, whether *kharāj* or tithe lands, and whether or not the different districts of the city are subject to the same rules.

[1] Māwardi, pp. 356-360.

Al-Māwardi distinguishes between *ithbāt* and *raf'*. *Ithbāt* means to enter a record in a register; *raf'*, to make a report to the registrar in order to have it recorded. *Ithbāt al-rufū'* would then mean the entering of such reports. *Ḥāl* means a statement of account. The French *état* renders it exactly. *Ikhrāj* means to prepare such a statement by reference to the registers.

If all the lands within the district are **tithe lands**, it is not necessary to register their area, since the tithe is fixed according to the amount of the produce. When there is a new crop, a report of it is made to the *dīwān* so that a record of it may be entered in the register of the tithes. In the report, the names of the owners of the lands are also mentioned, because the tithe is an obligation charged to the owner, and not to the land property. Moreover, when a crop and the name of the owner are reported to the *dīwān*, the amount of the crop and the method of irrigation used in cultivating it, whether running water or artificial irrigation, are indicated in order that the rate of the tithe to be charged may be determined.

If, however, all the lands of the city are **kharaj lands**, the areas are entered, because the *kharāj* is fixed according to area. If the *kharāj* is in the nature of a rental, the mention of the name of the landowner is not necessary, because his conversion to Islam does not make any difference so far as the payment of the *kharāj* is concerned. But if the *kharāj* is in the nature of *jizyah*, then it is necessary to enter the names of the landowners, and their religous affiliations, since the payment of the tax in this case depends on the religious status of the owner.

If part of the lands are tithe lands and part *kharāj* lands, the former are entered in the register of tithes, and the latter in the register of the *kharāj*, and each part is treated in accordance with the respective rules of its class as abovementioned.

The **details pertaining** to the kind of the *kharāj*, namely, whether it is of the proportional or the fixed kind of *kharāj*, are entered. If it is the proportional *kharāj*, then when a statement concerning the area of the land is prepared (*ukhrijat*) from the registers, the amount of the rate, like one-third or one-fourth of the produce, is also mentioned in the statement, and the amount of the produce is reported to the *dīwān* in order that the amount of the tax may be figured out accordingly. If the *kharāj* is paid in silver (*i. e.*, specie), two cases are possible. The *kharāj* may vary with the nature of the crop, or it may not vary. If it does not vary with the crop, then the area of the land is determined (*ukhrijat*) from the registers in order that the *kharāj* may be collected accordingly, and it is only necessary in this case to report to the *dīwān* the amount collected. But if the *kharāj* varies with the kind of crop grown on the land, the area is determined from the registers, and the kinds of the crops are reported to the registrar in order that the *kharāj* may be collected accordingly.

Furthermore, the **dhimmis of each city**, and the conditions under which they have been admitted into the status of *dhimmi* are indicated. If the amount of the *jizyah* is to vary according to the financial status of the *dhimmis* their names as well as their number are also recorded, in order that their financial status may be known; otherwise only their number is mentioned. Then every year a new examination is made, and the *dhimmis* who have come of age are recorded in the register and those who have died, or have become Moslems, are stricken out from it, the result being that only the *dhimmis* who are liable to the *jizyah* are registered.

If there are mines within the city limits, the **mines** and their kinds are mentioned. In the case of mines the tax is fixed according to what has been extracted from them, irrespective of the area of the land, and regardless of whether it is tithe or *kharāj* land. As already mentioned in the chapter on mines, there are various opinions as regards the kinds of mines which must pay tax, and also as regards the rate of the tax. If one of these points has been left undetermined by previous rulers, then the ruler for the time being decides the kind of mine that is to pay the tax, and the rate of the tax, and acts according to his opinion, provided he is a ***mujtahid***. But if the previous ***imāms*** have already expressed an opinion on these two points and acted according to that opinion, then the ruler for the time being follows their opinion only as regards the kinds of mines he is to tax.

If **frontier cities** situated on the border of the enemy's land (*dār al-ḥarb*) have treaties with the Moslem state whereby their goods are subject to a tax when they enter the Moslem territory, these treaties are recorded in the registers, and the amount of the tax rate, whether one-tenth, or one-fifth, or more or less, is indicated. Furthermore, if the rates are to differ with the nature of the goods, that fact is also mentioned. As regards the taxes levied on goods carried within Moslem territory from one place to another, the levy of a tax on such goods is prohibited by the *sharīʻah* and no *mujtahid* has ever allowed such a policy. Besides, it is only in accordance with a policy of justice, and the dictates of humanity. Such taxes are rarely levied, except in tyrannical cities. It is related that the Prophet said: "The worst of men are the toll collectors (*ʻash-shārūn*) who destroy".

When the governors (*wāli*) **change the laws** of the cities and the tax rates, the change is lawful, if the governors are of the class of *mujtahids* and the change made by them is one that is approved by the *sharīʻah*; and the tax is collected on the basis of it. In such case, when a statement of the account is prepared from the registers, it is allowable if only the new rate is taken into account, although it is better that both rates should be mentioned, because it is possible that the reasons which justified the change have meanwhile ceased to exist; in such case the tax would have to be paid according to the old rate. If, however, the change is not approved by the *sharī'ah,* and the governor who instituted the change is not a *mujtahid,* the change is null and void. When a governor wants a statement (*ḥāl*) of a tax account, the statement must mention also the rate previous to the change, unless the governor is already acquainted with it. In this last case it is sufficient to indicate that the rate used is the new rate.

SECTION II

The Duties of the Public Registrars[1]

The registrars of the *dīwān* are charged with the following six duties: the recording of laws; the settlement (*istīfā'*) of the accounts of taxes and dues; the recording of reports (*ithbāt al-rufū'*); the audit of the accounts of officials; the preparation of statements of accounts (*ikhrāj al-aḥwāl*); and the hearing of complaints. The parts pertaining to finance are as follows:

[1] Māwardi, pp. 370-75. To understand this section properly, the following distinctions must be borne in mind: There is, first, the department of the *dīwān,* which is charged with the settlement (*istīfā'*) and the audit (*muḥāsabah*) of accounts. This department is referred to by al-Māwardi, as *kātib al-dīwān* or *ṣāḥib al-dīwān,* the latter apparently applying to the head of the department. While an audit refers to the accuracy of an account, a settlement, on the other hand, refers, as it were, to the life career of the funds mentioned in an account,—namely, whether or not they have been properly disposed by the person who had laid hands on them, by their being turned over, for instance, to the treasurer, who is referred to as the *ṣāḥib bayt-al-māl.* The word *'āmilūn* (plural of *'āmil*) denotes the collectors who collect the taxes. They may turn them over directly to the treasurer, or to some authorized official (*'mmāl,* also plural of *'āmil*), who passes them on to the treasurer. There is, finally, the official who issues authorizations (*tawqī'*) for the payment of funds. He is referred to as *muwaqqi'.* On the other hand, the person in whose favor the authorization was issued is called *muwaqqa' lah* or *ṣāḥib al-tawqī'. Iḥtisāb* means to give credit for a sum. *Kharj ila* refers to a revenue, *kharj min,* to an expenditure.

The registrar of the *dīwān* sees to it that the laws passed during his tenure of office are recorded in the *dīwān* of the respective district (*nāḥiyah*) as well as in the *dīwān* of the public treasury, where a duplicate of all district records is kept. As regards laws passed before his time, he refers to their existing records, if those records have been written by trustworthy registrars, and if the records have been delivered to him under the seal of the persons entrusted with their safe keeping.

However, such reports do not constitute evidence in the usage of courts. Abu Hanīfah holds that the registrar (*kātib*) of the *dīwān* may not rely upon a written record unless he has heard its contents directly from the person who wrote the record and he meanwhile keeps it in his memory.[1] Abu Hanīfah arrived at this view by the analogy of legal testimony and judgment. However, such a view is impossible and absurd, for as testimony and judgment relate to private rights where the persons who would take a hand in (*mubāshir*), and look after (*qayyim*) them are many and it is not difficult for them to keep the facts in memory, it is not lawful in their case to rely upon writing alone. The rules and customs of the *dīwān*, however, are matters of public interest (*ḥuqūq 'āmmah*) which it is hard to keep in memory, for although they are many and widespread, the persons who would actually take a hand in them are few. Consequently, in their case, writing may be relied upon alone.

The settlement of the accounts of dues and taxes. Two cases are possible. The settlement may refer to the accounts of the collectors (*'āmilūn*) directly responsible for them, or it may refer to the accounts of the officials (*'ummāl*) who have received the taxes from the collectors. With respect to the settlement of accounts of the collectors

[1] *Cf. Kashf*, p. 771.

(*'āmilūn*), if the officials (*'ummāl*) admit having received from them the tax, their word is accepted. If the admission is in writing, the practice of the registrars is to consider such a written admission as evidence of the receipt of the tax if, by comparison with the well-known writing of the official, the writing is recognized to be his; whether or not he admits it. However, the opinion of the jurists on this point is that if the official denies that the writing is his, the writing alone cannot be held as evidence against him. If the official admits the writing to be his, but denies that he has actually received the tax, this written admission, as is otherwise the custom, constitutes evidence, according to al-Shāfi'i, in the matter of public dues alone, that the tax has been paid by the persons concerned (*mu'āmilūn*) and that the official received the same; but Abu Hanīfah here again differs from al-Shāfi'i.

As regards the settlement of the account of the officials, if it is a case of revenue for the public treasury (*kharj ila bayt-al-māl*), it is not necessary for the official to show an authorization from the proper authority (*tawqī' wali al-amr*), and the admission of the treasurer (*ṣāḥib bayt-al-māl*) that he received the money is sufficient for the acquittal of the official. If the admission of the treasurer is merely in writing and has not been confirmed by his oral admission, according to al-Shāfi'i, it is evidence that he received the money, although Abu Hanīfah holds the opposite view.

If, on the contrary, it is a case of a treasury expenditure instead of revenue, then the officials may not make the expenditure except upon a written authorization from the proper authorities. such an authorization, when genuine, being sufficient ground for the expenditure. There are, however, two possible courses (*wajhān*) in giving the official credit (*iḥtisāb*) for the amount included in the authorization. The first course, which is the one recommended by the *faqīhs,* is that if the person in whose favor the authorization of payment has been issued (*muwaqqa' lah*) admits having received payment of the amount contained in the authorization, the official who made the payment is given credit for the amount; otherwise he is not given credit for it, because the authorization, although it entitles the official to pay the money, is by no means evidence that he actually did pay it. The other course, which is the one followed in the practice of the *dīwān*, is to give the official credit for the amount in question so far as the public treasury is concerned, and if the person in whose favor the authorization was issued (*ṣāḥib al-tawqī'*) denies having received the amount, he institutes a suit against the official. The official in such case has to support his contention by presenting legal evidence, or, if he has no evidence, by demanding the oath, failing in which he has to repeat the payment.

If the public registrar (*ṣāḥib al-dīwān*) has reasons to doubt the fact of authorization, whether or not the persons in whose favor it was issued admits receipt of the amount involved, he does not give the official credit for it until he has inquired about the matter from the person who issued the authorization (*muwaqqi'*). If the latter admits having issued it, then the procedure is as above noted. If, however, he denies it, the official is not given credit for the amount involved. In this last case, the official recovers his loss by recourse to the persons to whom he made the payment, if such a recourse is still possible; otherwise the only remedy left to him is to demand the oath from the person alleged to have issued the authorization (*muwaqqi'*).

The Record of Reports in the Diwan. There are three kinds of reports (*rufū'*): (1) reports of areas and accounts (*a'māl*); (2) reports of receipts (*qabḍ*) and settlements (*istīfā'*); (3) reports of expenditure (*nafaqah*). As regards reports of area and account, if there are already in the *dīwān* previously established (*muqaddar*) records (*uṣūl*), their truth is determined by reference to those records, and if the reports are found to be in accordance with them, they are entered (*ithbāt*). If, however, there are no such records, then the entry is made in accordance with the statements of the person who made the report (*rāfi'*). As regards reports of receipt and settlement, they are entered in the registers, on the mere strength of the statement of the person who is making the report, since he is reporting against, and not for, his own interests. Finally, as regards reports of expenditure, the person making the report is really putting forth a claim (*da'wa*) and therefore his report is not entered unless substantiated by convincing proof. If he presents as evidence the authorization (*tawqī'*) of a superior officer the procedure is as explained above.

The Audit of the Accounts of Officials. The procedure in this connection differs according as the collector deals with tithe or *kharāj*. If he is a collector of *kharāj*, then it is his duty to make a report (*raf'*) of his account to the registrar, who is bound to verify the accuracy of the account. It is not, however, the duty of the collector of tithe to make a report of his account to the registrar, nor is it the duty of the registrar to audit his account, because the tithe, in al-Shāfi'i's opinion, is a kind of *ṣadaqah* whose disbursement so little is a prerogative of the authorities (*wulāt*), that should the tithe payer settle his tithe dues directly to the poor, his debt is discharged (*ajzā'at*) as between him and God. According to Abu Hanīfah, however, the collector of tithe is under obligation to make a report of his account, and the registrar to audit the same.

When the account of a collector has been audited by the registrar of the *dīwān*, if no difference of view has arisen between the two, the registrar is believed with respect to his audit,[1] but should the proper authority (*wali al-amr*) entertain doubts on this score, he may require the registrar to bring his evidence. If, thereupon, the proper authority's suspicions cease, no oath is administered to any one. In the contrary case, the authority in question may require the oath from the collector, but not from the registrar, since it is the collector who is subject to demand. If, however, the collector and the registrar have differed concerning the account, the collector is believed upon his oath if the disagreement bears on an item of revenue, since in this case the assertion is made by the registrar and the burden of proof rests on him. If, on the contrary, the dispute has to do with an item of expenditure, then the collector must prove his assertion. If, finally, the dispute concerns a matter of area, then the area is remeasured, if that is possible.

[1] The text here reads, "with respect to the balance of the account" (*fi baqāya al-ḥisāb*). The word "balance," however, was omitted as a meaningless, and probably later, addition.

CHAPTER XIV

Public Domain [1]

The concession (*iqṯā'*) of a piece of land by the sultan is allowed only as regards lands which he may administer and dispose of (*taṣarruf*), and concerning which his orders are valid. Consequently, his concession is not valid when exercised with regard to lands which are the property of known and definite persons. Concessions are of two kinds: concessions of ownership (*iqṯā' tamlīk*), and concessions of usufruct (*iqṯā' istiglāl*). Al-Shāfi'i,[2] speaking of this distinction, says that in the case of *iqṯā' irfāq,* as he calls *iqṯā' istiglāl,* the grantee has only the right of use (*intifā'*) as distinct from ownership (*raqabah*), and the right to prevent others from using it so long as he or his agent is using it; but that he forfeits his right by abandoning the thing granted, and that he may not sell it to others. The concessions referred to in this chapter with respect to waste and cultivated lands are concessions of ownership.

Concession of Waste Lands (*mawāt*).[3] According to al-Shāfi'i, the **term "waste" applies** to every piece of land which is not proper for cultivation (*'āmir*) and is not the

[1] Māwardi, pp. 330-37, 341-43.

[2] *Umm*, vol. iii, p. 266.

[3] Māwardi, pp. 330-2, 308-13; *Umm*, vol. iii, p. 265; *Mugni*, vol. ii, p. 334; *Wajīz*, p. 241; Anṣāri, vol. ii, p. 444; *Minhāj*, vol. ii, p. 171; *Hidāyah*, vol. ix, p. 2; *Baḥr*, vol. viii, p. 238; Zayla'i, vol. vi, p. 35; *Majma'*, vol. ii, p. 436; Yūsuf, p. 36; *Mabsūṭ*, part xxiii, p. 166; *Jāmi'*, vol. ii, p. 276; *'Alamkīriyyah*, vol. v, p. 574; *Durr*, p. 708; Dardīr, vol. ii, p. 181; Yahya, p. 61.

ḫarīm (complement or dependancy) of land proper for cultivation. According to Abu Yūsuf, a piece of land which cannot be utilized is not considered " waste " unless it is far enough from a town so that a person standing on this land at a point nearest to the town and shouting at the top of his voice cannot be heard from the town. Muḫammad Ibn al-Hasan, on the other hand, holds that a piece of land is waste if it can not be utilized, whether it is near or far from a town. According to al-Kāsāni [1] lands located within towns are never considered " waste."

A piece of land, in order to be waste land, must furthermore be the property of no one, for if a piece of land is known to have a present owner, whether a Moslem or a *dhimmi,* it is not considered waste, even if it has been literally waste for ages. On the contrary, a piece of land is considered waste if at present its owner is not known, whether the land has lain waste without an owner from time immemorial, or whether it was at one time under cultivation before it later went to waste, before or after Islam. This is the view of Abu Hanīfah. However, according to his disciple, Muḫammad, if the land is known to have had an owner at some time since the advent of Islam, whether or not the present owner is known, the land is not treated as waste, but belongs to the Moslem community at large. According to al-Shāfi'i, such lands, whether or not their present owners are known, are not waste, that is, they do not become private property by being developed for cultivation (*iḫyā'*), *etc.* According to al-Māwardi, the reason why lands which have lain waste from pre-Islamic times, such as the lands of 'Ad and Thamūd,[2] are treated as

[1] Vol. vi, p. 194.

[2] Ancient Arabian tribes. The adjective *'ādi,* derived from 'Ad, is used by the doctors in the sense of what has been from time immemorial (*qadīm*).

waste lands is the *ḥadīth*: "The lands which come from 'Ad (*'ādi al-arḍ*) belong to God and to His Prophet; then they are given to you (*i. e.,* the Moslems) from me." According to the Malikites,[1] waste lands are lands which have not become private property (*ikhtiṣāṣ*) through purchase or through some other method of acquisition, or by being developed (*iḥyā'*) for cultivation, *etc.*; or by being the *ḥarīm* of developed lands, such as the pasture lands which are the *ḥarīms* of a village, or such as the *ḥarīms* of springs, trees and houses; or by being given in concession (*iqṭā'*) by the *imām*; or finally by being reserved (*ḥima*) by the *imām* as pasture land, *etc.,* for common use.

Abu Yūsuf,[2] true to his definition of a "waste" land, does not allow to the *imām* the concession of waste lands which are near a town within the distance mentioned, because, he argues, such lands are apt to be used by the townspeople as meadows, *etc.* Muḥammad Ibn al-Hasan, however, allows the concession of such lands, if they are not used by the town folk in some way, *e. g.,* for getting wood or pasturing; on the contrary, he does not allow the enclosure of lands for private use, if they are used by the town people, no matter how far from the town the lands are situated. According to the Malikites,[3] the *imām* may give away in concession even such waste lands as are used by village people as pasture land and wood land (*muḥṭaṭab*).

When a piece of land coming under the description of waste as above explained **is developed** (*iḥyā'*) by a person, it becomes his property. According to the Hanifites, such person may be a Moslem or a *dhimmi,* but according to the Shafiites, and, as regards waste lands situated in the vicinity

[1] Kharashi, vol. v, p. 66; Dardīr, vol. ii, pp. 181-2.

[2] *Majma'*, vol. ii, p. 437.

[3] Dardīr, vol. ii, p. 181.

of towns, also the accepted Malikite views, only a Moslem may acquire the ownership of waste lands by development. The Malikites, however, allow the *dhimmis* equal rights as regards waste lands distant from towns.[1]

According to Abu Hanīfah, a person acquires property in a piece of land he developed only in case he had beforehand obtained the permission (*iqṯā'* or *idhn*) of the *imām* to develop it. According to his two disciples and to al-Shāfi'i, the permission of the *imām* is not necessary. Finally, according to the Malikites,[2] permission is necessary only as regards waste lands situated in the vicinity of towns. The ground for Abu Hanīfah's view is the *ḥadīth*: "A person owns only what pleases his *imām*". Besides, lands are a kind of booty obtained from unbelievers and like all booty, no part of it may be owned without permission from the *imām*. The ground for the opposite view is another *ḥadīth* to the effect that a person owns the land he has developed because lands, like game, are free property (*mubāḥ*).[3]

There is dispute as to the technical meaning of the word *iḥyā'* (development). According to the *'Ināyah*, as quoted in the *Baḥr*, *iḥyā'* consists in ploughing and irrigating the land; either one by itself being insufficient. According to the *Kāfi*, either one of them is sufficient. According to Abu Yūsuf, *iḥyā'* is building, or sowing, or ploughing, or irrigating. According to one report from Muḥammad Ibn al-Hasan, ploughing is not *iḥyā'*, unless followed by sowing. According to the *Mabsūṭ*,[4] *iḥyā* consists in rendering the land fit for cultivation by ploughing, or building water channels, or digging a canal leading to it. According to the *Majallah*,[5]

[1] *Majma'*, vol. ii, p. 436; *Minhāj*, vol. ii, p. 171; Dardīr, vol. ii, p. 183.

[2] Kharashi, vol. v, p. 70.

[3] *Hidāyah*, vol. ix, pp. 3-4.

[4] P. 168.

[5] Article 1051; also arts. 1275, 1276.

iḫyā' consists in rendering land fit for cultivation. According to al-Māwardi, the exact meaning of *iḫyā'* is fixed by reference to the purpose for which the land is developed in accordance with custom, since the Prophet has left it undetermined. Thus if the land is intended for residence, it is considered "developed" (*iḫyā'*) if a covered building is erected on it, since that is the minimum necessary for use as residence. If, on the other hand, the land is developed for cultivation, then three things are required: (1) The land must be marked off on all sides by heaping up earth. (2) The land must be irrigated, if it is dry, and drained if marshy. (3) The land must be tilled (*ḫarth*); but it is not necessary that it should be sown or planted, any more than that the house should be actually inhabited. Al-Shāfi'i, as a counterpart to his distinction between concession of ownership and concession of usufruct, distinguishes between the *iḫyā'* which results in the ownership of the thing developed, and the development which is not customarily called *iḫyā'* and produces a tithe of usufruct only. Thus if a nomad tribe puts up tents or wooden huts it is not a case of *iḫyā'*, and the tribe does not acquire the ownership of the ground but is only entitled to its use until it leaves the place. Finally, according to the Malikites, *iḫyā'* consists in providing a means of irrigation, or draining, or putting up a building, or plantng, or tilling, or clearing the land from trees, or leveling the ground. It does not consist in enclosing the land with a wall, or using it for grazing.

When the imam makes a **concession** (*iqṯā'*), **of waste land** to a person, such person acquires a title to the development of that land as over against others, and in this, al-Shāfi'i agrees with Abu Hanīfah. The concessionaire, however, does not acquire the ownership of the land before developing it. If he fails to do so, he does not own it, but he nevertheless has a title of possession (*yad*) to that land, as over against others. If his failure is due to an evident cause, the land is left in his possession until the disappearance of the cause. If he had no excuse for his failure, according to Abu Hanīfah he is not molested during three years from the date of concession, but, should he fail to develop the land within that time, the concession becomes null and void, and the land reverts to the status of waste. This term of three years is based on a precedent of Omar. According to al-Shāfi'i, Omar's precedent is not binding as it was meant for a special case, and the length of the term is determined by the possibility of development. Consequently, if the concessionaire fails to develop the land during a long enough term, he is required either to develop the land, or to forfeit his title to it in order that the land may be granted to others.

If, during these three years, the land is developed by some one other than the concessionaire, according to Abu Hanīfah, the land still belongs to the concessionaire. The case is otherwise, however, if it was developed after the three years. According to al-Shāfi'i, the land in either case belongs to the person who developed it.

According to the Malikites,[1] the concession (*iqṯā'*) by the *imām* of waste land in and of itself results in its becoming the property of the concessionaire, even if he fails to develop the land or neglects it after development. If, however, a piece of land was acquired by development (*iḫyā'*), it may not be allowed to lie waste for a long time, for should such land be meanwhile developed by a third party it becomes the property of the latter. According to a report from Ibn Rushd, if in the above case the third party developed the land shortly after its neglect by the first developer, the latter continues to own the land, but the third

[1] Dardīr, vol. ii, p. 182; Kharashi, vol. v, pp. 66, 69; 'Adawi, vol. v, p. 67.

party must be compensated for the standing (*qā'imah*) value of his development, if he was not aware of the fact of previous development; otherwise he is compensated only for the value of his development as removed from its position (*maqlū'a*).

According to al-Shāfi'i, when a person develops a piece of land he acquires a title of ownership not only to the land so developed, but also to such adjoining land as is indispensable for the full use of the land developed. For instance, he is entitled to a way, to a courtyard (*finā'*), to channels for drainage and water, *etc.* These rights are designated under the collective term of **harim**, which is defined by the *Rawḍ al-Ṭālib* [1] as the immediate environment necessary for the full use of a property. According to the *Hidāyah*, the *ḥarīm* of a land developed for planting trees is five cubits on every side.

If a person, instead of developing a piece of land, **contents himself with** the **initial stages of development** known as *taḥjīr* (literally, enclosure), marking off the land by placing stones all around it, in order to indicate his intention of development,[2] according to the *Minhāj*, he becomes entitled (*aḥaqq*) to this land as against others, but he may not sell it, and should another develop it the latter owns it. If the encloser unduly delays the development of the land, he is required by the sultan to develop it within a short time or forego his rights. According to the Hanifites, the encloser acquires a priority with respect to the land for three years, but only as a matter of religion (*diyānah*), so much so that if another person should develop it meanwhile he acquires the land. After the lapse of the three

[1] Anṣāri, vol. ii, p. 445.

[2] According to the Hanifites, *taḥjīr* consists in marking off the land by placing stones or sticking branches all around, or by burning the dry herbs grown on the land, *etc.*

years, the land is given to others in order that it may become a source of tax revenue. This term of three years is based on the precedent of Omar who desired to check the practice of enclosing land and not developing it later.[1]

According to the *'Alamkīriyyah* and the *Majallah,* if the *imām* permits the development of a piece of land on condition that the person developing it shall be entitled to possession alone, the land does not become his property.[2]

Cultivated Lands. These are of two kinds:

(a) Those whose **owners** are definite and **known** persons. The *imām* has no jurisdiction over these lands,[3] whether owned by Moslems or by *dhimmis,* if they are situated in the Moslem state, except in so far as they are subject to taxes. If, however, these lands are situated in the country of the enemy over which the Moslems have not as yet exercised rights of possession (*yad*) and the *imām* wishes to make a concession of them which will be valid when such lands shall have been conquered, it is lawful. There are instances of such concessions made by the Prophet himself. Thus Tamīm asked the Prophet to give him in concession the springs of the city of Damascus, before the city was yet conquered, and the Prophet granted his request. Again, the Prophet made concession of land in the Byzantine empire to al-Khushni upon his request. The same rule applies if a person is presented with wealth or

[1] Yahya, p. 66. The Hanifite texts are very confusing on the matter of enclosures. Most of them suggest, and some explicitly state, that an enclosure, to entitle to priority for three years, must have been based on a permit (*iqṭā'*). The *Mabsūṭ,* however, on which later works are largely based, clearly suggests the opposite, and the *Jāmi'* expressly states that permission is immaterial. The *Majallah,* finally, is conceived clearly in this same spirit. This is also in accordance with history, as appears from Yahya.

[2] *Cf.* Kharashi, vol. v, p. 69.

[3] *Cf. Umm,* vol. iii, p. 273.

women or children belonging to enemies. All these gifts and concessions are valid when the conquest is made. If the conquest is made in the way of peaceful agreement, the things made presents of are excluded from the effect of the terms of peace. If, however, the conquest is made by force of arms then the army is not compensated for these presents if they knew about them; otherwise the *imām* must satisfy them in some way. Abu Hanīfah says that the *imām* need not do so, when there is public benefit in excluding certain things from the spoils.

(b) Cultivated lands whose **owners** are **not known.** These are of three classes: (i) **Lands which are set apart** by the *imām* **for the public treasury** (*bayt-al-māl*) either because they came to belong to the state as its one-fifth share in the spoils of war, or because the *imām* reserved certain lands for the public treasury, the army being compensated for it otherwise. For example, Omar reserved for the public treasury from the lands of Sawād the lands owned by the Persian king (*kisra*) and by the members of his dynasty, and the lands whose owners had fled or perished. The rentals of these lands amounted to nine million *dirhams*, and were spent for the Moslem cause in general. Omar did not give any of these lands in concession. Later 'Uthmān, his successor, leased them (*iqṭā' ijārah*) because he thought that it would be better from the standpoint of yield to place them in private hands by *iqṭā'* rather than to have them lie idle, it being a condition of the lease that the lessees would pay the rights of the public (*ḥaqq al-fa'y*). This was therefore a case of concession of usufruct, not of ownership of the land, and in this way the rentals increased, until they reached, as is alleged, fifty million *dirhams*. 'Uthmān made his presents and gifts out of these sums. Things continued in this way until the year eighty-two, when during the rebellion of Ibn al-Ash'ath, the registers were burnt and each people took possession of the lands situated in their neighborhood.

It is not lawful to alienate the ownership of the public in these lands, because such lands by being reserved by the *imām* for the public treasury have become the property of all the Moslems and hence mortmain (*waqf*) forever.

The Malikite view of the matter is similar.[1] However, according to the Hanifites, who do not require the constitution of these lands into *waqf* property, it is allowable for the *imām* to give them away in concession.[3]

With regard to these lands, the *imām* has the right, with a view to insuring the best interests of the Moslems, to do one of the following two things: To have them cultivated on account of the public treasury (*yastagilluhu li bayt-al-māl*), as did Omar; or to leave them to persons who possess the ability to improve them, subject to payment of *kharāj* fixed according to the amount of the produce as did 'Uthmān, and in this case the *kharāj* collected from these lands is in reality their rental,[2] and is disbursed for works of

[1] Kharashi, vol. v, p. 69.

[2] Yūsuf, pp. 32-3.

[3] This practically amounted to a complete alienation of the ownership of the public treasury in these lands, the right of the state consisting simply in the *kharāj* collected from these lands. According to the *Mugni* (vol. iv, pp. 216-17; Māwardi, pp. 302-3), a Shafiite work, in the case of the lands of Sawād, for reasons of public interest, analogy was departed from in that they were leased by the calif Omar under a perpetual lease (*ijārah mu'abbadah*), the *kharāj* collected from the landholders being the rental. The author adds that although the landholders, being tenants, may not sell their landholdings, they may nevertheless lease them for short periods; furthermore, that the lands may not be taken away from their holders; finally, that the lease is not dissolved upon the death of the holders but devolves in favor of their heirs. Al-Shāfi'i (*Umm*, vol. iii, p. 240; compare *supra*, p. 377 fn.) at an earlier date had considered the nature of the landholder's title to these lands as a case of *qabālah*. It is, therefore, very probable that the claim of al-Māwardi that these lands continued to remain the

general utility, unless the lands were taken over by the state by virtue of its one-fifth share in the spoils, in which case the rental is disposed of to the beneficiaries of that share.

If the *kharāj* imposed in this case is a half-and-half proportion of the fruits or the crops, it is lawful in the case of dates, following the example of the Prophet who had entered into an agreement (*musāqāt*) with the people of Khaybar on the condition that they would pay to the Prophet half of the produce of their date trees. As regards crops (*zar'*), there is dispute among the doctors, those who do not allow the *mukhābarah* system objecting to it. Some say that the proportional *kharāj* may be levied on the crops even if the *mukhābarah* system in their respect is not lawful, because there is a public benefit in levying the proportional *kharāj* and therefore in their case the law concerning private relations may be departed from.

(ii) The **lands subject to the payment of kharaj.** The ownership of these lands may not be ceded, because

property of the state and that the cultivators were merely tenants, if at all true, was so only in theory. (*Cf.* Caetani, vol. v, pp. 392-433; Berchem, p. 5, fn.; Worms, *Journal asiatique*, 1842-4.) Turkish history offers two striking parallels in this line,—the so-called domanial lands (*arāḍi amīriyyah*), and the *waqf* (pious foundation) estates known as *ijāreteynli awqāf.* Although theoretically the ownership (*raqabah*) of these two classes of property is vested in the state (Young, vol. vi, p. 45) or in the *waqf* (*ibid.*, p. 115), respectively, and their holders are considered by the Turkish jurists as mere tenants (Husni, pp. 92-3), the latter nevertheless practically own them. The property rights of the state and the *waqf* were still further weakened by the laws of 1867 and 1875, which extended the right of inheritance to their holders to a considerable extent. However, the fact that in theory the present holders are only tenants constitutes a real handicap for the holders when they want to transfer or use their lands as security for loan. One of the many problems to the solution of which the Turkish Government has turned its attention since the recent restoration of the Constitutional Régime has been the complete assimilation of the domanial lands and the *waqf* properties to properties owned in fee simple (*milk*),—at least in their practical aspects.

either they are mortmain lands and then the *kharāj* levied on them is in reality a rental, and being mortmain they may not be alienated, or they are private property and in that case the *kharāj* levied on them is a sort of *jizyah*, and again they may not be alienated, since their ownership is vested in definite private persons. The Hanifite and Malikite views are to the same effect.[1]

(iii) Lands whose owners have died without leaving rightful heirs to inherit. Such lands devolve to the public treasury, as inheritance by the Moslems at large, and therefore they are spent in the interests of the Moslems at large. Abu Hanīfah says that such property is disbursed to the poor only as an alms from the deceased to them; al-Shāfi'i, however, does not agree with this view because, as he argues, by entering the public treasury these properties have lost their private character and have become the property of all the Moslems.[2]

Mines.[3] These are exposed or concealed. **Exposed mines** are those in which the mineral deposits are visible, like coal, salt, tar, naphtha, *etc.* These are like water, whose grant is not allowed; all persons being equally entitled to their use. The person who first lays hold on them owns them. The concession of exposed mines, therefore, has no

[1] *Cf.* Yūsuf, pp. 32-33; Kharashi, vol. v, p. 66.

[2] Al-Māwardi has probably in mind here such lands as were owned in fee simple (*milk*) by Moslems and upon their death devolved to the state. For such of them as were owned by *dhimmis*, according to the prevalent Shafiite view, become *fa'y* and may not be disbursed for purposes of public utility excepting the share of *maṣāliḥ* set apart from them. Abu Hanīfah's opinion, as quoted by al-Māwardi, also involves a certain contradiction; for, as we already saw, in the chapter on Public Treasury, according to the current Hanifite view, lands devolving to the state from *dhimmis* become *fa'y*, while those devolving from Moslems are disbursed to widows, *etc.*

[3] Māwardi, pp. 341-3; *Umm*, vol. iii, p. 265; Anṣāri, vol. ii, p. 452; *cf. Minhāj*, vol. ii, p. 178; *Tanbih*, p. 155.

legal effect and the grantee and others are equally entitled to them, and hence the concessionaire may not prevent others from helping themselves to the mines, and he may do the same himself. The Hanifite view is to the same effect.[1]

Concealed mines are those whose deposits are hidden under ground, and may be reached only by means of labor; such as mines of gold, silver, copper, iron, *etc.*, whether or not the ore extracted needs smelting and purification. Concerning the concession of such mines there are two views: One view is that, as in the case of exposed mines, their concession is not lawful, all men being alike entitled to them. The other view is that the concession is valid in consequence of what has been related of the Prophet, namely, that the Prophet made a grant of certain mines to Bilāl Ibn al-Harth. According to this second view, the grantee acquires a right of priority (*aḥaqq*) to these mines and may prevent others from encroaching on his right. As regards the legal status of the concession, some hold that the mines become the property (*raqabah*) of the grantee, it being a case of *iqṭā' tamlīk* (concession of ownership), irrespective of whether the grantee exploits the mines or leaves them idle, provided he has already had work done on them. Therefore, he may sell them and upon his death they devolve to his heirs. Others contend that it is a case of concession of usufruct alone (*iqṭā' irfāq*), and that, therefore, the grantee does not acquire the ownership of the mines but only the right to exploit them and to prevent others from using them during the time that he is working the mines, but as soon as he abandons the mines the concession ceases to be effective and the mines become common property (*mubāḥ*). Al-Shāfi'i,[2] in subscribing to this second view, observes

[1] *Durr*, p. 709.

[2] *Umm*, vol. iii, p. 267, l. —17.

that apparently the ground for it lies in the fact that mines are natural wealth lying in the ground and that no art attaches to them when a part of them is extracted and smelted by men, that consequently one should be entitled to them only in so far as he exploits them. Al-Shāfi'i further observes that the sultan, in giving a mine away, should expressly stipulate that the concessionaire shall pay the *zakāt* that will be due on the mines he is to operate, that he shall be entitled to the mine only so long as he operates it, and finally, that he may not sell it to others.

If a person improves a tract of land, whether or not such tract has been granted to him, and in the process of improvement mines are brought to light, whether they are exposed or concealed, they become the property of the improver forever, exactly as springs and wells would belong to the person who discovered or dug them up. According to the Malikites,[1] the *imām* has full authority over the disposal of mines.

Hima, or Reservations for Public Use.[2] **Hima** is the act of preventing the enclosure (*iḫyā'*) of waste lands for private ownership, in order to insure their perpetual reservation for common use, for the grass that grows on them and for grazing cattle. In fact the Prophet did reserve in Medina a stretch of land one by six miles large for the use of the horses of the Helpers (*anṣār*) and the Emigrants (*muhājir*). Al-Shāfi'i, following the precedents of the Prophet and Omar, says that a reservation must redound to the benefit of all the Moslems; that the poor people living near the reservation may graze their cattle on it, though not the rich people; that the *imām* grazes on the reservation grounds only those of his animals which are used in the holy war;

[1] Kharashi, p. 111.

[2] Māwardi, p. 322; *cf. Umm*, vol. iii, pp. 270-2; Anṣāri, vol. ii, p. 449; Kharashi, vol. v, p. 69; Dardīr, vol. ii, p. 182.

finally, that the grounds were and should be used for the grazing of the horses and camels used in the holy war, the cattle collected as *jizyah*, the remainder of the *ṣadaqah* cattle, and a few stray cattle.[1] As regards reservations made by the successors of the Prophet, if they have extended them to all the waste lands or the greater part of them, it is not lawful; or if they have made the reservation in favor of some of the Moslems, or the rich among them, it is also unlawful; but of they have made reservation in favor of all the Moslems, or the poor and the indigent, in one opinion, the reservation is not valid, inasmuch as the right to make reservations belonged to the Prophet alone, who in making the reservation above-mentioned, said: "There is no reservation except for God and His Prophet". According to the other opinion, the reservations made by the successors of the Prophet are valid, as were those made by the Prophet himself, inasmuch as the Prophet made these reservations for the benefit of Moslems, not for his own private interests, and, therefore, those who came in the Prophet's place as regards Moslem interests, are equally entitled to make reservations. Consequently, the meaning of the Prophetic saying: "There is no reservation except for God and His Prophet", is that there may be no reservation except for the benefit of the poor and the indigent, and in the interests of the Moslems in general, as contrasted with what used to be the case in the pre-Islamic times when the strong reserved the land for their own particular use.[2]

[1] According to a report from Mâlik (Zarqâni, vol. iv, p. 247), the number of such cattle pastured on reservation grounds during the califate of Omar was forty thousand.

[2] It is related that Kulayb Ibn Wâil used to take a dog to an elevated place and let him loose, and then reserve for his own use all the land for a distance as far as the yelping of the dog could be heard in every direction, the outlying land being used by others in common. This is alleged to have resulted finally in his murder. *Cf. Umm*, vol. iii, p. 270.

If the reservation has been made for the benefit of all, then all persons, rich or poor, Moslems, or *dhimmis,* have equal rights to pasture their horses and cattle in the reservation grounds. If, however, the reservation has been made for Moslems alone, then only Moslems, both rich and poor can use it. On the other hand, if the reservation has been made for the poor and the indigent alone, the rich and the *dhimmis* are barred from its use. It is not lawful to make a reservation for the rich alone, leaving out the poor, or for the *dhimmis* alone, leaving out the Moslems. Again, if a reservation has been made for the animals of *ṣadaqah* alone or for the horses of the soldiers alone, other cattle may not be pastured on the reservation grounds.

The restrictions established as to the persons who might use the reservation grounds continue in force, but if a reservation in favor of a special class should be sufficient for the whole population, then the whole population is allowed to use the reservation grounds, but a reservation made for all the people may not be restricted to the rich alone on the ground that the reservation grounds are not sufficient for all. As to whether in this last case the reservation may be restricted to the poor alone, there have been two different opinions.

When a piece of land has been already converted into a reservation and later a person, disregarding such reservation, encloses it for his own private use, in case the reservation is one that has been made by the Prophet himself, the act of enclosure is unlawful and the interloper is ousted from the land. Especially is this true when the reasons for which the reservation was made still exist, since the act of the Prophet may not be set aside. If, however, the reservation had been made by one of the *imāms* after the Prophet, then one view of the matter is that later enclosure is unlawful just as in the case of the reservations made by the Prophet himself, but the other view of the matter is that the reservation is overruled by the act of enclosure and the land becomes the private property of the person who enclosed it, since the Prophet said explicitly: " He who develops waste lands becomes their owner ". Moslem rulers are not allowed to take money for the use of pasture lands, whether waste or reservation lands, because the Prophet said: " The Moslems are partners in three things: water, fire, and grass ". Al-Shāfi'i [1] says that if a person who is not entitled to graze his cattle on the reservation grounds does so, the most that can be done is to prevent him from grazing his cattle, and that he is not punished or fined for it.

According to Abu Yūsuf,[2] **forests** belonging to no person may be used by every body for picking up fire-wood, and this is true if it is not known that the forest is private property. This applies also to **meadows** (*marj*) and wild fruits and honey; that is, every one is entitled to help himself to them. In the case of meadows, people are entitled to their use even if the meadows should be private property.[3] According to the Malikites,[4] one may not use grass growing on private meadows, but one may use grass (*kalā'*) growing on lands left uncultivated, provided it does not cause the land owners any damage.

Woodlands (*muhtatab*) **and pasture lands** in which the people of a village are known to pick fire-wood and pasture their cattle are the exclusive property (*milk*) of those people, and therefore they may exercise in their regard all the rights

[1] *Umm*, vol. iii, p. 272.

[2] Yūsuf, pp. 58-9.

[3] Apparently this is on account of the *hadīth* to the effect that in water, fire and grass all Moslems are partners.

[4] Kharashi, vol. v, p. 77.

of property and prevent others from their use. They should not, however, use this right if the woodlands and pasture lands in question are more than sufficient for their needs and consequently no prejudice would result in allowing their use to others.[1] The Malikites apparently agree with the Hanifites in granting the village people the exclusive use of their woodlands and pasture lands, for they consider them as the *ḥarīm* of the village. They nevertheless grant the *imām* the right to make concessions of such lands (*iqṭā'*) to individuals, should the public interest require it (*bi 'l-naẓar*).[2]

The doctors discuss **fishing and hunting** from a purely religious standpoint, *e. g.*, whether or not the devotional formula (*tasmiyah*): "In the name of God the merciful and the Clement" should be pronounced before the act of fishing or hunting, or when the meat of the game is "clean" for eating purposes, *etc.* The relation of the subject to the state is not discussed at all. It would appear from the general trend of the discussion that the matter escaped entirely the control of the state, except in so far as the failure of the Moslems to fulfill their religious duties, namely, the *farḍ, wājib, sunnah, etc.*, came under the cognizance of the *muḥtasib* or public inspector, who was appointed in order to see that those duties were performed and the delinquents punished.[3] These purely religious views will not therefore be discussed here beyond stating that in general fishing and hunting were allowed (*jā'iz*), as between the fisher or hunter, and God.[4]

[1] Articles 91, 97, 100 and 105 of the Ottoman Land Code (*Qānūn-nāmeh Arāḍi*) have been framed in practically the same spirit.

[2] Dardīr, vol. ii, pp. 181, 183.

[3] See Māwardi, pp. 404-32, also 375-403.

[4] It was already explained in Part I (chapter on Classification of the *Sharī'ah* Values) that the doctors distinguished between the predomi-

Water.[1] Following the *ḥadīth* according to which the Moslems are partners in water, fire and grass, water is considered as *res nullius* (*mubāḥ*) and belongs to the person who "occupies" (*iḥrāz*)[2] it, but it is not considered "occupied" until it has ceased to run, that is, until it is placed in a vessel or a water-tight well or basin. Consequently, water found in conduits, and rivers, or in wells and basins which are not water tight is considered as *res nullius* (*mubāḥ*) even if the conduits, river-beds, wells or basins should be private property.[3] *A fortiori* this is true of water found in lakes and seas. Such water therefore as has not been "occupied" is the common property of all, and every one is entitled to its use for drinking purposes (*shafah*), whether for himself or his animals, provided, however, the animals do not ex-

nantly religious and the predominantly worldly or legal values. The distinction often expressed in the Hanifite books by the use of the two words *diyānah* and *qaḍā'* is along the same line. Thus it may be one's religious duty to do a certain thing (*diyānah*) although one might not be forced judicially (*qaḍā'*) to do it. For details on hunting and fishin, see *Majma'*, vol. ii, p. 450; *Hidāyah*, vol. ix, p. 42; *Majallah*, art. 1292 *et seq*; *Minhāj*, vol. iii, p. 293; Dardīr, p. 173; Kharashi, vol. v, p. 77; Ibn Rushd, *B.*, p. 368. For details concerning *diyānah* and the state enforcement of the *sharī'ah* values, see *Tech. Dict.*, p. 503; Māwardi, pp. 118, 128, 134-40, 141-2, 160, 375, 376-8, 378-81, 404-8.

[1] *Mabsūṭ*, part xxiii, p. 161; *Majma'*, vol. ii, p. 440; Yūsuf, p. 53; *Hidāyah*, vol. ix, p. 12; *Durar*, p. 186; *Durr*, vol. ii, p. 710; *Baḥr*, vol. viii, p. 242; *'Alamkīriyyah*, vol. v, p. 580; Kāsāni, vol. vi, p. 188; *Jāmi'*, vol. ii, p. 281; *Majallah*, arts. 1262 et seq.; Māwardi, pp. 313-22; Anṣāri, vol. ii, p. 453; *Wajīz*, p. 243; *Minhāj*, vol. ii, p. 179; Kharashi, vol. v, p. 73.

[2] *Iḥrāz* legally means the act of occupying a thing which is common property and does not belong to any one person in particular (*mubāḥ*); it may be actual or hypothetical. The latter consists in preparing the means of actual occupation, as in the case of collecting rain in a vessel placed outdoors for that end. (*Majallah*, art. 1248.)

[3] Yūsuf, p. 55, l. 17; *Mabsūṭ*, part xxiii, pp. 164-5; Kāsāni, vol. vi, p. 188, l. —2; *Jāmi'*, vol. ii, p. 281; *Fatḥ al-Mu'īn*, vol. iii, p. 416; *cf.* *Majallah*, art. 1251; Māwardi, p. 319.

haust the entire supply of water. Moreover, it is not permissible to sell such water, or rent its use, since it is *res nullius*. The owner of the adjoining land, however, may prevent people from using it, if they can obtain drinking water elsewhere. In the contrary case, the owner of the land is asked either to grant a right of passage, or to fetch some water himself. If he fails to do so, he may be forced by use of arms. The right of drinking extends even to the case of water already "occupied", provided that the person who "occupied" it, has more water than he himself needs. In this last case, however, the person asking for water, in taking it by force, may not use arms, and, furthermore, is obliged to pay the price of the water he used.[1]

According to the Malikites,[2] the water of privately owned wells, basins, springs, and rivers is considered like privately owned water, such as water contained in a vessel. The owner of such water may prevent others from its use and may even sell it, although he is recommended to allow its free use. He is, however, obliged to allow its use, if there is danger of death from thirst.

This unconditional right to use, as regards water that has not been occupied by any one, such as water found in basins, wells, rivers, *etc.*, is limited only to use for drinking or cooking purposes, because use for irrigation or other similar purposes is conditioned upon the nature of the water as follows:

(1) Water of seas or the great natural rivers, such as the Euphrates, the Tigris, *etc.* Such water may be used by every one, for irrigation, turning mills, and otherwise. And every one may divert a river from them. According to the *Mabsūṭ*,[3] the use of the river is not allowed if the diversion of part of its water lessens its water to a degree

[1] *Mabsūṭ*, part xxiii, p. 166.

[2] Kharashi, vol. v, p. 73.

[3] Part xxiii, p. 178.

prejudicial to acquired interests, or if the use of its water for power involves the danger of overflow, should the dam later break.

(2) Water of small natural rivers. If the people of a village desire to divert part of the water of such a river to their lands, they may do so only if this does not prejudice the interests of the earlier settlers (*ahl*). According to al-Māwardi these latter may irrigate their lands whenever they need to do so, unless the level of the river is not high enough for irrigation, and needs to be dammed. In such case, the landowner situated highest up the river dams the river and draws off the water needed first, then the one next to him, and so on down the line. As regards the amount which each owner may draw off before allowing the water to go to the next owner, the Prophet is said to have allowed a level as high as the ankles, but al-Māwardi remarks that the Prophet's precedent was meant for the particular case in question, and that the amount varies with the nature of the land, the kind of crop, the time of sowing, the season, and the consideration whether the river is permanent or intermittent. The Hanifites, on the basis of a *ḥadīth* related by Ibn Mas'ūd, hold that, on the contrary, the right to dam the river first belongs to those situated lowest, and as, regards the *ḥadīth* in question, they dispose of it on the ground that it applies to cases where the water is abundant.[1] According to the Malikites,[2] the settlers situated higher up the stream irrigate their lands first until the water rises as high as the ankles. If, however, settlers situated lower had developed their lands earlier, and there is danger of their crops being destroyed should they come after those situated higher up the stream, they come before the latter.

(3) Water flowing in artificial beds, such as the water

[1] *Mabsūṭ*, part xxiii, p. 163.

[2] Kharashi, vol. v, p. 76.

of a river or canal dug by the people of a village, or the water of wells and pools. Such water is the exclusive right of the owners of the bed and others may not use it for irrigation, even if the water should be amply sufficient for all.

The expenses of dredging or repairing the natural rivers falls upon the public treasury, if there are funds in it; otherwise, it is assessed on the people. According to the Hanifites, in the case of the rivers which are owned, the expense is upon the owners, and if the river is not of the "private" (*khāṣṣ*) kind, the owners are forced to contribute to the expense. The doctors disagree as to the meaning of "private", some saying that the term may be applied to a river owned by forty persons, others, by one hundred, and still others, by one thousand. The view recommended by the *'Alamkīriyyah*[1] is that this matter should be left to the decision of the *mujtahids*. As regards the mode of assessment, according to Abu Hanīfah each landowner contributes equally to the expense only for the part fronting on his land and above it, not for the part below it, but according to his two disciples, the entire expense is assessed on all the partners in proportion to their shares. The argument of the latter is that each partner benefits from the entire river, since even those situated up the stream need the lower part of the stream for the drainage of the surplus water after the irrigation of their land. Abu Hanīfah's argument, on the other hand, is that the expense of dredging is assessed in consideration of the right of irrigation, and this right is not furthered by the dredging of lower parts of the river. As regards the drainage of the surplus, one need not concern himself about it. Moreover, one might turn off the stream at a point further up the stream, should that be necessary.[2]

[1] Vd. v, p. 579.

[2] *Mabsūṭ*, part xxiii, pp. 173-4.

For details on the subject of waters, consult the sources indicated, also *Durar al-Hukkām* (esp. vol. iii, pp. 516, 517, 537) and Bruno.

Markets, Schools, Mosques, Inns, Streets, and Other Public Domain.[1] The Hanifite texts do not consider this subject unless it be incidentally, *e. g.*, in connection with the treating of encroachments on public roads.[2] The Shafiite texts, on the other hand, devote to it special sections under such titles as Common Benefits (*manāfi' mushtarakah*), or *Irfāq* and *Irtifāq*, meaning by the latter two words the granting and the enjoyment of the use of a thing respectively, as contrasted with the ownership in that thing.[3]

The general principle applying to the public places in question is that the person who came first is entitled to their use on condition that he respects the rights of the others, and that his title lapses as soon as he gives up his use of them. In the case of the use of roads no fees may be charged by the *imām* or his governors. Here are a few details.

Any person may sit by the **road** for rest or for trade without a permit from the *imām*, and he may protect himself against the sun by a mat or the like, provided that in doing so he does not obstruct the traffic. Some say that the *dhimmis* do not enjoy this privilege, but others hold the contrary view. The *imām* may grant to a person the use of a part of the road for trade purposes, but he may not charge a fee for it, neither may he grant the ownership (*iqṭā' tamlīk*) of that part. According to al-Māwardi, in the absence

[1] Māwardi, pp. 325-9; Anṣāri, vol. ii, pp. 449-52; *Minhāj*, vol. ii, p. 176; *Wajīz*, p. 242.

[2] *Cf. Majma'*, vol. ii, p. 512; *Majallah*, arts. 1254 *et seq.*

[3] The information here given is derived almost entirely from the indicated Shafiite sources, since the Hanifite views on this subject are isolated and incidental. Suffice it to say that according to the latter, the general principle in regard to the use of common property (*mubāḥ*) is that every one is entitled to it on condition of not prejudicing the general public interest. The Malikite sources are equally silent. (*Cf.* Kharashi, vol. v, p. 71.)

of a grant on the part of the *imām*, if a person goes away from the place he occupied, he may not the next day claim priority on the basis of previous occupation, but the first comer is entitled to it. Mālik holds that when a person is well known as the occupant of a particular place, he is allowed a title to that place in order to avoid dispute. Al-Māwardi observes that although there is an advantage in this, it would nevertheless amount to transferring streets from the category of free things (*mubāḥ*) to that of private property (*milk*). The view expressed in the *Minhāj* concerning traders is like that held by Mālik, for according to it, the occupant of a place does not forfeit his title to it by mere departure, unless he gave up his trade, or his absence extends for a period long enough to result in a loss of his custom. However, a person who occupied part of the road for rest forfeits his right by merely walking away from it.

The person who sits habitually in a place in a mosque for rendering legal opinions (*fatwa*), or teaching, or following the lectures of a teacher is like the person who occupies a part of the road or market for trade. If, however, he is occupying the place for prayer, he forfeits his place by departing from it. Nevertheless, if he went away for a necessity and intends to come back, he does not forfeit his title for the prayer-meeting in question even if he did not leave his coat to indicate his intention. According to al-Māwardi, in the case of the great mosques and worshiping places, the *muftis, etc.*, may not occupy a place in them without the permission of the *imām*, if the custom is to that effect. According to Mālik, if a *mufti, etc.*, is known to sit in a certain place, he is entitled to it. Al-Māwardi holds that he forfeits his right by going away from it. Al-Anṣāri and al-Gazzāli, on the other hand, agree with Mālik.

According to al-Māwardi, people may use the courtyards of mosques and worshiping places, if this does not interfere with the religious functions; otherwise they are kept from them, and the *imām* may not allow them to use such places. There is divergence of view as to whether people need the permission of the *imām* for using such places. According to Mālik, as quoted by al-Kharashi, praying places (*masjid*) situated in the desert, may in the absence of other places be used for taking shelter in them and eating dry food such as dates. It is not, however, lawful to engage in irreverent practices while in such praying places, except when life is in imminent danger.

Nomad people who travel from place to place in the country, grazing their cattle, are entitled to the place where they camp until they leave. Such people may be allowed by the *imām* to settle in a place if this is not prejudicial to the interests of travelers.

As regards the **inns, watering places, schools,** and other public buildings or pious foundations of similar nature, their use belongs to the first comer, and may not extend beyond the customary length of time, unless the founder of the endowment stipulated to the contrary (*sharṭ wāqif*). When there is no stipulation, only the *faqīhs* may take up their residence in the schools, although the general public may visit them and enjoy their shelter for a short time. Except in the case of travelers' inns, where the travelers may not stay longer than three days and nights unless it be because of rain or bad weather, or fear of danger, the occupants of public buildings are not molested while they are pursuing the object for which the building is intended. Thus the students lodged in an educational institution (*madrasah*) are let alone until the end of their studies, or until they give them up. Such people do not forfeit their title by going away to attend to some necessary business.

CHAPTER XV

Summary and Conclusion

According to Mohammedan theory, as already explained, the revenue of a Mohammedan state falls into the two classes of religious and secular revenue. The religious revenue is derived from the Moslems and is chiefly made up of the so-called *zakāt* taxes. The secular revenue, on the other hand, is collected from non-Moslems especially and consists principally in the *jizyah*, the *kharāj*, and the fifth levied on spoils of war, mines, and treasure-trove.

According to the Hanifites, the *zakāt* taxes comprise the *zakāt* of animals (*sawā'im*), the *zakāt* of gold and silver, and the articles of trade, and finally, the *zakāt* of produce or tithe. Theoretically the *zakāt* applies to property only when it is productive. This theoretical limitation, however, is far less sweeping than might at first appear. In fact, animals which are pastured are considered productive for that very fact. Gold and silver are regarded as always productive in virtue of their very essence. Likewise agricultural produce is always assumed to be productive, since it is under all circumstances subject to *zakāt*. In all of these three cases, practically according to all of the three schools with which we have been mainly concerned, the *zakāt* is considered to apply to the physical identity (*'ayn*) of the object as distinct from its commercial value. On the contrary, articles (*'urūḍ*) which are not subject to *zakāt* on the basis of physical identity under one of the three heads mentioned, pay *zākat* on the basis of their commercial value, and it is only with reference to them that the theoretical limitation of productivity above referred to may be said to have had significance. Such articles are considered productive only in so far as they answer the technical description of articles of trade, that is, only in so far as they are acquired in the process of trade with the express or implied intention of trade. When due account of all theoretical limitations is taken, the three kinds of *zakāt* mentioned virtually reduce themselves to *zakāt* of flocks and herds, *zakāt* of commercial capital, and *zakāt* of agricultural produce or tithe, respectively. When it is further considered that flocks and herds and agricultural produce, on the one hand, and commercial capital, on the other, practically exhausted all the kinds of property then existing, it becomes apparent that *zakāt* in its various forms virtually constituted a general property tax. Allowance, of course, must be made for the above-mentioned qualification of productivity which resulted in the exemption of such potential trade articles as were intended for consumption, or at least failed to be articles of trade; as well as for the limitation of *nisāb* which caused the exemption of property falling short of the required minimum.

With respect to collection, the most important point to emphasize is the distinction between apparent and non-apparent property. While the *zakāt* of apparent property, namely, animals and agricultural produce, is collected and disbursed by the state, the *zakāt* of non-apparent property, namely, gold and silver and articles of trade, is disbursed to the beneficiaries of *zakāt* directly by the property owners themselves. The *zakāt* of non-apparent property came under state control only in so far as the owners passed with it the public collectors stationed on the public roads (*'āshirs*). Without attempting to anticipate the discussion of the relation between theory and practice reserved for Part III., let it be said here that this theoretical distinction between apparent and non-apparent property very strongly suggests that the Mohammedan experience with *zakāt* as a general property tax very closely followed that of other people, namely, that the greater part of the tax was ultimately borne by the owners of tangible as distinct from intangible, or in the present case, of apparent as distinct from non-apparent property.

The *zakāt* beneficiaries are specified in the Koran and in the main consist of those members of the Moslem community who need assistance, such as the poor, wayfarers, and debtors among them. The *zakāt* raised in a locality is disbursed to the *zakāt* beneficiaries of that locality. The *imām,* however, may under certain circumstances disburse the *zakāt* of one locality to the beneficiaries of another, for instance, on the ground that the latter are godlier. The *imām* may, moreover, disburse the entire proceeds to one class of beneficiaries to the exclusion of the others, or even to one single individual, provided that he does not disburse to any one beneficiary more than a certain maximum. This maximum is a very arbitrary standard which entirely ignores the special needs of the beneficiary.

To cite only a few of the important Shafiite and Malikite differences in the matter of *zakāt* taxes, the Shafiite definition of pasture animals (*sawā'im*), which according to the Hanifites are the only animals subject to *zakāt,* is broader, while the Malikites go even further and collect the *zakāt* on every animal, pastured and non-pastured. The Shafiites take *zakāt* largely out of state control by virtually assimilating apparent property to non-apparent property. The Malikites, on the contrary, require even the *zakāt* of non-apparent property to be paid to the state collector. In the matter of disbursement, the Shafiites consider the beneficiaries specified in the Koran as the real owners (*mustaḥiqq*) of the *zakāt* that has been collected, and consequently they reduce to the minimum the power of the *imām* to disburse the *zakāt* according to his own discretion. For instance, they do not allow an arbitrary exclusion of individual beneficiaries or classes of beneficiaries, nor do they allow the transfer of *zakāt* from one locality to another. The Malikites, unlike the Shafiites, give the *imām* in this respect considerable power, more in fact than the Ḥanifites. The amount which may be given to a beneficiary, according to both the Shafiites and the Malikites, is far less arbitrary than is the case with the Hanifites, and makes proper allowance for the peculiar circumstances of each case.

Of the secular revenue, the fifth levied on mines and treasure-trove hardly deserves discussion beyond the statement that mines and, in so far as it was not buried by Moslems, also treasure-trove, are considered a case of spoils of war, the fiction being that like the spoils of war they were originally the property of the infidels and became Moslem property by conquest. They are therefore treated like spoils of war.

The *jizyah* is a poll-tax levied on the male non-Moslem subjects of the Moslem state for their humiliation and as payment for the security of life and property which they enjoy; also, as the monetary equivalent of the military service which they owe the Moslem state, but for which their unbelief renders them unfit. Its rate varies according to the financial capacity of the tax payer. The tax is levied on such persons only as may lawfully be killed in war, namely, on persons other than women, children, and monks retired from the world, and it is abrogated upon their conversion to Islam.

Finally, the *kharāj* is a tax on land in proportion to its produce or fixed according to its area. The *kharāj* is levied on the so-called *kharāj* lands, and this is true even when the lands are owned by Moslems. The rates of *kharāj* are based on the precedent of the calif Omar, and where no precedent is available, on the tax-bearing capacity (*ṭāqah*) of the land. Although the actual *kharāj* rates may never exceed the particular rates assessed by Omar, they may be reduced below them, should the tax-bearing capacity of the land require it. However, the upper limit of this capacity has been fixed at the high point of one-half of the entire produce, because, as the Hanifite doctors are wont to put it, " a half-and-half division is the very quintessence of justice ". As a lower limit, one-fifth of the produce has been recommended. The fixed *kharāj* is levied on land irrespective of its cultivation, provided that it can be cultivated. The proportional *kharāj*, on the contrary, is levied only when a crop has been raised.

In the expenditure of secular revenue, the following two cases are possible: (1) The revenue is secured through the instrumentality of definite persons who thereby acquire special rights to it. The spoils of war, mines, and treasure-trove are of this type. They constitute the so-called booty revenue and belong to the persons who secured them, namely, the army, the miner, or the finder respectively, the state's share in them being only one-fifth. This fifth is disbursed according to a Koranic prescription. (2) It is not secured through the instrumentality of any particular person, and therefore inures to the benefit of Moslems at large. Such revenue constitutes the so-called *fa'y* revenue and is disbursed by the *imām* to meet the general expenses of the state, such as stipends of functionaries and soldiers, construction and repair of roads, *etc.* The *kharāj* and *jizyah* are the principal items of the *fa'y* revenue.

With respect to *fa'y* revenue, the Shafiites require one-fifth of it to be disbursed according to a Koranic prescription in the same way as the fifth of booty revenue levied as a tax by the state. The remaining four-fifths, according to al-Shāfi'i, is disbursed by the *imām* for the stipends of soldiers and for other military purposes, but according to later Shafiites, the *imām* may disburse it also for civil purposes. The Malikites, here, too, differ from the Shafiites and agree with the Hanifites, and in fact outdo the latter. For according to the Malikites, the *imām* has full discretion in the disbursement, not only of the entire *fa'y* revenue, but also of the fifth of booty revenue.

The outstanding feature of Mohammedan financial theory is, if one may put it so, its dual nature due to the distinction between religious and secular revenue above referred to. The standards used with respect to the former revenue, therefore, differ essentially from those used with respect to the latter. The *zakāt* taxes, for instance, are primarily a religious obligation as between every Moslem and God, and the function of the state as regards them resolves itself into one of police—namely, of seeing that the obligation is performed. The secular taxes, on the contrary, were purely civil obligations—in so far as a thing in those times could be purely civil and free of religious implication—which found their justification in the power of the stronger or at least in a *quid pro quo* relation. The *dhimmis* must pay the *jizyah,* because they have been conquered and deserve humiliation. This is the Koranic conception. It was later tempered by the additional justification that the *dhimmis* enjoy security of life and property, and should pay for it. This fundamental distinction between religious and secular revenue accounts for much of the difference in the theories concerning them. Since *zakāt* is primarily a religious obligation, the question of its discharge as between the tax payer and God is the fundamental question. The mere payment of the *zakāt* to the state could not therefore be sufficient by itself, unless it was also accompanied by its discharge as a religious obligation. This principle pushed to its logical conclusion would mean that the state could not collect the *zakāt* by force, should the *zakāt* payer refuse to settle it of his own free consent, for it is a well-known principle that a religious obligation can validly be discharged only when performed of one's own free will. We have already seen how the doctors reconciled this theoretical requirement with fiscal necessity. Again, the *zakāt* debt lapses upon the death of the property owner; debts of secular taxes do not. Indebtedness exempts from *zakāt*; it does not from secular taxes. The *zakāt* may often be disbursed by the owner directly to the *zakāt* beneficiaries; the secular taxes must always be paid to the state. The *zakāt* payer is believed when he claims to have himself disbursed his tax dues; the payer of secular taxes is not. The collectors of *zakāt* are not subject to audit; those of secular taxes are. There is an untaxable minimum in *zakāt*, but none in secular taxes.

Another marked characteristic of Mohammedan theory is its dialectical and legalistic nature. The examples that might be cited to support this assertion are legion, and it is a case where the only difficulty is that of selection. Here are a few illustrations of dialectical discussion: Goats pay *zakāt* like sheep, because the word *ganam* occurring in the Prophetic sayings (*ḥadīth*) means both; on the other hand, for instance, mules do not pay *zakāt* because they are not mentioned anywhere in the sources. The *zakāt* of camels, when paid in kind, is settled in females only, because the gender used in references to them in the sources is the feminine. Again, the differences of view as to the age of sheep acceptable in payment of *zakāt* in kind, all center in meanings of words. The *zakāt* may not be given to a slave because the word "give" used in the sources means to transfer the ownership of a thing, and the slave is legally incapable of owning property. The *zakāt* may not be disbursed to fewer than three, because the plural in which number the word is construed in the sources cannot apply to fewer than three. The *zakāt* may not be disbursed to a rich person and yet it may be disbursed to tyrannical rulers, for the latter, although they appear to be rich, in reality are poor in consequence of the fact that their property would not be sufficient to make proper restitution for all their misdeeds. The *zakāt* beneficiaries have a legal title on the *zakāt* proceeds, because the preposition *li* (to) occurring in the Koranic verse expresses such a title. Again, and perhaps this is the most absurd case of legalistic consistency,—if a *niṣāb* (taxable minimum) of property is destroyed before payment of the *zakāt* due on it, and the owner acquires a new *niṣāb*, *zakāt* is due on it upon the lapse of a year, if the first *niṣāb* was destroyed (*halāk*) accidentally? On the contrary, no *zakāt* need be paid on the acquired *niṣāb*, if the first *niṣāb* was destroyed (*istihlāk*) by the owner wilfully, for instance, for purposes of consumption, or by sale,—notwithstanding that the owner's intention may have been exactly to escape the *zakāt* on the new *niṣāb*. The reason for this seeming paradox is that in case of wilful destruction the *zakāt* on the *niṣāb* destroyed becomes a debt upon the owner who thereby escapes *zakāt* on the acquired *niṣāb*. In case of accidental destruction, however, the *zakāt* on the *niṣāb* destroyed lapses and the second *niṣāb*, being free of debt, becomes subject to the *zakāt*.[1]

Here are a few cases of legalistic discussion: The crossbreds do not pay *zakāt* if the mother was wild, because the sperm of the father has been in a legal sense destroyed by that of the mother, and so the offspring acquires the status of the mother. Cunning to escape *zakāt*

[1] *Baḥr*, p. 220.

before it has fallen due is lawful, since no encroachment upon acquired rights is yet involved. A *zakāt* debt of three bushels of good wheat may not be paid in terms of four bushels of inferior wheat of equal value, because this is a case of usury (*riba*). The insane do not pay *zakāt*, no matter how rich, because *zakāt* is an obligation (*taklīf*), and does not apply to a person who is not endowed with understanding (*'aql*). Should a person exchange his camels, on which *zakāt* is to fall due at the end of the year, for other camels, just a day before the completion of the year, he is not subject to *zakāt*, because camels are subject to *zakāt* in virtue of their physical identity, but the camels received in exchange are not the very same animals and therefore are subject to *zakāt* only after a year has elapsed after their acquisition. An animal is considered one of pasture only in case it has been pastured for at least slightly over half a year, since otherwise the quality of being a pasture animal would not have been predominant, and in law importance attaches to the predominant only. Non-Moslems do not pay a toll on pigs by themselves, because pigs are non-fungible (*qīmī*) goods, and to collect a toll on them on the basis of value would be tantamount to collecting a part of the pigs themselves, but pigs are prohibited to Moslems. Pigs, however, are subject to toll if found in connection with an article that by itself is fit to pay toll, such as wine, because in such case the pigs would merely be an appurtenance (*taba'*) of the wine, and it is a legal principle that what is not allowed by itself may be allowed incidentally (*bi 'l-taba'*).

Notwithstanding that dialecticism and legalism are the dominant notes of the entire discussion, here and there considerations of a practical nature are referred to, at least to reinforce the argument based on dialectical and legal reasoning. As one might expect, this happens most often with respect to matters, such as *kharāj* (land-tax), on which the sources are, relatively speaking, silent. Thus the *kharāj* is levied on a piece of land regardless of whether it is owned by a Christian or a Moslem. The *kharāj* rates are according to the tax-bearing capacity of the land. Indebtedness does not exempt from *kharāj* or *jizyah* as it does from *zakāt*. The *jizyah* rates vary with the financial means of the tax payer. The *zakāt* of animals (*sawā'im*) is given precedence over that of trade, because as al-Shāfi'i pleads, the property owners "often do not pay" their *zakāt* of trade, whereas the *zakāt* of animals is collected by the state itself and may not be so easily escaped. Again, with respect to the *zakāt* of gold and silver, a Hanifite doctor invokes administrative expediency to avoid incommensurate numbers.

It is hardly surprising that Mohammedan financial discussion is dialectical and legalistic. As already explained, Mohammedan financial theory is an integral part of *fiqh* or Mohammedan law. Mohammedan law in turn is derived from the revealed sources of the Koran and the Prophetic utterances and conduct (*sunnah*), and its avowed object (*gāyah*), as the doctors put it, is "beatitude in the two worlds." There is a body of revealed truth from which one must not stray, and to which one must adapt himself as best he can. Evidently the only element of flexibility in a situation of this sort lies in reading new meanings into the old letter, unless it be that the letter itself is ignored, and this has often been done and is being done. In fact, the layman at large prefers the latter course and leaves the task of casuistry to the doctors who are responsible for the theory and should also be responsible for its salvation.

It may not be amiss to conclude with a few generalizations as to the characteristics of the three schools that have most claimed our attention. The Hanifites, at least so far as financial theory is concerned, base their arguments more on dialectical and legal considerations than on precedent in the wide sense of the Koran, the Prophetic utterances and conduct, and the practice of the early califs. The Shafiites, on the other hand, put the emphasis on precedent at the expense of scholastic reasoning. Finally, the Malikites, while resembling the Shafiites in the neglect of scholastic methods, are yet not quite so keen on precedent. In short, the Hanifite treatment may be said to be a more or less abstract and schematic statement of the principles and rules of conduct pertaining to finance involved in the precedent mentioned, more for the sake of scholastic satisfaction than for practical reasons; the Shafiite treatment, on the other hand, is an ordered statement of those principles and rules of conduct with a view to attaining as faithful a statement of the divine law as possible; finally, the Malikite treatment is an attempt at a more or less ordered statement of those same principles, however, more with a view to practical exigencies and the solution of concrete actual problems, than is probably true of either of the other two schools.

Part III., where the origins of the Mohammedan tax system and its relation to theory will be discussed, will constitute a later monograph.

INDEX

This index is intended primarily as a glossary, giving therefore only the names which have not been explained every time they recur. It also facilitates reference to the topics treated, especially those that are not indicated in the table of contents or are difficult of access. Expressions in English should be looked up under the principal name, *e. g.*, article of trade, under article. Numbers indicate pages.

VITA

The author, Nicolas (son of) Prodromos Aghnides, was born of Greek parents at Kayabashi (suburb) of Nigdeh, vilayet of Koniah, Turkey, 1883. He received his first education in the Greek Community School of his native place. From 1900 to 1903 he attended the American missionary college at Marsovan, Turkey. During the next year he studied at the French school, École St. Joseph, Kadikeuy, Constantinople. Subsequently, he took up a law course in the Imperial Law School of Constantinople, where he was graduated in 1909. During 1910 he practiced at law. In 1911 after competitive examination he obtained a Turkish Government scholarship for study at Columbia University. He registered there in the Faculty of Political Science and received the degree of M. A. in 1913. In the same year he registered for the degree of Ph. D. He has taken courses chiefly under Professors E. R. A. Seligman, H. R. Seager, H. L. Moore, W. C. Mitchell, J. B. Clark, V. G. Simkhovitch, F. A. Fetter, J. Schumpeter, Karl F. Th. Rathgen, H. R. Mussey, R. E. Chaddock, F. H. Giddings, J. H. Robinson, J. T. Shotwell, W. A. Dunning, and John Dewey. He attended the Seminars of Professors E. R. A. Seligman and H. R. Seager.

Bei Fragen zur Produktsicherheit wenden Sie sich bitte an:
If you have any questions regarding product safety,
please contact:

Walter de Gruyter GmbH
Genthiner Straße 13
10785 Berlin
productsafety@degruyterbrill.com